HISTORICAL DICTIONARIES OF
LITERATURE AND THE ARTS

Jon Woronoff, Series Editor

Historical Dictionary of Contemporary American Theater

1930–2010

Volume 1: A–L

James Fisher

The Scarecrow Press, Inc.
Lanham • Toronto • Plymouth, UK
2011

Published by Scarecrow Press, Inc.
A wholly owned subsidiary of The Rowman & Littlefield Publishing Group, Inc.
4501 Forbes Boulevard, Suite 200, Lanham, Maryland 20706
http://www.scarecrowpress.com

Estover Road, Plymouth PL6 7PY, United Kingdom

British Library Cataloguing in Publication Information Available

Library of Congress Cataloging-in-Publication Data

Fisher, James, 1950–
  Historical dictionary of contemporary American theater, 1930–2010 / James Fisher.
      p. cm. — (Historical dictionaries of literature and the arts)
  Includes bibliographical references.
  ISBN 978-0-8108-5532-8 (cloth : alk. paper) — ISBN 978-0-8108-7950-8 (ebook)
  1. Theater—United States—History—20th century—Dictionaries. 2. Theater—United
States—History—21st century—Dictionaries. 3. American drama—20th century—
Dictionaries. 4. American drama—21st century—Dictionaries. I. Title.
  PN2266.3.F575 2011
  792.0973'0904—dc22   2010048180

∞™ The paper used in this publication meets the minimum requirements of
American National Standard for Information Sciences—Permanence of Paper
for Printed Library Materials, ANSI/NISO Z39.48-1992.

Printed in the United States of America

Contents

Editor's Foreword

This is the third act in the series of Historical Dictionaries of American Theater, the first—which has not appeared yet—deals with the very beginnings up to about 1880, the second with the period roughly from 1880 to 1930, and this volume with the period from 1930 to the present. There is no doubt that American theatre has been maturing over the whole time span and it has reached a peak of sorts at present, one that will presumably be exceeded in the future. For now, after many decades of experimentation and practice, and numerous plays as well as countless performances, theatre in the United States has ceased being peripheral, let alone provincial, but become largely independent, although it obviously borrows from other traditions and imports occasional foreign works. Moreover, the flow has if anything shifted with Broadway increasingly becoming a source of plays and practices emulated worldwide. During this time, not only has the output increased, it has become considerably more varied, taking on virtually any topic of general and particular interest (including many it had avoided in the past), such as politics, war, and sexuality.

Covering this period was no easy matter, since the chronology has to trace an evolution of about 80 years, and the list of acronyms has grown immeasurably. Fortunately, the introduction puts this all in context, while leaving the details to the dictionary section. This time it is even larger, with well over 1,700 entries. They include not only playwrights and actors, directors and producers, but also scene designers, costume designers, lighting specialists, critics and even agents. There are entries on all kinds of theatres, not only the big Broadway ones, but also those Off-Broadway and Off-Off Broadway, some in other large cities, and an impressive batch scattered around the nation. The number of plays is very impressive and the major themes are increasingly varied. Still, as before, this volume can and should be read in conjunction with other works on American theatre, and a very rich source of further reading can be found in the bibliography.

What is particularly notable about this *Historical Dictionary of Contemporary American Theater* is that it was written by one person, James Fisher. Prof. Fisher is head and professor of theatre at the University of North Carolina at Greensboro, following almost three decades at Wabash College, nearly half of this as department chair. Along with teaching, he has written numerous papers and articles on the topic and also coauthored the volume on *American Theater: Modernism.* Aside from this, he has crafted two plays of his own. Obviously, it would never have been possible to produce such a volume without extensive knowledge and experience, but also without an abiding passion for the theatre. These factors will make this a particularly useful volume to the many of us, including the editor, who are fascinated by American theatre and want to know how it has risen to become the very central player it is.

Jon Woronoff
Series Editor

Acknowledgments

As the author of *Historical Dictionary of Contemporary American Theater: 1930–2010* I am grateful to the staff of Scarecrow Press for their patience and support, with particular thanks to the series editor, Jon Woronoff, for his impressive grasp of the big picture as well as his remarkable memory for details. His promptness in responding to many queries as well as his insightful suggestions and edits has helped enormously. Gratitude is also due to April Snider, Jayme Bartles Reed, and other staff members at Scarecrow.

Further, I would like to express gratitude to and affection for Felicia Hardison Londré, my collaborator on *Historical Dictionary of American Theater: Modernism*, for too many kindnesses to enumerate here, but mostly for the privilege of learning from her vast store of knowledge of American theatre history, the model of her thorough scholarship and elegant writing, and especially for her warm, generous friendship and encouragement. Thanks go to my supportive colleagues and students in the Department of Theatre at the University of North Carolina at Greensboro for tolerating a department head too often distracted by the contemporary American theatre—and, similarly, I am grateful to my former coworkers and students at Wabash College where this volume was begun. My late parents, Clarkson S. and Mae H. Fisher; my brothers Dan, Scott, and Biff (and Biff's family); my in-laws, Daniel and Kathleen Warner; and brother- and sister-in law Dan Warner and Mary Russo have all been caring and encouraging of my work. There are several departed friends who, at various times in my life, gave vital support to me, both professionally and personally: Fredric Enenbach, Kathryn England, Kenneth W. Kloth, Erminie C. Leonardis, John C. Swan, and Lauren K. "Woody" Woods. Appreciation is also due to some very live friends who, similarly, helped me along the way, especially Peter Frederick, Herman Middleton, Philip C. Kolin, Kaizaad Kotwal, Diane and Jamey Norton, the Penland clan, Warren Rosenberg, and Bert Stern.

My children, Daniel and Anna, and my son-in-law Matthew Kohansky, fill my life with joy, and I am thankful for their encouragement, support, and love. Above all, my wife Dana has given me everything in life that matters, and her caring compassion, creativity, work ethic, and generosity in all things have taught me why I make theatre and teach. As such, this book is dedicated to Dana Warner Fisher.

Reader's Note

The plan of this volume follows the general format established for Scarecrow's series of Historical Dictionaries of Literature and the Arts—and, in particular, that of *Historical Dictionary of American Theater: Modernism*. Although only eight decades of the vast history of American theatre are covered in *Historical Dictionary of Contemporary American Theater: 1930–2010*, and despite the fact that the focus is narrowly on legitimate theatre, leaving musical and variety entertainments (not to mention film, radio, and television) aside, the impressive richness of the American stage between 1930 and 2010 necessitated somewhat selective coverage. To list every performer, designer, producer, or critic who made a mark on the theatre of this period, or to include an entry for every play of significance (and less important works reflecting the tastes of the times) and theatre companies and producing organizations might have doubled or tripled the length of this ample volume. Difficult choices of inclusion were made with an effort to understand the probable needs of prospective readers or researchers. Consideration was given to the relative influence of persons, institutions, and plays with attention paid to those boasting a potential for cross-referencing. Yet in doing so, the author's discretion was applied in terms of including names and titles that represented both significant and obscure developments, individuals, and plays with the hope of creating a portrait of a rapidly changing and increasingly diverse era.

The vastness and diversity of American theatre between 1930 and 2010 may be ascertained in the volume's bibliography, which is divided into subcategories. Other approaches to the material are offered in the chronology, in the introduction, and in selected overview entries on some broad topics (actors, directors, designers, critics, etc.). These overview entries aim to include important names relevant to that category and to provide a historical context and a survey of innovations and representative work. Many overview entries are also included to provide insight into critical movements either requiring some context or, as in the case of musical theatre, a major development which otherwise is not covered in individual entries in this volume (with a few notable exceptions). Developments in African-American, Chicano, Feminist, and Gay and Lesbian drama, Yiddish theatre, academic theatre, the Off-Broadway, Off-Off-Broadway, and regional theatre movements, and international stars performing in the United States (or important international dramatists—William Shakespeare, Henrik Ibsen, Anton Chekhov, George Bernard Shaw, Bertolt Brecht—whose works were profoundly influential between 1930 and 2010) are among the overview entries included.

Individual entries in *Historical Dictionary of Contemporary American Theater* are included on noteworthy dramatists, actors, directors, designers, producers, and critics, as well as important and representative individual plays, theatrical publications, companies, producing organizations, unions, technical developments, historical events, genres, archives, and regional activities, among others. Play entries include at least brief plot summaries, but may also emphasize important participants in the original production, critical response, pertinent anecdotes, information on noted revivals, and commentary intended to illuminate the play's influence. In cases where the influence or accomplishments of an individual entry begins prior to 1930 but extends well beyond, the entry included here will stress post-1930 activity and a separate individual entry is likely to be found in *Historical Dictionary of American Theater: Modernism* emphasizing pre-1930 accomplishments.

To facilitate use, there is ample cross-referencing. Names, titles, terms, etc., included in the *Modernism* volume will be indicated with an asterisk (Eugene O'Neill,* for example), while names, titles, etc., given an individual entry in this volume will be identified by **bold** type. To avoid a counterproductive excess of bolding, a number of commonly used and familiar terms (actor, director, producer, manager, star, tour, legitimate, amateur, film, and their various derivations) and entries that appear in both the *Modernism* and *Contemporary* volume are formatted using small caps (EUGENE O'NEILL). Individual entries that are included in both volumes will be represented with a dagger (e.g., **O'NEILL, EUGENE.**†). *See also* is used as well in order to report entries which are related but not specifically mentioned (and **bolded**) in the entry.

Finally, a bibliography of sources consulted in the writing of these entries will guide the reader to the vast storehouse of writing on this era of American theatre.

Acronyms and Abbreviations

AADA	American Academy of Dramatic Art
ACT	American Conservatory Theatre
AEA	Actors' Equity Association
AFA	Actor's Fund of America
AGVA	American Guild of Variety Artists
AIDS	Acquired Immune Deficiency Syndrome
AJT	American Jewish Theatre
ANT	American Negro Theatre
ANTA	American National Theatre and Academy
APA	Association of Producing Artists
APT	American Place Theatre
ART	American Repertory Theatre
ARTEF	The Workers' Theatre Group
ASF	Alabama Shakespeare Festival
ASFTA	American Shakespeare Festival Theatre and Academy
AST	Asolo State Theatre
ASTR	American Society for Theatre Research
ATA	American Theatre Association
ATCA	American Theatre Critics Association
ATHE	Association of Theatre in Higher Education
ATL	Actors Theatre of Louisville
ATW	American Theatre Wing
BA	Broadway Alliance
BAM	Brooklyn Academy of Music
BL	Broadway League
BPT	Body Politic Theatre
BTN	Black Theatre Network
CRC	Circle Repertory Company
CRT	Civic Repertory Theatre
CS	Center Stage
CSC	Classic Stage Company
CSF	Colorado Shakespeare Festival
CT	Crossroads Theatre
CTC	Children's Theatre Company

CTG	Center Theatre Group
DG	Dramatists Guild
DL	Drama League
DTC	Denver Theatre Center
ELT	Equity Library Theatre
EST	Ensemble Studio Theatre
ETC	Eureka Theatre Company
FSL	Folger Shakespeare Library
FTP	Federal Theatre Project
GT	Goodman Theatre
HGT	Hudson Guild Theatre
HST	Hartford Stage Company
HTC	Huntington Theatre Company
HUAC	House Un-American Activities Committee
INTAR	International Arts Relations, Inc.
IRT	Indiana Repertory Theatre
JCR	Jean Cocteau Repertory
JRT	Jewish Repertory Theatre
KC	Kennedy Center
KCRT	Kansas City Repertory Theatre
LATC	Los Angeles Theatre Center
LATP	League of American Theatre and Producers
LC	Lincoln Center
LCT	Louisville Children's Theatre
LHAT	League of Historic American Theatres
LORT	League of Resident Theatres
LWT	Long Wharf Theatre
LTC	Lookingglass Theatre Company
MT	Mercury Theatre
MTC	Manhattan Theatre Club
MTF	Mark Taper Forum
MRT	Milwaukee Repertory Theatre
NAG	Negro Actors Guild
NAT	National Actors Theatre
NATC	Naked Angels Theatre Company
NBT	National Black Theatre
NEA	National Endowment for the Arts
NEC	Negro Ensemble Company
NJSF	New Jersey Shakespeare Festival
NP	The Neighborhood Playhouse
NPC	National Playwrights Conference
NTC	National Theatre Conference
NTD	National Theatre of the Deaf

NYSF	New York Shakespeare Festival
NYTW	New York Theatre Workshop
OGT	Old Globe Theatre
OSF	Oregon Shakespeare Festival
OT	Open Theatre
OTC	Organic Theatre Company
PART	Pan Asian Repertory Theatre
PBP	Paper Bag Players
PH	Playwrights Horizons
PMA	Producing Managers Association
PMP	Paper Mill Playhouse
PRC	Playmakers Repertory Company
PS	Primary Stages
RCA	Radio Corporation of America
RKO	Radio Keith Orpheum
RSC	Royal Shakespeare Company
RTC	Roundabout Theatre Company
RTLC	Repertory Theatre of Lincoln Center
RTSL	Repertory Theatre of St. Louis
SAT	Studio Arena Theatre
SC	The Second City
SCR	South Coast Repertory
SCT	Seattle Children's Theatre
SFMT	San Francisco Mime Troupe
SRT	Seattle Repertory Theatre
SS	Syracuse Stage
SSDC	The Society of Stage Directors and Choreographers
SST	Second Stage Theatre
STC	Steppenwolf Theatre Company
TCG	Theatre Communications Group
TG	The Theatre Guild
TKTS	Tickets Booth
TTP	Tectonic Theatre Company
USF	Utah Shakespeare Festival
USITT	United States Institute for Theatre Technology
VGT	Victory Gardens Theatre
VSC	Vermont Stage Company
WCP	Westport Community Playhouse
WG	The Wooster Group
WTF	Williamstown Theatre Festival
YRT	Yale Repertory Theatre

Chronology

Pre-1930 The development of American theatre and drama from its true beginnings in the eighteenth century to the Wall Street economic crash of late 1929 reflects the evolution of the history of the United States and, most significantly, its culture. The rise of modernism in the second half of the nineteenth century encouraged American dramatists to move away from romantic, sentimental, and melodramatic plays toward a serious drama in the mode of Henrik Ibsen, George Bernard Shaw, Anton Chekhov, and other titans of modern drama. Some experimentation by U.S. playwrights in this direction began as early as 1890, as in James A. Herne's *Margaret Fleming* and the work of a few other dramatists, most notably Bronson Howard, William Vaughn Moody, Clyde Fitch, and Edward Sheldon, who also experimented with realistic techniques and franker subject matter drawn from previously taboo areas. A major turning point came in the decade following World War I in the plays of Eugene O'Neill who, inspired by classical drama, modernist concepts drawn from Friedrich Nietzsche, Sigmund Freud, and others, and Swedish playwright August Strindberg, experimented with a wide range of new forms including expressionism, symbolism, and realism. O'Neill's singular accomplishments inspired a generation of American playwrights who similarly contributed bold new concepts, supported by designers, directors, and actors similarly disposed toward realism and a new seriousness in subject matter. In the same era, a vigorous American musical theatre flourished and, along with O'Neill and his peers, a Golden Age of American Theatre commenced at the same moment the emergence of radio and sound films threatened the predominance of the live stage, as did a decade-long Great Depression resulting from the 1929 stock market crash.

1930 The Keith-Albee-Orpheum Circuit merges with Radio Corporation of America (RCA) to establish Radio-Keith-Orpheum (RKO). The League of New York Theatres & Producers is founded. Langston Hughes and Zora Neale Hurston collaborate on a race-themed drama, *Mule Bone*, but it is not produced. New Jersey's McCarter Theatre is founded. **26 February:** Marc Connelly's all-black *The Green Pastures*, based on biblical stories, opens and wins the Pulitzer Prize. **24 September:** *Once in a Lifetime* opens; it is the first of eight comedies George S. Kaufman writes in collaboration with Moss Hart. **3 November:** Maxwell Anderson's blank verse drama *Elizabeth the Queen* opens. **1 December:** Susan Glaspell's *Alison's House* opens in a production by Eva Le Gallienne's Civic Repertory Theatre (CRT) and wins the 1931 Pulitzer Prize.

1931 The Westport Country Playhouse begins operations in Westport, Connecticut. **26 January:** Lynn Rigg's *Green Grow the Lilacs* opens at the Guild Theatre; that same night, Eva Le Gallienne's Civic Repertory Theatre opens its biggest commercial success, *Camille*. **27 January:** Noël Coward's *Private Lives*, costarring Coward and Gertrude Lawrence, opens on Broadway following a successful London run. **9 February:** Katharine Cornell opens and scores a major personal success in *The Barretts of Wimpole Street*, merging producing with acting. **5 March:** Rachel Crothers's *As Husbands Go* opens. **28 September:** The Group Theatre offers its first production, Paul Green's *The House of Connelly*, under the direction of Lee Strasberg and Cheryl Crawford, with Stella Adler, Clifford Odets, Morris Carnovsky, and Franchot Tone among the cast on opening night. **26 October:** Eugene O'Neill's *Mourning Becomes Electra*, a trilogy inspired by Aeschylus' *Oresteia*, opens in a Theatre Guild production starring Alla Nazimova, Alice Brady, and Earle Larimore. **6 November:** Paul Muni rises to stardom when Elmer Rice's *Counsellor-at-Law* opens at the Plymouth Theatre. **26 December:** The musical satire *Of Thee I Sing*, with music by George Gershwin, lyrics by Ira Gershwin, and libretto by George S. Kaufman and Moss Hart, opens at the Music Box Theatre and becomes the first musical to win the Pulitzer Prize for Drama.

1932 **12 January:** Philip Barry's *The Animal Kingdom* opens starring British actor Leslie Howard, who becomes a major Broadway star. **25 April:** *Another Language* by Rose Franken opens. **19 May:** The Jerome Kern-Oscar Hammerstein musical, *Show Boat*, is revived with Paul Robeson scoring a personal success singing "Ol' Man River." **June:** Alfred Lunt and Lynn Fontanne sever their successful relationship with The Theatre Guild, but return three years later when Lunt joins the Guild's board of directors. **2 October:** Yiddish theatre star Maurice Schwartz wins critical acclaim in his own adaptation of Isaac Bashevis Singer's *Yoshe Kalb*, which moves from the Yiddish Art Theatre to Broadway in 1933. **6 October:** *When Ladies Meet*, the 26th play by Rachel Crothers in 26 years, opens at the Royale Theatre. **22 October:** George S. Kaufman and Edna Ferber's *Dinner at Eight* opens to critical acclaim using an innovative revolving stage technique. **12 December:** S. N. Behrman's comedy, *Biography,* opens at the Guild Theatre. **20 December:** Katharine Cornell, directed by her husband, Guthrie McClintic, opens in Thornton Wilder's translation of André Obey's *Lucrece*, Wilder's first Broadway endeavor; a week later, Cornell is pictured on the cover of *Time* magazine. **29 December:** Ben Hecht and Charles MacArthur score a Broadway hit with their comedy *Twentieth Century*, directed by George Abbott, which opens starring Eugenie Leontovich.

1933 Despite the deepening economic woes of the Great Depression, 151 productions are seen on Broadway during the 1933–1934 season. Eva Le Gallienne is forced to shutter her Civic Repertory Theatre due to financial strains exacerbated by the Depression. Robert Porterfield founds the Barter Theatre in Abington, Virginia, this year. **24 January:** Alfred Lunt and Lynn Fontanne costar with Noël Coward in Coward's risqué comedy, *Design for Living*, which opens at the Barrymore Theatre. **15 February:** James P. Hagan's comedy, *One Sunday Afternoon*, opens. **20 February:** Katharine Cornell opens at the Belasco Theatre in Sidney Howard's *Alien Corn*. **6 March:** Maxwell Anderson's drama, *Both Your Houses*, attacking political corruption, opens and wins the Pulitzer Prize. **13 April:** Bertolt Brecht and Kurt Weill's *Threepenny Opera* opens but receives mostly negative reviews and closes within two weeks. **12 September:** The Group Theatre stages its first major success with Sidney Kingsley's Pulitzer Prize-winning medical drama, *Men in White*. **2 October:** Eugene O'Neill's first comedy, *Ah, Wilderness!*, opens in a Theatre Guild production starring George M. Cohan, making his first appearance in a play by another writer. **20 October:** English dramatist Mordaunt Shairp's controversial gay-themed drama, *The Green Bay Tree*, opens on Broadway in a Jed Harris production with Laurence Olivier among the cast. **23 October:** Roland Young stars in his mother-in-law, Clare Kummer's, comedy, *Her Master's Voice*. **27 November:** Maxwell Anderson's blank verse historical drama, *Mary of Scotland*, opens at the Alvin Theatre starring Helen Hayes and Helen Menken. **29 November:** The non-profit, politically inspired Theatre Union opens its first production, *Peace on Earth*, at the Civic Repertory Theatre. **4 December:** Jack Kirkland's adaptation of Erskine Caldwell's novel *Tobacco Road* opens at the Masque Theatre, beginning its remarkable 3,182 performance run.

1934 **8 January:** Eugene O'Neill's *Days without End* opens to negative reviews causing O'Neill to give up active production of his new plays on Broadway for a dozen years. **24 February:** Sidney Howard's drama, *Dodsworth*, starring Walter Huston and Fay Bainter, opens to critical acclaim. **29 September:** George S. Kaufman and Moss Hart's *Merrily We Roll Along*, which tells its story in reverse, begins its run to a mixed critical reaction. **12 November:** Ireland's Abbey Theatre begins a New York season at the John Golden Theatre. **20 November:** Lillian Hellman's first play, *The Children's*

Hour, is successfully produced, although it causes controversy over hints of a lesbian relationship between the two leading characters. **20 December:** Costarring with Basil Rathbone, Katharine Cornell wins critical acclaim as Juliet in William Shakespeare's *Romeo and Juliet*, when it opens under the direction of her husband, Guthrie McClintic.

1935 The American National Theatre and Academy is founded by Cheryl Crawford and Robert Breen, and the New York Drama Critics Circle is formed. **7 January:** After a decade of innocuous juvenile roles, Humphrey Bogart becomes a Broadway star playing a John Dillinger-style gangster when *The Petrified Forest*, Robert E. Sherwood's drama of post-World War I disillusionments, premieres; that same night, Zöe Akins's *The Old Maid*, starring Judith Anderson and Helen Menken, opens at the Empire Theatre. **30 January:** George Abbott-John Cecil Holm's comedy, *Three Men on a Horse* scores a hit with critics and audiences at its first performance. **19 February:** The Group Theatre's production of Clifford Odets's drama *Awake and Sing!* wins critical acclaim as one of their most defining productions, with a cast including Stella and Luther Adler, John Garfield, Morris Carnovsky, Sanford Meisner, and Phoebe Brand, under Harold Clurman's direction; little more than a month later, Odets's *Waiting for Lefty* opens and also wins acclaim, as do two additional Odets plays produced by the Group that year. **26 July:** Hallie Flanagan is appointed head of the Federal Theatre Project of the Works Progress Administration of President Franklin D. Roosevelt's "New Deal" administration; among its many lofty goals, the Federal Theatre Project aims to employ theatre workers and bring all forms of plays to all parts of the United States. **26 September:** Maxwell Anderson's verse drama in a modern setting, *Winterset*, premieres and a strong cast includes Burgess Meredith, who wins critical kudos. **October:** Elmer Rice is appointed New York Regional Director of the Federal Theatre Project and within weeks announces the creation of the "Living Newspaper" unit and the Negro Theatre unit, among others. **10 October:** George Gershwin's "folk opera," *Porgy and Bess*, adapted from DuBose and Dorothy Heyward's 1927 play, *Porgy*, opens to mixed reviews—critics are confused, not sure if it is an opera or a musical. **24 October:** Langston Hughes's drama, *Mulatto*, begins a short run at the Vanderbilt Theatre with African American actress Rose McClendon in the cast. **28 October:** Sidney Kingsley's *Dead End*, a naturalistic drama of New York street life during the Great Depression, is produced to critical acclaim. **27 November:** George Abbott's direction of Sam and Bella Spewack's Hollywood spoof, *Boy Meets Girl,* opens for a long run. **26 December:** Helen Hayes scores her greatest critical success playing Queen Victoria, aging from 18 to 80, when Lawrence Housman's *Victoria Regina* begins its run.

1936   Eugene O'Neill wins the Nobel Prize for Literature, becoming the first and only American playwright so honored. **21 January:** Ruth Gordon and Raymond Massey win critical kudos following the opening of Edith Wharton's *Ethan Frome*, adapted by Owen and Donald Davis, at the National Theatre. **23 January:** Elmer Rice resigns as New York Regional Director of the Federal Theatre Project in reaction to attempts to censor "Living Newspaper" productions. **14 March:** The first "Living Newspaper" production, *Triple-A Plowed Under*, opens at the Biltmore Theatre, generating controversy for the inclusion of a Communist character; a week later, the Federal Theatre Project stages T. S. Eliot's *Murder in the Cathedral*, which wins critical approval, at the Manhattan Theatre. **24 March:** Robert E. Sherwood's *Idiot's Delight*, costarring Alfred Lunt and Lynn Fontanne, wins the Pulitzer Prize following its premiere. **9 April:** The Negro Unit of the Federal Theatre Project opens an all-black version of *Macbeth*, directed by Orson Welles, at the Lafayette Theatre in Harlem; set in nineteenth-century Haiti, critics label the production the "voodoo *Macbeth*." **18 April:** Irwin Shaw's surreal antiwar drama, *Bury the Dead*, opens at the Ethel Barrymore Theatre. **8 October:** John Gielgud appears in *Hamlet*, supported by Judith Anderson and Lillian Gish, winning kudos for his poetic approach to the character; the production racks up 136 performances, breaking John Barrymore's record of 101 (Leslie Howard brings his *Hamlet* to Broadway in a competing production on 10 November). **22 October:** George S. Kaufman and Edna Ferber's comedy-drama, *Stage Door*, depicting the threadbare lives of aspiring young actresses, wins positive reviews when it opens at the Music Box Theatre. **27 October:** Sinclair Lewis's *It Can't Happen Here*, produced by the Federal Theatre Project, premieres on Broadway and, simultaneously, in cities across the country. **19 November:** The Group Theatre stages the antiwar satire *Johnny Johnson*, under Lee Strasberg's direction, at the 44th Street Theatre. **14 December:** George S. Kaufman and Moss Hart's *You Can't Take It with You* begins its long run at the Booth Theatre and wins the Pulitzer Prize in 1937. **26 December:** Clare Boothe's *The Women*, a savagely satiric comedy on the frictions among New York society women, opens to mostly positive reviews at the Barrymore Theatre with a large female-only cast.

1937   The first outdoor drama, Paul Green's *The Lost Colony*, opens in Virginia. **8 January:** Orson Welles and John Housman open a Federal Theatre Project production of Christopher Marlowe's *Dr. Faustus*, with Welles directing. **9 January:** Maxwell Anderson's *High Tor* opens at the Martin Beck Theatre and wins the New York Drama Critics Circle Award. **5 March:** Margaret Webster directs Maurice Evans in *Richard II* at the St. James Theatre. **19 May:** The wacky John Murray and Alan Boretz backstage farce, *Room Service*, begins a long run under the direction of George Abbott.

16 June: Controversy surrounds the Federal Theatre Project production of Marc Blizstein's musical satire, *The Cradle Will Rock*, under Orson Welles's direction; its planned opening at Maxine Elliott's Theatre is blocked when the theatre is padlocked by authorities in an attempt to censor the show's content, but Welles and cast move to the vacant Venice Theatre and perform without scenery or costumes in defiance of the attempted censorship. **7 October:** *Susan and God*, starring Gertrude Lawrence, premieres to appreciative reviews; it is playwright Rachel Crothers's last Broadway play. **1 November:** Alfred Lunt and Lynn Fontanne open at the Shubert Theatre in Jean Giraudoux's comedy *Amphytrion 38*. **2 November:** Legendary star and playwright George M. Cohan scores a personal success playing President Franklin D. Roosevelt in Richard Rodgers and Lorenz Hart's musical satire, *I'd Rather Be Right*. **4 November:** Clifford Odets's drama *Golden Boy* wins critical acclaim in a Group Theatre production under Harold Clurman's direction. **11 November:** Orson Welles's Mercury Theatre, under the auspices of the Federal Theatre Project, presents a modern-dress version of *Julius Caesar*, offering parallels with the rise of fascism in Europe. **23 November:** *Of Mice and Men*, adapted (and directed) by George S. Kaufman from John Steinbeck's novel, opens at the Music Box Theatre and wins the New York Drama Critics Circle Award.

1938   The American Guild of Variety Artists is founded as a support organization, but by the following year it becomes a union. **17 January:** The Federal Theatre Project's "Living Newspaper" production, *One Third of a Nation*, written by Arthur Arent, premieres at the Adelphi Theatre. **3 February:** Veteran character actor Dudley Digges wins acclaim for his performance as an old man in a battle of wits with Death, when he opens in Paul Osborn's *On Borrowed Time*. **4 February:** Thornton Wilder's classic American drama, *Our Town*, begins its acclaimed run at Henry Miller's Theatre under Jed Harris's direction, winning a Pulitzer Prize for Drama, making Wilder the first American writer to win the Pulitzer in two categories (having previously won for Literature for his 1927 novel, *The Bridge of San Luis Rey*). **28 March:** Uta Hagen appears in her Broadway debut in a revival of Anton Chekhov's *The Seagull* at the Shubert Theatre, playing opposite Alfred Lunt and Lynn Fontanne, under the direction of Margaret Webster. **1 July:** The Playwrights Company is incorporated by founders Maxwell Anderson, S. N. Behrman, Sidney Howard, Elmer Rice, and Robert E. Sherwood. **22 September:** The zany musical revue *Hellzapoppin'*, starring Ole Olsen and Chic Johnson, is staged at the 46th Street Theatre for a remarkably long run of 1,404 performances. **10 October:** Maurice Evans opens in the title role of *Hamlet* in an uncut version of the play. **15 October:** Robert E. Sherwood's historical drama, *Abe Lincoln in Illinois,* begins a run at the Plymouth Theatre, winning a Pulitzer Prize and laudatory critical comments on Raymond Massey's portrayal of Lincoln. **19 October:** Dramatic actor Walter Huston makes his musical debut in Maxwell Anderson and Kurt Weill's *Knickerbocker Holiday*, which opens at the Barrymore Theatre; Huston delivers a memorable rendition of "The September Song." **December:** Clifford Odets appears on the cover of *Time* magazine, with a story emphasizing his work with The Group Theatre. **22 December:** Legendary actress Laurette Taylor returns to Broadway in triumph in a revival of Sutton Vance's *Outward Bound* following a decade-long struggle with alcoholism; Taylor's performance is seen at the Playhouse Theatre under Otto Preminger's direction. **28 December:** Thornton Wilder's *The Merchant of Yonkers* fails to find favor despite Jane Cowl in the lead and Max Reinhardt's direction when the gentle comedy opens at the Guild Theatre.

1939   The American Theatre Wing, a service and charitable organization, is founded by Rachel Crothers and other theatrical women. The Clarence Brown Theatre Company is established at the University of Tennessee and morphs into a repertory theatre in 1972. **3 January:** Ethel Waters receives mixed reviews for her performance as a self-sacrificing mother in DuBose and Dorothy Heyward's *Mamba's Daughters*, which opens at the Empire Theatre. **15 February:** Tallulah Bankhead scores a personal triumph as the avaricious Regina Giddens in Lillian Hellman's searing melodrama, *The Little Foxes*, which premieres under Herman Shumlin's direction at the National Theatre. **28 March:** Katharine Hepburn revives her fading career with a stellar performance in Philip Barry's high comedy set among the wealthy, *The Philadelphia Story*, when it is staged at the Shubert Theatre with Joseph Cotten, Van Heflin, and Shirley Booth in the supporting cast. **13 April:** William Saroyan's first play, *My Heart's in the Highlands*, opens at the Guild Theatre. **17 April:** Young British actor Laurence Olivier supports Katharine Cornell in S. N. Behrman's *No Time for Comedy*, a hit at the Biltmore Theatre. **May:** The New York World's Fair begins and has a negative impact on theatre ticket sales on Broadway. **30 June:** Funding for the Federal Theatre Project is terminated by the U.S. Congress, effectively halting all operations and productions. **16 October:** George S. Kaufman and Moss Hart's comedy, *The Man Who Came to Dinner*, begins a long run at the Music Box Theatre, affectionately satirizing Broadway and Hollywood personages such as Alexander Woollcott, Gertrude Lawrence, Harpo Marx, and others; Monty Woolley scores a personal success as the title character. **25 October:** William Saroyan wins the Pulitzer Prize (which he rejects) and the New York Drama Critics Circle Award for *The Time of Your Life*, when it is staged at the Booth Theatre. **8 November:** Howard Lindsay and Russel Crouse's comedy, *Life with Father*, adapted from Clarence Day's stories, opens at the Empire Theatre and runs for a phenomenal 3,224 performances, with Lindsay playing the title character. **27 November:** *Key Largo*, Maxwell Anderson's drama, debuts at the Barrymore Theatre under Guthrie McClintic's direction and with a cast including Paul Muni, Uta Hagen, and José Ferrer.

1940 Worsening war news in Europe has an impact on Broadway ticket sales. **9 January:** *The Male Animal*, a gentle comedy by Elliott Nugent (who also plays the lead) and James Thurber, opens at the Cort Theatre. **31 January:** John Barrymore appears in his final Broadway outing in the exploitive comedy *My Dear Children*, a slapdash affair filled with jokes echoing the alcoholic Barrymore's off-stage troubles. **6 March:** *The Fifth Column*, a rare play by Ernest Hemingway (in collaboration with Benjamin Glazer) focusing on the Spanish Civil War, premieres under Lee Strasberg's direction for a short run. **29 April:** Robert E. Sherwood's drama about the Soviet invasion of Finland, *There Shall Be No Night*, wins the Pulitzer Prize following its opening at the Alvin Theatre, with a cast including Alfred Lunt and Lynn Fontanne, Montgomery Clift, and Sydney Greenstreet. **5 June:** The American Negro Theatre is founded in Harlem by Abram Hill and Frederick O'Neal. **18 October:** The last collaboration of George S. Kaufman and Moss Hart, *George Washington Slept Here*, meets with a tepid response when it is staged at the Lyceum Theatre. **26 November:** Ethel Barrymore gives one of her most acclaimed performances as Scottish schoolteacher Miss Moffat when Emlyn Williams's drama, *The Corn Is Green*, opens at the National Theatre.

1941 **10 January:** Joseph Kesselring's absurd dark comedy, *Arsenic and Old Lace*, starring Josephine Hull, Jean Adair, and Boris Karloff, begins a 1,444 performance run at the Fulton Theatre. **11 January:** The pre-Broadway tryout of Tennessee Williams's *The Battle of Angels*, produced by the Theatre Guild and starring Miriam Hopkins, folds in Boston. **12 February:** Rose Franken's popular comedy, *Claudia*, starring Dorothy McGuire, premieres at the Booth Theatre. **24 March:** Under Orson Welles's direction, Richard Wright and Paul Green's drama of race prejudice, *Native Son*, adapted from Wright's novel, is staged at the St. James Theatre starring Canada Lee. **1 April:** *Watch on the Rhine*, Lillian Hellman's grim drama about a German antifascist in the United States who faces returning to work in the underground in his native country, premieres at the Martin Beck Theatre to appreciative reviews. **31 May:** The perennial *Tobacco Road* finally closes on Broadway after a record 3,180 performances. **October:** The Yiddish Art Theatre closes. **5 November:** English dramatist Noël Coward's *Blithe Spirit* opens to an enthusiastic response and a long run at the Morosco Theatre. **18 November:** Jerome Chodorov and Joseph Fields's light comedy of adolescent shenanigans, *Junior Miss*, opens for a long run at the Lyceum Theatre;

it is one of a series of such comedies that populate Broadway stages during the war years. **5 December:** The thriller *Angel Street*, by Patrick Hamilton, debuts at the John Golden Theatre for 1,293 performances. **7 December:** The Japanese attack American forces at Pearl Harbor, leading to the entry of the United States into World War II.

1942 American involvement in World War II profoundly affects the functioning of Broadway, the road, and other aspects of the business of theatre in the United States. **2 March:** The American Theatre Wing founds the Stage Door Canteen in a club under the 44th Street Theatre, with Broadway stars and other theatrical personnel serving as cooks and waiters for servicemen passing through New York. **18 May:** The dimming out of Broadway lights is established as a means of avoiding air raid threats. **20 May:** Eva Le Gallienne and Joseph Schildkraut star in Thomas Job's drama, *Uncle Harry*, which opens at the Broadhurst Theatre. **7 October:** Maxwell Anderson's tragic wartime romance drama, *The Eve of St. Mark*, premieres at the Cort Theatre. **November:** *New York Times* drama critic Brooks Atkinson leaves his duties to become a war correspondent in Asia. **10 November:** Katharine Hepburn stars at the St. James Theatre in Philip Barry's comedy, *Without Love*, costarring with Elliott Nugent. **18 November:** Thornton Wilder's innovative seriocomic play, *The Skin of Our Teeth,* premieres at the Plymouth Theatre with a cast including Fredric March, Florence Eldridge, Montgomery Clift, and Tallulah Bankhead; under Elia Kazan's direction, the play wins the Pulitzer Prize. **21 December:** Katharine Cornell produces a revival of Anton Chekhov's *The Three Sisters*, costarring Cornell, Ruth Gordon, and Judith Anderson, which opens at the Barrymore Theatre to admiring reviews.

1943 No Pulitzer Prize for Drama is awarded this year. **29 January:** Sidney Kingsley's *The Patriots*, a drama about the founding fathers, opens at the National Theatre. **3 March:** *Harriet* premieres at Henry Miller's Theatre starring Helen Hayes as Harriet Beecher Stowe. **14 April:** Arnaud d'Usseau and James Gow's *Tomorrow the World*, a drama about a young boy brainwashed to be a Nazi, begins its run at the Barrymore Theatre. **19 October:** Paul Robeson is acclaimed in the title role of William Shakespeare's *Othello*, when it opens at the Shubert Theatre; Robeson plays opposite Uta Hagen and critics uniformly praise the costarring of an African American and a white performer, once a taboo. **8 December:** John Van Druten's comedy, *The Voice of the Turtle*, starring Margaret Sullavan, debuts at the Morosco Theatre for an unexpectedly long run of 1,557 performances.

1944 The Donaldson Awards are created to honor Broadway's best work. **3 January:** Ruth Gordon stars in her own play, the comedy *Over 21*, at the

Music Box Theatre. **20 February:** The Equity Library Theatre (ELT) is founded. **12 April:** Lillian Hellman's antiappeasement drama, *The Searching Wind*, meets with mixed reviews at the Fulton Theatre despite a strong cast, including Dudley Digges, Montgomery Clift, Cornelia Otis Skinner, and Dennis King. **27 June:** Agatha Christie's murder mystery, *Ten Little Indians*, premieres at the Broadhurst Theatre. **30 August:** Philip Yordan's *Anna Lucasta*, about an African American prostitute, opens in an American Negro Theatre production. **19 October:** John Van Druten's warm comedy of a 1910s Norwegian-American family, *I Remember Mama*, begins a long run at the Music Box Theatre; the cast includes Marlon Brando in his Broadway debut. **1 November:** Mary Chase's whimsical comedy, *Harvey*, opens at the 48th Street Theatre starring Frank Fay and Josephine Hull and wins the Pulitzer Prize. **23 November:** Arthur Miller's first play, *The Man Who Had All the Luck*, closes after only four performances at the Forrest Theatre. **6 December:** Paul Osborn's *A Bell for Adano*, adapted from John Hersey's novel set in wartime Italy, stars Fredric March at the Cort Theatre.

1945 14 March: Howard Richardson and William Berney's Smokey Mountains fantasy, *Dark of the Moon*, debuts at the 46th Street Theatre. **31 March:** Tennessee Williams's "memory play," *The Glass Menagerie*, opens at the Playhouse Theatre following a pre-Broadway run in Chicago where the show nearly closes, reaping enthusiastic reviews for both Williams's play and Laurette Taylor's memorable performance, with Julie Haydon, Eddie Dowling, and Anthony Ross as the supporting cast. **12 April:** President Franklin D. Roosevelt dies in Warm Springs, Georgia, inspiring impromptu onstage tributes from Broadway actors at the conclusion of performances. **8 May:** VE (Victory in Europe) Day as the war in Europe ends with Germany's capitulation. **6 August:** The United States drops an atomic bomb on Hiroshima, Japan. **9 August:** The United States drops a second atomic bomb, this time on Nagasaki, Japan, leading to the capitulation of Japan. **August–September:** The surrender of Japan is announced on 15 August and the official surrender of Japan is signed on 2 September, ending World War II. **26 September:** Arnaud d'Usseau and James Gow's drama about a white woman in love with a black soldier, *Deep Are the Roots*, is staged at the Fulton Theatre starring Barbara Bel Geddes. **10 November:** Film star Spencer Tracy returns to Broadway for the first time since 1930 in Robert E. Sherwood's *The Rugged Path* at the Plymouth Theatre. **14 November:** Howard Lindsay and Russel Crouse's comedy, *State of the Union*, about a presidential candidate whose estranged wife revives his integrity, is staged at the Hudson Theatre and wins the Pulitzer Prize. **14 December:** Betty Field scores a personal triumph in the title role of Elmer Rice's comedy, *Dream Girl*, which premieres at the Coronet Theatre; Field was married to Rice at the time.

1946   9 January: Quoted in *Variety*, José Ferrer laments the limited opportunities for black actors on American stages and announces that he will not appear before segregated audiences; other white actors soon follow suit. **23 January:** Alfred Lunt and Lynn Fontanne star in Terence Rattigan's *O Mistress Mine* at the Empire Theatre. **4 February:** Judy Holliday receives enthusiastic reviews as Billie Dawn in Garson Kanin's comedy, *Born Yesterday*, which premieres at the Lyceum Theatre; film star Jean Arthur quit the production during its out-of-town tryout, providing Holliday with a star-making role. **20 May:** Laurence Olivier and the Old Vic Company appear for a season on Broadway, with Olivier impressing critics with his performances in a varied repertory, including *Oedipus Rex* and *The Critic*. **8 October:** José Ferrer wins critical acclaim as *Cyrano de Bergerac* at the Alvin Theatre. **9 October:** The last Eugene O'Neill play produced on Broadway during his lifetime, *The Iceman Cometh*, premieres at the Martin Beck Theatre with a cast including James Barton, Dudley Digges, and E. G. Marshall. **6 November:** Eva Le Gallienne, Margaret Webster, and Cheryl Crawford found the American Repertory Theatre, but financial stresses permit only a single season that begins on this date with a production of Shakespeare's *Henry VIII*. **18 November:** Ingrid Bergman wins acclaim in the title role of Maxwell Anderson's verse drama *Joan of Lorraine*, which opens at the Alvin Theatre under Margo Jones's direction. **20 November:** *Another Part of the Forest*, Lillian Hellman's prequel to her 1939 play *The Little Foxes*, is staged at the Fulton Theatre and wins acclaim for actress Patricia Neal. **3 December:** Ruth Gordon's nostalgic semi-autobiographical comedy, *Years Ago*, opens at the Mansfield Theatre.

1947   The American Theatre Wing establishes the Antoinette Perry "Tony" Awards to honor Broadway excellence. The Alley Theatre in Houston, Texas, is founded; Julian Beck and Judith Malina create The Living Theatre in New York; and actors Gregory Peck, Dorothy McGuire, and Mel Ferrer found the La Jolla Playhouse. **29 January:** Arthur Miller's *All My Sons* opens at the Coronet Theatre and wins the New York Drama Critics Circle Award. **5 March:** Eugene O'Neill's final drama, *A Moon for the Misbegotten*, folds during its pre-Broadway tryout in Detroit, Michigan, where the local censor calls it a slander on motherhood. **6 April:** The first Tony Awards ceremony is held. **1 October:** William Wister Haines's *Command Decision*, a drama of an Air Force officer nearly driven to suicide by the pressure of sending pilots to near certain death, premieres at the Fulton Theatre. **5 October:** The Actors Studio offers its first session. **20 October:** Judith Anderson wins acclaim from critics in Robinson Jeffers's free adaptation of Euripides' *Medea* at the National Theatre under the direction of John Gielgud; Marian Seldes makes her Broadway debut in the production appearing in a small role. **3 December:**

Tennessee Williams's searing drama, *A Streetcar Named Desire*, wins critical acclaim at the Barrymore Theatre and is awarded the Pulitzer Prize and the New York Drama Critics Circle Award under Elia Kazan's direction, with a cast including Jessica Tandy, Marlon Brando, Kim Hunter, and Karl Malden, all of whom are also acclaimed.

1948   Broadway actors and directors begin working with regularity in television shows originating from New York. **19 January:** Katharine Cornell is pictured on the cover of *Newsweek* magazine accompanying an article celebrating her numerous stage triumphs. **18 February:** Thomas Heggen and Joshua Logan's comedy-drama *Mister Roberts* begins its 1,157 performance run starring Henry Fonda, who receives critical kudos for his performance as a self-sacrificing officer on a Navy cargo ship during the last days of World War II. **6 October:** Tennessee Williams's *Summer and Smoke* premieres at the Music Box Theatre. **17 November:** Film star Madeleine Carroll opens in Fay Kanin's romantic comedy *Goodbye, My Fancy* at the Morosco Theatre. **18 November:** Moss Hart's backstage satire, *Light Up the Sky*, is staged at the Royale Theatre. **22 November:** A cover story in *Time* magazine on Tallulah Bankhead traces her long career and her recent Broadway success in a revival of Noël Coward's *Private Lives*. **8 December:** English actor Rex Harrison makes his Broadway debut playing Henry VIII in Maxwell Anderson's verse drama, *Anne of the Thousand Days*, at the Shubert Theatre.

1949   Small New York theatres begin to coalesce into what eventually becomes known as Off-Broadway through arrangements with Actors Equity Association and other theatrical unions. On Broadway, the top theatre ticket price is $6.60 on weekends. The Drama Desk Awards are established. **10 February:** Arthur Miller's *Death of a Salesman* premieres at Broadway's Morosco Theatre under Elia Kazan's direction, with Lee J. Cobb starring as the tragic central character, Willy Loman, with supporting performances by Mildred Dunnock, Arthur Kennedy, and Cameron Mitchell; the play, which is regarded by many as the quintessential American drama, wins the Pulitzer Prize and the New York Drama Critics Circle Award. **23 March:** Sidney Kingsley's naturalistic drama, *Detective Story*, opens at the Hudson Theatre. **19 May:** New York's Palace Theatre unsuccessfully attempts to revive vaudeville for the first time since 1933. **2 November:** Alfred Lunt and Lynn Fontanne star in S. N. Behrman's comedy, *I Know, My Love*, at the Shubert Theatre.

1950   **5 January:** Carson McCullers's *The Member of the Wedding*, starring Ethel Waters and Julie Harris, premieres at the Empire Theatre winning the New York Drama Critics Circle Award. **21 January:** T. S. Eliot's *The Cocktail Party* debuts at Henry Miller's Theatre. **26 January:** Katharine Hepburn appears to critical acclaim as Rosalind in *As You Like It* at the Cort Theatre. **15 February:** William Inge's first play, *Come Back, Little Sheba*, opens at the Booth Theatre in a Theatre Guild production featuring Shirley Booth and Sidney Blackmer. **24 April:** Film star Jean Arthur wins critical approval in a revival of *Peter Pan*, costarring Boris Karloff. **27 June:** U.S. President Harry S. Truman commits U.S. military troops to Korea and the Korean War begins. **16 August:** Washington, D.C.'s Arena Stage is founded. **10 November:** Clifford Odets's newest play, *The Country Girl*, stars Uta Hagen and Paul Kelly at the Lyceum Theatre.

1951 **13 January:** *Darkness at Noon*, Sidney Kingsley's anti-Communist drama, opens at the Alvin Theatre. **2 February:** New York's Circle in the Square Theatre, founded by José Quintero and Theodore Mann, presents its first production, Howard Richardson's *Dark of the Moon*. **3 February:** Maureen Stapleton wins critical kudos in Tennessee Williams's *The Rose Tattoo*, which opens at the Martin Beck Theatre. **8 March:** F. Hugh Herbert's risqué comedy, *The Moon Is Blue*, opens at Henry Miller's Theatre starring Barbara Bel Geddes and Barry Nelson. **8 May:** The World War II prisoner-of-war comedy-drama *Stalag 17*, written by Donald Bevan and Edmund Trzcinski, premieres at the 48th Street Theatre. **26 June:** J. Edward Bromberg, a member of The Group Theatre, refuses to cooperate when testifying before the House Un-American Activities Committee (HUAC). **October:** Judy Garland brings two-a-day vaudeville back to New York's Palace Theatre for an announced four-week run that turns into a record-breaking 19-week engagement; other performers follow suit, with none matching Garland's success. **24 October:** The husband-and-wife acting team of Hume Cronyn and Jessica Tandy win critical acclaim at the Barrymore Theatre in Jan de Hartog's *The Fourposter*, directed by José Ferrer. **28 November:** Julie Harris scores a personal success as Sally Bowles in John Van Druten's adaptation of Christopher Isherwood's "Berlin Stories," *I Am a Camera*, when it premieres at the Empire Theatre and wins the New York Drama Critics Circle Award. **13 December:** After a lengthy run and tour in *Mister Roberts*, Henry Fonda returns to Broadway in Paul Osborn's *Point of No Return*, which opens at the Alvin Theatre. **20 December:** British stars Laurence Olivier and Vivien Leigh, who are married, arrive to acclaim on Broadway playing the title characters in William Shakespeare's *Antony and Cleopatra* and George Bernard Shaw's *Caesar and Cleopatra*.

1952 Herbert Blau and Jules Irving found the Actors Workshop in San Francisco, an early regional theatre. **15 January:** Joseph Kramm's *The Shrike* opens at the Cort Theatre and wins the Pulitzer Prize. **20 February:** Helen Hayes garners appreciative reviews in Mary Chase's *Mrs. McThing* at the Martin Beck Theatre. **12 March:** John Garfield appears in a revival of Clifford Odets's *Golden Boy* at the ANTA Playhouse under Odets's direction. **10 April:** Elia Kazan testifies before the House Un-American Activities Committee, "naming names" of alleged Communists in theatre and films. **24 April:** Tennessee Williams's *Summer and Smoke* is revived at the Circle in the Square under José Quintero's direction, with Geraldine Page winning praise for her performance as Alma Winemiller. **15 October:** Shirley Booth wins critical praise in Arthur Laurents's comedy-drama *The Time of the Cuckoo* at the Empire Theatre. **29 October:** Frederick Knott's thriller, *Dial M for Murder*, debuts at the Plymouth Theatre starring Maurice Evans. **20 November:** Tom Ewell opens in George Axelrod's hit comedy, *The Seven Year Itch*, at the Fulton Theatre.

1953 The number of Broadway productions drops to around 50 during the 1953–1954 season. **22 January:** Arthur Miller's historical drama, *The Crucible*, depicting the seventeenth-century Salem, Massachusetts, witch trials, premieres at the Martin Beck Theatre with critics finding the play a metaphor for the anti-Communist witchhunts and blacklisting spearheaded by Sen. Joseph McCarthy and the House Un-American Activities Committee. **23 January:** Yiddish theatre star Menasha Skulnik makes the transition to Broadway, appearing in Sylvia Regan's comedy *The Fifth Season* at the Cort Theatre. **19 February:** William Inge's comedy-drama, *Picnic*, opens at the Music Box Theatre and wins the Pulitzer Prize and the New York Drama Critics Circle Award. **19 March:** Tennessee Williams's *Camino Real*, a symbolic drama featuring characters from literary history, is pilloried by critics in its Broadway premiere at the National Theatre, inspiring Williams to write a letter to the *New York Times* defending this highly experimental work. **30 September:** Robert Anderson's *Tea and Sympathy* opens at the Barrymore Theatre and scores a hit despite controversy over its homosexual theme. **5 November:** Josephine Hull wins critical approval in her last Broadway role as a little old lady taking on corporate interests in George S. Kaufman and Howard Teichmann's *The Solid Gold Cadillac* at the Belasco Theatre. **11 November:** Margaret Sullavan appears in Samuel Taylor's popular romantic comedy, *Sabrina Fair*, at the National Theatre. **29 December:** Novelist Jane Bowles's *In the Summer House* opens at the Playhouse to critical acclaim.

1954 Joe Papp founds the New York Shakespeare Festival, and the Milwaukee Repertory Theatre begins operations. **20 January:** With a cast including Henry Fonda and Lloyd Nolan, Herman Wouk's *The Caine Mutiny Court-Martial* opens at the Plymouth Theatre. **18 February:** Audrey Hepburn wins critical approval in Jean Giraudoux's *Ondine*, which opens at the 46th Street Theatre. **10 March:** Bertolt Brecht and Kurt Weill's *The Threepenny Op-*

era wins critical acclaim Off-Broadway at the Theatre de Lys with Weill's widow, Lotte Lenya, appearing in a leading role. **27 October:** Kim Stanley opens at the Playhouse Theatre in Horton Foote's *The Traveling Lady* and scores a personal success. **28 October:** N. Richard Nash's *The Rainmaker* opens at the Cort Theatre starring Geraldine Page and Darren McGavin. **8 December:** Maxwell Anderson's *The Bad Seed*, a thriller about a murderous child, opens at the 46th Street Theatre.

1955   The Williamstown Theatre Festival is founded at Williams College. **10 February:** Joseph Hayes's Tony Award-winning thriller, *The Desperate Hours*, opens at the Barrymore Theatre with a cast including Karl Malden, George Grizzard, and Paul Newman. **2 March:** William Inge's *Bus Stop*, starring Kim Stanley in a comedy-drama about travelers stranded in a Midwestern blizzard, premieres at the Music Box Theatre. **24 March:** Tennessee Williams's *Cat on a Hot Tin Roof* wins critical acclaim at the Morosco Theatre as well as a Pulitzer Prize and New York Drama Critics Circle Award; the cast includes Barbara Bel Geddes, Ben Gazzara, Burl Ives, and Mildred Dunnock. **21 April:** Jerome Lawrence and Robert E. Lee's *Inherit the Wind*, a fictionalized dramatization of the Scopes "Monkey" trial debate on evolution versus creationism, opens at the National Theatre starring Paul Muni, Ed Begley, and Tony Randall. **1 September:** Actor Philip Loeb commits suicide and his death is blamed, in part, on the fact that he had lost his leading role opposite star and writer Gertrude Berg in TV's popular series *The Goldbergs* due to the blacklist; Berg battles with television executives to save Loeb's job, but cannot. **29 September:** Arthur Miller's one-act, *A View from the Bridge*, premieres at the Coronet Theatre with a cast including Van Heflin and Eileen Heckart. **5 October:** Frances Goodrich and Albert Hackett's *The Diary of Anne Frank* wins the Pulitzer Prize, New York Drama Critics Circle Award, and Tony Award for its dramatization of the experience of a young Jewish girl caught up in the Holocaust. **20 October:** Andy Griffith scores a personal success as a genial country boy in the U.S. Army in Ira Levin's *No Time for Sergeants* at the Alvin Theatre. **9 November:** The Actors Studio production of Michael Gazzo's drama about drug addicts, *A Hatful of Rain*, opens at the Lyceum Theatre starring Shelley Winters and Ben Gazzara. **5 December:** Thornton Wilder's *The Matchmaker*, a revision of his 1938 flop *The Merchant of Yonkers*, begin its run at the Royale Theatre starring Ruth Gordon, who wins critical acclaim for her performance as the irrepressible Dolly Gallagher Levi under Tyrone Guthrie's direction.

1956   The Obie Awards are established by the *Village Voice* to honor theatrical achievement in Off-Broadway theatres, and the American Society for Theatre Research is founded. **12 January:** Orson Welles directs himself in a production of *King Lear* at the City Center. **8 February:** Paddy Chayefsky's *Middle of the Night* opens at the ANTA Theatre starring Edward G. Robinson in a rare return to Broadway. **15 February:** Tallulah Bankhead appears in a controversial limited-run City Center revival of Tennessee Williams's *A Streetcar Named Desire*, with some critics and audiences feeling Bankhead's camp persona overwhelmed the delicate role of Blanche DuBois. **19 April:** Samuel Beckett's "Theatre of the Absurd" play *Waiting for Godot* debuts on Broadway at the John Golden Theatre to puzzled responses from most critics and audiences; Bert Lahr, E. G. Marshall, Kurt Kasznar, and Alvin Epstein are the cast. **8 May:** A revival of Eugene O'Neill's *The Iceman Cometh*, directed by José Quintero, premieres at the Circle in the Square to critical acclaim for the play and actor Jason Robards, who begins a close association with O'Neill's plays. **29 June:** Arthur Miller marries film star Marilyn Monroe. **August:** Colleen Dewhurst scores an early success in Joe Papp's production of *The Taming of the Shrew*; this performance, as well as her role Off-Broadway in *The Eagle Has Two Heads*, brings Dewhurst an Obie Award. **31 October:** Jerome Lawrence and Robert E. Lee's comedy *Auntie Mame*, adapted from Patrick Dennis's novel, opens at the Broadhurst Theatre for a long run. **7 November:** Eugene O'Neill's *Long Day's Journey into Night* debuts with a cast including Fredric March, Florence Eldridge, Jason Robards, and Bradford Dillman, directed by José Quintero, at the Helen Hayes Theatre; O'Neill, who had left his widow instructions not to permit production until 25 years after his death, wins a posthumous Pulitzer Prize, as well as a New York Drama Critics Circle Award and a Tony Award. **18 December:** Uta Hagen stars in a rare Broadway production of a Bertolt Brecht play, in this case *The Good Woman of Setzuan*, at the Phoenix Theatre.

1957   **7 February:** Gore Vidal's satiric comedy, *Visit to a Small Planet*, opens at the Booth Theatre in a production directed by and starring Cyril Ritchard. **18 February:** The House Un-American Activities Committee indicts Arthur Miller for contempt of the U.S. Congress when he refuses to answer questions. **21 March:** Tennessee Williams's classically inspired drama, *Orpheus Descending*, revised from his 1940 flop *Battle of Angels*, opens at the Martin Beck Theatre under Harold Clurman's direction; critics are mixed, although appreciative of the performances of Maureen Stapleton and Cliff Robertson. **10 July:** Morris Carnovsky and Katharine Hepburn costar to acclaim in an American Shakespeare Festival production of *The Merchant of Venice*. **1 October:** English dramatist John Osborne's "angry young man" drama, *Look Back in Anger*, opens at the Lyceum Theatre, to mixed reviews. **28 November:** Ketti Frings's adaptation of Thomas Wolfe's *Look Homeward, Angel* opens at the Barrymore Theatre with a cast including Anthony Perkins, Jo Van Fleet, and Hugh Griffith. **5 December:** William

Inge's *The Dark at the Top of the Stairs*, starring Pat Hingle, Teresa Wright, and Eileen Heckart, wins critical approval in its first performance at the Music Box Theatre.

1958 Joseph Cino establishes the Caffe Cino, considered the epicenter of the Off-Off-Broadway theatre movement. **16 January:** Anne Bancroft plays opposite Henry Fonda in the two-character play, *Two for the Seesaw*, winning critical approval at the Booth Theatre. **30 January:** Dore Schary's historically based drama, *Sunrise at Campobello*, opens at the Cort Theatre with Ralph Bellamy playing Franklin D. Roosevelt in his struggle to return to politics after polio. **12 February:** Laurence Olivier is acclaimed for his performance as a bitter music hall performer in John Osborne's *The Entertainer*, at the Royale Theatre. **5 May:** Alfred Lunt and Lynn Fontanne appear in their last Broadway roles in Friedrich Dürrenmatt's *The Visit,* and the theatre in which they are appearing is renamed in their honor. **10 June:** Blacklisted actor Zero Mostel wins critical kudos at Off-Broadway's Rooftop Theatre in Padraic Colum's *Ulysses in Nighttown*, adapted from James Joyce. **2 October:** Eugene O'Neill's previously unproduced drama, *A Touch of the Poet*, opens at the Helen Hayes Theatre under the direction of Harold Clurman and starring Helen Hayes, Kim Stanley, and Eric Portman. **11 December:** Archibald MacLeish's Pulitzer Prize and Tony Award-winning verse drama, *J.B.*, debuts at the ANTA Theatre starring Raymond Massey, Christopher Plummer, and Pat Hingle, under Elia Kazan's direction.

1959 President Dwight D. Eisenhower breaks ground for the construction of the Lincoln Center for the Performing Arts in New York. The number of Broadway productions declines as the regional theatre movement, fueled by the founding of the Guthrie Theater in Minneapolis, Minnesota, grows. The Dallas Theatre Center is also established. **16 February:** Gertrude Berg and Cedric Hardwicke appear in Leonard Spigelgass's comedy of cultural understanding, *A Majority of One*, at the Shubert Theatre, winning a Tony Award for Berg. **10 March:** Tennessee Williams's *Sweet Bird of Youth*, directed by Elia Kazan and starring Geraldine Page and Paul Newman, opens at the Martin Beck Theatre to positive reviews. **11 March:** Lorraine Hansberry's *A Raisin in the Sun* debuts at the Barrymore Theatre and wins the New York Drama Critics Circle Award and much praise for the play and its cast including Sidney Poitier, Claudia McNeil, Ruby Dee, and Diana Sands; it is the first Broadway play by an African American woman. **15 July:** Jack Gelber's *The Connection*, a drama about drug addicts, is staged Off-Broadway in a Living Theatre production under Judith Malina's direction. **19 October:** Anne Bancroft and Patty Duke win critical acclaim as teacher Annie Sullivan and her pupil, Helen Keller, in William Gibson's Tony Award-winning play, *The*

Miracle Worker, at the Playhouse Theatre. **5 November:** Paddy Chayefsky's *The Tenth Man* opens at the Booth Theatre with a cast including Yiddish theatre actor Jacob Ben-Ami.

1960 The San Francisco Mime Troupe, a theatre collective inspired by left-wing politics and the traditions of *commedia dell'arte*, forms and inspires creation of other political, ethnic, and gender-themed companies. Asolo State Theatre in Sarasota, Florida, is founded by the Drama Department of Florida State University, and the Cincinnati Playhouse in the Park begins operations. The Association of Producing Artists is established by Ellis Rabb. *Back Stage*, a theatrical trade newspaper, begins publication. **14 January:** Edward Albee's one-act *The Zoo Story*, inspired by existential philosophy and Theatre of the Absurd techniques, is staged Off-Broadway at the Provincetown Playhouse, winning critical approval and a long run. **25 February:** Lillian Hellman's semiautobiographical period drama, *Toys in the Attic*, premieres at the Hudson Theatre starring Jason Robards, Maureen Stapleton, Irene Worth, and blacklisted actress Anne Revere. **31 March:** Gore Vidal's political drama, *The Best Man*, is staged at the Morosco Theatre. **10 November:** Tennessee Williams's *A Period of Adjustment*, a rare comedy from the playwright, debuts at the Helen Hayes Theatre. **30 November:** Tad Mosel's dark family drama, *All the Way Home*, opens at the Belasco Theatre and wins the Pulitzer Prize and New York Drama Critics Circle Award.

1961 Ellen Stewart founds La Mama Experimental Theatre Club, a major force in Off-Broadway theatre. Peter Schumann establishes the Bread & Puppet Theatre. **24 January:** Edward Albee's one-act absurdist play, *The American Dream*, is produced at Off-Broadway's York Theatre under Alan Schneider's direction. **22 February:** Neil Simon's first comedy, *Come Blow Your Horn*, scores a hit at the Brooks Atkinson Theatre. **4 April:** Kim Stanley wins praise from critics in Henry Denker's *A Far Country*, a drama based on a Sigmund Freud case, at the Music Box Theatre. **28 September:** Ossie Davis's comedy about friendship between the races in the "Jim Crow" South, *Purlie Victorious*, opens at the Cort Theatre with a cast including Davis, Ruby Dee, Godfrey Cambridge, and Alan Alda. **9 November:** Paddy Chayefsky's drama, *Gideon*, concerning the relationship of God and man, stars Fredric March under Tyrone Guthrie's direction at the Plymouth Theatre. **28 December:** Tennessee Williams's *The Night of the Iguana* premieres at the Royale Theatre and wins the New York Drama Critics Circle Award; the drama stars Margaret Leighton, Patrick O'Neal, and Bette Davis, in a rare stage appearance.

1962 26 February: Arthur Kopit's absurdist tragic-farce, *Oh Dad, Poor Dad, Mama's Hung You in the Closet and I'm Feelin' So Sad*, debuts Off-

Broadway at the Phoenix Theatre. **17 March:** The APA Repertory Company begins its first season. **5 April:** Jason Robards scores a personal success in Herb Gardner's *A Thousand Clowns*, at the Eugene O'Neill Theatre. **1 June:** Actors Equity announces that its members will no longer appear in any theatres requiring the audience to be segregated. **18 June:** Joe Papp's New York Shakespeare Festival's Delacorte Theatre opens in Central Park with a production of *The Merchant of Venice* starring George C. Scott. **13 October:** Edward Albee's first full-length play, *Who's Afraid of Virginia Woolf?*, generates controversy at the Billy Rose Theatre with a cast including Uta Hagen and Arthur Hill; the play shatters prior taboos on strong language and adult situations, causing it to be denied a Pulitzer Prize when the selection committee opts not to give the award, although the play is otherwise acknowledged with a Tony Award and a New York Drama Critics Circle Award. **8 December:** A New York newspaper strike begins and lasts for several months, undermining the runs of Broadway shows which can neither advertise nor be reviewed.

1963 The Open Theatre is founded by Joseph Chaiken and Peter Feldman. Baltimore's Center Stage and the Seattle Repertory Theatre are founded. **8 January:** George C. Scott, Colleen Dewhurst, and Rip Torn are acclaimed in a Circle in the Square revival of Eugene O'Neill's tragedy, *Desire Under the Elms*, under José Quintero's direction. **16 January:** Tennessee Williams's *The Milk Train Doesn't Stop Here Anymore* opens at the Morosco Theatre, but poor reviews close the play within two months. **11 March:** The Actors Studio Theatre revives Eugene O'Neill's *Strange Interlude* under José Quintero's direction and a cast including Geraldine Page, Franchot Tone, and Jane Fonda. **28 March:** A rare Broadway production of Bertolt Brecht's *Mother Courage and Her Children* is staged at the Martin Beck Theatre starring Anne Bancroft. **15 May:** Kenneth Brown's *The Brig* opens at the Living Theatre. **23 October:** Neil Simon's *Barefoot in the Park* begins a long run at the Biltmore Theatre under Mike Nichols's direction, with an acclaimed cast including Elizabeth Ashley, Robert Redford, and Mildred Natwick. **22 November:** President John F. Kennedy is assassinated in Dallas, Texas; on Broadway, theatres are dark that night and again on the following Monday, the day of Kennedy's funeral.

1964 The American Conservatory Theatre is founded by William Ball in Pittsburgh, Pennsylvania (although it later moves operations to San Francisco, California). Kentucky's Actors Theatre of Louisville is founded by Richard Block and Ewel Cornett, and the American Place Theatre is established by Wynn Handman and Sidney Lanier at New York's St. Clement's Church. The Eugene O'Neill Memorial Theatre Center is established in Connecticut and the South Coast Repertory is founded in California. **1 January:** Tallulah Bankhead opens at the Brooks Atkinson Theatre in her last Broadway appearance in a revised version of Tennessee Williams's *The Milk Train Doesn't Stop Here Anymore*, but critical apathy closes the play after five performances. **23 January:** Arthur Miller's *After the Fall* premieres at the ANTA Washington Square Theatre to predominantly negative reviews; critics fault Miller for what they consider a thinly veiled, self-serving portrait of his late wife, Marilyn Monroe. **23 March:** LeRoi Jones (later known as Amiri Baraka) stages his racially themed one-act *Dutchman* at the Cherry Lane Theatre. **9 April:** Richard Burton wins acclaim in *Hamlet*, in a modern-dress, "rehearsal concept" staging at the Lunt-Fontanne Theatre with a cast including Alfred Drake, Hume Cronyn, and Eileen Herlie under John Gielgud's direction. **23 April:** James Baldwin's race-themed drama, *Blues for Mr. Charlie*, opens at the ANTA Theatre under Burgess Meredith's direction in an Actors Studio production. **25 May:** Frank Gilroy's *The Subject Was Roses* premieres at the Royale Theatre, winning critical kudos for cast members Martin Sheen, Jack Albertson, and Irene Dailey, as well as a Pulitzer Prize, Tony Award, and New York Drama Critics Circle Award. **27 May:** Ann Jellicoe's Off-Broadway comedy, *The Knack*, begins a long run at the New Theatre. **22 June:** An Actors Studio revival of Anton Chekhov's *The Three Sisters*, starring Kim Stanley and Geraldine Page, opens at the Morosco Theatre under Lee Strasberg's direction. **2 July:** United States President Lyndon B. Johnson signs the Civil Rights Act. **12 October:** James Earl Jones wins critical kudos for his performance in the title role in *Othello*, in a New York Shakespeare Festival production at the Martinique Theatre. **11 November:** Eli Wallach, Anne Jackson, and Alan Arkin win praise in Murray Schisgal's dark comedy, *Luv*, at the Booth Theatre. **3 December:** Arthur Miller's drama *Incident at Vichy* is produced at the ANTA Theatre with a cast including Hal Holbrook, David Wayne, Joseph Wiseman, and Tony Lo Bianco. **18 December:** Two LeRoi Jones race-themed plays, *The Toilet* and *The Slave*, open at the St. Mark's Playhouse. **22 December:** Jason Robards is praised by critics for his performance in Eugene O'Neill's one-act *Hughie*, which begins performances at the Royale Theatre. **29 December:** Edward Albee's *Tiny Alice* opens to puzzled critical response at the Billy Rose Theatre, despite a distinguished cast including John Gielgud and Irene Worth.

1965 Public demonstrations against the Vietnam War grow in size and number. The first major Asian American theatre company, East West Players, is founded. Luis Valdez establishes El Teatro Campesino, a theatre company dedicated to improving conditions for Chicano farmworkers in California. The Long Wharf Theatre opens in New Haven, Connecticut. John Clark Donahue opens The Children's Theatre Company in Minneapolis, Minnesota. The National Theatre of the Deaf is founded by David Hays and the Roundabout Theatre begins operations in New York. The League of Resident Theatres is set up by Peter Zeisler. **28 January:** Arthur Miller's expanded version of his 1955 one-act drama, *A View from the Bridge*, opens at the Sheridan Square Theatre and has a long run with Robert Duvall, who receives critical praise for his performance as longshoreman Eddie Carbone. **10 March:** Walter Matthau and Art Carney open at the Plymouth Theatre in Neil Simon's comedy *The Odd Couple*. **8 April:** James Baldwin's first play, *The Amen Corner*, based on his novel *Go Tell It on the Mountain*, opens at the Ethel Barrymore Theatre. **26 April:** Terrence McNally's first Broadway play, *And Things That Go Bump in the Night*, flops at the Royale Theatre. **June:** President Lyndon B. Johnson signs legislation creating the National Endowment for the Arts. **15 June:** Hume Cronyn and Jessica Tandy win praise in a revival of *The Cherry Orchard* at the Guthrie Theatre in Minneapolis, Minnesota. **15 November:** Douglas Turner Ward's one-acts, *Happy Ending* and *Day of Absence*, are produced at the St. Mark's Playhouse. **8 December:** Film actress Lauren Bacall wins praise for her performance in Abe Burrows's comedy, *Cactus Flower*, at the Royale Theatre.

1966   The Yale Repertory Theatre is founded by Robert Brustein. **3 March:** James Goldman's *The Lion in Winter*, starring Rosemary Harris and Robert Preston, opens at the Ambassador Theatre. **21 April:** Dustin Hoffman wins praise from critics in the Off-Broadway production of Ronald Ribman's *The Journey of the Fifth Horse* at the American Place Theatre. **13 June:** Arnold Wesker's *The Kitchen* debuts at the 81st Street Theatre with a cast including Sylvia Miles and Rip Torn. **22 September:** Edward Albee's *A Delicate Balance* premieres at the Martin Beck Theatre with a cast including Hume Cronyn, Jessica Tandy, and Marian Seldes; the play is awarded the Pulitzer Prize. **5 October:** British dramatist Frank Marcus's lesbian-themed play, *The Killing of Sister George*, opens at the Belasco Theatre. **11 October:** Megan Terry's anti-Vietnam War musical play, *Viet Rock*, is staged at Yale University. **November:** The Roundabout Theatre Company stages its first production, a revival of August Strindberg's *The Father*. **7 November:** Jean-Claude van Itallie's *America Hurrah* opens at the La MaMa Experimental Theatre Club. **17 November:** Woody Allen's comedy *Don't Drink the Water* scores a hit at the Morosco Theatre.

1967   Joe Papp converts the old Astor Library into the New York Public Theatre with the goal of promoting diverse contemporary plays by new writers. Christopher Martin founds the Classic Stage Company and the Ensemble Studio Theatre is established to develop new American plays. Richard Schechner establishes the avant-garde The Performance Group and The

Play-House of the Ridiculous commences operations. **22 February:** Barbara Garson's satire of President Lyndon B. Johnson, *Macbird!*, debuts at the Village Gate Theatre. **23 February:** John Herbert's searing prison drama, *Fortune and Men's Eyes*, opens at the Actors Playhouse, generating controversy for its depiction of homosexuality. **13 March:** Robert Anderson's three one-acts with the overarching title *You Know I Can't Hear You When the Water's Running* is a popular success at the Ambassador Theatre. **14 April:** The Mark Taper Forum in Los Angeles, California, stages its first production. **16 October:** Eugene O'Neill's likeness appears on a U.S. postage stamp, the first time an American dramatist is so honored. **24 October:** Michael McClure's *The Beard* premieres Off-Broadway at the Evergreen Theatre under Rip Torn's direction; it creates considerable controversy for its use of nudity, strong language, and simulated sexual scenes. **31 October:** Ingrid Bergman returns to Broadway costarring with Colleen Dewhurst and Arthur Hill in an unfinished and previously unproduced Eugene O'Neill play, *More Stately Mansions*; the author had not wished it to be produced because it was unfinished.

1968 The Berkeley Repertory Theatre in California and the Alliance Theatre Company in Atlanta, Georgia, are established. Barbara Ann Teer founds the National Black Theatre. **2 January:** The Negro Ensemble Company stages its first production, Peter Weiss's *Song of the Lusitanian Bogey*, at St. Mark's Playhouse. **16 January:** Zoe Caldwell wins critical praise for her performance in the title role of Jay Presson Allen's adaptation of Muriel Sparks's novel, *The Prime of Miss Jean Brodie*, which opens at the Helen Hayes Theatre. **17 January:** Al Pacino appears in Israel Horovitz's *The Indian Wants the Bronx* at the Astor Place Theatre, scoring one of his first successes. **25 January:** Robert Anderson's *I Never Sang for My Father* premieres at the Longacre Theatre. **7 February:** Arthur Miller's *The Price,* about the sibling resentments of two middle-aged brothers, premieres at the Morosco Theatre. **14 February:** George C. Scott and Maureen Stapleton each play three characters when they open in Neil Simon's comedy, *Plaza Suite*, made up of three one-act plays set in the same hotel suite. **14 April:** Mart Crowley's drama depicting the lives of homosexual men, *The Boys in the Band*, is staged at the Theatre Four, running for over 1,000 performances. **13 June:** Rochelle Owens's *Futz!*, a one-act satire about the relationship of a boy and a pig, debuts at the Theatre De Lys. **3 October:** James Earl Jones and Jane Alexander win critical praise in Howard Sackler's *The Great White Hope* at the Alvin Theatre following a run at Washington, D.C.'s Arena Stage; the play wins the Pulitzer Prize, Tony Award, and New York Drama Critics Circle Award. **5 December:** Dustin Hoffman wins praise in Murray Schisgal's comedy, *Jimmy Shine*, at the Brooks Atkinson Theatre.

1969 Lanford Wilson and Marshall W. Mason found the Circle Theatre Company, eventually known as the Circle Repertory Theatre. **5 February:** Lonne Elder III's *Ceremonies in Dark Old Men* debuts at St. Mark's Playhouse in a Negro Ensemble Company production. **10 February:** Terrence McNally has a success with his comedy, *Next*, which is presented on a double bill with Elaine May's *Adaptation* at the Greenwich Mews Theatre. **12 February:** Woody Allen stars in his own comedy, *Play It Again, Sam*, which opens at the Broadhurst Theatre. **4 May:** Charles Gordone's *No Place to Be Somebody* wins the Pulitzer Prize, the first awarded to a black man and to an Off-Broadway production. **17 June:** The taboo-busting revue, *Oh! Calcutta!*, with skits exploring sexuality and nudity contributed by such noted writers as Samuel Beckett, Sam Shepard, and John Lennon, is staged to a controversial response at the Eden Theatre. **20 July:** NASA lands a man on the moon. **13 October:** Arthur Kopit's *Indians*, about the exploitation of Native Americans, begins a comparatively short run at the Brooks Atkinson Theatre. **21 October:** The long-running comedy, *Butterflies Are Free*, premieres at the Booth Theatre starring Blythe Danner, Keir Dullea, and Eileen Heckart. **28 December:** Neil Simon's comedy *Last of the Red Hot Lovers*, starring James Coco, opens at the Eugene O'Neill Theatre.

1970 Broadway productions continue to decline in number as Off-Broadway, Off-Off-Broadway, and regional theatres multiply. Newspapers report almost daily on controversies and attempts to censor the content of plays, whether in the areas of sexuality and nudity or politics and race. During the year, Joanne Alkalaitis founds the Mabou Mines theatre company and the Manhattan Theatre Club begins operation in New York. **7 April:** Paul Zindel's *The Effect of Gamma Rays on Man-in-the-Moon Marigolds* begins its run Off-Broadway at the Mercer-O'Casey Theatre and wins the Pulitzer Prize. **6 May:** Zoe Caldwell wins critical approval in the title role of Elinor Jones's *Colette*, adapted from Colette's writings, at the Ellen Stewart Theatre. **9 May:** Stars and producers read statements and ask audiences for moments of silence in memory of four students killed by National Guardsmen during protests of continued U.S. involvement in the Vietnam War at Kent State University. **30 June:** Bruce Jay Friedman's *Steambath*, directed by Anthony Perkins, opens at the Truck and Warehouse Theatre. **August:** Daniel Berrigan's *Trial of the Catonsville Nine* premieres at the Mark Taper Forum accompanied by FBI agents aiming to arrest Berrigan for destroying draft board records; Berrigan's play moves to Off-Broadway in February 1971. **13 December:** Maureen Stapleton gives an acclaimed performance in Neil Simon's *The Gingerbread Lady*, at the Plymouth Theatre, and wins a Tony Award.

1971   The John F. Kennedy Center for the Performing Arts is dedicated in Washington, D.C. Robert Moss founds Playwrights Horizons. The American Theatre Hall of Fame is established by Earl Blackwell, Gerald Ostreicher, James M. Nederlander, and Arnold Weissberger. A feminist group, Interart Theatre, is founded, and the Theatre of the New City, an Off-Off-Broadway company, is established. The Dell'Arte Players is founded in Blue Lake, California, by Carlo Mazzone-Clementi with an emphasis on mime and improvisation. **20 January:** Peter Brook's novel staging of *A Midsummer Night's Dream* transfers from London to New York's Billy Rose Theatre in a Royal Shakespeare Company production, winning critical kudos; increasingly, Broadway is dominated by such English transfers. **10 February:** John Guare's *The House of Blue Leaves* premieres at the Truck and Warehouse Theatre. **25 February:** Julie Harris, Estelle Parsons, and Nancy Marchand appear in Paul Zindel's *And Miss Reardon Drinks a Little* when it begins its run at the Morosco Theatre. **26 May:** Cliff Gorman is praised by critics for his performance in Julian Barry's *Lenny* based on the life of iconoclastic stand-up comic Lenny Bruce. **6 June:** Helen Hayes gives her farewell performance playing Mary Tyrone in a production of Eugene O'Neill's *Long Day's Journey into Night* in Washington, D.C. **7 November:** David Rabe's *Sticks and Bones*, a surreal drama about a Vietnam veteran returning to the United States, debuts at the Public Theatre before moving to Broadway, where it wins the Tony Award and a New York Drama Critics Circle Award. **11 November:** Neil Simon's *The Prisoner of Second Avenue* opens at the Eugene O'Neill Theatre. **14 November:** George Furth's *Twigs* stars Sada Thompson, who wins acclaim and a Tony Award playing three middle-aged sisters and their elderly mother, at the Broadhurst Theatre. **6 December:** The American Place Theatre is founded.

1972   The Alabama Shakespeare Festival is founded in Anniston, Alabama; John Housman establishes The Acting Company at the Juilliard School. The Indiana Repertory Theatre begins operations. Seattle, Washington's Intiman Theatre opens its doors. Ping Chong's first major work, *Lazarus*, opens at La MaMa Experimental Theatre Club. The Asian American Theatre Workshop is established in San Francisco, California. **21 February:** *Moonchildren*, Michael Weller's drama of "The Sixties" generation, premieres at the Royale Theatre with a cast including Edward Herrmann, James Woods, Christopher Guest, Jill Eikenberry, and Robert Prosky. **2 April:** Tennessee Williams's *Small Craft Warnings* opens at the Truck and Warehouse Theatre; during its run, Williams steps into the cast to play a role with the goal of boosting box office returns. **2 May:** *That Championship Season*, Jason Miller's searing drama about a reunion of high school basketball players turned unhappy grown men, premieres at the Public Theatre prior to a move to Broadway, where it wins the Pulitzer Prize and the Tony Award. **10 November:** Critic Eric Bentley's documentary drama, *Are You Now or Have You Ever Been*, chronicling the House Un-American Activities Committee anti-Communist witch hunt, is first performed at Yale University. **30 November:** Arthur Miller's biblical comedy, *The Creation of the World and Other Business*, opens at the Shubert Theatre to predominantly negative reviews and closes after 20 performances. **20 December:** Neil Simon's comedy about warring aging vaudevillians, *The Sunshine Boys*, scores a hit at the Broadhurst Theatre.

1973   **22 March:** Lanford Wilson's *Hot'l Baltimore* debuts Off-Off-Broadway in a Circle Repertory Company production before moving to the Circle in the Square Theatre for a long run. **27 March:** Joseph Walker's *The River Niger* opens in at Negro Ensemble Company production on Broadway at the Brooks Atkinson Theatre following an Off-Broadway run at St. Marks Theatre and wins the Tony Award. **4 June:** Mike Nichols directs an all-star cast, including George C. Scott, Nicol Williamson, Julie Christie, and Lillian Gish, in an acclaimed revival of Anton Chekhov's *Uncle Vanya* at the Circle in the Square Theatre. **25 June:** A discount ticket box office opens in Times Square, ultimately becoming known as TKTS. **8 November:** David Rabe's *In the Boom Boom Room* opens at the Vivian Beaumont Theatre. **27 November:** Neil Simon's adaptation of Anton Chekhov's stories, *The Good Doctor*, premieres at the Eugene O'Neill Theatre starring Christopher Plummer. **6 December:** Mark Medoff's *When You Comin' Back, Red Ryder?* is first performed at the Eastside Playhouse with Brad Dourif and Kevin Conway leading a strong cast. **29 December:** Eugene O'Neill's last play, *A Moon for the Misbegotten*, wins acclaim in a revival directed by José Quintero and starring Jason Robards and Colleen Dewhurst at the Morosco Theatre.

1974   The American Theatre Critics Association is founded. The Jewish Repertory Theatre begins operations. A feminist theatre group, At the Foot of the Mountain, is established in Minnesota. The Steppenwolf Theatre Company is formed in Chicago, Illinois. **2 January:** John Hopkins's gay-themed *Find Your Way Home* opens at the Brooks Atkinson Theatre, bringing Michael Moriarty a Tony Award for his performance. **5 May:** Terrence McNally's *Bad Habits* moves to Broadway's Booth Theatre following a successful Off-Broadway run. **23 May:** Miguel Piñero's harsh prison drama, *Short Eyes,* wins critical approval at the Vivian Beaumont Theatre following a run at the Public Theatre. **5 June:** A headline in *Variety* announces "Theatre Is Now a National Invalid" lamenting the falloff in theatre productions, the decline of Broadway, and the paucity of outstanding playwrights. **9 August:** Richard M. Nixon resigns the U.S. presidency in the midst of the Watergate scandal; Gerald R. Ford becomes the 38th President of the United

States **24 September:** Tennessee Williams's *Cat on a Hot Tin Roof* opens in a hit revival that wins acclaim for Elizabeth Ashley as "Maggie the Cat." **24 October:** *Equus*, Peter Shaffer's intense drama of a psychiatrist attempting to fathom the reasons why a young man blinds horses, opens at the Plymouth Theatre following a successful run in London; the play wins a Tony Award and a New York Drama Critics Circle Award.

1975 South Vietnam surrenders to North Vietnam, which essentially ends the Vietnam War. North Carolina's Playmakers Repertory Company (PRC) is established. **20 January:** Terrence McNally's farce, *The Ritz*, set in a gay steambath, opens at the Longacre Theatre. **26 January:** Edward Albee's *Seascape* premieres at the Shubert Theatre and wins the Pulitzer Prize. **4 May:** Ed Bullins's drama of a black man raping a white woman, *The Taking of Miss Janie*, debuts at the Mitzi E. Newhouse Theatre. **26 June:** George C. Scott scores a personal triumph in a Circle in the Square revival of *Death of a Salesman*, which he also directs with a cast including Teresa Wright, Harvey Keitel, and James Farentino. **29 September:** David Mamet's *Sexual Perversity in Chicago* debuts at St. Clements Church and wins an Obie Award. **30 December:** An all-star revival of George S. Kaufman and Edna Ferber's *The Royal Family* wins critical acclaim at the Helen Hayes Theatre, with a cast including Eva Le Gallienne, George Grizzard, Rosemary Harris, and Sam Levene.

1976 The multiethnic Mixed Blood Theatre Company is founded in Minneapolis, Minnesota. **3 February:** Katharine Hepburn returns to Broadway in Enid Bagnold's *A Matter of Gravity* with a cast including Christoper Reeve at the Broadhurst Theatre. **22 March:** Jack Heifner's *Vanities*, a comedy-drama about the lives of three cheerleaders from the day of President John F. Kennedy's assassination to the present day, debuts at the Westside Theatre. **28 April:** Julie Harris scores a personal triumph as Emily Dickinson in the one-woman play, William Luce's *The Belle of Amherst*, at the Longacre Theatre. **10 June:** Neil Simon's comedy, *California Suite,* opens at the Eugene O'Neill Theatre. **15 September:** Ntozake Shange's *for colored girls who have considered suicide/when the rainbow is enuf*, a poetic drama about the coming-of-age experiences of black women, premieres at the Public Theatre with Shange among the cast. **12 December:** Charles Fuller's *The Brownsville Raid* is staged at the Theatre De Lys in a Negro Ensemble Company production. **14 December:** *Sly Fox*, Larry Gelbart's adaptation of Ben Jonson's *Volpone*, opens at the Broadhurst Theatre starring George C. Scott.

1977 The Pan Asian Theatre Company and Theatre Rhinoceros, a gay theatre company, are founded. **16 February:** David Mamet's *American Buffalo*, directed by Ulu Grosbard, opens at the Barrymore Theatre to critics complaining of the play's strong language. **31 March:** Actor Michael Cristofer's *The Shadow Box*, a play about the lives of people turning to hospice care, wins the Pulitzer Prize and a Tony Award. **24 April:** Al Pacino wins critical approval when he appears at the Longacre Theatre in the title role of David Rabe's Vietnam-themed play, *The Basic Training of Pavlo Hummel*, revived on Broadway six years following its Off-Broadway premiere. **5 May:** Maria Irene Fornés's feminist drama, *Fefu and Her Friends*, debuts at the American Place Theatre. **21 May:** Albert Innaurato's comedy-drama about a college student contemplating his sexuality in Philadelphia, *Gemini*, moves to the Little Theatre following a successful Off-Broadway run. **6 October:** Directed by Mike Nichols, Hume Cronyn and Jessica Tandy appear in the Pulitzer Prize-winning two-character drama *The Gin Game*, by D. L. Coburn, at the John Golden Theatre. **20 October:** David Mamet's *A Life in the Theatre* premieres at the Theatre De Lys. Frank Langella scores a personal triumph in the title role of a revival of John Balderson and Hamilton Deane's *Dracula*, adapted from Bram Stoker's novel, at the Martin Beck Theatre in a production designed by Edward Gorey. **21 October:** Wendy Wasserstein's feminist play, *Uncommon Women and Others*, is staged at the Marymount Manhattan Theatre. **4 December:** Neil Simon's *Chapter Two*, a semiautobiographical play about a widower who falls in love again opens at the Imperial Theatre. **28 December:** Jason Robards returns to Eugene O'Neill's plays in a revival of O'Neill's *A Touch of the Poet*, costarring with Geraldine Fitzgerald, at the Helen Hayes Theatre.

1978 5 January: David Mamet's *The Water Engine* is produced at the Public Theatre. **2 February:** Harvey Fierstein's one-act, *The International Stud*, a comedy-drama about a drag queen, is staged at the La MaMa Experimental Theatre Club; the play is the first of three ultimately titled *Torch Song Trilogy*. **26 February:** Ira Levin's long-running thriller, *Deathtrap*, opens at the Music Box Theatre. **2 March:** Sam Shepard's *Curse of the Starving Class* arrives at the Public Theatre following a run at London's Royal Court Theatre the previous year, and it wins an Obie Award. **27 April:** Lanford Wilson's *Fifth of July*, about a gay disabled Vietnam veteran and his family, premieres in a Circle Repertory Company production. **1 May:** Barnard Hughes wins critical acclaim in the title role of Hugh Leonard's *Da* at the Morosco Theatre and wins the Tony Award and the New York Drama Critics Circle Award. **1 June:** Jack Lemmon returns to Broadway in Bernard Slade's *Tribute* at the Brooks Atkinson Theatre with more praise for Lemmon than the play. **3 October:** Henry Fonda and Jane Alexander win critical kudos in Jerome Lawrence and Robert E. Lee's *The First Monday in October* at the Majestic Theatre. **5 December:** Sam Shepard's *Buried Child*, a dark drama about a dysfunctional American family, opens at the Theatre De Lys and wins the Pulitzer Prize.

1979 The Second Stage Theatre is founded to produce worthy plays that experienced problems in their original productions. **28 January:** Veteran actress Constance Cummings wins praise and a Tony Award for her performance as a stroke victim in Arthur Kopit's *Wings* at the Lyceum Theatre, where it runs following its debut at the Public Theatre. **18 February:** Newspapers report that Asian American actors picket the Public Theatre demanding more opportunities. **28 February:** Ernest Thompson's *On Golden Pond*, a comedy-drama about an elderly couple facing the end of their lives, debuts at the Apollo Theatre starring Frances Sternhagen and Tom Aldredge. **25 March:** Luis Valdez's *Zoot Suit* moves to the Winter Garden Theatre following a successful run at the Mark Taper Forum; the musical play illuminates Chicano life in California. **17 April:** Scottish actor Tom Conti wins acclaim in Brian Clark's drama about a disabled man, *Whose Life Is It Anyway?*, at the Trafalgar Theatre. **19 April:** Bernard Pomerance's drama set in the nineteenth century concerning the life of deformed John Merrick, *The Elephant Man*, opens at the Booth Theatre and wins the Tony Award and the New York Drama Critics Circle Award. **3 May:** Lanford Wilson's *Talley's Folly*, a prequel to his *Fifth of July*, debuts in a Circle Repertory Company production and wins the Pulitzer Prize and the New York Drama Critics Circle Award. **6 June:** Michael Weller's *Loose Ends* premieres at the Circle in the Square Theatre. **2 December:** Martin Sherman's *Bent*, a grim drama about the persecution of homosexuals by the Nazis, begins a run at the Apollo Theatre. **13 December:** Samm-Art Williams's *Home*, concerning a black man's refusal to serve in Vietnam, is staged by the Negro Ensemble Company at St. Mark's Playhouse.

1980 Robert Brustein founds the American Repertory Theatre. The lesbian theatre company, Split Britches Theatre, is established. **31 January:** Edward Albee's *The Lady from Dubuque* premieres at the Morosco Theatre starring Irene Worth; the play, dismissed by critics, closes within two weeks. **30 March:** Mark Medoff's *Children of a Lesser God*, concerning a deaf woman who marries her teacher, opens at the Longacre Theatre and wins the Tony Award. **10 April:** A revival of Paul Osborn's failed 1939 comedy *Morning's at Seven* scores a major hit at the Lycem Theatre with a cast including veteran actresses Elizabeth Wilson, Nancy Marchand, Teresa Wright, and Maureen O'Sullivan. **30 April:** Neil Simon's *I Ought to Be in Pictures* debuts at the Eugene O'Neill Theatre. **8 June:** David Henry Hwang's *FOB* is staged at the Public Theatre. **8 October:** Steven Tesich's *Division Street* opens at the Ambassador Theatre for a short run starring John Lithgow. **17 December:** Peter Shaffer's *Amadeus*, exploring the rivalry of Wolfgang Amadeus Mozart and Antonio Salieri, transfers from London to the Broadhurst Theatre and wins a Tony Award. **21 December:** Beth Henley's *Crimes of the Heart*, about the relationship of three Southern sisters, opens at the Manhattan Theatre Club (MTC) and wins the Pulitzer Prize. **23 December:** Sam Shepard's *True West* is staged at the Public Theatre following a run at the Steppenwolf Theatre.

1981   5 February: Jane Lapotaire wins critical kudos in the title role of Pam Gems's *Piaf* at the Plymouth Theatre. **7 May:** Film star Elizabeth Taylor makes her Broadway debut in a well-received revival of Lillian Hellman's *The Little Foxes* at the Martin Beck Theatre; the supporting cast includes Maureen Stapleton and Anthony Zerbe. **21 October:** Christopher Durang's controversial satire of a nun and her pupils, *Sister Mary Ignatius Explains It All for You*, opens at Playwrights Horizons. **20 November:** Charles Fuller's *A Soldier's Play*, about a murder among black soldiers in World War II, is staged by the Negro Ensemble Company production at the Theatre Four and wins the Pulitzer Prize.

1982   Boston University establishes the Huntington Theatre Company (HTC), which becomes a not-for-profit theatre in 1986. **15 January:** Harvey Fierstein stars in his own *Torch Song Trilogy* at the Actors Playhouse, and later moves to Broadway's Little Theatre, where it wins the Tony Award. **3 February:** *Variety* reports that "B'Way Season Looms As Worst in Years: Hit Shows Scarce, Attendance Down." James Earl Jones and Christopher Plummer are praised by critics in a revival of *Othello* at the Winter Garden Theatre. **24 February:** A. R. Gurney's *The Dining Room* premieres at Playwrights Horizons. **30 March:** John Pielmeier's drama *Agnes of God*, concerning the murder of a baby in a convent, wins critical praise for its stars, Amanda Plummer, Geraldine Page, and Elizabeth Ashley, but little for the play. **2 May:** Zoe Caldwell is acclaimed for her performance in the title role of a revival of Robinson Jeffers's adaptation of *Medea* at the Cort Theatre with Judith Anderson, who played Medea in the original 1947 production, appearing as the Nurse. **4 May:** Athol Fugard's *Master Harold . . . and the Boys*, concerning race relations in South Africa, opens at the Lyceum Theatre. **11 November:** Hume Cronyn and Jessica Tandy return to Broadway in *Foxfire*, a drama about an Appalachian Mountain family written by Cronyn and Susan Cooper, at the Barrymore Theatre. **29 December:** Caryl Churchill's feminist play, *Top Girls*, makes its American debut at the Public Theatre.

1983   The first Asian American theatre company, MinaSama-No, is founded in Chicago, Illinois. **22 February:** A legendary theatrical flop, *Moose Murders*, opens and closes at the Eugene O'Neill Theatre. **27 March:** Neil Simon's *Brighton Beach Memoirs*, the first of three semi-autobiographical plays Simon writes, opens at the Alvin Theatre, wins the New York Drama Critics Circle Award, and runs for over 1,500 performances. **31 March:** Marsha Norman's dark drama about a suicidal woman, *'night, Mother*, premieres at the John Golden Theatre and wins the Pulitzer Prize. **4 April:** An all-star revival of George S. Kaufman and Moss Hart's *You Can't Take It with You* begins a run at the Plymouth Theatre; the cast includes Jason Robards, Colleen Dewhurst, James Coco, and Elizabeth Wilson—it is subsequently filmed for television. **26 May:** Sam Shepard's *Fool for Love* debuts in a Circle Repertory Company production. **22 November:** Tina Howe's *Painting Churches* is staged at the Lambs Theatre. **11 December:** Michael Frayn's backstage farce, *Noises Off*, a hit in London, begins a long run at the Brooks Atkinson Theatre.

1984   The number of Broadway productions for 1984–1985 drops to 31. **25 March:** David Mamet's *Glengarry Glen Ross*, a bleak drama about corruption among real estate salesmen, opens at the John Golden Theatre and wins the Pulitzer Prize. **29 March:** Dustin Hoffman is acclaimed in the title role in a revival of Arthur Miller's *Death of a Salesman* at the Broadhurst Theatre, with a cast including Kate Reid and John Malkovich. **27 May:** Beth Henley's *The Miss Firecracker Contest* debuts at the Manhattan Theatre Club. **31 May:** Chicago's Steppenwolf Theatre brings its revival of Lanford Wilson's *Balm in Gilead* to New York, winning critical kudos at the Circle Repertory Company. **7 August:** David Rabe's *Hurlyburly* moves from Off-Broadway to Broadway's Barrymore Theatre with a cast including William Hurt, Harvey Keitel, Sigourney Weaver, Judith Ivey, Christopher Walken, Cynthia Nixon, and Jerry Stiller. **September:** Charles Ludlam's camp pastiche *The Mystery of Irma Vep,* debuts Off-Off-Broadway in a Ridiculous Theatrical Company production. **11 October:** August Wilson's *Ma Rainey's Black Bottom* opens at the Cort Theatre and wins the New York Drama Critics Circle Award; Wilson's drama set in a 1920s' recording studio, is his first Broadway production. **1 November:** Larry Shue's farcical comedy, *The Foreigner*, is staged at the Astor Place Theatre; the play will have a long run and become a staple of regional, community, and university theatres.

1985   David Mamet and William H. Macy found the Atlantic Theatre Company. **21 January:** John DiFusco's *Tracers*, about Vietnam War veterans, is staged at the Public Theatre. **21 February:** Maria Irene Fornés's *The Conduct of Life*, dealing with the relationship of sexual power and violence, premieres at the Theatre for a New City. **28 March:** Neil Simon's semi-autobiographical comedy-drama set during World War II, *Biloxi Blues*, scores a hit at the Neil Simon Theatre and wins the Tony Award as well as critical praise for its star, Matthew Broderick. **21 April:** Larry Kramer's *The Normal Heart*, an indictment of the failure of various government, medical, and social institutions to respond adequately to the AIDS pandemic, begins a controversial run at the Public Theatre. **1 May:** William Hoffman's AIDS-themed drama, *As*

Is, debuts at the Circle Repertory Company. **16 May:** Christopher Durang's satiric comedy about a married couple, *The Marriage of Bette and Boo*, is staged at the Public Theatre. **19 June:** Charles Busch's camp satire *Vampire Lesbians of Sodom* begins an over 2,000 performance run at the Provincetown Playhouse. **27 August:** Wallace Shawn's *Aunt Dan and Lemon*, a controversial play about a woman fascinated with Nazism, debuts in London in a New York Shakespeare Festival production. **11 November:** *I'm Not Rappaport*, Herb Gardner's drama of the friendship between two old men, one black and one white, opens at the Booth Theatre and wins the Tony Award. **5 December:** Sam Shepard's drama of two families bound together by the violent marriage of their offspring, *A Lie of the Mind*, is staged by Shepard at the Promenade Theatre.

1986   9 March: Kevin Kline garners critical praise for his performance in *Hamlet* at the Public Theatre. **13 March:** Emily Mann's *Execution of Justice* about the trial of Dan White, the murderer of Harvey Milk, ekes out a short run on Broadway at the Virginia Theatre. **4 June:** Spalding Gray appears in his monologue drama, *Swimming to Cambodia*, at the Mitzi Newhouse Theatre for a short run. **19 November:** Tina Howe's *Coastal Disturbances* has a brief run at the Second Stage with praise for leading lady Annette Bening. **4 December:** The third of Neil Simon's semi-autobiographical plays, *Broadway Bound*, opens at the Broadhurst Theatre, with Linda Lavin winning acclaim for her performance.

1987   26 March: August Wilson's *Fences*, a drama set in 1940s' Pittsburgh about an ex-baseball player from the Negro leagues and his family, is critically acclaimed at the 46th Street Theatre and wins the Pulitzer Prize, a Tony Award, and the New York Drama Critics Circle Award. **15 April:** Alfred Uhry's *Driving Miss Daisy* debuts at Playwrights Horizons and ultimately wins the Pulitzer Prize. **28 May:** Eric Bogosian appears in his own play, *Talk Radio*, at the Public Theatre. **19 June:** Robert Harling's comedy-drama about the friendship of Southern women, *Steel Magnolias*, premieres at the Lucille Lortel Theatre following a run at the WPA Theatre. **13 October:** Terrence McNally's *Frankie and Johnny in the Clair de Lune* is staged at the Manhattan Theatre Club. **14 October:** John Malkovich and Joan Allen star in Lanford Wilson's *Burn This* at the Plymouth Theatre, following runs at the Mark Taper Forum and Circle Repertory Company. **1 September:** Rocco Landesman assumes the presidency of Jujamcyn Theatres.

1988   The Irish Repertory Theatre is founded in New York. **14 February:** The inter-active *Tony n' Tina's Wedding* begins its phenomenally long run. **20 March:** David Henry Hwang's *M. Butterfly* premieres at the Eugene O'Neill Theatre starring John Lithgow and B. D. Wong and wins the Best

Play Tony Award. **27 March:** August Wilson's *Joe Turner's Come and Gone*, the 1910s' entry in his 10-play series of decade-by-decade plays about African Americans, premieres at the Barrymore Theatre and wins the New York Drama Critics Circle Award. **14 June:** Jason Robards and Colleen Dewhurst appear in a revival of Eugene O'Neill's *Long Day's Journey into Night* at the Neil Simon Theatre under José Quintero's direction; the production plays in repertory with O'Neill's comedy, *Ah, Wilderness!* **20 October:** A. R. Gurney's *The Cocktail Party* debuts at the Promenade Theatre starring Nancy Marchand, following a run at the Old Globe Theatre in San Diego, California. **17 November:** Neil Simon's *Rumors* opens at the Broadhurst Theatre.

1989 The Asian American Ma-Yi Theatre Company and the National Asian-American Theatre Company are founded in New York. **5 January:** Richard Greenberg's *Eastern Standard*, a comedy about well-to-do Manhattanites, debuts at the John Golden Theatre following a run at the Manhattan Theatre Club (MTC). **16 February:** Jerry Sterner's *Other People's Money*, dramatizing hostile corporate takeovers, is staged at the Minetta Lane Theatre. **2 March:** Ken Ludwig's farce *Lend Me a Tenor* premieres at the Royale Theatre. **9 March:** Wendy Wasserstein's *The Heidi Chronicles* opens at Broadway's Plymouth Theatre following a run at Playwrights Horizons; starring Joan Allen, the play wins the Pulitzer Prize, a Tony Award, and the New York Drama Critics Circle Award. **19 March:** Constance Congdon's *Tales of the Lost Formicans*, a comedy-drama about aliens observing a troubled American family, debuts at the Actors Theatre of Louisville. **6 June:** Terrence McNally's *The Lisbon Traviata*, starring Nathan Lane as a gay opera buff, wins critical kudos at the Manhattan Theatre Club. **22 August:** A. R. Gurney's two-character *Love Letters*, about a lifelong correspondence of two lovers, begins a run at the Edison Theatre following its debut Off-Broadway; numerous well-known actors will play the roles, often as fundraisers for various theatres and causes. **15 November:** Aaron Sorkin's *A Few Good Men*, a military courtroom drama, opens at the Music Box Theatre; following an increasing trend. **14 December:** Robert Morse wins acclaim and a Tony Award playing Truman Capote in Jay Presson Allen's one-character play, *Tru*, at the Booth Theatre.

1990 The National Endowment of the Arts withdraws grants to four artists (subsequently known as the NEA Four) over what is deemed obscene works; the artists include performance artists Karen Finley, Holly Hughes, and Tim Miller. **9 February:** Eric Bogosian's *Sex, Drugs, Rock & Roll* debuts at the Orpheum Theatre with Bogosian the sole performer. **14 March:** Craig Lucas's romantic fantasy, *Prelude to a Kiss*, opens Off-Broadway prior to a transfer to Broadway. **21 March:** Kathleen Turner is praised by critics in a revival of Tennessee Williams's *Cat on a Hot Tin Roof* at the Eugene O'Neill Theatre. **22 March:** The Steppenwolf Theatre's acclaimed production of Frank Galati's adaptation of John Steinbeck's novel, *The Grapes of Wrath*, moves from Chicago to Broadway's Cort Theatre and wins the Tony Award. **16 April:** August Wilson's *The Piano Lesson*, set in the 1930s as an African American family decides what to do with an heirloom piano, premieres at the Walter Kerr Theatre, winning the Pulitzer Prize and the New York Drama Critics Circle Award. **14 June:** John Guare's *Six Degrees of Separation*, concerning a young black man attempting to convince a wealthy white couple that he is Sidney Poitier's son, opens at the Mitzi E. Newhouse Theatre.

1991 The Gulf War begins. With the goal of encouraging nonmusical plays, the Broadway Alliance is founded. The Signature Theatre Company is established in New York. **21 February:** Neil Simon's *Lost in Yonkers*, concerning two young boys left with a formidable grandmother and a mentally challenged aunt in the 1940s, premieres at the Richard Rodgers Theatre and wins the Pulitzer Prize and Tony Award. **17 March:** *The Substance of Fire*, Jon Robin Baitz's drama about a Holocaust survivor publishing scholarship on Nazi medical experiments, debuts at Playwrights Horizons. **14 April:** The Steppenwolf Theatre Company moves into a new state-of-the-art theatre space in Chicago, Illinois. **25 June:** Terrence McNally's *Lips Together, Teeth Apart* begins a run at the Manhattan Theatre Club. **10 December:** Tony Randall's National Actors Theatre offers a revival of Arthur Miller's *The Crucible* as its first production at the Belasco Theatre.

1992 New York's Mint Theatre Company, dedicated to reviving neglected American and English plays, is founded. **29 January:** Paula Vogel's *The Baltimore Waltz* premieres in a Circle Repertory Company production and wins an Obie Award. **24 March:** Neil Simon's *Jake's Women* receives tepid reviews at the Neil Simon Theatre. **29 March:** Herb Gardner's *Conversations with My Father* premieres at the Royale Theatre and wins acclaim for Judd Hirsch's Tony Award-winning performance. **12 April:** Jessica Lange and Alec Baldwin are critically praised for their performances in a revival of Tennessee Williams's *A Streetcar Named Desire* at the Barrymore Theatre. **13 April:** August Wilson's *Two Trains Running*, set in an African American restaurant in Pittsburgh in 1969, is staged at the Walter Kerr Theatre and wins the New York Drama Critics Circle Award. **12 May:** Anna Deavere Smith's solo performance of her *Fires in the Mirror*, concerning contemporary racial conflicts, begins a run at the Public Theatre. **20 October:** Larry Kramer's *The Destiny of Me*, a sequel to his AIDS-themed *The Normal Heart*, opens at the Lucille Lortel Theatre. **22 October:** Wendy Wasserstein's *The Sisters*

Rosensweig, a comedy-drama about three middle-aged sisters, debuts at the Mitzi E. Newhouse Theatre prior to a move to Broadway. **25 October:** David Mamet's controversial two-character drama, *Oleanna*, concerning political correctness and sexual harassment, begins performances at the Orpheum Theatre. **27 October:** John Leguizamo's *Spic-O-Rama*, a solo performance, opens at the Westside Theatre.

1993 Neil LaBute's first major play, *In the Company of Men*, is performed at Brigham Young University. **14 January:** Natasha Richardson, daughter of English actress Vanessa Redgrave, wins critical acclaim in the Roundabout Theatre Company's revival of Eugene O'Neill's *Anna Christie*, costarring with Liam Neeson. **25 February:** "New vaudevillians" Bill Irwin and David Shiner appear in *Fool Moon* at the Richard Rodgers Theatre and run for over 1,000 performances. **March:** Jane Martin's *Keely and Du*, an abortion-themed play, premieres at the Actors Theatre of Louisville's Humana Festival of New Plays; it is ultimately revealed that Jane Martin is a pseudonym for the ATL's artistic director, Jon Jory. **6 March:** Paul Rudnick's *Jeffrey*, a comedy about a gay man's life in the era of AIDS, debuts at the Minetta Lane Theatre starring John Michael Higgins. **4 May:** Tony Kushner's *Angels in America, Part One: Millennium Approaches*, an epic "gay fantasia" of life in America during the 1980s, opens at the Walter Kerr Theatre and wins the Pulitzer Prize, a Tony Award, and the New York Drama Critics Circle Award; the second play, *Perestroika*, opens a few months later and plays in repertory with *Millennium Approaches* and wins a Tony Award as well. **27 June:** Terrence McNally's *A Perfect Ganesh*, about the spiritual search in India of two aging women, debuts at the Manhattan Theatre Club starring Zoe Caldwell and Frances Sternhagen. **14 November:** Robert Schenkkan's *The Kentucky Cycle* is staged at the Royale Theatre; the play won a Pulitzer Prize while running at the Mark Taper Forum following a run in Seattle, but it fails to find a Broadway audience and closes within a month. **22 November:** Neil Simon's *Laughter on the 23rd Floor*, starring Nathan Lane as a television comedy writer during the 1950s, opens at the Richard Rodgers Theatre.

1994 Only 29 productions are seen on Broadway during 1994–1995. The Drama Dept., a nonprofit theatre collective with the mission of producing new plays or forgotten American classics, begins operation. **13 February:** Edward Albee wins a third Pulitzer Prize when his drama, *Three Tall Women*, premieres at the Vineyard Theatre prior to a move to Broadway, where it wins the New York Drama Critics Circle Award. **17 April:** Anna Deavere Smith appears in her solo play about the Los Angeles race riots sparked by the Rodney King beating, *Twilight: Los Angeles, 1992*, at the Cort Theatre. **4 June:**

The National Endowment of the Arts finally awards grants to the controversial "NEA Four," whose grants were revoked on claims of obscenity in 1990. **1 November:** Terrence McNally's AIDS-themed comedy, *Love! Valour! Compassion!*, debuts at the Manhattan Theatre Club before transferring to Broadway, where it wins the Tony Award. **12 December:** Tony Kushner's *Slavs! Thinking about the Longstanding Problems of Virtue and Happiness* is produced at the New York Theatre Workshop; the play is described as a coda to Kushner's *Angels in America* plays and is set in the collapsing Soviet Union at the time of the Chernobyl nuclear accident.

1995   6 April: Sarah Delaney's *Having Our Say*, about the close relationship of two elderly black sisters, debuts at the Booth Theatre. **9 April:** Neil Simon's *London Suite* opens to middling reviews and a short run. **July:** Pearl Cleage's *Blues for an Alabama Sky* premieres at the Alliance Theatre in Atlanta, Georgia. **24 August:** Nicky Silver's *The Food Chain* is staged at the Westside Upstairs Theatre. **1 October:** Carol Burnett returns to Broadway in Ken Ludwig's backstage farce, *Moon over Buffalo*, at the Martin Beck Theatre; Burnett costars with Philip Bosco. **24 October:** Uta Hagen wins critical approval in her final stage appearance in Nicholas Wright's *Mrs. Klein* at the Lucille Lortel Theatre. **5 November:** Terrence McNally's *Master Class*, starring Zoe Caldwell as Maria Callas, premieres at the John Golden Theatre and wins the Tony Award.

1996   Eve Ensler begins performing her controversial *The Vagina Monologues* and wins an Obie Award for this groundbreaking examination of women's bodies and attitudes about sexuality and rape. The Flea Theatre is established in an attempt to revive the glory days of Off-Off-Broadway theatre and wins a 2004 Drama Desk Award for distinguished achievement. **28 March:** August Wilson's *Seven Guitars*, set among African Americans in 1940s' Pittsburgh, premieres at the Walter Kerr Theatre and wins the New York Drama Critics Circle Award. **21 April:** Edward Albee's *A Delicate Balance* is revived at the Nederlander Theatre and wins acclaim for the play and its cast, including Rosemary Harris, George Grizzard, Elaine Stritch, and Mary Beth Hurt. **30 April:** Sam Shepard's Pulitzer Prize-winning play, *Buried Child*, opens on Broadway in a revival—his first on Broadway—in a Steppenwolf Theatre production. **22 August:** Al Pacino is lauded for his performance in a revival of Eugene O'Neill's *Hughie* at the Circle in the Square. **17 September:** The Atlantic Theatre Company revives David Mamet's *Edmond* to critical praise, despite the play's earlier failure.

1997   27 February: Alfred Uhry's *The Last Night of Ballyhoo*, concerning anti-Semitism at the time of the 1939 Atlanta premiere of *Gone With* *the Wind*, debuts at the Helen Hayes Theatre and wins the Tony Award. **9 March:** Naomi Wallace's *One Flea Spare*, a grim drama of the Black Plague, is staged at the Public Theatre and wins an Obie Award. **16 March:** Paula Vogel's *How I Learned to Drive*, focused on the moral questions surrounding an incestuous relationship between an uncle and his niece, premieres at the Vineyard Theatre and wins the 1998 Pulitzer Prize, the Drama Desk Award, and the New York Drama Critics Circle Award. **25 March:** Christopher Plummer wins critical praise playing John Barrymore in the solo play, *Barrymore*, at the Music Box Theatre. **27 March:** Horton Foote's *The Young Man from Atlanta* premieres at the Longacre Theatre and wins the Pulitzer Prize. **13 April:** Wendy Wasserstein's *An American Daughter* opens at the Cort Theatre starring Kate Nelligan, but critics are not appreciative. **20 May:** Donald Margulies' *Collected Stories* is staged at the Manhattan Theatre Club. **12 November:** Richard Greenberg's *Three Days of Rain* begins a run at the Manhattan Theatre Club with a cast including Patricia Clarkson, Bradley Whitford, and John Slattery. **7 December:** Tina Howe's *Pride's Crossing* opens at the Mitzi E. Newhouse Theatre and wins the New York Drama Critics Circle Award and a Drama Desk Award for actress Cherry Jones.

1998   **31 May:** Craig Lucas's *The Dying Gaul* opens at the Vineyard Theatre focusing on the moral compromises posed to a screenwriter and his script about AIDS. **25 June:** Warren Leight's *Side Man*, probing the lives of jazz musicians, is staged at the Criterion Center Stage Right and wins the Tony Award. **19 September:** Margaret Edson's *Wit* debuts at the Manhattan Class Company and wins the 1999 Pulitzer Prize, Drama Desk Award, and Outer Critics Circle Award. **5 October:** Joe DiPietro's comedy, *Over the River and through the Woods*, concerning a family striving to keep their son from leaving New Jersey, debuts at the John Houseman Theatre. **13 October:** Controversy, pickets, and bomb threats accompany a production of Terrence McNally's *Corpus Christi* at the Manhattan Theatre Club, but it wins the Drama Desk and New York Drama Critics Circle Award. **18 October:** Tracy Letts's *Killer Joe*, a black comedy about a violent trailer park family, begins a run at Soho Playhouse. **16 December:** Amy Freed's *Freedomland* opens at Playwrights Horizons. **19 December:** The United States Congress votes to impeach President Bill Clinton on charges of perjury and obstruction of justice; he is subsequently acquitted.

1999   The Classical Theatre Company of Harlem is founded at the Harlem School of the Arts. **25 February:** Tennessee Williams's early play set in a prison, *Not About Nightingales*, is staged at the Circle in the Square Theatre following a successful London production. **16 May:** Rebecca Gilman's *Spinning into Butter*, concerning the ramifications of a racial incident on a college campus, premieres at the Goodman Theatre in Chicago prior to its New York production. **4 November:** Donald Margulies' *Dinner with Friends* opens at the Variety Arts Theatre under Daniel Sullivan's direction and wins the 2000 Pulitzer Prize, the Outer Critics Circle Award, and the Lucille Lortel Award. **November:** Suzan-Lori Parks's *In the Blood* is produced at the Public Theatre with Charlayne Woodard heading the cast.

2000 **February:** The Tectonic Theatre Project debuts its production of *The Laramie Project*, which is based on interviews with the citizens of Laramie, Wyoming, in the aftermath of the hate crime murder of gay college student Matthew Shepard; the production is first performed at the Ricketson Theatre in a Denver Theatre Center production. **1 February:** Edward Albee's *The Play about the Baby* premieres at Century Center for the Performing Arts following a run at the Alley Theatre and wins the Lucille Lortel Award. **22 March:** Kenneth Lonergan's *The Waverly Gallery* opens at the Promenade Theatre starring Eileen Heckart, who wins an Obie and a Drama Desk Award. **9 April:** Arthur Miller's *The Ride Down Mt. Morgan*, previously produced in London and at the Public Theatre, is produced at the Ambassador Theatre to mixed reviews. **23 May:** David Auburn's *Proof* is staged at the Manhattan Theatre Club and wins the 2001 Pulitzer Prize, Tony Award, and the Drama Desk Award when it moves to Broadway's Walter Kerr Theatre. **14 September:** Pamela Gien's *The Syringa Tree*, a solo play performed by Gien, is presented at Playhouse 91 and wins an Obie Award. **2 November:** Charles Busch's *The Tale of the Allergist's Wife* opens at the Ethel Barrymore Theatre following an Off-Broadway run, winning the Outer Critics Circle John Gassner Award. **7 November:** The vote is so close in the United States presidential election that a victor cannot be determined for a month; ultimately, George W. Bush is declared winner.

2001 **1 May:** August Wilson's *King Hedley II* debuts at Virginia Theatre following runs at the Pittsburgh Public Theatre and in other regional theatres and is nominated for a Tony Award and a Drama Desk Award. **26 July:** Suzan-Lori Parks's *Topdog/Underdog* premieres at the Public Theatre, wins the 2002 Pulitzer Prize and the Drama Desk Award, and critical acclaim for actors Jeffrey Wright and Mos Def. **11 September:** Terrorists crash two airplanes into the World Trade Center, causing its twin towers to collapse; another plane crashes into the Pentagon in Washington, D.C., and a fourth crashes in a field in Pennsylvania; New York City is in a state of emergency for several days, shutting down theatres and many businesses, but a sign of renewal comes when Broadway and Off-Broadway theatres reopen a few days later. **30 October:** Rebecca Gilman's *The Glory of Living* is staged at the Manhattan Class Company under Philip Seymour Hoffman's direction.

November: Melissa James Gibson's play, *[sic]*, set among twenty-something artistic New Yorkers, opens at the Soho Repertory Theatre. **19 December:** Tony Kushner's Obie Award-winning *Homebody/Kabul*, an examination of the West's relationship to Afghanistan as seen through the eyes of an unhappy English family, begins a run at the New York Theatre Workshop (NYTW); critics hail it as prophetic since the play was written and in rehearsal prior to the 9/11 tragedies.

2002 **21 February:** Mary Zimmerman's Lookingglass Theatre Company production, *Metamorphoses*, moves to the Circle in the Square Theatre following runs in Chicago and Off-Broadway. **10 March:** Edward Albee's play about an unconventional love affair, *The Goat, or Who Is Sylvia?*, premieres at the John Golden Theatre and wins the Tony Award. **22 October:** Dael Orlandersmith's *Yellowman* opens at the Manhattan Theatre Club with the author in the cast. **18 December:** Neil LaBute's *The Mercy Seat* begins a run at the Manhattan Theatre Club.

2003 **27 February:** Richard Greenberg's *Take Me Out*, concerning the first "out" Major League baseball player, opens at the Walter Kerr Theatre following a successful run at London's Donmar Warehouse and wins the Tony Award and the Drama Desk Award. **25 September:** Theresa Rebeck and Alexandra Gersten-Vassilaros's *Omnium Gatherum* begins a run at the Variety Arts Theatre. **3 December:** Doug Wright's *I Am My Own Wife*, a solo show starring Jefferson Mays (who wins a Tony Award), debuts at the Lyceum Theatre and wins the Pulitzer Prize, the Tony Award, and the Drama Desk Award. **16 November:** Nilo Cruz's *Anna in the Tropics* wins the Pulitzer Prize.

2004 **17 February:** Craig Lucas's *Small Tragedy* debuts at Playwrights Horizons and wins an Obie Award. **2 March:** Charles Mee's *Wintertime* commences a run at the Second Stage Theatre under David Schweizer's direction. **11 May:** Christopher Shinn's *Where Do We Live Now?*, which he also directs, opens at the Vineyard Theatre and wins an Obie Award. **13 June:** Lynn Nottage's *Fabulation, or the Re-Education of Undine* is staged at Playwrights Horizons under Kate Whoriskey's direction. **17 November:** Neil LaBute's dark comedy, *Fat Pig*, focused on issues of physical attractiveness, opens at the Manhattan Class Company and wins the Outer Critics Circle Award. **6 December:** August Wilson's *Gem of the Ocean*, set in 1904, and, as such, the first in Wilson's 10-play cycle about African Americans in the twentieth century, premieres at the Walter Kerr Theatre.

2005 **31 March:** John Patrick Shanley's *Doubt* premieres at the Walter Kerr Theatre and wins the Pulitzer Prize and critical acclaim for its cast, including Cherry Jones and Brían F. O'Byrne. **19 September:** Rolin Jones's *The Intelligent Design of Jenny Chow* debuts at the Atlantic Theatre Company and wins an Obie Award. **29 November:** Christopher Durang's *Miss Witherspoon* opens at Playwrights Horizons directed by Emily Mann.

2006   2 February: David Lindsay-Abaire's *Rabbit Hole* opens at the Biltmore Theatre in a Manhattan Theatre Club (MTC) production and wins the Pulitzer Prize. **29 February:** Adam Rapp's *Red Light Winter* debuts at the Barrow Street Theatre and wins a special citation Obie Award for Rapp. **19 April:** Film star Julia Roberts makes her stage debut in the Manhattan Theatre Club revival of Richard Greenberg's *Three Days of Rain* at the Bernard B. Jacobs Theatre. **Summer:** Tony Kushner's adaptation of Bertolt Brecht's *Mother Courage and Her Children* is staged in Central Park in a New York Shakespeare Festival production starring Meryl Streep, Kevin Kline, and Austin Pendleton. **30 October:** Sarah Ruhl's *The Clean House* opens at the Mitzi E. Newhouse Theatre starring Jill Clayburgh. **13 November:** Douglas Carter Beane's *The Little Dog Laughed* moves to Broadway's Cort Theatre following an Off-Broadway run.

2007   8 May: The late August Wilson's *Radio Golf*, set in the 1990s and the last of his 10-play cycle on African American in the twentieth century, debuts at the Cort Theatre. **30 October:** Adam Bock's *The Receptionist* premieres at the Manhattan Theatre Club under Joe Mantello's direction. **10 November:** Broadway stagehands go on strike shutting down most shows for 19 days until the strike is settled. **10 December:** David Henry Hwang's *Yellow Face* opens at the Public Theatre following its first production at the Mark Taper Forum in association with the East West Players. **12 December:** Tracy Letts's *August: Osage County* moves to Broadway's Imperial Theatre following its initial acclaimed run at Chicago's Steppenwolf Theatre and wins the Pulitzer Prize, Tony Award, and Drama Desk Award.

2008   A major recession begins as several Wall Street financial houses teeter on the brink of collapse. **26 March:** Adam Bock's *The Drunken City* debuts at Playwrights Horizons. **14 May:** Neil LaBute's *reasons to be pretty* premieres at the Lucille Lortel Theatre in a Manhattan Theatre Club production prior to a transfer to Broadway; as with other LaBute works, it deals with present-day obsessions with physical appearance. **4 November:** African American Senator Barack Obama becomes the first African American elected United States president.

2009   8 January: Gina Gionfriddo's *Becky Shaw* is staged at the Second Stage Theatre following a run at Actors Theatre of Louisville, which commissioned the play. **10 February:** Lynn Nottage's *Ruined* premieres at the Manhattan Theatre Club, following a 2007 production at the Goodman Theatre, and wins the Pulitzer Prize, Obie Award, Outer Critics Circle Award, and Drama Desk Award. **9 March:** Moisés Kaufman's *33 Variations*, inspired by Beethoven and starring Jane Fonda, premieres at the Eugene O'Neill Theatre. **May:** Tony Kushner's *The Intelligent Homosexual's Guide to Capitalism and Socialism with a Key to the Scriptures* is produced at the Guthrie Theatre in Minneapolis, Minnesota, as part of a festival celebrating Kushner's work. **1 October:** Tracy Letts's race-themed *Superior Donuts* moves to the Music Box Theatre following a run at Chicago's Steppenwolf Theatre. **November:** The Signature Theatre stages Horton Foote's nine-play cycle of life in an early twentieth-century Texas town under the title *The Orphan's Home Cycle*. **19 November:** Sarah Ruhl's *In the Next Room (or The Vibrator Play)* opens at the Lyceum Theatre following a first production at the Berkeley Repertory Theatre. **December:** Melissa James Gibson's *This* is produced at Playwrights Horizons. **6 December:** David Mamet's *Race* opens on Broadway to mixed reviews, but has a successful run into the summer of 2010.

2010 Henry Miller's Theatre is renamed the Stephen Sondheim Theatre in celebration of Sondheim's 80th birthday. **11 March:** Geoffrey Naufft's *Next Fall*, concerning two gay lovers divided by religious belief, moves to Broadway's Helen Hayes Theatre following an Off-Broadway run; it wins the Outer Critics Circle John Gassner Award. **1 April:** John Logan's *Red*, starring Alfred Molina as the artist Mark Rothko, moves to the John Golden Theatre following a successful run at London's Donmar Warehouse; the play wins the Tony Award. **26 April:** Denzel Washington and Viola Davis win critical plaudits and Tony Awards in a revival of August Wilson's *Fences* at the Cort Theatre. **28 April:** Donald Margulies's *Collected Stories* opens in a Manhattan Theatre Club revival at the Samuel J. Friedman Theatre, winning critical kudos for Linda Lavin and Sarah Paulson. **Summer:** Al Pacino returns to the stage in a New York Shakespeare Festival revival of *The Merchant of Venice* at the Delacorte Theatre in Central Park; the production moves to Broadway in the fall. **27 June:** Kate Burton plays Katharine Cornell in A. R. Gurney's *The Grand Manner* at the Mitzi E. Newhouse Theatre under the direction of Mark Lamos. **10 September:** A revival of Lillian Hellman's *The Little Foxes* is directed by Ivo van Hove at the New York Theatre Workshop. **14 September:** A revival of Tony Kushner's *Angels in America* opens at the Signature Theatre, which devotes its 2010–2011 season to Kushner. **21 September:** Patrick Stewart and T. R. Knight star in a revival of David Mamet's *A Life in the Theatre* at the Schoenfeld Theatre. **7 October:** James Earl Jones and Vanessa Redgrave win acclaim in a revival of Alfred Uhry's *Driving Miss Daisy*.

Introduction

"The American theatre occupies five side streets, Forty-fourth to Forty-ninth, between Eighth Avenue and Broadway, with a few additional theatres to the north and south and across Broadway. In these thirty-two buildings every new play in the United States starts its life and ends it,"[1] wrote Arthur Miller in 1955, 25 years into the period covered in *The Historical Dictionary of American Theater: Contemporary*. Miller's statement underscores the fact that for much of the first two-thirds of the twentieth century, Broadway was the epicenter of American theatre and, as such, images and ideas about the turbulent and complicated times of the nation were, at least in dramatic terms, to be seen and heard in the five blocks of New York City Miller describes. This volume aims to present the plays and personages, movements and institutions, and cultural developments of the American stage from 1930 to 2010, a period of vast and almost continuous change from the seeming permanence suggested by Miller's statement to a wholly national phenomenon with theatres of importance all across the country. What Miller wrote was true in 1955 and it had been true since the nineteenth century; by 1960, this statement could be challenged; and, by the 1970s, it was simply no longer true.

"The Golden Age of Broadway," which stretches from approximately the end of World War I to the 1960s, produced a couple of generations of extraordinary playwrights, designers, performers, producers, and a host of innovations in the way plays are made and the techniques employed to perform them. By the mid-1950s, however, cultural and historical developments, economic forces, and rapid advances in technology remade American society, and along with it, the theatre. Broadway survived in an altered—and diminished—form into the twenty-first century, mainly as a shop window for plays and innovative productions usually created elsewhere, first in Off-Broadway and Off-Off-Broadway theatres and, subsequently, in regional theatres that were all major factors in decentralizing American theatre after the 1960s.

The roots of these changes are to be found in the history of the American theatre almost from its beginning, but the post-1930 stage in the United States emerged most fully as a result of the triumph of European modernism that had begun as early as the 1860s and influenced the American theatre from the 1890s in small ways and, after World War I, in significant ways.

The international cataclysm of World War I energized changes in all aspects of American life and the arts as the "lost generation" most profoundly influenced by that conflict brought their disillusionments and questioning of traditional values to the fore. The nation emerged as a great world power, and as its society and culture gained new sophistication and seriousness, the American stage came into its own in the 1920s. But the American economy, politics, and theatre were severely shaken by the Great Depression and took some time to emerge—fortunately, stronger than ever.

THE GREAT DEPRESSION

Despite the seemingly strict nature of realism in its adherence to the truth of life, throughout the second half of the twentieth century, and into the twenty-first, the form was influenced by more overtly theatrical styles prevalent before (including melodrama) and challenges to its predominance after. Realism ultimately was changed and expanded while existing side-by-side with other, newer forms. As the romantic and melodramatic theatre of the late nineteenth and early twentieth centuries slowly faded away after World War I, in its place came a fuller realization of what had been inherent in modernism. Modernism, and the realistic theatre born within it, was thoroughly absorbed into American drama by the 1940s with the emergence of Tennessee Williams and Arthur Miller, while dramatic forms and thematic content explored in the 1920s and during the Great Depression, also deepened and enriched the realistic genre. *The HDAT: Modernism* (2007), coauthored by myself and Felicia Hardison Londré, provides the personages, plays, theatres, movements, and terminology inherent in the modernist period and, as such, is an essential companion to the entries featured here. That volume concluded more or less in 1929 and this one begins with 1930.

The stock market crash in late 1929 brought on the Great Depression, an era that had a profound impact on all aspects of American life—including the theatre—in the 1930s. For all intents and purposes, the forces shaping contemporary theatre come into full focus with the stock market crash. The obviously harmful aspects of the nation's economic woes were seen at once in a decline in new productions on Broadway (although not as steep a decline as one might suppose), but most significantly in undermining experimentation and opportunities for new talents as producers grew wary of taking chances. Le Gallienne's bold adventure with the Civic Repertory Theatre ended for economic reasons in 1933 when the Depression was deepest, but the CRT's influence would be felt again in the 1950s as the regional theatre movement grew from a few theatres around the country operating much in the repertory style Le Gallienne pioneered.

President Franklin D. Roosevelt's election in 1932, and his vast "New Deal" program in response to the Depression, led to the establishment of the Works Progress Administration (WPA), a program aimed at putting a record number of unemployed Americans back to work. The Federal Theatre Project (FTP), a wing of the WPA, was created to employ theatrical personnel across the country and to bring a wide variety of theatre experiences to all Americans, but it also set off a divisive social debate regarding the nature of the arts in the United States that continues into the twenty-first century. The perceived social activism of FTP productions in the 1930s reflected the complex, confusing times, but while audiences were often responsive, some resisted art critical of traditional values, big business, gender and racial inequities, and all manner of authority, from religious institutions to the seats of power in the government. Theatre as entertainment and the theatre of social responsibility often overlapped to positive effect, but the division between "pop culture" and "serious art" became more pronounced by the mid-twentieth century.

During the 1930s, dramas advancing social concerns came to the fore more fully than ever before. This is vividly evident in The Group Theatre's production of Clifford Odets's *Waiting for Lefty* (1935), which espoused the necessity for unions, and FTP's "Living Newspapers," journalistic documentary-style dramas exploring the monopolizing of utilities, oppressive European dictators, the economic plight of farmers, race prejudice, the need for better housing for the poor, etc. While internal strife ended The Group Theatre, the "Living Newspapers" and other productions such as Marc Blitzstein's musical, *The Cradle Will Rock* (1937), set off controversy and ultimately led to the demise of the FTP, which was shut down in 1939 by a conservative U.S. Congress. In the late 1940s, some of those involved in creating works for the FTP or The Group Theatre, among others, were caught up in the anti-Communist witch hunts of the House Un-American Activities Committee (HUAC), often with damaging impact on their careers and, in some cases, personal tragedy.

Problems resulting from the content of plays were not the only difficulties challenging American theatre artists in the 1930s. The arrival of sound films and, to a lesser extent, commercial radio, led, over time, to a reduced number of new plays and musicals on Broadway, not to mention the diminishment of the road and stock and vaudeville theatres and companies. Audiences in the throes of the Depression had less disposable income—movies were cheap, while live theatre was comparatively expensive—yet a fairly sizable theatre-going public remained engaged throughout the Depression and into the 1940s as a generation of playwrights—Robert E. Sherwood, Clifford Odets, Lillian

Hellman, Thornton Wilder, and others—followed the inspiration of serious-minded dramatists like Eugene O'Neill, Elmer Rice, Maxwell Anderson, Susan Glaspell, and others.

Plays in the 1930s reflected the personal and societal struggles of the Depression and, increasingly, raised concerns over the gathering storm clouds of another world war taking shape with the energized fascism and Nazism in Europe. Sherwood's *The Petrified Forest* (1935) set the present moment in a larger historical context, as those profoundly affected by World War I faced, with mounting disillusionment, another worldwide catastrophe and the reality of the human penchant for violence. Even genial comedies vividly reflected the times, as in George S. Kaufman and Moss Hart's Pulitzer Prize-winning *You Can't Take It with You* (1936), in which a family of lovable and very American eccentrics rises above the era's deprivations and fears through a deep-seated belief in fundamental and eternal values of family and community. Odets's dramas produced by The Group Theatre, such as *Awake and Sing!* in 1935, reflected the moral dilemmas of the middle and lower classes striving to survive the depths of the Depression, and in many respects Odets was the iconic 1930s' playwright, who, as Harold Clurman wrote decades later, was important to his time (and as a representative of his time) for he "so directly communicates the very 'smell' of New York in the first years of the depression."[2] American plays of the 1930s gave the audience experiencing the Depression clarity and context for understanding the seemingly insurmountable dilemmas they were facing—and also provided escapism via comedies and great works of the Broadway musical theatre moving toward its pinnacle.

The dramas of the 1930s–1940s acknowledge the triumph of modernism that had begun to shape American theatre in the previous era. Realism in serious drama dominated by 1930—and American plays and acting techniques, not to mention the visual aspects, had fully embraced the tenets and techniques of realism, even as the boundaries of it expanded to accommodate non-realistic elements from expressionism to symbolism. After World War I, this is first evident in the overtly expressionist plays of the 1920s and, later, in such novel productions as *Our Town* (1938), in which Thornton Wilder's portrait of a turn-of-the-century New England small town is given universal resonance by the elimination of traditional scenery, with the play's environment created in its original production by a few chairs, a ladder, and some umbrellas. A stressing of basic humanistic values appear in this play, as in *You Can't Take It with You* and other 1930s plays in both dramatic and comic moods. The great moral questions of the times—and the enduring eternal values Kaufman and Hart and Wilder sought to stress—were central to the finest plays of the 1930s which mingled serious concerns with a high quotient of entertainment value.

O'Neill, who had withdrawn from active production of his new works in the early 1930s after a few works were dismissed by critics and audiences, quietly worked in seclusion during the 1930s, unsuccessfully attempting to complete an ambitious cycle of plays going generation-by-generation through an American family from the Revolution to the present-day. In the 1930s and early 1940s, despite ill health and depression, O'Neill did complete plays that are the crowning achievements of his canon of works, most notably *A Touch of the Poet* (1935), which was written for his cycle, *The Iceman Cometh* (1939), *Long Day's Journey into Night* (1939), widely regarded as his masterwork, the one-act *Hughie* (1940), and *A Moon for the Misbegotten* (1943). Fine productions of these plays in the 1950s and beyond would reinvigorate interest in O'Neill's achievement that continues into the twenty-first century.

As previously noted, the 1930s were a fertile period for musical theatre, which set the hard times to melodic music by Irving Berlin, George and Ira Gershwin, Cole Porter, Richard Rodgers and Lorenz Hart, and Jerome Kern and Oscar Hammerstein, the latter duo pioneering the integrated "book musical" with their masterwork, *Show Boat* (1927), in which music, plot, and character were unified to present a sweeping story of American life and theatre from the 1880s to the 1920s. This volume does not include entries on the musical theatre, but it is clear that *Show Boat*, like *You Can't Take It with You* and *Our Town*, suited the rapidly changing times and, like those plays, acknowledged life's eternal forces—birth and death, and the brevity of life, family, and bigotry—while stressing, in totality, an optimism for a brighter future, however narrow and tragic the present might seem. Life's vicissitudes were not ignored on the 1930s stage, but most dramatists seem convinced of a hopeful future and that the suffering of the present could lead not only to knowledge, but to greater concern for the well-being of others. This theme resonates through all of these plays and others, whether in the disillusionment of *The Petrified Forest* or the belief in family and community in *You Can't Take It with You* and *Our Town*. Wilder's play, one of the quintessential American works of the twentieth century, along with new techniques in scene, lighting, and costume design, represent the beginnings of American lyric realism, which would be fully realized in the mid-1940s in the works of the next generation of American dramatists.

WORLD WAR II AND THE COLD WAR

The outbreak of war in Europe in September 1939, followed by the entry of the United States into the escalating conflict in December 1941 as a direct result of the Japanese air attack on American forces at Pearl Harbor, radically altered American life once again. As the industrial build-up in support of the war effort began in earnest, the last vestiges of the Great Depression died away, although on the home front American citizens faced new deprivations through rationing as their grown sons and daughters faced the armies of totalitarian dictators in Europe and the South Pacific. Theatre reflected the anxieties of the time to a significant extent—although dramatists continued to seek and find reason for hope. Thornton Wilder's intellectual absurdist vaudeville, *The Skin of Our Teeth* (1942), acknowledged that natural and human catastrophes are tragically inevitable, but Wilder also underscored the resilience of the human species and what he viewed as their inherent desire to create a better world built on the knowledge of the past with optimistic expectations for the future. A forerunner of the Theatre of the Absurd and existentialist plays to come in the 1950s and 1960s, the cartoonish vaudeville style of *The Skin of Our Teeth* was also a striking departure from the prevalent realism of American drama, underscoring that both the modern and contemporary eras would see challenges to realism through such forms as surrealism, expressionism, epic theatre, and the Theatre of the Absurd, none of which would conquer realism, but all of which would—to a greater or lesser extent—expand the boundaries of the realistic tradition, remaking it in unique ways.

During the war years, Broadway experienced an uptick in the production of comedies and musicals, as audiences quite logically sought escape more than ever, with some works taking a nostalgic and rose-colored look at the American past, as in Howard Lindsay and Russel Crouse's remarkably long-running hit comedy, *Life with Father* (1939), or in the similarly long-running Richard Rodgers and Oscar Hammerstein musical, *Oklahoma!* (1943). Numerous innocuous comedies romanticizing and satirizing life during the war years became a Broadway cottage industry with such plays insisting that "normal" life goes on even in extraordinary times. Given the mounting tragedies of the war, it is not surprising that few plays of these years offered graphic depictions of the horrors of the frontlines. However, a number of serious dramas raised the moral dilemmas of war and assailed the aggression, prejudice, and fascism inherent in the Axis powers. Among these works, Lillian Hellman's *Watch on the Rhine* (1941), in its depiction of an anti-Nazi German citizen torn between remaining with his family in safety in the United States or returning to Germany and the dangerous work of the underground, celebrated the character's quiet heroism and the sacrifices being made by ordinary people. Other plays and films provided varied images of individual heroism or, more often, escapist fare.

Near war's end, new dramatists emerged with plays acknowledging the troubled times within the context of individual personal lives. Some also looked back to the previous decade without rose-colored glasses and measured the toll of the Depression and explored prewar attitudes. Tennessee Williams's "memory play," *The Glass Menagerie* (1944), is such a play, and it elevated stage language to poetry, as made clear in its opening monologue in which the play's central character, Tom Wingfield, Williams's alter ego, describes himself to the audience as the opposite of a "stage magician" who "gives you illusion that has the appearance of truth. I give you truth in the pleasant disguise of illusion."[3] In this semi-autobiographical work, Williams brought lyricism to ordinary speech, making use of a fragmented structure of short scenes, projected titles, and a central character able to step out of the play to address the audience directly (Wilder had similarly made use of a context-setting narrator in *Our Town*). Influenced by Anton Chekhov and D. H. Lawrence, the style and structure of *The Glass Menagerie* also owes a debt to another European influence, Bertolt Brecht, whose epic theatre called for breaking the fourth wall and the use of the various theatrical devices, along with projections, film, music, etc., to remove the play from the illusion of reality. Brecht's influence would eventually prove pervasive in American theatre productions and its techniques would inspire some American play-wrights after 1960.

Moment by moment and scene by scene, *The Glass Menagerie* is a realistic drama, but it is also something much more. Other dramatists followed suit with the help of directors and designers tuned to this refreshed and elaborated form of realism. For example, Arthur Miller's *Death of a Salesman* (1949) profited from Miller's use of flashbacks and imaginary sequences to depict the inner torment of its central character, Willy Loman, a tragically defeated traveling salesman. The original production profited from Jo Mielziner's evocative impressionistic setting in which ultra-modern high-rise New York City apartments seem to be crushing Loman's mortgaged little house. The play challenged positivist views of American-style capitalism in the midst of a postwar economic boom and, remarkably, despite its seeming discordance with the national mood, *Death of a Salesman* became the most talked-about play of its time. The audience for the play remembered the Depression and felt genuine concern for the play's prophetic notion that there were at least as many losers as winners in a materialistic society—and, more importantly, that the worth of a human being should not be based on economic success. When Loman is summarily fired he loses his grip, but not before frankly stating his plight: "I put thirty-four years into this firm, Howard, and now I can't pay my insurance! You can't eat the orange and throw the peel away—a man is not a piece of fruit!"[4] But Loman is discarded like an orange peel and Miller's play would continue to resonate for the next 60 years and beyond as the growth of corporations and their rising and falling fortunes would seem, at times, to overwhelmingly control American life. Later dramatists, including David

Mamet in *Glengarry Glen Ross* (1983), would advance this topic, as a group of real estate hucksters battled for survival in a company selling fraudulent land parcels and, apparently, the souls of their salesmen.

In the late 1940s, Williams brought American lyric realism to a peak with *A Streetcar Named Desire* (1947), while at the same time leading the way in smashing long-standing taboos against the frank exploration of sexuality and gender on the Broadway stage. In calling for an American national theatre years later, Harold Clurman wrote that *Streetcar* "would unquestionably be among the few worthy of a permanent place there."[5] Clurman was prophetic in one important sense; although no national theatre has yet been created, *Streetcar* found a permanent and central place in the canon of American drama, becoming an essential play frequently revived and produced in regional and university theatres. From the late 1940s into the 1960s, the previously taboo topics examined in *Streetcar*—sexual desire, rape, homosexuality—serve to underline Williams's importance in bringing such subjects into the light. The plays of his contemporaries, and those who came after, expanded on these topics in new ways as audiences became more accepting of bolder content.

The plays of Williams and Miller, and their like-minded contemporaries, usually found receptive audiences on Broadway, and as playwrights continued to stretch the boundaries in thematic content, character, and language, American actors rose to meet the challenges posed by these new works. The "Method," as it came to be known, resulting from The Group Theatre's experimentation with Constantin Stanislavsky's theories on acting, emerged from The Actors Studio and its leader Lee Strasberg. Other alumni of The Group, including Stella Adler, Robert Lewis, and Sanford Meisner, differed in their approaches from Strasberg and taught their own variations on Stanislavsky's theories, molding several generations of actors, including in the first wave such luminaries as Marlon Brando, Paul Newman, James Dean, Kim Hunter, Anne Bancroft, Kim Stanley, Maureen Stapleton, Julie Harris, Karl Malden, Geraldine Page, Eli Wallach, and Sidney Poitier. These actors would dominate Broadway and, ultimately, Off-Broadway, Off-Off-Broadway, and regional stages, not to mention postwar film and television. For better or worse, the "method" actor vanquished the romantic star actors of the pre-World War II era, but in truth, many of them became larger-than-life stars, too.

In the 1950s, in the wake of Williams and Miller, playwrights William Inge, Robert Anderson, the team of Jerome Lawrence and Robert E. Lee, and John Patrick, among others, pleased Broadway audiences with worthy dramas while also writing as frequently for movies and/or television. Few dramatists after the 1950s devoted themselves exclusively to the stage, a fact that further diminished the number of notable new plays each year. The most honored works of the period tended to be earnest evocations of humanistic values, as in Inge's *Picnic* (1953) or *Bus Stop* (1955), comedy-dramas exploring the longing for love and connection, or Albert Hackett and Frances Goodrich's *The Diary of Anne Frank* (1955), with its guardedly hopeful view that the best of human nature may even survive unimaginable horrors represented by the Holocaust. Lawrence and Lee's *Inherit the Wind* (1955) dramatized conflicts between faith and science in a fictionalized depiction of the Scopes "Monkey" trial of the 1920s, adding a political and spiritual dimension to arguments over evolution and creationism. O'Neill's last plays, including his semi-autobiographical masterpiece, *Long Day's Journey into Night*, were also first seen during the 1950s, and most of O'Neill's contemporaries offered their final works during the 1950s and 1960s.

A generation passed and among younger talents, Lorraine Hansberry became the first African American woman to contribute a critically acclaimed drama to Broadway with *A Raisin in the Sun* (1959). She and her play brought home for audiences issues of racism, serving as a harbinger of the great social changes roiling within the civil rights movement, and demonstrated, too, the theatre's growing openness to minorities traditionally closed out of mainstream theatre. Hansberry argued for plays by black writers, stressing that "the theatre is yet saddled with the notion that their [black playwrights] materials are necessarily parochial, and consequently without interest to the general theatergoing public."[6] Other minorities would slowly gain a footing during the 1960s and 1970s, as Asian, Chicano, and gay playwrights made significant inroads.

Technology, once again, brought major change during the 1950s. The widespread availability of network television from the late 1940s, like film and radio in the 1930s, dealt a severe blow to the fortunes of the live stage, while also providing lucrative income to theatre workers. Despite a continuing flow of dramas and comedies, not to mention musicals, Broadway, as the center of the American theatre, began a slow, steady decline in the 1950s as a diminished audience drawn away by television and put off by higher ticket prices led to fewer productions and shorter runs (or, perversely, phenomenally long runs for hit musicals and the occasional comedy). This decline contributed significantly to the emergence of Off-Broadway and Off-Off-Broadway theatre. The smaller theatres and more modestly produced plays featured in such theatres siphoned off a portion of the regular Broadway theatregoing audience by offering cheaper tickets, not to mention subject matter Broadway typically eschewed. Populated by small production companies and individual artists with specific cultural or political agendas, and featuring experimental techniques and playwrights from ethnic, racial, or gender minorities, these theatres found niche audiences seeking more adventurous experimental fare and attention to specialized and topical subjects. More importantly, these theatres also gave voice to various racial, ethnic, gender, and political activists who would contribute to the titanic social upheavals of the 1960s.

THE 1960s AND 1970s

The complacent, conformist attitudes often attributed to the United States during the administration of President Dwight D. Eisenhower in the 1950s masked deep fissures in the national psyche. These surfaced in growing unrest among various subsets of the population. Political divisions between conservative and liberal ideologies deepened in the second half of the twentieth century, and were most obviously exemplified by the controversies surrounding the anti-Communist witch hunts of the late 1940s and early 1950s. The House Un-American Activities Committee (HUAC) and various politicians on both sides of the political divide exploited the fears of the Cold War era and, in the process, persecuted those whose political sentiments in the depths of the Depression had led them to espouse various leftist political causes and organizations. Film and television writers, performers, and creative personnel found themselves blacklisted or compelled to testify and "name names" of those they knew to be Communist sympathizers. Friendships and creative alliances were damaged or destroyed, most notably the close professional and personal relationship between Arthur Miller and director Elia Kazan. Miller resisted cooperation with HUAC, while Kazan cooperated. The two men, whose collaboration on *Death of a Salesman* had provided the postwar American stage with its quintessential play, did not work together again for over a decade. Lesser-known artists saw their careers end in this period, but the theatre tended to be more welcoming to blacklisted talents and by 1960, even in film and television, some blacklisted artists returned to work even though deep-seated resentments remained.

After World War II, African Americans increasingly pushed back against segregation and other inequalities represented most obviously by "Jim Crow" laws in the South, and drew together to demand change. The civil rights movement grew in strength in the late 1950s under the leadership of Dr. Martin Luther King Jr., who called for non-violent resistance, boycotts, and peaceful demonstrations, while other black leaders like Malcolm X preferred to employ any means necessary to force change. Over time, and despite at times tragic consequences including the assassinations of King and Malcolm X among many violent acts, the movement brought about an end to segregation. The civil rights movement provided a model of resistance for other minorities to follow, including Chicano and Latinos, Asian Americans, and

Native Americans, as well as women and homosexuals who organized for change with increasing success after 1960. And, as involvement in the quagmire of the Vietnam War deepened, many Americans protested the war's continuance in much the same way.

The culture as a whole began reflecting changes in the 1950s ultimately categorized as part of "The Sixties" in the coming decade. The "Baby Boom" generation, children born in the aftermath of World War II, embraced rock'n'roll music from the mid-1950s, and their revolution in music, dress, and moral attitudes coalesced in the 1960s to symbolize radical changes and to provide either coherence to or escape from the shocking events of that turbulent era. The horrors of the Vietnam War were viewed nightly on television news, and race riots during the long, hot summers of the mid-1960s were simultaneously brought into every home via television. The assassination of President John F. Kennedy in 1963, and the subsequent murders of Malcolm X, King, and Senator Robert F. Kennedy tragically highlighted the uneasy mood of the times. A general loss of faith in "The Establishment," 1960s' youth-speak for the government, institutional, and corporate interests, and any form of authority exacerbated a generation gap separating "Baby Boomers" coming of age from their parents.

A sexual revolution and the search for alternative beliefs and ways of living that rejected the materialism of the previous generation deepened the gap, as did the younger generation's experimentation with drugs, participation in antiwar and civil rights demonstrations, women's liberation, and resistance to the military draft. "The Sixties" as an era extended into the mid-1970s, with cynicism about national leadership culminating in the Watergate scandal, leading to the resignation of U.S. President Richard M. Nixon. His successor, President Gerald R. Ford, expressed a desire to heal the nation's wounds that had accumulated since the end of World War II, and especially during the 1960s, but the legacy of these divisions continued even after the "Baby Boom" generation had themselves become "The Establishment."

Theatre was as divided as the country in the 1960s and 1970s. Broadway struggled to survive change, not only in the content and style of plays and musicals, but in rapidly evolving economic times. The expense of producing on Broadway skyrocketed in the mid-1960s and producers responded with fewer new productions and less adventurous choices. A "nostalgia craze" brought back vintage plays, musicals, and well-known performers who appealed to the older generation seeking escape from dizzying social changes they instinctively resisted, while producers tentatively introduced topical concerns in what they believed to be palatable form. New playwrights dealing with contemporary topics increasingly found themselves crowded out of Broadway theatres and new comedies and musicals on any topic were few and far between. Only Neil Simon seemed to weather the era with an unparalleled number of Broadway hits between 1960 and the late 1980s. Other nonmusical writers found Broadway success increasingly elusive. Some breakthroughs occurred on Broadway, as in the surprise success of Mart Crowley's *The Boys in the Band* (1968), a comedy-drama offering an examination of the lives of gay men in present-day New York, but little innovation in style or structure was to be found on Broadway. The "counterculture" musical, *Hair* (1968), featuring the attitudes of 1960s youth and making use of nudity, scored a Broadway hit, but it had moved from Off-Broadway's Public Theatre to Broadway. Such innovation was only palatable to Broadway producers if it could be proven that such style and content was a sure thing at the box office.

New plays—especially those reflecting current trends—found more welcoming venues in Off-Broadway and Off-Off-Broadway theatres. Keeping costs low in smaller theatres and other nontraditional spaces, Off-Broadway productions in New York provided venues for new talents, among them such enduringly significant dramatists as Edward Albee, Sam Shepard, Lanford Wilson, and Arthur Kopit. Many others followed in the 1970s and beyond, but over time the expense of mounting Off-Broadway productions also grew, so Off-Off-Broadway emerged with smaller theatres (under 100 seats), lower costs, and a greater opportunity for experimentation. Mainstream audiences and critics often failed to recognize the best work emanating from these theatres, but the writers themselves were unrepentant, as Albee made clear when he asserted in this era that Broadway theatre only "panders to the public need for self-congratulation and reassurance" and presents "a false picture of ourselves to ourselves, with an occasional very lovely exception," and that the new wave offered a theatre intended to "make a man face up to the human condition as it really is."[7] Albee's stinging condemnation of Broadway theatre suggests something of the gulf between the mainstream stage and the Off-Broadway avant-garde of a transitional era for the American stage.

Regional theatres functioned somewhat similarly to Off-Broadway in providing a more protected, less costly environment for the development of new plays and the production of classic works. The Guthrie Theatre of Minneapolis, Minnesota, for example, emphasized a repertory-style structure and emphasis on classics from its founding in 1959, but other theatres in cities across the country founded in subsequent decades developed varying missions, many aimed at providing opportunities for playwrights, new and old, to experiment with and perfect new work. Even such venerable figures as Tennessee Williams brought new plays to Off-Broadway and regional theatres in the 1970s, and small Off-Broadway-style companies appeared in major cities, also emphasizing new work and emerging artists. David Mamet, one of the major American dramatists of the late twentieth century, produced most of his early works in small theatres in Chicago, ultimately bringing plays to Broadway and Off-Broadway theatres from the 1980s and beyond. Mamet and his contemporaries recognized that their plays could take shape in fringe companies and regional theatres where a work could be nurtured without the high-pressure commercialism of Broadway and, when appropriate, a finished and well-received work could move to Broadway or Off-Broadway to reach a wider and more varied audience.

THE 1980s TO THE PRESENT

The transition that "The Sixties" represent polarized culture and politics in ways that remain deeply ingrained in the American cultural fabric. To a great extent, the conflicts became permanent as the political pendulum swung away from the liberal era of the 1960s to a more conservative one by the end of the 1970s. Ronald Reagan capitalized on this, and with his election to the U.S. presidency in 1980 he set off what was described as the "Reagan Revolution," a sweeping reversal of many "New Deal"-era social policies. Reagan stressed the idea of smaller government and deregulation of the corporate world, and the legacy of the Reagan era reverberates into the twenty-first century. Despite Reagan's enormous personal popularity, widespread mistrust of government and politicians continued. Reagan's administration, like those immediately preceding his, was tainted by scandal. In Reagan's case, the Iran-Contra arms deal marred his last years in the White House, as did his long silence on the AIDS pandemic.

The slow response of the medical establishment, the government, and the media to this health catastrophe had an almost immediate impact on the American theatre, as openly gay playwrights put the crisis on stage in the 1980s and 1990s in a wide range of works in which the personal circumstances of those affected by AIDS were seen in juxtaposition to societal attitudes, as indicated in William M. Hoffman's *As Is* (1985), or in angry assaults on antigay prejudice and the failures of national institutions to manage the crisis as depicted in Larry Kramer's scathing drama *The Normal Heart* (1985). Audiences were drawn to the topic, and gay-themed plays were some of the most honored works of the 1990s. Tony Kushner's Pulitzer Prize-winning two-play epic, *Angels in America* (1992), won numerous critical awards for its portrait of American life in the Reagan era and its importance in American history. Terrence McNally's *Love! Valour! Compassion!* (1994) won praise for its humanistic examination of gay life seen through the experiences of a diverse group of friends and was something of an updated *The Boys in the Band* while Paula Vogel's plays, including her Pulitzer Prize-winning

How I Learned to Drive (1997), were among the works of several lesbian playwrights and collectives shaping the feminist agenda at the dawn of the new millennium.

The major social changes since the 1960s, and the increased political activism of playwrights and producing organizations, as well as new techniques developed in Off-Broadway and Off-Off-Broadway theatres, were increasingly seen in numerous small and large theatre companies across the country as the regional theatre movement transformed American theatre. Companies of all sizes and missions found niche audiences in many cities and towns, often addressing local concerns, regional culture, and the need for revival of American and international classic plays. In a sense, the regional nature of American theatre in recent decades echoes the era of the road and stock theatres spread across the nation in the first half of the twentieth century. While regional theatres have risen and fallen since the movement began in the 1950s, the diversification of the American stage—its movement away from New York—provided the United States with an opportunity to nurture a truly national theatre. The potential existed for every community—small and large—to have high-quality theatre of both national and local significance.

In the decades following Reagan's presidency, the national political pendulum swung back and forth and during President George W. Bush's first term, the terrorist attacks on New York's World Trade Center and the Pentagon led to wars in Iraq and Afghanistan and a period of political divisiveness. These events set the stage for a remarkable 2008 primary and election season in which a woman, Hillary Clinton, and an African American man, Barack Obama, became the leading contenders for the Democratic nomination. Obama ultimately became the first African American president. These and other historical and cultural developments of the era between 1980 and 2010 were only some of the American stories told in dramatic form during that period. Despite momentous historic and political changes, theatre often kept its focus on the intimacies of personal lives, families, and values, with an emphasis on the individual's struggle for coherence, connection, and self-realization, and aimed to bring clarity to the confusions of changing values faced by families and in those relationships buffeted by moral, economic, and political conflict and uncertainty. America's prominence in world affairs, which marked the first half of the twentieth century, met with new and daunting challenges as a new millennium dawned.

Diversity in the content of American theatre after the 1960s resulted, in part, from geographic diversity supplied, also in part, by regional theatres with individual missions. The numbers of these theatres has fluctuated up and down since 1960, but in 2010 there were as many as 70 regional theatres functioning in the United States, even despite new economic challenges resulting from the recession of 2008. Increasingly since the emergence of regional theatres, serious drama, new playwrights, and innovative techniques have not originated on Broadway, but on these regional stages, as they had in Off- and Off-Off-Broadway theatres in the 1960s and 1970s and, increasingly, in academic theatre departments since the 1960s. Many of the foremost dramatists after 1980 (some of whom began their careers in the 1960s), including such leading figures as Lanford Wilson, Sam Shepard, Beth Henley, David Mamet, Wendy Wasserstein, August Wilson, and Tony Kushner, had comparatively fewer Broadway productions than playwrights of previous generations. Some pointedly rejected Broadway, presuming that their themes or theatrical experimentation would be of little or no interest to Broadway audiences or that they would face attempts by producers to dilute the content or style of their works to conform to mainstream sensibilities. By the late twentieth century, the rarity of new nonmusical plays on Broadway was all too obvious. Virtually every significant play produced on Broadway had begun its life elsewhere. The Broadway of the Golden Age was dead and in its place long-running musicals aimed at tourists dominated and non-musical plays were rare and, when they appeared, typically short-lived or unqualified successes from regional or international stages.

Millennial drama reflected the discomfitures of the times. Much had changed in the way theatre was made in America after 1960, but the content of plays, despite a greater freedom from taboos and more diverse images of America and American lives, continued to center around the individual, relationships, and family even while responding to topical issues and cultural developments and divisions. Playwrights who had emerged from the 1960s to the 1980s—Edward Albee, Sam Shepard, Lanford Wilson, David Mamet, August Wilson, Horton Foote, Beth Henley, Neil Simon, John Guare, Emily Mann, Christopher Durang, Maria Irene Fornés, Terrence McNally—continued to produce new works into the twenty-first century on a wide range of subjects, while a generation of dramatists who appeared beginning in the late 1980s resulted in the most culturally diverse group of American dramatists in the nation's history. Chicanos, Asians, Native Americans, women, gays, and physically challenged Americans continued to make inroads through the establishment of niche companies and by gaining a stronger foothold in regional theatres, on Off- and Off-Off-Broadway stages, and even, occasionally, on Broadway. This new and varied generation of playwrights, including such figures as Luis Valdez, David Henry Hwang, Tony Kushner, Richard Greenberg, Suzan-Lori Parks, Ping Chong, Rebecca Gilman, Jon Robin Baitz, Tracy Letts, Eve Ensler, John Patrick Shanley, Craig Lucas, Charles L. Mee, Anna Deavere Smith, Nicky Silver, Pearl Cleage, Paula Vogel, Donald Margulies, David Auburn, Charles Busch, Neil LaBute, Lynn Nottage, Sarah

Ruhl, Melissa James Gibson, and John Logan, among many others, are, in all of their diversity, a confirmation of a new order in American theatre at the end of the first decade of the twenty-first century.

Despite greater diversity of racial, ethnic, and gender plays and playwrights, all roads led back to constants of American theatre. For example, Tracy Letts's Pulitzer Prize-winning *August: Osage County* (2007) can be said to be little more than a continuation of the brand of tense and deeply personal family dramas typical of O'Neill, Williams, Miller, and other "Golden Age" American playwrights. John Patrick Shanley's *Doubt* (2004) and Tony Kushner's *The Intelligent Homosexual's Guide to Capitalism and Socialism with a Key to the Scriptures* (2009) stressed the moral, religious, and political tensions of the time, much as Odets and Miller had done in the 1930s and 1950s, respectively. August Wilson's 10-play "Pittsburgh Cycle," chronicling African American life in the twentieth century, focused around family and community, realizing the generation-by-generation approach O'Neill had envisioned but could not complete in the 1930s. Wilson finished the last of his cycle plays, *Radio Golf* (2005), shortly before his death, and like the next generation's Suzan-Lori Parks, whose stylistic experiments were more adventurous than Wilson's, these plays by African American writers looked at the seemingly eternal issues of race conflict. Parks's *Topdog/Underdog* (2001) and her other works serve as reminders of the full emergence of artists from traditional minority groups, of the unique aspects of such works, and of the continued struggles of African Americans, as well as women, gays, and other racial and ethnic groups to achieve equality in the new century, using theatre as one of several means of accomplishing their goal. In this, it seems clear that in the early twenty-first century, at least as far as American theatre is concerned, despite significant changes in the way theatre is made, and the boldness and diversity of the works created for American stages, in subject matter and in the desire of audiences to see their stories told in dramatic form, everything old was new again.

NOTES

1. Arthur Miller, "The American Theatre," *Holiday* (January 1955): 90.
2. Harold Clurman, "The Theatre of the Thirties," *Famous American Plays of the 1930s*. New York: Dell, 1959, pp. 7–17.
3. Tennessee Williams. *The Glass Menagerie,* in *Tennessee Williams: Plays 1937–1955*. New York: Library of America, 2000, p. 400.
4. Arthur Miller. *Death of a Salesman*, in *Arthur Miller: Collected Plays 1944–1961*. Edited by Tony Kushner. New York: Library of America, 2006, p. 213.

5. Harold Clurman, "Tennessee Williams," *The Divine Pastime: Theatre Essays.* New York: Macmillan, 1974, pp. 11–18.

6. Lorraine Hansberry, "Me Tink Me Hear Sounds in De Night," *Theatre Arts* (October 1960): 10.

7. Edward Albee, "Which Theatre is the Absurd One?," *New York Times Magazine* (25 February 1962): 30.

ABBOTT, GEORGE (1887–1995).[†] Beginning in the 1910s, George Francis Abbott, born in Forestville, New York, became the quintessential all-around theatre man, beginning an acting career in 1913 in *The Misleading Lady* and working steadily for a decade before making the transition to **Broadway**'s leading director/producer, particularly in comedies and musicals, and as a playwright. His earliest plays, written with collaborators, include *The Fall Guy* (1925; with James Gleason*), *A Holy Terror* (1925; with Winchell Smith*), and *Love 'Em and Leave 'Em* (1926; with J. V. A. Weaver) were moderately successful, but in collaboration with Philip Dunning,* Abbott scored his first major hit with *Broadway** (1926). At the same time, his directing career took off with Maurine Watkins's* *Chicago** (1926) and by the end of the 1920s, he was a much sought-after director, scoring another major success with BEN HECHT and CHARLES M ACARTHUR's *Twentieth Century* (1932). One of his most enduring plays, the expressionistic farce *Three Men on a Horse* (1935), coauthored with John Cecil Holm, won critical approval and commercial success, as did virtually everything Abbott staged and/or coauthored during the 1930s, including such popular comedies as *Boy Meets Girl* (1935), *Brother Rat* (1936), *Room Service* (1927), and *What a Life!* (1938).

He shifted to musical comedy in this era, working frequently with composer Richard Rodgers and lyricist Lorenz Hart on a series of highly popular MUSICALS, including *Jumbo* (1935), *On Your Toes* (1936), *The Boys from Syracuse* (1938), *Too Many Girls* (1939), and *Pal Joey* (1940). By the beginning of the 1940s, his status as the leading director of generally lighthearted musicals led to numerous hits into the 1960s, including *On the Town* (1944), *High Button Shoes* (1947), *Where's Charley?* (1948), *Call Me Madam* (1950), *A Tree Grows in Brooklyn* (1951), *Wonderful Town* (1953), *The Pajama Game* (1954), *Damn Yankees* (1955), *Fiorello!* (1969), and *A Funny Thing Happened on the Way to the Forum* (1962). The prolific "Mister Abbott," as he was called by Broadway coworkers, continued his remarkable career well into his nineties, although with diminished success with the exception of a 1983 revival of *On Your Toes*, which was well-received.

ABDOH, REZA (1963–1995). Born in Tehran, Iran, Reza Abdoh emigrated to Los Angeles, California, after some time in London, and began directing. Reviewers and audiences were amazed by the quality of his work when, at the age of 22, he staged *King Lear* and *Oedipus Rex* with the Dar a Luz Theatre Ensemble. Abdoh wrote many of the pieces he directed, most notably *The Hip-Hop Waltz of Eurydice* (1990), produced at the **Los Angeles Theatre Center**. **AIDS** cut short his impressive career.

ABE LINCOLN IN ILLINOIS. **Robert E. Sherwood**'s reverent drama on Abraham Lincoln's rise to the United States Presidency, and his troubled relationship with his wife, Mary Todd Lincoln, won a **PULITZER PRIZE** following its opening on 15 October 1938 in the first production of the **Playwrights' Company** at the Plymouth Theatre for a run of 472 performances. **Raymond Massey**'s masterful performance as Lincoln won considerable praise and he repeated his performance in the 1940 film version. Massey's preparation was so meticulous and obsessive that one **Broadway** wag commented that the actor would not be satisfied until he was assassinated. The play begins at the time of Lincoln's aborted romance with the doomed Ann Rutledge and continues through his courtship and marriage to the mercurial Mary Todd and his career as a lawyer in Springfield, Illinois, stressing his reluctance to pursue elected office and Mary's intense ambitions for him. Concluding with Lincoln's election and departure for Washington, the play foreshadows Lincoln's struggles with a deeply divided nation moving toward civil war and his wife's mental deterioration. *Abe Lincoln in Illinois* has had two major New York revivals, one in 1963 by the **Phoenix Theatre**, and another in 1993 produced by the **Lincoln Center Theatre** with **Sam Waterston** in a **Tony Award**-nominated performance.

ABEL, WALTER (1898–1987).[†] Born in St. Paul, Minnesota, Abel spent his long career mostly in character roles, moving easily among theatre, film, and television roles. His **Broadway** debut in Dorothy Donnelly's* *Forbidden* (1919) was followed by a supporting role in the first American production of **GEORGE BERNARD SHAW**'s *Back to Methuselah* (1922). He played the Sheriff in the original production of **EUGENE O'NEILL**'s *Desire under the Elms** (1924) and Orin Mannon in a short-lived 1932 revival of O'Neill's *Mourning becomes Electra*. When sound films began, Abel appeared with greater frequency on the screen, but returned to the stage to appear in several plays, including *When Ladies Meet* (1933), *Merrily We Roll Along* (1934), *The Wingless Victory* (1936), and appeared with **HELEN HAYES** in *The Wisteria Trees* (1950). Abel also appeared in *The Pleasure of His Company* (1958), *Night Life* (1962), *The Ninety Day Mistress* (1967), *Saturday Sunday Monday*

(1974), and, in his late seventies, made his last stage appearance in a **New York Shakespeare Festival** revival of *Trelawny of the "Wells"* (1975).

ABRAHAM, F[AHRID]. MURRAY (1939–). Born in Pittsburgh, Pennsylvania, the son of a Syrian American auto mechanic and a housewife, Abraham was raised in El Paso, Texas. He studied with **Uta Hagen** and debuted in Los Angeles in a production of Ray Bradbury's *The Wonderful Ice Cream Suit.* A versatile actor in a range of character roles and styles, Abraham made his first **Broadway** appearance in *The Man in the Glass Booth* (1968), which was followed by a varied series of plays both on Broadway and in **Off-Broadway** venues, including *6 Rms Riv Vu* (1972), *Bad Habits* (1974), and **Terrence McNally's** farce, *The Ritz* (1975), in which Abraham scored a success as a flamboyant regular at a gay bathhouse. He repeated his performance in the 1976 screen version. Abraham appeared with regularity in film and television, winning a 1984 Best Actor Academy Award as Antonio Salieri in the screen version of **Peter Shaffer's** *Amadeus.* He returned frequently to the stage, including roles in the 1976 flop *Legend, Tiebele, and Her Demon*, and he replaced **Ron Leibman** as Roy Cohn in **Tony Kushner's** two-play epic *Angels in America* (1993). This was followed by roles in a revival of *A Month in the Country* (1995), the MUSICAL *Triumph of Love* (1997), and *Mauritius* (2007). Other credits include the classics, with acclaimed performances in *Oedipus Rex, The Merchant of Venice*, and *Twelfth Night*, as well as modern classics, including *Waiting for Godot*. Abraham also teaches acting at Brooklyn College, and in stints at Harvard University and Columbia University.

ABUBA, ERNEST (1947–). Born in Honolulu, Hawaii, with a Filipino heritage, Abuba became involved as dramatist, actor, and director with the **Pan Asian Repertory Theatre.** His own plays focus on sociopolitical and cultural conflicts, including *The Dowager* (1978), *An American Story* (1979), *Cambodia Agonistes* (1990), *Papa-Boy* (1994), *Nightstalker* (1997), *Leir Rex* (1998), *Spleen* (2001), and *Kwatz! The Tibetan Project* (2004). On **Broadway**, Abuba appeared in *Pacific Overtures* (1976), ***Loose Ends*** (1979), *Zoya's Apartment* (1990), and *Shimada* (1992). *See also* ASIAN AMERICAN THEATRE.

ACADEMIC THEATRE.[†] From the middle of the nineteenth century there is little evidence that performances of plays were frequent on campuses or that the techniques of acting, directing, design, and playwriting were studied, although dramatic literature, particularly the classics, were studied. William O. Partridge, a Columbia University professor, called for the creation of classes and departments in theatre as early as 1886, but the first formalized instruction in theatrical techniques appears to be George Pierce Baker's* English 47 course at Harvard University which began in 1905. Within the first two decades of the twentieth century, the influence of Baker's course, including on such notable playwrights as EUGENE O'NEILL, PHILIP BARRY, and others, led faculty at various institutions to establish similar courses in theatre practice.

In 1914, Carnegie Institute of Technology established the first department of theatre under the guidance of Thomas Wood Stevens* and BEN IDEN PAYNE and in 1925 Baker created the Department of Drama at Yale University. By the end of the 1920s, many colleges and universities had departments of theatre or included theatre courses as part of English or Speech departments. In 1926, Paul Opp established Alpha Psi Omega, a national theatre fraternity for undergraduates working in theatre (and this evolved into an honor society that continues into the twenty-first century, with other similar societies following suit). The American Educational Theatre Association was founded in 1936 and theatre professors met annually to discuss mutual concerns, with its early membership of eighty university faculty expanding rapidly. Later called the **American Theatre Association (ATA)**, the organization disbanded in 1986 at a time it was serving over 1,600 college and university theatre departments. ATA was replaced by the **Association for Theatre in Higher Education (ATHE)**, which thrives into the twenty-first century, encouraging both scholarship and the practice of theatre in university and college settings.

According to the **National Endowment for the Arts (NEA)**, by 1977 2,500 colleges and universities were staging over 3,000 productions for annual audiences of more than nine million people. During the last decades of the twentieth century, academic theatre suffered from a general decline of professional opportunities for its graduates, but colleges and universities also become a venue for new playwrights to produce their works. The bonds between professional and academic theatres have multiplied since the 1960s and many theatre departments have developed major preprofessional university programs with close working relationships with professional repertory theatres in their region. Playwrights, as well as professional actors, directors, designers, and technicians have developed relationships with university theatres, teaching courses and doing short- and long-term residencies, such as **Edward Albee**'s long relationship with the University of Houston. The economic recession of 2009 threatened the survival of university programs, with many facing enormous budget cutbacks likely, in some cases, to radically alter programs.

ACCENT ON YOUTH. SAMSON RAPHAELSON's three-act comedy, produced by Crosby Gaige,* opened at the Plymouth Theatre on 25 December 1934 and chalked up 229 performances despite decidedly mixed reviews. The plot centers on playwright Steven Gaye, who has written a play about a middle-aged dramatist in love with a much younger woman. The production of the play is troubled, culminating in Gaye's desire to abandon it, but his young secretary, Linda Brown (played in the original production by **Constance Cummings**), salvages things by taking on the leading role. She becomes involved with her innocuous leading man and marries him, but later returns to Gaye when she realizes that despite their age difference, they are meant for each other. A longtime romantic staple of **summer** STOCK theatres, *Accent on Youth* was also filmed starring Sylvia Sidney and Herbert Marshall in 1935 and was musicalized for Bing Crosby and Nancy Olson under the title *Mr. Music* in 1950. Another adaptation, titled *But Not for Me,* starred Clark Gable and Carroll Baker in 1959. Despite its screen versions, *Accent on Youth* has had only one major **Broadway** revival, which opened for a limited run in April 2009, featuring a cast including David Hyde Pierce, Charles Kimbrough, Lisa Banes, Mary Catherine Garrison, and Byron Jennings.

ACCONCI, VITO (1940–). Born Vito Hannibal Acconi in New York to an Italian immigrant family, Acconci began his career as a poet before developing into an architect and performance artist with a narcissistic bent. He includes himself in some of his work, as in Seedbed, an installation/performance work at the Sonnabend Gallery in January 1971 in which he lay hidden under a ramp masturbating while his voices speaking his fantasies was heard as viewers walked across the ramp. The goal of an interchange between artist and audience was established, but later Acconci works tended to feature machinery and architectural elements.

ACTING/ACTORS.† Acting has always required a multiplicity of physical and vocal skills, a vibrant stage presence, and usually physical attractiveness, not to mention an intelligence tuned to encompass such practical concerns as memorization and, more importantly, interpretive and emotional acumen. The American stage has tended to be rich in talented actors in all eras, particularly from the early nineteenth century, a period in which the dominant acting style was of a bombastic nature, essentially influenced by the predominance of plays in the tradition of melodrama.* This led to a romantic school of acting, in which the actor built toward a crescendo of passion expressed vocally and physically. By the mid-nineteenth century, however, some actors gradually introduced greater REALISM into their performances. As early as the

1850s, Edwin Booth,* perhaps the most respected American actor of the era in **Shakespeare**'s plays, was turning away from the romantic style, adopting an economy of gesture, a comparatively conversational manner of delivery, and an immersion in character that influenced subsequent generations and pointed toward the future. Between the 1890s and 1910, Minnie Maddern Fiske* was especially noted for the apparent naturalness with which she assumed her characterizations in contemporary works, and she was fortunate in finding roles that allowed her use of subtler effects than many of her contemporaries adopted. The gradual acceptance of psychological realism in acting was powerfully reinforced with the advent of plays by modernist European dramatists HENRIK IBSEN and GEORGE BERNARD SHAW, and, in America, James A. Herne* and actor/playwright William Gillette,*with the latter moving away from elocutionary artifice toward a style of "under-acting" to create a more natural effect. Gillette's popularity reflected the audience's growing taste for increased reality, although the plays in which he appeared were more likely to belong to the melodramatic or romantic traditions. Many American actors until well into the mid-twentieth century continued with success in the romantic tradition, most notably stars like John Barrymore* and KATHARINE CORNELL, who may have been the last widely appeared romantic actress in roles in both the classics and contemporary works.

By the 1920s, the range of acting styles on **Broadway** expanded to include "celebrity" or star acting by those who stamped their roles indelibly with their own personalities rather than immersing themselves in the unique details of varied characters. A few examples are TALLULAH BANKHEAD, Billie Burke,* De Wolf Hopper,* Olga Nethersole,* and MAE WEST, although Bankhead most particularly occasionally rose to the challenge of creating a character unlike her own well-honed flamboyant persona. Other talented and compelling actors of the era, such as ETHEL BARRYMORE and Otis Skinner,* moved steadily toward a more complete immersion in character, although by contemporary standards would surely seem more part of the romantic tradition. The Barrymore name became synonymous with the acting profession. John and Ethel's brother, Lionel,* was also well-respected and all three succeeded on stage and screen. The threesome had descended from the Barrymore-Drew-Lane* family dynasty of actors first visible in the eighteenth century and continuing beyond them in the person of film star Drew Barrymore, John's granddaughter. In the first decades of the twentieth century, a proliferation of star actors were seen on Broadway, and although personalities and styles varied, audiences were drawn to the greatest of them even without regard for the quality of the play in which the star appeared. The Barrymores, Bankhead, Cornell, Skinner, and others dominated the productions in which they appeared and the play was often only a means by which they could impress audiences with their acting pyrotechnics. Even on New York's ethnic stages, star actors were essential in the first half of the twentieth century; for example, in the YIDDISH THEATRE on Second Avenue, Jacob Adler* became a major force and even performed on Broadway occasionally. His children, most notably **Stella** and **Luther Adler**, followed him onto the stage, but Stella, especially, was part of a movement that led the next generation away from the "grand manner" exemplified by her father and his contemporaries.

From 1920 to 1960, the married duo of **Alfred Lunt** and **Lynn Fontanne** were widely acclaimed, particularly before World WAR II, and their painstakingly rehearsed on-stage give-and-take with dialogue impressed audiences and CRITICS. Like the Barrymores and Cornell, their names became synonymous with great acting in the romantic tradition prior to the emergence of "method" acting after the mid-1940s. In truth, this revolution in American acting so simply labeled as "the method" had its roots in the 1923–1924 Broadway season (and tour) of the celebrated Moscow Art Theatre (MAT)* under the direction of Constantin Stanislavsky. In a varied REPERTORY featuring, among others, **Anton Chekhov**'s plays, the MAT impressed American actors and critics with the depth, naturalness, and ensemble acting style they demonstrated. The MAT visit occurred as American plays, led by the dramas of EUGENE O'NEILL, required a greater reality in the portrayal of characters than had been typical up to that time. As other dramatists followed O'Neill's model in their individual ways, the demand for more natural acting grew exponentially.

In 1931, the founding of The Group Theatre by **Harold Clurman**, **Lee Straberg**, and **Cheryl Crawford**, set off vast changes in American acting. The Group produced plays, including those of **Clifford Odets**, addressing the social dilemmas of the Great Depression in the Ibsenesque social problem play manner. The Group's estimable accomplishment in the plays they produced was paralleled by their concerted effort to develop an acting style suitable for such true-to-life plays, basing their central concepts on Stanislavsky's theories. This also commenced a complex conflict contributing to the breakup of The Group in 1940. A bitter rift among its various members over interpretations of Stanislavsky's ideas caused several members of The Group, most notably Strasberg, **Stella Adler**, **Sanford Meisner**, and **Robert Lewis**, to establish acting schools all based, to a great extent, on Stanislavsky, but each with unique variations. The result was that several subsequent generations of American actors were trained within these variations on the Stanislavsky system. The Group itself had either created or attracted to its productions a first generation of American actors to rival the predominant romantic acting style typical of the Barrymores, Cornell, and their peers, including **Luther Adler**, Phoebe Brand, **Morris Carnovsky**, **Lee J. Cobb**,

Howard da Silva, Frances Farmer, **John Garfield**, Sam Jaffe, Karl Malden, Sylvia Sidney, and **Franchot Tone**, most of whom would craft enduring careers on Broadway and in films. The Group also produced a major director, **Elia Kazan**, who between 1940 and 1960 staged some of the most important American dramas of the time with actors trained by such teachers as Strasberg, Adler, Meisner, and Lewis.

The Actors Studio, under Strasberg's direction (although it was founded by Kazan and Lewis), dominated in the post-World War II years, rivaled most successfully by Adler, who felt that Strasberg overemphasized Stanislavsky's ideas on emotional memory and undervalued the nurturing of an actor's imagination. The most celebrated "method actor" of the 1940s and 1950s, **Marlon Brando**, studied with both Strasberg and Adler, but seemed to profit most from Adler's teaching. Brando was fortunate in being cast as the animalistic Stanley Kowalski in **Tennessee Williams**'s PULITZER PRIZE-winning drama, *A Streetcar Named Desire* (1947), a role which permitted him ample opportunities to demonstrate the potency of the "method" in ways previously unseen. He became a major movie star and never returned to the live theatre after *Streetcar*. The Actors Studio alumni of Brando's generation, and the next, included some of the most acclaimed American actors from the 1950s into the twenty-first century, and most did return to the stage from screen success, some more frequently than others. The Studio's alumni includes Alec Baldwin, **Anne Bancroft, Ellen Burstyn**, Montgomery Clift, Robert De Niro, James Dean, Sally Field, Jane Fonda, Lee Grant, **Julie Harris, Dustin Hoffman, Kim Hunter, Anne Jackson**, Harvey Keitel, Martin Landau, Cloris Leachman, Marilyn Monroe, **Paul Newman, Al Pacino, Geraldine Page, Estelle Parsons**, Sean Penn, Sidney Poitier, **Anthony Quinn**, Eva Marie Saint, **Kim Stanley, Maureen Stapleton, Rip Torn, Christopher Walken, Eli Wallach, Shelley Winters**, and Joanne Woodward, among scores of others. After its first decade, the Studio established special units for dramatists, directors, and also developed finished productions. **Tennessee Williams, Edward Albee**, Norman Mailer, **Terrence McNally**, and **James Baldwin** were among writers involved at various times.

Other acting teachers emerged from the same generation. Meisner became associated with **The Neighborhood Playhouse**, where he taught, and **Herbert Berghof**, a director, set up the HB Studio in 1945. In 1948, Berghof's wife, actress **Uta Hagen**, joined the HB Studio as a teacher. Hagen subsequently wrote two books, *Respect for Acting* (1976) and *A Challenge for the Actor* (1991), widely admired and embraced by young actors. She spent the later part of her career teaching and returned to acting only infrequently, although notably in Albee's **Who's Afraid of Virginia Woolf?** (1962). Adler, Meisner, Lewis, and numerous other acting teachers also wrote books on the subject of acting. By the 1980s, acting training had become increasingly sectionalized, with voice, movement, stage combat, and other specialists sought out by aspiring actors.

In the first decade of the twenty-first century, American stages from Broadway to **regional** and **academic theatres**, were populated with an increasingly multicultural group of actors, although it has often been the case since the 1960s that after actors achieve a major success on Broadway or Off-Broadway, they are inclined to trade that success for more lucrative film and television work, rarely if ever returning to the stage. However, some movie and television stars have returned with frequency, including **Alan Alda, Joan Allen, Christine Baranski, Kathy Bates, Shirley Booth, Matthew Broderick, Kate Burton, Richard Burton, Hume Cronyn, Billy Crudup, Willem Dafoe, Blythe Danner, Viola Davis, Ruby Dee, Colleen Dewhurst, Olympia Dukakis, Charles Durning, José Ferrer, Henry Fonda, Morgan Freeman**, James Gandolfini, **Ben Gazzara, Lillian Gish, Ruth Gordon, Rex Harrison, Eileen Heckart, Katharine Hepburn, Philip Seymour Hoffman, James Earl Jones, Raúl Juliá, Kevin Kline, Jack Lemmon, John Lithgow, Patti LuPone, John Malkovich, Dorothy McGuire, Alfred Molina, Zero Mostel, Estelle Parsons, Anthony Perkins, Christopher Plummer, Jason Robards, George C. Scott, Gary Sinise, Kevin Spacey, Jean Stapleton, James Stewart, Meryl Streep, Jessica Tandy, Marisa Tomei, Lily Tomlin, Denzel Washington, Dianne Wiest**, B. D. **Wong**, and **Jeffrey Wright**, among many others. Conversely, some movie and television stars have attempted Broadway roles, including Scarlett Johansson, who won a **Tony Award** for a 2010 revival of *A View from the Bridge* on her first try, and Julia Roberts, whose stage debut in a 2006 revival of **Richard Greenberg**'s *Three Days of Rain* garnered tepid reviews, but filled theatre seats for its limited run.

The majority of stage actors are relatively unknown, laboring in Broadway, Off-Broadway, Off-Off-Broadway, regional, and semi-professional theatres, surviving in the twenty-first century by working jobs outside of theatre and/or combining theatre work with film, television, and radio jobs to supplement their income as the diminished number of productions and theatres in hard times fail to provide ample employment for even the most talented and experienced actors.

ACTING COMPANY, THE. Founded in 1972 by **John Houseman**, the company featured the first graduating class of the Juilliard School's Drama Division. Currently managed by producing director Margo Harley, the Acting Company continues a long tradition of touring performances of classic and new works to schools (high school and college) with young actors gaining significant experience. Many actors in the company at various times have risen to professional prominence, including **Kevin Kline, Patti LuPone**, Jesse L. Martin, Keith David, Lorraine Toussaint, David Ogden Stiers, **Jeffrey Wright**, Rainn Wilson, **Frances Conroy**, Lisa Banes, Dennis Boutsikaris, Derek Smith, David Schramm, Mary Lou Rosato, and others. Its stated goals include not only the training of young actors, but also the encouragement of new plays and the educating of a national audience.

ACTORS' EQUITY ASSOCIATION (AEA).† Founded in 1913 by a group of 122 actors in response to poor conditions and unethical practices by producers, this union for actors was preceded by the Actors' Society, which had formed in 1895 to fight for a minimum wage. Its disbanding in 1912 set the stage for the AEA, which negotiated unsuccessfully with producers until 1919 when a month-long strike by actors closed theatres in eight cities, forced the closing or prevented the opening of numerous productions, finally bringing an agreement with the PRODUCING MANAGERS' ASSOCIATION for a five-year contract. Over the subsequent decade, additional agreements established a minimum wage, rehearsal pay, and other issues. In the second half of the twentieth century and into the twenty-first, AEA established its headquarters in New York, with regional branches in Los Angeles, Chicago, and San Francisco, and reached a membership of over 40,000 actors. Despite occasional controversies and difficult financial issues, especially during the AIDS epidemic beginning in the early 1980s, AEA is concerned with the rights of actors and stage managers, in recent decades enhancing efforts in support of minorities, women, and disabled performers. In 2009, Mark Zimmerman served as AEA president, succeeding **Burgess Meredith, Frederick O'Neal, Theodore Bikel, Ellen Burstyn, Colleen Dewhurst, Ron Silver**, and Patrick Quinn, all of whom had served in AEA leadership over the years.

ACTORS' FUND OF AMERICA.† In 1882, Harrison Grey Fiske* lobbied through the *New York Dramatic Mirror** to establish a charitable organization to support the needs of elderly and infirm actors. Leading players and producers were among the founders who managed it beginning with a $500 contribution from distinguished actor Edwin Booth.* In 1902, a retirement home was established on Staten Island, but eventually moved to Englewood, New Jersey. By 2009, its budget had grown to $17 million annually and served over 6,000 individuals and actor **Brian Stokes Mitchell** served as president.

ACTORS STUDIO, THE. Established in 1947 by **Cheryl Crawford, Elia Kazan**, and **Robert Lewis** as a workshop for professional actors, its widespread influence on mid-twentieth century American theatre, film, and television is incalculable. Located for decades at 432 West 44th Street in New York, its limited membership was by invitation and within a year of its founding, when **Lee Strasberg** joined, it became the focus of "method" acting, an approach to acting with an emphasis on actors applying their own feeling and experiences to the content of a play's text in creating a character. The Studio's techniques were inspired by **The Group Theatre** of the 1930s, which based its acting work on the innovations of Constantin Stanislavsky* and the Moscow Art Theatre.* Scripts used were typically contemporary American and European plays in the tradition of REALISM.

Some of the finest mid-twentieth century American actors were members of the Actors Studio, including **Geraldine Page, Kim Stanley, Paul Newman**, Marilyn Monroe, Joanne Woodward, **Marlon Brando**, Montgomery Clift, Robert De Niro, **Estelle Parsons, Dustin Hoffman, Al Pacino, Ellen Burstyn, Shelley Winters**, and many others. After a decade, the Actors Studio established special units for dramatists and directors and to mount productions. **Tennessee Williams, Edward Albee**, Norman Mailer, **Terrence McNally**, and **James Baldwin** were among writers involved at various times. Following Strasberg's 1982 death, Burstyn and Pacino succeeded him as the Studio's directors. They continue as copresidents, along with Harvey Keitel, and Mark Rydell and Martin Landau directing the west coast Studio in West Hollywood, California. In 1994, the Studio added an M.F.A. program in acting, directing, and playwriting, and with a physical move to Pace University, and the popularity of television's *Inside the Actors Studio*, hosted by James Lipton, the Actors Studio continues its influence into the twenty-first century.

ACTORS THEATRE OF LOUISVILLE. Founded in 1964 by Richard Block and Ewel Cornett, this professional resident company in Louisville, Kentucky, progressed into one of the major **regional theatres** after 1969 when **Jon Jory** took over as producing director. The theatre's varied play selections and commitment to new works attracted the interest of the profession, particularly playwrights, who found the annual Humana Festival of New Plays (including full-length and short works) a welcoming venue for new work. For audiences, the Humana Festival provided opportunities to see new works by emerging dramatists, including such figures as **David Henry Hwang, Tony Kushner, Naomi Wallace, Craig Lucas, Jane Martin** (Jory's playwriting pseudonym), and numerous others. Actors Theatre has two major performance spaces, the Pamela Brown Auditorium (637 seats) and the Victor Jory Theatre (180 seats).

ACTOR'S WORKSHOP. Two San Francisco State College professors, **Herbert Blau** and **Jules Irving**, founded this **regional theatre** in San

Francisco in 1952. The goal was to permit actors, as individuals, to pursue their individual goals. Their original performance space was a loft, but within two years after its founding, Blau and Irving took over the Marines' Memorial Theatre, presenting classics and contemporary works, with particular emphasis on avant-garde movements and overtly political works. In 1965, when Blau and Irving left for posts at **Lincoln Center**, the workshop essentially ended despite occasional attempts to revive it.

ADAIR, JEAN (1873–1953). Born Violet McNaughton in Hamilton, Ontario, Canada, Adair had a long career in vaudeville and theatre (often billed as Jennet Adair), appearing first on **Broadway** in *It's a Boy!* (1922) and in Sophie Treadwell's *Machinal** (1928). In the 1930s, she appeared in many Broadway productions, most notably as Mrs. Fisher in a revival of *The Show Off** in 1932, *Murder at the Vanities* (1933), ***On Borrowed Time*** (1938), ***Morning's at Seven*** (1939), and costarred memorably with Josephine Hull as one of the charmingly murderous aunts in ***Arsenic and Old Lace*** (1941), reprising her role as Aunt Martha in the Frank Capra-directed film version in 1944. Her final appearances were in ***Detective Story*** (1949), ***Bell, Book and Candle*** (1950), and as Rebecca Nurse in **Arthur Miller**'s ***The Crucible***.

ADLER, LUTHER (1903–1984).[†] Born in New York as Lutha Adler, son of the great Yiddish theatre actor Jacob Adler* and his wife, Sarah Levitzka,* Adler was destined for the stage, where he succeeded as both an actor and a director. He began as a child working in Yiddish theatre, but later moved on to the Provincetown Players* and made his **Broadway** debut in *Humoresque* (1923), followed by a series of plays including Elmer Rice's *Street Scene** (1929), in which he played the pivotal role of the idealistic law student, Sam Kaplan. He joined **The Group Theatre** in 1935 and appeared in important roles for them, including in *Success Story* (1932), ***Alien Corn*** (1933), **Sidney Kingsley**'s Pulitzer Prize-winning ***Men in White*** (1933), *Gold Eagle Guy* (1934), *Case of Clyde Griffiths* (1936), ***Johnny Johnson*** (1936), *Thunder Rock* (1939), and a series of **Clifford Odets**'s greatest plays, ***Awake and Sing!*** (1935), ***Waiting for Lefty*** (1935), ***Paradise Lost*** (1935), ***Golden Boy*** (1937), and ***Rocket to the Moon*** (1938).

Following the demise of The Group Theatre, Adler never truly regained his momentum as an actor. He appeared for a short run in Rice's *Two on an Island* (1940), after which he directed *They Should Have Stood in Bed* (1942), which failed. He appeared in character roles in films, but his periodic returns to the stage were generally unsuccessful, including roles in The *Russian People* (1942), *Common Ground* (1945), *Beggars Are Coming to Town* (1945), *A Very Special Baby* (1956), *The Passion of Josef D.* (1964), and

Three Sisters (1964). He directed BEN HECHT's *A Flag Is Born* (1946) and his final appearance, as one of a long line of actors replacing **Zero Mostel** as Tevye in the MUSICAL *Fiddler on the Roof* (1964), brought him back to his Yiddish theatre roots.

ADLER, STELLA (1903–1992).[†] Born in New York as the daughter of YIDDISH THEATRE legend Jacob Adler* and his wife, Sara Levitzka,* Adler made her stage debut as a child with her father. Passionately interested in acting, she studied with **Richard Boleslavsky** at the American Laboratory Theatre.* She joined **The Group Theatre** in 1931 at the behest of **Harold Clurman**, who she married and later divorced. Adler's tall, formidable presence and powerful personality may have limited her as an actress, but she appeared with distinction in several of the Group's productions, including PAUL GREEN's *The House of Connelly* (1931) and, most notably, **Clifford Odets**'s *Awake and Sing!* and *Paradise Lost*, both in 1935. She directed two short-lived productions, *Manhattan Nocturne* (1943) and *Sunday Breakfast* (1952), and rarely acted after an acrimonious departure from The Group Theatre when she and fellow member **Lee Strasberg** clashed over her experiences studying with **Constantin Stanislavsky** in Paris in 1934. She returned to the Group with a differing interpretation of Stanislavsky's ideas than those promoted by Strasberg.

Adler made her final stage appearance in a **Tyrone Guthrie**-directed revival of Leonid Andreyev's *He Who Gets Slapped* (1945). Her lasting contribution was founding the Stella Adler Conservatory, a school for acting, in 1949. She imperiously presided over the conservatory until shortly before her death. Veering from Strasberg's insistence on Stanislavsky's idea of emotional memory, Adler encouraged generations of acting students (among them, **Marlon Brando**, Robert De Niro, **Elaine Stritch**, Martin Sheen, Harvey Keitel, and Warren Beatty) to develop their imaginations in order to transcend their own life experiences and to focus on the text as opposed to their own psyches. She wrote several books on acting and modern drama, much of which were drawn from her lectures at the conservatory, including *The Technique of Acting* (1988), *The Art of Acting* (2000), and *Stella Adler on Ibsen, Strindberg, and Chekhov* (2001).

AFRICAN AMERICAN THEATRE.[†] Black playwrights and managers were precious few in the United States prior to 1880, despite the brief triumph of the African Grove Theatre in New York in 1821. In serious drama, the options for black writers and performers were slimmer than in the MUSICAL THEATRE, but Chicago's Pekin Stock Company* (1906), New York's Negro Players* (1912), and the influential LAFAYETTE PLAYERS (1915) created more welcoming venues. On **Broadway**, the first appearances of blacks in serious drama came in the work of white playwrights, including Ridgely Torrence's* *Three Plays for a Negro Theatre* * (1917), EUGENE O'NEILL's *The Emperor Jones* * (1920), PAUL GREEN's PULITZER PRIZE-winning *In Abraham's Bosom* * (1926), DuBose and Dorothy Heyward's* *Porgy* * (1927), and MARC CONNELLY's *The Green Pastures* (1930), which also won a Pulitzer Prize. After 1930, change was slow but steady as socially conscious plays by African American writers began to appear, including Hall Johnson's *Run Little Chillun* (1933) and LANGSTON HUGHES's *Stevedore* (1934) and *Mulatto* (1935).

During the 1930s, the **Federal Theatre Project (FTP)** provided opportunity to black writers and performers through its Negro Units set up in 22 cities. From these emerged Theodore Browne's *Natural Man* (1937), Theodore Ward's *Big White Fog* (1938), and **Orson Welles**'s staging of a "voodoo" version of *Macbeth* in Harlem. During the 1940s, the **American Negro Theatre** nurtured black artists and produced white playwright **Philip Yordan**'s *Anna Lucasta* (1944), which was transferred to Broadway in a move ultimately causing dissolution of the company. Among notable African American productions post-1940, **Richard Wright**'s novel *Native Son* was dramatized in 1941 under the direction of Orson Welles and starred **Canada Lee** in an acclaimed performance. PAUL ROBESON scored a triumph in *Othello* (1943), which broke records for the length of the run of a **Shakespeare** play, and Theodore Ward's *Our Lan'* (1946), an historical drama about former slaves in the aftermath of the Civil War, won critical plaudits. After World **WAR** II, the growing civil rights movement encouraged black writers to address contemporary issues, bring forth such works as Louis Peterson's *Take a Giant Step* (1953), William Branch's *In Splendid Error* (1954), **Alice Childress**'s *Trouble in Mind* (1955), and **Loften Mitchell**'s *A Land Beyond the River* (1957).

The seismic appearance of **Lorraine Hansberry**'s *A Raisin in the Sun* (1959), the first drama by a black woman to succeed on Broadway, reaped awards and considerable critical praise, not to mention commercial success. It became a major film with much of its original cast in place, and it is frequently revived. The peak of the civil rights movement in the 1960s, as well as the other social upheavals of that era, energized African American theatre, as seen in such works as actor-playwright **Ossie Davis**'s *Purlie Victorious* (1961), **LeRoi Jones**'s (**Amiri Baraka**) controversial *Dutchman* (1964), **Lonnie Elder**'s *Ceremonies in Dark Old Men* (1969), and **Charles Gordone**'s *No Place to Be Somebody* (1969).

Mixed-race casting, pioneered at **Joseph Papp**'s **New York Shakespeare Festival**, opened up opportunities for black performers in a wide range of previously unavailable roles, from Shakespeare and the classics to musical theatre, as demonstrated by the great success of Pearl Bailey in an all-black version of *Hello, Dolly!* in 1967. Other all-black musicals appeared frequently, as well as works by white and black dramatists dealing with race. White playwright **Howard Sackler**'s *The Great White Hope* (1968) was a major success due, in large part, to actor **James Earl Jones**'s memorable performance as African American prizefighter Jack Jefferson. From the mid-1970s, African Americans established successful theatre companies for works by black writers, past and present. Among the most important new plays by black dramatists post-1975 are **Ntozake Shange**'s poetic *for colored girls who have considered suicide/when the rainbow is enuf* (1976), **Vinnette Carroll**'s *Your Arm's Too Short to Box with God* (1976), Philip Hayes Dean's one-man drama *Paul Robeson* (1978), **Charles Fuller**'s PULITZER PRIZE-winning *A Soldier's Play* (1981), and numerous works by **Ed Bullins**, **Adrienne Kennedy**, **Ron Milner**, Charlie Russell, Joseph Walker, Richard Wesley, and the much-praised **Suzan-Lori Parks**, among others.

Perhaps the most important black playwright to emerge in this period was **August Wilson**, whose 10-play series of African American life in the twentieth century was completed shortly before his 2005 death, and includes *Fences* (1983) and *The Piano Lesson* (1990), both of which won the Pulitzer Prize for Drama. At the millennium, several important artists emerged, including **George C. Wolfe**, director and playwright, who became artistic director of New York's **Public Theatre**, while young directors, Tisch Jones, **Tazewell Thompson**, and Ricardo Kahn, asserted themselves. New plays by young African American dramatists also appeared, including Brian Freeman's *Civil Sex* (2002) and Parks's *Topdog/Underdog* (2002), which won the Pulitzer Prize, and contributions by Cheryl L. West, **Anna Deavere Smith**, Carlyle Brown, Kia Corthron, and **Pearl Cleage**.

AFTER THE FALL. This two-act drama by **Arthur Miller**, opened on 23 January 1964 in a production by the **Repertory Theatre of Lincoln Center** at the **American National Theatre and Academy (ANTA)** Washington Square Theatre. With a notable cast including **Jason Robards** and Barbara Loden, Miller's partly autobiographical play centers on a middle-aged lawyer reflecting on the women in his past, most notably Maggie, his second wife, a suicidal actress riddled with deep emotional insecurities. Critics assailed what they felt was a betrayal of the late Marilyn Monroe, Miller's ex-wife, but the production ran for 208 performances as the first production of the Repertory Theatre of Lincoln Center. The **Roundabout Theatre** revived *After the Fall* in 2004 under **Michael Mayer**'s direction, featuring Peter Krause, Carla Gugino (**Theatre World Award** winner), and **Jessica Hecht**.

AGENTS.[†] Increasingly, after 1930, most theatrical personnel, especially actors, were represented by agents and agencies set up to help them locate work, to protect their interests in contract negotiations, and otherwise to promote their careers. As opportunities for stage actors diversified with the coming of motion pictures, radio, and television, agents grew in power, working with studios and networks, as well as theatrical producers, in casting shows and programs. A few agents during the **Broadway** golden age became well-known for various reasons. In the case of **Audrey Wood**, her fame derived from a single client, **Tennessee Williams**. Wood was the daughter of the first manager of the Palace Theatre and established the Liebling-Wood, Inc. agency with her husband, William Liebling, in 1937, finding Williams as a client shortly thereafter. Aside from Williams, whose career she nurtured from its beginning, Wood also represented **William Inge**, **Robert Anderson**, and **Arthur Kopit**. **Leland Hayward**, who was also a producer of note, represented a range of stars and literary figures (Ernest Hemingway, for example), many associated with both stage and screen, including at various times Fred Astaire, **Henry Fonda**, Greta Garbo, Judy Garland, **Katharine Hepburn** (with whom he had a personal relationship), Ginger Rogers, **James Stewart**, and **Margaret Sullavan** (one of his five wives). Singular agents like Wood and Hayward were ultimately replaced by major agencies representing working actors for theatre, as well as film, radio, and television.

AH, WILDERNESS! The only comedy by America's foremost dramatic playwright, EUGENE O'NEILL, *Ah, Wilderness!* opened on 2 October 1933 for an impressive 289 performance run at the Guild Theatre. This THEATRE GUILD production won kudos from critics for both O'Neill's play and the performance of the leading actor, the legendary GEORGE M. COHAN, who, in *Ah, Wilderness!*, appeared for the first time in a work he had not written (in a backhanded compliment from critics, some noted that it took O'Neill to show audiences what a truly great actor Cohan was).

Set in small-town Connecticut in 1906, this rose-colored depiction of O'Neill's adolescence portrays the family life O'Neill wished he had and serves as a complement to his later autobiographical play, *Long Day's Journey into Night* (1939), a tragic portrait of his family set six years after *Ah, Wilderness!* Neither is accurate autobiography, but both plays reflect the conflict within O'Neill over his family dynamics at the foundation of many of his dramas. Cohan played Nat Miller, an avuncular father figure who, along with his wife Essie, wryly observes the bittersweet coming-of-age of his adolescent son, Richard, a passionate reader of literature whose own passions are inflamed by the revolutionary sentiments expressed in his reading material. The heartaches of Richard's first romance and an alcoholic misadventure are set in counterpoint to his parents' mellow relationship and the bittersweet struggles of an aunt and uncle who have been unable to work out their relationship, despite deep feelings.

Ah, Wilderness! is frequently revived (on **Broadway** there were revivals in 1941, 1975, 1988, and 1998) and was filmed in 1935 and for television in 1976. It has been adapted into MUSICAL form twice, first as *Summer Holiday* (1948), an elaborate M-G-M musical featuring WALTER HUSTON and Mickey Rooney, and as a Broadway musical, *Take Me Along* (1959), with the emphasis shifted to the relationship of the uncle and aunt, played by Jackie Gleason and **Eileen Herlie**, with Walter Pidgeon as Nat and **Robert Morse** as Richard. The play has become a staple of **regional, academic**, and **community theatres**.

O'Neill planned a darker sequel to *Ah, Wilderness!*, set in the aftermath of World WAR I and featuring an embittered Nat, unable to cope with the rapidly changing society, and Richard, returning from the war with emotional and physical scars. He never completed the play, but left an outline of its plot among his papers.

AHERNE, BRIAN (1902–1986). Born William Brian de Lacy Aherne in King's Norton, England, Aherne spent most of his career on the American stage and in Hollywood films beginning in the silent era. His theatre work was frequently opposite KATHARINE CORNELL following their high successful appearance together as Robert Browning and Elizabeth Barrett in *The Barretts of Wimpole Street* in 1931. Also with Cornell, Aherne appeared as Mercutio in *Romeo and Juliet* in 1934, Warwick in *Saint Joan* in 1936, and as GEORGE BERNARD SHAW to Cornell's Mrs. Patrick Campbell in *Dear Liar* in 1960, Cornell's last stage appearance. Aherne also toured as Henry Higgins in *My Fair Lady*. Among his many film appearances are *Sylvia Scarlett* (1935), *The Great Garrick* (1937), *Juarez* (1939), and *My Sister Eileen* (1942), and during the 1950s and 1960s, he acted frequently on television.

AIDS ON THE AMERICAN STAGE. In 1981, as AIDS (acquired immune deficiency syndrome) was first reported as a **"gay** cancer," dramatists have responded to its toll on American life, most particularly the homosexual community. Gay-themed plays were still comparatively rare in mainstream drama—it had only been little more than a decade since **Mart Crowley**'s *The Boys in the Band* (1968), presented images of gay life. Stereotypical depictions of homosexuals abounded and gays were usually reduced to peripheral status in **Broadway** plays, although **Off-Broadway** and fringe venues had provided a platform for gay-themed works since the 1960s. Between 1960 and the 1980s, however, gay characters were seen in boulevard comedies like *Torch Song Trilogy* (1981), in occasional MUSICALS, or in broad stereotypes in straight plays. There were exceptions, including **Edward Albee**'s *Everything In the Garden* (1967), **LeRoi Jones**'s **(Amiri Baraka)** *The Toilet* (1964), and the grotesquerie of **Charles Ludlam**'s **Theatre of the Ridiculous**, but the outset of the AIDS pandemic set off significant changes in dramatic depictions of homosexuality.

With the arrival of the AIDS pandemic, gay-themed plays became either scathing indictments of American society's failures in responding to the AIDS crisis, as seen in **Larry Kramer**'s *The Normal Heart* (1985), *Just Say No* (1988), and *The Destiny of Me* (1992), or in dark depictions of historical oppression of gays, as in **Martin Sherman**'s *Bent* (1978), which dramatizes oppressions against homosexuals during the Holocaust. Gay-themed plays espousing tolerance had emerged prior to AIDS, as in **Harvey Fierstein**'s *Torch Song Trilogy*, but as the pandemic took hold, Fierstein offered *Safe Sex* (1987), a bill of three one-acts connected by a central theme: the impact of AIDS on both homosexuals and heterosexuals. Ludlam's death in the mid-1980s was only one among many losses of theatre artists early in the crisis and these deaths took on metaphorical significance as the next transition in gay drama fully emerged. Depictions of the personal struggles of gays and divisive social questions inflamed by AIDS became a theatrical cottage industry during the 1980s and into the 1990s. **William M. Hoffman**'s *As Is* (1985) plunged into the personal horrors of AIDS before it was recognized by most as the international pandemic it would become, but it was Kramer's *The Normal Heart* that inspired considerable controversy in its Broadway and West End productions. Like other AIDS dramas of the 1980s–1990s, *The Normal Heart* focuses, in part, on personal lives and ordinary individuals caught up in the crisis. The personal circumstances are set into an angry frontal assault on societal failures in response to the epidemic by government, the medical profession, religious and social organizations, and individuals trapped within a tradition of homophobia.

The next period of AIDS-related plays emerged in the early 1990s, as playwrights insisted on the centrality of gay individuals to American life. This view is central to **Tony Kushner**'s PULITZER PRIZE and **Tony Award**-winning *Angels in America* (1993) plays, *Millennium Approaches* and *Perestroika*, epic works which brushed aside tolerance pleas in depicting a range of gay characters — some "out" and others "in the closet" — grappling with political, moral, religious, and deeply personal issues in a dark social landscape at the height of Ronald Reagan's presidency. The toll of AIDS on the gay community was central to **Terrence McNally**'s bittersweet Pulitzer Prize-winning play *Love! Valour! Compassion!* (1994), in which a group of gay friends experience love and loss as the specter of AIDS hangs heavily over their lives. McNally wrote several plays dealing with the impact of AIDS, including *Lips Together, Teeth Apart* (1991) and a short play, *Andre's Mother* (1988), which was expanded into a film for television. McNally's *Corpus Christi* (1998) set off a firestorm of controversy in its **Manhattan Theatre Club** premiere for its depiction of Jesus Christ's life in the context of the present-day experiences of gay Texans. **Paul Rudnick**'s *The Most Fabulous Story Ever Told* (1998) similarly connected contemporary gay life, including AIDS, to biblical stories, and Rudnick's *Jeffrey* (1995) offered a broadly farcical chronicle of a gay Everyman in contemporary America. Emerging gay dramatists in the late 1990s–early 2000s, including **Paula Vogel**, **Richard Greenberg**, and others, were deeply influenced by AIDS, gay rights activism, and the openly gay dramatists who had come before them.

AKALAITIS, JOANNE (1937–). A noted American theatre director and writer born in Chicago, Illinois, Akalaitis founded New York's **Mabou Mines** in 1970, running the company for 20 years. For the **American Repertory Theatre**, she directed productions of Samuel Beckett's *Endgame* (the author attempted to halt her production), Jean Genet's *The Balcony*, and Harold Pinter's *The Birthday Party*, in the 1980s, and she directed numerous **regional theatre** productions and won five **Obie Awards**, including for her direction of *Cassandra* (1975), *Dressed Like an Egg* (1976), and *Through the Leaves* (1983), and Mabou Mines, under her guidance, won a Sustained Achievement Obie in 1985, as she herself did in 1992. The mother of two children, Juliet and Zachary, from her marriage to composer Philip Glass, she served as artistic director of the **New York Shakespeare Festival/Public Theatre** and has taught at the Juilliard School and Bard College.

AKERLIND, CHRISTOPHER (1962–). A native of Hartford, Connecticut, Akerlind studied at Boston University and at the Yale School of Drama under lighting designer **Jennifer Tipton**. He has won the **Tony Award** and the **Drama Desk Award** for lighting *The Light in the Piazza* (2006) and an **Obie Award** for sustained excellence, as well as numerous nominations. He spent 12 years as resident lighting designer for the Opera Theatre of St. Louis and worked consistently **Off-Broadway**, including with such collaborators as **Martha Clarke**, **Anne Bogart**, and **Charles Mee**. On **Broadway**, he designed *The Piano Lesson* (1990), a revival of *Philadelphia, Here I Come!* in 1994, *Seven Guitars* (1996), *The Tale of the Allergist's Wife* (2000), *Reckless* (2004), *In My Life* (2005), a revival of *A Touch of the Poet* in 2005, *Rabbit Hole* (2006), *Well* (2006), a revival of *Awake and Sing!* in 2006, *Shining City* (2006), *Talk Radio* (2007), a revival of *110 in the Shade* in 2007, and *Top Girls* (2008).

ALABAMA SHAKESPEARE FESTIVAL, THE (ASF). Established in 1972 as a summer theatre in Anniston, Alabama, the festival moved to a permanent facility in Montgomery, Alabama, in the 1980s, becoming one of the largest **Shakespeare** festivals in the world. Staging more than a dozen productions annually, featuring Shakespeare, but also including new works and international classics, the ASF also operates an M.F.A. training program for actors, designers, and stage managers. In the 1990s, artistic director Kent Thompson set up the Southern Writers' Project to foster regional work.

ALBEE, EDWARD (1928–). Born in Washington, D.C., Albee was adopted by the son of theatrical entrepreneur E. F. Albee* and named Edward Franklin Albee III. His adoption was not a happy one and he spent much of it in and out of numerous schools, including Trinity College. He gave up on his formal education and supported his interest in writing poetry with odd jobs until he was encouraged by THORNTON WILDER to abandon poetry for drama. His first play, a long one-act titled *The Zoo Story* (1959), was first produced in Germany, but it, as well as several subsequent one-acts written between 1959 and 1961, including *The Sandbox*, *Fam and Yam*, *The American Dream*, and *The Death of Bessie Smith*, won Albee a critical following.

In 1962, Albee's first full-length play, the controversial *Who's Afraid of Virginia Woolf?*, catapulted him to the forefront of American dramatists. The play won the **New York Drama Critics Award**, but was pointedly overlooked by the PULITZER PRIZE committee due to the play's use of strong language, sexual situations, and its scathing view of marriage. Many of Albee's plays from the 1960s to the 1980s failed to find critical favor or enthusiastic audiences, despite the obvious quality of his work, including his adaptation of **Carson McCullers**'s *The Ballad of the Sad Café* (1963), the highly experimental *Tiny Alice* (1964), and *Malcolm* (1966). In 1966, Albee's *A Delicate Balance* won a Pulitzer Prize, with speculation that it was a consolation prize for the overlooked *Who's Afraid of Virginia Woolf?* Despite critical brickbats, Albee's playwriting (and also his producing and directing) won him significant respect in the theatrical community—some of the finest actors of the era, including John Gielgud, **Irene Worth**, **Uta Hagen**, **Arthur Hill**, and others, welcomed the opportunity of working on an Albee play. Albee's *Everything in the Garden* (1967) and *All Over* (1971), were quick commercial failures, but he received a second Pulitzer Prize for his 1974 play *Seascape*.

For more than a decade, Albee's new plays were met with critical apathy, including *Listening* (1975), *Counting the Ways* (1976), *The Lady from Dubuque* (1979), *Box* (1980), his adaptation of Vladimir Nabokov's *Lolita* (1981), and *Finding the Sun* (1982). Returning to themes explored in *Who's Afraid of Virginia Woolf?*, Albee won plaudits for *Marriage Play* (1987) and his 1990 play, *Three Tall Women,* won him a third Pulitzer Prize. Since the early 1990s, Albee's output has not slowed, with *The Lorca Play* (1992), *Fragments* (1993), *The Play about the Baby* (1996), *The Goat, or Who Is Sylvia?* (2002), *Occupant* (2001), *Knock! Knock! Who's There!?* (2003), and *Me, Myself, and I* (2007) finding more appreciative critics and audiences that had been typical of Albee's work in the 1970s and 1980s. In 2004, Albee wrote a one-act, *At Home at the Zoo,* a prequel of sorts to *The Zoo Story,* presenting the two plays together under the title *Peter & Jerry.* In 2005, he published *Stretching My Mind,* a collection of his essays from 1960–2005, and he was presented with a **Tony Award** for Lifetime Achievement to add to the Gold Medal for Drama from the American Academy and Institute of Arts and Letter, a **Kennedy Center** Honor, and a National Medal of Arts award.

ALBERT, EDDIE (1908–2005). Born Edward Albert Heimberger in Rock Island, Illinois, Albert appeared on **Broadway** with note in the popular comedies *Brother Rat* (1936) and *Room Service* (1937), as well as the MUSICAL *The Boys from Syracuse* (1938), before turning to a long and successful career in films and television. He made occasional returns to the New York stage in Irving Berlin's musical *Miss Liberty* (1949) and in the flop *No Hard Feelings* (1973), and he replaced **Robert Preston** in *The Music Man* and **Jason Robards** in a revival of *You Can't Take It With You.*

ALBERTSON, JACK (1907–1981). Born in Malden, Massachusetts, Albertson labored in small and supporting roles in theatre, film and television for decades, including roles in *Meet the People* (1940), *Strip for Action* (1942), *Allah Be Praised!* (1944), *A Lady Says Yes* (1945), a revival of *The Cradle Will Rock* (1947), *Tickets, Please!* (1950), and *Top Banana* (1951). Late in his career, he scored major successes in **Frank D. Gilroy**'s *The Subject Was Roses* (1964) and in **Neil Simon**'s comedy about two aging vaudevillians,* *The Sunshine Boys* (1972).

ALDA, ALAN (1936–). Born in New York, the son of actor Robert Alda, Alda was noticed in several **Broadway** shows, including *Only in America* (1959), *Purlie Victorious* (1961), *Fair Game for Lovers* (1964), and *Café Crown* (1964), before scoring notable successes in the comedy *The Owl and the Pussycat* (1964) and the MUSICAL *The Apple Tree* (1966), for which he was nominated for a **Tony Award**. For nearly three decades, Alda worked in films and television, most notably in the long-running TV series *M*A*S*H,* but he returned to Broadway in **Neil Simon**'s *Jake's Women* (1992), for which he was nominated for a Tony, with occasional subsequent performances in *Art* (1998), *QED* (2001), *The Play What I Wrote* (2003), and to acclaim (and a Tony nomination) in a revival of **David Mamet**'s *Glengarry Glen Ross* in 2005.

ALDREDGE, THEONI V. (1932–2011). Born Theoni Athanasiou Vachlioti in Salonika, Greece, Vachlioti studied at the American School before moving to the United States. Her work for Chicago's GOODMAN THEATRE won her critical attention, and she married actor **Tom Aldredge** in 1953, taking his surname as her professional name. Aldredge designed in excess of a hundred **Broadway** plays and MUSICALS, winning **Tony Awards** for Best Costume Design for the musicals *Two Gentlemen of Verona* (1971) and *Annie* (1977), *Barnum* (1980), and *La Cage aux Folles* (1983), along with numerous other nominations. She frequently designed costumes for the **New York Shakespeare Festival**, and among her other credits are such noted productions as *Sweet Bird of Youth* (1959), *The Best Man* (1960), *Mary, Mary* (1961), *Mr. President* (1962), *Who's Afraid of Virginia Woolf?* (1962), *Anyone Can Whistle* (1964), *Any Wednesday* (1964), *Cactus Flower* (1965), *A Delicate Balance* (1966), *You Know I Can't Hear You When the Water's Running* (1967), *Little Murders* (1967), *I Never Sang for My Father* (1968), *That Championship Season* (1972), *Sticks and Bones* (1972), *A Chorus Line* (1975), *The Belle of Amherst* (1976), *Clothes for a Summer Hotel* (1980), *42nd Street* (1980), *Woman of the Year* (1981), *The Rink* (1984), and revivals of *Gypsy* (1989) and *Follies* (2001). Aldredge also worked in film, winning an Academy Award for her costumes for *The Great Gatsby* (1974). Her other film credits included *Network* (1976), *Annie* (1982), *Moonstruck* (1987), *The First Wives Club* (1996), and *The Mirror Has Two Faces* (1996).

ALDREDGE, TOM (1928–). A native of Dayton, Ohio, Thomas Ernest Aldredge attended the **Goodman Theatre School** at Chicago's DePaul University before embarking on a long career as a respected stage, film, and television actor. He married costume designer **Theoni V. Aldredge** in 1953 and both began to work in the New York theatre in the late 1950s. Aldredge made his **Off-Broadway** debut in *Electra* in 1957, followed by a shift to **Broadway** in *The Nervous Set* (1959). Aldredge won particular acclaim as curmudgeonly Norman Thayer, Jr., in *On Golden Pond* (1979) and he has been nominated for **Tony Awards** five times for his appearances in *Sticks and Bones* (1972), a 1975 revival of *Where's Charley?*, the Elizabeth Taylor revival of *The Little Foxes* in 1981, **Stephen Sondheim**'s musical *Passion* (1996), and a 2004 revival of the 1930s comedy *Twentieth Century*. Aldredge's other Broadway credits include *Everything in the Garden* (1967), *Indians* (1969), a 1973 revival of *The Iceman Cometh*, *Rex* (1976), *Vieux Carré* (1977), *Into the Woods* (1987), and revivals of *1776* in 1997, *The*

Crucible in 2002, and *12 Angry Men* in 2004. He also appeared frequently in films, including *Other People's Money* (1991), *What About Bob?* (1991), *Cold Mountain* (2003), *All the King's Men* (2006), and as Carmela Soprano's father in the acclaimed HBO-TV series *The Sopranos.*

ALDRICH, RICHARD STODDARD (1902–1986). Born in Boston, Massachusetts, Aldrich began his producing career as general manager for the American Laboratory Theatre* beginning in 1926. He worked closely with KENNETH MACGOWAN as a coproducer during the Great Depression, but in 1933, worked with **Alfred de Liagre, Jr.** He produced a few successful plays, including *Margin for Error* (1939) and *My Dear Children* (1940), before marrying legendary English stage star **Gertrude Lawrence** in 1940. After wartime service, Aldrich produced a successful revival of GEORGE BERNARD SHAW's *Pygmalion* starring Lawrence. He was managing director of the Cape Playhouse in Dennis, Massachusetts, for many years, as well as Washington, D.C.'s National Theatre. His postwar producing includes bringing the Old Vic, Habimah Players, and Dublin's Gate Theatre for appearances in New York, as well as the productions of new **Broadway** plays, including *Goodbye, My Fancy* (1948), *The Moon Is Blue* (1951), and *The Love of Four Colonels* (1953), and revivals of *Caesar and Cleopatra* (1949) and *The Devil's Disciple* (1951). Following Lawrence's death in 1952, Aldrich published *Mrs. A*, a memoir of their marriage, and produced three unsuccessful plays, *A Girl Can Tell* (1953), *Dear Charles* (1954), and *Little Glass Clock* (1956).

ALEXANDER, JANE (1939–). Born Jane Quigley in Boston, Massachusetts, to parents in the medical profession, Alexander attended Sarah Lawrence College and spent a year studying at the University of Edinburgh, where she became involved in the drama society. She married a young actor, Robert Alexander, and together they sought work in the New York theatre in the early 1960s. Her career was interrupted by the birth of a son, Jace, in 1964, a few years before the marriage ended. In 1975, she married **Edwin Sherin**, artistic director of Washington's **Arena Stage**. By that time, Alexander had won critical acclaim and a **Tony Award** for her performance as Eleanor Backman in **Howard Sackler**'s drama *The Great White Hope* (1967), opposite **James Earl Jones** as boxer Jack Jefferson. Alexander and Jones repeated their roles in an acclaimed 1971 film version *The Great White Hope* and she received an Oscar nomination (she received three additional Academy Award nominations for *All the President's Men* [1976], *Kramer vs. Kramer* [1979], and *Testament* [1983]).

Much of Alexander's later work was in film and television, although she interrupted her career for a stint as director of the **National Endowment**

of the Arts (NEA), enduring considerable controversy during the "culture wars" of the period (1993–1997). She later published a memoir of the experience, *Command Performance: An Actress in the Theatre of Politics* (2000). Her periodic returns to the **Broadway** stage have often brought her Tony nominations, including *6 Rms Riv Vu* (1972), *Find Your Way Home* (1973), *First Monday in October* (1978), *The Sisters Rosensweig* (1993), and *Honour* (1998), and she also appeared in *Goodbye Fidel* (1980), *Monday after the Miracle* (1982), and *Shadowlands* (1990), as well as revivals of *Hamlet* (1975), *The Heiress* (1976), *The Night of the Iguana* (1988), and *The Visit* (1992), for which she received another Tony nomination. Alexander's television work garnered her numerous Emmy Award nominations, including for the acclaimed miniseries *Eleanor and Franklin* (1976) and its sequel, *Eleanor and Franklin: The White House Years* (1977). She won Emmy Awards for *Playing for Time* (1980) and *Warm Springs* (2005). In 2004, Alexander and Sherin joined the faculty of Florida State University.

ALICE, MARY (1941–). A native of Indianola, Mississippi, Mary Alice Smith dropped her surname when she began a stage, film and television career. Her first **Broadway** credit was in the 1971 production of *No Place to Be Somebody* and she won an **Obie Award** in 1978 for her performances in *Nongogo* and *Julius Caesar*. She won considerable praise and a **Tony Award** as Best Featured Actress in a Play for the original Broadway production of **August Wilson**'s *Fences* (1987), playing opposite **James Earl Jones**. Most of her subsequent work was in film and television, but she returned to Broadway in a 1994 revival of *The Shadow Box* and *Having Our Say* (1995), which brought her a Tony nomination. She was twice nominated for Emmy Awards for her work on *I'll Fly Away*, winning the award in 1993. *See also* AFRICAN AMERICAN THEATRE.

ALIEN CORN. This three-act drama by SIDNEY HOWARD opened at the Belasco Theatre on 20 February 1933 starring KATHARINE CORNELL. She played Elsa, a promising German pianist compelled to work as a teacher to support her handicapped father, an embittered musician who had been interred as an alien in America. Two young men vie for Elsa's affections, a young political radical, played by LUTHER ADLER, and a wealthy married man, portrayed by James Rennie. When she rejects them, the radical commits suicide. Critics admired Cornell's performance and the subtlety of Howard's play, but at the height of the Great Depression, it managed to rack up only 98 performances.

ALISON'S HOUSE. This three-act drama by SUSAN GLASPELL opened at EVA LE GALLIENNE's CIVIC REPERTORY THEATRE on 1 December 1930 for only 41 performances, despite winning a PULITZER PRIZE. The play is set in Iowa, but is clearly based on Emily Dickinson's life in its portrait of a lonely spinster living on her brother's charity and writing poetry, although much of the focus is on family members, including Alison's sister, Elsa (Le Gallienne) and various family secrets revealed after Alison's death. Despite the fact that her poems expose the family, they ultimately decide to release them for publication. *Alison's House* has never had a major revival.

ALL MY SONS. This first important drama by **Arthur Miller**, which won the **New York Drama Critics Circle Award** and a playwriting **Tony Award**, opened at the Coronet Theatre on 29 January 1947 for a 328 performance run. Directed by **Elia Kazan** (who won a Tony), who produced the play in association with **Harold Clurman**, Walter Fried, and Herbert H. Harris, *All My Sons* featured evocative scenic and lighting design by **Mordecai Gorelik** and was bolstered by a cast including **Ed Begley**, **Arthur Kennedy**, and Karl Malden.

A family drama that explodes into a scathing critique of war profiteering and its ramifications centers on Joe Keller, an airplane parts manufacturer, who has sold defective parts to the government during World War II, resulting in the deaths of a number of pilots. Larry, Keller's son, a pilot in the war, has been reported missing in action, but a letter from him written before his loss arrives condemning his father's actions, which include allowing his partner to take the blame. Keller's surviving son, Chris, confronts Keller, who kills himself after finally recognizing his responsibility, noting that the lost pilots were "all my sons."

A film version was released in 1948 starring EDWARD G. ROBINSON and Burt Lancaster, and a PBS television production in 1986, featured **James Whitmore** and Aidan Quinn. **Richard Kiley** and Jamey Sheridan appeared in a short-lived 1987 **Broadway** revival, both garnering Tony Award nominations. **John Lithgow** and Patrick Wilson appeared in a 2008 Broadway revival that ran 101 performances partly on the strength of the publicity generated by the stage debut of film and television actress Katie Holmes.

ALL THE WAY HOME. This PULITZER PRIZE and **New York Drama Critics Circle Award**-winning drama in three acts, based on James Agee's *A Death in the Family*, was written by Tad Mosel and opened at the Belasco Theatre on 30 November 1960 for 334 performances with a strong cast, including **Arthur Hill** and **Colleen Dewhurst**. Directed by **Arthur Penn**, the play is set in 1915 in Knoxville, Tennessee, where questions of religious faith are tested in the marriage of Jay, an ambivalent man, and Mary, a devoutly Catholic woman. Along with their son, Rufus, they fall into conflict when

Mary resists telling Rufus that she is pregnant. When Jay is killed in a car accident visiting his ailing father, Mary's beliefs are challenged in carrying for Rufus and her new baby. **Robert Preston** and Jean Simmons appeared in a well-received 1963 big-screen version, and the play has also been filmed for television twice, in 1971 and 1981, the last a "live" television special starring Sally Field and **William Hurt**.

ALLEN, JAY PRESSON (1922–2006). Born in San Angelo, Texas, as Jacqueline Presson, Allen wrote plays, films and novels, produced for television, and was a stage director. She left home to become an actress, but turned to writing novels in the late 1940s. She married Lewis Allen in 1955 and he and others encouraged her to write, including her first unproduced play, *The First Wife*, which was filmed as *Wives and Lovers* (1963). Her next play, *The Prime of Miss Jean Brodie*, adapted from Muriel Spark's novel about an unconventional teacher at a girls' school, premiered in England in 1966, prior to a successful **Broadway** production in 1968. Allen scored again with *Forty Carats* (1968), a popular comedy about a 40-plus year-old woman who has an affair with a 20-something young man. She also wrote *A Little Family Business* (1982), which was a failure. Much of Allen's subsequent work was for the movies, including screenplays for *Marnie* (1964), *Cabaret* (1972), *Travels with My Aunt* (1972), *Funny Lady* (1975), *Just Tell Me What You Want* (1980), *Prince of the City* (1981), *Deathtrap* (1982), and others. She returned to theatre writing with *Tru* (1989) and wrote and directed *The Big Love* (1991), and was a respected "script doctor."

ALLEN, JOAN (1956–). A native of Rochelle, Illinois, Allen was educated at Northern Illinois University before beginning an acting career in theatre and film. She won a **Drama Desk Award** and a **Theatre World Award** for her **Off-Broadway** performance in *And a Nightingale Sang* (1984), and she was Drama Desk-nominated for *The Marriage of Bette and Boo* (1986). In her debut **Broadway** role in **Lanford Wilson**'s *Burn This* (1987), Allen won a **Tony Award**. She was nominated for a Tony and a Drama Desk Award as the title character in **Wendy Wasserstein**'s PULITZER PRIZE-winning *The Heidi Chronicles* (1989), but a burgeoning film career kept her away from Broadway until she returned in *Impressionism* (2009) and Off-Broadway prior to her appearance in *An Oak Tree* (2006). Allen became a major movie star and garnered three Academy Award nominations for her performances in *Nixon* (1995), *The Crucible* (1996), and *The Contender* (2000). On television, Allen was nominated for an Emmy Award for *The Mists of Avalon* (2001) and a Golden Globe Award for the television film *Georgia O'Keefe* (2009). Allen has been married to actor Peter Friedman since 1990.

ALLEN, WOODY (1935–). The personification of a modern-day New Yorker, Allen was born Allen Stewart Konigsberg and began his career as a television writer and stand-up comedian with a passion for American music, particularly jazz. Following several years writing for television, particularly for **Sid Caesar** (along with Mel Brooks, **Neil Simon**, **Larry Gelbart**, and others), Allen wrote the book to the musical revue *From A to Z* (1960), but found his first stage success with *Don't Drink the Water* (1966), followed by a major **Broadway** triumph with *Play It Again, Sam* (1969), which he wrote and starred in, essentially creating a version of the persona of the neurotic schlemiel he would perfect in his films which, like his plays, reflect his background (Jewish) and his intellectual curiosities and personal foibles. His Academy Award-winning film career as writer, director, and actor has been one of the most singular in Hollywood history, and New York cultural life, including the theatre, is often featured in his movies, but he returned to playwriting only once with *The Floating Light Bulb* (1981), produced at **Lincoln Center**. Allen is also an accomplished essayist and has published a number of short plays in several collections of his writings.

ALLEY THEATRE, THE (AT). Founded in 1947 by Nina Vance and her backers, Mrs. and Mrs. Robert Altfeld, the Alley Theatre began in an abandoned factory in Houston, Texas, before becoming fully professional in 1954. The AT grew in prosperity as Vance brought in name actors to attract audiences and won grant support and donations (and ultimately a **Tony Award** as an outstanding regional theatre). In 1968, the AT moved into a theatre complex containing two performance spaces (one thrust and one arena) and developed a reputation for producing American contemporary plays and developed close relationships with **Edward Albee** and other major writers. *See also* REGIONAL THEATRE MOVEMENT.

ALLIANCE OF RESIDENT THEATRES/NEW YORK (A.R.T). A service organization founded in 1972 by 49 **Off-Off Broadway** theatres, the A.R.T./New York was established to support the work of small theatres in which an emphasis on the city's cultural and artistic diversity was paramount. A.R.T. administers cash grants, loans, and can provide office and rehearsal space, as well as technical support, to theatre groups in the five boroughs of New York. As of 2009, the organization boasted membership of 425 not-for-profit theatres.

ALLIANCE THEATRE COMPANY. The Atlanta Municipal Theatre morphed into the Alliance Stage in 1968 with a production of *King Arthur*. By 1970, renamed the Alliance Theatre Company, artistic director Fred

Chappell and managing director Bernard Havard built a solid organization and garnered critical approval with adventurous work, including the world premiere of **Tennessee Williams**'s *Tiger Tail* and drawing major actors, including Richard Dreyfuss, Paul Winfield, **Morgan Freeman**, and **Jane Alexander** to its stage. Leadership changed, but the Alliance continued to attract attention with Sandra Deer's *So Long on Lonely Street*, which transferred to **Broadway**, as did **Alfred Uhry**'s PULITZER PRIZE-winning *Driving Miss Daisy*, which also toured to China and Russia. Since the 1990s, the theatre has premiered several important works, including **Pearl Cleage**'s *Blues for an Alabama Sky*, Uhry's *The Last Night of Ballyhoo*, Elton John and Tim Rice's *Aida*, **Carson McCullers**'s *The Heart Is A Lonely Hunter*, and Alice Walker's *The Color Purple*. In 2007, the Alliance was the recipient of the **Tony Award** for outstanding **regional theatre**.

ALSWANG, RALPH (1916–1979). Born in Chicago, Illinois, Alswang studied design at the GOODMAN THEATRE and the Chicago Art Institute. Under the mentorship of ROBERT EDMOND JONES, Alswang began designing on **Broadway** with *Comes the Revelation* (1942), and although he designed all manner of plays and MUSICALS, his signature style was the mode of REALISM. His numerous scene and/or lighting (and occasionally costume) designs include *Winged Victory* (1943), *Home of the Brave* (1945), *Strange Bedfellows* (1948), *King Lear* (1950), *The Rainmaker* (1954), *Time Limit!* (1956), *The Tunnel of Love* (1957), *Sunrise at Campobello* (1958), *Epitaph for George Dillon* (1958), *A Raisin in the Sun* (1959), *Come Blow Your Horn* (1961), *Beyond the Fringe* (1962), *Judy Garland "At Home at the Palace"* (1967), and *Piaf: A Remembrance* (1977). Alswang also consulted with architects designing New York's new Uris Theatre in 1970 and New Jersey's Garden State Arts Center.

ALTERNATIVE THEATRE. This term refers to **Off-Broadway** and **Off-Off-Broadway** theatre—and other "fringe" theatres—where experimentation and departures from the **Broadway** or regional theatre **repertory** and style is typical. The term was first applied in Great Britain after World WAR II, but in the United States, it is more likely to be used generically to identify any theatrical work out of the recognized mainstream. The term is also often applied to gender, ethnic and racial, or other "minority" theatre collectives applying experimental techniques to the task of raising consciousness about their chosen concerns.

AMBROSONE, JOHN (1961–). Following studies at SUNY Fredonia and Virginia Tech, Ambrosone began his career as a lighting designer, working in regional theatre in the United States, with international companies, and in opera and dance. From 1989 to 2002, Ambrosone was resident lighting designer for the **American Repertory Theatre (ART)**, where he designed lights for nearly 50 ART productions, after which he became head of lighting design at Virginia Tech. On **Broadway**, his lighting was seen in **David Mamet**'s *The Old Neighborhood* (1997) and **Off-Broadway** in **Adam Rapp**'s *Nocturne* (2000).

AMEN CORNER, THE. This first play by **James Baldwin**, following the critical success of his novel *Go Tell It on the Mountain,* was written and published in 1954, but not produced on Broadway until 8 April 1965 when it opened at the Ethel Barrymore Theatre for 84 performances. The play focuses on the importance of religion to African American families in contending with poverty and racial prejudice. *The Amen Corner* was musicalized by Garry Sherman and Peter Udell (with a book by Udell and Philip Rose) in 1983 as *Amen Corner,* but had a short run.

AMERICA HURRAH. A trilogy of short plays, *Interview, TV,* and *Motel,* by **Jean-Claude van Itallie** began as single entities produced at the **La Mama Experimental Theatre Club** in 1964-65 (with different directors, Peter Feldman, **Michael Kahn**, and **Tom O'Horgan**, and **Robert Wilson** contributing design elements) and a cast including James Coco, **Joseph Chaikin, Alvin Epstein**, Cynthia Harris, and Joyce Aaron. The three plays together under the title *America Hurrah,* opened **Off-Broadway** at the Pocket Theatre on 7 November 1966 and ran for 640 performances. **Critics** applauded the bill as a witty, observant view of contemporary life.

AMERICAN ACADEMY OF DRAMATIC ARTS (AADA).[†] Established in 1884 as the Lyceum Theatre School of Acting by Franklin Haven Sargeant, this first professional actor-training conservatory remains in operation into the twenty-first century. A not-for-profit educational institution, the AADA has provided a broadly practical education in acting to its students who, in their third year, may be selected to become part of a production company. In 1974, AADA established a Los Angeles campus. The AADA's impressive alumni of stage, film, and television actors includes SPENCER TRACY, EDWARD G. ROBINSON, WALTER ABEL, **Jason Robards**, GUTHRIE MCCLINTIC, HOWARD LINDSAY, **Anne Bancroft, Grace Kelly, Lauren Bacall, Judd Hirsch**, Nina Foch, **Agnes Moorehead**, Thelma Ritter, Gena Rowlands, **Rosalind Russell, Hume Cronyn, Colleen Dewhurst, Charles Durning, Garson Kanin, Ruth Gordon, Ron Leibman, Sam Levene, Philip Loeb, Lucille Lortel,** and Renee Taylor, among others.

AMERICAN BUFFALO. Emerging Chicago-based dramatist **David Mamet** rose to prominence with this two-act drama that premiered in a GOODMAN THEATRE showcase before opening on 16 February 1977 at **Broadway**'s Ethel Barrymore Theatre for 135 performances. The **New York Drama Critics Circle Award** winner for best play despite strong language offensive to some critics and audiences, *American Buffalo*, described by *New York Times* critic **Frank Rich** as "one of the best American plays of the last decade," focuses on a junk shop owner, played by J. J. Johnston who, along with two miscreants (played by **William H. Macy** and Bernard Erhard), plot to steal a valuable coin from a customer. Mamet's characteristically terse dialogue, stylized phrasing, and street-wise cynicism, and his recurring interest in masculinity, are plainly evident in this play, which was successfully revived **Off-Broadway** in 1981 with **Al Pacino**, who also appeared in a well-received 1983 Broadway revival. A 2008 Broadway revival, featuring **John Leguizamo**, Cedric the Entertainer, and Haley Joel Osment, ran a week. A 1996 film version, starring **Dustin Hoffman**, Dennis Franz, and Sean Nelson, was not well-received.

AMERICAN CONSERVATORY THEATRE, THE (ACT). Founded in Pittsburgh, Pennsylvania, by **William Ball** in 1964 (who remained in the post of artistic director until 1986), ACT opened with a production of *Tartuffe* staged at the **Pittsburgh Playhouse**. Operations were moved to the campus of Stanford University the following year for a time before becoming permanently established at San Francisco's Geary Theatre in 1966 (expanding to include a second theatre at the Marines' Memorial in 1968). Established as a seasonal **repertory**, ACT typically stages 10 plays annually, including American and European classics and the modern repertoire. In more recent years, ACT, which offers a conservatory program for actor training, has included premieres of contemporary works by **Robert Wilson**, **Eve Ensler**, **Philip Kan Gotanda**, and others. *See also* REGIONAL THEATRE.

AMERICAN DREAM, THE. An early one-act by **Edward Albee**, first staged on 24 January 1961 at New York's York Playhouse, it is a satire of American family life and, as Albee noted himself, "a stand against the fiction that everything in this slipping land of ours is peachy-keen." Focused on a middle-aged married couple (based on Albee's adoptive parents)—"Mommy" handily dominates the ineffectual "Daddy," while a neighbor, Mrs. Barker, explains to "Grandma" that the couple had adopted a son, but had mutilated the child in punishment when his actions did not please them. A virile young man appears seeking employment and Grandma realizes that he is the twin of the lost adopted child. This somewhat surreal work is often characterized as related to the Theatre of the Absurd movement and frequently revived by professional, university, and amateur theatres.

AMERICAN GUILD OF VARIETY ARTISTS (AGVA). Founded in 1938 as a professional support association, AGVA became a labor union the following year with the goal of advocating for the rights of performers in vaudeville, burlesque, rodeos, and carnivals, but as some of the venues vanished, AGVA emphasized membership from nightclubs and casinos, ice shows, and the concert stage. When actress Penny Singleton became AGVA president in 1969, following her active leadership in a 1967 strike in support of Radio City Music Hall's Rockettes, she became the first women president of an AFL-CIO union in the history of the United States.

AMERICAN JEWISH THEATRE (AJT). Stanley Brechner founded this company in 1974 to encourage new plays and MUSICALS expressing Jewish themes. Among plays produced were *The Prisoner of Second Avenue, Rags, The Puppetmaster of Lodz, The Yiddish Trojan Women, Yiddle With a Fiddle*, and *The Cocoanuts** before AJT shut down by the late 1990s. *See also* YIDDISH THEATRE.

AMERICAN NATIONAL THEATRE AND ACADEMY (ANTA). During the Great Depression, the United States Congress chartered ANTA as a "people's self-supporting national theatre." From its beginnings in 1935, under the leadership of **Cheryl Crawford** and Robert Breen as general directors, until after World War II, ANTA found the lack of financial support from the government and apathy from commercial producers a significant handicap. When ANTA purchased the Guild Theatre in 1950—renaming it the ANTA Theatre—it morphed into a producing organization, staging new works, including **Robinson Jeffers**'s *A Tower beyond Tragedy*, an adaptation of Aeschylus's *Oresteia* starring **Judith Anderson** as Clytemnestra. ANTA also produced well-received revivals of BEN HECHT and CHARLES MACARTHUR's *Twentieth Century* starring **José Ferrer** and Gloria Swanson in 1950 and **Mary Chase**'s *Mrs. McThing* starring HELEN HAYES in 1952, as well as *ANTA Album*, an annual benefit beginning in 1950. During the construction of the Vivian Beaumont Theatre at **Lincoln Center**, ANTA constructed a temporary theatre at Washington Square with the goal of establishing a repertory company for the new theatre. ANTA sold their theatre in 1981, but helped establish the National Theatre Conservatory in Colorado in 1984 and opened an ANTA West office in 1990s, as the New York office moved to Washington, D.C.

AMERICAN NEGRO THEATRE (ANT). Founded by writer Abram Hill and actor **Frederick O'Neal** at Harlem's Schomburg Library on 5 June 1940, ANT produced 19 plays prior to its demise in 1949. Intended as a **community theatre**, it added a studio training program in 1942, with students including **Sidney Poitier** and Harry Belafonte. Their most acclaimed production, Philip Yordan's *Anna Lucasta* (1944), had originally depicted a Polish family, but unable to secure a producer, Yordan, a white man, rewrote it depicting a black family. *Anna Lucasta* transferred to **Broadway** a few weeks after its opening, but this success provided little financial security for ANT and led to changes in the organization, including an emphasis on production of plays by white authors, with the result that **African Americans** came to see ANT merely as a means of breaking into show business.

AMERICAN PLACE THEATRE (APT). Initially established in New York's St. Clement's Church in New York following its founding in 1964 by **Wynn Handman** and Sidney Lanier, APT staged its first production, Robert Lowell's *The Old Glory*, there. Its goal of producing high-quality theatre by diverse American writers (with a board including **Tennessee Williams** and Myrna Loy) led APT to stage works from established writers including H. L. Mencken,* Joyce Carol Oates, **S. J. Perelman**, Sylvia Plath, Anne Sexton, and Robert Penn Warren, as well young dramatists including **Sam Shepard**, **Robert Ribman**, **Steven Tesich**, **Maria Irene Fornés**, **Ed Bullins**, Philip Hayes Dean, William Hauptman, Jonathan Reynolds, William Alfred, **Emily Mann**, and **Richard Nelson**, among others. A 1971 move to a new thrust stage space on the Avenue of the Americas allowed for growth and in recent years, APT has established a program, "Literature to Life," aimed at promoting literacy through drama and an internship program.

AMERICAN REPERTORY THEATRE (ART). Eva Le Gallienne, **Cheryl Crawford**, and **Margaret Webster** established ART in 1946 to create a place that could "be for the drama what a library is for literature or a symphony orchestra for music." In fact, it was, in many respects, an effort to revive Le Gallienne's repertory-style Civic Repertory Theatre (CRC), which had closed during the Great Depression. The three directors were able to attract established actors, including Walter Hampden, **Victor Jory**, and Ernest Truex for its company. The first season included productions of *King Henry VIII, What Every Woman Knows, John Gabriel Borkman, Androcles and the Lion, Pound on Demand, Yellow Jack,** and *Alice in Wonderland*, but critical and commercial apathy led to the closing of ART at the end of its inaugural season.

AMERICAN REPERTORY THEATRE (ART). With the lofty goal of seeking to "expand the boundaries of theater, exploring the best texts from across cultures and ages," ART was founded in 1980 by **Robert Brustein**, who served as its artistic director until 2002, when **Robert Woodruff** took over. Emphasizing a commitment to American plays, neglected classics, and fresh interpretations of standard works, ART has also established a training program for young artists in association with Harvard University. ART has staged premieres of plays by Edward Bond, Don DeLillo, **Christopher Durang**, Rinde Eckert, **Jules Feiffer**, Dario Fo, Carlos Fuentes, **Larry Gelbart**, Philip Glass, **David Henry Hwang**, Milan Kundera, **David Mamet**, **Charles L. Mee**, Heiner Müller, **Marsha Norman**, **David Rabe**, Franca Rame, **Adam Rapp**, **Ronald Ribman**, **Paula Vogel**, Derek Walcott, **Naomi Wallace**, and **Robert Wilson**, among many others, and has benefited from the contributions of international directors, designers, and actors who have participated in ART productions. *See also* REGIONAL THEATRE MOVEMENT.

AMERICAN SHAKESPEARE FESTIVAL THEATRE AND ACADEMY (ASFTA). Producer LAWRENCE LANGNER's idea of establishing this theatre led to the participation of Lincoln Kirstein and Joseph Verner Reed and the state of Connecticut incorporating it up as a not-for-profit organization. A Festival Theatre, modeled on historical evidence of **Shakespeare**'s Globe Theatre but with modern amenities, was built and the company produced a mostly Shakespearean **repertory** from 1955 until mismanagement led to its demise in the mid-1980s. Distinguished actors, including **Katharine Hepburn**, Fred Gwynne, **Morris Carnovsky**, **Will Geer**, **John Houseman**, **James Earl Jones**, **Christopher Plummer**, Lynn Redgrave, and **Christopher Walken**, appeared in festival productions during its existence.

AMERICAN SOCIETY FOR THEATRE RESEARCH (ASTR). Founded in 1956 with the purpose of supporting theatre historians in researching and disseminating their work on American theatre, the organization publishes the *ASTR Newsletter* and the journal *Theatre Survey*, as well as studies of theatre and drama in the United States.

AMERICAN THEATRE ASSOCIATION (ATA). Originally named the American Educational Theatre Association at the time of its founding in 1936 as an offshoot of the Speech Association of America, its principal founder, E. C. Mabie, was responding to what was deemed the underrepresentation of **academic** theatre in professional organizations, leading to a break from SAA in 1950. ATA fostered the development of specialized affiliate groups and published the *Educational Theatre Journal* (later known as *Theatre Journal*), but mismanagement led to its demise in the 1980s, to be replaced by the Association for Theatre in Higher Education.

AMERICAN THEATRE COMPANY (ATC). With the mission of producing new and classic American plays, this Chicago, Illinois-based company was founded in 1985 as the American Blues Theatre by Rick Cleveland, William Payne, Ed Blatchford, and Jim Leaming, with a goal of reaching a working-class audience. In 1993, the theatre settled into a permanent home in a warehouse in the Northcenter section of town, moving in 1997 to a full professional company mounting a four-play season. *See also* REGIONAL THEATRE MOVEMENT.

AMERICAN THEATRE CRITICS ASSOCIATION (ATCA). Established in 1974 to foster communication among theatre critics across the United States, its stated goals include advancing standards of **criticism,** supporting freedom of expression, and increasing awareness of theatre as a vital national resource. ATCA votes on an annual **Tony Award** for outstanding regional theatre. As an advocacy organization, it led a movement to secure release of two South African actors unjustly imprisoned.

AMERICAN THEATRE HALL OF FAME. Founded in 1971 by Earl Blackwell, Gerard Oestreicher, **James M. Nederlander**, and Arnold Weissberger, the annual inductees are chosen from those whose **Broadway** careers spanned at least 25 years. An annual ceremony is held at New York's Gershwin Theatre where plaques honoring the inductees are displayed. Inductees include theatre practitioners in all aspects of the field and the annual list features both living and posthumous inductees.

AMERICAN THEATRE WING (ATW). Rachel Crothers led several women in the theatrical profession in establishing ATW in 1939 to support the war effort, based on a model established by the Stage Women's War Relief* organization that had served a similar purpose during World War I. ATW set up New York's **Stage Door Canteen**, a club for service personnel where free food and entertainment was offered and served by actors of the **Broadway** stage. Following the end of the war, ATW set up educational seminars on aspects of theatre work, established scholarships, and most enduringly, created the Antoinette Perry **Tony Awards**, which, since 1947, annually honor achievement in Broadway theatre.

ANANIA, MICHAEL (1951–). A **Broadway** scene designer whose credits include a 1980 revival of *Canterbury Tales*, *Run for Your Wife* (1989),

A Change in the Heir (1990), *The Gathering* (2001), a revival of *I'm Not Rappaport* (2002), and *Jackie Mason's Laughing Room Only* (2003). He designed a revival of *The Most Happy Fella* (2006) for the New York City Opera and **Charles Busch**'s *Die Mommie Die!* (2007) **Off-Broadway**, and he frequently designs for **regional theatres**, including the **Paper Mill Playhouse** in New Jersey, where he was resident designer for 20 years.

AND MISS REARDON DRINKS A LITTLE. This two-act comedy-drama by **Paul Zindel**, following his acclaimed **Off-Broadway** play *The Effect of Gamma Rays on Man-in-the-Moon Marigolds,* opened on 2 February 1971 at the Morosco Theatre for 108 performances. Featuring a strong cast, including **Julie Harris**, **Estelle Parsons**, **Nancy Marchand**, Rae Allen, Bill Macy, Virginia Payne, and Paul Lieber, the play centers on three middle-aged sisters dealing with the recent death of their difficult mother and their extreme differences: Catherine is an alcoholic, Anna is a hypochondriac teacher accused of an inappropriate relationship with a student, and Ceil is an unhappy social climber. Catherine and Ceil are locked in a battle of wills over committing Anna to a mental facility; Catherine prevails, despite the interference of a neighbor couple, and Ceil abandons her sisters to care for themselves.

ANDERS, GLENN (1890–1981).[†] A native of Los Angeles, California, Anders began as a journeyman actor in a California STOCK company in 1910, worked in vaudeville,* and had considerable experience touring with E. H. Sothern* and Julia Marlowe* after 1912. In the 1920s, Anders appeared in important roles in several notable **Broadway** dramas, including *Hell-Bent Fer Heaven** (1924), *They Knew What They Wanted** (1924), *The Constant Nymph* (1926), *Strange Interlude** (1928), and *Dynamo** (1929). After 1930, he appeared in *Hotel Universe* (1930), *Another Language* (1932), *The Masque of Kings* (1936), *Skylark* (1939), *Soldier's Wife* (1944), *Light Up the Sky* (1948), *The Remarkable Mr. Pennypacker* (1953), and *Time Remembered* (1957). He appeared a few times on television and in films, most notably on the big screen in D. W. Griffith's *Sally of the Sawdust* (1925) and **Orson Welles**'s *The Lady from Shanghai* (1947).

ANDERSON, JUDITH (1898–1992). Born in Adelaide, Australia, as Frances Margaret Anderson, where she gained her first theatrical experiences, Anderson's career truly began at New York's 14th Street Theatre prior to a tour of *Dear Brutus* (1920), playing opposite William Gillette* and considerable experience in stock. Her **Broadway** performances included *Cobra* (1924), *Behold the Bridegroom** (1927), and as LYNN FONTANNE's replacement in EUGENE O'NEILL's *Strange Interlude** (1928) and on tour in O'Neill's

Mourning Becomes Electra in 1931. She typically won critical plaudits in modern dramas, including *As You Desire Me* (1931), *Come of Age* (1934), and *The Old Maid* (1935), prior to scoring a success as Gertrude to John Gielgud's Hamlet in 1936. Much of her subsequent stage work was in the classics, including as Lady Macbeth opposite **Maurice Evans** in 1941, and as Olga in *The Three Sisters* (1942) with Katharine Cornell and **Ruth Gordon**.

Anderson won a Best Actress **Tony Award** for her most acclaimed performance in the title role **Robinson Jeffers**'s *Medea* (1947), freely adapted from Euripides. In 1950, she played Clytemnestra in *A Tower beyond Tragedy*, Jeffers's adaptation of Aeschylus's *Oresteia*. She worked frequently in films and television after 1940, but returned to Broadway for *John Brown's Body* (1953), *In the Summer House* (1953), *Comes a Day* (1958), and, at age 84, played the nurse opposite **Zoe Caldwell**'s Medea in a revival of the Jeffers adaptation, winning a Best Supporting Actress Tony nomination. Her distinguished film career included her most memorable screen role as the obsessed housekeeper Mrs. Danvers in *Rebecca* (1940), as well as supporting roles in *King's Row* (1942), *Edge of Darkness* (1943), *And Then There Were None* (1945), *The Furies* (1950), *The Ten Commandments* (1956), and *Cat on a Hot Tin Roof* (1958), and she continued to act in the television soap opera *Santa Barbara* until she was nearly 90. A theatre space on New York's **Theatre Row** was named for her in 1984, but has since been torn down.

ANDERSON, LAURIE (1947–). Born in Glen Ellyn, Illinois, as Laura Phillips Anderson, she was trained as a sculptor at Columbia University, but emerged as a **performance artist** and composer deeply influenced by conceptual art and a range of avant-garde writers and composers. Her performances, which are highly MUSICAL, emphasize ordinary street sounds (like car horns) and a range of visual media (video, projections, sculpture) in challenging gender stereotypes, language, and the human voice. Among her major works are *Automotive* (1972), *Duets on Ice* (1974), *United States* (1978), *Empty Places* (1988), *The Nerve Bible* (1994), and *Songs and Stories from Moby Dick* (1999).

ANDERSON, MAXWELL (1888–1959).[†] Born James Maxwell Anderson in Atlantic, Pennsylvania, he attended college at the University of North Dakota and Stanford University prior to working as a schoolteacher and newspaperman. Enamored of theatre, his first play, *The White Desert* (1923), flopped, but the following year, in collaboration with Laurence Stallings,* he wrote *What Price Glory** (1924), perhaps the finest American play about World War I. Following a few poorly received collaborations with Stallings, Anderson went solo with *Saturday's Children** (1927), a long-running comedy about marriage. An interest in the sensational Sacco and Vanzetti case led Anderson to coauthor (with Harold Hickerson) *Gods of the Lightning** (1928), but it failed to find favor. A comedy, *Gypsy* (1929), won some critical approval, but a short run. His shift to writing in blank verse for *Elizabeth the Queen* (1930), which starred LYNN FONTANNE, led to critical respect and he frequently worked in the form after that time. He won a PULITZER PRIZE for his 1933 political satire, *Both Your Houses*, prior to two more historical dramas, *Mary of Scotland* (1933) and *Valley Forge* (1934). He returned to Sacco and Vanzetti with a daring experiment in applying blank verse to a play with a contemporary setting in *Winterset* (1935), winning a **New York Drama Critics Circle Award** for Best Play.

Anderson's *The Wingless Victory* (1936) took on the then explosive subject of interracial marriage and *High Tor* (1937) focused on a man's desire to escape the ordinariness of contemporary life. In a change of pace, Anderson contributed the libretto and lyrics to a MUSICAL, *Knickerbocker Holiday* (1938), with music by Kurt Weill; the collaboration produced a classic number from the musical stage, "The September Song." In 1938, Anderson led his fellow dramatists in forming **The Playwrights' Company**, a producing organization aimed at supporting the development of American playwrights. As World War II loomed, Anderson turned his attention to contemporary events, although he frequently retained his blank verse style, with *Key Largo* (1939), *Candle in the Wind* (1941), and *Storm Operation* (1944).

Following the end of the war, Anderson's *Truckline Café* (1946) focused on the problems of an ex-soldier returning home to an unfaithful wife. He returned to historical subjects with *Joan of Lorraine* (1946) and *Anne of the Thousand Days* (1948) and another musical, *Lost in the Stars* (1949), again collaborating with Kurt Weill. Anderson's classically-inspired *Barefoot in Athens* (1951) failed, but his dramatization of William March's novel about a psychopathic child, *The Bad Seed* (1954), was a critical and commercial hit on stage and screen. Critics consistently applauded Anderson's striving to create a modern equivalent of classical tragedy and his attempts to restore poetry to the stage, but some noted that he fell short of the mark in both goals, despite an admirable output of diverse plays.

ANDERSON, ROBERT (1917–2009). Born Robert Woodruff Anderson in New York, Anderson was educated at Harvard University and launched his career by winning the 1944 National Theatre Conference award for his play *Come Marching Home*. After writing sketches for a failed 1950 musical revue,* *Dance Me a Song*, Anderson scored a major critical and box office success with *Tea and Sympathy* (1953), a play about a prep school student accused of **homosexuality** who sleeps with an unsympathetic teacher's unhappy wife. The play's success continued with the popular 1956 film version, which featured the original Broadway leads, Deborah Kerr, John Kerr, and Leif Erickson. Anderson wrote comparatively few subsequent plays, including *All Summer Long* (1954), *Silent Night, Lonely Night* (1959), and *Solitaire/Double Solitaire* (1971), but only his bill of one-acts, *You Know I Can't Hear You When the Water's Running* (1967) and *I Never Sang for My Father* (1968) achieved much critical approval. He wrote a few television dramas and screenplays, including his plays *Tea and Sympathy* and *I Never Sang for My Father*, as well as *The Nun's Story* (1959) and *The Sand Pebbles* (1966).

ANDERSONVILLE TRIAL, THE. Saul Levitt's two-act drama of the trial of Henry Wirz, the Confederate commander of the notoriously brutal Andersonville Prison during the Civil WAR, opened on 29 December 1959 for 179 performances under the direction of **José Ferrer**. **George C. Scott** was nominated for a **Tony Award** for his performance as Judge Advocate Chipman, a figure at the center of the trial of Henry Wirz (**Herbert Berghof**), with Albert Dekker, Ian Keith, and Russell Hardie among the all-male supporting cast. A 1970 PBS-TV production starred Richard Basehart, Martin Sheen, William Shatner, and Cameron Mitchell and won an Emmy Award and a Peabody Award.

ANGEL STREET. Patrick Hamilton's three-act psychological thriller opened at the John Golden Theatre on 5 December 1941 for a remarkable 1,295 performances under the direction of Shepard Traube. Set in 1880 London, Manningham (Vincent Price), a cultured sophisticate, is slowly driving his new wife (**Judith Evelyn**) to madness. The supporting cast featured included **Leo G. Carroll**. *Angel Street* was revived on **Broadway** in 1948 starring **José Ferrer**, **Uta Hagen**, and **Richard Whorf**, and in 1975 with Michael Allinson and Dina Merrill, again under the direction of Traube. A 1940 British film version, renamed *Gaslight*, and with character name changes, starred Anton Walbrook and Diana Wynyard. Another film version also called *Gaslight* (1944), was directed by George Cukor and has become a film classic thanks to the performances of **Charles Boyer**, **Ingrid Bergman**, **Joseph Cotten**, and a young **Angela Lansbury**. Bergman won an Academy Award for her performance, with Oscar nominations going to Boyer and Lansbury. Evelyn recreated her **Broadway** performance opposite Henry Daniell in a 1946 television adaptation.

ANGELS IN AMERICA. **Tony Kushner**'s epic work is actually two long plays which did not reach Broadway until 1993, although both works had received prior productions at San Francisco's **Eureka Theatre**, where artistic director **Oskar Eustis** had commissioned it; the **Mark Taper Forum**; and the National Theatre of Great Britain, where it was honored with an **Olivier** Award as Best Play. When *Millennium Approaches*, the first part, finally opened at the **Walter Kerr** Theatre on Broadway on 4 May 1993, it won a PULITZER PRIZE, a **Tony Award**, and a **Drama Desk Award** as Best Play of the year. When the second part, *Perestroika*, joined *Millennium Approaches* in repertory on Broadway on 23 November 1993, it won a Tony Award and Drama Desk Award as Best Play. The Broadway production, directed by **George C. Wolfe**, featured a cast of eight—**Ron Leibman, Stephen Spinella, Joe Mantello, Jeffrey Wright**, Marcia Gay Harden, **Kathleen Chalfant**, Emily McLaughlin, and David Marshall Grant—with most of them playing multiple and cross-gender roles.

Mixing drama and comedy, *Angels* weaves together diverse strands of late twentieth-century American life. Set in the mid-1980s shortly after Ronald Reagan's re-election to the U.S. presidency, *Angels in America* follows two fictional couples and one icon from post-World War II American history, Roy Cohn, the conservative New York lawyer who served as an aide to Wisconsin's Senator Joseph McCarthy during the Communist "witch hunts" of the 1950s. In and around the personal crises of these characters, *Angels in America* explores late twentieth-century attitudes about American history, **sexuality**, **race**, **religion**, and the opposing poles of conservative and liberal politics. Kushner was inspired in part by Walter Benjamin's essay, "Theses on the Philosophy of History," which, in turn, was inspired by Paul Klee's "Angelus Novus," a painting depicting the Angel of History being blown into the future by the winds of progress while glancing back at the rubble of history. Using that image as a thematic inspiration, Kushner employs an epic theatre style drawn from his admiration for **Erwin Piscator**'s epic theatre theories and **Bertolt Brecht**'s plays, weaving his variation of epic form with American lyric realism in the manner of **Tennessee Williams**.

A majority of critics found *Angels* to be a one of the most significant dramas of the late twentieth century, and applauded its theatricalized exploration of the perplexing and challenging issues of the last half of the twentieth century, while also offering a model for an overt brand of American political drama. This most-honored play of its time became one of the most honored television films of the era when *Angels in America* was filmed in 2003 as a six-hour miniseries for HBO-TV by director **Mike Nichols**, with a cast including **Al Pacino, Meryl Streep**, Emma Thompson, Patrick Wilson, and **Mary-Louise Parker**, winning an Emmy Award and a Golden Globe and numerous awards for the actors and director. **The Signature Theatre** announced plans to revive both parts of *Angels in America* on **Broadway** in 2010, its first New York revival to be directed by **Michael Grief**.

ANGELOU, MAYA (1928–). The much-admired poet and autobiographer best known for her first memoir, *I Know Why the Caged Bird Sings* (1969), was born Marguerite Ann Johnson in St. Louis, Missouri. Angelou occasionally acts, receiving a **Tony Award** nomination for her role in *Look Away* (1973) and has appeared in several films. Early in her writing career she authored several plays, including *Cabaret for Freedom* (1960), *Best of These* (1966), *The Clawing Within* (1966), *Least of These* (1966), *Adoja Amissah* (1967), *Ajax* (1967), *Gettin' Up Stayed on My Mind* (1967), *And Still I Rise!* (1976), and *Moon on a Rainbow Shawl* (1988).

ANIMAL KINGDOM, THE. PHILIP BARRY's three-act comedy, produced by GILBERT MILLER, opened on 12 January 1932 for 183 performances at the Broadhurst Theatre. A personal triumph for British actor **Leslie Howard**, *The Animal Kingdom* offered the mildly shocking thesis that Howard's character, Tom Collier, may have a more honorable relationship with his mistress than with his wife. In typical Barry fashion, the well-drawn characters are revealed through witty dialogue and a well-constructed plot as in his best-remembered plays, *Holiday** (1928) and *The Philadelphia Story* (1939). Tom marries Cecilia Henry, although he is far more simpatico with a lady friend, Daisy Sage, a fact that his friends and family know better than Tom. When Cecilia proves to be a demanding and possessive wife, Tom finally realizes that he will be better off with Daisy. Howard repeated his performance in the 1932 film version, costarring with Myrna Loy, and Wendell Corey played Tom in a 1952 television adaptation, with **Robert Preston** doing the same on *The Alcoa Hour* anthology series in 1957.

ANNA IN THE TROPICS. Set in 1929 among cigar-making workers in Ybor City, Florida, this PULITZER PRIZE-winning play by **Nilo Cruz** opened on 16 November 2003 for 113 performances at the Royale Theatre, directed by **Emily Mann** with a cast including Jimmy Smits, Priscilla Lopez, and Daphne Rubin-Vega. The reading of Tolstoy's *Anna Karenina* to the cigar workers begins to parallel the lives of the children of Santiago and Ofelia, two lifelong workers in the cigar factories. The dreams of one daughter, Marela, and the unhappy marriage of another, Conchita, are set against the fears of progress as machines in the factory change lives. The play had premiered at the New Theatre in Coral Gables, Florida, before critical acclaim inspired the **Broadway** production.

ANNA LUCASTA. A three-act drama by Philip Yordan, *Anna Lucasta* opened on 30 August 1944 for 957 performances at the Mansfield Theatre, following its premiere at the **American Negro Theatre (ANT)**, where it ran for a few weeks. Yordan, a white man, had originally written the play about a Polish family, but switched them to **African Americans** in order to get the play produced by the ANT. Its relatively simple plot concerns the title character, played by Hilda Simms, a Pennsylvania girl banished by her family who goes to New York and becomes a prostitute. A sincere attempt to reform leads her to fall in love with Rudolf (**Earle Hyman**), a Southerner. When Anna learns that Rudolf knows her past, she flees to Pennsylvania, but he follows and assures her of his love. The cast also included such rising talents as **Alice Childress**, **Rosetta LeNoire**, **Canada Lee**, and **Frederick O'Neal**. A 1947 revival had only a short run, but a switch to a white cast for a 1949 film version, scripted by **Arthur Laurents**, provided a starring role for Paulette Goddard, while Yordan restored the African American setting for his 1959 screenplay for a film starring Eartha Kitt, Sammy Davis, Jr., and other members of the original stage cast.

ANNE OF THE THOUSAND DAYS. This blank-verse drama in two acts by MAXWELL ANDERSON was produced by **The Playwrights' Company** and **Leland Hayward**, and opened at the Shubert Theatre on 8 December 1948 for a 288 performance run starring **Rex Harrison** as Henry VIII. The play focuses on Henry's break with his wife, Catherine of Aragon, and his growing relationship with his mistress, Anne Boleyn. He divorces his wife and marries Anne, who gives birth to a daughter, Elizabeth, but cannot provide the son and heir Henry demands. Anne chooses death over exile so that her daughter might one day ascend to the throne. Harrison and scene designer Jo MIELZINER won **Tony Awards** for their contributions. A lavishly produced 1969 film version, starring **Richard Burton** and Geneviève Bujold, was nominated for ten Academy Awards.

ANNIVERSARY WALTZ. This surprisingly popular three-act comedy by **Jerome Chodorov** and Joseph Fields opened on 7 April 1954 at the Broadhurst Theatre for 615 performances. The innocuous plot involves a happy couple, played by Macdonald Carey and Kitty Carlisle, who reveal to their grown children that they had a sexual relationship prior to marriage, setting off all sorts of minor distresses. The play became a perennial for **summer** STOCK and **community theatres**.

ANOTHER LANGUAGE. **Rose Franken**'s three-act play opened at the Booth Theatre on 25 April 1932 for 344 performances and featured MARGARET WYCHERLY as Mrs. Hallam, a domineering mother of four sons, who meets her match in Stella (**Dorothy Stickney**), the wife of the youngest son, Victor, portrayed by GLENN ANDERS. Matters come to a head when Stella embarks on an affair with Jerry (John Beal), her nephew and Mrs. Hallam's grandson. The revelation of the affair, and the subsequent family confrontation led by Mrs. Hallam, backfires, with Victor and Jerry realizing the matriarch's domination. Following its February 1933 closing, it was revived at the Waldorf Theatre for 89 performances with much of the original cast, but with PATRICIA COLLINGE taking over the role of Stella.

ANOTHER PART OF THE FOREST. The critical and commercial success of **Lillian Hellman**'s *The Little Foxes* in 1939 led Hellman to return to its characters, as well as its indictment of the excesses of capitalism, in *Another Part of the Forest* (1946), which opened at New York's Fulton Theatre on 20 November 1946 for 182 performances under Hellman's direction. A prequel of sorts to *The Little Foxes*, the play examines the previous generation of the rapacious Hubbard family, with the holdover characters of Regina, Ben, Oscar, and Birdie seen as their youthful selves in 1880. The tone of *Another Part of the Forest* differs from the melodramatic* *The Little Foxes*—in this case, Hellman creates what some critics described as a Jonsonian picaresque comedy of villains outsmarting one another.

Marcus, the play's self-made man and patriarch of the Hubbard clan, builds a fortune in the aftermath of the Civil WAR, clawing his way up from abject backwoods poverty. His children claw at each other to gain the old man's favor. The Hubbard family background provides something of an explanation for how Regina and her brothers came to so completely lack a moral compass that might temper their drive for financial success in *The Little Foxes*. The cast included Patricia Neal, Jean Hagen, Leo Genn, **Mildred Dunnock**, Margaret Phillips, and **Paul Ford** working in an evocative period scene and lighting design by JO MIELZINER. A 2010 Pecadillo Theatre Company revival **Off-Broadway** at St. Clement's Theatre was received with mixed reviews.

ANTHONY, JOSEPH (1912–1993). A Milwaukee, Wisconsin, native, Joseph Deuster was educated at the University of Wisconsin before joining the **Pasadena Playhouse** as an actor, changing his name. He acted in **Federal Theatre Project (FTP)** productions and on **Broadway** in, among other productions, **Tennessee Williams**'s *Camino Real* (1953), but his career as an "actor's director" established him beginning in 1948. His productions, which included straight plays and MUSICALS, included *The Rainmaker* (1954), *The Most Happy Fella* (1954), *The Lark* (1955), *The Marriage-Go-Round* (1958), *The Best Man* (1960), *Mary, Mary* (1961), *Rhinoceros* (1961), *110 in the Shade* (1963), *Slow Dance on the Killing Ground* (1964), *Jimmy* (1969), and *Finishing Touches* (1973). He received six **Tony Award** nominations as a director, but never won.

ANTIN, ELEANOR (1935–). A native New Yorker, Antin is a noted **performance artist**, filmmaker, and installation artist whose subjects are typically historical, including ancient Rome, the Crimean WAR, and Jewish history. She created an on-stage persona, Eleanora Antinova, a neglected black ballerina of Diaghilev's Ballets Russes, appearing as the character in both scripted and improvised performances. She is also a visual artist and photographer, and has been on the faculty of the University of California, San Diego, since 1975.

ANTOON, A. J. (1944–1992). Born Alfred Joseph Antoon in Lawrence, Massachusetts, he graduated from Boston College and the Yale School of Drama before working closely with **Joe Papp** at the **New York Public Theatre**, becoming the first director ever nominated for Best Director **Tony Awards** for two productions in a single year, *Much Ado about Nothing* and the PULITZER PRIZE-winning *That Championship Season*, in 1972. For *That Championship Season*, he also picked up a **Drama Desk Award**. Subsequent productions include *The Good Doctor* (1973), *Dance of Death* (1974), *Trelawny of the "Wells"* (1975), *The Effect of Gamma Rays on Man-in-the-Moon Marigolds* (1978), *The Rink* (1984), for which he won a Tony, *Sherlock's Last Case* (1987), and *Song of Singapore* (1991). He died of complications from **AIDS**.

ANY WEDNESDAY. A popular two-act comedy by Muriel Resnik opened on 18 February 1964 for an impressive 982 performance run at the Music Box Theatre. Pampered by a loving wife, pompous, lecherous business tycoon John Cleves secretly spends Wednesdays with his eccentric mistress, Ellen Gordon, played by **Sandy Dennis**, who won a Best Actress **Tony Award** for her performance. When one of Cleves's abused employees finds out that Ellen's expenses are a tax write-off for Cleves, both wife and mistress find Cleves's self-justifying reaction appalling. *Any Wednesday* became a staple of STOCK and dinner theatres, and was a popular 1966 film starring **Jason Robards**, Jane Fonda, and Dean Jones.

ARCENAS, LOY (1953–). Born in the Philippines, Arcenas received **Drama Desk Award** nominations for his scene designs for **Off-Broadway** productions of *Reckless (*1989), *Simpatico* (1994), and *Ballad of Yachiyo* (1998). On **Broadway**, he has designed settings for *Prelude to a Kiss* (1990), *Once on This Island* (1990), a revival of *The Glass Menagerie* (1994), *Love! Valour! Compassion!* (1995), a revival of *The Night of the Iguana* (1996), *High Society* (1998), and *Chita Rivera: The Dancer's Life* (2005). Arcenas also designed *A Man of No Importance* (2002) and *Dessa Rose* (2005) at

Lincoln Center and works closely with the Filipino American troupe **Ma-Yi Theatre Company** and occasionally directs, including *Flipzoids* (1996), for **Theatre for the New City**.

ARDREY, ROBERT (1908–1980). A native of Chicago, Illinois, Ardrey became a noted playwright and screenwriter, although his training was as an anthropologist. His plays include *Star Spangled* (1936), *Casey Jones* (1938), *God and Texas* (1938), *How to Get Tough about It* (1938), *Thunder Rock* (1939), *Jeb* (1946), *Sing Me No Lullaby* (1954), and *Shadow of Heroes* (1958), none of which found much success, but his screenplays fared better, including *Song of Love* (1947), *The Three Musketeers* (1958), *Madame Bovary* (1949), and *The Four Horsemen of the Apocalypse* (1962). His books in the area of behavioral science include *African Genesis* (1961) and *The Territorial Imperative* (1966).

ARENA STAGE. Zelda Fichandler and Edward Mangum established this Washington, D.C.-based **repertory theatre** devoted to a combination of classics and contemporary plays in 1950. Modeled on England's Old Vic, Arena Stage was the first regional theatre to receive a **Tony Award**. For several years, the company performed in an abandoned cinema and a brewery converted for theatrical use, but ultimately evolved into a cultural force in the nation's capital. Funds were raised for a permanent home with three theatre spaces: the Arena, the Kreeger, and the Old Vat. Among its premiere productions, **Howard Sackler**'s *The Great White Hope* (1968), **Arthur Kopit**'s *Indians* (1969), and **Michael Weller**'s *Moonchildren* (1972) all moved to **Broadway**. In 1973, the company toured the Soviet Union and Hong Kong.

ARENT, ARTHUR (1904–1972). Born in Jersey City and educated at New York University, Arent made his mark in theatre with the **Federal Theatre Project (FTP)**'s **Living Newspaper** Unit, which he supervised and during the mid-1930s he contributed to the scripts for the unit's most noted and controversial works, including *Ethiopia, Triple-A Plowed Under, 1935, Injunction Granted, Power*, and *One-Third of a Nation*. He also wrote the book for the MUSICAL *Pins and Needles* (1937). Arent went to Europe planning to write an antiWAR living newspaper, but conditions there changed his perspective. After the war, he wrote screenplays for films, wrote radio shows, and wrote for television drama anthology shows.

ARKIN, ALAN (1934–). Brooklyn-born Alan Wolf Arkin, son of a teacher and a painter/writer, moved with his family to Los Angeles, California, where his father had hoped to take a scene design job, but a strike of Hollywood workers ended his hopes. Arkin's parents were accused of being Communists during the Red Scare of the early 1950s and encouraged their son's dramatic aspirations. Arkin studied with Benjamin Zemach, a protégé of **Constantin Stanislavsky**, and attended Bennington College. Arkin appeared on **Broadway** in *From the Second City* (1961), *Enter Laughing* (1963), and *Luv* (1964). He also directed for Broadway and **Off-Broadway**, including *Eh?* (1966), *Hail Scrawdyke!* (1966), *The Sunshine Boys* (1972), *Molly* (1973), and *Taller Than a Dwarf* (2000). On stage, he excelled in comic roles, but in films also appeared with distinction in more dramatic characters and became a versatile character actor in films, including *The Russians Are Coming, The Russians Are Coming* (1966), *Wait Until Dark* (1967), *The Heart Is a Lonely Hunter* (1968), *Catch-22* (1970), *Last of the Red Hot Lovers* (1972), *The Seven-Per-Cent Solution* (1976), *Glengarry Glen Ross* (1992), and *Little Miss Sunshine* (2006), for which he won a Best Supporting Actor Academy Award, as well as many television shows.

ARMSTRONG, WILL STEVEN (1930–1969). In his short life, Armstrong, who was born in New Orleans, Louisiana, designed atmospheric scenery for a number of **Broadway** productions, including a revival of *The Great God Brown** in 1959, *The Andersonville Trial* (1959), *Caligula* (1960), *Kwamina* (1961), *Subways Are for Sleeping* (1961), *One Flew Over the Cuckoo's Nest* (1963), *Nobody Loves an Albatross* (1963), *Ready When You Are, C.B.!* (1964), *Forty Carats* (1968), and he won a **Tony Award** for his scene design of *Carnival!* (1962). He also won an **Obie Award** for *Ivanov* in 1958 and also designed for the **American Shakespeare Festival**.

ARNONE, JOHN (1949–). A native of Dallas, Texas, Arnone began his theatrical work as an actor, but became a scene designer in 1976, capturing attention for his designs for *Vanities* (1976). He was a founding member of New York's Lion Theatre Company and won an **Obie Award** for *K* (1977) and another for sustained excellence in 1991. Among his **Broadway** credits, Arnone created scene designs for *Patio/Porch* (1978), *Lone Star & Pvt. Wars* (1979), a revival of *The Homecoming* (1991), *Twilight: Los Angeles, 1992* (1994), *Sacrilege* (1995), the revivals of *Grease* (1994) and *How to Succeed in Business without Really Trying* (1994), *Sex and Longing* (1996), *Minnelli on Minnelli* (1999), *The Ride Down Mt. Morgan* (2000), *The Full Monty* (2000), *The Goat, or Who Is Sylvia?* (2002), *Fortune's Fool* (2002), *Lennon* (2005), and *The Grand Manner* (2010). Arnone won a **Tony Award** and a **Drama Desk Award** for *The Who's Tommy* (1993). He has also done much work with major **regional theatres** and designed films, including *Sex, Drugs, Rock & Roll* (1991), and television productions.

ARONSON, BORIS (1900–1980).[†] Born in Kiev, Ukraine, Aronson studied art and design in Moscow and Berlin before moving to New York in 1923. He designed scenery for the Unser Theatre and the Yiddish Art Theatre* before joining EVA LE GALLIENNE'S CIVIC REPERTORY THEATRE in 1927, where he designed several productions. For **Broadway**, he designed more than 75 productions, including many of the most important plays and MUSICALS from the 1930s to the 1970s: *Three Men on a Horse* (1935), *Awake and Sing!* (1935), *Paradise Lost* (1935), *The Merchant of Yonkers* (1938), *The Gentle People* (1939), *Cabin in the Sky* (1940), *Clash by Night* (1941), *Truckline Café* (1946), *Love Life* (1948), *Detective Story* (1949), *I Am a Camera* (1951), *The Crucible* (1953), *Bus Stop* (1955), *A View from the Bridge* (1955), *The Diary of Anne Frank* (1955), *Orpheus Descending* (1957), *J.B.* (1958), *A Loss of Roses* (1959), *Do Re Mi* (1960), *Fiddler on the Roof* (1964), and *The Price* (1968). He designed several of **Stephen Sondheim**'s early musicals. His characteristically evocative, highly imaginative designs owed much to his roots in Russian theatre (and his admiration for painter Marc Chagall), which he effectively merged with American realism and Broadway style. He won **Tony Awards** for his designs of *Season in the Sun* (1950), *The Country Girl* (1950), *The Rose Tattoo* (1951), *Cabaret* (1966), *Zorba* (1968), *Company* (1969), *Follies* (1971), and *Pacific Overtures* (1976), and was nominated for several more. Aronson was married to his assistant, Lisa Jalowetz.

ARONSTEIN, MARTIN (1936–2002). Born in Pittsfield, Massachusetts, Aronstein moved to New York with his family when he was 12 and studied at Queens College. After attending a performance at the **New York Shakespeare Festival**, he asked a stage technician if help was needed, beginning his career working as an apprentice there, ultimately becoming lighting designer for the festival. He was also resident lighting designer for the **Repertory Theatre of Lincoln Center**. Subsequently, he was nominated for five **Tony Awards** for *Ain't Supposed to Die a Natural Death* (1971), *Much Ado about Nothing* (1972), *In the Boom Boom Room* (1973), *Medea* (1982), and *Wild Honey* (1986), for which he also received a Drama Desk nomination. His first **Broadway** production, *Arturo Ui* (1963) led to nearly 100 productions of plays and MUSICALS for Broadway, including *The Milk Train Doesn't Stop Here Anymore* (1964), *Tiny Alice* (1964), *The Impossible Years* (1965), *The Royal Hunt of the Sun* (1965), *Cactus Flower* (1965), *Slapstick Tragedy* (1966), *George M!* (1968), *Play It Again, Sam* (1969), *The Gingerbread Lady* (1970), *And Miss Reardon Drinks a Little* (1971), *Moonchildren* (1972), *Sugar* (1972), *Measure for Measure* (1973), *The Ritz* (1975), *Kennedy's Children* (1975), *The Grand Tour* (1979), *Division Street* (1980), and *Noises Off* (1983). In the late 1970s, he moved to California and designed regularly for the **Mark Taper Forum** and the Ahmanson Theatre, winning the Los Angeles Drama Critics Circle's Angstrom Award for lifetime achievement in lighting.

ARSENIC AND OLD LACE. The otherwise unknown Joseph Kesselring had his only **Broadway** success with *Arsenic and Old Lace*, a macabre farce, but theatrical legend reveals that the play's producers, HOWARD LINDSAY and RUSSEL CROUSE, reworked Kesselring's thriller, *Bodies in Our Cellar*, into a long-running comedy hit which opened at the Fulton Theatre on 10 January 1941 for a remarkable 1,444 performances. This darkly farcical comedy is about Abby and Martha Brewster (JOSEPHINE HULL and **Jean Adair**), two sweet little old ladies, who spend their days serving poisoned wine to lonely old men as a Christian act. Abby and Martha's genially deranged brother who believes he is Teddy Roosevelt buries the bodies in the basement of their Victorian mansion, believing the deceased to be yellow fever victims from the Panama Canal. Mortimer Brewster, their sane nephew, marries the girl next door, but his honeymoon is interrupted when he discovers his aunts' homicidal proclivities. Planning to commit them and Teddy to a friendly insane asylum, Mortimer runs afoul of his brother, Jonathan, an escaped murderer (who uncannily resembles the horror film star Boris Karloff and who conveniently played the role on Broadway) who unexpectedly returns to the family home to hide out. Farcical situations abound before Mortimer learns that he was adopted and, as such, is free of the insanity running (or "galloping," as he puts it) through the Brewster clan. Critics were at a loss to explain how so much humor could be generated by such murderous goings-on, but the play has had an enduring life on professional and amateur stages, including a 1986 **Broadway** revival, and in a classic 1944 screen version directed by Frank Capra.

ARTEF. The Workers' Theatre Group (ARTEF is a Yiddish acronym), founded in 1925 as the dramatic wing of *Freiheit*, the Yiddish-language community daily newspaper. The group produced YIDDISH THEATRE classics and contemporary radical agitprop works on Jewish issues through most of the 1930s before essentially disbanding in 1937, although occasional productions were done after that until about 1940. Their most noted productions included Jacob Mostel's *Strike*, Shmuel Godiner's *Jim Kooperkop*, Avrum Vevioka's *Diamonds*, and several of Maxim Gorky's plays.

AS HUSBANDS GO. RACHEL CROTHERS's three-act comedy, in a JOHN GOLDEN production, opened on 5 March 1931 at John Golden's Theatre for 149 performances. A domestic comedy about two Iowa ladies on a toot in

Paris where a romantic fling for Lucile, the married one (Lily Cahill), follows her back to Dubuque. The play was revived in 1933, racking up an additional 148 performances. A 1934 film version, starring Helen Vinson and Warner Baxter, was scripted by S. N. BEHRMAN from Crothers's play.

AS IS. Originally produced by the **Circle Repertory Company** and the Glines at the Circle Theatre in March 1985, **William M. Hoffman**'s drama about the **AIDS** epidemic opened on **Broadway** on 1 May 1985 at New York's Lyceum Theatre for a 285 performance run, receiving a **Drama Desk Award** and a **Tony Award** nomination as Best Play. Directed by **Marshall W. Mason**, with a cast featuring Jonathan Hadary, it was one of the first mainstream plays to address the issues of AIDS, focusing on a group of New York friends affected by the pandemic in its early days. *New York Times* critic **Frank Rich** applauded Hoffman for writing this difficult subject with "charity and humor." A year after the Broadway production, Hoffman adapted the play for a television film directed by **Michael Lindsay-Hogg**, again with Hadary in the lead, supported by Robert Carradine and **Colleen Dewhurst**.

ASHLEY, ELIZABETH (1939–). Born in Ocala, Florida, Ashley made her **Broadway** debut in the comedy *Take Her She's Mine* (1961), winning a Best Featured Actress **Tony Award**, but scored a more notable success (and a Best Actress Tony nomination) playing newlywed Corie Bratter in **Neil Simon**'s *Barefoot in the Park* (1963) and although she spent much of her career in films and television, Ashley made frequent returns to the stage, most notably in an acclaimed performance, also Tony-nominated, as "Maggie the Cat" in a 1974 revival of **Tennessee Williams**'s *Cat on a Hot Tin Roof*. Her other Broadway appearances include *Ring around the Bathtub* (1972), a 1975 revival of *The Skin of Our Teeth*, *Legend* (1976), a 1977 revival of *Caesar and Cleopatra*, *Hide and Seek* (1980), *Agnes of God* (1982), *Garden District* (1995), a 2000 revival of *The Best Man*, *Enchanted April* (2003), and *Dividing the Estate* (2008). Ashley also took over the role of Mattie Fae in *August: Osage County* in 2009 and she played the title role in *Mrs. Warren's Profession* at the **Shakespeare Theatre Company** in Washington, D.C. in 2010. She was married to two noted actors, George Peppard and James Farentino.

ASIAN AMERICAN THEATRE. Actors with Asian roots and Asian American characters appeared in plays from nearly the beginning of the American theatre, but as with many ethnic minorities, frequently in small and stereotypical roles, or the characters were played by non-Asian actors. By the 1960s, an Asian American theatre movement began with the formation of several companies, most notably **East West Players** in Los Angeles, California; Asian American Theatre Workshop in San Francisco, California; Theatrical Ensemble of Asians (subsequently renamed Northwest Asian American Theatre) in Seattle, Washington; and **Pan Asian Repertory Theatre** in New York. These four troupes, all of whom shared the common goal of elevating the profile of Asian American writers and performers on stage, in films, and television, dominated until the 1980s when a steady growth of Asian American troupes spiked to 40 companies across the country by the mid-1990s.

In the 1970s, the first important group of Asian American playwrights began making their mark, including Wakako Yamauchi, Momoko Iko, Edward Sakamoto, Hiroshi Kashiwagi, and Frank Chin, following by the most acclaimed, **David Henry Hwang**, whose play *M. Butterfly* became the first Asian American play produced on Broadway in 1988, winning the **Tony Award** as Best Play. Hwang has had an enduringly successful career and set the stage for such playwrights as **Philip Kan Gotanda**, Velina Hasu Houston, Diana Son, Sung Rno, Hn Ong, Chay Yew, Rick Shiomi, and Ralph Peña.

The evolution across these three generations of Asian American dramatists saw themes move from cultural identity and family life to works in which Asian American experience formed the background for plays on a range of broader topics. More experimental Asian American artists moving into multimedia and solo performances include **Ping Chong**, Dan Kwong, Denise Uyehara, Jude Narita, and Lan Nishikawa, as well as improvisation and comedic groups, including Slant Performance Group and 18 Might Mountain Warriors.

ASOLO STATE THEATRE. Now known as the Asolo **Repertory** Theatre, this Sarasota, Florida-based theatre was founded in 1960 by the Florida State University drama department as a summer acting company for students. By 1965, the theatre had become the first State Theatre of Florida, adding an M.F.A. training program in the 1970s and moving from its first home at the Ringling Museum to the newly constructed Asolo Center for the Performing Arts in 1990. The company is a true repertory with a resident company and rotating performances. *See also* REGIONAL THEATRE MOVEMENT.

ASSOCIATION FOR THEATRE IN HIGHER EDUCATION. *See also* AMERICAN THEATRE ASSOCIATION.

ASSOCIATION OF PRODUCING ARTISTS (APA). Actor-director **Ellis Rabb** founded APA in 1960, staging plays in Bermuda, New Jersey, and Milwaukee, Wisconsin, before settling at the Folksbiene Playhouse in New York, later becoming the resident company of the University of Michigan. In 1964, APA merged with the **Phoenix Theatre**, achieving acclaim with diverse productions of classics and modern works, including **George M. Cohan**'s

The Tavern,* Luigi Pirandello's *Right You Are If You Think You Are*, Maxim Gorky's *The Lower Depths*, and Molière's *Scapin*. Despite critical success, the troupe was forced to move back to the University of Michigan, but they returned to **Broadway** with an acclaimed revival of GEORGE S. KAUFMAN and **Moss Hart**'s *You Can't Take It with You* in 1965. The success of this production allowed APA to remain in New York at the Lyceum Theatre where they produced a **repertory** including noted productions of Anton Chekhov's *The Cherry Orchard*, directed by EVA LE GALLIENNE and starring **Uta Hagen**, and George *Kelly*'s* *The Show-Off* * starring HELEN HAYES in 1967. Internal strife and the departure of Rabb's wife, **Rosemary Harris**, from the company, ended its tenure by the end of the 1960s.

AT THE FOOT OF THE MOUNTAIN. Founded in 1974, this **feminist** theatre troupe in Minneapolis, Minnesota, is the oldest women-centered theatre company in the United States. The company won critical plaudits for the use of experimental techniques, ritual drama, and strongly articulated feminist politics.

ATKINSON, BROOKS (1894–1984).[†] Born in Melrose, Massachusetts, Justin Brooks Atkinson was the son of a journalist and educated at Harvard University. He worked as a reporter for the *Springfield Daily News* and as an English instructor at Dartmouth University prior to service in the United States Army during World WAR I. Following the war, he became assistant drama critic of the *Boston Evening Transcript* before serving as book review editor for the *New York Times* in 1922. He ascended to the post of drama **critic** at the *Times* in 1925, continuing in that position until 1942 when he became a news correspondent during World War II in China and Russia. In 1946, he returned to the role of *New York Times* drama critic and continued until 1960, when he became critic-at-large for the *Times*, continuing until 1965. He authored more than a dozen books on a range of topics, including collections of his **Broadway** theatre reviews and most notably his aptly named 1970 book *Broadway*, in which he revisits his encounters with New York theatre between 1925 and 1965. Widely respected by the theatrical community, Atkinson won a PULITZER PRIZE in 1947 for his writings on the Soviet Union and, subsequently, numerous awards for his drama criticism. In 1960, New York's Mansfield Theatre was renamed the Brooks Atkinson Theatre.

ATKINSON, JAYNE (1959–). An actress born in Bournemouth, England, Atkinson studied at Northwestern University and the Yale School of Drama. She made her **Off-Broadway** debut in *Bloody Poetry* (1986), but won attention on **Broadway** in revivals of *All My Sons* (1987), *Ivanov* (1997), *The Rainmaker* (1999), *Our Town* (2002), and *Blithe Spirit* (2009), and Matthew Barber's *Enchanted April* (2003), for which she received **Tony** and **Drama Desk Award** nominations. Other Drama Desk nominations include her Off-Broadway performances in *The Art of Success* (1990) and *The Shriker* (1997). *The Rainmaker* brought her another Tony nomination. She replaced **Mary-Louise Parker** as Li'l Bit in *How I Learned to Drive* (1997), and she toured in *Lionheart* (2005), a solo piece in which she played Eleanor of Aquitaine.

ATLANTIC THEATRE COMPANY. Playwright **David Mamet** and actor **William H. Macy** established this company in 1985 dedicated to ensemble acting, staging over 100 productions, including many of Mamet's plays and the **Tony Award**-winning productions of *The Beauty Queen of Leenane* (1998) and *Spring Awakening* (2006). The company also established the Atlantic Acting School in 1983 as a conservatory and undergraduate program in conjunction with New York University. Neil Pepe serves as artistic director and the ensemble includes such noted actors as Kathryn Erbe, Felicity Huffman, Kristen Johnson, Camryn Manheim, Rebecca Pidgeon, Mary Steenburgen, and director **Scott Zigler**, as well as Mamet and Macy.

AUBURN, DAVID (1969–). Born in Chicago, Illinois, Auburn spent most of his youth in Ohio and Arkansas before returning to his birthplace to attend the University of Chicago. He also studied on a fellowship from Amblin Entertainment and attended the Juilliard School's playwriting program where he studied with **Marsha Norman** and **Christopher Durang**. His earliest play, *Skyscraper*, was produced **Off-Broadway** in 1997 and he published a short piece, *What Do You Believe about the Future?* (1996) in *Harper's* magazine. He won critical acclaim, as well as a PULITZER PRIZE and a **Tony Award** for *Proof* (2000) starring **Mary-Louise Parker,** and he scripted a 2005 screen version starring Gwyneth Paltrow and Anthony Hopkins. Also for film, he wrote *The Lake House*, released in 2006, and directed and wrote another film, *The Girl in the Park* (2007).

AUGUST: OSAGE COUNTY. This three-act sardonic comedy-drama by **Tracy Letts** began its life at the **Steppenwolf Theatre** in June 2007 before opening at New York's Music Box Theatre on 29 April 2008 for an impressive 648 performances. The play focuses on an extended and deeply dysfunctional Pawhuska, Oklahoma, family, the Westons, in which issues ranging from the matriarch's drug abuse, the patriarch's suicide, and alcoholism, incest, the problems of aging, **race**, and infidelity prevail, although some members of the family are capable of great love. A British production opened at London's National Theatre in November 2008, with other international productions, a national tour, and a screen version in the works in 2010. The play swept the year's awards, winning a PULITZER PRIZE, **Tony Award, Outer Critics Circle Award, New York Drama Critics Award, Drama Desk Award,** and **Drama League Award,** making it the most honored play in many years.

AUNT DAN AND LEMON. **Wallace Shawn**'s controversial drama had its first production at the Royal Court Theatre in London in a **New York Shakespeare Festival** production on 27 August 1985, but did not have a New York production until a 2003 **Off-Broadway** revival at the Acorn Theatre. In the play, Lemon, a reclusive, ailing young woman fascinated by Nazism, is befriended by Dan, a charismatic figure who shares tales of her love affairs with women and her application of Henry Kissinger's notion of *realpolitik* (an amoral ruthlessness as Dan sees it) leads to a view of relationships in terms of dominance and submission. Although a subsequent illness, during which she is tended by a compassionate nurse, changes Dan's attitudes, Lemon comes to embrace Dan's previous notions, praising not only Kissinger, but also Adolf Hitler, with *New York Times* critic **Ben Brantley** warning that the play's uncomfortably haunting power rested in the "gentle, poisonous voice" of Lemon.

AUNTIE MAME. Patrick Dennis's popular novel was dramatized by **Jerome Lawrence** and **Robert E. Lee** and won critical approval and a long run at the Broadhurst Theatre, where it opened on 31 October 1956 for 639 performances. Some critics felt that **Rosalind Russell**'s *tour de force* performance as the eccentric aunt of an orphaned boy carried the play, but *Auntie Mame* has proven an enduringly popular vehicle for many leading ladies, including Greer Garson and Beatrice Lillie, both of whom replaced Russell, with Lillie eventually starring in the London production. Russell also appeared in the lavish 1958 film version and composer/lyricist Jerry Herman adapted the play as a MUSICAL, *Mame* (1966), in which **Angela Lansbury** scored a personal success in the leading role. First set in the 1920s, the play spans several decades of Auntie Mame's life raising her nephew, Patrick. Through many ups-and-downs, the indefatigable Mame stays true to her mantra of living a full life. Despite her freewheeling and unorthodox ways, Patrick grows up to be a stable young man as Mame takes Patrick's young son, Michael, on a world tour.

AUTUMN GARDEN, THE. **Lillian Hellman**'s three-act drama opened at New York's Coronet Theatre on 7 March 1951 for 101 performances, directed by **Harold Clurman** and produced by **Kermit Bloomgarden**. The cast featured **Fredric March, Florence Eldridge**, Ethel Griffies, Kent Smith, and Jane Wyatt in a **Chekhovian**-style drama set in a once-grand New Orleans boarding house where the problems of the boarders, and the family running the boarding house, are the central concern of Hellman's rueful take on family, marriage, and the crossroads of midlife. The play has never been revived on **Broadway**, but it has had frequent productions in regional and university theatres, including critically acclaimed stagings at the **Williamstown Theatre Festival** (2007) and Chicago's Eclipse Theatre (2008).

AVNER THE ECCENTRIC (1948–). Born in Atlanta, Georgia, as Avner Eisenberg, he attended the University of Washington before studying with Jacques Lecoq for two years. When he returned to the United States, he joined the faculty of Carlo Mazzone Clementi's **Dell'Arte School of Physical Comedy** in Blue Lake, California. As a performer, Eisenberg, who combines clowning, MIME, juggling, and other such skills in solo appearances and plays as diverse as *The Comedy of Errors* and *Waiting for Godot*. An exemplar of the "New Vaudeville"* movement, Eisenberg has also appeared on film, most notably playing "The Jewel" in *The Jewel of the Nile* (1984).

AWAKE AND SING! **Clifford Odets** was catapulted to the forefront of American drama in 1935 with the authorship of several plays for production by **The Group Theatre**, most particularly this three-act drama that premiered at the Belasco Theatre on 19 February 1935 for 184 performances (after a hiatus of several months, the production returned for 24 additional performances in September). Directed by **Harold Clurman**, this classic work of the Great Depression is set in 1933 in the Bronx home of the Berger family.

Bessie Berger, the matriarch, played memorably by **Stella Adler**, is domineering and self-centered, aimed on controlling the lives of her family members, particularly her grown children, with her eye firmly fixed on improving the family's reduced financial situation. The children, Hennie, unwed and pregnant, and Ralph (**John Garfield**, then billed as Jules), an ambitious dreamer, want to live their own lives out of their mother's control. Hennie ultimately runs away with Moe Axelrod (**Luther Adler**), a disabled World War I veteran who can provide financial security. In support of Ralph, his philosophizing grandfather, Jacob (**Morris Carnovsky**), makes the young man beneficiary of a $3,000 life insurance policy before staging his suicide as an accidental fall from a roof. In response to his grandfather's sacrifice, Ralph becomes a radical political activist. **Sanford Meisner** and Phoebe Brand were also in the original cast.

Awake and Sing! has had **Broadway** revivals in 1938, 1939, 1984, and 2006, the last winning a **Tony Award** as Best Revival of a Play. This production spawned a 2007 revival in London's West End with **Stockard Channing** as Bessie. **Off-Broadway** revivals were seen in 1970, 1979, 1993, and 1995, and a 1972 PBS-TV adaptation starred **Walter Matthau** and Felicia Farr.

AWARDS. Acknowledging outstanding work in American theatre has been a long-standing tradition. Since 1917, the PULITZER PRIZE committee made up of theatre critics and academics annually named an American play as the year's best, but other awards, like the **Donaldson Award**, established by *Billboard* magazine in 1944, offered awards for best play, MUSICAL, performances, stage debuts, costumes, and set designs. After the establishment of the ANTOINETTE PERRY **Tony Awards**, which have been presented annually since 1947, the Donaldson Award came to seem superfluous and was discontinued in 1955. **Off-Broadway** has acknowledged various categories of theatrical achievement with the annual **Obie Awards**, established by the *Village Voice* in 1955. Off-Broadway accomplishments are also celebrated by the **Lucille Lortel Awards** each year.

The **Drama League Awards**, established in 1935, acknowledge both **Broadway** and Off-Broadway work. The **Theatre World Award**, founded in 1945 and chosen by New York-based drama critics, names promising actors making outstanding stage debuts in New York each year, both on Broadway and Off-Broadway. Several awards from drama critics, including the **New York Drama Critics Circle**, **Outer Critics Circle**, **Drama Desk Award**, and others also acknowledge the quality of New York theatre, while most major American cities have developed their own awards for outstanding work in their region, such as Chicago's Sarah Siddons and Joseph Jefferson Awards or Washington, D.C.'s HELEN HAYES Award. The theatrical union, ACTORS' EQUITY, presents the annual PAUL ROBESON Award to a distinguished theatrical personage and other organizations acknowledge achievement of particular racial and ethnic groups, such as New York's Latin ACE Awards.

AXELROD, GEORGE (1922–2003). Born in New York City, Axelrod was the son of a silent movie actress, Beatrice Carpenter, and a father who worked in real estate. Following military service during World WAR II, Axelrod wrote scripts for radio and television before his first **Broadway** effort, the book for a MUSICAL revue,* *Small Wonder* (1948). He scored an enormous commercial success with his risqué comedy, ***The Seven Year Itch*** (1952), which ran for over 1,100 performances. He collaborated on a screenplay for *The Seven Year Itch* with legendary director Billy Wilder, whose 1955 film version provided Marilyn Monroe with one of her most iconic performances as a restless married man's fantasy woman. Axelrod had a second stage hit with *Will Success Spoil Rock Hunter?* (1955), followed by a movie version in 1957. Axelrod had a mild Broadway success with *Goodbye Charlie* (1959), which starred **Lauren Bacall**, and he produced **Gore Vidal**'s comedy, *A Visit to a Small Planet* (1957). Axelrod also directed, including Harry Kurnitz's *Once More with Feeling* (1958) and **Neil Simon**'s *The Star-Spangled Girl* (1966). He spent much of the remainder of his career writing screenplays, including his Academy Award-nominated script for *Breakfast at Tiffany's* (1961). His other films include *The Manchurian Candidate* (1962) and *How to Murder Your Wife* (1965), and he directed several films.

AYERS, LEMUEL (1915–1955). A New York native, Ayers was educated at Princeton University and the University of Iowa prior to designing settings for producer Leonard Sillman's revivals of *Journey's End* and *They Knew What They Wanted** in 1939. He designed settings and/or costumes for numerous **Broadway** productions, including *Macbeth*, a 1941 production starring **Maurice Evans** and **Judith Anderson**, *Angel Street* (1941), *The Pirate* (1942), *Harriet* (1943), *Oklahoma!* (1943), *Song of Norway* (1944), *Bloomer Girl* (1944), *Cyrano de Bergerac* (1946), *St. Louis Woman* (1946), *Inside U.S.A.* (1948), *Kiss Me, Kate* (1948), *Out of This World* (1950), *Camino Real* (1953), a revival of GEORGE BERNARD SHAW's *Misalliance* in 1953, *Kismet* (1953), and *The Pajama Game* (1954), among others. He won a **Tony Award** for his costumes for *Kiss Me, Kate*, as well as one for producing the show.

AZENBERG, EMANUEL (1934–). The Bronx, New York-born "Manny" Azenberg was won over to a life in the theatre when, in his youth, he saw **John Garfield** in Jan de Hartog's *Skipper Next to God* in 1948. After studying at New York University and a stint in the military, Azenberg first worked as a company manager for a number of productions, beginning with the flop *The Legend of Lizzie* (1959). He became a close friend of **Neil Simon** a few years later and, once established as a producer, Azenberg produced all of Simon's plays beginning in 1972, including *The Sunshine Boys* (1972), *The Good Doctor* (1973), *God's Favorite* (1974), *California Suite* (1976), *Chapter Two* (1977), *They're Playing Our Song* (1979), *I Ought to Be in Pictures* (1980), *Fools* (1981), a revival of *Little Me* in 1982, *Brighton Beach Memoirs* (1983), *Biloxi Blues* (1985), *Broadway Bound* (1986), *Rumors* (1988), *Lost in Yonkers* (1991), *Jake's Women* (1992), *The Goodbye Girl* (1993), *Laughter on the 23rd Floor* (1993), *Proposals* (1997), *45 Seconds from Broadway* (2001), and revivals of *The Odd Couple* in 1985 and 2005. Among the over 60 productions of plays and MUSICALS since the early 1970s, Azenberg has produced *Ain't Supposed to Die a Natural Death* (1971), *Scapino*

(1974), *The Wiz* (1975), *Ain't Misbehavin'* (1978), *Whose Life Is It Anyway?* (1979), **Children of a Lesser God** (1980), *"Master Harold"... and the Boys* (1982), *The Real Thing* (1984), a revival of **A Moon for the Misbegotten** in 1984, the PULITZER PRIZE-winning *Sunday in the Park with George* (1984), a 1985 revival of *A Day in the Death of Joe Egg*, *Rent* (1996), a 1999 revival of **The Iceman Cometh**, *The Dinner Party* (2000), and revivals of *Private Lives* in 2002 and *Macbeth* in 2008.

B

BABE, THOMAS (1941–2000). A playwright and screenwriter, Babe was born in Buffalo, New York, and studied at Harvard, Cambridge, and Yale universities, completing a law degree at Yale. Many of his plays were written during a long collaboration with **Joe Papp** at the **New York Shakespeare Festival**, where he scored his first success with *Kid Champion* (1975), focusing on America's national myths on the relationships of fathers and daughters. Among his subsequent works are *Rebel Women* (1976), *Prayer for My Daughter* (1978), *Fathers and Sons* (1978), and ***Taken in Marriage*** (1979), which starred **Meryl Streep**, **Colleen Dewhurst**, **Kathleen Quinlan**, **Elizabeth Wilson**, and Dixie Carter. Subsequent works included *Salt Lake City Skyline* (1980), *Buried Inside Extra* (1984), *Planet Fires* (1985), *Carrying School Children* (1987), and *Demon Wine* (1987). Babe also directed on occasion, taught playwriting for many years at New York University, and worried about the survival of theatre, explaining, "The startling vanishment of the playwright is not only a fact, but his and her persistence in an era of incivility and social chaos is something of a miracle."

BACALL, LAUREN (1924–). Born Betty Joan Perske in New York, this sultry beauty studied at the AMERICAN ACADEMY OF DRAMATIC ART and debuted in a bit role in *Johnny 2 X 4* (1942) and *Franklin Street*, a show that closed during its tryout that same year. She worked as a model and her fortunes improved as the result of her first screen teaming with her future husband, Humphrey Bogart, in *To Have and Have Not* (1945). She became a major movie star, often playing opposite Bogart. Following his death, Bacall returned to **Broadway** in *Goodbye, Charlie* (1959) and two years later married **Jason Robards** (they were subsequently divorced in 1969). Bacall appeared in the popular **Abe Burrows** comedy *Cactus Flower* (1965) opposite **Barry Nelson**, but won a Best Actress in a MUSICAL **Tony Award** for *Applause* (1970). She appeared in another musical, *Woman of the Year* (1981), again winning a Tony, and a revival of **Noël Coward**'s *Waiting in the Wings* (1999).

BACK STAGE. Founded in 1960 by Ira Eaker and Allen Zwerdling, this New York-based weekly theatrical trade publication aimed at supplying actors and other show business professionals with casting information, news, feature articles, reviews, and financial information. A Los Angeles version of *Back Stage* was begun in 1993 and the two papers merged in 2005. *See also* PERIODICALS.

BAINTER, FAY (1891–1968).[†] Born in Los Angeles, California, where she began acting as a child, Bainter made her first New York stage appearance in *The Rose of Panama* (1912), a MUSICAL. She toured with Minnie Maddern Fiske* in *Mrs. Bumpstead-Leigh** (1914) before achieving her first important successes in *Arms and the Girl* (1916) and *The Willow Tree* (1917). She attained stardom in *East Is West** (1918), beginning a very active period of contemporary and classical roles, including **Noël Coward's** *Fallen Angels* (1927), *Lysistrata* (1930), and *The Admirable Crichton* (1931). After 1930, she appeared frequently in character roles in films, but made periodic returns to the stage, including playing Mimi in the road company of Cole Porter's *The Gay Divorce* (1932) and as Fran Dodsworth in SIDNEY HOWARD's *Dodsworth* (1934). She also appeared on **Broadway** in *The Next Half Hour* (1945), but most of her stage work, including a stint as Mary Tyrone in the 1957–1958 national tour of EUGENE O'NEILL's *Long Day's Journey into Night,* was done in STOCK or on tour. Her memorable films roles include supporting roles in *Jezebel* (1938), *Woman of the Year* (1942), and *The Children's Hour* (1961).

BAITZ, JON ROBIN (1961–). This socially conscious, politically engaged dramatist was born in Los Angeles, California, and raised in South America before returning to California to attend Beverly Hills High School. He worked for theatrical producers who inspired his first play, *Mizlansky/Zilinsky* (1985), a one-act (in 1997 expanded and revised as *Mizlansky/Zilinsky or "Schmucks"*). His first full-length play, *The Film Society* (1989), premiered in Los Angeles before moving to **Off-Broadway** starring **Nathan Lane**, where it won a **Drama Desk Award**. His subsequent plays, which deal with such topics as business ethics, politics, and the Holocaust has inspired critics to compare him to **Arthur Miller**. His plays also include *The Substance of Fire* (1991) and *The End of the Day* (1992), which were also well-received by critics and audiences. In 1991, Baitz wrote *Three Hotels*, about his parents, for a PBS American Playhouse broadcast and later revised it for the stage, receiving a Drama Desk nomination. Baitz adapted HENRIK IBSEN's *Hedda Gabler* in 1999 and subsequent plays include *A Fair Country* (1996). He has written for television and film and also acts, including a supporting role in *One Fine Day* (1996).

BAKER, PAUL (1911–2009). A native of Hereford, Texas, Baker graduated from Trinity University in 1932 and took a position teaching drama at Baylor University, where he met his wife, Kitty Cardwell, who taught art and **children's theatre**. In 1939, he received a Rockefeller grant to allow him to seek a degree at the Yale School of Drama and 1941 he received another Rockefeller to write about a 1936 trip he made to study European theatre design and production. After military service during World WAR II, Baker returned to teach and in 1959, helped found the **Dallas Theatre Center**, which was closely tied to the Baylor drama program (serving as its graduate program, where students interacted with a resident company of actors). However, when he produced *Long Day's Journey into Night* without cuts in 1962, a patron complained of the language and the Baylor administration insisted he shut down the production. In response, he moved his department to Trinity University and began to work closely with a graduate student, Preston Jones, who later wrote the plays that formed *A Texas Trilogy* beginning in 1973. They continued to work together until Jones's untimely death in 1979. Baker staged over 60 new scripts and American premieres at the DTC. He retired from Trinity in 1976 and from the board of the DTC in 1982. In 2009, at the age of 97, Baker was honored by the DTC, along with its other directors, for his contributions to Texas theatre. He died later that year.

BALDWIN, JAMES (1924–1987). Born in Harlem, New York, as James Arthur Baldwin, he moved to Greenwich Village at age 17 to pursue a writing career. Being **African American** and **gay**, Baldwin chafed at American prejudices and moved to Paris in 1948, winning fame writing novels, short stories, essays, and two plays, *The Amen Corner*, which was produced at Howard University in 1954 prior to a **Broadway** production in 1965, and *Blues for Mister Charlie* (1964), both works in which he focused on issues of race. *See also* AFRICAN AMERICAN THEATRE.

BALL, WILLIAM (1931–1991). This prolific director of theatre and opera, and founder of the **American Conservatory Theatre (ACT)** was born in Chicago, Illinois, and studied theatre at the Carnegie Institute of Technology. He began his career as an actor and assistant designer for **Margaret Webster** and started ACT in Pittsburgh in 1965. Disagreements with local financial benefactors led Ball to take ACT on the road before settling in San Francisco. He produced over 300 productions, directing 87, and won particular acclaim for revivals of *Cyrano de Bergerac* (1974) and *The Taming of the Shrew* (1976), both of which were broadcast on PBS. The ACT received a **Tony Award** for excellence in regional theatre in 1979. Ball was a flamboyant and provocative artist who ran afoul of **Edward Albee** when taking liberties the playwright did not appreciate with his *Tiny Alice* (1964) in 1969. Ball resigned from ACT in 1986 due to financial and artistic disagreements. He won a **Drama Desk Award** for his **Off-Broadway** revival of *Ivanov* and his sole **Broadway** productions were revivals of *Tartuffe* in 1965 (for which he was Tony-nominated), *Tiny Alice* in 1969, and *The Three Sisters* in 1969. Ball was the author of a 1984 book, *A Sense of Direction: Some Observations on the Art of Directing.*

BALLARD, LUCINDA (1906–1993). Born in New Orleans, Louisiana, Ballard worked as assistant to NORMAN BEL GEDDES and Claude Bragdon* before beginning her much-honored career as a costume designer on stage and screen. She debuted on **Broadway** with costumes for a 1937 revival of *As You Like It*, followed by numerous MUSICALS and ballets, including *I Remember Mama* (1944), for which she won a **Donaldson Award**, *Annie Get Your Gun* (1946), and others before winning the first **Tony Award** for her work for the 1946–1947 season, including *Happy Birthday, Street Scene,* * *Another Part of the Forest, John Loves Mary*, and *The Chocolate Soldier*. She subsequently designed dozens of Broadway productions, including *Allegro* (1947), *A Streetcar Named Desire* (1947), *Love Life* (1948), *The Fourposter* (1951), *Mrs. McThing* (1952), *My Three Angels* (1953), *Silk Stockings* (1955), *Cat on a Hot Tin Roof* (1955), *Orpheus Descending* (1957), *The Dark at the Top of the Stairs* (1957), *J. B.* (1958), *The Sound of Music* (1959), *A Loss of Roses* (1959), and *The Gay Life* (1961), for which she won a Tony. She designed costumes for the films *Portrait of Jennie* (1948) and *A Streetcar Named Desire* (1951), as well as numerous ballets.

BALSAM, MARTIN (1919–1996). This versatile character actor of stage and film was born Martin Henry Balsam in the Bronx, New York. He studied at the Dramatic Workshop of The New School with **Erwin Piscator** before appearing on **Broadway** in the flop *Ghost for Sale* (1941). He joined the Army during World WAR II, restarting his stage career after the war when he was selected by **Lee Strasberg** and **Elia Kazan** to appear on **The Actors Studio** television show in 1947. On Broadway, he appeared in *The Wanhope Building* (1947), a revival of *Macbeth* (1948), *Sundown Beach* (1948), *The Liar* (1950), *The Rose Tattoo* (1951), *Camino Real* (1953), *The Middle of the Night* (1956), and *Nowhere to Go but Up* (1962). Beginning in the 1950s, he appeared more frequently in film and television, but he returned to Broadway twice, winning a **Tony Award** for **Robert Anderson**'s *You Know I Can't Hear You When the Water's Running* (1968) and garnering a **Drama Desk Award** nomination in **Ronald Ribman**'s *Cold Storage* (1977). He also won an Academy Award as Best Supporting Actor for *A Thousand Clowns* (1965), and appeared in such notable films as *On the Waterfront* (1954), *12 Angry Men* (1957), *Psycho* (1960), *Breakfast at Tiffany's* (1961), *Catch-22* (1970), *Murder on the Orient Express* (1974), and *All the President's Men* (1976), as well as dozens of television shows.

BALTIMORE WALTZ, THE. **Paula Vogel**'s connected series of tragicomic scenes centered on a European trip by a brother and sister opened in a **Circle Repertory Company** production on 29 January 1992 for 55 performances under the direction of **Anne Bogart**. Vogel won an **Obie Award**, as did Bogart and **Cherry Jones**, who played Anna, a terminally ill woman dying of a fictional disease, ATD (Acquired Toilet Disease), an obvious reference to **AIDS**. Driven to seek casual sex with as many men as possible before her death, Anna travels to Europe with her brother, Carl (Richard Thompson) and a mysterious Third Man (an allusion to the classic film) played by **Joe Mantello**. The play was produced the following year by the **Yale Repertory Theatre** and was revived **Off-Broadway** in a **Signature Theatre Company** production directed by **Mark Brokaw** on 5 December 2004 for a month-long run.

BANCROFT, ANNE (1931–2005). Born Anna Maria Louisa Italiano in the Bronx, New York, this versatile stage and film actress studied at the HB Studio, the AMERICAN ACADEMY OF DRAMATIC ARTS, the **Actors Studio**, and the American Film Institute's Directing Workshop for Women at the University of California at Los Angeles. She appeared in live television in New York before appearing in films, beginning with *Don't Bother to Knock* (1952). After a series of undistinguished movies, she turned her attentions to stage work, winning plaudits and a **Tony Award** in her first **Broadway** play, *Two for the Seesaw* (1958). She won a second Tony for *The Miracle Worker* (1959), playing Helen Keller's teacher, Annie Sullivan, a role she repeated on screen, winning an Academy Award. On Broadway, Bancroft also appeared with distinction in a revival of *Mother Courage and Her Children* in 1963, *The Devils* (1965), a revival of *The Little Foxes* in 1967, *A Cry of Players* (1968), and was again Tony-nominated for *Golda* (1977). Her final Broadway appearance in *Duet for One* (1981), was short-lived, but she appeared on screen with frequency until the end of her life, winning four more Academy Award nominations starring in such films as *The Pumpkin Eater* (1964), *The Graduate* (1967), *The Turning Point* (1977), and *Agnes of God* (1985), as well as several films written and directed by her husband, Mel Brooks.

BANKHEAD, TALLULAH (1903–1968).[†] This deep-voiced, drawling Huntsville, Alabama, native became a symbol of the tempestuous, flamboyant actress, but Bankhead often transcended this stereotype to become a dominant figure of the **Broadway** theatre. If not the greatest actress of her age, Bankhead was undoubtedly one of its most fascinating, publicized for both her on-stage brilliance and her off-stage antics. She debuted in *Squab Farm* (1918), but spent much of her early career replacing stars and moved to London and for over a decade dazzled English audiences.

Returning to the Broadway stage in the mid-1930s with the cache of her London triumphs, Bankhead created a range of memorable roles, including Mary Clay in *Forsaking All Others* (1933), Judith Traherne in *Dark Victory** (1934), Monica Grey in *Something Gay* (1935), and Muriel Flood in *Reflected Glory* (1936). Her definitive characterization of the avaricious Regina Giddens in **Lillian Hellman**'s drama, *The Little Foxes* (1939), secured her prominence. Bankhead also had personal triumphs in revivals of SOMERSET MAUGHAM's *Rain** in 1935 and **Noël Coward**'s *Private Lives* in 1946, but she met with resounding failure when she played Cleopatra in a 1937 production of Shakespeare's *Antony and Cleopatra*, a performance that inspired critic JOHN MASON BROWN to write that she "barged down the Nile as Cleopatra and sank." Bankhead's off-stage antics, including addressing everyone as "Darling," were employed effectively by **Thornton Wilder** in his creation of Sabina Fairweather in *The Skin of Our Teeth* (1942), a role that brought Bankhead the Best Actress award from the **New York Drama Critics**.

Bankhead's raucous sense of humor made her a popular figure in radio and on early television, but audiences, including a vocal **gay** following, found it increasingly difficult to take Bankhead seriously on stage. When she appeared in a disastrous New York revival of **Tennessee Williams**'s *A Streetcar Named Desire*, most critics were merciless and portions of the audience hooted at Bankhead's increasingly campy delivery. Williams publicly rebuked Bankhead (although he subsequently apologized via the press), but this did not stop him from featuring her in his *The Milk Train Doesn't Stop Here Anymore* (1964), a failure and her last Broadway appearance. Other later performances include roles in *Foolish Notion* (1945), *The Eagle Has Two Heads* (1947), *Dear Charles* (1954), and *Midgie Purvis* (1961), the last winning her critical approval despite the play's short run. Bankhead occasionally appeared on screen, but scored only one significant film success in Alfred Hitchcock's *Lifeboat* in 1944, for which she received the Best Actress Award from the New York Film Critics.

BARAKA, AMIRI (1934–). The son of a postman and a social worker, Everett LeRoi Jones was born in Newark, New Jersey, and, at various times, studied philosophy and religion at Rutgers University, Columbia University, and Howard University, never completing a degree. He joined the Air Force, but an anonymous accusation that he was a Communist led to a dishonorable discharge. After some time in Cuba around 1960, he wrote about jazz and became interested in the Beat poets. He won critical acclaim and an **Obie Award** for *Dutchman* (1964), followed by other plays including *The Slave* (1964), *A Black Mass* (1966), and *Slave Ship* (1967). The assassination of Malcolm X in 1966 led him declare himself a "black cultural nationalist" and he took a Muslim name, Amiri Baraka. He established the Black Arts Repertory Theatre/School in Harlem in 1965 and Spirit House in Newark in 1966. His political views shifted to those of a "revolutionary socialist," views he depicted in *The Motion of History* (1975), which he subsequently published with other plays. Baraka has also appeared in films. *See also* AFRICAN AMERICAN THEATRE.

BARANSKI, CHRISTINE (1952–). A native of Buffalo, New York, Christine Jane Baranski studied at the Juilliard School and began her New York acting career in the **Off-Broadway** production of *Coming Attractions* (1980) prior to her **Broadway** debut in *Hide & Seek* that same year. She won an **Obie Award** for a 1984 production of *A Midsummer Night's Dream* and also appeared in *Hurlyburly* in 1985, *The House of Blue Leaves* in 1986, and *The Loman Family Picnic* in 1993. In 1984, she won a **Tony Award** and **Drama Desk Award** in **Tom Stoppard**'s *The Real Thing*. She won another Tony for *Rumors* (1989) and won a **Drama Desk Award** for *Lips Together, Teeth Apart* in 1992. An actress known for her versatility, Baranski also appears in occasional musicals, including a 2006 revival of *Mame* at the **Kennedy Center** and in concerts and various benefits. She appears frequently in films and on television, where she won an Emmy Award for the comedy series *Cybill* in 1995 and *The Good Wife*, which has brought her additional critical acclaim beginning in 2009. Her subsequent **Broadway** appearances include *Nick & Nora* (1991), *Short Talks on the Universe* (2002), and a hit revival of *Boeing-Boeing* (2008).

BAREFOOT IN THE PARK. **Neil Simon**'s **Tony Award**-nominated light romantic comedy about the period of adjustment for a newlywed couple in their first apartment in early 1960s New York City opened on 23 October 1963 for an impressive 1,530 performances at the Biltmore Theatre, winning critical approval for director **Mike Nichols** and stars **Elizabeth Ashley** and Robert Redford (who repeated his performance in the 1967 screen adaptation). The cast also included **Mildred Natwick**, **Kurt Kasznar**, and Herbert Edelman. An exuberant young bride, Corie Bratter (Ashley), impulsively rents a fifth floor walk-up apartment to the frustration of her button-down husband, Paul (Redford), and Corie's mother, Mrs. Banks (Natwick). Corie reads Paul's frustration as a lack of adventurousness, leading to several misadventures led by Corie and a flamboyant neighbor, Victor Velasco (Kasznar), all of which end with the newlyweds happily finding common ground. Simon's play was enduringly popular in STOCK, **community**, and university theatres, and was revived on **Broadway** in 2006 under the direction of **Scott Elliott** and starred Amanda Peet, Patrick Wilson, Jill Clayburgh, and **Tony Roberts** for 109 performances at the Cort Theatre.

BARNES, CLIVE (1927–2008). Born in London, England, Clive Alexander Barnes studied at Oxford University and began working as a dance and drama CRITIC in 1950 for *Dance and Dancers* magazine and other publications before becoming drama critic for *The Times* in 1961. Barnes moved to the United States in 1965 to take a position as dance critic for the *New York Times* and becoming drama critic in 1967. Barnes tended to prefer new "cutting edge" drama to commercial theatre and found British drama preferable to American theatre, opinions he expressed with a characteristic wit. He left the *New York Times* in 1977 and became drama and dance critic for the *New York Post*, a position he kept until his death.

BARNES, HOWARD (1904–1968). British-born son of American parents, Barnes attended Yale University, Queen's College at Oxford, and the Sorbonne prior to taking a position as assistant film CRITIC for the *New York World*. In 1928, he moved to the *New York Herald-Tribune*, where he worked under the wing of Percy Hammond.* After Hammond's retirement, Barnes took over a chief drama critic in 1942, continuing in that post until 1951.

BARR, RICHARD (1917–1989). Washington-born producer-director Richard Alphonse Barr attended Princeton University, where he performed in plays and was given his first professional acting opportunity (for no pay) by **John Houseman, Orson Welles**, and **the Mercury Theatre**, for whom he acted in the controversial radio broadcast of *The War of the Worlds* in 1938. He also assisted Welles during the filming of *Citizen Kane* (1941) before serving in the Air Force during World WAR II. After the war, he directed **Broadway** revivals, including **José Ferrer** in *Volpone* in 1948, **Richard Whorf** in *Richard III* in 1949, and Francis Lederer in *Arms and the Man* in 1950 before turning to producing in partnership first with **Clinton Wilder** and later with **Charles Woodward**, as well as serving as president of the **League of American Theatres and Producers**. As a producer, mostly **Off-Broadway**, Barr was significant in bringing **Edward Albee**'s plays to the stage, not to mention **Sam Shepard, William Hanley, Paul Zindel, LeRoi Jones, John Guare, Terrence McNally, A. R. Gurney**, and **Jean-Claude Van Itallie**, and promoted the production of plays by major avant-garde European playwrights, including Samuel Beckett and Eugene Ionesco. Among his notable Broadway credits are several of Albee's plays, including *Who's Afraid of Virginia Woolf?* (1962), *Tiny Alice* (1964), *Malcolm* (1966), *A Delicate Balance* (1966), *Everything in the Garden* (1967), *All Over* (1971), *Seascape* (1975), and *The Lady from Dubuque* (1980), and a 1969 all-star revival of *The Front Page,** *The Grass Harp* (1971), *The Last of Mrs. Lincoln* (1972), *Noël Coward in Two Keys* (1974), and *Sweeney Todd* (1979), among others.

BARRECA, CHRISTOPHER (1957–). Born in Massachusetts, Barreca studied at the University of Connecticut and received an M.F.A. in Design from Yale University. He was nominated for a 1998 **Drama Desk Award** for his **Off-Broadway** design of **Richard Greenberg**'s *Three Days of Rain*. Barreca's **Broadway** credits include *Our Country's Good* (1991), *Search and Destroy* (1992), Stephen Lang's *Hamlet* (1992), *Marie Christine* (1999), and *The Violet Hour* (2003). Barreca has designed for numerous **regional theatres**, including the **Mark Taper Forum, South Coast Repertory**, Baltimore's **Center Stage, Dallas Theatre Center**, and the **American Conservatory Theatre**, and in the early 1980s cofounded the American IBSEN Theatre in Pittsburgh, where he worked with **Charles Ludlam** and Travis Preston. Barreca has also designed opera and is head of design at CalArts.

BARRETTS OF WIMPOLE STREET, THE. One of KATHARINE CORNELL's most notable acting triumphs came in Rudolf Besier's three-act drama of the life of Elizabeth Barrett, which opened on 9 February 1931 at the Empire Theatre under the direction of GUTHRIE MCCLINTIC with designs by JO MIELZINER. The drama depicts the romance of Barrett and Robert Browning (**Brian Aherne**) over the objections of her father (McKay Morris). Cornell toured in the play and returned to **Broadway** twice in revivals of it in 1935 and 1945, all three times appearing opposite Aherne. When the play was filmed in 1934, Norma Shearer, **Fredric March**, and **Charles Laughton** played the leads and a remake in 1957 starred Jennifer Jones, Bill Travers, and John Gielgud.

BARRY, PHILIP (1896–1949).[†] Son of prosperous Irish-American parents from Philadelphia, Pennsylvania, Barry was a sickly child who filled his lonely days with books. He entered Yale University in 1914 and made an impression in the school's literary activities. Rejected for military service at the time of America's entry into World WAR I, Barry instead worked for the State Department in London. Barry continued his education at Yale after the war and began to write plays before enrolling in George Pierce Baker's* playwriting class at Harvard University. Barry had an initial **Broadway** success with *You and I** (1923), originally titled *The Jilts*, a work that established his style of mixing sophisticated, witty high comedy with social commentary.

Barry's lasting contribution stems from this combination, a formula that permitted him to create a twentieth-century American equivalent of the British comedy of manners. Many of his plays feature the "Barry girl," seen most vividly in Tracy Lord (played by **Katharine Hepburn** in its original production) of *The Philadelphia Story* (1939). The "Barry girl" is typically a pampered, headstrong young woman who both profits from and rejects the social expectations that wealth and privilege provide. *The Philadelphia Story* has proven the most durable of Barry's dramatic accomplishment, a work that is frequently revived and provided the source for the 1956 M-G-M film, *High Society*, with music and lyrics by Cole Porter. Among his other pre-World War II plays, *Holiday** (1928) and *The Animal Kingdom* (1932), were particularly well-received and became popular films.

Barry's dramatic output also includes *White Wings** (1926), *Paris Bound** (1927), *Cock Robin* (1928; coauthored by ELMER RICE), *Hotel Universe* (1930), *Tomorrow and Tomorrow* (1931), *The Joyous Season* (1934), *Bright Star* (1935), *Here Come the Clowns* (1938), *Liberty Jones* (1941), *Without Love* (1942), *Foolish Notion* (1945; adapted from Jean-Pierre Aumont's play *My Name Is Aquilon*), *Second Threshold* (1951; unfinished at the time of Barry's death, the script was completed by ROBERT E. SHERWOOD). The popularity of Barry's high comedy declined after World War II, but he remains the singular proponent of witty, sophisticated, and socially conscious comedy.

BARRYMORE, ETHEL (1879–1959).† Born in Philadelphia, Pennsylvania, to actors Maurice Barrymore* and Georgiana Drew,* Barrymore, along with her brothers John* and Lionel,* went on the stage at an early age, appearing with her grandmother, Mrs. John Drew,* in *The Rivals*, after which she appeared with William Gillette* in *Secret Service** and with Henry Irving's company at the Lyceum Theatre in London. Her 1901 New York debut in Clyde Fitch's* *Captain Jinks of the Horse Marines** made her a star and her career on stage and in films extended over more than 50 years. Over time, she mellowed from a great beauty in ingénue* roles into a versatile character actress capable of moving easily from comedy to drama and from classics to contemporary works.

Barrymore's regal bearing and impressive voice helped to make her a favorite of critics in *Alice-Sit-By-the-Fire* (1905), *Our Mrs. McChesney**

(1915), *The Lady of the Camellias* (1917), *Déclassé** (1919), *The Constant Wife* (1926), and *The Kingdom of God* (1928). When sound films arrived, Barrymore appeared more frequently on screen in such films as *Rasputin and the Empress* (1932), which was the only time she appeared on film with her brothers Lionel and John, and she won a Best Supporting Actress Academy Award for *None but the Lonely Heart* (1944). She also received Oscar nominations for *The Spiral Staircase* (1946), *The Paradine Case* (1948), and *Pinky* (1950).

Barrymore returned to **Broadway** in 1938 as a 101-year-old woman in Mazo de la Roche's *Whiteoaks*, but many critics regarded her performance as Miss Moffat, a compassionate Scottish teacher, in Emlyn Williams's *The Corn Is Green* (1940), Barrymore's greatest. Her last New York appearance in Ladislaus Bush-Fekete and Mary Helen Fay's *Embezzled Heaven* (1944) was only a modest success and she appeared in *The Joyous Season* on tour in 1945 before retiring from the stage. Barrymore continued to make films and also appeared on radio and television in her later years, retiring after her last film role in *Johnny Trouble* (1957).

BARTER THEATRE. This Abingdon, Virginia, theatre was founded by Robert Porterfield in 1933 at the height of the Great Depression, getting its name from Porterfield's idea of allowing audience members to purchase tickets with goods, usually food, which supported the theatre's company. In 1946, the theatre became the State Theatre of Virginia and was responsible for launching the theatrical careers of such actors as Gregory Peck, Ernest Borgnine, Patricia Neal, **Ned Beatty**, **Hume Cronyn**, Frances Fisher, **Kevin Spacey**, and others. Following Porterfield's 1971 death, Rex Partington took over as artistic director, followed by Richard Rose in 1992. *See also* REGIONAL THEATRE MOVEMENT.

BARTON, JAMES (1890–1962). This versatile comedian and character actor, who began his career in vaudeville* and BURLESQUE, was born in Gloucester, New Jersey, to vaudevillian parents who took him onstage at the age of two. He toured the country for years before making his **Broadway** debut in the revue* *The Passing Show* of 1919. He scored a success playing a feckless comedian in the touring production of *Burlesque** (1927), but he had two dramatic success, first replacing HENRY HULL in *Tobacco Road* (1933) in 1934, a role he played for over five years, and as Hickey in the original Broadway production of EUGENE O'NEILL's *The Iceman Cometh* (1946). He occasionally appeared on screen from the early sound era, including in the role of Kit Carson in the film version of **William Saroyan**'s *The Time of Your Life* (1948), and later in episodic television during the 1950s. Barton continued in vaudeville and MUSICAL THEATRE, including *Paint Your Wagon* (1951), making his last Broadway appearance in *The Sin of Pat Muldoon* (1957).

BARTON, LUCY (1891–1979). A native of Ogden, Utah, Barton graduated from the Carnegie Institute of Technology in 1917 and completed a master's degree at New York University in 1943. She began teaching theatre at the University of Texas at Austin in 1947 before becoming Head of the Department of Drama at the University of Alabama. Barton's lasting achievement is her textbook, *Historic Costume for the Stage* (1935), along with its complementary volume, *Period Patters* (1945).

BASIC TRAINING OF PAVLO HUMMEL, THE. The first of **David Rabe**'s trilogy of Vietnam War plays, this drama opened **Off-Broadway** in a **New York Shakespeare Festival** production directed by **Jeff Bleckner** on 19 May 1971 at the **Public Theatre** with a cast including William Atherton in the title role, **Edward Hermann**, and Garrett Morris. This **Drama Desk Award**-winning play depicts an emotionally disturbed soldier, Hummel, who has been drafted in the Army and goes through basic training before being injured several times. The play has a surreal quality in which Hummel interacts with Ardell, who serves as a Greek chorus figure and Hummel's conscience. Finding determination to be a soldier, Hummel continues in the Army despite his injuries, with fatal results. The play was produced on **Broadway**, where it opened on 24 April 1977 for 117 performances with **Al Pacino** in the title role, for which he won a **Tony Award** and Drama Desk Award.

BATES, KATHY (1948–). Born Kathleen Doyle Bates in Memphis, Tennessee, she moved to New York in 1970, following graduation from Southern Methodist University. In regional theatre, she won critical plaudits in the premiere of **Lanford Wilson**'s *Lemon Sky* (1970) at Buffalo's **Arena Theatre**. She acted **Off-Broadway** in *Casserole* (1975), *A Quality of Mercy* (1975), and won strong notices as Joanne in **Jack Heifner's** *Vanities* (1976) before scoring a notable success in **Terrence McNally**'s *Frankie and Johnny in the Clair de Lune* (1987), a play McNally wrote for her. On **Broadway**, Bates appeared in *Goodbye Fidel* (1980), stepped in as a replacement in *Fifth of July* (1980), *Come Back to the 5 & Dime Jimmy Dean, Jimmy Dean* (1982), and *'night, Mother* (1983), which brought her a **Tony Award** nomination. She has spent most of her career working in films, winning an Academy Award and Golden Globe Award for *Misery* (1990) and subsequent Oscar nominations for *Primary Colors* (1998) and *About Schmidt* (2002). Bates has also appeared on screen in *Fried Green Tomatoes* (1991), *Dolores Claiborne* (1995), *Titanic* (1997), *The Bridge of San Luis Rey* (2004), *Revolutionary*

Road (2008), and *Chéri* (2009), as well as numerous television shows, including seven Emmy Award-nominated appearances.

BAY, HOWARD (1912–1986). The son of two teachers, Bay was born in Centralia, Washington, and his design work was first noticed in the **Federal Theatre Project (FTP) "living newspaper"** productions of *One Third of a Nation* (1937) and *Power (1937)*. Shortly thereafter, he embarked on a long career designing scenery, lighting, and/or costumes for over 100 plays and MUSICALS for **Broadway**, winning critical acclaim and **awards** for his inventive solutions to difficult creative problems and the flair with which he adapted his techniques to the needs of each individual work. Bay won **Tony Awards** for his designs of *Toys in the Attic* (1960), and *Man of La Mancha* (1965) and a Tony nomination for *Cry for Us All* (1970). His design credits include some of the most important plays and musicals produced on Broadway between the 1930s and the late 1970s, including *The Little Foxes* (1939), *The Corn Is Green* (1940), *Uncle Harry* (1942), *One Touch of Venus* (1943), *Carmen Jones* (1943), *Ten Little Indians* (1944), a revival of *Show Boat* in 1946, *The Big Knife* (1949), *Come Back, Little Sheba* (1950), *The Autumn Garden* (1951), *The Shrike* (1952), *The Desperate Hours* (1955), *Look Back in Anger* (1957), *The Music Man* (1957), and *Milk and Honey* (1961). Bay taught for many years at Brandeis University and authored *Stage Design* (1974).

BEATTY, JOHN LEE (1948–). A native of Palo Alto, California, Beatty attended Brown University and Yale University to train as a scene designer. He began his work **Off-Broadway** in the 1970s with such companies as the **Manhattan Theatre Club** and **Circle Repertory Company** before amassing over 80 **Broadway** design credits, receiving **Drama Desk Award** nominations for *Knock Knock* (1976) and *The Innocents* (1976). He won a **Tony Award** and Drama Desk Award for *Talley's Folly* (1979), Drama Desk Awards and Tony nominations for *Fifth of July* (1980) and a revival of *Dinner at Eight* in 2003, a Drama Desk Award for a revival of *Twentieth Century* in 2004, and numerous nominations for both awards. Among his many other Broadway designs are *Faith Healer* (1979), *Fools* (1981), *Crimes of the Heart* (1981), *Angels Fall* (1983), *Burn This* (1987), *A Small Family Business* (1992), revivals of *Anna Christie** and *Abe Lincoln in Illinois** (both in 1993), *The Last Night of Ballyhoo* (1997), *Proof* (2000), *45 Seconds from Broadway* (2001), *Doubt* (2005), *The Color Purple* (2005), and revivals of *Accent on Youth* and *Brighton Beach Memoirs* in 2009. Beatty received a 1993 **Lucille Lortel Award** for career achievement and was inducted into the **Theatre Hall of Fame** in 2003.

BEATTY, NED (1937–). A native Kentuckian born in Louisville, Ned Thomas Beatty was educated at Transylvania University, although he did not complete a degree. He began his career in local theatre, including the newly established **Actors Theatre of Louisville**, where he appeared in *Death of a Salesman* in 1966. He made his **Broadway** debut as an understudy and replacement in *The Great White Hope* (1968), but spent most of his career in television and films, appearing in over 100 motion pictures, garnering an Oscar nomination for *Network* (1976). In 2003, he returned to Broadway as Big Daddy in a revival of *Cat on a Hot Tin Roof* and won a **Drama Desk Award** for his performance.

BEAUFORT, JOHN DAVID (1912–1992). A Canadian by birth, Beaufort moved to the United States in 1922 and studied at Boston University and Rollins College. He joined the staff of the *Christian Science Monitor* in 1930 as a copy boy and became an assistant reviewer in 1935 until he served as a war correspondent during World WAR II. After the war, he became chief of the *Monitor*'s news bureau, but by the mid-1960s, he served as drama CRITIC and arts and entertainment editor for the remainder of his career. He was also president of the **Drama Desk** in the late 1960s.

BECK, JULIAN (1925–1985). A native New Yorker, Beck studied for a time at Yale University, but dropped out to become a painter. He met **Judith Malina** in 1943 and, following their marriage they founded the **Living Theatre**, a group inspired by the Theatre of Cruelty techniques of Antonin Artaud. Beck described that mission as an insistence on "experimentation that was an image for a changing society. If one can experiment in theatre, one can experiment in life." Among their most notable productions, **Jack Gelber**'s *The Connection* (1959) provided an example of the Living Theatre philosophy, as actors portraying junkies wandered through the audience begging for money to supply their habit. Beck also appeared in films and wrote poetry.

BECKY SHAW. Gina Gionfriddo's play, a PULITZER PRIZE finalist, was described by *New York Times* critic **Charles Isherwood** as a "comedy of bad manners," focused on a five psychologically complex thirty-somethings (played by David Wilson Barnes, Emily Bergl, Kelly Bishop, Annie Parisse, and Thomas Sadowski) exploring contemporary attitudes about love, sex, and ethics in present-day New York. It opened at **Second Stage Theatre** on 8 January 2009 under the direction of Peter DuBois. The play had premiered in 2008 at the **Actors Theatre of Louisville** Humana Festival of New Plays.

BEDFORD, BRIAN (1935–). Born in Morley, West Yorkshire, England, Bedford studied at the Royal Academy of Dramatic Art and although he has appeared in film and television, has devoted his career to the stage. He is a much-honored interpreter of the characters of **Shakespeare** and Molière, winning a **Tony Award** and a **Drama Desk Award** for the latter's *The School for Wives* (1971). He has also been nominated for *Two Shakespearean Actors* (1992), *Timon of Athens* (1994), *The Molière Comedies* (1995), *London Assurance* (1997), and *Tartuffe* (2003). He made his **Broadway** debut in *Five Finger Exercise* (1959) and won a 1965 **Obie Award** for his performance in *The Knack*, as well as Drama Desk Awards for *The Misanthrope* in 1969, *Private Lives* in 1970, *Jumpers* in 1974, and *Two Shakespearean Actors* in 1992. His other **Broadway** credits include *Lord Pengo* (1962), *The Private Ear and The Public Eye* (1963), *The Astrakhan Coat* (1967), *The Unknown Soldier and His Wife* (1967), *The Seven Descents of Myrtle* (1968), and a revival of *The Cocktail Party* (1968). Much of his work has been done in regional theatres, including 27 seasons he has spent acting and directing for Canada's Stratford Shakespeare Festival, where he played Lady Bracknell in *The Importance of Being Earnest* in 2009, reprising the role on Broadway in 2011.

BEGLEY, ED (1901–1970). This character actor of stage, film, and television was born Edward James Begley in Hartford, Connecticut. He began his career in radio and acted on **Broadway** in a few less-than-successful plays before he won particular critical approval as Joe Keller in **Arthur Miller**'s *All My Sons* (1947). He also met with critical plaudits as Matthew Harrison Brady, a character based on William Jennings Bryan, in *Inherit the Wind* (1955), for which he won a **Tony Award**. In a display of versatility, Begley later switched to the role of Henry Drummond during the run. His other Broadway appearances include *All Summer Long* (1954), *A Shadow of My Enemy* (1957), *Semi-Detached* (1960), *Advise & Consent* (1960), *Zelda* (1969), and his last as Dr. Gibbs in a 1969 revival of *Our Town*. Begley appeared with distinction in numerous films and won a Best Supporting Actor Academy Award for *Sweet Bird of Youth* (1962). He made numerous television appearances as well and was the father of actor Ed Begley, Jr.

BEHRMAN, S. N. (1893–1973).[†] Samuel Nathaniel Behrman was born in Worcester, Massachusetts, and studied playwriting under George Pierce Baker* at Harvard University. Between 1927 and 1964, he had a steady stream of drawing room comedies with an edge of social **criticism** produced on **Broadway**, including *The Second Man** (1927), *Serena Blandish* (1929), *Meteor** (1929), *Brief Moment* (1931), ***Biography*** (1932), *Rain from Heaven* (1934), ***End of Summer*** (1936), *Amphitryon 38* (1937), *Wine of Choice*

(1938), *No Time for Comedy* (1939), *The Pirate* (1942), *Jacobowsky and the Colonel* (1944), *Dunnigan's Daughter* (1945), *I Know My Love* (1949), *Jane* (1952), *The Cold Wind and the Warm* (1958), *Lord Pengo* (1962), and *But for Whom Charlie* (1979). Behrman also contributed the libretto for the MUSICAL *Fanny* (1954) and his *Jacobowsky and the Colonel* was adapted as a musical by Jerry Herman in 1979. Behrman wrote or contributed to numerous screenplays, including *Hallelujah, I'm a Bum* (1933), *The Scarlet Pimpernel* (1934), *A Tale of Two Cities* (1935), *Waterloo Bridge* (1940), *Quo Vadis* (1951), and several of his own plays.

BEL GEDDES, BARBARA. *See* GEDDES, BARBARA BEL.

BEL GEDDES, NORMAN. *See* GEDDES, NORMAN BEL.

BELL, BOOK, AND CANDLE. **John Van Druten**'s comedy/fantasy, which he also directed, concerned the romantic machinations of a young witch living in present-day New York opened on 14 November 1950 at the Ethel Barrymore Theatre for a 233 performance run. Critics credited much of the play's success to a bright cast including **Rex Harrison**, Lili Palmer, and **Jean Adair**, but *Bell, Book, and Candle* became a perennial success on STOCK, **community,** and university theatre stages and was adapted to the screen in 1958 starring Kim Novak and **James Stewart**, followed by a 1976 television version and a remake set for release in 2010.

BELL FOR ADANO, A. **Paul Osborn**'s three-act drama, based on a novel by John Hersey, opened on 6 December 1944 at the Cort Theatre for 296 performances, produced by **Leland Hayward. Fredric March** appeared as an Italian American serving in the United States military during the Second World WAR who helps the villagers of Adano, which he has helped liberate from the fascists, get a new bell for their church. The play's idealism and sentimentality appealed to audiences as World War II drew to a close.

BELLAMY, RALPH (1904–1991). Born in Chicago, Illinois, Ralph Rexford Bellamy toured in a STOCK **Shakespeare** company immediately following graduation from high school. He worked in stock and tours for five years before his earliest performances on **Broadway** in *Town Boy* (1929) and *Roadside* (1930), which preceded a switch to film work, where he became a reliable leading man and character actor. He appeared in such screen classics as *The Awful Truth* (1937), *Carefree* (1938), *His Girl Friday* (1940), *The Wolf Man* (1941), and *Rosemary's Baby* (1968), subsequently being awarded an honorary Academy Award in 1987. Bellamy made periodic returns to Broadway, including in *Tomorrow the World* (1943), *Pretty Little Parlor* (1944), which he also produced and directed, *State of the Union* (1945), *Detective Story* (1949), and he won a **Tony Award** playing Franklin D. Roosevelt in his final Broadway appearance in **Dore Schary**'s *Sunrise at Campobello* (1958), repeating his performance in a 1960 film version. He also appeared in over 100 television shows.

BENNETT, RICHARD (1873–1944).[†] A native of Deacon's Mills, Indiana, Bennett began his long acting career in *The Limited Mail* (1891). After a decade of STOCK and touring productions, Bennett costarred with Maude Adams* in *What Every Woman Knows* (1908). His greatest stage successes in the 1920s included EUGENE O'NEILL's *Beyond the Horizon** (1920), *He Who Gets Slapped* (1922), and SIDNEY HOWARD's *They Knew What They Wanted** (1924). Bennett, who fathered screen actresses Joan and Constance Bennett, was praised for his intellectual, graceful performances. He appeared in films and made his last stage appearances in *Solid South* (1930) and as the insane Judge Gaunt in MAXWELL ANDERSON's *Winterset* (1935), a role he repeated on screen. Bennett also appeared on film in **Orson Welles**'s *The Magnificent Ambersons* (1942).

BENT. **Martin Sherman**'s **Tony Award**-nominated play about the historical persecution of **homosexuals** starred Ian McKellen when it premiered in 1979 in London prior to a **Broadway** production starring Richard Gere (who won a **Theatre World Award**), which opened at the New Apollo Theatre on 2 December 1979 for 241 performances under the direction of Robert Allan Ackerman, with scene design by **Santo Loquasto**. Gere played Max, a wealthy, apolitical Berliner ostracized by his family because of his homosexuality. He brings home a young man who, it turns out, is hunted by the Nazis. When the SS arrives and kills the man, Max and his boyfriend, Rudy, are forced to flee. They are eventually arrested by the Gestapo and in the process of being separated, Rudy calls to Max, who is forced to either beat Rudy to death or acknowledge his own homosexuality. The Gestapo force Max to prove his heterosexuality by having intercourse with the corpse of a young female. To prevent the harshest treatment, which he has determined is reserved for gays (who are forced to wear pink triangles), Max claims to be a Jew. Max becomes acquainted with Horst, played by Tony-nominated **David Dukes**, who teaches Max dignity. Resisting his captors, Horst is shot and Max responds by putting on Horst's pink triangle and commits suicide by grabbing an electrified fence. *Bent* was filmed in 1997.

BENTLEY, ERIC (1916–). A native of Bolton, Lancashire, England, Eric Russell Bentley became an American citizen in 1948 and worked as drama CRITIC for the *New Republic* from 1952 to 1956 and taught at Columbia University beginning in 1953. Also a playwright, his docudrama *Are You Now or Have You Ever Been* (1979), chronicled the anti-Communist "witchhunt" of the House Un-American Activities Committee, and his translation of **Bertolt Brecht's** *Mother Courage and Her Children* received a **Tony Award** nomination in 1963. Bentley also directed his own translation of Brecht's *The Good Woman of Setzuan* in 1956 on **Broadway**. Bentley notably translated the works of Brecht and Luigi Pirandello, and authored several books on modern theatre, including *The Playwright as Thinker* (1946), *The Life of the Drama* (1964), *The Brecht Commentaries 1943–1980* (1981), and *Thinking About the Playwright* (1987). Following two marriages, Bentley declared his **homosexuality** in 1969 and wrote a play *Lord Alfred's Lover* (1979) about Oscar Wilde. In 2006, Bentley was presented with a lifetime achievement **Obie Award**.

BERG, GERTRUDE (1898–1966). Born Gertrude Edelstein in New York, this actress and writer attended Columbia University and wrote skits for her father's resort in the Catskill Mountains before becoming a radio pioneer depicting a present-day Jewish family in a 15-minute episodic comedy, *The Rise of the Goldbergs*, beginning in 1929. The show expanded in length and Berg herself played the family matriarch, Molly Goldberg, a warm-hearted, wise mentor for not only her own family, but her richly ethnic neighborhood. The show, which Berg also scripted, moved to television in 1949 and a stage version, *Me and Molly* (1948), ran a season on **Broadway**. Berg won the first Best Actress Emmy Award in 1951. When the show ended, Berg returned to the stage, winning a **Tony Award** and a Sarah Siddons Award for her performance in *A Majority of One* (1961). Her final stage appearance in *Dear Me, The Sky is Falling*, which was based on one of her stories, ran for 145 performances. A MUSICAL, *Molly*, based on her characters from *The Goldbergs*, appeared on Broadway in 1973.

BERGHOF, HERBERT (1909–1990). This influential director, actor, and teacher was born in Vienna, Austria, where he studied at the Vienna State Academy of Dramatic Arts and under MAX REINHARDT. He moved to the United States in 1941 and appeared in a number of **Broadway** productions including *The Man Who Had All the Luck* (1944), revivals of *Little Women** in 1944, *Ghosts* and *Hedda Gabler* in 1948, *Miss Liberty* (1949), *The Deep Blue Sea* (1952), *The Andersonville Trial* (1959), and *In the Matter of J. Robert Oppenheimer* (1969). Berghof directed *Waiting for Godot* (1956), *Protective*

Custody (1957), *The Infernal Machine* (1958), *Do You Know the Milky Way!* (1961), *Poor Murder* (1976), and *Charlotte* (1980) on Broadway. Aside from his work as an actor director, in 1945 Berghof founded his own acting school, the HB Studio, and when he married actress/teacher **Uta Hagen** in 1957, she taught there as well.

BERGMAN, INGRID (1915–1982). This luminous and legendary screen actress, born in Stockholm, Sweden, also made occasional stage appearances, including her first in a revival of Ferenc Molnar's *Liliom* in 1940. She won a **Tony Award** for MAXWELL ANDERSON's *Joan of Lorraine* (1946) and her periodic returns to **Broadway** included the American premiere of EUGENE O'NEILL's *More Stately Mansions* (1967) and revivals of *Captain Brassbound's Conversion* (1972) and *The Constant Wife* (1975). In films, Bergman won three Academy Awards for *Gaslight* (1945), *Anastasia* (1957), and *Murder on the Orient Express* (1975), and was nominated four other times. Her other notable performances on film include *Casablanca* (1942), *For Whom the Bell Tolls* (1943), *The Bells of St. Mary's* (1945), *Spellbound* (1945), *Notorious* (1946), *Joan of Arc* (1948), *The Visit* (1964), and *Cactus Flower* (1969).

BERGNER, ELISABETH (1897–1986). Born Elisabeth Ettel in Drohobycz, Austro-Hungary, she worked as a model and film actress before fleeing the rise of the Nazis in 1933. In London and on **Broadway**, she scored a success playing an unwed mother in *Escape Me Never* (1935), followed by work in film, including playing Rosalind to **Laurence Olivier**'s Orlando in *As You Like It* in 1936. Between film roles and London appearances, Bergner appeared on Broadway in *The Two Mrs. Carrolls* (1944), a revival of *The Duchess of Malfi* in 1946, and *The Cup of Trembling* (1948), and she directed *The Overtons* (1945). She is believed to be the model for the character of flamboyant actress Margo Channing in *All about Eve* (1951).

BERKELEY REPERTORY THEATRE (BRT). A not-for-profit theatre founded in 1968 by Michael Leibert in Berkeley, California, this respected organization started in a small storefront space, but won critical acclaim for the high quality of its productions and its permanent acting ensemble. In 1980, the BRT moved to a 400-seat facility prior to Leibert's departure in 1983. His successor, Sharon Ott, dropped the permanent acting company while shifting the focus to edgier contemporary plays and reinterpretations of classics. Ott left in 1997 as the BRT won a **Tony Award** as outstanding regional theatre. Tony Taccone, who had been associate artistic director since 1988, took over and the theatre added a new space, the Theatre Next Door in 2001. New plays by such writers as **Philip Kan Gotanda, José Rivera, Tony Kushner**, and **Han Ong** premiered at the BRT. *See also* REGIONAL THEATRE MOVEMENT.

BERKSHIRE THEATRE FESTIVAL (BTF). Founded in 1928, the BTF is among the oldest regional theatres functioning in the United States. A stated mission of supplying a home for the next generation of American theatre artists began when EVA LE GALLIENNE appeared in *The Cradle Song* as the opening production. Producing work by American and European dramatists continued as the BTF became a not-for-profit theatre in 1967 under artistic director George Tabori, who was subsequently followed by Peter Cookson and **Arthur Penn**. In 2010, artistic director Kate Maguire led the growing operation. *See also* REGIONAL THEATRE MOVEMENT.

BERLIN, PAMELA (1952–). Born in Newport News, Virginia, Berlin attended Radcliffe College planning a career in medicine, but was drawn into the arts. She continued her education at Southern Methodist University, completing an M.F.A. in directing in 1977. She moved to New York in 1979 and worked as a stage manager prior to joining the **Ensemble Studio Theatre (EST)** where she rose to literary manager. For EST and **Off-Broadway**, she directed *The Self-Begotten* (1982), *Ordway Ames-gay* (1982), *To Gillian on Her 37th Birthday* (1984), *Elm Circle* (1984), *Crossing Delancey* (1985), *Mama Drama* (1987), ***Steel Magnolias*** (1987), *Peacetime* (1992), *Snowing at Delphi* (1993), and *Endpapers* (2002). On **Broadway**, Berlin directed *The Cemetery Club* (1990). She served as president of the **Society of Stage Directors and Choreographers** from 2001–2007 and directs many **regional theatre** productions.

BERLIND, ROGER S. (1930–). This notable theatrical producer graduated from Princeton University in 1954 and was among the founders of the investment firm Carter, Berlind, Potoma & Weill in 1960. He began producing for the stage in 1976, and his shows have won numerous **Tony Awards** and PULITZER PRIZES. His productions include many major MUSICALS between 1976 and 2009 and such non-musical works as *The Merchant* (1977), ***Amadeus*** (1980), *The Real Thing* (1984), revivals of *A Day in the Death of Joe Egg* in 1985 and ***Long Day's Journey into Night*** in 1986, *Artist Descending a Staircase* (1989), *Lettice and Lovage* (1990), *Death and the Maiden* (1992), a revival of *Hamlet* in 1995, *Skylight* (1996), a revival of ***A View from the Bridge*** in 1997, *The Judas Kiss* (1998), *The Blue Room* (1998), *Closer* (1999), *Amy's View* (1999), *The Ride Down Mt. Morgan* (2000), *Copenhagen* (2000), ***Proof*** (2000), revivals of *Dance of Death* in 2001 and *Medea* in 2002,

Anna in the Tropics (2003), a revival of *Who's Afraid of Virginia Woolf?* in 2005, *Doubt* (2005), *Well* (2006), *The History Boys* (2006), revivals of *Faith Healer* in 2006 and *The Caine Mutiny Court-Martial* in 2006, *Shining City* (2006), *The Vertical Hour* (2006), *The Year of Magical Thinking* (2007), *Deuce* (2007) *Rock 'n' Roll* (2007), *Is He Dead?* (2007), a revival of *Equus* in 2008, and *To Be or Not to Be* (2008).

BERN, MINA (1911–2010). Born Mina Bernholtz in Lodz, Poland, Bern was relocated to a displaced persons camp in Uganda by the Nazis during World WAR II. After the war, she performed in Israel before moving to New York in 1949. Despite the fact that the YIDDISH THEATRE on Second Avenue was in steep decline in that era, Bern became a popular performer over the subsequent decades, appearing on **Broadway**, often with her husband Ben Bonus, in *Let's Sing Yiddish* (1966), *Sing, Israel, Sing* (1967), *Light, Lively, and Yiddish* (1970), and *Those Were the Days* (1990). Bern was presented with a sustained excellence **Obie Award** in 1999, and she appeared in small roles in several films, including *Crossing Delancey* (1988), *Avalon* (1990), *I'm Not Rappaport* (1996), *Celebrity* (1998), and *Flawless* (1999).

BERNSTEIN, ALINE (1880–1955). Born Aline Frankau in New York, where her father was an actor, Bernstein began her career as a founding member of the NEIGHBORHOOD PLAYHOUSE in 1915 prior to costume designing for the THEATRE GUILD. In 1926, EVA LE GALLIENNE asked her to design for the CIVIC REPERTORY COMPANY (CRC). After 1930, she worked frequently with production **Herman Shumlin**, beginning with *Grand Hotel* (1930). Their association continued through the 1930s and included her work on **Lillian Hellman**'s *The Children's Hour* (1934), *Days to Come* (1936), *The Little Foxes* (1939), and *The Searching Wind* (1944). In all, Bernstein designed costumes (and, on occasion, settings) for 50 **Broadway** productions. She won a **Tony Award** for *Regina* (1950), the musical version of *The Little Foxes*, and her other Broadway designs include *Reunion in Vienna* (1931), *The Late Christopher Bean* (1932), a revival of *Camille* in 1935, *The Male Animal* (1940), *Harriet* (1943), *The Eagle Has Two Heads* (1947), *The Happy Time* (1950), and **Arthur Miller**'s adaptation of HENRIK IBSEN's *An Enemy of the People* (1950).

BERRY, GABRIEL (1951–). Born in Omaha, Nebraska, Berry worked as a designer with numerous experimental theatre artists after she began her career in 1979, including **Meredith Monk, JoAnne Akalaitis, Anne Bogart, Peter Sellars, Maria Irene Fornés**, and **Andrei Serban**, and was the first American to win an individual medal at the International Design

Quadrennial in Prague in 1995. She is resident costume designer for **La Mama Experimental Theatre Club** and is an associate at the **New York Shakespeare Festival**, the **New York Theatre Workshop**, and designs frequently for the **American Repertory Theatre**, among other **regional theatres** and **Off-Broadway**, where her design of *'Tis Pity She's a Whore* brought her a **Drama Desk Award** nomination. She also received an **Obie Award** for sustained excellence. Berry's only **Broadway** costume designs were for *Cuba & Teddy Bear* (1986).

BEST MAN, THE. **Gore Vidal**'s three-act drama set backstage at a political party's convention opened on 31 March 1960 at the Morosco Theatre for a 520 performance run under the direction of **Joseph Anthony** with scene design by Jo MIELZINER. This **Tony Award**-nominated play featured a strong cast, including **Melvyn Douglas**, LEE TRACY, Frank Lovejoy, and Leora Dana. The play focuses on the unsavory machinations of two rival candidates for the presidential nomination, William Russell and Joseph Cantwell, overseen by the outgoing President, Arthur Hockstader. The play was filmed in 1964 starring **Henry Fonda**, Cliff Robertson, and Tracy reprising his role as Hockstader, and it was revived on **Broadway** in 2000 with an all-star cast, including Chris Noth, **Spalding Gray**, **Charles Durning**, Christine Ebersole, **Elizabeth Ashley**, Michael Learned, and Jonathan Hadary.

BIG APPLE CIRCUS. This unique not-for-profit one-ring CIRCUS, founded by Michael Christensen and Paul Binder, constructs its performance around a theme ("Grandma Goes West," "Carnevale in Venice," etc.) and was honored in 2000 as a "Living Landmark" by New York City's Landmark Conservancy.

BIG WHITE FOG. The Chicago Unit of the **Federal Theatre Project (FTP)** staged **Theodore Ward**'s probing drama on **African American** politics for 10 weeks in 1938. The family-centered play examines the involvement of the father in Marcus Garvey's nationalist movement and his son's interest in Communism. As the Great Depression deepens and Garvey's movement collapses, the family's struggles intensify. Following the FTP production, the Negro Playwrights Company presented the play in New York at the Lincoln Square Theatre, where it opened on 22 October 1940, as its premiere production. The cast featured **Canada Lee**, Hilda Offley, and Frank Silvera, and it was performed until December 1940. Powell Lindsay directed and Perry Watkins, the first black member of the **Union of Scenic Artists**, created the scene designs.

BIKEL, THEODORE (1924–). This versatile performer at home in both dramas and musicals was born Theodore Meir Bikel in Vienna, Austria. His family fled Vienna at the rise of the Nazis, and Bikel eventually studied at the Royal Academy of Dramatic Art, after which **Laurence Olivier** hired him as understudy for Stanley and Mitch in the West End production of *A Streetcar Named Desire* in 1948. After working in several films, including his debut in *The African Queen* (1951), and plays in Europe, Bikel moved to the United States in 1954, where he appeared in movies and occasional **Broadway** productions, including playing Captain von Trapp in the MUSICAL *The Sound of Music* (1959) opposite **Mary Martin**, garnering his second **Tony Award** nomination (his first was for *The Rope Dancers* in 1957). He was nominated for an Academy Award for his performance in *The Defiant Ones* (1958) and appeared on Broadway in *Tonight in Samarkand* (1955), *The Lark* (1955), *Café Crown* (1964), *Pousse-Café* (1966), and a revival of *The Inspector General* (1978). He appeared **Off-Broadway** in Arje Shaw's *The Gathering* (1999) and served as President of ACTORS' EQUITY ASSOCIATION from 1973–1982.

BILLINGTON, KEN (1946–). This prolific lighting designer was born in White Plains, New York, and has designed over 70 **Broadway** shows, as well as many **Off-Broadway** and regional theatre productions. Billington also served as principal lighting designer for Radio City Music Hall from 1979 to 2004 and won a **Tony Award** and a **Drama Desk Award** for his lighting for the revival of *Chicago* in 1997. He has also been nominated for Tonys seven additional times for a revival of *The Visit* (1974), *Working* (1978), *Sweeney Todd* (1979), *Foxfire* (1983), *The End of the World* (1984), *The Drowsy Chaperone* (2006), and a 2008 revival of *Sunday in the Park with George.* His **Off-Broadway** credits include *Diamonds* (1984), *Lips Together, Teeth Apart* (1991), *Absent Friends* (1991), *Sylvia* (1995), and *London Suite* (1995), among others. He also works in television.

BILOXI BLUES. The second of **Neil Simon**'s "Brighton Beach" trilogy won a Best Play **Tony Award**. This comedy/drama about the experience of Simon's alter ego, Eugene Morris Jerome, during basic training during World WAR II, opened on 28 March 1985 at the Neil Simon Theatre, where it ran for 524 performances. **Matthew Broderick** won critical approval as Eugene, with Barry Miller as his Jewish radical bunkmate, and **Penelope Ann Miller** as Eugene's first love, Daisy Hannigan. Simon explores the seriocomic aspects of military life, including the enlisted men's battle of wills with a disturbed sergeant and the **ethnic** and **sexual** prejudices of the time. Broderick and Miller repeated their **Broadway** performances in a 1988 screen adaptation directed by **Mike Nichols**.

BIOGRAPHY. S. N. BEHRMAN's witty three-act comedy of a woman confused by the opposing poles of conservative and liberal politics of the 1930s opened on 12 December 1932 at the Guild Theatre for 267 performances. This THEATRE GUILD production directed by PHILIP MOELLER and designed by JO MIELZINER starred **Ina Claire** as Marion Froude, an egotistical woman composing her biography for a radical publication edited by Richard Kurt, with whom she falls in love. When Marion's ex-lover Leander Nolan, a political conservative, fears that her writings might undermine his run for the U.S. Senate, Marion is persuaded to destroy her biography and end her relationship with Kurt. A film adaptation, under the title *Biography of a Bachelor Girl*, was released in 1935

BISHOP, ANDRÉ (1948–). André Bishop Smolianinoff was born in New York, the son of an investment banker. He attended Harvard University prior to beginning his career as artistic director and literary manager of **Playwrights Horizons** in 1978, leading the organization to produce new works by emerging contemporary playwrights as artistic director from 1981 to 1991, including the PULITZER PRIZE-winners *Driving Miss Daisy* (1987) and *The Heidi Chronicles* (1989). In 1991, Bishop became artistic director of the **Lincoln Center Theatre**. Among the works premiered at Lincoln Center during Bishop's tenure are *The Light in the Piazza* (2005), *Contact* (2000), *The Coast of Utopia* (2006), *Rock 'n' Roll* (2007), and *Dividing the Estate* (2008), as well as revivals of *Carousel* in 1994, *The Heiress* in 1995, *A Delicate Balance* in 1996, *Henry IV* in 2004, *South Pacific* in 2008, and *Joe Turner's Come and Gone* in 2009.

BLACK THEATRE NETWORK (BNT). This not-for-profit organization emerged from the Afro-Asian Theatre Project of the **American Theatre Association** in 1965, which was followed by the African Theatre Project and the Black Theatre Project before becoming the BTN in 1986. The BTN mission is the preservation of black theatre as a unique art form and offers student design and writing competitions and recognition awards for theatre professionals. *See also* AFRICAN AMERICAN THEATRE; ASIAN AMERICAN THEATRE.

BLACKMER, SIDNEY (1895–1973). A native of Salisbury, North Carolina, Blackmer left home in his youth to work in theatre and film in New York, including playing a bit part in the silent screen serial *The Peril of Pau-*

line in 1914. He debuted on **Broadway** in *The Morris Dance* (1917), before joining the military during World WAR I, resuming his career after the war in such plays as *The Mountain Man* (1921), *The Love Child* (1922), *Scaramouche* (1923), *Love in a Mist* (1926), *Mima* (1928), *Round Trip* (1945), and *Portrait in Black* (1947). He won a **Tony Award** for the role of Doc in **William Inge**'s *Come Back, Little Sheba* (1950). On Broadway, his subsequent appearances were in *The Brass Ring* (1952), ***Sweet Bird of Youth*** (1959), and *A Case of Libel* (1963), and he replaced Walter Pidgeon in the MUSICAL *Take Me Along* (1959). Among his films were roles in *Heidi* (1937), *In Old Chicago* (1937), *Duel in the Sun* (1946), *The High and the Mighty* (1954), *High Society* (1956), and *Rosemary's Baby* (1973). His first wife was actress Lenore Ulric.*

BLAU, HERBERT (1926–). Born in Brooklyn, New York, Blau graduated from New York University and emerged as a director, theorist, CRITIC, author, and teacher who led in the evolution of postmodern theatre. Blau and **Jules Irving** founded the San Francisco Actors Workshop in 1952 where they produced works by Samuel Beckett and **Bertolt Brecht**. In 1965, Blau and Irving became coartistic directors of the **Repertory Theatre of Lincoln Center**, but Blau resigned in 1967 to found the California Institute of the Arts in 1968. He ultimately joined the faculty of the University of Washington and wrote numerous books on contemporary theatre and postmodern concepts, including *The Impossible Theatre: A Manifesto* (1964), *Take Up the Bodies: Theatre at the Vanishing Point* (1982), *Blooded Thought: Occasions of Theatre* (1982), *The Eye of Prey: Subversions of the Postmodern* (1987), *The Audience* (1990), *To All Appearances* (1992), *Nothing in Itself* (1999), *The Dubious Spectacle* (2002), and *Sails of the Herring Fleet* (2003), the last focusing on the work of Samuel Beckett.

BLECKNER, JEFF (1943–). This much-honored director of stage and television was born in Brooklyn, New York, and began his directing career **Off-Broadway** with *The Unseen Hand/Forensic* (1970), two one-acts by **Sam Shepard**. Bleckner won a **Drama Desk Award** and an **Obie Award** for his direction of **David Rabe**'s *The Basic Training of Pavlo Hummel* (1971). The next year, his direction of Rabe's *Sticks and Bones* (1972) brought him another Drama Desk Award and a **Tony Award** nomination. On **Broadway**, he has also directed *The Secret Affairs of Mildred Wild* (1972) and a revival of *The Goodbye People* in 1979. He has directed in numerous **regional theatres**, but has devoted much energy to television drama, which brought him Emmy Awards for an episode of *Hill Street Blues* in 1981 and *Concealed Enemies* (1984).

BLESSING, LEE (1949–). Born Lee Knowlton Blessing in Minneapolis, Minnesota, Blessing studied at the Graduate Writers' Workshop at the University of Iowa before writing numerous plays, including the best known, *A Walk in the Woods* (1987), which was nominated for a **Tony Award**. His more than 30 plays include *Independence* (1984), *Eleemosynary* (1988), *Cobb* (1989), *Fortinbras* (1991), *Lake Street Extension* (1992), *Patient A* (1993), *Down the Road* (1993), *The Rights* (1994), *Going to St. Ives* (1996), *The Winning Streak* (2000), *Snapshot* (2002), *Whores* (2002) *Flag Day* (2004), *A Body of Water* (2005), *The Scottish Play* (2005), *Lonesome Hollow* (2006), *Moderation* (2007), *Great Falls* (2008), *Perilous Nights* (2008), *Into You* (2009), *Heaven's My Destination* (2009), and *When We Go Upon the Sea* (2010), most produced **Off-Broadway** or in **regional theatres**. He was playwright-in-residence with the **Signature Theatre** in 1992 and heads the graduate playwriting program at Rutgers University.

BLOOM, CLAIRE (1931–). Born in Finchley, England, Patricia Claire Blume was trained for the stage at the Guildhall School of Music and Drama and the Central School of Speech and Drama. She worked with the Oxford Stage Company and made her London debut in *The Lady's Not for Burning* (1947) prior to playing Ophelia in *Hamlet* in 1948, the year she began her film career, including playing opposite Charlie Chaplin in *Limelight* (1952). She has appeared in numerous film roles and on stage in England and the United States, touring America with the Old Vic in 1956. On **Broadway**, she made notable appearances in *Rashomon* (1959), revivals of *A Doll's House* and *Hedda Gabler* in 1971, winning **Drama Desk Awards** for both, *Vivat! Vivat! Regina* (1972), and revivals of *The Innocents* in 1976 and *Electra* in 1998, the last bringing her a **Tony Award** nomination. Bloom's other notable movie roles include playing Lady Anne opposite **Laurence Olivier** in *Richard III* (1955), *The Spy Who Came in from the Cold* (1965), *Clash of the Titans* (1981), and *Crimes and Misdemeanors* (1989). Bloom married three times, to actor Rod Steiger, producer Hillard Elkins, and novelist Philip Roth.

BLOOMGARDEN, KERMIT (1904–1976). Born in Brooklyn, New York, Bloomgarden began his distinguished producing career with a flop, *Heavenly Express* (1940). Between 1940 and the mid-1970s, Bloomgarden produced many notable American plays of the time, including **Lillian Hellman**'s *Another Part of the Forest* (1946), beginning a long association including productions of Hellman's *The Autumn Garden* (1951), a revival of *The Children's Hour* in 1952, *The Lark* (1955), *Toys in the Attic* (1960), and *My Mother, My Father, and Me* (1963). Bloomgarden also produced the **Broadway** productions of *Deep Are the Roots* (1945), *Command Decision* (1947),

Death of a Salesman (1949), *The Crucible* (1953), *A View From the Bridge* (1955), *The Diary of Anne Frank* (1955), *The Most Happy Fella* (1956), *Look Homeward, Angel* (1957), *The Music Man* (1957), *The Gang's All Here* (1959), *The Gay Life* (1961), *Anyone Can Whistle* (1964), *Illya Darling* (1967), *Hot L Baltimore* (1973), and *Equus* (1974).

BLUE MAN GROUP. An act that evolved over time in the late 1980s, this unique entertainment involving three bright blue performers interacting with a variety of media, props, music, and art is a multisensory experience that has led from the Astor Place Theatre, where it began a long run in 1991, to inspire multiple companies performing throughout the world. *See also* PERFORMANCE ART.

BLUES FOR AN ALABAMA SKY. **Pearl Cleage**'s two-act drama set in Harlem in 1930 opened at the **Alliance Theatre** in Georgia in July 1995 under the direction of Kenny Leon, with scene design by Rochelle Barker, costumes by Susan E. Mickey, and lighting design by Judy Zanotti. **Phylicia Rashad** played Angel, a singer at Harlem's fabled Cotton Club who is struggling with issues of race, displacement, abandonment, politics, and sexuality. Taking a skeptical view of the era of the Harlem Renaissance, Cleage underscores the struggles of artists and discrimination facing **gays**. Commenting on the play and her work, Cleage said, "I will always write about Black people and our efforts to build a community where we can live safely. . . . These will always be my themes, regardless of the forum." *See also* AFRICAN AMERICAN THEATRE.

BLUES FOR MISTER CHARLIE. **James Baldwin**'s drama written to honor murdered civil rights activist Medgar Evers was dedicated by the author to the four little **African American** girls murdered in a church bombing in Birmingham, Alabama. Produced by the **Actors Studio** and directed by **Burgess Meredith**, it opened on **Broadway** at the **American National Theatre and Academy (ANTA)** Playhouse on 14 April 1964, where it ran for 148 performances. A searing view of racial attitudes and emotions, incidents in the play were taken from the real-life murder of Emmett Till, with the plot focusing on a preacher's son who is murdered for an innocent conversation with a white woman in Blacktown and Whitetown, USA, two fictional hamlets through which Baldwin depicts racial conflict. The large cast included **Diana Sands**, who was nominated for a **Tony Award**, Joe Don Baker, **Pat Hingle**, **Rip Torn**, Ralph Waite, Ann Wedgeworth, and Al Freeman, Jr.

BLYDEN, LARRY (1925–1975). Born Ivan Lawrence Blieden in Houston, Texas, Blyden began his **Broadway** acting career as a replacement, taking over the role of Ensign Pulver in *Mister Roberts* (1948). He was a versatile performer and appeared regularly in both MUSICAL and non-musical works, including *Wish You Were Here* (1952), **Oh, Men! Oh, Women!** (1953), *Flower Drum Song* (1962), for which he garnered a **Tony Award** nomination, *Foxy* (1964), **Luv** (1964), *The Apple Tree* (1966), and *Absurd Person Singular* (1974), the last bringing him another Tony nomination. Blyden also appeared as a replacement in **You Know I Can't Hear You When the Water's Running** (1967). He directed *Harold* (1962) and *The Mother Lover* (1969) on Broadway and produced and acted in a revival of *A Funny Thing Happened on the Way to the Forum* in 1972, winning a Tony. He was married to dancer Carol Haney.

BOESING, MARTHA (1936–). A native of Exeter, New Hampshire, Boesing graduated from Abbot Academy in Andover, Massachusetts, before beginning her work with the Firehouse Theatre in the 1960s, which raised her political engagement in **feminist** issues. She rose to prominence as founder and artistic director of **At the Foot of the Mountain (AFOM)**, a women's theatre collective, beginning in 1974, a group she led for a decade and for whom she wrote plays dealing with women's issues, including *River Journal* (1975), *Raped* (1976), *The Moontree* (1976), *The Story of a Mother* (1977), and *The Web* (1982), which she developed collaboratively with the AFOM group. She has directed and written plays for numerous regional theatre companies and her post-AFOM plays include *Standing on Fishes* (1991), *My Other Heart* (1993), *Hard Times Come Again No More* (1994), *These Are My Sisters* (1996), *After Long Silence* (1999), and *A Place of Her Own* (2007).

BOGART, ANNE (1951–). This acclaimed and controversial director, author, and educator was born in Newport, Rhode Island, to a Navy family. She studied at Bard College and received an M.A. from New York University's Tisch School of the Arts in 1977. As a choreographer and director, Bogart gained notoriety radically rethinking the staging of canonical dramatic works, receiving a 1984 Bessie Award for her production of *South Pacific* set in a veterans' mental hospital. She was artistic director of the **Trinity Repertory Theatre** in 1989–1990 and cofounded the Saratoga International Theatre Institute (SITI) with Tadashi Suzuki in 1992.

In 1995, Bogart was named the first "Modern Master" at the **Actors Theatre of Louisville** "Classics in Context" Festival. She won Best Director **Obie Awards** for *No Plays No Poetry but Philosophical Reflections Practical Instructions Provocative Opinions and Pointers from a Note Critic and Playwright* (1988) and **Paula Vogel**'s *The Baltimore Waltz* (1990). Among her productions of note are her staging of **Eduardo Machado**'s *In the Eye of* *the Hurricane* at the 1991 Humana Festival and the premiere of Vogel's *Hot 'N' Throbbing* (1994) at the **American Repertory Theatre**.

Bogart heads the Graduate Directing Program at Columbia University and her books include *A Director Prepares: Seven Essays on Art and Theatre* (2001), *The Viewpoints Book: A Practical Guide to Viewpoints and Composition* (2005), and *And Then, You Act: Making Art in an Unpredictable World* (2007). Thinking about the nature of theatre, Bogart wrote on her blog in 2009, "In our present moment of economic and cultural upheaval, theatre is probably the most important activity one can imagine doing or coming into contact with. Why? The answer is simple: Theatre provides innovative and alternate models for how people might function together. We need this now. The theatre is the only art form that concerns itself predominantly with social issues. Can we get along? Can we get along in this room? Can we get along as a society? How might we get along better?"

BOGOSIAN, ERIC (1953–). The son of a hairdresser and an accountant of Armenian heritage, Bogosian was born in Woburn, Massachusetts. He attended Oberlin College prior to beginning his theatrical career in New York as a playwright and actor. After writing several plays and one-person shows, Bogosian won a **Drama Desk Award** for *Drinking in America* (1986), followed in 1987 by the work that raised him to prominence, *Talk Radio*, which was filmed by Oliver Stone a year later, a work typical of Bogosian's themes of the contradictions and discordances of millennial American life. *Talk Radio* was produced on **Broadway** in 2006, garnering a **Tony Award** nomination as Best Play. Subsequent works, including three **Obie Award** winners, include *Sex, Drugs, and Rock & Roll* (1990), *Notes from the Underground* (1993), *Pounding Nails in the Floor with My Forehead* (1994), and the much-produced *subUrbia* (1994), which was adapted to the screen in 1996. He continued to write for the theatre, but increasingly acted in film and television after the late 1990s, including as a regular on the TV series *Law & Order: Criminal Intent* from 2006–2009. Among his more recent plays are *Griller* (1998), *Wake Up and Smell the Coffee* (2000), *Humpty Dumpty* (2004), *Wasted Beauty* (2005), and *1+1* (2008). He also writes novels, including *Perforated Heart* (2009).

BOLAND, MARY (1880–1965). Born Marie Ann Boland in Philadelphia, Pennsylvania, Boland became one of the most durable comic actresses of the **Broadway** stage in the first half of the twentieth century. She made her first New York appearance in *Strongheart** (1905), before producer Charles Frohman* selected her as John Drew's* leading lady in a series of plays, most notably *Jack Straw* (1908) and *Much Ado About Nothing* (1913). Boland later appeared in *Clarence** (1919), in which she played the first of a long line of dizzy society matrons she would play for the next 30 years on stage and screen. During the 1920s, she appeared in *The Torch-Bearers** (1922) and when sound films began, Boland spent much of her time in movies returning to the stage in *Ada Beats the Drum* (1930), *The Vinegar Tree* (1930), *Face the Music* (1932), *Jubilee* (1935), as a replacement in *Hellzapoppin'* (1938), and *Open House* (1947). She was particularly well-received as Mrs. Malaprop in a 1942 revival of *The Rivals* and in her last appearance, as a domineering mother in *Lullaby* (1954), although both were short-lived productions.

BOOTH, SHIRLEY (1898–1992). A native New Yorker born as Thelma Booth Ford, Booth began her acting career in STOCK with the Poli Stock Company in 1919 prior to her **Broadway** debut in *Hell's Bells* (1925). Between the mid-1920s and the late 1940s, she worked consistently on Broadway in both successes and failures, including such plays as *Laff That Off* (1925), *The War Song* (1928), *Coastwise* (1931), a revival of *The Mask and the Face* in 1933, ***Three Men on a Horse*** (1935), *Excursion* (1937), ***The Philadelphia Story*** (1939), ***My Sister Eileen*** (1940), ***Tomorrow the World*** (1943), and *Hollywood Pinafore* (1945).

Booth's performance as Grace Woods in ***Goodbye, My Fancy*** (1948) won her a **Tony Award**, but her most notable stage success came as the slatternly housewife Lola in **William Inge**'s ***Come Back, Little Sheba*** (1950), for which she won another Tony. She repeated the role in the 1952 screen version and won an Academy Award, a Golden Globe Award, a New York Film Critics Award, and a Special Mention Award from the Cannes Film Festival. Following a well-received performance as the floozy Aunt Cissy in the MUSICAL *A Tree Grows in Brooklyn* (1952), Booth won another Tony as the lonely spinster Leona Samish in ***The Time of the Cuckoo*** (1952).

Booth appeared in several films during the 1950s, including the screen version of **Thornton Wilder**'s ***The Matchmaker*** (1958), but returned to the Broadway stage in *By the Beautiful Sea* (1954), *The Desk Set* (1955), *Miss Isobel* (1957), *Juno* (1959), and *A Second String* (1960). In the early 1960s, Booth won two Emmy Awards for her performance in the title role of the long-running television situation comedy, *Hazel*, but returned to the Broadway stage twice, in the failed musical *Look to the Lilies* (1970) and a revival of **Noël Coward**'s *Hay Fever* in 1970.

BOOTHE, CLARE (1903–1987). Born in New York, Boothe, later known as Clare Boothe Luce following her marriage to publisher Henry Luce, was a playwright, political figure, and journalist whose plays include *Abide with*

Me (1935), *Kiss the Boys Good-bye* (1938), and ***Margin for Error*** (1939), although she is most remembered for her scathing satire of New York society women in the aptly titled ***The Women*** (1936), which had a long run on **Broadway**, was revived in 1973 and 2001, and which became a classic all-star film directed by George Cukor in 1939 (remade in 2008).

BORN YESTERDAY. **Garson Kanin** directed his three-act comedy, which was produced by **Max Gordon**, with scene designs by DONALD OENSLAGER. It opened on 4 February 1946 at the Lyceum Theatre for 1,642 performances and made a star of **Judy Holliday** as the irrepressible Billie Dawn, mistress of Harry Brock, a wealthy, politically powerful, and cruelly vulgar junkman. Brock sees Billie as "dumb" and hires Paul Verrall, a writer, to educate her. Paul does such a good job with the naturally bright Billie that she begins to see through Brock's bullying and misdeeds (including using her as a cosigner on some shady deals) and, with Paul's assistance, stifles Brock's ruthless excesses. Screen star Jean Arthur was originally set to play Billie, but withdrew during the play's tryouts, clearing the way for Holliday, who repeated her performance in the 1950 film version, winning a Best Actress Academy Award. *Born Yesterday* was revived on **Broadway** in 1989 starring **Madeline Kahn**, who was nominated for a **Tony Award**, and a movie remake starring Melanie Griffith was released in 1993. Another Broadway revival was announced for 2011.

BORSCHT BELT. This term refers to resort hotels and camps in the Catskill and Adirondack mountains enjoyed by predominantly Jewish New Yorkers escaping the heat of the city during the summer months. From around 1900 to the 1960s, these resorts served as a circuit for comedians, vaudevillians,* BURLESQUE performers, and actors who learned their craft providing entertainment, described by their audience as *tummlers* (funmakers). Many stage performers, including **Sid Caesar**, Mel Brooks, Milton Berle, Red Buttons, Danny Kaye, Jerry Lewis, and others, began their careers working the Borscht Belt. *See also* YIDDISH THEATRE.

BOSCO, PHILIP (1930–). Born Philip Michael Bosco in Jersey City, New Jersey, the son of a carnival worker and a policewoman, Bosco studied at the Catholic University before embarking on a distinguished acting career mostly on stage beginning in 1954, although he has made infrequent appearances in film and television. He made his first **Broadway** appearance in a flop, *Rape of the Belt* (1960), but despite the play's fate, Bosco received a **Tony Award** nomination. He demonstrated his versatility in an impressive array of classic and contemporary plays, including the MUSICAL *Donnybrook!* (1961) and revivals of plays by **Shakespeare**, GEORGE BERNARD SHAW, Jean Giraudoux,

Bertolt Brecht, Edmond Rostand, Molière, HENRIK IBSEN, **Arthur Miller**, and **Tennessee Williams** during the 1960s and 1970s.

Bosco also made notable appearances in new plays, including *In the Matter of J. Robert Oppenheimer* (1969), *Enemies* (1972), *Whose Life Is It Anyway?* (1979), *Eminent Domain* (1982), and *The Loves of Anatol* (1985). Despite several Tony Award and **Drama Desk Award** nominations, Bosco did not win either until 1989 for his performance in the farce *Lend Me a Tenor*, when he won both. He appeared in highly successful revivals of *The Inspector Calls* in 1994 and *The Heiress* in 1995 and played opposite **Carol Burnett** in the hit comedy *Moon Over Buffalo* (1995). Bosco also won critical approval for his performances in *Copenhagen* (2000), a revival of *12 Angry Men* in 2004, *Chitty Chitty Bang Bang* (2005), and a revival of *Heartbreak House* in 2006. Despite his frequent appearances on Broadway, Bosco also acted with distinction in numerous **regional theatres**.

BOTH YOUR HOUSES. This three-act satiric drama by MAXWELL ANDERSON, produced by the THEATRE GUILD, won a PULITZER PRIZE. It assailed Congressional corruption and pork barrel politics at the height of the Great Depression. It opened at the Royale Theatre on 5 March 1933 for 120 performances under the direction of Worthington Miner. Alan McClean (Shepperd Strudwick) is expelled from college for exposing financial misdeeds, so his journalist father backs the young man for a Congressional run and garners support from some industrialists. When Alan is elected, he exposes corrupt practices of his backers. Embittered by his attempt to stop a pork barrel bill, he proposes an ironic bill in which all of the Congressmen are awarded money for their pork projects. Instead of embarrassment, Alan's colleagues pass the bill and applaud his political acumen. The cast also included **Morris Carnovsky**, Russell Collins, J. Edward Bromberg, and Jerome Cowan.

BOVASSO, JULIE (1930–1991). Born in Brooklyn, New York, to an Italian American family, Bovasso studied at the High School of Music and Art and City College. She founded the Tempo Playhouse at St. Mark's Place in 1953 and won the first **Obie Award** for acting in 1956 for her performance in Jean Genet's *The Maids* at the outset of a long career in which she emphasized experimental work on the stage while appearing in more conventional material in films and television. She also won a **Drama Desk Award** and an **Outer Critics Circle Award** in Genet's *The Screens* in 1972. Bovasso was an admired teacher of acting in New York at the New School for Social Research, Brooklyn College of the City University of New York, and Sarah Lawrence College. Bovasso also wrote plays, including *The Moon Dreamers* (1967), *Schubert's Last Serenade* (1971), *The Nothing Kid* (1974), *Super Lover*

(1975), and *Angelo's Wedding* (1985), and often directed as well, working frequently at **La MaMa Experimental Theatre Club**. In 1969, she won triple Obies as playwright, director, and actress for *Gloria and Esperanza*. In films, she appeared notably in *Saturday Night Fever* (1977), *Staying Alive* (1983), *Wise Guys* (1986), and *Moonstruck* (1987).

***BOY MEETS GIRL*.** **Sam and Bella Spewack**'s farce in three acts was produced and directed by GEORGE ABBOTT at the Cort Theatre, where it opened on 27 November 1935 for 669 performances. Set in Hollywood, the play centers on two wisecracking screenwriters, Robert Law (Allyn Joslyn) and J. Carlyle Benson (Jerome Cowan), who resist writing a film script for a cowboy star. When a pregnant waitress at the studio needs help, Law and Benson write her baby into the script, which leads to a hit movie and a romantic outcome for the waitress. When Warner Bros. filmed the play in 1938, James Cagney and Pat O'Brien gave memorable performances as Law and Benson. *Boy Meets Girl* was revived on **Broadway** in 1943 and 1976, but both revivals were failures despite the fact that the play was popular for many years in STOCK, **community**, and university theatre productions.

BOYER, CHARLES (1897–1978). The quintessential Frenchman, Boyer was born in Figeac, Lot, Midi-Pyrenees, France who worked in a hospital during World WAR I, where he performed for the soldiers. Boyer studied for a time at the Sorbonne before beginning a stage career in the 1920s. He also appeared in several silent films and made the transition to sound which, ultimately, led from France to Hollywood. In the mid-1930s, Boyer became a major screen star, often in suave, sophisticated roles, in such films as *The Garden of Allah* (1936), *Conquest* (1937), *Algiers* (1938), *Love Affair* (1939), *Gaslight* (1944), *Arch of Triumph* (1948), and many others. After a decade of film work, Boyer, who endeavored to move beyond the romantic roles he typically played on screen, debuted on **Broadway** in *Red Gloves* (1948), followed by an acclaimed performance in *Don Juan in Hell* (1951), for which he and the rest of the cast were presented with a special **Tony Award**. He was also nominated for a Tony in the title role of *Lord Pengo* (1963) and appeared in *Kind Sir* (1953) with **Mary Martin**, *The Marriage-Go-Round* (1958) opposite Claudette Colbert, and *Man and Boy* (1963). Late in his career, he appeared in the 1967 film version of **Neil Simon**'s *Barefoot in the Park*.

***BOYS IN THE BAND, THE*.** **Mart Crowley**'s two-act comedy-drama won praise for depicting more realistic images of **homosexuals** and **criticism** for indulging in outmoded stereotypes when it opened on 14 April 1968 at **Off-Broadway**'s Theatre Four for 1,000 performances following a brief

Playwrights Unit staging the previous January. A gay tolerance play in which all characters on stage are homosexual men from various backgrounds and with diverse attitudes about their lives, the lasting value of *The Boys in the Band* may be its warning against a life lived in the closet—or in the attempts of gay men to hide their secret homosexual lives behind a "straight" public façade—and in comparatively progressive views of the gay lifestyle and the particular dilemmas facing effeminate gays unable to hide their sexual orientation. The original cast featured Kenneth Nelson as Michael, who is hosting a birthday party for Harold, played by Leonard Frey, leading to a confrontation is which Harold bluntly assesses Michael's internal conflict between his sexuality and his desire to be straight. **Clive Barnes**, writing at the time of the play's premiere, found it to be "by far the frankest treatment of homosexuality I have ever seen on the stage," noting that it "is not a play about a homosexual, but a play that takes the homosexual milieu, and the homosexual way of life, totally for granted and uses this as a valid basis of human experience." A 1970 film version directed by William Friedkin retained members of the original cast and the play was revived at the Lucille Lortel Theatre in 1996, but has had numerous productions in regional, amateur, and university theatres, including a 2010 Off-Broadway revival by the Transport Group in a site-specific production in a penthouse apartment. Crowley wrote a sequel, *The Men from the Boys* (2002), which revisited the characters later in life. *See also* GAY AND LESBIAN THEATRE.

BRADY, ALICE (1892–1939).[†] Born in New York, the daughter of theatrical producer William A. Brady* and a French dancer, Rose Marie Rene, Brady attended the Convent of St. Elizabeth in Madison, New Jersey before studying opera at the New England Conservatory of Music. Her father disapproved of her desire to be an actress and she made her debut without his knowledge with Robert Mantell* in a New Jersey production of *As You Like It*. She subsequently won plaudits as Meg in *Little Women** (1912) and acted in silent films. Her father, who finally acquiesced to her stage career, produced Owen Davis's* *Forever After** (1918) for her and she appeared successfully in *Zander the Great* (1923), *Bride of the Lamb* (1926), *Bless You Sister* (1927), *A Most Immoral Lady* (1928), *The Game of Love and Death* (1929), *Karl and Anna* (1929), and *Love, Honor, and Betray* (1930). She joined the THEATRE GUILD in 1928 and won the opportunity of playing her most significant stage role, Lavinia Mannon in EUGENE O'NEILL's tragic trilogy, *Mourning Becomes Electra* (1931). She made her final **Broadway** appearance in *Mademoiselle* (1932), written by her stepmother, Grace George,* and in the Los Angeles production of S. N. BEHRMAN's *Biography* (1934). She was otherwise occupied with an impressive array of character roles in

Hollywood films, including *The Gay Divorcee* (1934), *My Man Godfrey* (1936), and *Young Mr. Lincoln* (1939). She won a Best Supporting Oscar for her performance in *In Old Chicago* (1937) before cancer prematurely ended her career.

BRANCH, WILLIAM (1927–   ). The son of an A.M.E. Zion minister, Branch was born in New York, but spent his teen years in Charlotte, North Carolina, and started to write plays. He studied at Northwestern University and Columbia University prior to working as an actor, appearing in the national tour of *Anna Lucasta* (1944) and other productions. Branch became a writer and educator, teaching at various times at the University of Maryland-Baltimore County and Cornell University, and his plays, which protest the status of **African Americans** in mid-twentieth-century America, including *A Medal for Willie* (1951), *In Splendid Error* (1945), *A Wreath for Udomo* (1960), adapted from Peter Abraham's novel, and *Baccalaureate* (1975). Branch won a 1992 American Book Award for his editorship of *Black Thunder: An Anthology of Contemporary African American Drama.* In a 2004 interview, Branch commented on issues of **race** and racism in America and the theatre: "racism, which is endemic to the whole of American society, certainly was not absent from theatre anymore than from any other institution of American life. And that goes for today as well as in the past. Even though things are somewhat better than the past, racism is not dead—certainly not dead in the theatre either. There is a long, long way to go before there is anything like equality of opportunity in the theatre."

BRANDO, MARLON (1924–2004). Born Marlon Brando, Jr. in Omaha, Nebraska, to a pesticide manufacturer and an actress who were divorced in his adolescence, Brando had a turbulent time in his teens due, in part, to his mother's alcoholism. He attended the Shattuck Military Academy in Faribault, Minnesota, where he won approval in theatre productions, but he was expelled in his last year. After some odd jobs, Brando attended the **American Theatre Wing** Professional School, the Dramatic Workshop of The New School, and **The Actors' Studio** prior to his **Broadway** debut as Nels in *I Remember Mama* (1944). He won critical approval in *Truckline Café*, revivals of *Antigone* and *Candida* with KATHARINE CORNELL, and *A Flag Is Born*, all in 1946, winning a **Theatre World Award** that year. He became a major star playing the intensely brutish, overtly sexual Stanley Kowalski in **Tennessee Williams**'s PULITZER PRIZE-winning drama, *A Streetcar Named Desire* (1947). His highly praised performance, which brought "method acting" to the forefront of American acting techniques, led to Hollywood, where he debuted in *The Men* (1950), followed by his Academy Award-nominated performance in the 1951 film version of *A Streetcar Named Desire*. He subsequently won two Academy Awards, for *On the Waterfront* (1954) and *The Godfather* (1972), famously refusing to accept the award for the latter in protest of the nation's treatment of **Native Americans**. He acted in, and occasionally directed, films, but never returned to the Broadway stage. A tumultuous and ultimately tragic personal life may have prevented a full realization of his significant talents, but Brando's name became synonymous with the finest American acting of the second half of the twentieth century.

BRANTLEY, BEN (1954–). Born in Durham, North Carolina, Brantley attended Swarthmore College and began a journalistic career with the *Winston-Salem Sentinel* in 1976 before becoming an editorial assistant at the *Village Voice* in 1975, followed by an editorship at *Women's Wear Daily* in 1978. He became their European editor in 1983 and, after 1985 worked as a freelance writer, contributing to such publications as *ELLE*, *Vanity Fair*, and the *New Yorker*. He became a drama CRITIC for the *New York Times* in 1993, rising to chief theatre critic in 1996 following **Frank Rich**'s move to the editorial pages. Brantley edited *The New York Times Book of Broadway: On the Aisle for the Unforgettable Plays of the Last Century* (2001) and he received the George Jean Nathan Award for Dramatic Criticism in 1996.

BREAD & PUPPET THEATRE. Peter Schumann, who had run the New Dance Group in Germany, founded the Bread & Puppet Theatre in 1961 in New York with the assistance of his wife, Elka Schumann, and numerous volunteers (including Paul Zaloom, Grace Palley, and others) from American and international politically inspired theatres. Radically leftwing in its content, the Bread & Puppet's name refers to the offering of fresh bread with garlic butter distributed free at performances, public demonstrations and parades, and in the annual CIRCUS presented (until 1998) on a remote farm in Glover, Vermont, which became the theatre's base of operations. The Bread & Puppet was particularly prominent in its engagement in antiWAR protests in the Vietnam era, with its papier-mâché, larger-than-life big-headed **puppets** (including Schumann himself as Uncle Sam on enormous stilts), a visual icon not only of antiwar sentiments, but also the theatre's poor theatre, communal approach in their creative techniques. Bread & Puppet volunteers were arrested during the 2000 Republican National Convention as the result of unfounded rumors of terrorist plots. In December 2001, the theatre presented *The Insurrection Mass with Funeral March for a Rotten Idea: A Special Mass for the Aftermath of the Events of September 11th*, a protest of American policies following 9/11.

BRECHT ON THE AMERICAN STAGE. In the decade following World War II, the plays and theatrical techniques of Bertolt Brecht, the influential German dramatist, director, and dramatic theorist, began to have a profound impact on practices in American theatre, particularly in antiREALISM staging techniques, acting styles, and political theatre. Prior to World War II, Brecht's plays had not been particularly well-known in the United States; his *Threepenny Opera* had its American premiere at the Empire Theatre in 1933, but failed to find an audience. Brecht, who had fled Germany at the rise of the Nazis, first visited New York in 1935 when the THEATRE UNION presented his play *Mother* at the CIVIC REPERTORY THEATRE, but this production was also short-lived. Brecht settled in the United States for a time, returning to Berlin following the end of World War II. No other Broadway productions of Brecht appeared until 1947, when **Charles Laughton**, playing the title role, brought his staging of Brecht's *Galileo* to **Broadway**, where it folded after a mere six performances, although the production generated some approval from CRITICS. A well-received production of *Threepenny Opera* appeared on Broadway in 1954 following a successful **Off-Broadway** run.

Following this production, Brecht's works were seen with somewhat greater frequency, especially Off-Broadway and in university theatres where, by the mid-1960s, Brecht's political viewpoints seemed in sync with the turbulent times. Critic and playwright **Eric Bentley**, who had become acquainted with Brecht prior to the playwright's death in 1956, wrote about Brecht's work and translated and published many of Brecht's plays in the United States. While Brecht's plays beyond *Threepenny Opera*, which was revived successfully in 1976, 1989, and 2006, have never found great popularity on Broadway stages, a few productions of note appeared, including a 1956 Bentley-directed production of *The Good Woman of Setzuan* featuring **Uta Hagen** in the title role, a 1963 production of *Mother Courage and Her Children* starring **Anne Bancroft** and directed by Jerome Robbins, the **Repertory Theatre of Lincoln Center** productions of *The Caucasian Chalk Circle* (which Brecht had written with a Broadway production in mind) in 1966, *Galileo* in 1967, and *The Good Woman of Setzuan* in 1970, and a **Jujamcyn** production of *Happy End* in 1977.

Off-Broadway and **regional theatre**, not to mention **academic** theatres, have provided more fertile fields for Brechtian productions, with some notable productions, including a critically lambasted 2002 production of *The Resistible Rise of Arturo Ui* starring **Al Pacino**, with **Billy Crudup**, Steve Buscemi, Chazz Palminteri, **Charles Durning**, **Linda Emond**, and John Goodman. **Tony Kushner**'s adaptation of Brecht's *Mother Courage and Her Children*, starring **Meryl Streep**, **Kevin Kline**, and **Austin Pendleton**, fared better in 2006 in a **New York Shakespeare Festival/Public Theatre** produc-tion. Kushner, a vocal proponent of Brecht's theatre, had earlier adapted *The Good Woman of Setzuan*, which premiered at the **La Jolla Playhouse** and, in New York, at the tiny Wings Theatre Off-Broadway in 1999.

BREUER, LEE (1937–). This noted director, filmmaker, educator, and writer was born in Los Angeles, California, and studied at the University of California at Los Angeles before initiating his career with the San Francisco **Actors' Workshop** in the early 1960s. In 1965, he traveled to Europe to work with the Berliner Ensemble and the Polish Theatre Lab. Back in the United States, Breuer found a base for his life's work as founding artistic director of New York's **Mabou Mines** in 1970, with founding members Philip Glass, **Ruth Maleczech, JoAnne Akalaitis, David Warrilow**, and Frederick Neu-man. He first won note for his staging of the plays of Samuel Beckett, includ-ing productions of *Play* in 1970 and *Come and Go* in 1971, prior to writing, directing, and occasionally acting in his own plays, which include *The Red Horse Animation* (1970), *The B-Beaver Animation* (1974), *The Saint and the Football Players* (1976), *The Lost Ones* (1977), *The Shaggy Dog Animation* (1978), *Animations* (1979), *A Prologue to A Death in Venice* (1980), *Sister Susie Cinema* (1980), *The Gospel at Colonus* (1982), *Hajj* (1983), *The War-rior Ant* (1988), *Lear* (1990), *MahabharANTa* (1992), *Red Beads* (2005), *Ecco Porco* (2009), and *Summa Dramatica* (2009). His controversial *Doll-house*, adapted from HENRIK IBSEN's *A Doll's House*, and *Peter and Wendy* (2007) each won two **Obie Awards**, and Breuer has been the recipient of numerous **awards** and grants in support of his work.

BRIG, THE. Kenneth H. Brown's play, produced by the **Living Theatre** and directed by **Judith Malina**, opened on 15 May 1963 for 239 performances. Set in 1957, it depicts a day in the hellish existence for inmates of a Marine prison in Japan. Ostensibly because Malina and her husband, **Julian Beck**, who had designed the production, had not paid their taxes, the United States government and the theatre's landlord, locked the company out of their per-formance space. Despite this impairment (not to mention critical resistance to the play's content), the cast and audience members climbed over the barred entrance to see the final performance. The production moved briefly to the Midway Theatre before a tour of Europe. This controversial play was filmed in 1964 and a Living Theatre revival with Malina directing appeared in 2007.

BRIGHT ROOM CALLED DAY, A. **Tony Kushner**'s three-act drama, writ-ten as a response to **Bertolt Brecht**'s *The Private Life of the Master Race*, premiered in a workshop production by Theatre 22 in April 1985 under Kushner's direction. Staged by **Oskar Eustis**, it had a fully realized premiere at San Francisco's Eureka Theatre in October 1987 and returned to New York in January 1991 for a **New York Shakespeare Festival/Public Theatre** production directed by **Michael Greif**. The play centers on a group of filmmakers and artists in Berlin in 1932–1933 observing the rise of the Nazis—all react differently to the mounting evil, some fleeing the country, others joining the underground, and one, Agnes Eggling (**Frances Conroy**), becoming immobile as darkness descends. Agnes is observed from another time by a 1980s' political radical, Zillah Katz, who equates Ronald Reagan's presidency, which she angrily resists, with Hitler's Germany. Many critics condemned the play, finding this comparison extreme and the play's scope pretentious, but a few recognized Kushner as a writer of promise, a promise fulfilled in little more than a year as Kushner's epic *Angels in America* (1993) caused many of these same critics to reverse their estimation of his abilities.

BRIGHTON BEACH MEMOIRS. The first of **Neil Simon**'s semi-autobiographical trilogy of "Brighton Beach" plays, this two-act comedy-drama opened on 27 March 1983 at the Alvin Theatre for 1,299 performances, winning the **New York Drama Critics Circle Award** for Best Play. **Matthew Broderick** won a **Tony Award** and a **Theatre World Award** as Simon's alter ego, Eugene Morris Jerome, an adolescent aspiring to become a writer, but contending with an extended family caught up in the economic struggles of the Great Depression in 1937. The show's director, **Gene Saks**, also won a Tony and during the run of the production, **Broadway**'s Alvin Theatre was renamed the Neil Simon Theatre. The play was filmed in 1986 with Jonathan Silverman as Eugene. A 2009 revival received good reviews, but folded in a week.

BRISSON, FREDERICK (1912–1984). The son of Danish performer Carl Brisson born in Copenhagen, Denmark, Brisson was educated in England. In the United States from the 1930s, Brisson became a **Broadway** producer. Among the diverse plays and MUSICALS he produced himself or with partners were *The Pajama Game* (1954), *Damn Yankees* (1955), *New Girl in Town* (1957), *The Pleasure of His Company* (1958), *The Gazebo* (1958), *Five Finger Exercise* (1959), *Under the Yum Yum Tree* (1960), *The Caretaker* (1961), *First Love* (1961), *Alfie!* (1964), *Generation* (1965), *The Flip Side* (1968), *Coco* (1969), *Twigs* (1971), *Jumpers* (1974), *So Long, 174th Street* (1976), *Mixed Couples* (1980), and *Dance a Little Closer* (1983). Brisson also produced several films, mostly screen adaptations of the plays and musicals he produced on Broadway. He married actress **Rosalind Russell** in 1941, earning him the unflattering nickname "The Lizard of Roz."

BROADWAY. Labels ostensibly describing groupings of theatres in New York City offer a means of determining the type of theatre experience available in each. Broadway is a collection of mostly large playhouses surrounding the **Times Square** area of Manhattan exceeding 300 seats. Broadway was the center of American theatre from the late nineteenth century to at least the 1960s—and has remained a showcase for MUSICALS, comedies, dramas, solo performers, **international stars and companies**, and revivals, although since the late 1960s, fewer and fewer new works are created directly for Broadway. Increasingly, most productions in Broadway theatres have been nurtured in **Off-Broadway**, **Off-Off Broadway**, **regional**, and **academic** theatres, as opposed to the period between World WAR I and the late 1950s, when many new musicals and plays were prepared directly for Broadway.

BROADWAY ALLIANCE, THE. This producing organization established in 1991 to provide a means on **Broadway** for producing new non-MUSICAL works, nurtured productions of **Steven Tesich**'s *The Speed of Darkness* (1991), Timberlake Wertenbaker's *Our Country's Good* (1991), Abraham Tetenbaum's *Crazy He Calls Me* (1992), and Richard Baer's *Mixed Emotions* (1993) before its demise. The organization intended to make use of the less desirable Broadway houses, keeping rents and ticket prices low for the new plays.

BROADWAY BOUND. **Neil Simon**'s **Tony Award**-nominated play, the third of his "Brighton Beach" trilogy, opened on 4 December 1986 at the Broadhurst Theatre for 756 performances. As with the two prior plays in the trilogy, ***Brighton Beach Memoirs*** (1983) and ***Biloxi Blues*** (1985), Simon centers the action on his alter ego, Eugene Morris Jerome, played by Jonathan Silverman, an aspiring writer who has returned home from military service during World WAR II as his parents' and grandparents' marriages break apart. With his brother, Stanley, Eugene aspires to success as a radio comedy writer. **Linda Lavin** won Tony and **Drama Desk Awards** as Eugene's weary mother and John Randolph did the same as Eugene's grandfather. The play was filmed for television in 1992 starring Silverman, **Anne Bancroft**, and **Hume Cronyn**. A **Broadway** revival was planned in 2009, but when Simon's *Brighton Beach Memoirs*, with which it was to run in repertory, closed a week after opening, *Broadway Bound* was cancelled.

BROADWAY LEAGUE, THE. *See* LEAGUE OF AMERICAN THEATRES AND PRODUCERS.

BRODERICK, JAMES (1927–1982). An admired character actor and father of **Matthew Broderick**, James Wilke Broderick was born in Charleston, New Hampshire. He was educated at the University of New Hampshire, where he was a pre-med student. When he acted in a university production of GEORGE BERNARD SHAW's *Arms and the Man*, his teacher recommended him to the NEIGHBORHOOD PLAYHOUSE, where began his professional career in theatre, television, and film. On **Broadway**, Broderick appeared in *Maggie* (1953), *Johnny No-Trump* (1967), a revival of *The Time of Your Life* in 1969, and *Let Me Hear You Smile* (1973), none particularly successful. He had better luck appearing in numerous early television dramas during the 1950s and 1960s and he was nominated for an Emmy Award for the television series *Family* in 1978. In films, he appeared in *The Group* (1966), *Alice's Restaurant* (1969), *The Taking of Pelham One Two Three* (1974), and *Dog Day Afternoon* (1975), among others.

BRODERICK, MATTHEW (1962–). The son of actor **James Broderick** and writer Patricia Biow Broderick, this versatile actor was born in New York, and studied acting at the HB Studio prior to winning a role in the original **Off-Broadway** production of **Harvey Fierstein**'s *Torch Song Trilogy* (1978), which launched a career that has encompassed theatre, film, and television. He was cast as Eugene Morris Jerome, **Neil Simon**'s alter ego, in *Brighton Beach Memoirs* (1983), winning a **Tony Award**, and appeared again as Eugene in the second of Simon's "Brighton Beach" trilogy, *Biloxi Blues* (1985), repeating the role on screen in 1988. As film work absorbed much of his time, Broderick managed to return to **Broadway** in revivals of *How to Succeed in Business Without Really Trying* in 1995, which won him a second Tony, *Night Must Fall* in 1999, *The Foreigner* in 2004, *The Odd Couple* in 2005, and *The Philanthropist* in 2009, but scored a notable success as Leo Bloom in the musical version of Mel Brooks's *The Producers* (2001), which brought him a Tony nomination. He repeated his performance in the 2005 screen version. Broderick married actress Sarah Jessica Parker in 1997 and he has appeared in nearly 50 films, including *Ferris Bueller's Day Off* (1986), *Glory* (1989), *The Cable Guy* (1996), *Election* (1999), and a television remake of *The Music Man* in 2003.

BROKAW, MARK (1959–). Born in Aledo, Illinois, he worked in theatre at the Celebration Company, a small group in Urbana, Illinois, before training at the Yale School of Drama as a director. Brokaw, who specializes in minimal scenery in the productions he directs, began his career at **Second Stage** directing *The Good Times Are Killing Me* (1991). **Off-Broadway**, Brokaw has also directed *As Bees in Honey Drown* (1997) and revivals of *Out of This World* in 1995 and *On a Clear Day You Can See Forever* in 2000, and he was nominated for **Drama Desk Awards** for **Paula Vogel**'s PULITZER PRIZE-winning *How I Learned to Drive* (1997) and *Lobby Hero* (2001). On **Broadway**, he staged *Reckless* (2004), a revival of *The Constant Wife* with Lynn Redgrave and **Kate Burton** in 2005, *Cry-Baby* (2008), and *After Miss Julie* (2009).

BROOKLYN ACADEMY OF MUSIC (BAM). A theatre by this name was built in 1861 on Montague Street in Brooklyn, New York, but burned in 1903. Replaced in 1908, the facility with four theatres was considered the first such multistage complex in America. Despite its name, BAM has also presented a wide range of performing arts events encompassing American theatre, dance, and music, as well as foreign troupes and performers. During the management of Harvey Lichtenstein in the 1960s and 1970s, BAM adopted a progressive approach to performances given there, stressing **alternative theatre** groups and artists. Following Lichtenstein's departure in 1999, BAM generally continued as a venue for major groups and artists with an innovative bent.

BROTHER RAT. John Monks, Jr. and Fred F. Finklehoffe's three-act comedy produced and directed by GEORGE ABBOTT opened on 16 December 1936 for 577 performances at the Biltmore Theatre. This slight piece concerned a Virginia Military Institute student, played by **Eddie Albert**, who is secretly married. As the school's best pitcher, he hopes to win $200 for winning a ballgame to help support his wife when he finds out she is expecting a baby. However, the imminent birth and the interference of friends, played by Frank Albertson and **José Ferrer**, unnerve him and he loses the game, although the birth of the baby wins him a $300 prize as the first father at school. Albert, Albertson, and Ferrer, all newcomers, gave bright performances and despite the play's slim plot, a film version appeared in 1938 with Albert repeating his role with a young Ronald Reagan taking over Ferrer's part. The film proved so popular that it inspired two sequels.

BROTHER/SISTER PLAYS, THE. **The New York Public Theatre** presented **Tarell Alvin McCraney**'s *The Brother/Sister Plays* in November 2009 under the direction of **Tina Landau**. The bill of three plays (all of which had premiered individually in various theatres), *In the Red and Brown Water, The Brothers Size*, and *Marcus or the Secret of Sweet*, were described by *Village Voice* critic **Michael Feingold** as concerning "the Jungian notion that **community** is destiny: The collective unconscious is always at work, making the same types recur in each generation." Focused on the impact of poverty on **African Americans** in present-day Louisiana, the work won critical approval for McCraney's language and use of diverse influences including West African Yoruban mythology, the plays of Federico García Lorca, and the music of Motown.

BROTHERS. Kathleen Collins's memory drama on racial issues, produced by the Women's Project, opened at the **American Place Theatre** in April 1982. The two brothers of the title are black men that "should have been born white," as the author contends, because they "spent their entire lives trying to jump out of their skins." One brother, who became a politician during the Kennedy era, and the other an Olympic athlete, do not appear in the play, but they are present through the recollections of the women in their lives, who in a series of monologues explore a range of issues facing **African Americans** in the mid-to-late twentieth century. Billie Allen directed a cast including Trazana Beverly.

BROWN, ARVIN (1940–). Born in Los Angeles, California, Brown spent most of his career as a director on the other coast as artistic director of the **Long Wharf Theatre (LWT)** in New Haven, Connecticut. His first production at LWT, a revival of ***Long Day's Journey into Night***, was presented in 1966 and an **Off-Broadway** remounting won him a **Drama Desk Award** in 1971 (he was nominated again for a double bill, *A Memory of Two Mondays/27 Wagons Full of Cotton* in 1976). Many of Brown's LWT productions have moved to **Broadway** or Off-Broadway, including *The National Health*, which brought him a **Tony Award** nomination in 1975, as did a revival of ***Ah, Wilderness!*** in 1976. Brown's other Broadway productions include *The Shadow Box* (1977), ***The Gin Game*** (1977), revivals of ***Watch on the Rhine*** in 1980, *A View from the Bridge* in 1983, *American Buffalo* in 1983, *A Day in the Death of Joe Egg* in 1985, ***All My Sons*** in 1987, *Private Lives* in 1992, *Chinese Coffee* in 1992, and ***Hughie*** in 1996, as well as new works, including *Open Admissions* (1984), *Requiem for a Heavyweight* (1985), *Love Letters* (1989), *The Twilight of the Golds* (1993), and *Broken Glass* (1994). Brown was married to actress Joyce Ebert until her death in 1997. Following his departure from the LWT, Brown has directed television and film.

BROWN, BLAIR (1947–). Daughter of a U.S. Intelligence agent and a teacher, Bonnie Blair Brown was born in Washington, D.C. She attended the National Theatre School of Canada and acted at the Stratford **Shakespeare** Festival and in numerous regional theatres. In 1976, she appeared as Lucy Brown in the **New York Shakespeare Festival/Public Theatre** revival of *Threepenny Opera* and made her first significant **Broadway** appearance in

David Hare's *Secret Rapture* (1989). Despite frequent film and television roles, Brown has appeared in **regional theatre** and as a Broadway replacement in two MUSICALS, a revival of *Cabaret* in 1998 and *James Joyce's The Dead* in 2000 and won a **Tony Award** for her performance in *Copenhagen* (2000). Her other New York appearances include *Arcadia* (1995), and *The Clean House* (2004) and she directed *A Feminine Ending* (2007). She was nominated five times for an Emmy Award for the television series *The Days and Nights of Molly Dodd* and was nominated for two Golden Globe Awards for the film *Continental Divide* (1981) and the television movie *Kennedy* (1983).

BROWN, JOHN MASON (1900–1969).[†] Born in Louisville, Kentucky, Brown attended Harvard University, after which he worked as a reporter on the *Louisville Courier-Journal* beginning in 1917. He became associate editor and drama **critic** for *Theatre Arts Monthly* in 1924, a post he kept for four years. In 1929, he took a position with the *New York Evening Post* and wrote a column, "Two on the Aisle," during the 1930s. In 1941, Brown moved to the *New York World-Telegram*, but America's entry into World WAR II interrupted his career when he joined the United States Navy. After leaving the navy, Brown became associate editor and drama critic for the *Saturday Review*, contributing a regular column, "Seeing Things." He resigned from the PULITZER PRIZE Committee in protest for its refusal to award the prize to **Who's Afraid of Virginia Woolf?** in 1963 and authored several books, including *The Modern Theatre in Revolt* (1929), *Two on the Aisle* (1938), *Seeing Things* (1946), *Dramatis Personae* (1963), and *The Worlds of Robert E. Sherwood* (1965).

BROWN, TONY (1951–) and KARI MARGOLIS (1955–). As coartistic directors of Margolis/Brown Adaptors, subsequently known as the Margolis Brown Theatre Company, these two met in Paris in 1975 where they were studying MIME with Etienne Decroux. They established their multimedia movement-based theatre and school, which has received numerous grants and honors, in 1983 in New York, but moved to Minneapolis between 1993 and 2005, when they moved again to the Catskill Mountains. Among their thirteen large-scale productions, created with their students, are *Autobahn* (1984), *Deco Dance* (1986), *Bed Experiment One* (1987), *Decodanz: The Dilemma of Desmodes and Diphylla* (1991), *Kopplevision and Other Digital Dieties* (1991), *Vanishing Point* (1995), *Bed Experiment II* (1997), *Vidpires!* (1998), *American Safari* (2001), and *Sleepwalkers* (2002),

BROWNE, ROSCOE LEE (1925–2007). The son of a Baptist minister, Browne was born in Woodbury, New Jersey, and attended Lincoln University as an undergraduate, followed by graduate studies at Middlebury College, Columbia University, and the University of Florence. After a period of working for the Schenley Import Corporation, Browne quit to become an actor, landing a role in *Julius Caesar* with the **New York Shakespeare Festival** in 1961, the same year he appeared in his first film, *The Connection* (1961). From that time until his death, Browne appeared with regularity in the theatre, film, and television, often in roles requiring dignity and his sonorous voice. He won a 1965 **Obie Award** in Robert Lowell's *Benito Cereno* and two Los Angeles Drama Critics Circle Awards for Derek Walcott's *The Dream on Monkey Mountain* (1970 and **August Wilson**'s *Joe Turner's Come and Gone* (1989). **Off-Broadway**, he appeared in Jean Genet's *The Blacks* (1961). On **Broadway**, he was nominated for a **Tony Award** for Wilson's *Two Trains Running* (1992), and also appeared in *The Cool World* (1960), *General Seeger* (1962), *Tiger, Tiger Burning Bright* (1962), *The Ballad of the Sad Café* (1963), a revival of *Danton's Death* in 1965, *A Hand is on the Gate* (1966), which he also directed, and the MUSICAL *My One and Only* (1983). He won an Emmy Award in 1986 as a guest star on *The Cosby Show*.

BRUSTEIN, ROBERT (1927–). Born Robert Sanford Brustein in New York, this critic, producer, educator, and occasional playwright attended Amherst College and Columbia University, completing his Ph.D. in 1957. He became drama **critic** for the *New Republic* in 1959 and founded the **Yale Repertory Theatre** during his long tenure as Dean of the Yale Drama School from 1965 to 1979. That year, Brustein moved from Yale to Harvard University, where he founded the **American Repertory Theatre (ART)**. At ART, Brustein adapted 11 plays, including works by Aristophanes, Thomas Middleton, HENRIK IBSEN, **Anton Chekhov**, August Strindberg, and Luigi Pirandello. He also wrote *Shleimel the First* (1994), adapted from Isaac Bashevis Singer's stories, which he directed at ART. He has written 15 books, including *The Theatre of Revolt: An Approach to Modern Drama* (1964), *Revolution as Theatre: Notes on the New Radical Style* (1971), *Making Scenes: A Personal History of the Turbulent Years at Yale, 1966–1979* (1981), *Dumbocracy in America: Studies in the Theatre of Guilt, 1987–1994* (1994), *Cultural Calisthenics: Writing on Race, Politics, and Theatre* (1998), *Letters to a Young Actor: A Universal Guide to Performance* (2005), and *The Tainted Muse: Prejudices and Preconceptions in Shakespeare's Works and Times* (2008), as well as multiple collections of his theatre reviews.

BRYGGMAN, LARRY (1938–). Born Arvid Laurence Bryggman to Swedish American parents in Concord, California, Bryggman attended the City College of San Francisco and studied at the **American Theatre Wing**.

He made his **Off-Broadway** stage debut in *A Summer Ghost* (1962) and first appeared on **Broadway** as a replacement in *Ulysses in Nighttown* (1974). He has acted in productions at the **Manhattan Theatre Club, Lincoln Center Theatre, Second Stage**, the **Atlantic Theatre Company**, and the **New York Shakespeare Festival/Public Theatre**, and on Broadway in *The Basic Training of Pavlo Hummel* (1988), **Al Pacino**'s *King Richard III* (1979), *Prelude to a Kiss* (1990), a revival of *Picnic* in 1994, *Proof* (2000), and a revival of *12 Angry Men* in 2004. *Picnic* and *Proof* brought him **Tony Award** nominations and he won a 2005 **Drama Desk Award** in an Atlantic Theatre Company production of **David Mamet**'s *Romance*. Bryggman appeared on the television soap opera *As the World Turns* from 1969 to 2004, winning two Daytime Emmy Awards.

BUFMAN, ZEV (1930–). Born in Tel-Aviv, Israel, Bufman began his career as a cabaret performer in Israel in 1950, before acting in productions in California. He ultimately became a producer in the late 1950s in California, moving to **Off-Broadway** and **Broadway** in the 1960s, where he produced *Your Own Thing* (1968). As a Broadway producer or coproducer, he has presented *Vintage '60* (1960), revivals of *Pajama Tops* in 1963 and *Marat/ Sade* in 1967, *Spofford* (1967), *Jimmy Shine* (1968), *Paul Sills' Story Theatre* (1970), revivals of *Peter Pan** in 1979, *Oklahoma!* in 1979, *West Side Story* in 1980, and *Brigadoon* in 1980. Much publicity surrounded his production of a revival of **Lillian Hellman**'s *The Little Foxes* in 1981, since it marked the Broadway debut of movie star Elizabeth Taylor. Most of Bufman's subsequent productions were also revivals, including *Private Lives* in 1983, which starred Taylor and her ex-husband **Richard Burton**, *A View from the Bridge* in 1983, *The Corn is Green* in 1983, and *Blithe Spirit* in 2009, garnering multiple **Tony Award** and **Drama Desk Award** nominations for outstanding revivals. New works produced by Bufman after 1980 include *Joseph and the Amazing Technicolor Dreamcoat* (1982), *Peg* (1983), *Requiem for a Heavyweight* (1985), *The News* (1985), and *Jerry's Girls* (1985).

BUG. **Tracy Letts**'s black comedy premiered at the Gate Theatre in London on 20 September 1996 prior to production at Chicago's Red Orchid Theatre, where it opened on 20 August 2001 and a 2004 production **Off-Broadway** at the Barrow Street Theatre. The play deals with the relationship of Agnes, a disaffected waitress, and Peter, who may be an AWOL Gulf WAR veteran. Agnes is in hiding from her abusive ex-husband and Peter assails the war in Iraq and other areas in which he believes the American government conspires. His conspiracy theories and paranoia exacerbate Agnes's descent into insanity. A film version was released in 2006.

BULLINS, ED (1935–). A native of Philadelphia, Pennsylvania, Bullins served in the U.S. Navy from 1952 to 1955 before completing B.A. at Antioch College and an M.F.A. at San Francisco State University. His debut as a playwright in 1965 came **Off-Broadway** with a bill of three one-acts, *How Do You Do?*, *Clara's Ole Man*, and *Dialect Determinism, or The Rally*. After some time as a member of the Black Panther Party, Bullins, who followed the principles of the black aesthetic movement, joined the New Lafayette Theatre and continued his playwriting career with *Goin' a Buffalo* (1966), *In the Wine Time* (1968), *The Corner* (1968), *In New England Winter* (1969), *The Duplex* (1970), *The Fabulous Miss Marie* (1971), *The Taking of Miss Janie* (1975), *Home Boy* (1976), and *Daddy* (1977), most of his works focusing on merging his black nationalist politics and lyrical language to explore racial tensions in the United States in the 1960s and 1970s. He won two **Obie Awards** in the early 1970s and a 1975 **New York Drama Critics Circle Award** for *The Taking of Miss Janie*. **The Negro Ensemble Company** staged Bullins's *Boy X Man* (1997). Bullins moved to San Francisco in 1982 and worked with the Northeastern University Center for the Arts in Boston in the 2000s. *See also* AFRICAN AMERICAN THEATRE.

BULOFF, JOSEPH (1900–1985). This theatre and film actor and director was born in Wilno, Lithuania, and began his theatrical career with the Vilna Troupe. In the United States after 1928, Buloff acted in YIDDISH THEATRE in New York and Chicago and was a founding member of the New York Art Theatre. He began performing in English on **Broadway** in *Don't Look Now* (1936), followed by performances in *Call Me Ziggy* (1937), *To Quito and Back* (1937), *The Man from Cairo* (1938), *Morning Star* (1940), was a replacement in *My Sister Eileen* (1940), and *Spring Again* (1941), prior to his memorable performance as peddler Ali Hakim in the original production of the groundbreaking MUSICAL *Oklahoma!* (1943). Later roles included *The Whole World Over* (1947), *Once More with Feeling* (1958), *Moonbirds* (1959), *The Wall* (1960), and *The Fifth Season* (1975), which he also directed. Buloff also directed HELEN HAYES in *Mrs. McThing* (1952) and appeared **Off-Broadway** in *A Chekhov Sketchbook* (1962) and *Hard to Be a Jew* (1974), for which he won a **Drama Desk Award**. He also played Gregory Solomon in the 1979 and 1982 revivals of **Arthur Miller's** *The Price*. During the 1950s and 1960s, Buloff worked frequently acting and directing in Israel.

BURDEN, CHRIS (1946–). This avant-garde performance artist was born in Boston, Massachusetts, and was educated at Pomona College and the University of California at Irvine. His most famous **performance art** piece, *Shoot* (1971), involved Burden being shot in his left arm by an assistant.

Burden was compelled to see a psychiatrist after this performance and it inspired considerable controversy, with various views suggesting that it was either a pro or con statement about the right to bear arms and the Vietnam WAR. During the 1970s, Burden's performance pieces, which combined his central conceit of personal danger as part of the performance and aspects of sculpture, video, assemblage, and language, included *Trans-Fixed* (1974), in which Burden reclined on a Volkswagen Beetle and had nails hammered into his hands as though he was being crucified. Other pieces in that era included *Five Day Locker Piece* (1971), *Deadman* (1972), *TV Hijack* (1972), *B.C. Mexico* (1973), *Fire Roll* (1973), *White Light/White Heat* (1974), *Doomed* (1975), and *Honest Labor* (1979). He joined the faculty of the University of California at Los Angeles in 1978, but resigned in 2005 when a student performance piece modeled on Burden's involved the firing of a loaded gun. That same year, Burden's *Ghost Ship*, a self-navigating yacht, took a 300-mile journey without a crew thanks to onboard computers, and was funded by the Arts Council of England.

BURIED CHILD. **Sam Shepard**'s three-act drama was first performed in San Francisco at the Magic Theatre on 27 June 1978 prior to performances at New York's **Theatre for the New City** on 19 October 1978 before transferring to the Theatre de Lys. The play was awarded the PULITZER PRIZE and was followed by numerous major revivals, including at the **Yale Repertory Theatre** and the **Circle Repertory Theatre** in 1979, in London in 1980, and in a **Steppenwolf Theatre** revival directed by **Gary Sinise** that moved to **Broadway**'s Brooks Atkinson Theatre in 1996 where it garnered five **Tony Award** nominations for a cast including James Gammon, Terry Kinney, and **Lois Smith**. *Buried Child* depicts a nuclear American family in disintegration, reflecting the demise of national myths of family values and economic opportunity presented in a postmodern modified realistic style including elements of surrealism and symbolism.

BURLESQUE.[†] Most commonly thought today to refer to bump-and-grind shows featuring strippers and comics, burlesque in the nineteenth century derived from eighteenth-century travesties, or satires, of well-known works. Two burlesque circuits formed at the beginning of the twentieth century, the Empire and the Columbia Wheel, both of which came to feature the suggestive dress (or undress to the point of **nudity**) and the bawdy, low comedy that differentiated burlesque from vaudeville. After 1930, striptease artists were particularly appreciated, with the Minsky Theatre's "ecdysiast" **Gypsy Rose Lee** translating her burlesque fame into legitimate stage and film opportunities. Other strip women remained in burlesque for long, lucrative careers, including Ann

Corio, who later created *This Was Burlesque*, an entertainment mythologizing the form. Other performers rose from burlesque, most particularly comedians, including **Bobby Clark**, Willie Howard, Fanny Brice, Phil Silvers, Abbott and Costello, and Jackie Gleason, while many other performers were not able to leap the chasm separating legitimate stages and burlesque houses. The world of burlesque at its height in the 1930s was captured in the classic **Arthur Laurents**, Jule Styne, and **Stephen Sondheim** MUSICAL, *Gypsy* (1959), based on the memoirs of Gypsy Rose Lee. Choreographer Bob Fosse also created a short-lived musical about burlesque, *Grind* (1985), but it paled in comparison to the popularity of *Sugar Babies* (1979), a revue pastiche created out of burlesque sketches and popular music of the 1920s–1930s.

BURN THIS. **Lanford Wilson**'s play commissioned by the **Circle Repertory Company** and directed by **Marshall W. Mason**, opened on 19 February 1987 at Theatre 890 before moving to **Broadway** on 14 October 1987 at the Plymouth Theatre where it ran for 437 performances with a cast featuring **John Malkovich**, **Joan Allen** (who won a **Tony Award**), Jonathan Hogan, and Lou Liberatore. The play begins in the aftermath of the funeral of Robbie, a **gay** dancer, who drowned in a boating incident. His friends, some of whom were present, gather to attempt to deal with their shared tragedy and measure their own varied lives against Robbie's. Malkovich and Liberatore appeared in the 1990 West End production with Juliet Stevenson and Michael Simkins. In 2002, a **Signature Theatre** revival featured Edward Norton, Catherine Keener, Ty Burrell, and Dallas Roberts, with Norton winning an **Obie Award** for his performance.

BURROWS, ABE (1910–1985). This **Broadway** writer, play doctor, and humorist was born Abram Solman Borowitz in New York City. Burrows attended City College and New York University before working for a Wall Street accounting firm. When he met an aspiring writer, Frank Galen, in 1938, the two partnered to write comedy for radio personalities, including Ed Gardner of the popular *Duffy's Tavern* show, Danny Kaye, and Joan Davis. He turned to the Broadway stage with the triumph of *Guys and Dolls* (1950), which won the **Tony Award** and the **New York Drama Critics Circle Award**. During the 1950s, he wrote the libretto and/or lyrics for a series of MUSICALS, including Cole Porter's *Can-Can* (1953) and *Silk Stockings* (1955), among others. He won a PULITZER PRIZE and Tonys as writer and director for *How to Succeed in Business without Really Trying* (1962). Although his work was mostly in musicals, he also wrote comedies, including *Reclining Figure* (1954), *Cactus Flower* (1965), and *Four on a Garden* (1971), all of which he also directed, as well as some film and television scripts. He also directed

Golden Fleecing (1959), *Forty Carats* (1968), and *No Hard Feelings* (1973), the last of which only ran for one performance. Burrows's son became the television writer James Burrows.

BURSTYN, ELLEN (1932–). This Oscar and **Tony Award**-winning actress was born Edna Rae Gilooly in Detroit, Michigan, and began her career under the name Ellen McRae as a showgirl on Jackie Gleason's variety show on television and made her **Broadway** debut in the comedy *Fair Game* (1957). Burstyn joined the **Actors Studio** in 1967 and spent much of the next decade working in television and, eventually, feature films, winning a Best Actress Academy Award in the title role of *Alice Doesn't Live Here Anymore* (1974), having previously received nominations for *The Last Picture Show* (1971) and *The Exorcist* (1973). The following year, she returned to Broadway in **Bernard Slade**'s *Same Time, Next Year* (1975), winning a Tony and a **Drama Desk Award** for her performance in this two-person comedy-drama. She repeated her performance in the 1978 film version, receiving an Oscar nomination (she received two more Academy Award nominations for *Resurrection* [1980] and *Requiem for a Dream* [2000]). Burstyn was the first woman elected president of ACTORS' EQUITY ASSOCIATION (1982–1985) and in 2000 she became coartistic director (with **Al Pacino** and Havey Keitel) of the Actors Studio following **Lee Strasberg**'s death. Her other Broadway appearances include *84 Charing Cross Road* (1982), as a replacement in *Shirley Valentine* (1989), *Shimada* (1992), *Sacrilege* (1995), and *Oldest Confederate Widow Tells All* (2003).

BURTON, KATE (1957–). The daughter of celebrated Welsh actor **Richard Burton** and producer Sybil Christopher, Katherine Burton was born in Geneva, Switzerland, and studied at Brown University and the Yale School of Drama. Beginning her acting career following her graduation from Yale, she won a **Theatre World Award** in 1983 for three performances, in *Winners* **Off-Broadway** and in revivals of *Present Laughter* with **George C. Scott** and *Alice in Wonderland* with EVA LE GALLIENNE on **Broadway**. She was subsequently nominated for a **Drama Desk Award** for *Some Americans Abroad* (1990) and for **Tony Awards** for three revivals: *The Elephant Man* in 2002, *Hedda Gabler* in 2002, and *The Constant Wife* in 2006. Her other Broadway appearances include *Doonesbury* (1983), *Wild Honey* (1986), *Jake's Women* (1992), a revival of *Company* in 1995, and she was a replacement in several productions, including *An American Daughter* in 1997, *The Beauty Queen of Leenane* in 1998, and *Spring Awakening* in 2007. She has worked frequently Off-Broadway and in **regional theatres**, recently appearing at Boston's **Huntington Theatre** in

The Cherry Orchard in 2007 and *The Corn Is Green* in 2009, among many others. In 2010, she played KATHARINE CORNELL at **Lincoln Center** in **A. R. Gurney**'s *The Grand Manner*.

BURTON, RICHARD (1925–1984). Born Richard Walter Jenkins in Pontrhydyfen, Wales, 12th of 13 children of a working-class household. His father was an alcoholic mine worker and his mother died when Burton was two years old. An ability in literature and memorization in school led to his acting in school productions, including GEORGE BERNARD SHAW's *The Apple Cart*, which led his teacher, Philip Burton, to encourage him and eventually adopt him as his ward (and who provided him with a stage name). With Burton's assistance, he was able to attend Exeter College before serving in the RAF between 1944 and 1947 as a navigator.

Beginning in the late 1940s, Burton began acting with some regularity in England, including radio roles for the BBC and in Emlyn Williams's *Druid's Rest* in 1944. In 1949, he was cast by John Gielgud in Christopher Fry's *The Lady's Not For Burning*, which he acted in to critical approval in London and New York. He also began to work in films, establishing himself as a major film actor during the 1950s. In 1951, he won stage stardom as Prince Hal in **Shakespeare**'s *Henry IV, Part 1* at Stratford and the next year became a Hollywood star opposite Olivia de Havilland in *My Cousin Rachel*. He played Hamlet and Coriolanus at the Old Vic in 1953, but films roles took an increasing amount of his time. He was a hard drinker off-stage and although he married producer Sybil Christopher in 1949, he had several publicized affairs, including his *Hamlet* costar **Claire Bloom** and, with much greater scandal, movie star Elizabeth Taylor, who he subsequently married twice (both marriages ended in divorce). Burton appeared infrequently on **Broadway**, but usually with distinction. In 1958, he received a **Tony Award** nomination for *Time Remembered*, appearing with a strong cast including HELEN HAYES, GLENN ANDERS, and Susan Strasberg.

Burton won a Tony in 1961 for the MUSICAL *Camelot*, in which he played the legendary King Arthur (Burton also appeared in the 1980 revival). Burton was nominated for a Tony again in 1964 for *Hamlet*, in a unique rehearsal-style production (which was subsequently filmed for television) and with a notable cast, including **Hume Cronyn, Alfred Drake, George Rose, George Voskovec, Eileen Herlie, Barnard Hughes**, and **John Cullum**. Burton took over the role of Dysart from Anthony Hopkins in the Broadway production of *Equus* (1974), a role he repeated on film in 1977, and in 1976 he was awarded a special Tony for his career achievements. He made his final Broadway appearance in a revival of *Private Lives* in 1983, appearing with his ex-wife Elizabeth Taylor. Burton's nearly 70 film and television roles include his seven Oscar-nominated roles in *My Cousin Rachel* (1952), *The Robe* (1953), *Becket* (1964), *The Spy Who Came in from the Cold* (1965), **Who's Afraid of Virginia Woolf?** (1966), **Anne of the Thousand Days** (1969), and *Equus* (1977). He also appeared in the films **Look Back in Anger** (1958), *Cleopatra* (1963), **The Night of the Iguana** (1964), and *The Taming of the Shrew* (1967). He was the father of actress **Kate Burton**.

BURY THE DEAD. **Irwin Shaw**'s harrowing one-act antiWAR drama was performed on a double bill at the Ethel Barrymore Theatre on 18 April 1936, where it subsequently ran for 97 performances. The play's relatively short run is explained, in part, by Shaw's outspoken pacifism and leftist politics, and the play's grim portrayal of soldiers killed in battle who, in the surreal drama, refuse to be buried. *Bury the Dead* did not name its particular war, choosing instead to implicate all wars, but Shaw seems inspired to a great extent by the carnage of World War I in the immediate past, and the current news of the Spanish Civil War. On a war-torn field where graves are being prepared for soldiers killed during the "Second Year of War That Is to Begin Tomorrow," six of the dead arise to argue against the horror and waste of war. Shocked officers insist that "Wars can be fought and won only when the dead are buried and forgotten," but these six dead soldiers refuse to be forgotten and the burial detail, persuaded by the arguments they make, break ranks and refuses to bury the dead. When the wives and lovers of the dead soldiers appear to support their position, frightened officers demand that the dead be machine-gunned into oblivion. Bullets prove ineffective as the dead soldiers go forth into the world to argue against the folly of war. This play, and a few other Shaw dramas, *Siege* (1937), **The Gentle People** (1939), and *Sons and Soldiers* (1943), won various degrees of critical approval, but his other theatrical works were less appreciated, and Shaw abandoned drama for a successful career as a novelist.

BUS STOP. **William Inge**'s three-act comedy-drama opened on 2 March 1955 at the Music Box Theatre for 478 performances under **Harold Clurman**'s direction. The **Tony Award**-nominated play is set in a blizzard in Grace's roadside café where passengers on a bus are trapped for the night. **Kim Stanley** won acclaim as small-time "chanteuse" Cherie who improbably finds love with Bo Decker (Albert Salmi), a rowdy cowboy, who must learn to put aside his pride to win her heart. Other characters, including the café owner (**Elaine Stritch**), a teenaged waitress (Phyllis Love), the local sheriff (Lou Polan), an alcoholic ex-professor on the run from his past (Anthony Ross), the randy bus driver (Patrick McVey), and the cowboy's understanding buddy (Crahan Denton) share thoughts on life and love over the course of their long night together. The play became a perennial of STOCK, **community**, and university theatres, and was revived at the **Circle in the Square** starring **Billy Crudup** and **Mary-Louise Parker** in 1996. The 1956 film version retained most of the characters but changed many elements of the play. It was directed by **Joshua Logan** and featured Marilyn Monroe in her most memorable dramatic performance as Cherie.

BUSCH, CHARLES (1954–). Charles Louis Busch was born in New York City and attended Northwestern University. A playwright and stage and film actor, Busch's drag persona combines elements of vintage movie goddesses and characters from melodramas,* which served him well in the play that brought him to prominence, *Vampire Lesbians of Sodom* (1984), in which he also appeared. Busch's other plays include *Theodora, She-Bitch of Byzantium* (1984), *Sleeping Beauty, or Coma* (1984), *Times Square Angel* (1984), *Pardon My Inquisition, or Kiss the Blood Off My Castanets* (1986), *Psycho Beach Party* (1987), *The Lady in Question* (1989), *Red Scare on Sunset* (1991), *You Should Be So Lucky* (1994), *Flipping My Wig* (1996), *Queen Amarantha* (1997), *Shanghai Moon* (1999), *Die, Mommie, Die!* (1999), *Our Leading La*dy (2006), *The Third Story* (2009), and *The Divine Sister* (2010). These plays were all produced **Off-Broadway**, but Busch's *The Tale of the Allergist's Wife* (2000) scored on **Broadway**, racking up 777 performances and a **Tony Award** nomination as Best Play, and he collaborated on the libretto for the Boy George musical, *Taboo* (2003). His *Psycho Beach Party* and *Die, Mommie, Die!* were filmed in 2000 and 2003, respectively, and Busch has appeared in movies and television programs written and directed by others. He appeared in a 1993 revival of Jean Genet's *The Maids* and has appeared in three productions of *Auntie Mame* in 1998, 2003, and 2004, playing the title character. His most recent film, which he wrote, directed, and stars in, *A Very Serious Person*, was released in 2006 and a documentary about his life and work, *The Lady in Question Is Charles Busch*, was released in 2005.

BUTTERFLIES ARE FREE. Leonard Gershe's popular two-act comedy opened at the Booth Theatre on 21 October 1969 for 1,128 performances under the direction of Milton Katselas. The play centers on Don Baker (Keir Dullea), a young blind man attempting to strike out on his own despite the challenges, which include not only his lack of sight but the overprotectiveness of his domineering mother (**Eileen Heckart**). She is a successful author who writes children's books about a blind hero, "Little Donny Dark," and she is upset that Don has found himself an apartment and intends to live on his own. Making matters worse is Don's flower-child neighbor, Jill Tanner, played by **Blythe Danner**, who won a **Tony Award**. Jill provides Don his first romantic (and sexual) experience, and she helps him find the strength to defy his mother's wishes and live an independent life. Steven Schwartz contributed a song "Butterflies Are Free," which Don sang during the play, and silent screen legend Gloria Swanson took over the role of Mrs. Baker during the play's long **Broadway** run. A 1972 film version featured Eddie Albert, Jr., Goldie Hawn, and Heckart reprising her Broadway role.

BUTTON, JEANNE (1930–). A pioneering **Broadway** costume designer, Button studied at the Carnegie Institute of Technology and the Yale School of Drama prior to her first New York design for LANGSTON HUGHES's *Tambourines to Glory* (1963). Her credits include *The Watering Place* (1969), a revival of *King Henry V* in 1969, *The Robber Bridegroom* (1975), **Wings** (1979), a revival of *King Richard III* in 1979, *Home* (1980), *The Dresser* (1981), revivals of *Arsenic and Old Lace* in 1986 and *Broadway** in 1987, and *The Twilight of the Golds* (1993). **Off-Broadway** Button designed numerous productions, winning a Hewes Design Award for *MacBird* (1967), and she also designed for numerous **regional theatres**. Button taught at Yale, New York University, and Tulane University prior to her retirement in 2000.

C

CACTUS FLOWER. **Abe Burrows**'s genial comedy, a typical example of a genre of lightly romantic, topical situation comedies with a small cast that proliferated on **Broadway** in the 1950s and 1960s, prior to long lucrative lives in **summer** STOCK and dinner theatres, opened on 8 December 1965 at the Royale Theatre for 1,234 performances in a **David Merrick** production directed by Burrows. To be sure, *Cactus Flower* was a better-than-average example of its genre, thanks to the wit of Burrows's script and a bright cast, including **Lauren Bacall**, Brenda Vaccaro, and **Barry Nelson** in a romantic triangle, with Nelson, as a randy dentist, chasing the too-young-for-him hippie Vaccaro while his loyal assistant, Bacall, patiently waits for him to recover from his infatuation. The actors won critical praise and the play was filmed in 1969 starring **Ingrid Bergman**, **Walter Matthau**, and Goldie Hawn in an Academy Award-winning performance.

CAESAR, ADOLPH (1933–1986). Born in Harlem, New York, Caesar studied theatre at New York University, joined the navy, and worked as an announcer before becoming involved with the **Negro Ensemble Company (NEC)** in 1970, working as a director, actor, and choreographer. He appeared in the NEC's production as **Joseph A. Walker**'s *The River Niger* (1972), his own play, *Square Root of Soul* (1976), and **Charles Fuller**'s *The Brownsville Raid* (1976). Caesar also acted with various **repertory** theatres, including the **American Shakespeare Company** and the Minnesota Theatre Company. He took roles in a few films, including *Che!* (1969) and *The Hitter* (1979), and acted in a recurring role on the soap opera *General Hospital* for a time. His only **Broadway** appearance, in a short-lived revival of *Mary Stuart* in 1971, was little noted, but when Caesar won a **Drama Desk Award** as the tough-as-leather Sergeant Waters in the NEC's production of Fuller's *A Soldier's Play* (1982), repeating his performance in the film version, retitled *A Soldier's Story,* in 1984, for which he received Academy Award and Golden Globe nominations. He followed this with a fine performance as Old Mister in the Steven Spielberg-directed film *The Color Purple* (1985), prior to his sudden death from a heart attack. *See also* AFRICAN AMERICAN THEATRE.

CAFFE CINO. This coffeehouse in Greenwich Village (31 Cornelia Street) is regarded as a seminal space in the evolution of **Off-Off Broadway** beginning in late 1958. The owner, a retired dancer, Joseph Cino, encouraged poets and actors to offer readings and performances and, over time, plays were performed, beginning with an abridged version of *The Importance of Being Earnest*. During the early 1960s, a significant number of ultimately influential writers saw their earliest works done on the small Cino stage, including **Lanford Wilson, John Guare, Maria Irene Fornés, Robert Patrick, Tom Eyen, William M. Hoffman, Megan Terry, Leonard Melfi, Jean-Claude Van Itallie,** and others. Its liberal production policies permitted experimentation and for a few years it was a highly energized environment, especially for writers and actors. A fire destroyed Caffe Cino in 1965, but it was rebuilt. Cino committed suicide in 1967, but Caffe Cino continued for a time with Michael Smith, a CRITIC for the *Village Voice*, attempting to keep it going, but its moment had passed.

CAINE MUTINY COURT-MARTIAL, THE. Herman Wouk adapted his own novel about a naval court-martial, which opened at the Plymouth Theatre on 20 January 1954 for 415 performances in a SHUBERT production under the direction of **Charles Laughton**. **Henry Fonda**, John Hodiak, and Lloyd Nolan starred in the drama of Lt. Barney Greenwald's (Fonda) court-martial for leading a mutiny on the *USS Caine*, commanded by erratic Captain Queeg (Nolan). **Broadway** revivals were seen in 1983 and 2006 and a 1954 film version, with the title shortened to *The Caine Mutiny*, provided Humphrey Bogart, as Queeg, with one of his best roles. A 1988 television adaptation was directed by Robert Altman.

CALDWELL, ZOE (1934–). This much-honored stage actress and sometime director was born Ada Zoe Caldwell in Melbourne, Australia, and began her career in England with the Union Theatre Company in 1958, prior to her 1960 London debut with the Royal Court Theatre. She performed in her native Australia and Canada, playing Bianca in *Othello* with PAUL ROBESON in 1959. She joined the **Guthrie Theatre**'s company in 1963. Caldwell made her **Broadway** debut in John Whiting's *The Devils* (1965), but won a **Tony Award** and a **Theatre World Award** the next year for **Tennessee Williams**'s *Slapstick Tragedy* (1966). She won a Tony again two years later for the title role in *The Prime of Miss Jean Brodie* (1968), the same year she married producer **Robert Whitehead**. In the 1970s, Caldwell also appeared in **Arthur Miller**'s *The Creation of the World and Other Business* (1972), a revival of *Dance of Death* in 1974, and *An Almost Perfect Person* (1977), which she also directed.

In the 1980s, Caldwell won a Tony and a **Drama Desk Award** for a revival of the **Robinson Jeffers**'s adaptation of *Medea* (1982) and played **Lillian Hellman** in a one-woman play, *Lillian* (1986). The 1990s brought Caldwell another Tony and Drama Desk Award for **Terrence McNally**'s *Master Class* (1996). **Off-Broadway**, Caldwell won a Drama Desk Award for *Colette* (1970) and appeared in McNally's *A Perfect Ganesh* (1993). Her directing credits include *Park Your Car in Harvard Yard* (1991) and several **Shakespeare** productions, including stepping in during the rehearsal period to direct Glenda Jackson and **Christopher Plummer** in a 1988 revival of *Macbeth*. In England, Caldwell directed Vanessa Redgrave and Eileen Atkins in *Vita & Virginia* (1994) at the Union Square Theatre and she was awarded an OBE in 1970. She has appeared on television and in films, including **Woody Allen**'s *The Purple Rose of Cairo* (1985) and a 1983 television film of *Medea*.

CALHERN, LOUIS (1895–1956). Born Carl Henry Vogt in Brooklyn, New York, Calhern was raised in St. Louis, Missouri, and joined a touring STOCK company prior to World WAR I. He moved to New York and worked as a prop man and extra in stock and BURLESQUE, but the war interrupted his work. After the war, he appeared in a few silent films, but acted steadily on **Broadway** in *Roger Bloomer** (1923), *The Song and Dance Man* (1923), *Cobra* (1924), a revival of *Hedda Gabler* in 1926, *The Woman Disputed* (1926), *Gypsy* (1929), *The Love Duel* (1929), and others. With the dawn of sound on film, Calhern began to work frequently in films, while returning to Broadway on occasion for such plays as *Brief Moment* (1931), *Jacobowsky and the Colonel* (1944), and in his most notable success, *The Magnificent Yankee* (1946), in which he played Oliver Wendell Holmes. Calhern repeated his performance in the 1950 film version. His subsequent Broadway roles included *The Survivors* (1948), a revival of *The Play's the Thing* in 1948, and he played the title role in *King Lear* in 1950. He appeared in over 70 films during his long career, several of which are classics, including *Duck Soup* (1933), *The Life of Emile Zola* (1937), *Heaven Can Wait* (1943), *Notorious* (1946), *The Red Pony* (1949), *Annie Get Your Gun* (1950), *The Asphalt Jungle* (1950), *Executive Suite* (1954), and *High Society* (1956). Calhern married three actresses, **Ilka Chase**, Julia Hoyt, and Natalie Schafer, but all ended in divorce.

CALL, EDWARD PAYSON (1928–). Born in Connecticut, Call attended the University of Maryland and began his career as production manager at the **Circle in the Square** in 1958. He moved to the **Guthrie Theatre** from 1963 to 1970, directing a revival of **Bertolt Brecht**'s *The Resistible Rise of Arturo Ui* in 1968 that played briefly on **Broadway**. Call became the first artistic director of the **Denver Theatre Center** from 1979 to 1983, which he structured much like the Guthrie. He later became an artistic associate at the Arizona Theatre Company from 1987 to 1989 and he has directed for numerous **regional theatres** and staged *Little Black Sheep* (1975) for the **New York Shakespeare Festival**; the production had a brief run on **Broadway**. *See also* REGIONAL THEATRE MOVEMENT.

CAMINO REAL. At the height of his career, following triumphs with *The Glass Menagerie* and *A Streetcar Named Desire*, **Tennessee Williams** indulged himself in this most experimental of his early plays. Even admiring CRITICS and audiences found it a strange and disturbing oddity when it opened on **Broadway** at the Martin Beck Theatre on 19 March 1953 under **Elia Kazan**'s direction. Set against a stream of historical and cultural landmarks, and drawing on the classics of literature for many of its characters, *Camino Real* appropriated elements from Spanish folklore, Christian tradition, and classic Hollywood films to impressionistically illuminate the lives of the defeated and discarded beings found along the camino real.

Kilroy (**Eli Wallach**), the play's protagonist and an embodiment of the mythical All-American G.I., arrives in a fantastic plaza where the privileged and powerful mingle with the poor and weak. In this imaginary netherworld populated with humanity's castoffs, Williams's characters reveal his fascination with the perilous struggle of the sensitive, the artistic, and the damaged to survive in a harsh and godless world. "The violets in the mountains have broken the rocks," exclaims Cervantes's Don Quixote, as Williams's literary misfits (also including Casanova, Marguerite Gautier, Lord Byron, and Proust's Baron de Charlus), discover that a romantic outlook is necessary to survive life's brutal realities. Part epic theatre, part absurdist carnival, *Camino Real* profits from Williams's mastery of poetic imagery, language, and symbols, all set in bold relief against the play's otherworldly landscape. He had originally written the play in one-act form in 1948 as *Ten Blocks on the Camino Real*.

Following the performance of scenes at **The Actors Studio**, director Kazan encouraged Williams to expand the play into a full-length work. Most critics found the play obscure, and audiences generally seemed to share their confusion. Williams challenged the negative critical response in a *New York Times* essay and was deeply disappointed by the play's cold reception. Since 1953, however, *Camino Real's* theatricality, lyricism, and literary underpinnings have won for it a growing critical appreciation and occasional productions. Following its New York run, *Camino Real* was produced in London in 1957 prior to a New York revival directed by **José Quintero** in 1960. In 1966, an NET television adaptation starring **Lotte Lenya** and a young Martin

Sheen won critical plaudits. *Camino Real* was revived again at Los Angeles's **Mark Taper Forum** in 1968 and at **Lincoln Center** in 1970, with a strong cast led by **Al Pacino**, Jean-Pierre Aumont, and **Jessica Tandy**. England's Royal **Shakespeare** Company produced *Camino Real* in 1998 as its first-ever production of a Williams play. And in 2010, Target Margin Theatre produced *The Really Big One*, a play about the making of the original production of *Camino Real*. Numerous **regional theatres** across the United States continue to perform the play, and a major movie version was under consideration in the first years of the new millennium.

CANBY, VINCENT (1924–2000). Chicago, Illinois-born Canby was known mostly as a film CRITIC for the *New York Times*, beginning in 1969, but he also wrote theatre criticism for the *Times* Sunday paper beginning in 1993, VARIETY, and other publications. He became chief theatre critic at the *Times* in 1994. New York's **Ensemble Studio Theatre** produced one of his plays, *End of War* (1978).

CANTOR, ARTHUR (1920–2001). Born in Boston, Massachusetts, Cantor began as a press agent for such **Broadway** plays as *Goodbye, My Fancy* (1948), *Anne of the Thousand Days* (1948), *Miss Liberty* (1949, *Darkness at Noon* (1951), *The Most Happy Fella* (1956), *Auntie Mame* (1956), and *Long Day's Journey Into Night* (1956), among many others, before branching out as a producer responsible for presenting over 100 plays and MUSICALS in New York and London between the late 1950s and a few years before his death. He was also a theatre owner (**Coconut Grove Playhouse**, Tappanzee Playhouse) and he headed the theatre division of Mercury Records and was joint managing director of H. M. Tennent, Ltd. in London. Among his numerous Broadway productions are *The Tenth Man* (1959), *Toys in the Attic* (1960), *All the Way Home* (1960), *Gideon* (1961), *A Thousand Clowns* (1962), *In Praise of Love* (1974), a revival of *Private Lives* in 1975, *On Golden Pond* (1979), *A Little Family Business* (1982), *Pack of Lies* (1985), *Starlight Express* (1987), and a revival of *The Three Sisters* in 1996.

CAPALBO, CARMEN (1925–2010). A native of Harrisburg, Pennsylvania, Capalbo began his career running **Off-Broadway** theatres, including the Cherry Lane Theatre, where he staged productions of *Juno and the Paycock*, *Awake and Sing!*, and *Shadow and Substance* in 1946. At the Theatre de Lys he produced a hit revival of *Threepenny Opera* in 1954, which moved to **Broadway** and won a special **Tony Award**, and from then until the early 1970s, he staged and/or produced Broadway productions of *The Potting Shed* (1957), *A Moon for the Misbegotten* (1957), *The Cave Dwellers* (1957), and

Seidman and Son (1962), and others, as well as production sat the **Paper Mill Playhouse**, Paramus Playhouse, and others. He also worked in television and directed touring productions.

CARICATURES. In the United States, caricatures and their makers emerged in the mid-nineteenth century, mostly as political cartoonists like Thomas Nast. Early theatre caricatures appear in the 1850s, when Edwin Forrest and P. T. Barnum were caricatured in *The Comic History of the Human Race* (1851). W. J. Gladding published caricatures of a dozen leading American actors in 1868, but were not published widely until much later. James Montgomery Flagg published caricatures of theatre personages in a range of newspapers and magazines, while Alfred J. Frueh did the same and collected his work in *Stage Folk* (1922). The major newspapers in New York covering theatrical activity frequently made use of artists to capture stage performances and performers, including William Auerbach-Levy and Reginald March, and several women caricatured for magazines, including Peggy Bacon and Irma Selz.

After the 1930s, the leading theatre caricaturists included Sam Norkin, who worked for the *New York News* beginning in 1940, and Miguel Covarrubias, but **Al Hirschfeld** became the unofficial Dean of American Caricaturists. He began his career with the *New York Herald-Tribune* in 1926 with a caricature of French actor/playwright Sacha Guitry, then appearing on **Broadway**. By 1928, he began providing regular theatre caricatures to the *New York Times* and remained with the paper for over 70 years. During that long era, Hirschfeld created unforgettable images of virtually every major figure and play presented in New York, as well as films and movie personalities as well. For an actor to be caricatured by Hirschfeld was tantamount to immortality. In the same era, **Sardi's Restaurant** on W. 44th Street became a mecca for theatre folks who awaited opening night reviews until the wee hours of the morning. The restaurant began hanging caricatures of noted actors on the restaurant walls, which remain covered with images of the greats and near-greats of mid-twentieth-century Broadway. In the latter part of the twentieth century, designers of posters for Broadway and **Off-Broadway** theatre productions moved from using photographs to caricatures, with a few artists, such as Paul Davis and James McMullan, developing highly recognizable styles.

CARIOU, LEN (1939–). This Canadian actor was born Leonard Joseph Cariou in St. Boniface, Manitoba, where he began acting and directing in plays in school before he attended St. Paul's College. He began his professional career with the Stratford (Ontario) **Shakespeare** Festival and the **Guthrie Theatre** in Minneapolis. On **Broadway**, Cariou is best known for appearing in MUSICALS, including *Applause* (1970), for which he won a

Theatre World Award, *A Little Night Music* (1973), for which he received a **Tony Award** nomination, *Sweeney Todd* (1979), for which he won a Tony and a **Drama Desk Award**, and *Dance a Little Closer* (1983), but he also appeared in a range of non-musical plays. These include a 1969 revival of *King Henry V*, *Night Watch* (1972), *Don't Call Back* (1975), *Cold Storage* (1977), *The Speed of Darkness* (1991), *The Dinner Party* (2000), and he stepped in as a replacement in ***Proof*** (2000). Cariou has also appeared with frequency on television and in films, including as a regular on *Blue Bloods* beginning in 2010.

CARNOVSKY, MORRIS (1897–1992). The long, varied career of Carnovsky, who was born in St. Louis, Missouri, began even before he attended college, when he worked for a time in YIDDISH THEATRE. He attended Washington University in his hometown before making his **Broadway** debut in *The God of Vengeance* (1922). For several years in the 1920s, he acted for THE THEATRE GUILD in *Saint Joan* (1923), *Ned McCobb's Daughter** (1926), *The Brothers Karamazov* (1927), *Right You Are If You Think You Are* (1927), *Marco Millions** (1928), *Uncle Vanya* (1929), *The Apple Cart* (1930), ***Hotel Universe*** (1930), ***Elizabeth the Queen*** (1930), and ***Both Your Houses*** (1933), among others, prior to joining **The Group Theatre** in 1931. He appeared in key roles, usually characters older than himself, in most of the Group's most noted productions, including ***The House of Connelly*** (1931), ***Men in White*** (1933), ***Awake and Sing!*** (1935), ***Paradise Lost*** (1935), ***Johnny Johnson*** (1936), ***Golden Boy*** (1937), ***Rocket to the Moon*** (1938), and *Night Music* (1940), among others. He married Group Theatre actress Phoebe Brand in 1941 and developed his own approach to method acting, digressing from **Lee Strasberg**'s approach and instead merged REALISM with techniques permitting greater effectiveness in poetic and more theatrical roles. After The Group Theatre disbanded, Carnovsky appeared on Broadway and in films, as well as with the **American Shakespeare Festival**, tackling the leads in such major **Shakespeare**an plays as *King Lear*, *The Merchant of Venice*, and *The Tempest*, playing these and other roles at the festival and in other Shakespeare festivals and in **academic** theatres. On Broadway after 1940, he appeared in ***My Sister Eileen*** (1940), *Café Crown* (1942), *Counterattack* (1943), the **Arthur Miller** adaptation of HENRIK IBSEN's *An Enemy of the People* in 1950, *Tiger at the Gates* (1955), *The Lovers* (1956), *Nude with Violin* (1957), *The Cold Wind and the Warm* (1958), *Rhinoceros* (1961), and *A Family Affair* (1962).

CAROLINA PLAYMAKERS. University of North Carolina at Chapel Hill Professor Frederick Henry Koch founded this group in 1918 modeled on a similar one, the Dakota Playmakers, he had founded at the University of North Dakota in 1910. Koch's goal was a company focused on writing and performing works native to the region. Success led to the publication of some of these works in a series, Carolina Folk-Plays, and writers Thomas Wolfe and PAUL GREEN were among the contributors. In the 1970s, the Playmakers abandoned the original mission (although they occasionally produce regional work) and evolved as a **repertory theatre** in association with UNC-Chapel Hill. *See also* PLAYMAKERS REPERTORY COMPANY; REGIONAL THEATRE MOVEMENT.

CARROLL, LEO G. (1892–1972). This dignified character actor, familiar to audiences for his many film and television appearances, was born in Weedon, England. Despite his long career on screen, Carroll frequently worked on **Broadway**, where he debuted in *Rutherford & Son* (1912), and was seen in such plays as *The Vortex* (1925), *The Constant Nymph* (1926), *Speak Easy* (1927), *The Perfect Alibi* (1928), *Too True to Be Good* (1932), a revival of *The Mask and the Face* in 1933, *The Green Bay Tree* (1933), *The Masque of Kings* (1936), *Save Me the Waltz* (1938), *Angel Street* (1941), *The Late George Apley* (1944), and revivals of *You Never Can Tell* in 1948, and *On Borrowed Time* in 1953. Carroll's numerous film appearances include *A Christmas Carol* (1938), *Wuthering Heights* (1939), *Father of the Bride* (1950), and *The Bad and the Beautiful* (1952), and several directed by Alfred Hitchcock, including *Rebecca* (1940), *Suspicion* (1941), *Spellbound* (1945), *The Paradine Case* (1947), *Strangers on a Train* (1951), and *North by Northwest* (1959). He also played the title role in the popular television comedy *Topper* from 1953 to 1955 and received two Emmy Award nominations for the series *The Man from U.N.C.L.E.* in the 1960s.

CARROLL, VINNETTE (1922–2002). The first **African American** woman to direct on **Broadway** was born in New York. She studied at Long Island University, New York University, and Columbia University prior to more specialized theatrical training under **Erwin Piscator**, **Lee Strasberg**, and STELLA ADLER in the late 1940s. Deeply involved in the life of the black community, she taught high school, worked at the Harlem Y.M.C.A., directed the Ghetto Arts Program, and served as artistic director of the Urban Arts Corps in Greenwich Village, where the first of her own plays were performed. She scored a particular success with her MUSICAL adaptation of seven sermons, *Trumpets of the Lord*, in 1964. It moved to **Broadway** in 1969, but failed to find an audience. Also an actor, Carroll appeared on Broadway in the 1956 revival of *A Streetcar Named Desire*, *Small War on Murray Hill* (1957), *Jolly's Progress* (1959), and a revival of *The Octoroon* in 1961. She won an **Obie Award Off-Broadway** for *Moon in a Rainbow Shawl* (1962), but her directing skills led back to Broadway with *Don't Bother Me, I Can't Cope* (1972), which brought her a **Tony Award** nomination. Her next production, *Your Arms Too Short to Box with God* (1976), brought her Tony nominations for directing and her libretto. Carroll's final Broadway production, *But Never Jam Today* (1979), had a short run. Late in her life, she established a **repertory** company in Fort Lauderdale, Florida. *See also* AFRICAN AMERICAN THEATRE.

CASSIDY, CLAUDIA (1900–1996). Born in Shawneetown, Illinois, Cassidy studied at the University of Illinois in Urbana, and in 1925 became music and theatre CRITIC for the *Chicago Journal of Commerce*, where she worked until 1941 when she was given the opportunity to set up the music and drama departments of the *Chicago Daily Sun*, a new daily newspaper. She wrote a daily column, "On the Aisle," and although her music reviews was frequently challenged, she championed theatre talents, most particularly praising the Chicago tryout of **Tennessee Williams**'s *The Glass Menagerie* in late 1944. Cassidy became Chicago's most powerful critic from the 1940s to her retirement in 1965, and a theatre in the Chicago Cultural Center was ultimately named in her honor.

CAT ON A HOT TIN ROOF. **Tennessee Williams** received his second PULITZER PRIZE in 1955 for this intense family drama, a characteristic Williams play in which his mastery with language, character, symbol, and dramatic form are in full evidence. In its original production directed by **Elia Kazan**, scene designer JO MIELZINER heightened *Cat*'s pared-down realism and intensity by choosing only a few carefully selected furnishings (particularly an ornate bed and a bar) to create its Southern gothic environment. *Cat on a Hot Tin Roof* opened for a long and critically applauded run at New York's Morosco Theatre on March 24, 1955. Under Kazan's direction, the cast featured **Barbara Bel Geddes**, **Ben Gazzara**, **Mildred Dunnock**, and Burl Ives in a memorable performance as Big Daddy.

A significant disagreement between Williams and Kazan inspired a rewriting of the play's third act. In Williams's original, Big Daddy does not reappear after dominating *Cat*'s second act. Kazan persuaded Williams to find a way to bring Big Daddy back in the third act fearing that his omission would disappoint the audience. This rewritten version was used for the original production, but in the subsequently published script Williams included both versions of the third act, inviting readers to decide on the most effective approach. The play owes much to Freud's theories and the works of two of Williams's favorite writers, **Anton Chekhov** and D. H. Lawrence.

Cat on a Hot Tin Roof is set on the vast Pollitt plantation on the Mississippi Delta where family patriarch, Big Daddy, is celebrating his sixty-fifth birthday with his wife, Big Mama, and their two adult sons, Gooper and Brick. The joyful mood of the party is heightened by news that Big Daddy's recent ailments are not, as feared, stomach cancer, but merely a "spastic colon." The party's merriment is set against an undercurrent of marital strife, greed, and lingering fears about Big Daddy's health. Earlier, Brick, a former star athlete, attempted to jump hurdles in a drunken state. The resultant broken ankle has made him a captive in his bedroom where Maggie, Brick's wife and a former beauty queen, exploits his immobility in an attempt to end their estrangement. Describing herself as a "cat on a hot tin roof," Maggie fears that Brick, the favored son of Big Daddy, will be disinherited should he fail to produce an heir. In fact, Brick, who displays no interest in Big Daddy's fortune or the feverish family machinations surrounding the battle for the estate, refuses to touch Maggie. Brick seeks only the "click" that comes when he has imbibed enough alcohol to render him senseless to the endless squabbles around him. His alcohol consumption is also an attempt to blot out the disturbing revelation that Skipper, his now deceased team roommate, harbored **homosexual** desires for him. Questioning his own **sexuality**, Brick is mired in an alcohol-induced melancholic haze from which Maggie has been struggling to release him.

The play's homosexual element was removed entirely from *Cat*'s 1958 film version starring Elizabeth Taylor, **Paul Newman**, and Ives recreating his stage role, but it was critically well-received and popular. Two television films have also appeared: a 1976 version with Natalie Wood, Robert Wagner, and **Laurence Olivier** (as Big Daddy) and a 1985 production with Jessica Lange, Tommy Lee Jones, **Rip Torn**, and **Kim Stanley**. *Cat* has often been revived on stage, most notably three times on **Broadway**. The first New York revival in 1974 starred **Elizabeth Ashley**, Keir Dullea, and Fred Gwynne; the next, in 1990, featured an acclaimed performance by Kathleen Turner, supported by Daniel Hugh Kelly and **Charles Durning**; and, in 2003, Ashley Judd, Jason Patric, and **Ned Beatty** again returned *Cat* to the New York stage.

CENSORSHIP.[†] The censoring of various aspects of theatrical endeavor has existed from the theatre's beginnings and in the United States it began with the Puritans, who were likely to view the stage as a den of idleness and iniquity. Over time, the censorious focused on particular thematic content, certain forms of human behavior (particularly **sexuality**), politics, and language. In the mid-nineteenth century, performances featuring scantily clad women both titillated and outraged audiences, but after 1880 the focus shifted to the content of realistic social problem plays, with frequent closings (and arrests) associated with the earliest American productions of the plays of HENRIK IBSEN, GEORGE BERNARD SHAW, and others. James A. Herne's* *Margaret Fleming** (1890), written in the Ibsenite mode, was not permitted performances in New York and Boston, and New York productions of Shaw's *Mrs. Warren's Profession* in 1905, Clyde Fitch's* *Sapho* (1900), and George Scarborough's* *The Lure* (1913) also ran afoul of local authorities. While MUSICALS, revues,* and BURLESQUE were able to employ certain degrees of **nudity** and risqué subject matter, the serious stage met with frequent difficulty.

The most important American playwright post-World WAR I, EUGENE O'NEILL, caused controversy with several of his plays, including *Desire under the Elms** (1924), *All God's Chillun Got Wings** (1924), and *Strange Interlude** (1928). As late as 1947, the pre-Broadway production of O'Neill's ***A Moon for the Misbegotten*** was challenged by out-of-town CRITICS on moral grounds and in Detroit, for example, several words had to be deleted before a performance could be permitted. The antiwar sentiments of Laurence Stallings* and MAXWELL ANDERSON's *What Price Glory** (1924) led to calls for censorship, as did the plays of Mae West,* whose sexually liberated *Sex** (1926), in which she also played the lead, led to her arrest for indecency, and her play *The Drag* (1927), depicting a homosexual "drag" party, was closed by authorities before it reached **Broadway**. West's exploits led to the enactment of the Wales Padlock Law* of 1927, which permitted the authorities to arrest personnel, lock theatres, and ban productions viewed as indecent. This law was rarely enforced, but it remained on the books until the 1960s and was significant in forcing producers to tread carefully in sensitive areas.

Out of New York, local tastes and standards have frequently led to attempts to censor dramatic works, while in New York in the middle of the twentieth century, playwrights as diverse as **Tennessee Williams**, **William Saroyan**, **Lillian Hellman**, and **Arthur Miller**, among others, pushed at the boundaries of acceptability in everything from sexuality to politics. From the late 1950s, as civil rights, **feminism**, opposition to the Vietnam War, and other social upheavals changed American society and playwrights challenged spoken and unspoken taboos. **Edward Albee** broke the language barrier with ***Who's Afraid of Virginia Woolf?*** (1962), which was denied the PULITZER PRIZE due to its use of various expletives and the sexual indiscretions of its characters. Curiously, Albee indulged in a kind of censorship when he halted a 1972 production of *Who's Afraid of Virginia Woolf?* and sued the **American Conservatory Theatre** over its interpretation of ***Tiny Alice*** (1964). Living playwrights have since occasionally objected to cross-gender casting and other "radical" interpretations of their work. *Hair*, the "tribal rock musical" of 1967, broke the nudity barrier in New York and when attempts were made to ban it in Boston, the Supreme Court overturned the ban.

Since 1980, fundamentalist Christians and political conservatives have pressured the **National Endowment of the Arts (NEA)**, as well as theatre companies and producers of plays over a range of issues, including nudity, sexuality, strong language, and political themes. As **gay** and **lesbian** writers moved to the fore after 1980, and especially in the wake of the **AIDS** pandemic, conservatives focused their penchant for censorship on homosexual themes, assailing such plays as **Larry Kramer**'s *The Normal Heart* (1985), **Tony Kushner**'s *Angels in America* (1993), and others, while **Terrence McNally**, whose *Corpus Christi* (1998), which relates to Jesus Christ's life and the lives of gay men in Texas, was scheduled for performances at the **Manhattan Theatre Club (MTC)**. When a furor erupted over the play's subject matter, the MTC withdrew the play, inspiring a second uproar against censorship that resulted in the reinstatement of the production, which played despite demonstrations and bomb threats. The regional theatre movement that began in the late 1950s shifted the center of American theatre away from New York and, as such, many censorship battles are played out regionally. At the beginning of the twenty-first century, such conflicts arise with some frequency, often resulting from the deep political divisions in the United States.

CENTER STAGE. Founded in 1963 by a group of theatre-interested local citizens, Baltimore's Center Stage is the state theatre of Maryland. Emphasizing modern American and European plays, including premieres of **Eric Overmyer**'s *On the Verge* (1985), David Felshuh's *Miss Evers' Boys* (1992), Elizabeth Egloff's *The Lover* (1996), and **Lynn Nottage**'s *Intimate Apparel* (2002), the theatre was structured on the **repertory** model of the **Guthrie Theatre**. Despite a catastrophic fire in 1974 and occasional controversy, including over its production of Daniel Berrigan's *The Trial of the Catonsville Nine* in 1971, Center Stage has thrived, first under the longtime leadership of Peter Culman (1977–1991) and, more recently, Stan Wojewodski, Jr. *See also* REGIONAL THEATRE MOVEMENT.

CENTER THEATRE GROUP. Founded in 1966, this not-for-profit theatre company guides the programs of the Ahmanson Theatre and the **Mark Taper Forum**, theatre spaces constructed in 1957 as part of the Music Center of Los Angeles. Both spaces have been venues for encouraging new and classic American plays and MUSICALS. The Ahmanson has premiered six **Neil Simon** plays, as well as works by **Edward Albee**, **August Wilson**, **John Guare**, **Wendy Wasserstein**, **A. R. Gurney**, and **Terrence McNally**, among others, while the Mark Taper Forum, which has presented nearly 200 productions, has offered premieres of works (including three PULITZER PRIZE-winners) by **Lanford Wilson**, August Wilson, **Tony Kushner**, **Luis Valdéz**, **Anna**

Deavere Smith, **Eduardo Machado**, and **Jon Robin Baitz**. The Forum received a 1977 **Tony Award** as an outstanding **regional theatre**. A third theatre space, the Kirk Douglas Theatre, opened in 2004 and has presented premieres by Baitz and **Charles L. Mee**.

CEREMONIES IN DARK OLD MEN. **Lonne Elder III**'s tragic-comic play set in a Harlem barbershop where bootleg alcohol is secretly sold, was produced in 1969 by the **Negro Ensemble Company** and won its author a **Drama Desk Award**. Directed by **Douglas Turner Ward**, who also appeared in the cast (and in a 1985 revival), the play is set in the 1950s and explores problems facing a splintered **African American** family as some members attempt to free themselves of the psychological and societal constraints on their lives. Reviewing a 1985 revival, CRITIC **Mel Gussow** wrote in the *New York Times* that "Though the play has its digressionary moments and a few questionable motivations, it is marked by the breadth of its vision of interdependent, mutually harmful lives, and it is written with humor and a depth of understanding."

CERVERIS, MICHAEL (1960–). Born in Bethesda, Maryland, but raised in Huntington, West Virginia, Cerveris attended Phillips Exeter Academy and Yale University. He has appeared successfully in MUSICALS, *The Who's Tommy* (1993), which brought him a **Theatre World Award** and a **Tony Award** nomination, *Titanic: The Musical* (1997), revivals of **Stephen Sondheim**'s *Assassins* in 2004, for which he won a Tony, and *Sweeney Todd* in 2005, which brought him a Tony nomination, and *Lovemusik* (2007), for which he received nominations for a Tony and a **Drama Desk Award**. He has also appeared notably in non-musical theatre, including **Signature Theatre**'s revival of **Lanford Wilson**'s *Fifth of July* in 2003, *Cymbeline* in 2007, and *Hedda Gabler* in 2009. He has also appeared frequently in films and on television.

CHAIKEN, JOSEPH (1935–2003). This Brooklyn, New York-born director, playwright, and teacher became ill with rheumatic fever in childhood, involving isolated care and lifelong health issues. He began study at Drake University, but decided to study with various New York acting teachers and to begin a career in theatre as an actor, working in small roles at the Metropolitan Opera, on **Broadway**, where he debuted in *Dark of the Moon* (1958), and with **The Living Theatre**. In 1963, he founded **The Open Theatre**, which began as an experimental laboratory aimed at developing a post-method, post-Theatre of the Absurd approach and subsequently evolved into a performance ensemble. The Open Theatre won particular acclaim for its productions of **Jean-Claude Van Itallie**'s *America Hurrah* (1966) and *The Serpent* (1970), emphasizing sound and movement and improvisation techniques drawn from the theories of **Viola Spolin** and Nola Chilton. Chaikin played Hamm in The Open Theatre's production of *Endgame* in 1969, and the company performed Susan Yankowitz's *Terminal* (1970) and toured in Europe and America. During the 1970s, Chaikin founded The Winter Project with some members of The Open Theatre and others, and began to work closely with **Sam Shepard**, collaborating with him on *Tongues* and *Savage/Love* in 1978, with both plays premiering at San Francisco's **Magic Theatre**. Chaikin and Shepard were commissioned to write *When the World Was Green* (1996) for the Olympics in Atlanta, Georgia. Chaikin suffered a stroke during heart surgery in 1984 and despite some impairment, he continued to direct with an emphasis on disability-themed works at such varied regional theatres as the **Mark Taper Forum**, the **New York Shakespeare Festival**, and the **Trinity Repertory Theatre**. Chaikin won six **Obie Awards** and two **Drama Desk Awards**. *See also* ALTERNATIVE THEATRE.

CHALFANT, KATHLEEN (1945–). Born Kathleen Ann Bishop in San Francisco, California, Chalfant studied acting with **Wynn Handman** and had a long acting career in **regional theatre** and **Off-Broadway** prior to her involvement in **Tony Kushner**'s *Angels in America* (1993), in which she played multiple, cross-gender roles, garnering nominations for **Tony Awards** (for each of the two *Angels* plays) and a **Drama Desk Award** nomination. She also appeared on **Broadway** in *Racing Demon* (1995), but Off-Broadway she received another Drama Desk nomination for *Nine Armenians* (1997) and won an **Obie Award**, Drama Desk Award, **Lucille Lortel Award**, and an **Outer Critics Circle Award** for Margaret Edson's *Wit* (1999). She also won an Obie for Alan Bennett's *Talking Heads* (2003) and appeared in **Sarah Ruhl**'s *Dead Man's Cell Phone* (2008) at **Playwrights Horizons**. In 2009, Chalfant acted a major role in the premiere of Kushner's *The Intelligent Homosexual's Guide to Capitalism and Socialism with a Key to the Scriptures* at the **Guthrie Theatre** and Off-Broadway in **Beth Henley**'s *Family Week* (2010). Chalfant also appears frequently in television drama and films.

CHANEY, STEWART (1910–1969). Kansas City, Missouri-born scene designer Chaney studied at Yale University under George Pierce Baker.* During the 1930s and 1940s, he was one of **Broadway**'s most prolific designers (occasionally designing lights and costumes as well as scenery). Between 1934 and 1964, Chaney, who excelled at stylish, highly detailed realistic designs, was responsible for designing nearly 80 productions, including *The Old Maid* (1935), *Parnell* (1935), *Life With Father* (1939), *Blithe Spirit*

(1941), *The Voice of the Turtle* (1943), *Jacobowsky and the Colonel* (1944), *The Late George Apley* (1944), *An Inspector Calls* (1947), *Life with Mother* (1948), *I Know My Love* (1949), *The House of Bernarda Alba* (1951), *The Moon Is Blue* (1951), and numerous revivals.

CHANG, TISA (1941–). Born in Chungking, China, Chang graduated from Barnard College and studied acting with **Uta Hagen**, emerging as an actor and director. She debuted in a production of *The World of Susie Wong* in Buffalo, New York, in 1962 and on **Broadway** in *Lovely Ladies, Kind Gentlemen* (1970). She also appeared in *The Basic Training of Pavlo Hummel* (1972) and a few tours. Chang began her directing work at **La MaMa Experimental Theatre Club**, but is most known for founding the **Pan Asian Repertory Theatre (PART)** as a means of creating more opportunities for **Asian American** performers, directors, and writers. The PART has premiered new works by R. A. Shiomi and **Ernest Abuba** and has also staged numerous cross-cultural productions of classic works. Chang has also appeared in a few films and television shows. *See also* ASIAN AMERICAN THEATRE.

CHANNING, CAROL (1921–). A legendary performer in American MUSICAL THEATRE, Channing was born in Seattle, Washington, and studied at Bennington College prior to her **Broadway** debut in *No for an Answer* (1941). She won critical notice in *Lend an Ear* (1948), but found stardom in *Gentlemen Prefer Blondes** (1949). She appeared in other MUSICALS during the 1950s, including succeeding **Rosalind Russell** in *Wonderful Town* (1954), *The Vamp* (1955), and *Show Girl* (1961), but she occasionally moved away from musicals, as in a tour of GEORGE BERNARD SHAW's *The Millionairess* in 1963. Channing scored another notable hit, and won a **Tony Award**, in the title role of *Hello, Dolly!* (1964), a musical based on **Thornton Wilder**'s *The Matchmaker*, a show she has returned to in tours and revivals for decades. In non-musicals, Channing appeared opposite Sid Caesar in **Abe Burrows**'s *Four on a Garden* (1971) and toured with **Mary Martin** in *Legends* (1986), although the production never opened in New York. She was presented with a special Tony in 1968 and a lifetime achievement Tony in 1995.

CHANNING, STOCKARD (1944–). Born Susan Antonia Williams Stockard in New York, she attended the Madeira School and Radcliffe College and following the end of her marriage to Walter Channing, she kept the name. She began acting with the Theatre Company of Boston and appeared in that troupe's **Off-Broadway** production of *Adaptation/Next* (1969) prior to her **Broadway** debut in *Two Gentlemen of Verona—The Musical* (1971). In this same period, she appeared in films and television, but returned to Broadway with some frequency and demonstrating versatility in her ability to stand out in drama, comedy, and MUSICALS. During the 1970s and 1980s, she appeared on Broadway in *No Hard Feelings* (1973), replaced Lucie Arnaz in *They're Playing Our Song* (1979) and Liza Minnelli in *The Rink* (1984), *The Golden Age* (1984), and won a **Tony Award** in a revival of *A Day in the Death of Joe Egg* (1985). She was nominated again the next year for ***The House of Blue Leaves*** (1986).

Channing won a **Drama Desk Award** Off-Broadway for her performance in *Woman in Mind* (1988). Film and television work occupied Channing for a time, but she returned to Broadway, notably in ***Six Degrees of Separation*** (1990), which brought her Tony and Drama Desk nominations, and *Four Baboons Adoring the Sun* (1992), garnering a Tony nomination. Off-Broadway, she was Drama Desk-nominated for *Hapgood* (1995) and she returned to Broadway in three revivals, ***The Little Foxes*** in 1997, ***The Lion in Winter*** in 1999, and *Pal Joey* in 2008, the last two bringing her Tony nominations. She appeared in the hit film *Grease* (1978) and garnered an Academy Award nomination for the film version of *Six Degrees of Separation* in 1993. Her numerous television appearances include a long-running stint as Abbey Bartlet, the First Lady, in *The West Wing* (1999–2006), which brought her six Emmy Award nominations, and she won an Emmy for *The Matthew Shepard Story* (2002).

CHAPMAN, JOHN (1900–1972). Born John Arthur Chapman in Denver, Colorado, he worked for the *Denver Times* (1917–1919) prior to joining the staff of the *New York Daily News* in 1920, becoming drama editor in 1929 and replacing Burns Mantle* as theatre CRITIC in 1943, continuing in that post until shortly before his death. For the *Daily News*, he wrote a column, "Mainly about **Broadway**," and edited the *Best Play* series of books from 1947 to 1953 started by Mantle.

CHAPTER TWO. **Neil Simon**'s semi-autobiographical two-act comedy-drama, produced by **Emanuel Azenberg** and directed by Herbert Ross, premiered in October 1977 at Los Angeles's Ahmanson Theatre prior to opening on **Broadway** on 4 December 1977 at the Imperial Theatre for 857 performances. Based in part on Simon's own experiences following the early death of his first wife, Joan, and his remarriage to actress Marsha Mason (who played Jennie Malone, the character based on herself), the play was among Simon's first attempts to go beyond the successful formula he had used for nearly two decades writing New York-based witty and light domestic comedies depicting an optimistic view of life. In the play, novelist George Schneider, played by **Judd Hirsch**, is in deep mourning for the death of his wife, Barbara. His brother, Leo, attempts to introduce him to other women, finally succeeding with Jennie, a recently divorced actress being pushed into new relationships by her friend, Faye. Leo and Faye flirt with an extramarital affair, while George and Jennie fall in love. They are married, but George has serious difficulties fully accepting a new relationship, although with Jennie's support, he is finally able to move forward with his life. Simon's formula remained unchanged with *Chapter Two* with the exception that he probed more deeply into the experiences of loss and psychological problems than had been typical of his work. CRITICS were mostly approving, but a subsequent film version in 1979 made little impact despite the presence of the Broadway production's star, Mason (who was nominated for an Academy Award and a Golden Globe Award), along with the addition of film star James Caan.

CHASE, ILKA (1900–1978). New York-born actress who moved easily from sophisticated comedy to drama and sometime novelist, Chase attended boarding schools in England, France, and the United States prior to her **Broadway** debut in *The Red Falcon* (1923). Chase's subsequent notable roles included **The** *Animal Kingdom* (1932), *Forsaking All Others* (1933), *Days without End* (1934), *Small Miracle* (1934), *Revenge with Music* (1934), as the venal Sylvia Fowler in *The Women* (1936), *Keep Off the Grass* (1940), *In Bed We Cry* (1944), and in 1963 she returned to Broadway to replace **Mildred Natwick** as Mrs. Banks in *Barefoot in the Park* (1963). She appeared in several films, including reprising her role in *The Animal Kingdom* (1932) and in *Now, Voyager* (1942), *Miss Tatlock's Millions* (1948), and *Ocean's Eleven* (1960), and in many television programs. She was briefly married to **Louis Calhern** in 1926.

CHASE, MARY (1907–1981). A Denver, Colorado, native, Mary Ellen McDonough Coyle lived in her hometown all of her life, despite writing 14 plays and a screenplay, as well as children's stories. She worked for the *Rocky Mountain News* for several years beginning in 1924, but left when she married reporter Robert L. Chase. Her first **Broadway** play, *Now You've Done It* (1937), was short-lived, but she won a PULITZER PRIZE and a remarkably long run with her winsome comedy, *Harvey* (1944), which was frequently revived on Broadway, STOCK, and in **community** and university theatres, and became a classic 1950 film. Of Chase's remaining plays, only *Mrs. McThing* (1952), which profited from the presence of HELEN HAYES in the cast, found success, although *The Next Half Hour* (1945), *Bernardine* (1952) and *Midgie Purvis* (1961), which starred TALLULAH BANKHEAD, appeared on Broadway for a short run.

CHAYEFSKY, PADDY (1923–1981). Playwright, screenwriter, and novelist Sidney Aaron Chayefski was born in the Bronx, New York, to Ukranian Jewish parents. He attended Fordham University, where he studied languages, and picked up the nickname Paddy while serving in the United States Army during World WAR II. Injured in the war, he spent some time in an English hospital and wrote the libretto and lyrics for a MUSICAL *No T.O. for Love* (1945), which was produced by Army Special Services, but moved to London's West End. Back in the United States after the war, Chayefsky wrote successfully for radio and television, becoming known as an overtly socially conscious writer. Chayefsky adapted his 1953 television drama, *Marty*, for the big screen in 1955, and it won several Academy Awards, including Best Screenplay. Encouraged by this success, he adapted several of his teleplays either for **Broadway** or the movies (or both). On Broadway, *The Middle of the Night* (1956) scored a hit with EDWARD G. ROBINSON in the lead and was filmed with **Fredric March** in 1959. This was followed by another hit with *The Tenth Man* (1959), for which Chayefsky received a **Tony Award** nomination, as he did for *Gideon* (1961) the following year. Chayefsky's *The Passion of Josef D.* (1964), which he also directed, failed and he spent the remainder of his career writing for films, including two that brought him Best Screenplay Academy Awards, *The Hospital* (1971) and *Network* (1976), and he was nominated for an Oscar for *The Goddess* (1958). Chayefsky's television drama, *The Catered Affair* (1951), became a 1956 film and, ultimately, a Broadway musical, *A Catered Affair* (2008).

CHEKHOV ON THE U.S. STAGE. Among the titans of modern drama, Anton Chekhov (1860–1904) profoundly influenced American drama if, for nothing else, through the strong influence he exerted on playwrights, most particularly one of America's greatest, **Tennessee Williams**, who frequently spoke of his admiration for Chekhov's work and, in his last years, freely adapted Chekhov's *The Seagull* (1896), a play he had long admired, as *The Notebook of Trigorin* (1981). Other American playwrights, including **Clifford Odets, Lillian Hellman, Arthur Miller, Lanford Wilson, Beth Henley**, and **Tony Kushner**, have been influenced by Chekhov. Although the earliest U.S. production of Chekhov dates to 1908, his works did not attract much attention until the 1923–1924 visit of the Moscow Art Theatre (MAT)* to New York, where their **Broadway** season repertory included Chekhov's *Uncle Vanya* (1899), *Three Sisters* (1900), and *Ivanov* (1887). Many American theatre artists were deeply moved by the plays and the quality of the MAT's acting company, which ultimately influenced American acting mostly through **The Group Theatre** which, between 1931 and 1940, developed a "method" for acting based on the concepts of the MAT's director **Constantin Stanislavsky** as seen through Chekhov's plays. The Group attempted to produce *Three Sisters* in 1939, but the production did not come off due to internal problems with the company.

EVA LE GALLIENNE was another strong proponent of Chekhov's plays, including Chekhovian dramas in the seasons of her CIVIC REPERTORY THEATRE between 1926 and 1933, staging the first American productions of *Three Sisters* in 1926, *The Cherry Orchard* in 1928, and *The Seagull* in 1929. After 1930, productions of Chekhov's plays increased in frequency, with leading actresses appreciating the uncommonly good female roles in his plays. JED HARRIS produced *Uncle Vanya* starring LILLIAN GISH and OSGOOD PERKINS in 1930 and three great actresses, **Judith Anderson, Ruth Gordon**, and KATHARINE CORNELL, appeared in GUTHRIE MCCLINTIC's production of *Three Sisters* 1942, which resonated with audiences during World WAR II. After the war, **Joshua Logan** adapted *The Cherry Orchard* and reset it in the American South as *The Wisteria Trees* (1950) starring HELEN HAYES. A notable **Circle in the Square** production of *Uncle Vanya* in 1973 featured a powerhouse cast, including **George C. Scott**, Nicol Williamson, Julie Christie, **Elizabeth Wilson**, Gish, and **Cathleen Nesbitt** under **Mike Nichols**'s direction. Nichols also directed **Meryl Streep, Kevin Kline**, and **Philip Seymour Hoffman** in a 2001 production of *The Seagull* for the **New York Shakespeare Festival/Public Theatre**.

During the 1960s and 1970s, Chekhov's plays were often adapted or featured bold interpretations, with modern dress or multi-**racial** casting, as in the **Public Theatre**'s all-black production of *The Cherry Orchard* in 1973. Radical staging experimentation was also applied, as in **Andrei Serban**'s production of *The Cherry Orchard* in 1977, which abandoned realistic scenery for isolated elements designed by **Santo Loquasto** and extremely physical acting from its stars, **Irene Worth**, Streep, and **Raúl Juliá**. Serban's approach was adopted and adapted by others, but by the late 1980s, a trend toward fragmented **realism** toned down more radical approaches for a time. Experimentation continued into the new millennium, as in **The Wooster Group's** *Brace Up!* (1990), a multimedia production influenced by Japanese cinema taken from Chekhov's plays. Chekhov as source material emerged in **Neil Simon**'s *The Good Doctor* (1973), an adaptation of several Chekhov short stories which also served several contemporary dramatists in *Orchards* (1985), a collection of original one-acts based on Chekhov's stories by such distinguished American playwrights as **David Mamet, Maria Irene Fornés, Wendy Wasserstein, John Guare**, and others. Mamet adapted Chekhov's plays with distinction, as have several other American dramatists. By the 1990s, Chekhov's plays and adaptations of his work were fully assimilated into American theatre. Broadway, **Off-Broadway**, **regional**, and **academic** theatres frequently present Chekhov. Most recently on Broadway, Derek Jacobi and **Laura Linney** appeared in a revival of *Uncle Vanya* in 2000, and Kristin Scott Thomas and Peter Sarsgaard won critical acclaim for a 2008 revival of *The Seagull*.

CHEKHOV, MICHAEL (1891–1955). Born Mikhail Aleksandrovich Chekhov in St. Petersburg, Russia, he gained fame in the United States for his development of acting techniques and his work as an actor, director, and writer. Nephew of **Anton Chekhov**, he was a student of **Constantin Stanislavsky** at the Moscow Art Theatre.* After a break with Stanislavsky, Chekhov moved to England where his work, including the establishment of a school, was interrupted by the outbreak of World WAR II. He moved his operations to Connecticut and worked on developing his acting techniques. By the 1950s, his students included **Elia Kazan**, Marilyn Monroe, **Anthony Quinn**, Clint Eastwood, Mala Powers, Yul Brynner, Patricia Neal, Jack Palance, and others. Chekhov's book, *To the Actor* (1953), was widely influential. Aside from teaching, Chekhov acted in several films, including Alfred Hitchcock's *Spellbound* (1945), which brought him an Academy Award nomination, and directed **Broadway** productions of *Revisor* (1935), *The Possessed* (1939), and a revival of *Twelfth Night* in 1941.

CHICANO THEATRE. Terms like Chicano, Hispanic, Latino, etc., are variant in meaning, but ultimately, in relation to theatre, all intersect and share mutual concerns. Spanish-speaking theatre in America dates back to 1598 when Juan de Oñate's explorers performed a **religious drama** near what is now El Paso, Texas. Along the border between the United States and Mexico, Spanish and mestizo culture incorporated theatrical performances for centuries. In the twentieth century, MUSICAL performances, zarzuela, and serious dramas were seen in Chicano **communities** from the border to Chicago. As with all theatre, the Great Depression diminished much activity, but renewed energy emerged by the 1960s in response to vast social changes.

    Luis Valdéz joined with César Chávez, who led the farmworkers' strike in California. Valdéz created what he called *actos*, short propaganda plays aimed at expressing the issues of unionizing and other problems facing the workers. Valdéz ultimately established **El Teatro Campesino** (Farm Workers' Theatre) on the model he had observed from his time performing with **The San Francisco Mime Troupe**, merging many styles of theatre, from *commedia dell'arte* and other forms of broad comedy with drama and agit-prop techniques. El Teatro Campesino inspired other such groups to spring up around the country during the 1960s and 1970s, including two other California troupes, Teatro de la Gente (People's Theatre) founded in 1970, and

Teatro de la Esperanza (Theatre of Hope) founded by Jorge Huerta in 1971. The following year, Teatro Bilingüe (Bilingual Theatre) was founded by Joe Rosenberg in Kingsville, Texas, and as many as 100 Chicano theatres may have been in operation at the height of this period.

Many festivals included theatrical performances and a national organization, El Teatro Nacional de Aztlá (TENAZ), was established in 1971 to aid the interaction of this disparate, geographically separated theatre. Chicano theatres sprang up in response to issues in a given community and the difficulty of actors, directors, designers, and writers of Hispanic heritage to find opportunities. These troupes were initially handicapped by a lack of playwrights, but during the 1980s and 1990s young playwrights began to emerge, including Josefina Lopéz, Lalo Cervantes, Rodrigo Duarte-Clark, Estela Portillo Trambley, **Cherrie Moraga**, Milch Sánchez-Scott, Oliver Mayer, Carlos Morton, Octavio Solis, and **Nilo Cruz**, whose *Anna in the Tropics* (2001) won a PULITZER PRIZE.

CHILDREN OF A LESSER GOD. Exploring the relationship between a deaf woman and a hearing man, this two-act drama by **Mark Medoff** was written in response to Medoff's acquaintance with Phyllis Frelich, a deaf woman, who inspired the play while he was teaching at New Mexico State University. **The Mark Taper Forum** premiered the play in 1979 prior to its move to **Broadway**, where it opened on 30 March 1980 at the Longacre Theatre for 887 performances. Starring Frelich as Sarah Norman and John Rubinstein as James Leeds in **Tony Award**-winning performances under **Gordon Davidson**'s direction, the play won a Tony, a **Drama Desk Award**, and the **Outer Critics Circle Award** for Best Play. CRITICS applauded the play's attention to the challenges of disability, emphasizing Sarah's refusal to allow her deafness to prevent her from a full life, as Leeds learns over the course of the play. A 1986 film version brought star Marlee Matlin an Academy Award and a Golden Globe Award as Best Actress.

CHILDREN'S HOUR, THE. **Lillian Hellman**'s first play was produced by **Herman Shumlin** and was both condemned and acclaimed for its story of two women teachers, who are accused of having a **lesbian** relationship by a schoolgirl. The play opened at the Maxine Elliott Theatre on 20 November 1934 for 691 performances. Blackmailing a weak-willed fellow student into supporting her accusations, a misbehaving student tells her grandmother the two teachers have a sexual relationship. As this news spreads, the lives of the two teachers are destroyed, leading to the suicide of one. Hellman, writing in the tradition of HENRIK IBSEN and GEORGE BERNARD SHAW, believed the stage had a moral purpose and could serve as a political platform. In recognizing that a play for the commercial **Broadway** stage must provide entertainment, she leaned toward the well-made problem play style, enriching it with bold, multidimensional characterizations and what some critics have labeled as melodramatic* embellishments. *The Children's Hour* results from these inspirations and concerns, leading Hellman to make use of the idea that even a child could wield the destructive power of a lie and that this notion could serve as the catalyst for a play. Neither the 1936 or 1961 screen versions of the play are completely successful in capturing Hellman's play, as both shy away from the lesbian accusation, but a 1952 Broadway revival starring **Kim Hunter** and Patricia Neal had a successful run. *See also* GAY AND LESBIAN THEATRE.

CHILDREN'S THEATRE. Plays for children in the United States date back to the nation's founding, but as an articulated movement, its true birth is closer to the end of the nineteenth century when such plays as Frances Hodgson Burnett's* *Little Lord Fauntleroy* (1889) drew large audiences of children and pantomimes, MUSICAL entertainments, CIRCUS, and Wild West shows also attracted their attention. In 1903, Alice Minnie Herts founded the Children's Educational Theatre on New York's Lower East Side, catering to immigrant children as an aid to learning English and the ways of American culture. Other cities established similar programs during the first decades of the twentieth century. Various service clubs and women's groups, most particularly Junior League chapters, also contributed by offering drama classes aimed at children. The Chicago chapter of the Junior League created a Play Bureau to encourage the growth of children's theatre.

On **Broadway** by the 1920s, plays for children appeared with greater regularity, encouraged by the earlier popularity of the Burnett's plays, *Little Lord Fauntleroy* and *The Little Princess* (1903) and Maude Adams's* triumph in J. M. Barrie's frequently revived *Peter Pan** (1905). Constance D'Arcy Mackay* published *How to Produce Children's Theatre* in 1915, which provided concepts for children's theatre with educational goals. In 1923, Clare Tree Major founded a touring company with the mission of performing plays for children and teenagers that continued operations into the mid-1950s. EVA LE GALLIENNE's adaption of *Alice in Wonderland* (1932), written by Le Gallienne and Florida Friebus, for her CIVIC REPERTORY THEATRE, revived on Broadway in 1947 and 1982, also encouraged STOCK companies and, ultimately, regional theatres to include family-oriented fare in their theatre seasons, as did the **Federal Theatre Project**, which offered numerous children's plays during its all-too-brief existence (1935–1939).

In this same period, a seminal figure in American children's theatre, **Winifred Ward**, who, among other accomplishments, developed guidelines for educators and professionals in the making of children's theatre (theatre for child spectators), which she specifically distinguished from creative drama (theatre in which children participate). Ward, a professor at Northwestern University and noted for her work in speech therapy with World WAR I shell shock victims, was central in the founding of a professional organization, the American Alliance for Theatre and Education, which guided the development of professionals and educators in the broad field of children's theatre and creative dramatics. By 1935, Sara Spencer founded the Children's Theatre Press, the first to specialize in plays for children, and during the 1930s and 1940s, **Charlotte Chorpenning**, a prolific dramatist in this field working with Chicago's GOODMAN THEATRE, articulated rules for writing children's plays, with an emphasis on a well-made play structure and source material drawn from fairy tales. Her concepts predominated for many years.

Vast cultural changes after World War II, and particularly in the 1960s, opened up great experimentation in children's theatre, beginning with the popularity of **The Paper Bag Players**, founded in 1958, utilizing an improvisatory, poor theatre approach that encouraged audience participation. **TheatreworksUSA**, established in 1962, similarly broke away from the formalized approach articulated by Chorpenning. In more recent decades, particularly since the late 1970s, previously taboo subjects moved to the forefront in theatre for youth, with a range of dramatists, including **Aurand Harris**, Suzan L. Zeder, Laurie Brooks, and James Still, among others, dealing with such topics as racial prejudice, divorce, **sexuality**, and death. In this period, professional companies performing exclusively theatre for young people (the preferred description by the late twentieth century) works emerged, including **The Children's Theatre Company** of Minneapolis in the 1960s, Metro Theatre of St. Louis, and the Seattle (Washington) Children's Theatre in the 1970s, and others, all part of a growing movement in which varied productions, new plays and publications, and professional organizations proliferated, with degree programs in theatre for youth becoming part of the curriculums of many universities and conservatories.

CHILDREN'S THEATRE COMPANY, THE (CTC). Based in Minneapolis, Minnesota, this theatre for youth company was founded in 1965 by John Clark Donahue, and by the mid-1970s it had its own facility. Along with productions, the CTC offers classes in various aspects of theatre training, and its overall mission is to create high-quality and varied theatre for young audiences. Their repertoire combines adaptation of classic fairy tales, children's stories, and folklore, but original scripts are performed as well. Their production of the MUSICAL *A Year with Frog and Toad* (2003), moved to **Broadway**, and the company won the **regional theatre Tony Award**, the first children's company so honored.

CHILDRESS, ALICE (1920–1994). A native of Charleston, South Carolina, Childress moved to Harlem as a child. After high school, she studied with the **American Negro Theatre (ANT)**, where she acted in productions, including ANT's *Anna Lucasta* (1944) when it moved to **Broadway**. She turned to playwriting in 1949 when her first play, *Florence*, was produced **Off-Broadway** in 1950. Her play *Trouble in Mind* (1955) won an **Obie Award**. Childress's other plays include *Just a Little Simple* (1950), *Gold through the Trees* (1952), *Wedding Band: A Love/Hate Story in Black and White* (1966), *String* (1969), *Wine in the Wilderness* (1969), *Mojo: A Black Love Story* (1980), *Sea Island Song* (1977), and *Moms: A Praise Play for a Black Comedienne* (1987). She also wrote several novels, including *A Hero Ain't Nothin' But a Sandwich* (1973), which she adapted as a film aimed at young adults. She viewed her work as portraying the have-nots of society and wrote, the "gift of understanding is often given to those who constantly battle against the negatives of life with determination." *See also* AFRICAN AMERICAN THEATRE.

CHODOROV, EDWARD (1904–1988). Born in New York, and elder brother of **Jerome Chodorov**, who was also a playwright and screenwriter, Chodorov studied at Brown University, after which he worked as an assistant stage manager. He began writing plays in 1931 with *Wonder Boy*, but it flopped on **Broadway**. His next play, *Kind Lady* (1935), which starred Grace George* and won approval, and subsequent works, which he also directed, included *Those Endearing Young Charms* (1943), *Decision* (1944), *Common Ground* (1945), and his most successful comedy, *Oh, Men! Oh, Women!* (1953). That same year, he was blacklisted for failing to cooperate with the House Un-American Activities Committee (HUAC), which ended his work in films. He had produced or scripted several, including adaptations of his own plays, as well as such films as *The Mayor of Hell* (1933), *Undercurrent* (1946), and *The Hucksters* (1947). *See also* CENSORSHIP.

CHODOROV, JEROME (1911–2004). A New York-born playwright and screenwriter, Chodorov was the younger brother of **Edward Chodorov**. He partnered with Joseph Fields to write films and they also collaborated on **Broadway** plays, including *Schoolhouse on the Lot* (1938), which flopped, and *My Sister Eileen* (1940), which was a major hit. Chodorov and Fields scored again with *Junior Miss* (1941) prior to service in World WAR II. Following the war, Chodorov reteamed with Fields for *The French Touch*

(1945) and *Pretty Penny* (1949), both of which failed (the latter closed on the road). Their fortunes improved with the MUSICAL *Wonderful Town* (1953), for which they provided a **Tony Award**-winning libretto based on their play, *My Sister Eileen*. They also contributed the libretto for *The Girl in Pink Tights* (1954) and their comedy *Anniversary Waltz* (1954) was a long-running hit comedy that had a long life in STOCK and **community theatres**.

Chodorov and Field's *The Ponder Heart* (1956) was less successful, and Chodorov spent more of his time directing works by others, including *Make a Million* (1958), *The Gazebo* (1958), *Christine* (1960), and *Blood, Sweat, and Stanley Poole* (1961). Without Fields, Chodorov also wrote the libretto for *I Had a Ball* (1964) and the comedy *3 Bags Full* (1966), which failed, as did his collaboration with Norman Panama on *A Talent for Murder* (1981). Like his brother, Chodorov was blacklisted during the McCarthy era, essentially ending screenwriting opportunities, which had previously included several films, including screenplays for *Junior Miss* and *My Sister Eileen*.

CHONG, PING (1946–). Born in Toronto, Canada, of Chinese heritage, he was raised in New York's Chinatown and studied art and film at the School of Visual Arts and Pratt Institute, after which he joined **Meredith Monk**'s the House Foundation. His own work focuses on collisions of East and West culture and matters of diversity, as in his first production, *Lazarus* (1972). Merging his thematic concerns with techniques involving multidisciplinary elements, he has created most of his productions with Ping Chong & Company (originally known as the Fiji Theatre Company), which he founded in 1975 to "explore the meaning of contemporary theatre and art on a national and international level" through the creation of innovations in the collaboration of theatre and art to explore "the intersections of history, **race**, art and technology" in contemporary society. Beginning in 1992, Chong and his company began creating 30 pieces as part of a project called *Undesirable Elements*, a series of oral history theatre works examining issues of culture and identity. Among his works are three **puppet theatre** productions: *Kwaidan* (1998), *Cathay: Three Tales of China* (2005), and *Obon: Tales of Rain and Moonlight* (2002). Chong is the recipient of two **Obie Awards**, one of which acknowledged sustained achievement. *See also* ASIAN AMERICAN THEATRE.

CHORPENNING, CHARLOTTE (1873–1955). A pioneer in **children's theatre** in the United States born Charlotte Barrows in Eldora, Iowa, Chorpenning studied at Radcliffe College and between 1915 and 1919 she was playwright-in-residence for several organizations in Winona, Minnesota prior to writing and directing for the Children's Theatre of Chicago's GOODMAN

THEATRE from 1932 to 1951. Among her works, most of which were based on popular fairy tales, are *The Emperor's New Clothes* (1932), *Jack and the Beanstalk* (1935), *The Prince and the Pauper* (1938), *Rip Van Winkle** (1938), *Cinderella* (1940), *Little Red Riding Hood, or Grandmother Slyboots* (1943), *Rumpelstiltskin* (1944), and *Alice in Wonderland* (1946), among others. Her children's plays were widely considered superior to others available prior to the 1950s, particularly in her emphasis on the universal truths inherent in fairy tales, and the American Alliance for Theatre and Education established an annual **award** in her name to acknowledge outstanding writers of children's plays.

CHRISTIANS, MADY (1900–1951). Marguerita Maria Christians was born in Vienna, Austria, and performed in German-language theatre in New York as a child, but returned to Austria. Back in the United States after 1931, she appeared in over a dozen **Broadway** productions, scoring a memorable success as the title character in **John Van Druten**'s *I Remember Mama* (1944). She played Gertrude to **Maurice Evans**'s Hamlet in 1939 and played the loyal wife Sara Muller in **Lillian Hellman**'s *Watch on the Rhine* (1941). Her other Broadway appearances include *A Divine Drudge* (1933), *Alice Takat* (1936), *Save Me the Waltz* (1938), revivals of *Heartbreak House* in 1938 and *King Henry IV, Part I* in 1939, *Return Engagement* (1940), *The Lady Who Came to Stay* (1941), *Message for Margaret* (1947), and a revival of August Strindberg's *The Father* in 1949. Christians also appeared in European silent films beginning in 1916 and in Hollywood movies, including *Come and Get It* (1936), *Heidi* (1937), *Tender Comrade* (1943), and *All My Sons* (1948).

CHRISTIANSEN, RICHARD (1931–). This future drama CRITIC was introduced to theatregoing in his childhood, and he performed in high school plays. He began his journalistic career writing obituaries and reviews of **community theatre** for the *Chicago Daily News* in 1963. When the *Daily News* folded in 1978, Christiansen moved over to the *Chicago Tribune* and beginning in the 1960s he tracked the evolution of Chicago theatre, noting the superior work of the **Steppenwolf** and GOODMAN THEATRES and the playwrights and actors nurtured within the Chicago fringe theatres. At the time of Christiansen's 2002 retirement, **David Mamet** wrote that his monument "is the current health and world reputation of Chicago Theatre." In 2004, Christiansen published *A Theatre of Our Own: A History and a Memoir of 1001 Nights in Chicago*, recounting the evolution of Chicago theatre in the second half of the twentieth century. A Chicago theatre named for him, the old Biograph at Victory Gardens Theatre, was dedicated in 2010.

CHRISTIE, AUDREY (1911–1989). Born in Chicago, Illinois, where she studied dance, Christie developed a long career as a character actress. She began in vaudeville,* but made her **Broadway** debut in *Shady Lady* (1933) and for the next three decades moved easily between comedies and MUSI-CALS, including *Sailor, Beware!* (1933), *The Women* (1936), *I Married an Angel* (1938), *Return Engagement* (1940), *Banjo Eyes* (1941), *Without Love* (1942), *The Voice of the Turtle* (1943), and *Light Up the Sky* (1948). Later in her career, she replaced original cast members in *The Desk Set* (1955), *Come Blow Your Horn* (1961), and *Mame* (1966). Christie also occasionally appeared in films, including *Keeper of the Flame* (1942), *Carousel* (1956), *Splendor in the Grass* (1961), *The Unsinkable Molly Brown* (1964), and *Mame* (1974), and numerous television programs.

CINCINNATI PLAYHOUSE IN THE PARK. One of America's first **regional theatres**, this not-for-profit organization opened in 1960. The previous year, Gerald Covell, a college student, organized local business and political figures to establish a professional theatre in Cincinnati. The original space, the Eden Park Shelterhouse, offered fewer than 200 seats and the first production, directed by David Marlin Jones, was Meyer Levin's *Compulsion*. An additional 12 plays were produced that season. Numerous noted actors have appeared during the Playhouse's 50 years, including **Sam Waterston**, Henry Winkler, Lynn Redgrave, **Anthony Perkins**, Raúl Esparza, **Swoosie Kurtz**, **Mercedes Ruehl**, **Estelle Parsons**, Patty Duke, and others. In 1968, the Robert S. Marx Theatre was opened with a production of **Tennessee Williams**'s *Camino Real*. The Playhouse has grown in scope and ambition, premiering new works, moving productions to **Broadway**, touring, offering acting classes, and **children's theatre**.

CIRCLE IN THE SQUARE. Founded in 1950 under the direction of **José Quintero** in association with **Theodore Mann** (who remains artistic director), the Circle in the Square was initially a wing of the Loft Players of Woodstock, New York. The theatre opened in a tiny arena space at 5 Sheridan Square with *Dark of the Moon* (1951). Firmly established the following year with a revival of **Tennessee Williams**'s *Summer and Smoke* with **Geraldine Page**, the theatre grew in stature again in 1956 with a revival of *The Iceman Cometh*, a production significant in renewed interest in EUGENE O'NEILL's work. The production featured **Jason Robards** as Hickey at the start of a long association with the plays of O'Neill and in collaboration with Quintero. **George C. Scott**, **Colleen Dewhurst**, Cicely Tyson, **James Earl Jones**, Vanessa Redgrave, **Philip Bosco**, **Dustin Hoffman**, and other noted actors were among young talents who began their careers in Circle productions.

When the Sheridan Square theatre was torn down in 1960, Circle in the Square operations moved to a space on Bleecker Street in Greenwich Village until 1972, when a theatre facility was constructed for the organization in the Paramount Plaza office tower. Circle in the Square has retained its commitment to the plays of O'Neill and Williams, but has revived many great American plays, as well as MUSICALS, modern European plays, and occasional classics. The Circle in the Square Theatre School, established in 1961, is the only accredited conservatory associated with a **Broadway** theatre, and offers a two-year training program in acting.

CIRCLE MIRROR TRANSFORMATION. Annie Baker's comedy produced by **Playwrights Horizons** in December 2009, featured a strong cast, including Reed Birney, Tracee Chimo, Peter Friedman, Deirdre O'Connell, and Heidi Schreck under **David Zinn**'s direction. The play centers on a New England **community** center drama class where the class experiments and games unleash passions among the participants. *New York Times* critic **Charles Isherwood** described it as "rich, unforgettable theatre . . . [an] unheralded gem."

CIRCLE REPERTORY COMPANY (CRC). Originally named the Circle Theatre Company, the CRC was founded in 1969 by playwright **Lanford Wilson**, directors **Marshall W. Mason** and Rob Thirkield, and actress Tanya Berezin with the idea of establishing a company of actors, writers, and designers who could regularly collaborate to create new plays. The CRC performed in a second-floor loft at **Broadway** and 83rd Street (prior to an early 1970s move to the Sheridan Square Playhouse, followed by a new facility in 1982 at 99 7th Avenue South. Most of Wilson's major plays were produced by the CRC, including *The Hot L Baltimore* (1972), *The Mound Builders* (1974), *Fifth of July* (1977), the PULITZER PRIZE-winning *Talley's Folly* (1979), *A Tale Told* (1980), *Angels Fall* (1983), *Burn This* (1987), and *Redwood Curtain* (1992). Among the work of other dramatists, **Mark Medoff**'s *When You Comin' Back, Red Ryder?* (1973), Edward J. Moore's *The Sea Horse* (1974), **Jules Feiffer**'s *Knock Knock* (1976), **Albert Innaurato**'s *Gemini* (1977), **Sam Shepard**'s *Fool for Love* (1982), **Larry Kramer**'s *The Destiny of Me* (1992), **William M. Hoffman**'s *As Is* (1984), **Craig Lucas**'s *Reckless* (1987) and *Prelude to a Kiss* (1989), **William Mastrosimone**'s *Sunshine* (1989), and **Jon Robin Baitz**'s *Three Hotels* (1992), among others, also premiered there. Plays produced initially at CRC won numerous **Tony**, **Obie**, and **Drama Desk Awards**, but it closed down operations in 1996.

CIRCUS.[†] The modern American circus has its roots in the eighteenth century when Philip Astley, an Englishman, established one that emphasized equestrians and other animal entertainments. By the 1780s, clowns became a familiar element in such performances and with the opening of equestrian John Bill Ricketts's show in Philadelphia, which he billed as a "circus," the form grew in popularity and evolved in content. European managers brought performances to the United States in the early nineteenth century, with an American lion tamer, Isaac A. Van Amburgh, gaining worldwide repute, appearing in European theatres.

By the mid-nineteenth century, circus was a major aspect of American show business, with such entertainments seen on wagons, in theatres, showboats,* and tents. Several extended families spent generations in the circus business and they, along with such managers as William W. Cole and Adam Forepaugh, established increasingly elaborate circuses. After the Civil WAR, the legendary showman P. T. Barnum expanded his interests to include circuses beginning in 1871. With various partners, most particularly James A. Bailey, his innovations included the use of three "rings" for simultaneous acts and the Barnum & Bailey Circus, billed as "The Greatest Show on Earth," toured the world in the 1890s. Challenged by the Ringling Brothers, who had begun a small circus in the 1880s, after Bailey's 1906 death, the Ringlings purchased the Barnum & Bailey circus and, after 1918, merged it with their show to create the enduring Ringling Bros. and Barnum & Bailey Circus.

Over time, circuses increasingly modernized, moving from wagons to trucks and railroad transportation. The Ringling Bros. and Barnum & Bailey Circus established a model emulated, usually on a significantly smaller scale, by other circuses. After a catastrophic fire in Hartford, Connecticut, in 1944, which killed 168 people, the Ringling circus faced various problems until the mid-1950s, when owner John Ringling North decided to abandon traditional circus tents for large civic and sports arenas. Even in such different venues, the show itself largely remained the same until the 1980s, when managers and performers influenced by various postmodern concepts, developed new styles, including the **Pickle Family Circus** and most particularly Canada's **Cirque du Soleil**, both influenced by France's Big Apple Circus in which street performers and spectacular effects revitalized the form, although the increased spectacle brought ticket prices to a level matching **Broadway** MUSICALS. *See also* BIG APPLE CIRCUS; CLARK, BOBBY.

CIRQUE DU SOLEIL. Established in 1984 in Quebec City, Canada, by Guy Laliberté, the Cirque du Soleil, inspired in part by France's Big Apple Circus, revitalized interest in circus, although it bears little resemblance to the traditional CIRCUS in the style of the Ringling Bros. and Barnum & Bailey Circus. Abandoning the circus tent and the use of animals, Cirque du Soleil performances mix a variety of theatrical devices, with emphasis on acrobatics, **mime**, music, dance, masks and makeup, high-tech lighting and multimedia devices structured around a theme. By the early 2000s, Cirque du Soleil boasted no less than five resident shows playing in Las Vegas venues and touring productions. One Cirque du Soleil production making use of the music of the Beatles beginning in 2006 was particularly well-received.

CIULEI, LIVIU (1923–). Born in Bucharest, Romania, Ciulei studied at the Royal Conservatory of Music and Theatre, beginning his career as an actor. In 1948, and continuing in the 1970s, he evolved as an actor and director (of theatre and film), a scene and costume designer, and a teacher at the Lucia Sturza Bulandra Theatre in his birthplace, but increasingly after the mid-1970s, he directed in Europe and Canada prior to accepting the artistic directorship of the **Guthrie Theatre** in Minneapolis in 1980. Ciulei staged a range of plays by **Shakespeare**, HENRIK IBSEN, **Bertolt Brecht**, and others, with particular acclaim for a 1987 production of Euripides' *The Bacchae*. After leaving the Guthrie in 1986, Ciulei freelanced in **regional theatres,** including the **New York Shakespeare Festival**, where his production of *Hamlet* brought him a **Drama Desk Award**, the **Circle in the Square** for whom he directed a revival of *The Inspector General*, and the **Arena Stage**, and he taught at Columbia University and New York University prior to retiring in 2003.

CIVIC REPERTORY THEATRE (CRT). One of several attempts to establish a **repertory theatre** in New York City patterned on the English repertory system, the CRT was a signal forerunner of the American repertory movement that flourished after the late 1950s. Established by EVA LE GALLIENNE, who directed and/or acted in most of its productions, the CRT articulated a mission of bringing important world drama to American audiences at reasonable prices, while also addressing the need for American actors to develop their craft playing diverse classical and contemporary roles in a repertory structure. Financially troubled from its start, but sustained by Otto Kahn's* philanthropy, the CRT suffered from its original location at the Fourteenth Street Theatre, situated away from most **Broadway** theatres.

The CRT survived for 10 tumultuous, financially strained seasons, producing 37 plays in all, including much-admired productions of *The Good Hope, Peter Pan,** *Hedda Gabler, Romeo and Juliet*, and *Camille*. Emphasis was placed on modernist classics, especially works by **Anton Chekhov** and HENRIK IBSEN (five Ibsen dramas were produced during CRT's tenure), but also premieres of three new American plays, notably SUSAN GLASPELL'S PULITZER PRIZE play, *Alison's House** (1931). The CRT company included ALLA

NAZIMOVA, BURGESS MEREDITH, and Jacob Ben-Ami,* but Le Gallienne proved the dominant attraction. The CRT's emphasis on women professionals provided important early opportunities to designers Aline Bernstein* and **Irene Sharaff**, among others. Le Gallienne's desire to keep ticket prices low consigned the CRT to persistent budget strains exacerbated by the Great Depression. A surprise hit with Le Gallienne's 1932 adaptation of *Alice in Wonderland* provided a temporary reprieve when it transferred to a Broadway for an extended run. Unable to keep the company afloat despite this success, Le Gallienne disbanded the CRT in 1933, but not before inspiring THE THEATRE GUILD and **The Group Theatre**, among other serious-minded producing organizations. Along with **Cheryl Crawford** and **Margaret Webster**, Le Gallienne attempted to resuscitate the CRT model as the **American Repertory Theatre** in 1946, but it lasted only one season.

CLAIRE, INA (1893–1985). Born Ina Fagan in Washington, D.C., this stylish, charming actress with a flair for comedy first performed in silent films, vaudeville,* *The Ziegfeld Follies* (the 1915 and 1916 editions) and MUSICALS, prior to her debut in the non-musical hit comedy *Polly With a Past** (1917). She followed this with a series of light comedies including *The Gold Diggers** (1919) and *Our Betters* (1928) before her most notable success in S. N. BEHRMAN's *Biography* (1932) in which her particular talents were most effectively utilized. Her subsequent **Broadway** appearances include *End of Summer* (1936), *Barchester Towers* (1937), *Once Is Enough* (1938), *The Talley Method* (1941), *The Fatal Weakness* (1946), and *The Confidential Clerk* (1954). She appeared in a dozen films, including some of her stage vehicles, along with *The Royal Family** of Broadway* (1930), *The Greeks Had a Word for Them* (1932), *Ninotchka* (1939), and *Claudia* (1943).

CLARENCE BROWN THEATRE COMPANY. Established in 1939 as the Loft Theatre as part of the theatre department at the University of Tennessee, the Clarence Brown Company, named for the noted film director and UT alumnus whose family supported it, emerged as a professional **repertory theatre** in 1972 run by Ralph Allen and British actor Anthony Quayle. Quayle appeared in several productions for the theatre, including a 1976 revival of *Rip Van Winkle** that transferred to the **Kennedy Center** and opposite **Mary Martin** in *Do You Turn Somersaults?* (1978), which transferred to **Broadway**, as did Christopher Isherwood and Don Bachardy's *A Meeting by the River* (1979) and, most successfully, Allen's tribute to BURLESQUE, *Sugar Babies* (1979), which starred Mickey Rooney and Ann Miller and racked up 1,208 performances and 8 **Tony Award** nominations. *See also* REGIONAL THEATRE MOVEMENT.

CLARK, BOBBY (1888–1960). This Springfield, Ohio-born comedian and vaudevillian partnered with Paul McCullough (1883–1936), to perform in CIRCUS, vaudeville,* and MUSICALS on **Broadway** and in London. McCullough was straight man to Clark, who memorably wore painted-on eyeglasses, smoked a cigar, and carried a cane. Following McCullough's suicide in 1936, Clark continued as a single and, improbably starred in revivals of William Congreve's *Love for Love* in 1940, Richard Brinsley Sheridan's *The Rivals* in 1942, and Molière's *The Would-Be Gentlemen* in 1946, as well as Vernon Sylvaine's farce, *All Men Are Alike* (1941). Clark and McCullough also appeared in numerous films from the dawn of the sound era and, on his own, Clark continued in character roles and appeared on television.

CLARK, PEGGY (1915–1996). Born Margaret Brownson in Baltimore, Maryland, Clark was attracted to theatre in childhood and was educated at Smith College and Yale University prior to beginning a career as a lighting designer (although she occasionally designed settings and costumes). Ultimately, she became a seminal figure in establishing lighting as an independent area of design and was the first woman to serve as president of the **United Scenic Artists**. She designed over 150 **Broadway** productions, including many of the major MUSICALS of the era, as well as the **Robinson Jeffers**'s adaptation of *Medea* (1947), *The Trip to Bountiful* (1953), *In the Summer House* (1953), *No Time for Sergeants* (1955), *Auntie Mame* (1956), *Nude with Violin* (1957), *Mary, Mary* (1961), *Romulus* (1962), a revival of *The Rose Tattoo* in 1966, *Last of the Red Hot Lovers* (1969), and *How the Other Half Loves* (1971).

CLARKE, MARTHA (1944–). A Baltimore, Maryland, native who studied dance in childhood, Clarke attended the Juilliard School where she was taught by Anthony Tudor, Louis Horst, and Anna Sokolow. Clarke cofounded Pilobolus in 1972 and Crowsnest in 1978 where she blended dance and theatre influenced by Martha Graham's modern dance and the theatrical techniques used by **The Living Theatre** and Jerzy Grotowski. After some early small projects, Clark moved toward greater spectacle in *The Garden of Earthly Delights* (1984), *Vienna Lusthaus* (1986), *Endangered Species* (1990), *Dämmerung* (1993), and *An Uncertain Hour* (1995), works that alternately dealt with forbidden pleasures and the catastrophes of WAR. Clarke choreographed Lee Breuer's *DollHouse* (2003) and *A Midsummer Night's Dream* in 2004 at the **American Repertory Theatre**, and worked closely with such playwrights as **Richard Greenberg**, **Charles L. Mee**, and **Alfred Uhry**. In 2006, her adaptation of stories by Luigi Pirandello, *Kaos*, was staged at the

New York Theatre Workshop and Clarke received the first **Tony Randall** Foundation Award. Clarke is also the recipient of a **Drama Desk Award**, two **Obie Awards**, and the Los Angeles Drama Critics Circle Award, as well as the MacArthur Fellowship.

CLASSIC STAGE COMPANY, THE. *See* CSC REPERTORY THEATRE.

CLASSICAL THEATRE OF HARLEM (CTH). Founded in 1999 as a not-for-profit theatre by two white men, Alfred Preisser and Christopher McElroen, at the Harlem School of the Arts. Emphasizing the Harlem community, the theatre presents a wide range of plays performed by mostly black actors. Its productions include their first, *Macbeth* (2000), as well as works by **Bertolt Brecht**, **August Wilson**, Stanislaw Witkiewicz, **Adrienne Kennedy**, Derek Walcott, and Jean Genet, whose play *The Blacks* brought four **Obie Awards** to the CTH in 2003 and the CTH has also been acknowledged with a 2004 **Drama Desk Award** for Artistic Excellence, a 2006 **Lucille Lortel Award**, and a 2008 **American Theatre Wing** Award. *See also* AFRICAN AMERICAN THEATRE.

CLAUDIA. **Rose Franken**'s three-act comedy opened at the Booth Theatre on 12 February 1941 for 722 performances in a JOHN GOLDEN production directed by Franken with scene design by DONALD OENSLAGER. A bright cast led by **Dorothy McGuire**, **Donald Cook**, Frances Starr, and Olga Baklanova enacted Franken's examination of an immature young woman, Claudia, whose impetuous actions frustrate her architect husband, David. When Claudia discovers that her mother is dying, she is transformed by the news. McGuire and Baklanova played their roles again in a 1943 film version and it was popular enough to inspire a sequel, *Claudia and David* (1946), again starring McGuire.

CLAYBURGH, JIM (1949–). This postmodernist designer who stresses environmental design schemes studied at New York University and joined **The Performance Group** in 1972, where he designed several productions. Clayburgh was also a founding member of **The Wooster Group**, becoming their resident designer and technical director in 1976 and continuing to 1995 when he moved to Brussels. With The Wooster Group, he worked in close collaboration with director **Elizabeth LeCompte**, using simplified, flexible elements, reconsidering the intersection of the spaces for audience and actors. Among his Wooster Group designs were the acclaimed production of EUGENE O'NEILL's *The Hairy Ape** (1997).

CLEAGE, PEARL (1948–). Born in Springfield, Massachusetts, daughter of a pastor prominently involved in the civil rights movement, Cleage was raised in Detroit, Michigan, and attended Howard University and Spelman College prior to beginning a writing career. She has written several collections of essays and novels, including *What Looks Like Crazy on an Ordinary Day* (1997), *I Wish I Had a Red Dress* (2002), and *Baby Brother's Blues* (2007), and her plays include ***Blues for an Alabama Sky*** (1995), *Flyin' West* (1992), and *Bourbon at the Border* (1997). Of the experience of being a black writer, Cleage has said, "The pull of what the audience wants is always a danger. I have to answer the questions that I have and not reassure the audience about the questions they have. There's always a temptation to lean toward what people want, and a black audience always wants the black person to win." *See also* AFRICAN AMERICAN THEATRE.

CLEAN HOUSE, THE. **Sarah Ruhl**'s first play of note premiered at the **Yale Repertory Theatre** in 2004 and won the Susan Smith Blackburn Prize and was nominated for a PULITZER PRIZE. Subsequent productions at the **South Coast Repertory** in early 2005, the **Goodman Theatre** in 2006, and at **Lincoln Center**, also in 2006, generated critical interest in Ruhl's whimsical comedy-drama of a Brazilian cleaning woman who would rather be a stand-up comedian. *The Clean House* deals with death, but ultimately emphasizes forgiveness and the notion that human beings are not inherently selfish, despite appearances.

CLEVELAND PLAY HOUSE. Founded in 1915, this theatre opened in 1916 with *The Garden of Semiramis* under the leadership of Raymond O'Neill. The amateur group produced 16 plays—all foreign classics by authors that included Kalidasa, Claudel, Andreyev, Molière, and Goldoni—in the few years before it turned professional in 1921. The story of those early years is the subject of a book titled *The Cleveland Play House: How It Began* (1965) by Julia M. Flory, one of the founders. In 1921, the Board of Trustees recognized the need for a professional operation and chose Frederic McConnell as director. In a converted church, he produced seasons of as many as 20 plays, though the repertoire remained predominantly European. Working with Play House president Charles S. Brooks, McConnell opened two theatres (one seating 160, the other 500) in the gardens of the Francis Drury estate. An additional, larger complex opened in 1949. McConnell was succeeded as director by K. Elmo Lowe, who guided the Play House through financial challenges prior to his retirement in 1969. After a difficult transition period, Richard Oberlin was named director in 1972. Oberlin modernized many aspects of the business operation, launched innovative community programs, and in 1983 oversaw the opening of a new Play House complex. Cleveland Play House today holds the record as the longest continuously operating **regional theatre** in the United States.

CLOSE, GLENN (1947–). Born in Greenwich, Connecticut, this celebrated stage and film actress began her **Broadway** career in the **Phoenix Theatre** revivals of *Love for Love, The Rules of the Game*, and *The Member of the Wedding* (1974–1975), followed by the MUSICAL *Rex* (1976), establishing a pattern of alternating musical and non-musical projects. After appearing in *The Crucifer of Blood* (1978), she received her first **Tony Award** nomination for *Barnum* (1980). She won a Tony in 1984 for **Tom Stoppard**'s *The Real Thing*, directed by **Mike Nichols**. She increasingly worked in films after 1980, but returned to the Broadway stage periodically in *Benefactors* (1985) and *Death and the Maiden* (1992), winning another Tony for the latter. In 1995, she won a Tony and a **Drama Desk Award** as Norma Desmond in the Andrew Lloyd-Webber musical *Sunset Boulevard*. She also appeared in several **Off-Broadway** plays, including *Uncommon Women and Others* (1977), and she won an **Obie Award** for *The Singular Life of Albert Nobbs* (1982). Close's film work has brought her five Academy Award nominations for *The World According to Garp* (1982), *The Big Chill* (1983), *The Natural* (1984), *Fatal Attraction* (1987), and *Dangerous Liaisons* (1988). Close has also worked frequently in television, winning Emmy Awards for *Serving in Silence: The Margarethe Cammermeyer Story* (1995) and for the dramatic series *Damages*, which also brought her a Golden Globe Award in 2008.

CLURMAN, HAROLD (1901–1980). One of the three original founders of **The Group Theatre**, Harold Edgar Clurman was born in New York to a Jewish American family. Inspired by the YIDDISH THEATRE, he began a long and distinguished career as a director and CRITIC. After some time in Paris in his early twenties, where he roomed with Aaron Copland and was further inspired by Jacques Copeau, who he assisted on and translated *The Brothers Karamazov*, and performances of the Moscow Art Theatre,* Clurman returned to New York in 1924 and began a theatrical career in bit parts and as a stage manager and play reader for THE THEATRE GUILD while studying the **Constantin Stanislavsky** system for acting with **Richard Boleslavsky**.

Discussing his ideas of theatre with **Cheryl Crawford** and **Lee Strasberg** led Clurman to a long series of midnight talks for actors and directors which culminated in the founding of The Group Theatre in 1931. In encouraging the playwriting of **Clifford Odets**, Clurman found the dramatic voice of The Group and he directed five of Odets's plays, *Awake and Sing!* (1935), *Paradise Lost* (1935), *Golden Boy* (1937), *Rocket to the Moon* (1938), and

Night Music (1940). In 1940, he married a member of The Group, STELLA ADLER, daughter of his Yiddish theatre idol Jacob Adler.* After the demise of The Group in 1940, he chronicled their history in *The Fervent Years* (1945).

While continuing his directing work, Clurman became drama critic for the *New Republic* from 1948–1952 and, later, the *Nation* from 1953–1980. His **Broadway** credits include *Truckline Café* (1947), ***The Member of the Wedding*** (1950), ***The Autumn Garden*** (1951), ***The Time of the Cuckoo*** (1952), ***Bus Stop*** (1955), *Tiger at the Gates* (1955), *Pipe Dream* (1955), *The Waltz of the Toreadors* (1957), ***Orpheus Descending*** (1957), ***A Touch of the Poet*** (1958), *The Cold Wind and the Warm* (1958), *A Shot in the Dark* (1961), and ***Incident at Vichy*** (1964). He taught at Hunter College from 1964 to 1980 and wrote several books, most notably *On Directing* (1968) and IBSEN (1977), as well as collections of his criticism.

COATES, GEORGE (1952–). Born in Rhode Island, Coates moved to California and worked for a time as an actor with the National **Shakespeare** Company. In 1977, he founded George Coates Performance Works as a not-for-profit theatre in Berkeley, California, where he aimed to develop new and original forms of theatre stressing multimedia technology and merging music and theatre with movement. At a variety of American and European theatres and music centers, Coates and his collaborators have created **music-theatre** spectacles, including *2019 Blake* (1977), *The Way of How* (1981), *Are/Are* (1982), *Seehear* (1983), *RARE AREA* (1985), *Actual Sho* (1987), *Right Mind* (1989), *The Architecture of Catastrophic Change* (1990), *Invisible Site: A Virtual Show* (1991), *The Desert Music: A Live Show* (1992), *Box Conspiracy* (1993), *Nowhere NowHere* (1994), *The Bandwidth Addict* (1995), *Twisted Pairs* (1997), *Wittgenstein: On Mars* (1998), *Blind Messengers* (1998), *Triangulated Nation* (1999), *Valerie Solanas' Lost Play: Up Your Ass* (2000), and *Crazy Wisdom* (2001). Coates says, "My art form is synthesis and live art. My job is to disorganize thinking. I think one job of the artist is multimedia is to 'get lost.' If we don't know where we are going, we will find things that we didn't know we needed when we began looking."

COBB, LEE J. (1911–1976). This versatile, bearlike actor—the first to play the role of Willy Loman in **Arthur Miller**'s *Death of a Salesman* (1949)—was born Leon Jacob in New York. He studied at New York University. He joined **The Group Theatre** in 1935, appearing in their productions of ***Waiting for Lefty*** (1935), *Till the Day I Die* (1935), ***Johnny Johnson*** (1936), ***Golden Boy*** (1937), ***The Gentle People*** (1939), and *Thunder Rock* (1939). He also appeared in productions for the **Theatre Union**, including *Mother* (1935) and *Bitter Stream* (1936), and in THE THEATRE GUILD's failed production of Ernest Hemingway's *The Fifth Column* (1940). **Lee Strasberg** directed Cobb in **Clifford Odets**'s *Clash by Night* (1941) prior to World WAR II. While in the service, Cobb appeared in *Winged Victory* (1943). After the war, Cobb returned to films.

On **Broadway**, *Death of a Salesman* was Cobb's greatest success, although the demands of this tragic role took a toll, and after several months he left the production. He later appeared in a 1952 revival of *Golden Boy*, *The Emperor's Clothes* (1953), and as King Lear in the **Repertory Theatre of Lincoln Center** production in 1968, his last **Broadway** appearance. Cobb appeared in films and received Academy Award nominations for *On the Waterfront* (1954) and *The Brothers Karamazov* (1958). His other film appearances include *Golden Boy* (1939), *The Song of Bernadette* (1943), *Call Northside 777* (1948), *12 Angry Men* (1957), *Come Blow Your Horn* (1963), *In Like Flint* (1967), and *The Exorcist* (1973), and Cobb appeared in numerous television shows, most notably a 1966 TV production of *Death of a Salesman*.

COBURN, CHARLES (1877–1961). Charles Douville Coburn was born in Macon, Georgia. Coburn and his wife, Ivah Wills Coburn* (1882?–1937), founded the Coburn **Shakespeare**an Players in 1906, a troupe that toured performing Shakespeare and the classics. With his wife's assistance, he also established the Mohawk Drama Festival (1934) at Union College in Schenectady, New York. Coburn appeared notably on **Broadway** in *The Yellow Jacket** (1916), *The Imaginary Invalid* (1917), *The Better 'Ole* (1918), *The Farmer's Wife* (1924), *Trelawny of the "Wells"* (1925), *Ghosts* (1927), *Diplomacy* (1928), *The Plutocrat* (1930), *Kultur* (1933), *The First Legion* (1934), *Three Wise Fools* (1936), a revival of *The County Chairman** in 1936, *Around the Corner* (1936), and *Sun Kissed* (1937).

From the beginning of sound films, Coburn emerged as one of the screen's most beloved character actors playing befuddled fathers (and grandfathers) and benign or corrupt businessmen, including *Idiot's Delight* (1939), *The Lady Eve* (1941), *The Devil and Miss Jones* (1941), *Kings Row* (1942), *Heaven Can Wait* (1943), *Knickerbocker Holiday* (1944), *The Paradine Case* (1947), and *Gentlemen Prefer Blondes** (1953). He played Falstaff in his last **Broadway** role for THE THEATRE GUILD in *The Merry Wives of Windsor* in 1946, but continued in STOCK for several seasons playing Grandpa in GEORGE S. KAUFMAN and **Moss Hart**'s *You Can't Take It with You*.

COCKTAIL PARTY, THE. Inspired by Euripides' *Alcestis*, **T. S. Eliot**'s allegorical comedy of manners was first performed at the Edinburgh Festival in 1949, followed by runs in London and on **Broadway**, where it won the **Tony Award** as Best Play when it opened at Henry Miller's Theatre on 21

January 1950 for 409 performances. What appears to be a drawing room comedy in the English comic theatre tradition becomes a darker existentialist meditation on human interaction as seen through a married couple and a mysterious stranger who is revealed to be a psychiatrist (**Rex Harrison**). A 1968 Broadway revival starred **Brian Bedford, Frances Sternhagen**, and Sydney Walker and a 2010 revival was staged **Off-Broadway** by The Actors Company Theatre.

COCONUT GROVE PLAYHOUSE. Advertised as "**Broadway** by the Bay" in Miami, Florida, this theatre was constructed in 1926 as a movie theatre, but eventually converted to live theatre and played host to the January 1956 American premiere of Samuel Beckett's *Waiting for Godot* with a cast including **Bert Lahr** and **Tom Ewell**. Retired Floridians resisted Beckett's play, but otherwise welcomed a variety of theatre including appearances by such leading players as **George C. Scott, Hume Cronyn, Jessica Tandy**, TALLULAH BANKHEAD, **Maureen Stapleton, Colleen Dewhurst**, Ethel Merman, Liza Minnelli, Beatrice Arthur, **Linda Lavin**, and others. In 1964, the theatre was used by The Miami Actors Company and in 1982 **José Ferrer** took over artistic management and succeeded in making the theatre one of the leading regional stages. In more recent years, artistic director Arnold Mittleman resigned under a cloud following accusations of misappropriating funds, and the theatre was shut down in 2007.

COE, RICHARD (1914–1995). A native of New York, where he was born Richard Livingston Coe, he became a leading theatre and film CRITIC for the *Washington Post*. He started with the paper in 1936, ascending to the rank of drama critic in 1946, continuing until his retirement in 1980. A critic known for his constructive reviews, Coe is credited with advising critics on possible improvements to a number of plays and MUSICALS that had tryouts in Washington, D.C. during his tenure. He was also vocal in support of ending segregation at Washington's National Theatre, and in 1963 the Directors Guild of America named him critic of the year. **Marian Seldes** described Coe "as one of the most admired critics in America."

COHAN, GEORGE M. (1878–1942).[†] Born in Providence, Rhode Island, to vaudevillian* parents, George Michael Cohan went on the stage as a toddler and continued to perform to the end of his life. He gained his first success as part of the Four Cohans, his family's variety act, but by the late 1890s he became a major figure of the burgeoning **Broadway** theatre as composer, lyricist, librettist, producer (often with his longtime partner, SAM H. HARRIS), director, and star of a series of popular MUSICALS and revues.* In 1911, he opened the George M. Cohan Theatre, and he occasionally veered from the musical form to write straight plays, including two durable hits, *The Tavern** (1921) and *Seven Keys to Baldpate** (1923).

When his own plays and musicals declined in popularity in the mid-1920s, Cohan notably acted in two works written by others. The first, EUGENE O'NEILL'S only comedy, **Ah, Wilderness!** (1933), starred Cohan as Nat Miller, the avuncular father of a turn-of-the-century middle-class Connecticut family dealing with the growing pains of its 16-year-old son. Cohan won rhapsodic reviews for the comic richness of his performance. He followed this with another personal triumph in a musical satire of Franklin D. Roosevelt's New Deal, *I'd Rather Be Right*, with a book by GEORGE S. KAUFMAN and **Moss Hart**, with music by Richard Rodgers and lyrics by Lorenz Hart. As FDR, the 60-year-old Cohan delighted audiences with his spry dancing and comic shenanigans. Despite the spoof, Roosevelt presented Cohan with the Congressional Medal of Honor for his World WAR I anthem, "Over There," and he was also the subject of a lavish film biography, *Yankee Doodle Dandy* (1942), produced by Warner Bros. and starring James Cagney in an Academy Award-winning performance, released shortly before Cohan died of cancer.

COHEN, ALEXANDER H. (1920–2000). A theatrical producer whose productions appeared with regularity in New York and London, Cohen was born in New York. He had an inauspicious start after investing in a failure, *Ghost for Sale* (1941), prior to scoring a success with **Angel Street** (1941), a long-running hit. He produced all manner of theatre, from dramas to MUSICALS, as well as solo artists and European theatre productions. Among his most successful productions were *King Lear* in 1950, *Make a Wish* (1951), *My Three Angels* (1953), *At the Drop of a Hat* (1959), *Beyond the Fringe* (1962), a revival of *The School for Scandal* in 1963, John Gielgud's *Ages of Man* (1963), the **Richard Burton** *Hamlet* in 1964, a revival of *Ivanov* in 1966, *The Homecoming* (1967), **Little Murders** (1967), *The Unknown Soldier and His Wife* (1967), *Dear World* (1969), *Home* (1970), **6 Rms Riv Vu** (1972), *Ulysses in Nighttown* (1974), *Comedians* (1976), Richard Rodgers's musical version of **I Remember Mama** (1979), *A Day in Hollywood/A Night in the Ukraine* (1980), *84 Charing Cross Road* (1982), *Accidental Death of an Anarchist* (1984), and *Waiting in the Wings* (1999). He also produced solo **Broadway** appearances of such international performers as Maurice Chevalier, Marlene Dietrich, Yves Montand, Marcel Marceau, and **Mike Nichols** and **Elaine May**. In addition, with his second wife and coproducer **Hildy Parks**, he conceived the television broadcast of the annual **Tony Awards** in 1967 and produced many telecasts, and he produced the first and third editions of *Night of 100 Stars* as a benefit for the ACTORS' FUND OF AMERICA from Radio City Music Hall.

COLLECTIVES. The history of collective theatre groups in America depends to a great extent on how the term is defined. Most theatre companies are essentially collectives, a group of theatre artists held together by an articulated mission. STOCK companies were essentially collectives, but the term generally refers to a situation in which all members of the creative body of a group participate with equality in decision making and the creative process. A number of such groups formed during the post-World WAR II era **Off-Broadway** and **Off-Off Broadway**. Collective theatre thus came to mean experimental or **alternative theatre** and, as such, the postwar notion of collectives springs from the founding of **The Living Theatre** in 1948, with **Julian Beck** and **Judith Malina**, its founders, clearly expressing a desire to work collectively to experiment with theatrical techniques and to commit to a sociopolitical mission.

Other such groups followed suit, including **The Performance Group**, The Manhattan Project, **The Wooster Group**, **Mabou Mines**, etc., all of which could be described as collectives. Outside of New York, a range of collectives appeared in the late 1950s, including such enduring groups as **The San Francisco Mime Troupe**, founded in 1959 by R. G. Davis; **The Bread & Puppet Theatre**, established by Peter Schumann in the 1960s; **El Teatro Campesino**, a **Chicano** farmworkers theatre established by **Luis Valdéz** in 1965; and the all-black troupe, Free Southern Theatre, which came to the fore during the civil rights movement. After the 1970s, some **feminist** writers, directors, and actors adopted the collective approach, including **At the Foot of the Mountain**, Women's Experimental Theatre, **Spiderwoman Theatre**, and **Split Britches**, among others. By the late twentieth century, collective theatre could be defined as an approach through which artists wishing to experiment in techniques and present challenging themes could work outside of the constraints of mainstream theatres; such groups necessarily developed distinct styles and despite the "collective" aspect, groups that survived were typically founded and guided by one or two dominant members of the group with a strong vision of its goals.

COLLINGE, PATRICIA (1892–1974).[†] Born in Dublin, Ireland, Collinge made her stage debut in London before moving to the United States in 1908. Her varied and long career on stage and screen spanned playing ingénues* in *The Show Shop** (1914) and the title role in *Pollyanna** (1915), a major popular success that she played for three years in New York and on tour. During the 1920s, she appeared with distinction in several important revivals. Also a writer, Collinge's play *Dame Nature* (1938), in which she also appeared, had a short **Broadway** run. After 1930, she appeared on stage in a few failures, including *The Lady with a Lamp* (1931) and *To See Ourselves* (1935), but had successes with C. L. Anthony's *Autumn Crocus* (1932) and **Rose Franken**'s *Another Language* (1932). Collinge won critical approval for her performance as the abused Birdie in **Lillian Hellman**'s *The Little Foxes* (1939), a role she repeated in the 1941 film version. She also appeared on screen in *Shadow of a Doubt* (1943) and *The Nun's Story* (1959), and on television dramas. Her later stage work included playing one of the murderous old ladies of *Arsenic and Old Lace* (1941) as a replacement during the show's long run. Her last important stage appearance as the duplicitous Aunt Lavinia in Ruth and Augustus Goetz's long-running stage adaptation of Henry James's *Washington Square* titled *The Heiress* (1947) was well-received, but she had short runs in a revival of J. M. Barrie's* *Mary Rose* in 1951 and **John Van Druten**'s *I've Got Sixpence* (1952).

COLLINS, PAT (1932–). For **Broadway**, Collins designed lighting for numerous productions since her first, a revival of *Threepenny Opera* in 1976, which brought her a **Tony Award** nomination. She won a **Drama Desk Award** for *Execution of Justice* (1986) and a Tony for *I'm Not Rappaport* (1986) on Broadway, and picked up another Tony nomination for *Doubt* (2005) and Drama Desk nominations for **Off-Broadway** productions of *Penguin Touquet* (1981) and *Woman in Mind* (1988). Among her other Broadway credits are the legendary flop *Moose Murders* (1983), *The Boys of Winter* (1985), *Death and the King's Horseman* (1987), *Ain't Misbehavin'* (1988), *The Heidi Chronicles* (1989), *The Sisters Rosensweig* (1993), revivals of *A Delicate Balance* in 1996 and *A Moon for the Misbegotten* in 2000, *Proof* (2000), *Sight Unseen* (2004), and *Dr. Seuss' How the Grinch Stole Christmas* (2006). Collins has also designed lighting for over 100 international opera productions, and her work has been seen regularly in major **regional theatres**.

COLORADO SHAKESPEARE FESTIVAL. Considered one of the finest **Shakespeare** Festivals in the United States, it was founded at the University of Colorado in their outdoor Mary Rippon Theatre where, beginning in 1944 an annual summer Shakespeare production was offered. From this beginning, the festival began in 1958 with three productions, *Julius Caesar, Hamlet*, and *The Taming of the Shrew*. By 1975, the festival achieved the rare distinction of having produced the entire Shakespearean canon.

COLORED MUSEUM, THE. **The Crossroads Theatre** in New Brunswick, New Jersey, provided the 1986 premiere of director/playwright **George C. Wolfe**'s satire of racial attitudes and **African American** culture under the direction of Lee Richardson. Wolfe received the Dramatists Guild Award for the play, and it moved to **New York Shakespeare Festival/Public Theatre** for a successful run. Wolfe's satiric voice ranges across **African American** history, from slave ships to Josephine Baker and a comically ruthless deconstruction of **Lorraine Hansberry**'s *A Raisin in the Sun* in a sketch called "The Mama-on-the-Couch Play." *The Colored Museum* was also produced by London's Royal Court Theatre and by many **repertory** and university theatres in the United States.

COME BACK, LITTLE SHEBA. **William Inge**'s first play, a drama in two acts, opened in a THEATRE GUILD production at the Booth Theatre on 15 February 1950 for 190 performances. Its stars, **Sidney Blackmer** and **Shirley Booth**, both won **Tony Awards** for their performances, although critics were divided on the play's merits. Focused on the relationship of Doc, an alcoholic who, despite his name, never completed his medical training, and his slovenly wife, Lola, a dreamer who is obsessed with her lost dog, Little Sheba. Doc resents the boyfriend of their boarder, Marie, a college coed, without realizing his sexual feelings for her. Marie's impending marriage causes Doc to go on a bender, but he returns to Lola without any resolution of their unhappy relationship. Booth repeated her performance in a 1952 film version, winning an Academy Award and a Golden Globe Award playing opposite Burt Lancaster as Doc. A 2008 **Manhattan Theatre Club** revival starred Kevin Anderson and S. Epatha Merkerson, who received a Tony nomination for her performance.

COME BLOW YOUR HORN. **Neil Simon**, one of the most prolific and popular American playwrights of the 1960s to 1980s, scored his first **Broadway** success with this three-act comedy, which opened on 22 February 1961 at the BROOKS ATKINSON Theatre for 677 performances. Alan Baker (Hal March) is a happy-go-lucky playboy at odds with his parents, who disapprove of his lifestyle, and Connie, a girlfriend who intends a more serious commitment from him than a casual **sexual** encounter. When Alan's younger brother, Buddy (Warren Berlinger), runs away from home and into Alan's bachelor pad, Alan comes to a reckoning with his parents (**Lou Jacobi** and **Pert Kelton**) and Connie. A 1963 screen version starred Frank Sinatra, Tony Bill, Barbara Rush, **Lee J. Cobb**, and MOLLY PICON.

COMMAND DECISION. William Wister Haines's three-act drama, which he had first written in the form of a novel, opened 1 October 1947 at the Fulton Theatre for 409 performances in a **Kermit Bloomgarden** production directed by John O'Shaughnessy with scene design by JO MIELZINER. Set in the headquarters of the Fifth American Bombardment Division in England during World WAR II, Brigadier General Dennis, played by Paul Kelly in a **Tony Award**-nominated performance, has a tense relationship with his officers, including one, played by James Whitmore (who won a Tony and a **Theatre World Award**), who sees Dennis as power hungry and recklessly sending too many men on what amount to suicide missions. Dennis also resists orders when he believes more important targets can be taken out. When Dennis leaves for a new assignment in the South Pacific, he admits the constant stress of his job nearly drove him to suicide, the fate of his predecessor.

COMMUNITY THEATRE.[†] Community theatre, which might generally be defined as theatre created by and for a given community, came to mean amateur theatre in the post-World WAR II era. However, the small, often experimental operations that emerged in the Little Theatre movement* of the early twentieth century were often essentially professional operations. Typically intended to promote new playwrights and experimental theatre techniques without commercial pressure, little theatres proliferated, although few were long-lived. The designation as a movement came after the 1915 openings of the most important of these theatres, including the Washington Square Players,* Provincetown Players,* and NEIGHBORHOOD PLAYHOUSE. Percy MacKaye* may be the first American theatre artist to promote the notion of such theatres in his book, *The Playhouse and the Play* (1909), but earlier initiatives, notably Jane Addams's Hull House Players* in Chicago, Illinois, in 1897 established a model. Chicago became a hotbed of little theatres between 1900 and 1925, with many—for example, Maurice Browne's* Chicago Little Theatre (1919)—operating only briefly. Others, like Detroit's Arts and Crafts Theatre run by Samuel J. Hume,* did significant work in introducing modernist European trends to the U.S.

Some little theatres focused on producing new plays, as in the case of the Provincetown Players, who gave early opportunities to EUGENE O'NEILL and SUSAN GLASPELL. Others, like the Detroit Arts and Crafts Theatre, stressed European plays and techniques, particularly those in the social problem play style perfected of HENRIK IBSEN and GEORGE BERNARD SHAW. Still others devoted attention to the cultures of immigrant groups in their community, while some, like New York's LAFAYETTE PLAYERS and Cleveland's Karamu House,* elevated the quality of theatrical opportunities for **African Americans**. The Little Theatre Movement laid the foundation for the rise of community theatres in the 1930s and after, which in turn prepared audiences for the great network of professional **regional** resident non-profit theatres that developed in the 1960s. In most cases, after the 1960s, most community theatres were wholly amateur, with perhaps the exception of a professional artistic director and/or designer. Community theatres range in quality and, unfortunately, have often been stigmatized, as in the screen comedy *Waiting for Guffman* (1996), which depicts a hapless community theatre group and their backstage shenanigans. However, most community theatres deliver high-quality performances and, in many cases, provide the only theatre available in smaller towns.

CONDUCT OF LIFE, THE. **Maria Irene Fornés**'s 19-scene play opened at the **Theatre for the New City** on 21 February 1985 under her direction. In the play, an ambitious officer in a Latin American army under a repressive regime creates a power structure in his own home, in which he has a wife and a young mistress he has abducted. As a male, the officer is seen as a dictator in his bedroom, easily able to dominate both women though **sex** and violence in a metaphor of the unchanging nature of power structures in a male-dominated society. CRITICS resisted the play, with Herbert Mitgang writing in the *New York Times*, describing it as a "numbing" experience, although **feminist** groups and Hispanic theatre companies gave the play life after its initial run. *See also* CHICANO THEATRE.

CONGDON, CONSTANCE (1944–). Born in Rock Rapids, Iowa, but raised in Colorado, Congdon completed an M.F.A. from the University of Massachusetts in 1982 and embarked on a playwriting career that has reaped more than 30 plays. She is best known for *Tales of the Lost Formicans* (1988), for which she won an Oppenheimer **Award** for its satire of a troubled family in suburbia observed by aliens. Congdon's other plays include *Gilgamesh* (1977), *Fourteen Brilliant Colors* (1977), *The Bride* (1980), *Native American* (1984), *No Mercy* (1985), an adaptation of Mark Twain's *The Gilded Age* (1986), *A Conversation with Georgia O'Keefe* (1987), *Casanova* (1989), *Time Out of Time* (1990), *Losing Father's Body* (1992), and several **children's** plays, including *Automata Pieta* (2000). Congdon teaches at Amherst College and **Tony Kushner** describes her as "one of the best playwrights this language has produced."

CONKLE, E. P. (1899–1994). Ellsworth Prouty Conkle was born in Peru, Nebraska, and studied under George Pierce Baker* at Yale University, earned a Ph.D. at the University of Iowa, and, as a teacher of playwriting there, counted **Tennessee Williams** among his students. From 1939 to 1973, he taught at the University of Texas at Austin. Author of over 50 plays, he excelled at capturing the folksy humor of small-town Midwestern life of a generation earlier. *Sparkin'* was his best-known one-act in that vein. The full-length *Prologue to Glory* (1938) concerning the early life of Abraham

Lincoln was produced on **Broadway** by the **Federal Theatre Project** and became the basis for a later CBS radio series titled *Honest Abe*.

CONKLIN, JOHN (1937–). Scene and sometime costume designer on **Broadway**, in **regional theatres**, and in opera, Conklin was educated at Yale University and did his earliest work at the **Williamstown Theatre Festival**. He worked with the **Hartford Stage Company** and in other regional theatres, as well as on **Broadway**, where he was nominated for a **Tony Award** for *The Au Pair Man* in 1974 and a **Drama Desk Award** for a 1974 revival of *Cat on a Hot Tin Roof*. **Off-Broadway**, Conklin was Drama Desk-nominated for a revival of *'Tis Pity She's a Whore* in 1992. He began to teach design at New York University in 1980 while continuing his own work as a designer. On Broadway, his other productions include *Tchin-Tchin* (1962), *Tambourines to Glory* (1963), *Scratch* (1971), *Lorelei* (1974), *The Leaf People* (1975), *Rex* (1976), a revival of *Romeo and Juliet* in 1977, *Bully* (1988), and revivals of *The Bacchae* in 1980, *The Philadelphia Story* in 1980, *Awake and Sing!* in 1984, and *A Streetcar Named Desire* in 1988. After 1990, he more exclusively worked on operas with major U.S. and European companies and other regional theatres. In 1992, he wrote, directed, and designed *The Carving of Mount Rushmore* for **Actors Theatre of Louisville**, a work demonstrating his interest in history, art, and architectural structures.

CONKLIN, PEGGY (1906–2003). Born Margaret Eleanor Conklin in Dobbs Ferry, New York, in impoverished circumstances, she graduated from high school and set out for New York City to be an actress. Her first **Broadway** opportunities were in the choruses of the MUSICALS *Treasure Girl* (1928) and *The Little Show* (1929). Within a short time, she appeared in roles in comedies and dramas, usually in ingénue roles, including *Old Man Murphy* (1931), *Mademoiselle* (1932), and *The Pursuit of Happiness* (1933) before scoring a notable success as the yearning heroine Gabby Maple in ROBERT E. SHERWOOD's *The Petrified Forest* (1935), playing opposite LESLIE HOWARD and Humphrey Bogart. Conklin continued to act on Broadway in such plays as *Co-respondent Unknown* (1936), *Yes, My Darling Daughter* (1937), *Casey Jones* (1938), *Miss Swan Expects* (1939), *Mr. and Mrs. North* (1941), *Feather in a Gale* (1943), *Alice in Arms* (1945), *The Wisteria Trees* (1950), *Picnic* (1953), and *Howie* (1958). Conklin also appeared in films and television dramas during the 1950s.

CONNECTION, THE. Realistically depicting the down-and-out lives of drug addicts, **Jack Gelber**'s two-act play opened on 15 July 1959 for 722 performances in a production of **The Living Theatre**. The simple plot involves an addict, Leach, awaiting the return of his supplier, Cowboy. Cowboy returns instead with the idealistic Sister Salvation, who hopes to reform the addicts, but she realizes there is nothing she can do. The play made use of a framing device in which characters are able to step out of the play to provide some context and a jazz score by Freddie Redd enhanced the environment. *The Connection* won a Best Play **Obie Award** despite audience puzzlement, both in New York and in London. The production was filmed in 1961 and raised **censorship** issues over its content and language. The play was revived in 1980 at New York's Henry Street Settlement and **The Living Theatre** revived it in 2008 under the direction of **Judith Malina**, who also played Sister Salvation.

CONNELLY, MARC (1890–1981).[†] Born in McKeesport, Pennsylvania, Marcus Cook Connelly's long career as a playwright, occasional actor, producer, and director began with amateur theatricals in his hometown. His first **Broadway** contribution was as librettist of a failed MUSICAL, but his career truly began in collaboration with GEORGE S. KAUFMAN for *Dulcy** (1921), *To the Ladies** (1922), *Merton of the Movies** (1922), and *Beggar on Horseback** (1924), among others. Working solo, Connelly won the PULITZER PRIZE for *The Green Pastures* (1930), which he also directed, a long-running adaptation of Roark Bradford's folk tales of **African American** life that ran for well over 600 performances. In 1934, Connelly collaborated with Frank B. Elser on *The Farmer Takes a Wife*, which provided **Henry Fonda** with his first important Broadway role. Connelly's forays into acting included playing the Stage Manager in **Thornton Wilder**'s *Our Town* for a 1944 revival and in *Tall Story* (1959). As a director (and producer), *Having Wonderful Time* (1937) was the peak, although most of his subsequent solo and collaborative writing projects were unsuccessful, including his last play, *The Stitch in Time* (1981), which folded before opening shortly after Connelly's death.

CONROY, FRANCES (1953–). A respected actress in theatre, film, and television, Frances Conroy was born in Monroe, Georgia, and studied at Dickinson University, THE NEIGHBORHOOD PLAYHOUSE, and the Juilliard School. She began her career with the Juilliard's touring organization, **The Acting Company**, and worked steadily in **regional theatre**. **Off-Broadway** she appeared in *Othello* with Richard Dreyfuss and **Raúl Juliá** in 1980, receiving a **Drama Desk Award** nomination prior to her **Broadway** debut in **Edward Albee**'s *The Lady from Dubuque* (1980). She appeared Off-Broadway in **Tony Kushner**'s *A Bright Room Called Day* (1991) and on Broadway in a 1988 revival of *Our Town* and received another Drama Desk nomination for *The Secret Rapture* (1989). She also received Drama Desk nominations for *In the Summer House* (1994) and *The Rehearsal* (1997) and **Tony Award** and Drama Desk nominations for *The Ride Down Mt. Morgan* (2000). Conroy's other Broadway appearances include *Some Americans Abroad* (1990), *Two Shakespearean Actors* (1992), *Broken Glass* (1994), and revivals of *The Little Foxes* in 1997 and *Ring Round the Moon* in 1999. Her work on television includes her acclaimed work on the HBO-TV series *Six Feet Under* (2001–2005) which brought her a Golden Globe Award, Screen Actors Guild Award, and four Emmy Award nominations, and she has appeared in many films.

CONTEMPORARY THEATRE, INC., A. This Seattle, Washington-based theatre was founded in 1965 by University of Washington School of Drama director Gregory Arthur Falls with the goal of providing the Seattle-area theatrical **community** with quality contemporary theatre. It has staged over 100 productions and although it struggled with significant financial problems in the early 2000s, the theatre has survived and produced premieres or New York transfers of plays by Martin McDonagh, Philip Glass, Pamela Gien, **Alan Arkin**, and **Elaine May**, and others.

CONWAY, KEVIN (1942–). New York-born actor and director trained by **Uta Hagen**, Conway has appeared in numerous film and television roles, often as a menacing figure, as well as making frequent stage appearances. **Off-Broadway**, Conway has appeared in *Muzeeka* (1968), *One Flew Over the Cuckoo's Nest* (1973), *When You Comin' Back, Red Ryder?* (1973), which brought him a **Drama Desk Award**, and *Other People's Money* (1989). Conway won another Drama Desk Award, as a director, for *Mecca* (1980). On **Broadway**, he debuted in **Arthur Kopit**'s *Indians* (1969), followed by *Moonchildren* (1972), revivals of *The Plough and the Stars* in 1973 and *Of Mice and Men* in 1974, *The Elephant Man* (1979), *On the Waterfront* (1995), and in a revival of *Dinner at Eight* in 2002. His film appearances include *Slaughterhouse-Five* (1972), *Portnoy's Complaint* (1972), *Paradise Alley* (1978), *Rambling Rose* (1991), and *The Quick and the Dead* (1995), and he has appeared frequently on television.

COOK, DONALD (1901–1961). A native of Portland, Oregon, Cook debuted on **Broadway** in *Seed of the Brute* (1926), with numerous subsequent appearances, including *New York Exchange* (1927), *Paris Bound** (1927), *Rebound* (1930), *Skylark* (1939), *Claudia* (1941), *Foolish Notion* (1945), *Made in Heaven* (1946), *Portrait in Black* (1947), a revival of *Private Lives* costarring with TALLULAH BANKHEAD in 1948, *The Moon Is Blue* (1951),

King of Hearts (1954), *Champagne Complex* (1955), and *Goodbye Again* (1956), among others. Cook appeared in over 50 films, most notably as the upright brother of James Cagney's hoodlum in *The Public Enemy* (1931) and as Helen Morgan's husband in *Show Boat* (1936), as well as *Baby Face* (1933), *Viva Villa!* (1934), and in the role of Ellery Queen in *The Spanish Cape Mystery* (1935), as well as television dramas in the 1950s.

COPPERFIELD, DAVID (1956–   ). David Seth Kotkin was born in Metuchen, New Jersey, to Jewish parents prior to attending Fordham University. A fan of **Broadway musicals**, and interested in magic since childhood, he renamed himself David Copperfield and began to appear on stages and television as an illusionist in increasingly elaborate productions. He won an Emmy Award for specials in which he made everything from a jet to the Statue of Liberty disappear. His act merges music, magic, dance, and often a story. He brought a stage show to Broadway titled *David Copperfield: Dreams and Nightmares* (1996), but most frequently appears in Las Vegas and on tour.

CORIO, ANN (1909–1999). Born Anna Corea in Hartford, Connecticut, to an Italian immigrant family of 14 children, Corio worked as a showgirl beginning as a voluptuous teenager. Within a few years, she became one of the leading striptease artists working in BURLESQUE, including Minsky's Burlesque in New York and the Howard Theatre in Boston. When crusading New York mayor Fiorello La Guardia clamped down on burlesque theatres, Corio moved to Los Angeles and worked in small roles in B-films, including *Jungle Siren* (1941). As she aged and the era of burlesque became nostalgia, Corio directed, wrote, and appeared in a **Broadway** production, *This Was Burlesque* (1965), a rose-colored memoir of her career. A revised version of the show returned to Broadway in 1981, and Corio appeared again, despite being in her 70s.

CORNELL, KATHARINE (1893–1974).[†] Among the most versatile, respected stage actresses of the first half of the twentieth century, Cornell moved with ease from comedy to drama, from the classics to contemporary plays. Her father had been a theatre manager, but Cornell was born in Berlin, Germany, where her father had moved to study medicine. Her first significant stage appearance was with the prestigious Washington Square Players* in 1916, but she spent a lengthy apprenticeship in STOCK before scoring a personal success on **Broadway** in *Nice People** (1921). Cornell's performance in the title role of the 1924 revival of GEORGE BERNARD SHAW's *Candida* elevated her stature (and she frequently appeared in revivals and tours in it) and was followed by a series of roles that gained her the reputation of one of the era's finest actresses with leading roles in *The Green Hat* (1925), *The Letter** (1927), *The Age of Innocence* (1928), *Dishonored Lady* (1930), and her greatest triumph, the role of Elizabeth Barrett in **The Barretts of Wimpole Street** (1931), with which she became a manager in partnership with her husband, director GUTHRIE MCCLINTIC, whom she had married in 1921. McClintic enhanced Cornell's stature as a leading lady in the romantic tradition—and she dominated the Broadway stage (and on tour) prior to World War II. She continued with success afterward, although her style was less favored after the rise of "method acting." Although ironically she worked with and encouraged the careers of several of the new wave actors, including **Marlon Brando**.

Like her contemporaries HELEN HAYES and TALLULAH BANKHEAD, Cornell committed herself to lengthy, arduous tours with her successes—in 1934 she played *The Barretts of Wimpole Street* in nearly 80 cities in little more than half a year, demonstrating that the road still had viability despite the damage done by the popularity of sound films. Cornell frequently claimed not to enjoy acting, but she was widely admired for her graceful, impassioned performances. Her career continued without abatement through roles in Shaw's *Saint Joan* (1936) and *The Doctor's Dilemma* (1941), S. N. BEHRMAN's *No Time for Comedy* (1939) with a young **Laurence Olivier** in support, and a critically admired 1942 revival of **Anton Chekhov**'s *The Three Sisters* in which she played Masha opposite **Ruth Gordon** (Natalya) and **Judith Anderson** (Olga).

During the war years, Cornell performed her most celebrated roles for American military personnel during long, arduous, and dangerous tours before returning to Broadway in *Antigone* (1946), *Antony and Cleopatra* (1947), *The Constant Wife* (1951), *The Prescott Proposals* (1953), *The Dark Is Light Enough* (1955), and *Dear Liar* (1960), her final role playing Mrs. Patrick Campbell. Cornell lost interest in performing after McClintic's 1961 death and spent her final years in retirement. Little-known today because she eschewed film roles, Cornell appeared only once—and briefly—on screen, playing herself in an all-star WARtime film, *Stage Door Canteen* (1943), in which she touchingly obliges an admiring young soldier by delivering a speech from *Romeo and Juliet*. In 2010, Cornell was the central character (played by **Kate Burton**) in **A. R. Gurney**'s **The Grand Manner** at **Lincoln Center**.

CORPUS CHRISTI. Terrence McNally's **Drama Desk, New York Drama Critics Award**, and **Outer Critics Critics Circle Award**-winning modern-day passion play opened at the **Manhattan Theatre Club (MTC)** on 13

October 1998 under the direction of **Joe Mantello**. The mere announcement of a play depicting Jesus Christ and his apostles as a group of **gay** men in present-day Texas set off a storm of controversy led by the Catholic League. Death threats directed at McNally and bomb threats at the MTC caused the theatre to withdraw the play, which set off another controversy from artists demanding that it proceed as a matter of artistic freedom. The MTC relented and the play was performed despite protesting picketers. *See also* CENSORSHIP.

COSTUME DESIGN. *See* DESIGN/DESIGNERS.

COTTEN, JOSEPH (1905–1994). Born Joseph Cheshire Cotton in a well-to-do family in Petersburg, Virginia, Cotten attended the Hickman School of Speech and Expression in Washington, D.C. He worked in advertising and as a theatre CRITIC, which led him toward work as an actor. He appeared on **Broadway** in *Absent Father* (1932), *Jezebel* (1933), and *Loose Moments* (1935), but he rose to prominence in 1937 as a member of **Orson Welles's Mercury Theatre**, appearing in their revivals of *Julius Caesar* in 1937, *Shoemaker's Holiday* in 1938, and *Danton's Death* in 1938. When Welles went to Hollywood to film *Citizen Kane* (1941), Cotten was a central member of the cast and played the lead in Welles's second film, *The Magnificent Ambersons* (1942), and they occasionally worked together over subsequent decades. As a result of these films, Cotten became a major film star, appearing in such classics as *Shadow of a Doubt* (1943), *Gaslight* (1944), *Since You Went Away* (1944), *Duel in the Sun* (1946), *The Farmer's Daughter* (1947), *Portrait of Jennie* (1948), *The Third Man* (1949), *Hush, Hush, Sweet Charlotte* (1964), and *A Delicate Balance* (1973). He also returned with some frequency to Broadway, starring opposite **Katharine Hepburn** in *The Philadelphia Story* (1939), and appearing in *Sabrina Fair* (1953), *Once More with Feeling* (1958), and *Calculated Risk* (1962).

COUNSELLOR-AT-LAW. ELMER RICE's three-act drama of a day in the life of a personally and professionally embattled lawyer opened on 6 November 1931 for 292 performances at the Plymouth Theatre under the direction of Rice. PAUL MUNI scored a personal success as George Simon, a successful New York society lawyer who has risen from poverty as the child of Jewish American immigrants. His marriage crumbles as he struggles with his conscience over whether he wants to work for his spoiled clients or to help the disenfranchised in his old neighborhood. The play won critical approval and it was revived successfully in 1942 with Muni again heading the cast for 258 performances. John Barrymore,* in one of his finest screen performances, appeared as Simon in the 1933 film version directed by William Wyler.

COUNTRY GIRL, THE. **Clifford Odets**'s drama of an alcoholic actor, his wife, and a young idealistic director opened on 10 November 1950 for 235 performances at the Lyceum Theatre under Odets's direction, with scenery by **Boris Aronson**, who won a **Tony Award**. **Uta Hagen** also won a Tony as Georgie, the loyal wife of the self-destructive actor Frank Elgin (Paul Kelly), who has been given one last chance to redeem his career and self-respect by director Bernie Dodd (Steven Hill). Bernie becomes enamored of Georgie while struggling to hold Elgin together for the sake of the play and his life. Despite feelings for Bernie, Georgie stands by Elgin. A 1954 film version starred Bing Crosby, **Grace Kelly** (in an Academy Award-winning performance), and William Holden, and the play has been revived on **Broadway** twice, in 1972 starring **Jason Robards** (in a Tony-nominated performance), **Maureen Stapleton**, and **George Grizzard**, and in 2008 with **Morgan Freeman**, Frances McDormand (in a **Drama Desk Award**-nominated performance), and **Peter Gallagher**.

COWARD, NOËL (1899–1973). English-born playwright, actor, composer, librettist, and producer, Coward was one of the signal figures of London and New York stages from the 1920s to the 1960s. Most of his works, which included high comedies, dramas, operettas,* and MUSICALS, were first performed in England, but most appeared on **Broadway**, occasionally with Coward appearing in them as well, most memorably partnered with **Gertrude Lawrence** in *Private Lives* in 1931 and *Tonight at 8:30* in 1936. Coward also appeared on Broadway in *The Vortex* (1925), *This Year of Grace* (1928), *Design for Living* (1933), costarring with ALFRED LUNT and LYNN FONTANNE, *Nude with Violin* (1957), and *Present Laughter* (1958). He was nominated for a **Tony Award** for his direction of *High Spirits* (1964), a musical based on his play *Blithe Spirit*, which had appeared on Broadway in 1941, for his libretto for *The Girl Who Came to Supper* (1964), and he was given a special Tony in 1970 for "his multiple and immortal contributions to the theatre." Coward was knighted in 1970. His plays and musicals are frequently revived on Broadway and in **regional** and university theatres.

COWL, JANE (1884–1950).[†] Born in Boston, Massachusetts, Cowl made her **Broadway** debut in David Belasco's* *Sweet Kitty Bellairs** (1903), after which she appeared in several Belasco productions. She attained stardom in the long-running thriller *Within the Law** (1912), beginning a long and admired stage career. Also a dramatist, Cowl acted in plays she wrote or cowrote, including *Lilac Time* (1917) and *Smilin' Through* (1920). She scored a major success in a revival of *Romeo and Juliet* (1923) and won critical approval in **Noël Coward**'s *Easy Virtue* (1925) and ROBERT E. SHERWOOD'S

The Road to Rome* (1927). After 1930, her notable appearances were in Katherine Dayton and GEORGE S. KAUFMAN's *First Lady* (1935), **Thornton Wilder**'s failed *The Merchant of Yonkers* (1938), and **John Van Druten**'s *Old Acquaintance* (1940). Her final Broadway appearances, in *Ring around Elizabeth* (1941) and *The First Mrs. Fraser* (1947), were failures. Cowl appeared in two silent films and late in her career five sound films, including *Payment on Demand* (1951), released after her death.

CRADLE WILL ROCK, THE. This MUSICAL allegory by Marc Blitzstein, produced by **John Houseman** for the **Federal Theatre Project (FTP)** with **Orson Welles** directing, has taken on legendary status due to its opening-night battle between government authorities attempting to shut it down (ostensibly on the grounds of "budget cuts") and Welles, Houseman, and company who were determined to open the production. On opening night, 16 June 1937, when the Maxine Elliott Theatre was padlocked, preventing access to scenery and costumes, Welles and Houseman rented the vacant Venice Theatre and, despite threats from ACTORS' EQUITY that the cast could not perform onstage, the actors delivered their performances from the audience and all over the theatre, with the result that it became one of the most talked-about productions in FTP's history (it reopened on 3 January 1938 for 108 performances at the Windsor Theatre) although it also contributed to a mounting desire on the part of conservative political forces to close down this Works Progress Administration program of the New Deal. Subsequently revived on **Broadway** in 1947, on television in 1960, **Off-Broadway** in 1964, and in a 1983 tour of **The Acting Company** (which played in London in 1985, winning leading lady **Patti LuPone** an **Olivier** Award), the original production and its off-stage battles were dramatized in Tim Robbins's 1999 all-star film, *Cradle Will Rock. See also* CENSORSHIP.

CRAVEN, FRANK (1875–1945).[†] Born in Boston, Massachusetts, Craven acted from childhood and toured widely prior to branching out as a playwright. From the 1910s, he wrote many of his own vehicles: *Too Many Cooks** (1914), *This Way Out* (1917), *The First Year** (1920), *Money From Home* (1927), and *The Nineteenth Hole* (1927). With the dawn of sound films, Craven went into motion pictures, appearing in *State Fair* (1933), *City for Conquest* (1940), *In This Our Life* (1942), and *Keeper of the Flame* (1942). He returned to **Broadway** occasionally, most notably to originate the role of the Stage Manager in **Thornton Wilder**'s *Our Town* (1938), an acclaimed performance he repeated in the 1940 film version. His other later Broadway appearances include *Village Green* (1951), *The Flowers of Virtue* (1942), and *Mrs. January and Mr. X* (1944).

CRAWFORD, CHERYL (1902–1986). An Akron, Ohio, native, Crawford studied drama at Smith College and moved to New York, becoming a major American producer and director after appearing as an actress in two **Broadway** productions, *Juarez and Maximilian* (1926) and *The Brothers Karamazov* (1927). Her initial fame came in collaboration with **Harold Clurman** and **Lee Strasberg** when they founded **The Group Theatre** (1931–1940) and although she directed, including **Sidney Kingsley**'s PULITZER PRIZE-winner, *Men in White* (1933), she decided to focus on producing, scoring a notable success with The Group's *Golden Boy* (1937). She partnered with EVA LE GALLIENNE in 1946 to found the **American Repertory Theatre**, which only lasted a season, and in 1947, with **Elia Kazan** and **Robert Lewis**, she established **The Actors Studio**, which subsequently trained some of the most important American actors after **Lee Strasberg** became artistic director in 1951. Among Crawford's more notable Broadway productions are a revival of *Porgy and Bess* in 1942, *One Touch of Venus* (1943), *Brigadoon* (1947), *Love Life* (1948), *The Tower Beyond Tragedy* (1950), *The Rose Tattoo* (1951), *Paint Your Wagon* (1951), *Camino Real* (1953), *Oh, Men! Oh, Women!* (1953), *Sweet Bird of Youth* (1959), *Period of Adjustment* (1960), *Marathon '33* (1963), *Jennie* (1963), *Celebration* (1969), *Yentl* (1975), *The Love Suicide at Schofield Barracks* (1972), and *So Long on Lonely Street* (1986). Crawford's autobiography, *One Naked Individual: My Fifty Years in the Theatre* (1977), chronicled her work in theatre and her extraordinary coworkers.

CRIMES OF THE HEART. **Beth Henley**'s PULITZER PRIZE-winning comedy-drama opened on 8 December 1980 at the **Manhattan Theatre Club** following a production at the **Actors Theatre of Louisville** in 1979. The play reopened on **Broadway** at the John Golden Theatre on 4 November 1981 for 535 performances under the direction of Melvin Bernhardt, receiving a **New York Drama Critics Circle Award** and a Best Play **Tony Award** nomination. Set in Hazlehurst, Mississippi, the play focuses on three very different troubled sisters, all of whom are facing various problems and repressions, but come together in support of one who has shot and wounded her philandering, abusive husband. Despite their troubles, the sisters remain closely bonded. The play was revived **Off-Broadway** at the **Second Stage Theatre** in 2001 and at the **Roundabout Theatre Company** in 2008, a production directed by Kathleen Turner that had begun at the **Williamstown Theatre Festival** in 2007. A film version in 1986 starred Diane Keaton, Jessica Lange, Sissy Spacek, and **Sam Shepard**.

CRISTOFER, MICHAEL (1945–). Born Michael Ivan Procaccino in Trenton, New Jersey, this playwright, screenwriter and sometime actor worked in films and television from 1974 before serving for nearly a decade as the coartistic director of River Arts Repertory in Woodstock, New York, where he participated in productions of new works by American playwrights and adapted movies into stage plays. He also directed Joanne Woodward in an adaptation of HENRIK IBSEN's *Ghosts*. Cristofer rose to prominence in 1977 when his play, *The Shadow Box*, about three terminally ill people, won a PULITZER PRIZE and **Tony Award**. The television film version, directed by **Paul Newman**, won a Golden Globe Award and an Emmy nomination. He also directed a 1980 television film of *The Shadow Box* and *Gia* (1998), for which he won a Directors Guild of America Award and an Emmy Award nomination, *Body Shots* (1999), and *Original Sin* (2001) and wrote screenplays for *Falling in Love* (1984), *The Witches of Eastwick* (1992), *The Bonfire of the Vanities* (1990), and *Breaking Up* (1997), based on his play of the same name written in 1993. His other plays include *Americomedia* (1973), *Ice* (1976), *Black Angel* (1978), *C. C. Pyle and the Bunyon Derby* (1978), *The Lady and the Clarinet* (1980), *Execution of the Caregiver* (1993), *Amazing Grace* (1995), and *Tabarjaby* (2006). Cristofer returned to the stage as an actor in 2009, appearing in the premiere of **Tony Kushner**'s *The Intelligent Homosexual's Guide to Capitalism and Socialism with a Key to the Scriptures* at the **Guthrie Theatre**, and in a **Broadway** revival of **Arthur Miller**'s *A View from the Bridge* in 2010.

CRITICS, CRITICISM.[†] Dramatic criticism in the United States dates to before the American Revolution when reviews of plays, often anonymous, appeared in various publications before and after the WAR. Washington Irving is often identified as the first true critic for reviews he wrote on New York theatre for the *Salmagundi* (1807) and *Select Reviews* (1815). A slang term calling theatre critics "aisle sitters" emerged sometime in the nineteenth century since critics were typically given aisle seats so that they could rush from the theatre to their newspaper office in time to bang out a review that could appear in the morning edition. A critic might be barred from a particular theatre for publishing some comment at which the theatre manager or producer might take offense. Augustin Daly* attempted to have the *San Francisco Evening Post* critic ejected from the theatre where his company was performing, because a prior review had failed to mention the star, Ada Rehan,* and in the 1960s, **Broadway** producer **David Merrick** invited several ordinary citizens with the same names as the New York critics to see a performance of one of his productions, after which he published their glowing comments in newspaper advertisements to make it appear the real critics were unanimous in their praise.

Reputations of critics are usually based on their ability to respond to developing trends and this was certainly true of the leading American critics of the later half of the nineteenth century, including William Dean Howells,* Edward Dithmar,* and James Hunecker, who both admired the emergence of REALISM in European drama and lauded U.S. playwrights moving in that direction. In the twentieth century, the major American critics in the first decades were greatly influenced by Howells, Dithmar, and Hunecker, most particularly GEORGE JEAN NATHAN, ALEXANDER WOOLLCOTT, Percy Hammond,* all of whom began their careers—in some cases very long careers—in the first two decades of the twentieth century. The next generation, Burns Mantle,* BROOKS ATKINSON, John Anderson,* **Gilbert Gabriel**, **John Mason Brown**, **Richard Watts, Jr.** wrote for the many New York newspapers. In periodicals, leading critics included STARK YOUNG, JOSEPH WOOD KRUTCH, ROBERT BENCHLEY, ROSAMOND GILDER, KENNETH MACGOWAN, and EDITH J. R. ISAACS, and others led the charge prior to 1930. After 1930, some reviewers, most particularly Atkinson, writing in the *New York Times*, continued, although he was increasingly inclined to resist changing social mores reflected in the drama and new techniques, particularly after World War II.

Critics in other major cities exerted more than regional influences after 1930, among them Henry Taylor Parker, **Claudia Cassidy**, **Elliot Norton**, and **Richard Coe** were admired, and later in the twentieth century they were succeeded by such critics as **Kevin Kelly**, **Richard Christiansen**, **Dan Sullivan**, **Sylvie Drake**, and Peter Marks. In the postwar era, **Walter Kerr**, a learned theatre historian, brought a stronger contextualizing voice to the *New York Times*, while the impact of modern European theatre and vast social changes were more fully acknowledged by critics like **Harold Clurman**, **Eric Bentley**, **Robert Brustein**, **Stanley Kauffmann**, **Henry Hewes**, **Wolcott Gibbs**, **Brendan Gill**, **Edith Oliver**, **Louis Kronenberger**, **T. E. Kalem**, **Jack Kroll**, and others. **John Simon**, perhaps the most controversial critic since the 1960s, is admired for the quality of his writing, but he has frequently met with outrage for nasty attacks on the personal appearance of performers whose features fail to please him. After the 1980s, critics focused on new developments in theatre continued to attract a readership, including **Michael Feingold**, **Julius Novick**, **Michael Kuchwara**, Alisa Solomon, Charles McNulty, although the seriously diminished number of newspapers and, ultimately, magazines in the late twentieth century made it challenging for theatergoers to find criticism.

For Broadway, **Off-Broadway**, and **Off-Off Broadway**, the *New York Times* critic still held considerable power over the fortunes of productions.

Frank Rich, the *Times* critic from 1980–1993, was much admired for the erudition of his writing, and he was succeeded by **Ben Brantley** and **Charles Isherwood**. In **periodicals**, **John Lahr** excels as critic for the *New Yorker*, also writing occasional profiles of major theatrical and film figures, but Lahr is one of the few remaining magazine critics provided ample space for an in-depth review. Academic periodicals often feature theatre reviews by scholars; however, many are quarterly publications and by the time a review appears, the production has usually long since closed.

Media criticism dates to the early days of commercial radio after World War I—and television news programs, particularly in the 1950s and 1960s, featured short theatre reviews, although these are now rare and most media reviewers cover only film. Internet sites offer criticism and bloggers write about theatre, but with no discernible impact on the development of contemporary theatre.

CROMER, DAVID (1965–). Born in Skokie, Illinois, Cromer studied at Columbia College in Chicago, although he did not complete a degree, after which he made a name for himself as an actor and director in Chicago-area theatre in the 1990s. He directed a scaled-down production of **Thornton Wilder**'s *Our Town*, in which he also played the Stage Manager, for Chicago's **Steppenwolf Theatre**, and it moved **Off-Broadway** in 2009 to critical kudos. Cromer has numerous credits in **regional theatre** and in Chicago, including **Austin Pendleton**'s *Orson's Shadow* (2005). His 2008 Off-Broadway revivals of ELMER RICE's *The Adding Machine** brought him **Obie** and **Lucille Lortel Awards** and a **Drama Desk Award** nomination. In 2009, Cromer's critically praised **Broadway** revival of **Neil Simon**'s *Brighton Beach Memoirs* folded after only a week of performances, and he directed *When the Rain Stops Falling* (2009) at **Lincoln Center**. Of Cromer's work, André Bishop has said, "To me, he has all the skills of an old-time Broadway director with all the emotion and inner life of the new breed."

CRONYN, HUME (1911–2003). Born in London, Ontario, Canada, as Hume Blake Cronyn, he attended Ridley College and McGill University in Montreal. His family intended him to follow a law career, but he chose to study acting with MAX REINHARDT and at the AMERICAN ACADEMY OF DRAMATIC ART. He made his **Broadway** debut in the flop *Hipper's Holiday* (1934), after which he replaced an actor in the hit *Boy Meets Girl* (1935). From 1935 to 1941, Cronyn appeared in *High Tor* (1937), *There's Always a Breeze* (1938), *Escape This Night* (1938), *Off to Buffalo* (1938), a revival of *The Three Sisters* in 1939, *The Weak Link* (1940), *Retreat to Pleasure* (1940), and *Mr. Big* (1941). Cronyn spent time in Hollywood as a character actor for much of the 1940s, appearing in character roles in such notable films as *Shadow of a Doubt* (1943), *Phantom of the Opera* (1943), *Lifeboat* (1944), and *The Postman Always Rings Twice* (1946), and he received a Supporting Actor Academy Award nomination for *The Seventh Cross* (1944).

Cronyn married British-born actress **Jessica Tandy** in 1942, after which they frequently acted together on stage and screen. He returned to Broadway in 1948 for a flop, *The Survivors* (1948), and two other failures, *Now I Lay Me Down to Sleep* (1950) and *Hilda Crane* (1950), but he and Tandy won critical praise and a long run in ***The Fourposter*** (1951). Throughout the 1950s, he remained busy, including acting in such plays as *Madam, Will You Walk* (1953), which he also directed, *The Honeys* (1955), *A Day By the Sea* (1955), *The Man in the Dog Suit* (1958), and *Triple Play* (1959), which he also directed. Cronyn and Tandy were part of the **Guthrie Theatre** company for a time and, after 1960, his Broadway appearances were in increasingly distinguished plays and productions.

Cronyn was nominated for a **Tony Award** for *Big Fish, Little Fish* (1961) and won a Tony for his performance as Polonius in the **Richard Burton** *Hamlet* (1964). He was nominated again for Tonys for *A Delicate Balance* (1967) and ***The Gin Game*** (1978). Other Broadway appearances included *The Physicists* (1964), *Promenade All* (1972), *Noël Coward in Two Keys* (1974), *Foxfire* (1982), which he cowrote with Susan Cooper, and *The Petition* (1986). Cronyn's later film appearances include ***Sunrise at Campobello*** (1960), *Cleopatra* (1963), *The World According to Garp* (1982), *Cocoon* (1985), and *Marvin's Room* (1996).

Cronyn also appeared in numerous television dramas beginning at the dawn of the medium in virtually all of the important "anthology" series from the earliest days of television. Cronyn won three Emmy Awards for the television movies *Age-Old Friends* (1989), ***Broadway Bound*** (1992), and *To Dance with the White Dog* (1993) and he shared a Writer's Guild Award with Susan Cooper for the TV film *The Dollmaker* (1984). Cronyn and Tandy were presented with a special **Drama Desk Award** in 1986 and a Lifetime Achievement Tony in 1994, shortly before her death. Cronyn continued working as an actor until shortly before his death at age 91.

CROSSROADS THEATRE, THE. Established by cofounders Ricardo Khan and L. Kenneth Richardson in New Brunswick, New Jersey, in 1978 with a commitment to plays examining the **African American** experience, Crossroads received the 1999 **Tony Award** for Outstanding Regional Theatre. Among the plays premiered at Crossroads, standouts include **George C. Wolfe**'s *The Colored Museum* (1986) and *Spunk* (1989), and other productions include works by **August Wilson, Pearl Cleage, Ntozake Shange**, Mbongeni Ngema, **Ruby Dee**, Rita Dove, and others.

CROTHERS, RACHEL (1878–1958).† Born in Bloomington, Illinois, Crothers attended Illinois State Normal School and studied drama in New York and Boston before beginning a theatrical career that made her the most renowned American female playwright (and director) prior to **Lillian Hellman**. Between 1903 and 1937, she had 28 plays produced on **Broadway**. Her early experience acting in a tour with Hortense Rhéa's* company in Hall Craine's* 1898 play *The Christian** contributed to her understanding of stagecraft. Most of her comedy-dramas depict the difficulties faced by **women**, particularly those trying to earn their way as artists. Her plays reflect the influence of Freud and cover such topics as marriage, divorce, prostitution, women in the workplace, and the gender double standard of her time.

Noteworthy among Crothers's plays, many of which she directed, are *Nora* (1903), *The Three of Us** (1906), *A Man's World** (1910), *The Herfords* (1911; revised in 1920 as *He and She*), *Ourselves* (1913), *Nice People** (1921), *Everyday* (1921), *Mary the Third* (1923), *Expressing Willie** (1924), *A Lady's Virtue* (1925), *The Book of Charm* (1925), *What They Think* (1925), *Venus* (1927), *Exceeding Small* (1928), *Let Us Be Gay** (1929), **As Husbands Go** (1931), *Caught Wet* (1931), **When Ladies Meet** (1932), and *Susan and God* (1937), the last her most acclaimed and commercially successful play.

Crothers often lectured on the drama and she also directed Paul Vincent Carroll's *The Old Foolishness* (1940) on Broadway, but it flopped. Crothers was a significant force in several philanthropic theatrical organizations during both world WARS, including the United Theatre Relief Committee, the Stage Relief Fund,* the Stage Women's War Relief Fund,* and the **American Theatre Wing** for War Relief. A number of Crothers's plays were filmed in both the silent and sound eras, most notably *Susan and God* in 1940, which starred Joan Crawford and **Fredric March**. Of Crothers's achievement, Ethan Mordden writes that she "may have been the first famous American to be called a 'radical **feminist**' decades before the term became current."

CROUSE, RUSSEL (1893–1966). Born in Findlay, Ohio, where he began his working life as a journalist, Crouse turned to acting in the 1920s and did public relations work for THE THEATRE GUILD. After coauthoring two modestly successful MUSICALS, *The Gang's All Here* (1931) and *Hold Your Horses* (1934), he entered a career-long collaboration with HOWARD LINDSAY with Cole Porter's musical *Anything Goes* (1934). They followed this hit with librettos for the musicals *Red, Hot and Blue!* (1936) and *Hooray for What!* (1937). The Crouse-Lindsay team was acknowledged for their craftsmanship and unerring instincts for what mainstream **Broadway** audiences sought in entertainment.

Crouse and Lindsay scored their greatest and most enduring success with the nostalgic comedy *Life with Father* (1939), which ran for years (with Lindsay in the lead) and became the longest-running Broadway play of the time. Crouse and Lindsay also produced several plays, including **Joseph Kesselring**'s hit *Arsenic and Old Lace* (1941), which they were rumored to have rewritten.

In 1945, Crouse and Lindsay received the PULITZER PRIZE for the comedy-drama *State of the Union*, and they contributed librettos for several musicals, including *Call Me Madam* (1950), *Happy Hunting* (1956), *The Sound of Music* (1959), and *Mr. President* (1962), as well as *Life with Mother* (1948), a short-lived sequel to *Life with Father*, and *The Great Sebastians* (1956), which starred ALFRED LUNT and LYNN FONTANNE. Crouse acted in the Crouse-Lindsay comedy *Tall Story* (1959) and served as president of the Authors' League of America. Crouse was the father of actress Lindsay Crouse.

CROWLEY, MART (1935–). Born in Vicksburg, Mississippi, Crowley was educated at Catholic University, after which he worked in television production. Actress Natalie Wood hired him as her personal assistant, which provided time during which he wrote his first play, the groundbreaking comedy-drama *The Boys in the Band* (1968), the first **homosexual**-themed play to succeed on **Broadway**, where it ran for over 1,000 performances and was made into a 1970 film. Crowley's next play, *Remote Asylum* (1970), was not well-received, but his next, *A Breeze from the Gulf* (1973), received a nomination for the Los Angeles Drama Critics Circle Award. In 1979–1980, Crowley was a script editor and producer of the television series *Hart to Hart* and he wrote the television films *Pony* (1986), *Bluegrass* (1988), *People Like Us* (1990), and a *Hart to Hart* reunion movie (1996). Thirty-five years after the premiere of *The Boys in the Band*, Crowley completed a sequel, *The Men from the Boys* (2002). *See also* GAY AND LESBIAN THEATRE.

CRUCIBLE, THE. Arthur Miller's grim drama of the 1692–1693 Salem witch trials in Massachusetts written as a metaphor for the era of the House Un-American Activities Committee (HUAC) "witch hunt" opened on 22 January 1953 for 197 performances at the Martin Beck* Theatre in a **Kermit Bloomgarden** production. Critical reaction acknowledged the contemporary parallels with HUAC and the blacklisting of the era in this seeming historical drama.

Miller researched the actual Salem trials and his characters names are taken from the surviving records, including John Proctor (**Arthur Kennedy**),

Miller's protagonist, a forthright, independent-minded farmer living with his sin of briefly straying from his marriage with a servant girl, Abigail Williams (Madeleine Sherwood), who is displeased when John terminates their affair. Proctor's wife Elizabeth (**Beatrice Straight**) has forgiven him this transgression, but coldness has descended on their relationship. When Abigail and some local girls are caught dancing at night in the woods, they defend themselves by making accusations of witchcraft. When authorities (WALTER HAMPDEN, **E. G. Marshall**, Phillip Coolidge, Fred Stewart) believe their story, Abigail realizes the power that the lie can wield. Ultimately, trials convict innocent individuals of witchcraft, a circumstance manipulated by landowners who are able to profit from the removal of their neighbors from their property, by the local minister who would otherwise have lost his post, and by government officials seeking political gain. Some of the accused refuse to admit their supposed crimes even when faced with torture or execution. When Abigail and an easily manipulated servant girl in the Proctor home manage to implicate John and Elizabeth, Proctor refuses to surrender his good name by signing a confession. Despite the fact that the authorities have considerable evidence to discredit Abigail, the situation continues to spin out of control. Proctor goes to his death refusing to lie to save his skin.

The Crucible, which was only a moderate success in its original production directed by JED HARRIS, has been revived on **Broadway** four times, in 1964 featuring Farley Granger and Denholm Elliott in a short-lived **American National Theatre and Academy (ANTA)** production; in a 1972 **Repertory Theatre of Lincoln Center** production with Robert Foxworth, **Philip Bosco**, Martha Henry, and Pamela Payton-Wright; in a 1991 **National Actors Theatre** production starring Martin Sheen, Maryann Plunkett, **Fritz Weaver**, Michael York, and **Martha Scott**; and in a 2002 **Jujamcyn** production directed by Richard Eyre with a cast including **Liam Neeson**, **Laura Linney**, **Tom Aldredge**, **Brian Murray**, and **John Benjamin Hickey**. In 1957, the play was also adapted by Jean-Paul Sartre for the film *Les Sorcières de Salem,* and Miller wrote an Academy Award-nominated screenplay for a 1996 movie adaptation starring Daniel Day-Lewis, Winona Ryder, **Joan Allen**, and Paul Scofield. A 1967 television production starred **George C. Scott**, **Colleen Dewhurst**, and Tuesday Weld. Composer Robert Ward adapted the play as a PULITZER PRIZE-winning opera.

CRUDUP, BILLY (1968–). William Gaither Crudup was born in Manhasset, New York, and was educated at the University of North Carolina at Chapel Hill and the Tisch School of the Arts at New York University. He made his **Broadway** debut as Septimus Hodge in **Tom Stoppard**'s *Arcadia* (1995) at **Lincoln Center**, winning a **Theatre World Award** and an **Outer Critics**

Circle Award, followed by revivals of *Bus Stop* in 1996, playing Bo Decker opposite the Cherie of **Mary-Louise Parker**, *The Three Sisters* in 1997, and *The Elephant Man* in 2002, which brought him a **Tony Award** nomination. He received another Tony nomination for Martin McDonagh's *The Pillowman* (2005) and won a Tony as Belinsky in Stoppard's *The Coast of Utopia* (2006). He has appeared consistently in films, most notably in *Everyone Says I Love You* (1996), *Inventing the Abbotts* (1997), *Almost Famous* (2000), *Big Fish* (2003), *Stage Beauty* (2004), *The Good Shepherd* (2006), and *Public Enemies* (2009).

CRUZ, NILO (1960–). Born in Matanzas, Cuba, Cruz moved with his family to the "Little Havana" area of Miami, Florida, when he was 10 years old. He became a naturalized citizen of the United States and attended Miami-Dade Community College before moving to New York City. While studying with **Maria Irene Fornés** she recommended him to **Paula Vogel**, who was teaching on the Brown University faculty. Cruz entered Brown and completed an M.F.A. in 1994. In 2001, while working as playwright-in-residence at the New Theatre in Coral Gables, Florida, he completed his play *Anna in the Tropics*, which was awarded the 2003 PULITZER PRIZE for Drama (making him the first Cuban American so honored) and the Steinberg Award for Best New Play. *Anna in the Tropics* moved to **Broadway** in 2003 under **Emily Mann**'s direction and starring Jimmy Smits and Daphne Rubin-Vega, garnering a Best Play **Tony Award** nomination. Cruz's other plays, which all deal with the history and culture of Latinos, include *Dancing on Her Knees* (1994), *Night Train to Bolina* (1995), *A Park in Our House* (1995), *Two Sisters and a Piano* (1998), *A Bicycle Country* (1999), *Hortensia and the Museum of Dreams* (2001), *Lorca in a Green Dress* (2003), *Ybor City* (2003), *Capriccio* (2003), *Beauty of the Father* (2004), and *A Very Old Man with Enormous Wings* (2005). *See also* CHICANO THEATRE.

CSC REPERTORY THEATRE. With a commitment to re-imagining classic plays for a contemporary American audience, Christopher Martin founded the Classic Stage Company, ultimately known as the CSC **Repertory**, in 1967. The company performed in several small spaces until 1974 when it found a permanent home on 13th Street. Martin left the CSC in 1985 and the late 1980s proved a transition period during which the theatre repertoire expanded to include modern classics and occasional new plays. **Carey Perloff** became artistic director in 1987, succeeded in 1992 by **David Esbjornson**. Barry Edelstein became artistic director in 1998, followed in 2003 by **Brian Kulick**, under whose leadership the CSC reemphasized its roots in classical theatre and expanded to add a Young Company with family-oriented productions.

CULLUM, JOHN (1930–). A Knoxville, Tennessee, native who was educated at the University of Tennessee, Cullum won recognition in **Broadway** MUSICALS beginning with *Camelot* (1960), *On a Clear Day You Can See Forever* (1965), for which he received a **Theatre World Award** and a **Tony Award** nomination, *1776* (1969), *Shenandoah* (1975), and *On the Twentieth Century* (1978), winning Tonys for the last two, but he also appeared with regularity in non-musical theatre, including in supporting roles for the **New York Shakespeare Festival** in the early 1960s. He appeared as Laertes in the 1964 **Richard Burton** *Hamlet,* and he stepped into the lead in *Deathtrap* (1979) during its run.

Cullum also appeared in *The Rehearsal* (1963), *Vivat! Vivat Regina!* (1972), *The Trip Back Down* (1977), a 1983 revival of *Private Lives, Doubles* (1985), *The Boys in Autumn* (1986), a 1986 revival of *You Never Can Tell*, and he played Joe Keller in a **Roundabout Theatre** revival of *All My Sons* in 1997. Other **Off-Broadway** appearances include *Whistler* (1982), for which he won a **Drama Desk Award**, *Sin: A Cardinal Deposed* (2004), for which he was Drama Desk-nominated, *The Other Side* (2005), *Cymbeline* (2008), and *The Conscientious Objector* (2008), for which he was again Drama Desk-nominated.

Cullum stepped into the Broadway cast of *August: Osage County* (2009) during its run. His other musical appearances include taking over the title role in *Man of La Mancha* (1966) during its run, *Aspects of Love* (1994), a 1994 revival of *Show Boat*, *Urinetown* (2001), *Dr. Seuss' How the Grinch Stole Christmas!* (2006), and a revival of *110 in the Shade* in 2007, for which he was nominated for a Tony. Cullum has also appeared in numerous film and television roles, including his Emmy Award-nominated role in the TV series *Northern Exposure* (1990–1995).

CULTURE CLASH. Founded on Cinco de Mayo 1984 for Ric Montoya, Richardo Salinas, and Herbert Siguenza, this **Latino** comedy sketch troupe with a strong political voice has performed in many **regional** and university theatres. Their sketch material is taken from interviews with Latino Americans with the goal of expressing cultural changes and frictions through bold satire and impersonations. Typically, they focus on the **community** in which they are performing to express local concerns as well as more universal issues of significance in what they label their "performance collage." *See also* ALTERNATIVE THEATRE; CHICANO THEATRE.

CUMMINGS, CONSTANCE (1910–2005). Born Constance Halverstadt in Seattle, Washington, she debuted on **Broadway** in her late teens, prior to accepting a film contract. In Hollywood, although she appeared with such leading men as PAUL MUNI, SPENCER TRACY, Harold Lloyd, and WALTER HUSTON, her roles were limited to ingénues and a few years after she married British playwright and screenwriter Benn W. Levy in 1933, Cummings gave up her Hollywood career and, after a few more roles on Broadway, including *Accent on Youth* (1934), *Young Madame Conti* (1937), a revival of *Madame Bovary* (1937), and *If I Were You* (1938), she moved to England and began working in British films and theatre, including the classic 1945 film version of **Noël Coward**'s *Blithe Spirit* and a wide range of stage roles from Shakespeare to **Bertolt Brecht**, most notably her acclaimed 1971 stage performance as Mary Tyrone in *Long Day's Journey Into Night* costarring with **Laurence Olivier**. Cummings made only occasional returns to Broadway for *One-Man Show* (1945), *Rape of the Belt* (1960), as Gertrude in a 1969 revival of *Hamlet* starring Nicol Williamson and Francesca Annis, and she won a **Tony Award** and a **Drama Desk Award** for her acclaimed portrayal of an ex-aviatrix suffering from a stroke in *Wings* (1979), a role she repeated in a 1983 television film. **Off-Broadway**, she appeared in a revival of *The Chalk Garden* in 1982, reaping a Drama Desk nomination.

CURCHACK, FRED (1948–   ). New York-born Curchack received a B.A. and an M.A. from Queens College before moving to Texas, where he emerged as a **performance artist** who has created many original theatre pieces, including over 20 **solo** works involving multimedia elements. His major works, for which he received a 1991 Guggenheim Fellowship, are inspired by a wide range of sources, from **Shakespeare**, the source for two of his most effective works, *Stuff as Dreams Are Made On* (1990) and *What Fools These Mortals Be* (1992), as well as Asian theatre, dance, and Jerzy Grotowski's techniques. Curchack is on the faculty of the University of Texas at Dallas and continues his solo performing with the recent *Gauguin's Paradise* (2004) and *Milarepa* (2009). *See also* ALTERNATIVE THEATRE.

CURSE OF THE STARVING CLASS. **Sam Shepard**'s family tragicomedy was commissioned by **Joe Papp** for the **New York Shakespeare Festival/Public Theatre**, but opened first at London's Royal Court Theatre on 21 April 1977. In a rare and controversial decision, an **Obie Award** was given to Shepard before the play opened in New York, which it ultimately did on 2 March 1978. A bizarre assault on a consumerist society, the play depicts the deeply dysfunctional Tate family struggling to hold their farm together. The Public Theatre cast, under the direction of **Robert Woodruff**, included **Olympia Dukakis**, Pamela Reed, Kenneth Welsh, James Gammon, and Michael J. Pollard. The play was revived at the **Yale Repertory Theatre** in 1980, followed by another with **Kathy Bates** and Bill Pullman at

International Arts Relations, Inc. (INTAR) in 1985, and a film version, starring Bates and James Woods, was released in 1995. In 2008, the play was revived by the **American Conservatory Theatre** with original cast member Pamela Reed, who had played Emma, the Tate's daughter, in the original production moving into the role of Ella, the burned-out matriarch of the family.

CURTIS, PAUL J. (1927–). Born Paul James Curtis in Boston, Massachusetts, he studied with **Erwin Piscator** at the New School for Social Research before establishing the first MIME theatre and school in America with the American Mime Theatre in 1952. He has explained its mission through his students, noting, "Most of the people who study with us have no intention of being American mimes. It's too limited. You couldn't possibly get enough work. But all kinds of performers study with us. For example, we've had a great many magicians study here simply to improve their performing skills. We've also had clowns and CIRCUS performers. We've even had singers." Curtis also established International Mimes and Pantomimists, an organization for performers in the field.

D

DA COSTA, MORTON (1914–1989). Born Morton Tecosky in Philadelphia, Pennsylvania, and began his career as an actor in the ensemble of **Thornton Wilder**'s *The Skin of Our Teeth* (1942). He switched to directing in 1948 with a revival of *The Alchemist* at New York's City Center and subsequently directed both MUSICALS and straight plays, including such notable productions as a revival of *Dream Girl* in 1951, *Plain and Fancy* (1955), *No Time for Sergeants* (1955), *Auntie Mame* (1956), *The Music Man* (1957), for which he received a **Tony Award** nomination, *The Wall* (1960), *Sherry!* (1967), an all-star revival of *The Women* (1973), *A Musical Jubilee* (1975), and *Doubles* (1985). He directed *Saratoga* (1959) and *Maggie Flynn* (1968), for which he also contributed librettos. Da Costa also directed films, including *Auntie Mame* (1958) and *The Music Man* (1962), the latter earning him an Academy Award nomination.

DA SILVA, HOWARD (1909–1986). This versatile Jewish American actor was born Howard Silverblatt in Cleveland, Ohio, and labored as a steelworker prior to changing his name and beginning a theatre and film career. His earliest appearances for EVA LE GALLIENNE'S CIVIC REPERTORY THEATRE included secondary roles in such productions as *Alison's House* (1931) and *Alice in Wonderland* (1932), after which he appeared in **The Group Theatre**'s production of *Golden Boy* (1937), the **Federal Theatre Project**'s controversial *The Cradle Will Rock* (1937), as Jack Armstrong in *Abe Lincoln in Illinois* (1938), a role he repeated in the 1940 film version, and as the murderous Jud Fry in *Oklahoma!* (1943).

Alternating between theatre and film (and later television) roles, Da Silva also appeared on **Broadway** in *Diary of a Scoundrel* (1956), *Compulsion* (1957), *Fiorello!* (1959), for which he received a **Tony Award** nomination, *Romulus* (1962), *In the Counting House* (1962), *Dear Me, The Sky Is Falling* (1963), *The Unknown Soldier and His Wife* (1967), and *1776* (1969). Da Silva directed *Sandhog* (1954), *Purlie Victorious* (1961), *The Advocate* (1963), *My Sweet Charlie* (1966), and he wrote the libretto for *The Zulu and the Zayda* (1965) and with Arnold Perl conceived *The World of Sholom Aleichem*

(1982). On screen, Da Silva's many films include *The Sea Wolf* (1941), *Sergeant York* (1941), *Reunion in France* (1942), *Keeper of the Flame* (1942), *The Lost Weekend* (1945), *They Live by Night* (1948), *David and Lisa* (1962), *1776* (1972), *The Great Gatsby* (1974), and *Mommie Dearest* (1981), and he won an Emmy Award in 1978 for the television film *Verna: USO Girl*.

DAFOE, WILLEM (1955–). The sixth of eight children, Dafoe was born in Appleton, Wisconsin, the son of a doctor and a nurse. He was educated at the University of Wisconsin-Milwaukee, but never graduated. Instead, he joined an experimental group, **Theatre X**, and toured the United States and Europe in their productions of *Offending the Audience*, *Phaedre*, and *Razor Blades* before moving to New York, where he joined **The Performance Group**, appearing in their productions of *Cop* (1978) and *The Balcony* (1979). Dafoe met and began a personal relationship with **Elizabeth LeCompte** and both became founding members of the experimental theatre collective, **The Wooster Group**. He has appeared in many Wooster productions, most notably a revival of EUGENE O'NEILL's *The Hairy Ape** in 1996. Also for Wooster, he appeared in *North Atlantic* (1985), *Miss Universal Happiness* (1985), and *To You, The Birdie* (2002), among others. He was nominated for Academy Awards for *Platoon* (1987) and *Shadow of the Vampire* (2000). Dafoe's other notable films include *To Live and Die in L.A.* (1985), the controversial *The Last Temptation of Christ* (1988), *Mississippi Burning* (1988), *Born on the Fourth of July* (1989), *Wild at Heart* (1990), *Tom and Viv* (1994), *The English Patient* (1996), *American Psycho* (2000), *Spider-Man* (2002), and *Once Upon a Time in Mexico* (2003), and he has also appeared on television.

DALE, JIM (1935–). Born James Smith in Northamptonshire, England, Dale served in the Royal Air Force and trained as a dancer prior to beginning a stage, film, and television career in London with the National Theatre at the Old Vic. Since touring to the United States with the Young Vic with his acclaimed adaptation (with Frank Dunlop) of Molière's *Les Fourberies de Scapin*, retitled *Scapino!* (1974), for which he won a **Drama Desk Award** and **Tony Award** nomination, Dale has mostly worked in the United States, appearing on **Broadway** in the title role of the MUSICAL *Barnum* (1980), for which he won a Tony and a Drama Desk Award. He also received nominations for both in revivals of *A Day in the Death of Joe Egg* in 1985 and *Candide* in 1997. Dale replaced Robert Lindsey in *Me and My Girl* (1986) and won a Drama Desk Award for *Threepenny Opera* in 2006, which also brought him a Tony nomination and an **Outer Critics Circle Award**. **Off-Broadway**, Dale appeared in *Privates on Parade* (1989), *Travels with My Aunt* (1995), for which he won a **Lucille Lortel Award**, and *Comedians* (2003), garnering yet another Drama Desk nomination. Dale has appeared in movies, including numerous entries in England's famous *Carry On* film series, television, won two Grammy Awards for his audio book reading of the *Harry Potter* book series, and was nominated for an Academy Award and a Golden Globe Award for coauthoring the title song of the film *Georgy Girl* (1966).

DALLAS THEATRE CENTER. Baylor University professor **Paul Baker** founded the Center in 1959 with the support of several Dallas, Texas, citizens who supplied the Kalita Humphreys Theatre designed by Frank Lloyd Wright. Baker established a permanent acting company dedicated to staging both classics and contemporary plays and a graduate program. Other theatres spaces were added and although Baker's original model for the theatre evolved over time, the center has thrived as a major **regional theatre** with the expectation of moving to a new five-theatre complex in 2009. *See also* REPERTORY THEATRE.

DALRYMPLE, JEAN (1902–1998). Producer, manager, and writer, Dalrymple was born in Morristown, New Jersey, and began her theatre career performing on the vaudeville* circuit with a partner, Dan Jarrett. Giving up performing, she took a job working as a press agent for producer JOHN GOLDEN and married drama CRITIC **Ward Morehouse**. In 1940, Dalrymple set up her own publicity firm and in 1945 she produced her first **Broadway** play, *Hope for the Best*, followed by *Brighten the Corner* (1945) and a hit revival of *Burlesque** in 1946. As executive director of the **American National Theatre and Academy (ANTA),** she oversaw production of numerous productions, mostly revivals of American and European classics. She became director of the New York City Center Light Opera Company and the City Center Drama Company in 1953 (although she had been centrally involved with both since 1943) and produced a range of musicals and plays. She also wrote a few plays, including *The Quiet Room* (1958).

DANIELS, JEFF (1955–). A native of Athens, Georgia, Jeffrey Warren Daniels grew up in Chelsea, Michigan, and attended Central Michigan University where he studied theatre prior to dropping out to move to New York City. He debuted there in *The Shortchanged Review* (1979) at the **Second Stage**. On **Broadway**, he understudied several roles in *Gemini* (1977) and was seen in **Lanford Wilson**'s *Fifth of July* (1980), for which he was nominated for a **Drama Desk Award**, **A. R. Gurney**'s *The Golden Age* (1984), Wilson's *Redwood Curtain* (1993), and *God of Carnage* (2009), which brought him a **Tony Award** nomination. **Off-Broadway**, Daniels won an **Obie Award** for the **Circle Repertory Theatre** production of *Johnny Got His Gun* (1983) and garnered a Drama Desk nomination for *Lemon Sky* (1986). That same year, Daniels moved back to his hometown and started the Purple Rose Theatre, a not-for-profit organization, and he wrote original plays for this **regional** company. He has appeared in numerous films, receiving Golden Globe Award nominations for *The Purple Rose of Cairo* (1985), *Something Wild* (1986), and *The Squid and the Whale* (2005), and he also appeared in *Terms of Endearment* (1983), *Gettysburg* (1993), *Dumb and Dumber* (1994), *The Squid and the Whale* (2005), *Good Night, and Good Luck* (2005), and *State of Play* (2009). Daniels has also frequently appeared on television.

DANIELS, WILLIAM (1927–). Born William Davis Daniels in Brooklyn, New York, he studied at Northwestern University and married Bonnie Bartlett, with whom he frequently acts. He became a member of **The Actors Studio** and appeared in the **Off-Broadway** premiere of **Edward Albee**'s *The Zoo Story* (1960), winning an **Obie Award**. On **Broadway**, Daniels appeared in *The Legend of Lizzie* (1959), *A Thousand Clowns* (1962), *One Flew Over the Cuckoo's Nest* (1963), *On a Clear Day You Can See Forever* (1963), *Daphne in Cottage D* (1967), and, most notably, as founding father John Adams in the musical *1776* (1969), a role he repeated in the 1972 film version (the **Tony Award** committee ruled Daniels ineligible for a Best Actor nomination because his name was not billed above the title; he refused to accept a Best Featured Actor nomination). Daniels has appeared in many films, most memorably playing **Dustin Hoffman**'s father in *The Graduate* (1967), and he starred on the long-running drama series, *St. Elsewhere* (1982–1988), for which he won two Emmy Awards. Daniels also served as president of the Screen Actors Guild from 1999 to 2001.

DANNER, BLYTHE (1943–). Philadelphia, Pennsylvania-born Blythe Katharine Danner graduated from Bard College in 1965 before beginning her acting career with the Theatre Company of Boston and the Trinity Square Theatre. She won a **Theatre World Award** in 1969 in the **Repertory Theatre of Lincoln Center** revival of Molière's *The Miser*. Within months, she won a **Tony Award** playing a free-spirited hippie in Leonard Gershe's hit comedy *Butterflies Are Free* (1969). On **Broadway**, she also received Tony nominations for *Betrayal* (1980) and revivals of *A Streetcar Named Desire* in 1988 and *Follies* in 2001, and appeared in revivals of *Twelfth Night* in 1972, *The Philadelphia Story* in 1980, *Blithe Spirit* in 1987, and *The Deep Blue Sea* in 1998. **Off-Broadway**, Danner received **Drama Desk Award** nominations for revivals of *The New York Idea* in 1977 and *Suddenly Last*

Summer in 2007, and also appeared in *Much Ado about Nothing* in 1989 and *Sylvia* (1995), and several productions with the **Williamstown Theatre Festival**. She has appeared in numerous films, including *1776* (1972), *The Great Santini* (1979), *Brighton Beach Memoirs* (1986), *Another Woman* (1988), *Prince of Tides* (1991), and *Meet the Fockers* (2004), and on television she has won two Emmy Awards for her appearances on *Huff* (2004). Danner is the mother of Academy Award-winning film star Gwyneth Paltrow and director Jake Paltrow.

DARK AT THE TOP OF THE STAIRS, THE. **William Inge**'s three-act drama opened on 5 December 1957 at the Music Box Theatre for 468 performances in a production directed by **Elia Kazan**, garnering a Best Play **Tony Award** nomination. Set in 1920s Oklahoma, the Flood family is struggling financially as Rubin (**Pat Hingle**), a harness salesman, is losing income due to the growing popularity of automobiles. Among the children of Rubin and his wife Cora (Teresa Wright) is Reenie, whose date for a school dance, a young Jewish boy, is harassed by anti-Semitic students and commits suicide. This and family problems, including Rubin's job loss and problems for Cora's sister Lottie, played by **Eileen Heckart**, come to a head, with bittersweet results. A film version, starring **Robert Preston**, **Dorothy McGuire**, and Academy Award-nominated Shirley Knight as Reenie, was released in 1960.

DARK OF THE MOON. This two-act "legend with music" by Howard Richardson and William Berney, opened on 14 March 1945 at the 46th Street Theatre for 318 performances. Adapted from the old song about Barbara Allen (Carol Stone), this atmospheric fantasy focuses on John, a witch boy, who lives in the Smoky Mountains away from mortals, but when he falls in love with Barbara he pleads with a Conjur Woman to make him human. The Conjur Woman agrees with the proviso that Barbara must remain true to him for a year or her spell will be broken. When Barbara gives birth to a witch child the midwives kill it. When her relatives compel her to sleep with another man, the spell ends, Barbara dies, and John returns to the mountains as a witch boy. *Dark of the Moon* had a long stage life in STOCK, **community**, and university theatres.

DARKNESS AT NOON. **Sidney Kingsley**'s drama, which he also directed, was adapted from a 1941 novel by Arthur Koestler and brought a **Tony Award** to veteran film actor Claude Rains and a **New York Drama Critics Circle Award** to Kingsley. The play opened on 13 January 1951 for 186 performances at the Alvin Theatre in a **Playwright's Company** production. Set in a Russian prison in 1937, this propagandistic anti-Communist play centers on Rubashov, an old Bolshevik guard and revolutionary, who is tried for treason by the totalitarian Stalin government and repudiates his Marxist beliefs. Rains was supported by a strong cast including **Kim Hunter**, Walter J. Palance (soon to be known as Jack), who won a **Theatre World Award**, Lois Nettleton, Alexander Scourby, and Philip Coolidge.

DAVIDSON, GORDON (1933–). Born in Brooklyn, New York, Davidson was educated at Cornell University and Case Western Reserve University and began his directing career in regional theatres, including New Jersey's **Paper Mill Playhouse**, Virginia's **Barter Theatre**, and others, as well as stage managing for Martha Graham. He eventually worked with **John Houseman** at the **American Shakespeare Festival** and became producing director of Los Angeles's Ahmanson Theatre from 1989–2005 and artistic director of the **Mark Taper Forum (MTP)** from 1967–2005, directing numerous productions. On **Broadway**, he won a **Drama Desk Award** for *In the Matter of J. Robert Oppenheimer* (1969) and a **Tony Award** for *The Shadow Box* (1977), garnering Tony nominations for *The Trial of the Catonsville Nine* (1972) and *Children of a Lesser God* (1980), and MTP productions under his supervision won numerous awards. Davidson retired in 2005.

DAVIS, BETTE (1908–1989). Screen legend Davis was born in Lowell, Masschusetts, where she dreamed of a theatrical career after seeing actress Peg Entwhistle play Hedda Gabler. She made her **Broadway** debut in a flop, *The Earth Between* (1929), but fared better in *Broken Dishes* (1929) and *Solid South* (1930), after which she left the stage for Hollywood. After several undistinguished films, Davis made her first mark costarring with George Arliss* prior to winning two Best Actress Academy Awards (and nine nominations) during her long career under contract to Warner Bros., where many of her most successful movies, including *Dark Victory* (1939), *The Letter** (1940), and *The Little Foxes* (1941), were screen versions of stage successes. When her contract with Warner Bros. ended in 1949, Davis scored another screen triumph playing theatre actress Margo Channing in *All about Eve* (1950) in a characterization many viewed as inspired by TALLULAH BANKHEAD. Davis made a few Broadway appearances while continuing her film work, including singing and clowning in the MUSICAL revue* *Two's Company* (1952), on Broadway and on tour with her then-husband Garry Merrill in the two-hander *The World of Carl Sandburg* (1960), and playing Maxine Faulk in the premiere of **Tennessee Williams**'s *The Night of the Iguana* (1961). Her final stage appearance in *Miss Moffat* (1974), a musical adaptation of Emlyn Williams's *The Corn is Green*, closed in Philadelphia during its out-of-town tryout.

DAVIS, OSSIE (1917–2005). Born Raiford Chatman Davis in Cogdell, Georgia, this acclaimed **African American** actor and playwright studied at Howard University, but quit to pursue acting in New York. He found work with the Rose McClendon* Players in Harlem in 1939 and debuted on **Broadway** in *Jeb* (1946). He toured in the company of *Anna Lucasta* in 1947 and returned to Broadway in *The Leading Lady* (1948), *The Smile of the World* (1949), *The Wisteria Trees* (1950), revivals of *The Royal Family** and *The Green Pastures* in 1951, *Remains to Be Seen* (1951), *Touchstone* (1953), and *Jamaica* (1957), the last bringing him a **Tony Award** nomination. He succeeded **Sidney Poitier** as Walter Lee Younger in *A Raisin in the Sun* (1959), playing opposite his wife, **Ruby Dee**, whom he had married in 1948. In 1961, Davis appeared in his own hit play, *Purlie Victorious* (1961), and later acted in *The Zulu and the Zayda* (1965) and replaced Cleavon Little in *I'm Not Rappaport* (1985). Davis's *Purlie Victorious* was adapted as the MUSICAL *Purlie* (1970) and garnered a Tony nomination. He appeared in many films, including *No Way Out* (1950), *The Hill* (1965), *The Scalphunters* (1968), *School Daze* (1988), *Do the Right Thing* (1989), *Jungle Fever* (1991), *Malcolm X* (1992), and *I'm Not Rappaport* (1996). Davis also appeared frequently on television, receiving four Emmy Award nominations for *Teacher, Teacher* (1969), *King* (1978), *Miss Evers' Boys* (1997), and *The L Word* (2004).

DAVIS, VIOLA (1965–). Raised in Central Falls, Rhode Island, Davis had been born in St. Matthews, South Carolina. She was a drama student at Rhode Island College prior to attending the Juilliard School. Mixing stage and screen work, Davis has emerged as a much-admired actor in both realms. Her first **Broadway** appearance in **August Wilson**'s *Seven Guitars* (1996) brought her a **Theatre World Award** and **Drama Desk** and **Tony Award** nominations. She was also Drama Desk-nominated for *Everybody's Ruby* (1999). She won a Tony as Best Supporting Actress for Wilson's *King Hedley II* (2001) and **Lynn Nottage's** *Intimate Apparel* (2004). Despite appearing in numerous television dramas and such films as *The Substance of Fire* (1996), *Out of Sight* (1998), *Traffic* (2000), *Antwone Fisher* (2002), and *Solaris* (2002), Davis did not have a true breakthrough until she played the distressed mother of a molested child in *Doubt* (2008), which brought her an Academy Award nomination and a Golden Globe Award as Best Supporting Actress. In 2010, Davis returned to Broadway opposite **Denzel Washington** in a revival of Wilson's *Fences*, garnering Tony, Drama Desk, and **Outer Critics Circle Awards** for her performance. *See also* AFRICAN AMERICAN THEATRE.

DAYS WITHOUT END. EUGENE O'NEILL's "modern miracle play" in four acts produced by THE THEATRE GUILD, opened at the Henry Miller Theatre on 8 January 1934 for 57 performances. O'Neill, who had previously experimented with masks and spoken asides to reveal the inner natures of his characters, divided his protagonist, John Loving, into two separate characters, John (Earle Larimore*) representing his better self and Loving (Stanley Ridges) as his darker side. Giving up God for love, the embittered, isolated Loving reveals his true nature to his wife Elsa and their priest, causing Elsa to become seriously ill from the shock of his revelations. Realizing the sins of Loving, and to save Elsa, John renews his faith in Catholicism and thus destroys Loving. Most critics rejected this play and O'Neill, disheartened by their response and the production's short run, resolved not to produce further new works on **Broadway** and he kept his resolution until the 1946 production of *The Iceman Cometh. See also* RELIGIOUS DRAMA.

DE LIAGRE, ALFRED, JR. (1904–1987). Born Alfred Gustav Etienne de Liagre, Jr. in Passaic, New Jersey, he studied with **Monty Woolley** at Yale University. In 1930, he began his career as a stage manager at the Woodstock Playhouse before becoming a producer in 1933 with a **Broadway** production of *Three-Cornered Moon*, after which he mounted over 30 productions in New York and England, sometimes with coproducers. De Liagre's other Broadway productions, some of which he also directed, include *Yes, My Darling Daughter* (1937), *Mr. and Mrs. North* (1941), *The Voice of the Turtle* (1943), *Galileo* (1947), *The Madwoman of Chaillot* (1948), *The House of Bernarda Alba* (1951), *The Golden Apple* (1954), a revival of *The Skin of Our Teeth* in 1955, *Janus* (1955), *J.B.* (1958), *Big Fish, Little Fish* (1961), *Tiny Alice* (1969), and revivals of *Our Town* in 1969, *Harvey* in 1970, and *On Your Toes* in 1983, and *Breaking the Code* (1987). **Katharine Hepburn** called De Liagre "the last of the great gentlemen producers."

DEAD END. **Sidney Kingsley**'s naturalistic drama depicting the hardships of contemporary urban life is set on a New York street dead-ending into the Hudson River. *Dead End* shocked some critics with its frank depiction of the human and economic realities of the Great Depression when it opened on 28 October 1935 at the Belasco* Theatre for a 684 performance run. *Dead End*'s producer, NORMAN BEL GEDDES, also designed the acclaimed REALISTIC setting of a divided city street with a new luxurious apartment house for the rich butted up against a tenement. The theatre's orchestra pit served as the East River, with tenement children leaping into the water throughout the play. *Dead End* opens with Gimpty, a handicapped architect unable to find employment who sits all day sketching ideas and observing the goings on at the end of the street.

Tommy (Billy Halop), a young tough, is torn between his sister Drina (Elspeth Eric), who strives to keep him out of trouble, and the gang of wayward boys he leads. The future of the gang members is embodied in Baby Face Martin (Joseph Downing), once a resident of the street and now a notorious gangster wanted for murder. The desperate Martin is on the lam from the law and returns secretly to visit his long-suffering mother (Marjorie Main), who will have nothing to do with him. At the same time, Tommy and his gang (Leo Gorcey, Huntz Hall, **Gabriel Dell**, David Gorcey) plan and execute the theft of a watch from a pampered boy living in the apartment house. The boy's father attempts to retrieve the watch, but is stabbed by Tommy who, to Drina's great distress, is arrested as the police corner Martin and kill him in a shootout. Gimpty, who is attracted to the sensitive Drina, comforts her as the rapid pace of the city continues oblivious to the lives at the dead end.

Dead End bears some resemblance to ELMER RICE's PULITZER PRIZE-winning *Street Scene** (1929), a naturalistic melodrama* set on the steps of a tenement exploring the varied lives intersecting in the New York melting pot. *Dead End* was filmed in 1937 by director William Wyler and provided a vehicle for emerging film star Humphrey Bogart as Baby Face Martin and introduced several of the stage cast members to film success, including Marjorie Main, who played Martin's mother in both the stage and screen versions, and the Dead End Kids. They appeared again in *Angels with Dirty Faces* (1938), which, like *Dead End*, proved popular with audiences and inspired a series of Dead End comedies (also referred to as East Side comedies) that were made into the late 1940s.

DEAD END KIDS: A HISTORY OF NUCLEAR POWER. **Mabou Mines** won an **Obie Award** for this cautionary play, conceived and directed by **JoAnne Akalaitis**, on nuclear energy. Using techniques of vaudeville,* nightclub performance, stand-up comedy, magic, and the classroom, it opened at the **New York Shakespeare Festival/Public Theatre** on 11 November 1980. Akalaitis culled material from scientists, government documents, media, visual images, and other sources to create a collage on the benefits and fears of nuclear power. Jeremy Gerard, writing in the *New York Times*, called it a "provocative, haunted tour through the history of nuclear power."

DEAR RUTH. **Norman Krasna**'s two-act comedy opened on 13 December 1944 at Henry Miller's Theatre for 680 performances under the direction of **Moss Hart**. A judge's 15-year-old daughter, Miriam (Lenore Lonergan) endeavors to aid the war effort by writing letters to a soldier overseas, but uses her older sister's name, Ruth (Virginia Gilmore), and sends the very attractive

Ruth's photo as well. When the soldier (John Dall) turns up unexpectedly on leave, he arrives just after Ruth has accepted a marriage proposal. Ruth, however, falls in love with the soldier, dumps her new fiancé, and her judge father performs a hasty marriage ceremony so that the couple can have a honeymoon before he returns to duty. A popular 1947 screen version starred Joan Caulfield, Mona Freeman, and William Holden.

DEATH OF A SALESMAN. **Arthur Miller**'s two-act drama—or modern tragedy, as he described it—opened on 10 February 1949 at the Morosco Theatre for 742 performances under **Elia Kazan**'s direction and with a memorable scene design by JO MIELZINER. Both play and production were widely acclaimed, winning both a **Tony Award** as Best Play and the PULITZER PRIZE for Drama, among other kudos, and sold in excess of 200,000 copies when published by the Book-of-the-Month Club. **Lee J. Cobb** played Miller's iconic American character, Willy Loman, an aging traveling salesman unraveling emotionally, although his supportive wife Linda (**Mildred Dunnock**) attempts to offer comfort and protect him.

Willy's illusions of the economic success he had spent his life striving for are crumbling before him. In desperation, he turns to his boss, Howard, in hopes that he can get off the road and have a desk job. Instead, this young son of his original employer unsympathetically fires Willy, setting off a series of illusory flashbacks (although Kazan referred to these as "daydreams" in which "Willy is justifying himself") in which Willy drifts away lost in significant moments in his past that are muddled with intrusions from the present. Some of Willy's illusions provide comforting happy moments from the past, but most are critical transitional encounters, including visions of his financially successful older brother, Ben, who has carved a fortune out of some far-off adventure. The imaginary Ben ultimately gives Willy his approval to commit suicide as Willy concocts the misguided notion that his insurance money would provide his favored son Biff, played by Tony Award-winning **Arthur Kennedy**, a chance to succeed. The triumph of *Death of a Salesman* was remarkable on several counts, not least in its depiction of the dark side of capitalism—or, at least, the illusions it can create in those who view material success (the vaunted "American dream") as fulfillment. The play's grim view of capitalism was in stark contrast to America's post-World War II economic boom; in every respect, *Death of a Salesman* seemed to counter contemporary currents of American life—on the surface, more a play about the Great Depression of the 1930s, *Death of a Salesman* still managed to speak to its audience in 1949, perhaps as a cautionary tale.

In the subsequent 60 years since its premiere, *Death of a Salesman* has had numerous revivals, film and television productions, and a healthy life in print frequently taught in high school and colleges. It has had three major **Broadway** revivals: in 1975 at the **Circle in the Square**, directed and starring **George C. Scott**; in 1984 starring **Dustin Hoffman** and **John Malkovich** in a **Drama Desk Award**-winning performance; and in 1999 featuring **Brian Dennehy** in a Tony-winning performance. A 1951 film version starring **Frederic March** was nominated for several Academy Awards. Cobb and Dunnock appeared in a 1966 television production and a 1985 television film version was based on the 1984 Hoffman-Malkovich revivals. In 2000, Dennehy also appeared in another television film version.

DEATHTRAP. **Ira Levin's** two-act mystery-drama-comedy, directed by **Robert Moore**, opened on 26 February 1978 for an impressive 1,793 performances, garnering a **Tony Award** nomination as Best Play. John Wood starred as a celebrated, but burned-out mystery writer who hatches a plan to steal a promising manuscript from a young writer (**Victor Garber**) and pass it off as his own. **Marian Seldes**, Marian Winters, and Richard Woods provided able support—and various red herrings—in Levin's well-plotted thriller laced with elements of comedy and drama. Michael Caine and Christopher Reeve starred in a 1982 film version directed by Sidney Lumet.

DEE, RUBY (1924–). This versatile actress and pioneer in **African American** theatre was born Ruby Ann Wallace in Cleveland, Ohio, and studied at Hunter College. In 1948, she married **Ossie Davis** and often acted with him. On **Broadway**, Dee took over the title role in the **American Negro Theatre**'s production of *Anna Lucasta* (1944) and toured with the production, and appeared in *Jeb* (1946), *A Long Way from Home* (1948), and *The Smile of the World* (1949) before originating the role of Ruth Younger in **Lorraine Hansberry**'s *A Raisin in the Sun* (1959), repeating her performance in the 1961 screen version. She also appeared with her husband in his play, *Purlie Victorious* (1961), and in *Checkmates* (1988). She received an **Obie Award** and a **Drama Desk Award** for *Boesman and Lena* (1971) and a Drama Desk Award for *Wedding Band* (1973), and her other **Off-Broadway** and **regional theatre** credits include playing Cordelia in *King Lear* (1965) opposite **Morris Carnovsky** (as well as other Shakespearean roles), and has appeared in all-black versions of *Long Day's Journey into Night* (1982) and *The Glass Menagerie* (1989).

Also a playwright, Dee's plays include *Twin Bit Gardens* (1976), *Take It from the Top* (1979), *Zora Is My Name* (1983), *The Disappearance* (1993), and *Two Hah Hahs and a Homeboy* (1995). In 1998, she performed her own solo play, *My One Good Nerve*, and was elected to the **Theatre Hall of Fame** in 1988. In movies, she has appeared in *The Jackie Robinson Story* (1950),

St. Louis Blues (1958), *Do the Right Thing* (1989), *Jungle Fever* (1991, and *American Gangster* (2008), which brought her an Academy Award nomination and a Screen Actors Guild Award. For her work in television, Dee received a 1991 Emmy Award for the TV film *Decoration Day* and five other nominations. Dee received a Screen Actors Guild Lifetime Achievement Award in 2001.

DEEP ARE THE ROOTS. **Arnaud D'Usseau** and James Gow's melodrama* of the oppressions experienced by a black war hero's return to his Southern hometown opened on 26 September 1945 in a **Kermit Bloomgarden** and George Heller production at the Fulton Theatre for 477 performances under the direction of **Elia Kazan** with settings by **Howard Bay**. Gordon Heath played Brett Charles, the soldier, and the **race**-themed play caused some controversy over not only its condemnation of Southern racism, but also the depiction of an underlying **sexual** tension between Brett and the white daughter (**Barbara Bel Geddes**) of a senator. *See also* AFRICAN AMERICAN THEATRE.

DELICATE BALANCE, A. **Edward Albee**'s PULITZER PRIZE-winning drama opened on 22 September 1966 at the Martin Beck Theatre for 132 performances under the direction of Alan Schneider. The impressive cast for Albee's assault on the complacency of well-heeled and materialistic suburbanites included **Hume Cronyn**, **Jessica Tandy**, Rosemary Murphy, and **Marian Seldes**. The play chronicles the hollow, anxious lives of Agnes and Tobias, and Agnes's alcoholic sister Claire, who lives with them. Harry and Edna, another couple, arrive unexpectedly, as does the bitter daughter of Agnes and Tobias, whose marriage has just ended in divorce. The characters express a desire to escape an unknown terror, although none can quite name the source of their fear. A film version, directed by Tony Richardson, produced as part of the American Film Theatre starred **Katharine Hepburn**, Paul Scofield, **Joseph Cotten**, **Kate Reid**, and Lee Remick, and a stellar 1996 revival offered **George Grizzard**, **Rosemary Harris**, **Elizabeth Wilson**, **Mary Beth Hurt**, and **Elaine Stritch** in a production that ran longer than the original.

DELL, GABRIEL (1919–1988). Born Gabriel Marcel Dell Vecchio in New York, Dell is best remember as a key member of the Dead End Kids, beginning with his **Broadway** debut in **Sidney Kingsley**'s *Dead End* (1935). Dell, as part of the Dead End Kids, appeared in the screen version of *Dead End* in 1937 and a long series of nominal sequels (sometimes called the East Side Kids or the Bowery Boys) stressing broad comedy. Dell also studied at **The Actors Studio** and appeared in several Broadway productions, including *Tickets Please* (1950), *Ankles Away* (1955), *Marathon '33* (1963), *Anyone Can Whistle* (1964), ***The Sign in Sidney Brustein's Window*** (1964), *Something Different* (1967), *Fun City* (1972), and *Lamppost Reunion* (1975), garnering a **Tony Award** nomination for the last. He also replaced **Alan Arkin** in *Luv* (1964) and Peter Falk in ***The Prisoner of Second Avenue*** (1971) and appeared in **Off-Broadway** productions, including *Fortuna* (1962), *The Rogue's Trial* (1966), *Adaptation* (1969), and *Where Do We Go from Here?* (1974). On television, he was a member of the STOCK company of *The Steve Allen Show*, where he proved adept at sketch comedy, and he appeared in television and feature films as well, including *Angels with Dirty Faces* (1938), *Crime School* (1938), *They Made Me a Criminal* (1939), and others.

DELL'ARTE PLAYERS COMPANY. Founded in 1971 by Carlo Mazzone-Clementi and Jane Hill in Berkeley, California, the company was based in Blue Lake, California, where workshops in physical theatre were first offered in 1972. Techniques based on *commedia dell'arte*, MIME, and other movement systems predominate in their actor training, but the company also began producing plays, including nearly 40 original pieces, in 1977 under the guidance of artistic directors Joan Schirle, Michael Fields, and Donald Forrest. *See also* REGIONAL THEATRE MOVEMENT.

DENHAM, REGINALD (1894–1983). Born in London, England, this theatre and film director and writer was, at one time, married to Moyna Macgill, the mother of **Angela Lansbury**. He spent much of his career directing on **Broadway**, beginning in 1929 with *Rope's End*, and spanning nearly 40 years, including such productions as *Ladies in Retirement* (1940), which he also wrote with Edward Percy, ***The Two Mrs. Carrolls*** (1944), *Wallflower* (1944), which he cowrote with Mary Orr, *Portrait in Black* (1947), ***Dial "M" for Murder*** (1952), ***The Bad Seed*** (1954), ***Janus*** (1955), and *Hostile Witness* (1966), among many others.

DENNEHY, BRIAN (1938–). A native of Bridgeport, Connecticut, Brian Mannion Dennehy joined the Marine Corps. He studied at Columbia University and Yale University prior to beginning an acting career in theatre, film, and television. On **Broadway**, he has appeared in *Translations* (1995) and revivals of ***Inherit the Wind*** in 2007 and *Desire under the Elms** in 2009. Dennehy won Best Actor **Tony Awards** for two other revivals, ***Death of a Salesman*** in 1999 (he also won an Olivier Award when the production moved to London) and ***Long Day's Journey into Night*** in 2003. In regional theatre, Dennehy has frequently appeared in Chicago, most notably with the

Goodman Theatre, and he has appeared in plays by **Shakespeare**, Samuel Beckett, and EUGENE O'NEILL. In 2010, Dennehy appeared on Broadway in a double-bill of O'Neill's *Hughie* and Beckett's *Krapp's Last Tape*. He has been nominated for six Emmy Awards and won a Golden Globe Award for the television production of *Death of a Salesman* in 2000.

DENNIS, SANDY (1937–1992). Born in Hastings, Nebraska, Sandra Dale Dennis studied at Nebraska Wesleyan University and the University of Nebraska prior to moving to New York. She began her career on the soap opera *The Guiding Light* in 1956, but preferred theatre work as a committed method actress and recipient of a 1961 **Theatre World Award**. Dennis understudied and went on as a replacement in *The Dark at the Top of the Stairs* (1957) prior to appearing in *Face of a Hero* (1960) and *Complaisant Lover* (1961). She won consecutive **Tony Awards** for her performances in *A Thousand Clowns* (1962) and *Any Wednesday* (1964), and her subsequent performances include *Daphne in Cottage D* (1967), *How the Other Half Loves* (1971), *Let Me Hear You Smile* (1973), *Absurd Person Singular* (1974), *The Supporting Cast* (1981), and *Come Back to the 5 & Dime Jimmy Dean, Jimmy Dean* (1982). Dennis also replaced **Ellen Burstyn** in *Same Time, Next Year* (1975). On screen, she won a Supporting Actress Academy Award for *Who's Afraid of Virginia Woolf?* (1966) for her second film and also appeared in *Sweet November* (1968), for which she was nominated for a Golden Globe Award, *The Out-of-Towners* (1970), *Nasty Habits* (1977), *The Four Seasons* (1981), *Another Woman* (1988), and *The Indian Runner* (1991).

DENVER THEATRE CENTER (DTC). Begun by Helen G. Bonfils, **Broadway** producer Donald R. Seawell, and others in the early 1950s as a **community theatre**, their work ultimately involved a partnership to produce plays on Broadway and in London. Their success led to expanding beyond **community theatre** for Denver and plans were made to build a new space, with guidance from **Tyrone Guthrie** and observance of the model provided by the **Guthrie Theatre** of Minneapolis, Minnesota. Housed in the Helen G. Bonfils Theatre Complex in the Denver Center for the Performing Arts, DTC truly began operations as a professional company in the Complex's three theatre spaces in 1979, with concurrent productions of *The Caucasian Chalk Circle, Moby Dick Rehearsed*, and *The Learned Ladies. See also* REGIONAL THEATRE MOVEMENT.

DERWENT, CLARENCE (1884–1959). Born in London, England, Derwent acted in Great Britain for 13 years before making his New York debut in 1915 opposite Grace George* in the American premiere of GEORGE BER-

NARD SHAW's *Major Barbara*. He enjoyed a long distinguished career in both countries, playing perhaps as many as 500 roles. Having performed in all but three of **Shakespeare**'s plays, he claimed Shylock in *The Merchant of Venice* as his favorite. On **Broadway**, among his many appearances, Derwent acted in *The Three Musketeers* (1928), *Serena Blandish* (1929), *Topaze* (1930), *The Late Christopher Bean* (1932), *The Amazing Dr. Clitterhouse* (1937), *Kind Lady* (1940), *The Pirate* (1942), *Lute Song* (1946), *The Eagle Has Two Heads* (1947), *Laura* (1947), and *The Madwoman of Chaillot* (1948). He served two terms as president of the ACTORS' EQUITY ASSOCIATION and was president of the **American National Theatre and Academy (ANTA)** from 1952 until his death.

DESIGN/DESIGNERS. For present-day theatre productions, whether on **Broadway**, **Off-Broadway**, **Off-Off-Broadway**, **regional**, and **academic theatre**, the visual elements—scenery, costumes, lighting, properties, special effects, etc.—are typically each created by individual designers supported by assistants and crews carrying out the realization of the design. In the early nineteenth century, following the rise of antiquarianism, a movement leading to the creation of an historically accurate *mise-en-scène* for a play (as opposed to the generic settings often employed), scene painters concerned themselves mostly with a visually appealing scene not unlike a life-sized picture postcard of a genuine location. The earliest American publication on scene painting was *A Practical Guide to Scene Painting and Painting in Distemper* (ca. 1883) by F. Lloyds, who described techniques, equipment, and scenic elements, but with improvements in technology, particularly in lighting with the arrival of electric lights, and greater attention to costuming, the necessity for specialized designers increased by 1900.

Scene, costume, and lighting design emerged as individual areas of concern, each requiring a designer during the early twentieth century, with other areas, including sound, props, and special effects, ultimately also requiring specialized designers. As the visual aspects of theatre diversified in such a way, the director emerged as an essential figure responsible for, among other things, collaborating with the designers to achieve a unified production. Ironically, by the 1930s, many scene designers also chose to provide costume and/ or lighting designs as well (often in a desire to more easily achieve a holistic visual scheme), but only a few designed multiple areas with any regularity.

Evolving from new theories and the experimentation of European designers, most notably Adolphe Appia and Edward Gordon Craig, a New Stagecraft* developed with an emphasis on departures from the prevailing "painted REALISM" typical of the nineteenth-century stage. In the first decade of the twentieth century, the concepts of Appia and Craig, and others, which had been developing since the 1880s, increasingly won widespread acceptance in European productions, but did not reach America until shortly before World WAR I, first and most decisively in the work of ROBERT EDMOND JONES. In general terms, the New Stagecraft, as practiced by Jones, involved a freer, more impressionistic use of color and line, with the unifying element of lighting, all with the goal of creating a visual environment in which everything seen contributed to a revelation of the text's themes, characters, and mood, and were thoroughly unified with the contributions of the actor and director, as well as the playwright. The seminal production featuring the New Stagecraft in the United States was Jones's 1915 design for an English translation of Anatole France's *The Man Who Married a Dumb Wife*, staged by British director Harley Granville Barker. It was a simple design, selective in its use of central elements of structure and furnishing, and like the work of Appia and Craig in Europe, Jones's designs provided a path away from what Craig derisively described as the limitations of "photographic realism" in the *mise-en-scène*.

Jones's style, inspired by European design, was otherwise singular and his prolific designing career, which stretched from the 1910s to the 1950s, encompassed every conceivable genre, from **Shakespearean** productions of *Richard III* in 1920 and *Hamlet* in 1922 starring John Barrymore* to most of EUGENE O'NEILL's plays of the 1920s and 1930s and even an occasional MUSICAL. Other like-minded designers followed in Jones's path, including most notably LEE SIMONSON, DONALD OENSLAGER, MORDECAI GORELIK, and JO MIELZINER. By the 1940s, as stage technology continued to improve and as American plays and musicals invited bolder design choices, a few designers, especially Mielziner, dominated. His designs for two of the greatest American plays of the era, **Tennessee Williams**'s *A Streetcar Named Desire* (1947) and **Arthur Miller**'s *Death of a Salesman* (1949), in large part through his contributions, confirmed the triumph of American lyric realism. The European influence continued to be significant, as seen in the evocative and diverse scene designs of Russian-born **Boris Aronson**, who spent his career designing for Broadway into the 1970s after cutting his teeth as a designer during the 1920s and early 1930s in Moscow. Transplanted German designers also had an impact on Broadway and in opera, including **Harry Horner**, **Herman Rosse**, and **Wolfgang Roth**.

From World War II to 1980, two generations of highly individual scene designers brought visual innovations as stage technology and available materials for stage use significantly improved in quality and variety. These scene designers, many of whom also designed costumes and/or lighting—and occasionally directed or produced—included **Lemuel Ayers**, **Howard Bay**, **John Lee Beatty**, **Stewart Chaney**, **John Conklin**, **William and Jean Eckart**,

Ben Edwards, Karl Eigsti, Eldon Elder, Charles Elson, Frederick Fox, Ralph Funicello, Neil Peter Jampolis, George Jenkins, Albert R. Johnson, Marjorie Bradley Kellogg, Peter Larkin, Eugene Lee, Ming Cho Lee, Samuel Leve, William Ivey Long, Santo Loquasto, David Mitchell, Tanya Moiseiwitsch, Beni Montresor, Robert O'Hearn, Lester Polakov, William Ritman, Douglas W. Schmidt, Oliver Smith, Serge Soudekine, Raymond Sovey, Fred Voelpel, Robin Wagner, Tony Walton, Peter Wexler, and Ed Wittstein, among others. Many of these designers continue to contribute into the twenty-first century and many have been extraordinarily prolific on Broadway, although increasingly after 1960 many worked in Off-Broadway, Off-Off-Broadway, regional, and university theatres, and also designed for opera, ballet, films, and television. Scene designers of the era between 1980 to 2010 were more likely to do their work away from Broadway, most often in regional and Off-Broadway theatres. Among these are such leading figures as Michael Anania, Loy Arcenas, John Arnone, Christopher Barreca, Gabriel Berry, Jim Clayburgh, David Gallo, David Hays, Robert Israel, Heidi Ettinger Landesman, Adrianne Lobel, Thomas Lynch, James Noone, Neil Patel, Kevin Rigdon, David Rockwell, Douglas Stein, Paul Steinberg, Tony Straiges, Julie Taymor, George Tsypin, Michael Yeargan, and David Zinn. Each have added innovations, particularly as computer-related technologies, emerged and offered new possibilities. Many among these designers—Julie Taymor, for example—are likely to blur the lines among the various areas of design and, in Taymor's case, she also directs and writes with distinction.

In the area of costume design, it is more likely that the designer focuses exclusively on costumes; however, like scene designers, they are inclined to work successfully in film (as in the case of Broadway's Irene Sharaff) or in opera and dance, as well as regional and university theatres. Since 1930, most have contributed to Broadway, including such leading costume designers as Theoni V. Aldredge, Lucinda Ballard, Aline Bernstein, Rolf Gérard, Jane Greenwood, Willa Kim, Florence Klotz, Franne Lee, Robert Mackintosh, Mainbocher, Motley, Nancy Potts, Carrie Robbins, Ann Roth, Rouben Ter-Artunian, Susan Tsu, and Patricia Zipprodt, while post-1970s costume designers are more likely to have their work seen Off-Broadway and in regional theatres, as well as film and television. Among these are Susan Hilferty, Ann Hould-Ward, Michael Krass, Martin Pakledinaz, Robert Perdziola, Dunya Ramicova, Paul Tazewell, Jennifer Von Mayrhauser, and Catherine Zuber, to name a few.

Lighting design, particularly since World War II on Broadway, has tended to be dominated by few major names, among them Jules Fisher, Tharon Musser, Jean Rosenthal, Thomas R. Skelton, and Jennifer Tipton, but most of these artists also branched out to embrace opportunities away from Broadway, ultimately, in regional theatres. Other major lighting designers of the era between 1930 and 2010 include **Martin Aronstein, Ken Billington, Peggy Clark, Pat Collins, Peggy Eisenhauer, Beverly Emmons, Abe Feder, Paul Gallo, John Gleason, Gilbert Hemsley, Mark Henderson, Peter Kaczorowski, Leo Kerz, Roger Morgan, Richard Nelson, Dennis Parichy,** and **Richard Pilbrow,** among many others.

American designers have also developed new theatre technologies—computerized equipment for drafting, lighting, and sound—and consulted on theatre architecture, including such designers as **Herbert J. Krapp,** Edward Kook, and, most notably, **George Izenouer.** Many, beginning with Robert Edmond Jones, have written theoretical works on theatre and design (Jones's seminal *The Dramatic Imagination* has remained in print since its original publication in 1941) and the most noted and prolific of the scene and costume designers have had collections of their designs published which, in the cases of Jones, Simonson, Oenslager, Mielziner, and Aronson, provides a remarkable visual history of the American theatre between World War I and 1980.

DETECTIVE STORY. **Sidney Kingsley**'s slice-of-life drama of a day in a police station opened on 23 March 1949 at the Hudson Theatre for 581 performances. HOWARD LINDSAY and **Russel Crouse** produced, Kingsley directed, and BORIS ARONSON provided scene designs for this realistic large-cast play featuring **Ralph Bellamy** as a harried detective. The cast included veterans **Jean Adair**, Alexander Scourby, **Joseph Wiseman**, and Horace McMahon, while bright newcomers including Lee Grant and **Maureen Stapleton** made strong impressions. A 1951 film version directed by William Wyler featured members of the **Broadway** cast, including McMahon, Wiseman, and Grant, who garnered an Academy Award nomination, with Kirk Douglas replacing Bellamy.

DEVIL AND DANIEL WEBSTER, THE. As part of the American Lyric Theatre Repertory, this play with music (some critics labeled it a "folk opera") by Stephen Vincent Benét and Douglas Stuart Moore, adapted from Benét's 1937 short story, opened on 18 May 1939 for 6 performances under the direction of **John Houseman** with scene designs by ROBERT EDMOND JONES. Despite its brief **Broadway** life, Benét's story, which was inspired by Faust and Washington Irving's story "The Devil and Tom Walker," and the play have had an enduring life on stages and on screen. The play centers on Jabez Stone, a New Hampshire farmer with little luck, who sells his soul to the devil, known as Mr. Scratch. When Stone ultimately repents his decision, he calls upon Daniel Webster to defend him, although Mr. Scratch will only agree if he can summon a jury of historic villains from the bowels of hell to serve as a jury. An atmospheric 1941 RKO film version, sometimes called *All That Money Can Buy*, starring WALTER HUSTON, in an Academy Award-nominated performance, as Mr. Scratch, has attained classic status, in part through Bernard Herrmann's Oscar-winning score, although an updated 2007 remake failed to find favor.

DEWHURST, COLLEEN (1924–1991). Born in Montreal, Canada, this much-honored actress of theatre, film, and television was raised in Whitefish Bay, Wisconsin, and attended Milwaukee-Downer College. She labored long in **Off-Broadway** theatres, beginning in a minor role in a 1952 revival of *Desire under the Elms.** She won a **Theatre World Award** for *Children of Darkness* (1958) and a **Drama Desk Award** for *Hello and Goodbye* (1970) Off-Broadway, but much of her most noted work was done on **Broadway**, where she won a **Tony Award** for *All the Way Home* (1960) and garnering Tony nominations for *Great Day in the Morning* (1962), *The Ballad of the Sad Café* (1963), *More Stately Mansions* (1967), *All Over* (1971), and a revival of *Mourning Becomes Electra* in 1972 (for which she won a Drama Desk Award).

Dewhurst appeared in another highly acclaimed revival, EUGENE O'NEILL's *A Moon for the Misbegotten* in 1973, continuing a long association with O'Neill's work. She won a Tony and a Drama Desk Award for her performance of Connecticut farm girl Josie Hogan and appeared in a 1975 television production based on the revival. Dewhurst appeared with some frequency in films and television (winning four Emmy Awards and eleven nominations), but returned to the stage, receiving a Tony nomination for a revival of *Who's Afraid of Virginia Woolf?* in 1976 and Drama Desk nominations for *The Queen and the Rebels* (1982) and a revival of O'Neill's *Long Day's Journey into Night* in 1988, this last being part of a two-play **repertory** with O'Neill's *Ah, Wilderness!*, both of which starred Dewhurst with her *A Moon for the Misbegotten* costar, **Jason Robards**, who, like Dewhurst, was much-admired in productions of O'Neill's plays.

Dewhurst's other noted Broadway appearances include a revival of *The Good Woman of Setzuan* in 1970, *An Almost Perfect Person* (1977), and the all-star 1983 revival of *You Can't Take It with You*. Dewhurst was twice married to and divorced from actor **George C. Scott** and is the mother of actor Campbell Scott. From 1985 to her death, Dewhurst was president of the ACTORS' EQUITY ASSOCIATION.

DEXTER, JOHN (1925–1990). A British theatre, opera, and film director, Dexter was born in Derby, England, and following service in the British army during World WAR II, he began his theatre career as an actor, but in 1957 joined the Royal Court Theatre as associate director prior to taking a similar position with the National Theatre of Great Britain in 1963 and, eventually, becoming its director. Despite the fact that much of his career was spent in England, he directed several **Broadway** productions, winning **Tony Awards** and **Drama Desk Awards** for his productions of *Equus* (1974) *and M. Butterfly* (1988). On Broadway, he also staged *Do I Hear a Waltz?* (1965), *The Royal Hunt of the Sun* (1965), *Black Comedy/White Lies* (1967), for which he was Tony-nominated, *The Unknown Soldier and His Wife* (1967), and revivals of *The Misanthrope* in 1975, *The Glass Menagerie* in 1983, and *Threepenny Opera* in 1989.

DIAL "M" FOR MURDER. Frederick Knott's hit thriller about a man's plan to murder his wife opened at the Plymouth Theatre on 29 October 1952 for 552 performances under the direction of **Reginald Denham**. John Williams won a **Tony Award** as Inspector Hubbard, who works to determine who is the guilty party—husband Tony Wendice (**Maurice Evans**) or wife Margot (Gusti Huber). Alfred Hitchcock directed a 1954 film version in which Williams repeated his performance and costarred with **Grace Kelly** and Ray Milland.

DIARY OF ANNE FRANK, THE. **Frances Goodrich** and **Albert Hackett** adapted the diary of an optimistic young Jewish girl lost in the Holocaust into a two-act PULITZER PRIZE, **New York Drama Critics Circle Award**, and **Tony Award**-winning drama that opened on 5 October 1955 in a **Kermit Bloomgarden** production at the Cort Theatre for 717 performances under the direction of **Garson Kanin** with scene design by BORIS ARONSON. Covering a period from July 1942 to August 1944, the play chronicles the struggles of the Frank family and a few other Jewish neighbors to live hidden in an Amsterdam attic as the occupying Nazi forces search for them and other hidden "undesirables." Thirteen-year-old Anne, the daughter of the family, played by **Theatre World Award** winner and Tony Award-nominated Susan Strasberg, maintains an unyielding optimism and goes through growing pains under these extraordinary circumstances. The original cast, which included JOSEPH SCHILDKRAUT as Otto Frank, with **Jack Gilford**, Gusti Huber, **Lou Jacobi**, and others, received critical acclaim. The play, in a revised version by Wendy Kesselman and **James Lapine**, returned to **Broadway** in 1997 for 221 performances and a 1959 film version won three Academy Awards, including one for **Shelley Winters** in a supporting role, with Schildkraut, Huber, and Jacobi repeating their Broadway performances. In addition, there were two television film versions (1967, 1980) and two TV series (1987, 2008) based on the play also appeared.

DIGGES, DUDLEY (1879–1947).† Born in Dublin, Ireland, Digges worked with the Irish National Theatre before moving to the United States in 1904. He played opposite Minnie Maddern Fiske* in *The Rising of the Moon* (1908) and George Arliss* in *Disraeli* (1911) joining THE THEATRE GUILD in 1919. For the Guild, Digges distinguished himself in the original productions of *The Adding Machine** (1923), *Outward Bound** (1924), *Marco Millions** (1928), and *Dynamo** (1929), as well as a range of American productions of important European works. Digges also staged several Guild productions and when he left the Guild in 1930, he gave notable performances in **Paul Osborn**'s *On Borrowed Time* (1938), GEORGE S. KAUFMAN and **Moss Hart**'s *George Washington Slept Here* (1942), and a revival of GEORGE BERNARD SHAW'S *Candida* in 1942. He served as vice-president of ACTORS' EQUITY ASSOCIATION and appeared in nearly 50 films, including the screen version of EUGENE O'NEILL's *The Emperor Jones** (1933). Given his association with several O'Neill plays in the 1920s, it was fitting that Digges had his final **Broadway** role as Harry Hope in *The Iceman Cometh* (1946), a performance that won him critical plaudits.

DINING ROOM, THE. **A. R. Gurney, Jr.**'s comedy of manners in 18 scenes was produced by **Playwrights Horizons** in their Studio Theatre, where it opened on 24 February 1982 for 511 performances. Gurney makes use of a single well-appointed dining room set in which the stories of several New England families overlap in a depiction of the decline of upper-middle class white families in the late twentieth century. The play derives some mocking comedy from particular characters, but also laments the passing of a certain kind of social stability inherent in their lives. The original cast featured **William H. Macy**, Lois de Banzie, **Remak Ramsay**, and John Shea. Despite the play's success, a 1984 television film version failed to excite much critical enthusiasm.

DINNER AT EIGHT. GEORGE S. KAUFMAN and EDNA FERBER's brittle comedy-drama opened on 22 October 1932 in a SAM H. HARRIS production at the Music Box Theatre for 232 performances. Kaufman and Ferber capture a moment among New York City's elite as its denizens face the hard economic realities of the Great Depression. Their rarified world would soon vanish and the only characters with a chance of survival must be resourceful and demonstrate strong moral character. Several of the play's characters are in dire financial straits, but none are as desperate as Larry Renault, a played-out roué and ex-matinee idol, who has fallen into a casual month-long affair with the shipping magnate Oliver Jordan's (Malcolm Duncan) socialite daughter, Paula (Marguerite Churchill), whose feelings for him are made of equal parts desire and pity. Paula's mother, Millicent (Ann Andrews), a flighty social climber, plans a dinner for England's Lord and Lady Ferncliffe and has invited Renault, unaware of his illicit relationship with Paula. The tribulations of the various guests, including stage star Carlotta Vance (Constance Collier), are seen as they all prepare to attend the party. Paula tries to stem Renault's out-of-control drinking, but his impatience with her entreaties causes her to back off. When Renault is offered a minor role in an upcoming **Broadway** play, he is too proud to accept and, with nowhere to turn, commits suicide.

Conway Tearle* scored a personal success as Renault and the entire production was praised, with the *New York Herald Tribune* critic calling it "one of the best of the shrewdly literate Broadway dramas." A revival in 1966 with an all-star cast (Darren McGavin played Renault) ran for 127 performances, and a 2002 **Lincoln Center** production won plaudits for Byron Jennings as Renault, but the play lives most vividly in the cultural imagination through its lavish 1933 screen adaptation, and the character of Renault similarly merged with the brilliant, self-destructive John Barrymore,* who gave one of his finest screen performances under director George Cukor.

DINNER WITH FRIENDS. This Pulitzer Prize-winning play by **Donald Margulies** was first performed in 1998 at the Humana Festival of New American Plays at the **Actors Theatre of Louisville** prior to its **Off-Broadway** production, which opened on 4 November 1999. In the play, happily married Gabe and Karen (Matthew Arkin, Lisa Emery) observe the collapse of the marriage of their friends, Tom and Beth (Kevin Kilner, Julie White), which ultimately forces them to assess their own marriage. Along with the Pulitzer, the play also won the **Lucille Lortel Award** and an **Outer Critics Circle Award**, among other acknowledgments. A 2001 television film version received two Emmy Award nominations and starred Dennis Quaid, Andie MacDowell, Greg Kinnear, and Toni Collette.

DIRECTING/DIRECTORS. The director as the dominant force in theatrical production was a concept and a reality that began to emerge in the last decades of the nineteenth century. The position of the actor-manager of the eighteenth century and first three-quarters of the nineteenth century slowly evolved into a dominant interpretive force commanding overall responsibility for every facet of a theatre production. As pioneered by Georg II, Duke of Saxe-Meningen, in 1870s Europe, the modern director guides actors, designers, and technicians to achieve an aesthetically unified production, and as new technologies provided greater visual opportunities and the New Stagecraft* of *fin de siècle* Europe demanded a strong force to guide the growing number of collaborators, the contemporary director emerged.

At the beginning of the twentieth century, American theatre practitioners largely embraced this model, although program credit for directing did not become standard until after World WAR I. The prior control of actor-managers, particularly those who were star actors, continued into the twentieth century as the star often remained the strongest presence in a commercial theatre production. Artistically inclined producers such as GEORGE M. COHAN (who often directed, while also producing, acting, and writing) or Florenz Ziegfeld, Jr.* (strictly a producer, albeit one whose taste and artistic vision contributed significantly to the quality of his productions) employed directors as little more than glorified stage managers while they continued to control all aspects of production. Indeed, in England, the practice of directing continued to be ascribed to a "producer" for several decades after the term "director" became current in American theatre. In addition, many producers until well into the mid-twentieth century were also directors.

The rise of REALISM in U.S. drama, first evident in James A. Herne's* social problem play *Margaret Fleming** (1890), and in the painstakingly detailed stage productions of David Belasco,* along with significant advances in stage technology, increased the need for a strong director to guide actors through the intricacies of challenging plays and to supervise increasingly complex technical productions. By the 1910s, with the emergence of the Little Theatre movement,* and particularly after World War I, the formation of ambitious producing organizations (the Provincetown Players,* the THEATRE GUILD, **The Group Theatre**, etc.) required directors with a fervent artistic vision coupled with sensitive interpretive skills, not to mention a strong organizational bent. The Russian-born theatre artist Theodore Komisarjevsky worked in the United States from 1934 and was among several international directors instrumental in demonstrating directorial artistry as distinct from producing or management, although some notable American-born directors were already at work on **Broadway** in the 1920s, including GEORGE ABBOTT, GEORGE M. COHAN, JED HARRIS, EVA LE GALLIENNE, and PHILLIP MOELLER, although Cohan and Le Gallienne were closer to the star actor-managers of the pre-World War I era and all were, at various times, producers. In fact, many leading actors, as well as producers, also directed in the 1920s and 1930s.

Some of the most acclaimed directors between 1920 and 1960 were also playwrights, including **Abe Burrows, Moss Hart, Garson Kanin, George S. Kaufman**, and **Arthur Laurents**, and some, like **Eddie Dowling** and

Richard Whorf, were better known as actors (or producers) or, in the cases of **Herbert Berghof** and **Lee Strasberg**, acting teachers. **Harold Clurman** doubled as a director and a CRITIC/teacher for a long career extending from the 1930s, when he rose to prominence with The Group Theatre, to the 1970s. Other directors became associated with a particular actor; for example, **Guthrie McClintic** guided the long and distinguished career of his wife, KATHARINE CORNELL, although he occasionally directed plays without her involvement. Without question, Abbott, known to his colleagues by the affectionate and respectful moniker "Mister Abbott," was the "brand name" Broadway director between the mid-1920s and the 1960s, although Kaufman was easily as versatile a director as Abbott; both men staged plays in every genre typical of Broadway, from the most serious dramas to MUSICALS. In Kaufman's case, the achievement is especially impressive since he was also a prolific Pulitzer Prize-winning playwright.

The Group Theatre was not the only entity in the 1930s to inspire directors like Clurman, Strasberg, and others. **The Federal Theatre Project** provided important early opportunities to a number of directors, none more so than **Orson Welles**, who rose to fame and notoriety as a director (and actor) with the FTP, most famously for his staging of Marc Blitzstein's musical satire, *The Cradle Will Rock* (1937), which caused considerable controversy, but also for novel productions of SHAKESPEARE, including his all-black "voodoo" *Macbeth* (1936) and a modern-dress version of *Julius Caesar* (1937), creating a parallel with the rise of European fascism. The 1930s also produced the most acclaimed Broadway director from the 1940s to the 1960s, **Elia Kazan**. Both Welles and Kazan spent at least as much time directing films as theatre once they had achieved fame. Welles's returns to the stage were particularly rare after the early 1940s. Kazan, however, returned consistently to Broadway and was associated with some of the most important new American plays produced in the mid-twentieth century, most particularly the works of **Tennessee Williams** and **Arthur Miller**. Many stage directors in the wake of Welles and Kazan were influenced by their work on stage and screen, and most also worked as often in film (and television after the late 1940s) as theatre.

Some directors arriving on the scene between the 1940s and the 1970s devoted themselves to Broadway's more popular fare (**Morton Da Costa, Vincent J. Donehue, Robert Moore, Gene Saks, Dore Schary**), while others were identified with serious drama (**William Ball, Gene Frankel, Jules Irving, Daniel Mann, Marshall W. Mason, Arthur Penn, José Quintero, Stuart Vaughan**) or more experimental and avant-garde works either on Broadway or, more likely, **Off-Broadway** and **Off-Off-Broadway** (**Julian Beck, Herbert Blau, Tom O'Horgan, Alan Schneider, Robert Wilson**).

Others, including **Joseph Anthony, José Ferrer, Gerald Freedman, Joseph Hardy, Albert Marre, Jack O'Brien, Ellis Rabb, Mel Shapiro, Edwin Sherin, Daniel Sullivan, David Wheeler,** and **Garland Wright,** demonstrated versatility, moving between commercial works and serious drama. Among the most versatile of the era, there are two standouts: **Joshua Logan,** although he is perhaps more remembered for his work in musicals (some of which he coauthored, such as the PULITZER PRIZE-winning *South Pacific*), and **Mike Nichols,** who began as a performer before becoming a celebrated film and stage director who continued to work with distinction for five decades in all genres.

Women directors were comparatively rare until the late 1960s and into the twenty-first century, although in the nineteenth and early twentieth centuries, several star actress/managers had taken strong directorial control of their productions. EVA LE GALLIENNE, following on the model established by the most notable among such women, Minnie Maddern Fiske,* established herself as a director (and actress) with her Civic Repertory Theatre,* while other women, including British director **Margaret Webster,** who often directed Shakespeare's plays on Broadway and in other American theatres, were increasingly accepted. Women playwrights, including RACHEL CROTHERS, and later, **Elaine May,** often directed their own works, and by the 1940s, women directors including **Antoinette Perry** and **Margo Jones,** along with Webster, directed with some frequency. By the 1970s, more significant inroads were made when **Julie Taymor** became the first director to win a **Tony Award** (ironically named for Antoinette Perry), one sign of greater acceptance on Broadway, although Off-Broadway and Off-Off-Broadway theatres had been more welcoming to women directors since the 1950s, including such pioneers as **Julie Bovasso** (who was more known as an actress and a sometime writer), **Elizabeth LeCompte, Judith Malina,** and others. **African American** women directors were even more rare in the twentieth century, although **Vinnette Carroll** won acclaim as the first black woman director on Broadway in 1972, staging Miki Grant's musical, *Don't Bother Me, I Can't Cope.* **Regional theatres,** feminist companies, and other theatres away from the New York mainstream provided increased opportunities to women directors after 1980, including, among others, **Pamela Berlind, Anne Bogart, Tina Landau, Carey Perloff, Lisa Peterson,** and **Mary Zimmerman.**

African American directors were few prior to the 1960s, but in the later decades of the twentieth century several rose to distinction, including **Gilbert H. Moses, III, Harold Scott** (who became the first African American to serve as artistic director of a major regional theatre, the **Paper Mill Playhouse**), and **Douglas Turner Ward.** Most notable among black directors were **Lloyd Richards,** who directed the premieres of most of **August Wilson**'s plays and headed the Yale School of Drama, and **George C. Wolfe**, who won acclaim as a playwright (*The Colored Museum*) and as artistic director of **The Public Theatre**.

International and foreign-born directors worked with regularity in American theatre, on Broadway and elsewhere, from the 1920s, but more frequently after World War II, including, between the 1930s to 2010, Peter Brook, **Michael Chekhov, Liviu Ciulei, Reginald Denham, John Dexter, Michael Grandage, Peter Glenville, Ulu Grosbard, Tyrone Guthrie, Adrian Hall, Peter Hall, Nicholas Hytner, Michael Langham, Vivian Matalon, Des McAnuff, Trevor Nunn, Ben Iden Payne, Erwin Piscator, Max Reinhardt, Michael Saint-Denis, Andrei Serban, John Tillinger, Matthew Warchus**, Margaret Webster, and **Bretaigne Windust**.

After 1970, most American stage directors not only worked frequently in film and television, but most either emerged from or developed long relationships with regional theatres and, on occasion, **academic theatres**. More importantly, many post-World War II directors were increasingly influenced by film techniques (as were playwrights) and were inspired by many modern and contemporary international stage techniques, from Asian theatre to the epic theatre of **Bertolt Brecht**. Directors continued to associate themselves either with particular artists and companies or with a genre of theatre, but most followed the model established by earlier major directors like Abbott and Kaufman, becoming skilled in all forms of theatre and often writing/adapting plays, acting, and producing and/or serving as artistic directors of companies. From 1970 to 2010, these directors include such diverse figures as **A. J. Antoon, Jeff Bleckner, Lee Breuer, Mark Brokaw, Arvin Brown, Carmen Capalbo, David Cromer, Gordon Davidson, Scott Elliott, Scott Ellis, David Esbjornson, Oskar Eustis, Robert Falls, Gene Feist, Frank Galati, Michael Greif, Gerald Gutierrez, Jon Jory, Michael Kahn, Moisés Kaufman, Brian Kulick, Mark Lamos, James Lapine, Wilford Leach, Michael Mayer, Gregory Mosher, Stephen Porter, John Rando, Peter Sellars, Bartlett Sher, Robert Woodruff, Jerry Zaks**, and **Scott Ziegler**, among others. Some worked on Broadway and others devoted themselves exclusively to one or another theatre company, either in New York or other major cities, and some worked frequently in film and television, but all continued a long American directorial tradition dating back at least as far as 1920.

DISNEY THEATRICAL PRODUCTIONS. Set up by the Walt Disney Company in 1994, this production organization produces **Broadway** versions of Disney-owned screen properties. Thus far, it has only produced MUSICALS based on Disney films, but among its contributions to the New York theatre was the careful restoration of the New Amsterdam Theatre on 42nd Street, once the home of the *Ziegfeld* Follies*.

DOCUMENTARY THEATRE. Since the classical period, much theatre has been based on history and topical events, but this term refers most directly to a brand of contemporary theatre based, in part, on the epic theatre style pioneered by **Erwin Piscator** and **Bertolt Brecht** in Germany before World WAR II. Adherents to the epic style, including Rolf Hochhuth, Peter Weiss, and Heinar Kipphardt, like Brecht, turned to the historical to make political arguments about the impact of that history and current events. In the pre-World War II years in America, this approach with modifications was adopted by the **Federal Theatre Project** for their **Living Newspaper** productions, in which current issues taken from the headlines were presented in theatrical form, using direct quotes from documents, government officials, and others pertinent to the topic of a particular work.

The documentary form was not much used by American playwrights in the first decades after the war. However with the social unrest of the 1960s, documentary theatre—sometimes referred to as docudramas—achieved a vigorous new life, particularly **Off-Broadway** and **Off-Off Broadway**, in such works as Martin Duberman's *In White America* (1964), Daniel Berrigan's *Trial of the Catonsville Nine* (1970), **Eric Bentley**'s *Are You Now or Have You Ever Been* (1972), all of which looked back at American history in response to more current issues. Many courtroom dramas, including *Inherit the Wind* (1955) and *In the Matter of J. Robert Oppenheimer* (1968), draw heavily on the historical record while fictionalizing as well. This balance of fact and fiction has blurred, even as more artful presentations of the historical record have appeared, and the necessity of following the historical record closely is at least partially challenged even as the work retains its documentary ambience, including Steve Dobbins's *The Dan White Incident* (1983), **Robert Wilson**'s *CIVIL WarS* (1984), **Spalding Gray**'s *Swimming to Cambodia* (1985), **Emily Mann**'s *Execution of Justice* (1986), **Anna Deavere Smith**'s *Fires in the Mirror* (1991), **Ping Chong**'s *The Undesirable Elements* (1992), Marc Wolf's *Another American: Asking and Telling* (1999), the **Tectonic Theatre Project**'s *The Laramie Project* (2001), Michael Rohd's *Witness Our Schools* (2004), and **Doug Wright**'s *I Am My Own Wife* (2004).

Gary Fisher Dawson has written a study surveying American documentary drama in *Documentary Theatre in the United States: An Historical Survey and Analysis of Its Content, Form, and Stagecraft* (Greenwood Press, 1999). Another sort of documentary theatre are **solo performances** depicting historical personages in which the subject's own words are used, such as in *Mark Twain Tonight!* (1966), as well as numerous subsequent plays adopting a similar approach and focusing on such diverse figures as Harry S. Truman in *Give 'Em Hell, Harry* (1975), Emily Dickinson in *The Belle of Amherst* (1976), Theodore Roosevelt in *Bully!* (1978), PAUL ROBESON in *Paul*

Robeson (1978), and Golda Meir in *Golda's Balcony* (2003), and others, many of which succeeded on **Broadway**, on tour, and in **regional theatres**.

DODSON, OWEN (1914–1983). Born in Brooklyn, New York, Owen Vincent Dodson graduated from Bates College and the Yale School of Drama before teaching at Howard University. A playwright, poet, and novelist, Dodson trained a number of important **African American** theatre practitioners, including **Ossie Davis**, **Amiri Baraka**, **Earle Hyman**, **Richard Wesley**, **Phylicia Rashad**, and Debbie Allen. As a playwright, he acknowledged debts to HENRIK IBSEN and LANGSTON HUGHES, and his work has mostly been produced in university theatres, including *Divine Comedy* (1938), *Garden of Time* (1939), *Amistad* (1939), *Doomsday Tale* (1941), *Gonna Tear Them Pillars Down* (1942), *The Ballad of Dorrie Miller* (1943), *New World A-Coming* (1944), *The Third Fourth of July* (1946; coauthored with Countee Cullen), *Bayou Legend* (1946), *Medea in Africa* (1959; coauthored with Countee Cullen), *Till Victory Is Won* (1965), *The Story of the Soul* (1978), and *Freedom, The Banner* (1983). Writing of Dodson's significance in the Harlem Renaissance, James V. Hatch notes that Dodson "is the product of two parallel forces—the Black experience in America with its folk and urban routes, and a classical humanist education."

DODSWORTH. **Sidney Howard**'s three-act drama adapted from Sinclair Lewis's novel was produced by **Max Gordon** and opened on 24 February 1934 at the Shubert Theatre for 147 performances under the direction of Robert B. Sinclair, with settings by JO MIELZINER. WALTER HUSTON starred as the title character, a wealthy automaker who has retired to take his wife Fran (FAY BAINTER) on a European grand tour. Instead of renewing their relationship and enjoying the cultural riches of Europe, the spoiled and childish Fran indulges in meaningless affairs. The unhappy Dodsworth meets Edith Cortright (Nan Sunderland), whose grace and compassion encourages him to stay in Europe with her while Fran, surprised by Dodsworth's resolve to start his life over, faces her culpability in the end of their relationship. Huston repeated his performance in a 1936 film version, reaping an Academy Award nomination, as did Howard's screenplay.

DONALDSON AWARD. These theatre **awards** were created in 1944 to honor the memory of W. H. Donaldson, the founder of *Billboard** magazine. Several categories were created, including best play, best MUSICAL, best debut performances, and best costumes and set design. The Donaldson Awards continued annually until 1955, a few years after the ANTOINETTE PERRY **Tony Awards** rendered the Donaldsons redundant.

DONAT, PETER (1928–). A native of Kentville, Nova Scotia, Canada, Pierre Collingwood Donat moved to the United States in 1950 and found work as an actor with the Provincetown Playhouse,* the **Margo Jones** Theatre, and several STOCK theatres, playing everything from **Shakespeare** and SHAW to contemporary American plays. The nephew of Academy Award-winning actor Robert Donat, after a long apprenticeship in **repertory** and stock theatre, he found a semi-permanent home at San Francisco's **American Conservatory Theatre** beginning in 1968, winning praise for many performances, including the title role in *Cyrano de Bergerac* in 1972 and Dysart in *Equus* in 1975. Donat has given numerous film and television performances and appeared on **Broadway** in *The First Gentlemen* (1957), for which he won a **Theatre World Award**, a revival of *The Country Wife* in 1957, *The Entertainer* (1958), *The Chinese Prime Minister* (1964), and *There's One in Every Marriage* (1972).

DONEHUE, VINCENT J. (1915–1966). Born in Whitehall, New York, Vincent Julian Donehue began his career as an actor, appearing on **Broadway** in *Jeremiah* (1939), *Christmas Eve* (1939), and *The Old Foolishness* (1940), but switched to directing in 1953, scoring major successes staging *Sunrise at Campobello* (1958), for which he won a **Tony Award**, and *The Sound of Music* (1959), for which he received a Tony nomination. Adept at both drama and MUSICALS, he also directed *The Trip to Bountiful* (1953), *The Traveling Lady* (1954), *All in One* (1955), *Daughter of Silence* (1961), *Lord Pengo* (1962), *Jennie* (1963), and *Catch Me If You Can* (1965). Donehue also directed for television during the 1950s and 1960s, most notably the 1960 TV production of *Peter Pan** in 1960 and on the big screen he directed *Lonelyhearts* (1958) and the screen version of *Sunrise at Campobello* in 1960.

DONNELLY, DONAL (1931–2010). This Anglo-Irish actor was born in Bradford, West Yorkshire, England, but raised in Ireland. He attended the Synge Street Christian Brothers School before beginning a stage and film career touring in Anew McMaster's Irish Repertory Company. On **Broadway**, he was nominated for a **Tony Award** in Brian Friel's *Philadelphia, Here I Come!* (1966), after which he replaced the lead in *A Day in the Death of Joe Egg* (1968). He received a **Drama Desk Award** nomination for *Faith Healer* (1979) and won a **Theatre World Award** and a Drama Desk Award as part of the ensemble of *Dancing at Lughnasa* (1991). Donnelly's other Broadway appearances include *The Mundy Scheme* (1969), *Execution of Justice* (1986), *Sherlock's Last Case* (1987), *Ghetto* (1989), and *Translations* (1995), and replaced Keith Baxter as Milo Tindle in *Sleuth* (1970) and also stepped in as a replacement in *The Elephant Man* (1979). He appeared in many television shows and films, including most notably *The Knack . . . and How to Get It* (1965).

DOUBT: A PARABLE. **John Patrick Shanley**'s PULITZER PRIZE and **Tony Award**-winning play premiered at the **Manhattan Theatre Club** on 23 November 2004 prior to transferring to **Broadway**'s **Walter Kerr** Theatre on 31 March 2005 for 525 performances under the Tony-winning direction of **Doug Hughes**. Set in 1964, the play is set at a parochial school in the Bronx (designed by **John Lee Beatty**) where the principal, the rigid Sister Aloysius (**Cherry Jones** in a Tony-winning performance) suspects that a priest, Father Flynn (Brían F. O'Byrne), has had an inappropriate relationship with the school's first black student. Despite lacking hard evidence, Sister Aloysius enlists the somewhat unwilling assistance of Sister James (Heather Goldenhersh) and the boy's mother, Mrs. Muller (Adriane Lenox in a Tony-winning performance). Shanley's play transcends the question of whether or not Father Flynn has done what Sister Aloysius believes he has done, but instead centers on the nature of uncertainty and a range of inherent questions of morality, **race**, and **religious** belief. A 2008 film version was nominated for five Academy Awards and starred **Meryl Streep**, **Philip Seymour Hoffman**, Amy Adams, and **Viola Davis**.

DOUGHGIRLS, THE. Joseph Fields's three-act comedy produced by **Max Gordon** opened at the Lyceum Theatre on 30 December 1942 for 671 performances. Directed by GEORGE S. KAUFMAN, the play is set in a Washington, D.C. hotel suite where three women, all unmarried although they have been living with men, are compelled to live together due to the wartime housing shortage in the nation's capital. Virginia Field, Doris Nolan, and Arleen Whelan played the three women, with **Arlene Francis** as a Russian sniper who moves in with them. The personal relationships of the women cause a variety of complications, all resolved despite critical complaints at the risqué aspects of the plot. Despite this, wartime audiences clearly enjoyed this lighthearted romp expertly staged by Kaufman. A 1944 film version, starring Ann Sheridan, Alexis Smith, and Jane Wyman, ramped up the comedy, but diluted the moral ambiguities by providing the girls with husbands or more chaste relationships.

DOUGLAS, MELVYN (1901–1981). Born Melvyn Edouard Hesselberg in Macon, Georgia, Douglas's long acting career encompassed stage and screen. He began his career in stock companies, including that of Jessie Bonstelle,* before establishing his own theatre in Madison, Wisconsin. Douglas debuted on **Broadway** in 1928 in *A Free Soul* and shortly thereafter began a successful film career. On Broadway, Douglas won a Best Actor **Tony Award** for *The Best Man* (1960) and also appeared in *Tonight or Never* (1930), *No More Ladies* (1934), *Within the Gates* (1934), *Two Blind Mice* (1949), *The Bird Cage* (1950), *Glad Tidings* (1951), which he also directed, *Time Out for Ginger* (1952), a revival of *The Waltz of the Toreadors* in 1958, *Juno* (1959), *The Gang's All Here* (1959), and *Spofford* (1967).

Douglas also replaced PAUL MUNI in *Inherit the Wind* (1955). In the movies, Douglas won a Best Supporting Actor Academy Award twice, for *Hud* (1963) and *Being There* (1979), and received an Oscar nomination for *I Never Sang for My Father* (1970). Other notable films include *Counsellor-at-Law* (1933), *Captains Courageous* (1937), *Ninotchka* (1939), *A Woman's Face* (1941), *The Sea of Grass* (1947), *Billy Budd* (1962), *The Candidate* (1972), *The Seduction of Joe Tynan* (1979), and *Ghost Story* (1981). On television, Douglas was nominated for an Emmy Award for a TV production of *Inherit the Wind* in 1965 and he won an Emmy for *Do Not Go Gentle into That Good Night* (1967).

Douglas's second wife, actress **Helen Gahagan**, famously went into politics as a three-term Congresswoman who ran against Richard Nixon, who accused her of Communist leanings, stating that she was "pink right down to her underwear." In response, Gahagan labeled Nixon "Tricky Dick." Douglas's granddaughter Illeana Douglas is a successful film and television actress.

DOWD, HARRISON (1897–1964). Born in Madison, Connecticut, Dowd was a poet, pianist, and actor. In 1918, he made his **Broadway** debut in *Chu Chin Chow*. With the Provincetown Players* in 1919, he played Pierrot in *Aria da Capo.** He also appeared in productions of *A Trip to Scarborough* (1929), *The Dragon* (1929), *Night of Love* (1941), *Harriet* (1943), a revival of *Little Women** in 1944, *The Assassin* (1945), *A Temporary Island* (1948), *Dinosaur Wharf* (1951), *See the Jaguar* (1952), in support of ALFRED LUNT and LYNN FONTANNE in *The Visit* (1958), *Caligula* (1960), and *Night Life* (1962).

DOWLING, EDDIE (1889–1976). This actor, playwright, and producer was born Joseph Narcisse Gaucher in Woonsocket, Rhode Island, of Canadian parentage. He began his acting career in 1909 in a STOCK production of *Quo Vadis?* in Providence, Rhode Island. He toured in the *Ziegfeld* Follies of 1918* and married actress/comedienne Ray Dooley. Much of Dowling's early **Broadway** work was in MUSICALS, including *Sally, Irene and Mary* (1922), *Honeymoon Lane* (1926), *Sidewalks of New York* (1927), for which he also wrote the book, music, and lyrics, and others before becoming a producer of such diverse plays as the **Maurice Evans** production of *Richard II* in 1937,

Shadow and Substance (1938), and *Here Come the Clowns* (1938). As World WAR II approached, Dowling continued to produce (and sometimes direct and act, but he distinguished himself directing and starring as Joe in **William Saroyan**'s *The Time of Your Life* (1939) and **Tennessee Williams**'s *The Glass Menagerie* (1945), in which he played Williams's alter ego, Tom Wingfield opposite the legendary LAURETTE TAYLOR. He also directed Saroyan's *Love's Old Sweet Song* (1940) and EUGENE O'NEILL's *The Iceman Cometh* (1946). Dowling also appeared in a few early "talkies" between 1929 and 1931.

DRAKE, ALFRED (1914–1992). Born Alfredo Capurro in New York, he won his most lasting fame in MUSICALS, but his acting career was far more varied. His first **Broadway** appearances were in the ensembles of several Gilbert and Sullivan operettas* of the Civic Light Opera Company in 1935, but he was first noticed as part of the exuberant young company of *Babes in Arms* (1937) and several other musicals before winning critical acclaim as the cowboy Curly in *Oklahoma!* (1943) and Fred Graham/Petruchio in *Kiss Me, Kate* (1948). Drake won a **Tony Award** for *Kismet* (1954) and subsequent nominations for *Kean* (1962) and *Gigi* (1974). Drake's non-musical Broadway appearances were in *Out of the Frying Pan* (1941), a short-lived revival of *As You Like It* in 1941, *Yesterday's Magic* (1942), *The Gambler* (1952), *Love Me Little* (1958), *Lorenzo* (1963), *Those That Play the Clowns* (1966), *Song of the Grasshopper* (1967), and a revival of *The Skin of Our Teeth* in 1975. Most notably on Broadway, Drake played Claudius to **Richard Burton**'s Hamlet in 1964. For the **American Shakespeare Theatre** he appeared as Othello and as Benedick opposite **Katharine Hepburn**'s Beatrice in *Much Ado about Nothing* in 1957. In 1990, Drake was awarded a lifetime achievement Tony Award.

DRAKE, SYLVIE (1930–). Egyptian-born drama critic, Drake was raised in her birthplace of Alexandria prior to studying in England, where she achieved an Oxbridge Higher Certificate in England and French literature. In the United States after 1949, she worked at the **Pasadena Playhouse** and in television as an actress, writer, and director. In 1969, she began contributing theatre reviews to the *Los Angeles Canyon Crier* and the *Los Angeles Times* before joining the *Times* as a columnist and CRITIC in 1971. In 1991, Drake replaced **Dan Sullivan** as the *Times's* chief critic. Prior to her retirement in 1993, after which she served as an artistic associate at the **Denver Center Theatre.**

DRAMA DEPT. Established in 1994 as a not-for-profit theatre collective, with Douglas Carter Beane supervising activities, the Drama Dept. aimed to produce one or two productions a year, focusing on either forgotten American classics or new plays. Among the collective's membership are Cynthia Nixon, Sarah Jessica Parker, **B. D. Wong**, **Billy Crudup**, **Mark Brokaw**, Stephen Flaherty, **Richard Greenberg**, **Nicky Silver**, and others. Beane's *As Bees in Honey Drown* (1997) was one of the new works, along with **Charles Busch**'s *Shanghai Moon* (1999), Isaac Mizrahi's *Les MIZrahi* (2000), David and Amy Sedaris's *The Book of Liz* (2001), and others, with revivals of such diverse works as *Uncle Tom's Cabin* in 1998, which generated some controversy, GEORGE S. KAUFMAN and Ring Lardner's* *June Moon** in 1997, and the Irving Berlin-**Moss Hart** revue* *As Thousands Cheer* in 1998. *See also* REPERTORY THEATRE.

DRAMA DESK, THE/ DRAMA DESK AWARDS. The Drama Desk was founded in 1949 (chartered a not-for-profit organization in 1974) with a membership of theatre critics and journalists. Theatre professionals speak at monthly lunches held by the Drama Desk, but its main mission is the acknowledgment of outstanding theatre work in New York with the annual Drama Desk Awards, which have been presented since 1955 in a range of categories.

DRAMA LEAGUE, THE. Originally established in 1909 by an Evanston, Illinois, women's literary group called the Riley Circle, the League expanded within a few years to include thousands of members across the United States. Beginning in 1911, the League published a monthly periodical, *The Drama*, kept its membership abreast of activities with bulletins, sponsored theatre tours of the Irish Players, the Hull-House Players,* and such noted actors as Minnie Maddern Fiske* and George Arliss,* published play collections, offered summer educational activities, and held annual conventions. In 1931, the national League disbanded, but some local organizations continued, including the New York Drama League, which presented **awards** and sponsored support for young playwrights and directors.

DRAMATIC CRITICISM. *See* CRITICS, CRITICISM.

DRAMATIC THEORY. The evolution of dramatic theory, which could be said to date back to Aristotle, began in earnest in the United States in the late nineteenth century when playwrights, CRITICS, and **academics** began regularly writing and speaking on the nature of theatre and drama, including such figure as Dion Boucicault,* Bronson Howard,* David Belasco,* Edward Harrigan,* William Dean Howells,* and James A. Herne,* who threw down the gauntlet in support of an American drama based on REALISM in the mode of HENRIK IBSEN's plays.

By the early twentieth century, the influence of the New Stagecraft* in European drama moved centrally into the theorizing in the United States, with such figures as Brander Matthews,* Sheldon Cheney,* KENNETH MACGOWAN, GEORGE JEAN NATHAN, JOSEPH WOOD KRUTCH, and others dominated in the pre-World WAR II era, with leading playwrights (EUGENE O'NEILL, MAXWELL ANDERSON, **Thornton Wilder**), designers (ROBERT EDMOND JONES, LEE SIMONSON, MORDECAI GORELIK), and directors, actors and acting teachers (**Harold Clurman, Lee Strasberg**, STELLA ADLER) debating, usually in print, the nature of contemporary American drama and its techniques of performance. Following World War II, most major dramatists (**Tennessee Williams, Arthur Miller, Edward Albee**, and others) contributed to a growing body of essays on dramatic theory.

New trends in both European and American theatre were espoused after the war by such critics and practitioners as **Eric Bentley**, Northrup Frye, **Richard Schechner, Herbert Blau, Richard Foreman**, Marvin Carlson, Martin Esslin, **Robert Brustein**, and others, while **feminist** theorists began to have a significant impact after the 1970s, with such figures as Sue-Ellen Case, Elin Diamond, Alisa Solomon, Judith Butler, and others contributing various viewpoints on gender and **sexuality** in contemporary theatre. Queer theory came to the fore in the early 1990s, with writers including Laurence Senelick, Solomon, and various playwrights, from **Charles Ludlam** to **Tony Kushner**, contributing concepts. Most late twentieth-century and early twenty-first-century drama critics, particularly in such major publications as the *New York Times* or the *New Yorker*, explore dramatic theory, including **Frank Rich, Ben Brantley, Charles Isherwood, John Lahr**, and others, as well as a range of scholars in academic publications on theatre and drama, film, and other media. *See also* GAY AND LESBIAN THEATRE.

DRAMATISTS GUILD, INC., THE. This professional organization was founded in 1920 to protect the interests of writers of plays and MUSICALS. In the early twenty-first century, the Guild's membership exceeded 7,500 and continued in its original mission to protect the rights of playwrights. The Guild publishes the *Dramatists Guild Quarterly* and organizes auditions, readings, symposia and other activities for its membership.

DRAPER, RUTH (1884–1956). Born in New York, Draper carved out a unique niche in American and international theatre as a monologist and writer, creating over 35 sketches in which she performed over 50 characters she had imagined from her world travels. Beginning her career as an actress in *A Lady's Name* (1916), Draper soon discovered that her gifts as a mimic permitted her to create personas, accents, and attitudes from all walks of life and that skill in improvisation allowed her to depart from her text and make each performance original. As a monologist, she debuted at London's Aeolian Hall in 1920 and on **Broadway** in 1929 and died only hours after giving her final performance in New York in December 1956. She toured widely, with frequent returns to Broadway in 1932, 1934, 1936, 1940, 1947, 1954, and her final performances. Draper's monologues were recorded, but apparently no sound film of her in performance survives. Draper was the aunt of actor Paul Draper.

DREAM GIRL. ELMER RICE made a rare foray into light comedy in this two-act semi-fantasy, which he also directed. It was produced by the **Playwright's Company** at the Coronet Theatre where it opened on 14 December 1945 for 348 performances. Stylishly produced with scene and lighting designs by JO MIELZINER and costumes by **Mainbocher**, the play starred **Betty Field** (Rice's wife) as Georgina Allerton, an unsuccessful novelist and book store owner, who escapes her drab existence through daydreams, including an encounter with a radio psychiatrist. Eventually, she meets Clark Redfield (Wendell Corey), a book reviewer with aspirations to be a sports writer, and Clark proposes marriage if Georgina can control her dreams. Betty Hutton played Georgina in a 1948 film version and **Judy Holliday** took on the role in a 1951 New York City Theatre Company revival and in 1965 a musical adaptation starred **Julie Harris**.

DREXLER, ROSALYN (1926–). A playwright, screenwriter, novelist, and pop artist, Drexler was born and educated in New York and had her first major **solo** exhibition of art works in 1960, but won three **Obie Awards** for her productions of *Home Movies* (1964), *The Writer's Opera* (1979), and *Transients Welcome* (1985). Drexler's other plays include *Skywriting* (1965), *The Investigation* (1966), *Hot Buttered Roll* (1966), *The Line of Least Existence* (1968), *Softly and Consider the Nearness* (1972), *Was I Good?* (1972), *The Bed Was Full* (1972), *The Ice Queen* (1973), *She Who Was He* (1974), *Travesty Parade* (1974), *Graven Image* (1979), *Vulgar Lives* (1979), *The Tree Artist* (1981), *Starburn* (1983), *The Mandrake* (1983), *Dear* (1983), *Room 17C* (1983), *Lobby* (1984), *Delicate Feelings* (1984), *A Matter of Life and Death* (1986), *What Did You Call It?* (1986), and *The Heart That Eats Itself* (1987). Drexler also won an Emmy Award for writing *The Lily Show . . . A Lily Tomlin Special* on CBS-TV in 1974. In 2004, Drexler stated, "I was born an artist. I've always been an artist."

DREYFUSS, HENRY (1904–1972). A scenic and industrial designer, Dreyfuss was born in Brooklyn, New York, and studied under NORMAN BEL

GEDDES prior to opening his own design firm. On **Broadway**, he designed *Hold Everything!* (1928), ***The Last Mile*** (1930), *Fine and Dandy* (1930), *Pagan Lady* (1930), *The Gang's All Here* (1931), *Shoot the Works* (1931), *The Cat and the Fiddle* (1931), *Strike Me Pink* (1933), and *Paths of Glory* (1935) before shifting to industrial designs of everything from telephones, fountain pens, and alarm clocks to the "Democracity" model city of the future at the 1939 New York World's Fair.

DRIVING MISS DAISY. **Alfred Uhry**'s PULITZER PRIZE-winning comedy-drama opened on 15 April 1987 in **Playwrights Horizons** production at the **John Houseman** Theatre for 1,195 performances. The play also won the **Outer Critics Circle Award** and received a **Drama Desk Award** nomination, while the play's leading actors, **Dana Ivey** and **Morgan Freeman**, won **Obie Awards** for their respective performances as Daisy Werthan, an elderly Southern Jewish woman, and Hoke Colburn, her **African American** chauffeur. Miss Daisy resists having a chauffeur, but her protective son insists, and the play spans the years from 1948 to 1973 in Atlanta, Georgia, as the attitudes of its central characters reflect racial and other cultural changes filtered through the evolving personal relationship between them. The London production starred Wendy Hiller and a much-honored 1989 film version starred **Jessica Tandy** in an Academy Award-winning performance as Miss Daisy and Freeman repeating his stage role as Hoke. A 2010 **Broadway** revival, directed by **David Esbjornson**, starred **James Earl Jones** and Vanessa Redgrave.

DUKAKIS, OLYMPIA (1931–). Born in Lowell, Massachusetts, to immigrant Greek parents, Dukakis began a long career as an actress, teacher, and director following her graduation from Boston University. Dukakis labored in **regional theatres** and **Off-Broadway** for many years, cofounding Boston's Charles Street Playhouse in 1957 and the Edgartown Summer Theatre in 1960 before debuting Off-Broadway in *The Breaking Wall* (1960) and on **Broadway** as understudy in *The Aspern Papers* (1962). On Broadway, Dukakis appeared in *Abraham Cochrane* (1964), *Who's Who in Hell* (1974), *Social Security* (1986), and she was nominated for a **Drama Desk Award** for her solo performance in *Rose* (2000), which she had premiered at the National Theatre of Great Britain in 1999. Off-Broadway, Dukakis won **Obie Awards** for *A Man's a Man* (1963) and ***The Marriage of Bette and Boo*** (1985) and she has appeared in such **repertory** theatres as the **Williamstown Theatre Festival** and the **Hartford Stage**, where she played Mrs. Goforth in a revival of **Tennessee Williams**'s *The Milk Train Doesn't Stop Here Anymore* in 2008. Dukakis served as artistic director of New Jersey's Whole Theatre

Company from 1976 to 1990 and won film stardom through her Academy Award and Golden Globe Award-winning performance in *Moonstruck* (1987). Among her many films are *Working Girl* (1988), *Steel Magnolias* (1989), *Mighty Aphrodite* (1995), *Mr. Holland's Opus* (1995), and *The Great New Wonderful* (2005). Dukakis is also a three-time Emmy Award nominee. She is married to actor **Louis Zorich** and is the cousin of 1988 Democratic presidential candidate Michael Dukakis.

DUKES, DAVID (1945–2000). Son of a highway patrolman, David Coleman Dukes was born in San Francisco, California, and began his acting career on **Broadway** appearing in the **Phoenix Theatre** productions of *The School for Wives, The Great God Brown,** and *Don Juan* in 1971–1972. He appeared in the **Roundabout Theatre**'s revival of *The Play's the Thing* (1973) and Phoenix revivals of *The Visit, Chemin de Fer, Holiday,* Love for Love*, and *The Rules of the Game* in 1973–74, garnering **Drama Desk Award** nominations for the last two. As a replacement, he stepped into the role of Henry Carr in *Travesties* (1975), replaced **Frank Langella** in a revival of *Dracula** in 1977, and also took over the role of Salieri in *Amadeus* in 1980. Dukes's performance as Horst in **Martin Sherman**'s controversial *Bent* (1979) brought him Drama Desk and **Tony Award** nominations. He originated leading roles in *Frankenstein* (1981) and *Broken Glass* (1994), but replaced in *M. Butterfly* in 1988 and *Someone Who'll Watch over Me* in 1992. He appeared in over 30 films and on television, garnering an Emmy nomination for *The Josephine Baker Story* (1991) and he appeared as the potential rapist of Edith Bunker in one of the most talked-about episodes of *All in the Family* in 1977.

DUNNOCK, MILDRED (1901–1991). Born in Baltimore, Maryland, Dunnock attended Goucher College and did not begin a theatrical career until she was in her thirties. She debuted on **Broadway** in *Life Begins* (1932) and appeared in all manner of plays, from **Shakespeare** to modern dramas and even a MUSICAL (*Lute Song* in 1946). She appeared with ETHEL BARRYMORE in *The Corn Is Green* (1940) and during the 1940s also appeared in a revival of *Richard III* in 1943, *Only the Heart* (1944), *Foolish Notion* (1945), *Another Part of the Forest* (1946), *The Hallams* (1948), and *The Leading Lady* (1948) prior to her most acclaimed performance as Linda Loman in the premiere of **Arthur Miller**'s PULITZER PRIZE-winning drama *Death of a Salesman* (1949), repeating her performance in a 1951 film version (garnering an Academy Award nomination) and a 1966 television production (earning an Emmy Award nomination). Dunnock appeared in another Pulitzer Prize-winner, **Tennessee Williams**'s *Cat on a Hot Tin Roof* (1955) in the role of Big Mama. Dunnock also appeared in Broadway revivals of HENRIK IBSEN's

Peer Gynt and *The Wild Duck* in 1951, *In the Summer House* (1953), *Child of Fortune* (1956), *Pictures in the Hallway* (1959), *Farewell, Farewell Eugene* (1960), *The Milk Train Doesn't Stop Here Anymore* (1963), *Traveller without Luggage* (1964), *Days in the Trees* (1976), and a revival of *Tartuffe* in 1977. Off-Broadway, Dunnock directed *Graduation* (1965) and won a 1971 **Drama Desk Award** for *A Place without Doors*. She also appeared for several seasons with the **American Shakespeare Festival** and in numerous films, including *The Corn Is Green* (1945), *Viva Zapata!* (1952), *Baby Doll* (1956), for which she was Oscar-nominated, *The Nun's Story* (1959), *The Story on Page One* (1959), *Butterfield 8* (1960), and *Sweet Bird of Youth* (1962). Dunnock appeared frequently on television dramas and continued acting into her late 80s.

DURANG, CHRISTOPHER (1949–). Montclair, New Jersey, was the birthplace of Christopher Ferdinand Durang, who was educated at Harvard University and the Yale School of Drama before emerging in 1971 as a major **Off-Broadway** playwright and sometime actor. His outrageously comic, often satiric works challenge images of **homosexuality**, Roman Catholicism, child abuse, and many aspects of contemporary American culture. His plays, particularly those challenging the Catholic Church, have generated controversy. Durang received **Obie Awards** for *The Marriage of Bette and Boo* (1973), *Sister Mary Ignatius Explains It All for You* (1979), and *Betty's Summer Vacation* (1999), and was nominated for a **Tony Award** for his libretto for the MUSICAL *A History of the American Film* (1976). Among his other works are *Titanic* (1974), *The Nature and Purpose of the Universe* (1975), *'Dentity Crisis* (1978), *The Vietnamization of New Jersey* (1978), *The Idiots Karamazov* (1980), *Beyond Therapy* (1981), *The Actor's Nightmare* (1981), *Baby with the Bathwater* (1983), *Laughing Wild* (1987), *Sex and Longing* (1996), *Adrift in Macao* (2002), *Mrs. Bob Cratchit's Wild Christmas Binge* (2002), *Miss Witherspoon* (2005), *Why Torture Is Wrong, and the People Who Love Them* (2009), and numerous one-act parodies performed as an evening under the title *Durang/Durang* (1994). In 2010, Durang, in collaboration with Barrie Humphreys (aka Dame Edna Everage) and Michael Feinstein, wrote *All about Me*, featuring Humphreys and Feinstein on Broadway for a brief run at Henry Miller's Theatre. With **Marsha Norman**, Durang cochairs the playwriting program at the Juilliard School.

DURHAM, JIMMIE (1940–). This Wolf Clan Cherokee Indian was born in Washington, Arkansas, and worked as a visual artist until he moved to Geneva in 1968 to study at the L'École des Beaux-Arts. Back in the United States in 1973, Durham became involved in the American Indian movement and other organizations working for **Native American** concerns. In the late 1970s, Durham established himself in New York where he made art to confront stereotypes of Native Americans. Along with visual art, Durham created performance art works, including *My Land* (1965), *Thanksgiving* (1982), *Manhattan Giveaway* (1985), and *Savagism & You* (1991), all challenging traditional identities of Native Americans and the relationship between Indians and whites.

DURNING, CHARLES (1923–). A native of Highland Falls, New York, Durning was drafted into the United States Army during World WAR II, participated in the D-Day invasion, and was awarded a Silver Star and three Purple Hearts. Known mostly for his work in films and television, Durning has also appeared regularly on **Broadway**, winning a **Drama Desk Award** for his performance in the PULITZER PRIZE-winning drama *That Championship Season* (1972) and a **Tony Award** and a Drama Desk Award for his performance in a 1990 revival of *Cat on a Hot Tin Roof*. Durning also appeared in *Drat! The Cat!* (1965), *Pousse-Café* (1966), *The Happy Time* (1968), *Indians* (1969), *In the Boom Boom Room* (1973), *The Au Pair Man* (1973), and revivals of *Inherit the Wind* in 1996, *The Gin Game* in 1997, and *The Best Man* in 2000. Among his many films, Durning was twice nominated for Academy Awards for *The Best Little Whorehouse in Texas* (1982) and *To Be or Not to Be* (1983), and also appeared in *Dog Day Afternoon* (1975), *Tootsie* (1982), *Mass Appeal* (1984), *Home for the Holidays* (1995), and *O Brother, Where Art Thou?* (2000). For his work in television, he received nine Emmy Award nominations and won a Golden Globe Award for *The Kennedys of Massachusetts* (1990).

D'USSEAU, ARNAUD (1916–1990). Born in Los Angeles, California, as the son of film director and producer Leon D'Usseau, he followed in his father's footsteps, writing for the screen, but was also a collaborator on a few plays. None managed long runs, but his first two plays, *Tomorrow the World* (1943), concerning a German child indoctrinated with Nazism adopted by an American couple, and *Deep Are the Roots* (1945), about an **African American** WAR hero returning to the South after the war, won critical approval. Both were written with James Gow, as was *The Legend of Sarah* (1950), which ran for less than a month on **Broadway**. In collaboration with DOROTHY PARKER, D'Usseau wrote *Ladies of the Corridor* (1953), which also had a moderately successful run on **Broadway**. D'Usseau also wrote several Hollywood films before being blacklisted during the McCarthy era. He spent a number of years writing under pseudonyms in Europe before returning to the United States to teach writing at New York University and the School of Visual Arts.

DUTCHMAN. **LeRoi Jones (Amiri Baraka)** faced controversy and won an **Obie Award** for this drama which was first produced by the Playwrights Unit before moving to the Cherry Lane Theatre in March 1964. The action focuses on a white woman, Lula, who encounters Clay, a black man, on a New York subway train. Lula, eating an apple in the manner of the biblical Eve, chooses her Adam when she engages Clay in a sexually charged conversation mixed with insults and racial slurs before she stabs him in front of other passengers who do not stop her. In fact, she orders the other passengers to throw his body from the train at the next stop as she approaches another black male as she had with Clay. Many critics found the play shocking, but it was filmed in 1967 starring Shirley Knight and Al Freeman, Jr., and has endured as an example of **Off-Broadway** drama circa the mid-1960s. *Dutchman* was revived at the Cherry Lane Theatre in 2007 starring Dulé Hill. *See also* AFRICAN AMERICAN THEATRE.

DYING GAUL, THE. **Craig Lucas**'s play opened at the **Vineyard Theatre** on 31 May 1998 under the direction of **Mark Brokaw** and with a cast including Tony Goldwyn and **Linda Emond**. In the play, a young writer has written an autobiographical screenplay about the death from **AIDS** of his lover. A studio executive likes the script, but demands that the protagonist be changed from a **gay** man to a straight woman, which sets off moral compromises. A 2005 film version starred Patricia Clarkson, Peter Sarsgaard, and Campbell Scott.

E

EAST LYNNE COMPANY, THE. This not-for-profit theatre company in Jersey City, New Jersey, was established by Warren Kliewer in 1980 and is unique in its mission of producing classic American plays rarely staged, including nineteenth-century works by Washington Irving, David Belasco,* and William Dean Howells,* and early twentieth-century plays by such figures as RACHEL CROTHERS. The theatre moved to Cape May, New Jersey, and under the artistic directorship of Gayle Stahlhuth since 1999, the theatre continues to focus on rarely produced American classics. *See also* REGIONAL THEATRE MOVEMENT.

EAST WEST PLAYERS. Based in Los Angeles, California, this not-for-profit company became the first **Asian American** theatre in 1965. Founded by Asian performers and writers frustrated by a lack of access to mainstream stages, its initial goal was to encourage integration of Asian American artists into the American theatre. Their earliest productions cast Asians in well-known Caucasian works by playwrights including Carlo Goldoni and **Bertolt Brecht**, but in the 1970s when actor Mako took over as artistic director the company's goal became encouraging new plays by Asian American writers, including **David Henry Hwang**, Wakako Yamauchi, and Valina Houston. In 1993, longtime company member Tim Dang became artistic director, continuing its mission of presenting Asian American plays and performers. *See also* REPERTORY THEATRE.

EASTON, RICHARD (1933–). This Canadian-born actor studied at the Central School of Speech and Drama in London, but has spent much of his career on United States stages, following a stint as an original company member of the Stratford Festival in Ontario, Canada. His first **Broadway** appearance, in a 1957 revival of *The Country Wife*, was followed by a string of **Shakespeare**an roles, including *King Henry IV* in 2003 at **Lincoln Center**. He won a Best Actor **Tony Award** for **Tom Stoppard's** *The Invention of Love* (2001), and has also appeared in revivals of *The Rivals* in 2004 and *Entertaining Mr. Sloane* in 2006. Easton also appears frequently at the **Old**

Globe Theatre in San Diego, California, where he is on the faculty of the University of San Diego.

ECCENTRICITIES OF A NIGHTINGALE. *See SUMMER AND SMOKE.*

ECKART, WILLIAM (1920–2000) and JEAN (1921–1993). This highly successful husband and wife became a design team following their training at Yale University. They were mostly identified with MUSICALS (for which they received three **Tony Award** nominations), including *The Golden Apple* (1954), *Damn Yankees* (1955), *Once Upon a Mattress* (1959), *Fiorello!* (1959), *Anyone Can Whistle* (1964), and *Mame* (1966). They also designed *Oh, Men! Oh, Women!* (1953), ***Take Her, She's Mine*** (1961), ***Never Too Late*** (1962), ***Oh Dad, Poor Dad, Mama's Hung You in the Closet and I'm Feeling So Sad*** (1963), and a revival of *Of Mice and Men* in 1974, as well as opera, ballet, industrial, and television productions.

EDELSTEIN, BARRY (1965–). Born in New Jersey, Edelstein, who acted in high school plays in Fair Lawn, New Jersey, studied at Tufts University and was a Rhodes Scholar at Oxford. He emerged as a significant director with his 1997 revival of *All My Sons* at the **Roundabout Theatre**. That same year, he became artistic director of the **Classic Stage Company**, where he staged a range of classic and contemporary works until 2003. He directed Gwyneth Paltrow in a production of *As You Like It* at the **Williamstown Theatre Festival** and is on the faculty of the University of Southern California.

EDMONDS, RANDOLPH (1900–1983). A significant force in academia, Edmonds was widely regarded as a pioneer in **African American** theatre education. In 1935, he founded the first theatre department at Dillard University, a traditionally black school. To encourage other all-black institutions to establish programs, Edmonds founded the National Association of Drama and Speech Arts. He also wrote upwards of 50 plays, some of which he produced and were published in the collections *Shades and Shadows* (1930), *Six Plays for the Negro Theatre* (1934), and *The Land of Cotton and Other Plays* (1942).

EDWARDS, BEN (1916–1999). A native of Union Springs, Alabama, Edwards attended the Feagin School of Dramatic Arts in New York and won acclaim as a scene designer leading to a 1998 lifetime achievement **Tony Award** (he had been nominated numerous times, but had never won a Tony). Influenced by the work of ROBERT EDMOND JONES, he worked at Virginia's

Barter Theatre in 1935 prior to designing numerous **Broadway** productions beginning in 1938, including revivals of *Pygmalion* and *Diff'rent** in 1938, **Robinson Jeffers**'s free adaptation of *Medea* (1947), *The Time of the Cuckoo* (1952), *Anastasia* (1954), *The Honeys* (1955), *The Ponder Heart* (1956), *The Waltz of the Toreadors* (1957), *The Dark at the Top of the Stairs* (1957), *The Disenchanted* (1958), *Purlie Victorious* (1961), *A Shot in the Dark* (1961), *The Ballad of the Sad Café* (1963), the **Richard Burton** revival of *Hamlet* in 1964, *The Royal Hunt of the Sun* (1965), *Where's Daddy?* (1966), *Purlie* (1970), *A Matter of Gravity* (1976), *A Texas Trilogy* (1976), *The West Side Waltz* (1981), *A Few Good Men* (1989), and often in collaboration with director **José Quintero**, productions of several of EUGENE O'NEILL's plays, including the American premiere of *More Stately Mansions* in 1967 and revivals of *A Moon for the Misbegotten* in 1974, *Anna Christie** in 1977, *A Touch of the Poet* in 1977, *The Iceman Cometh* in 1985, and *Long Day's Journey into Night* in 1988. Beginning in the 1960s, he often worked closely with his wife, costume designer **Jane Greenwood**.

EFFECT OF GAMMA RAYS ON MAN-IN-THE-MOON MARIGOLDS, THE. **Paul Zindel's** breakthrough 1964 play, which premiered at the **Alley Theatre** in Houston, Texas, won a PULITZER PRIZE and **Drama Desk Award** when it opened on 7 April 1970 at the Mercer-O'Casey Theatre **Off-Broadway**. This two-act play, under the direction of Melvin Bernhardt, reminded some critics of the work of **Tennessee Williams**, was also a personal triumph for **Sada Thompson** as Beatrice Hunsdorfer, an unhappy, domineering widow, who ekes out a living caring for an elderly woman. One of her two daughters, Tillie, is a brilliant science student and her class project, to study the impact of the exposure of radiation on flowers serves as a metaphor for Beatrice's toxic influence on her children. A number of noted actresses, including Joan Blondell and **Shelley Winters**, played Beatrice in various productions and the play was revived on **Broadway** in 1978 with Winters, but it managed only a brief run. A 1972 film version was directed by **Paul Newman** and starred Joanne Woodward.

EHLE, JENNIFER (1969–). Daughter of writer John Ehle and actress **Rosemary Harris**, Ehle was born in Winston-Salem, North Carolina, and trained at the North Carolina School of the Arts and London's Central School of Speech and Drama. She has acted in both England and America, gaining notice playing Elizabeth Bennett in the 1995 BBC-TV adaptation of Jane Austen's *Pride and Prejudice*. Ehle, who inherited her mother's grace and dignity on stage, won two **Tony Awards**, for a revival of *The Real Thing* in 2000 and *The Coast of Utopia* (2007). She played opposite **Kevin Spacey** in the Old Vic's revival of *The Philadelphia Story* in 2005 and in the **Second Stage Theatre**'s production of Douglas Carter Beane's comedy *Mr. and Mrs. Fitch* (2010) opposite **John Lithgow**, and she has appeared in several films, including *Wilde* (1997), *Sunshine* (1999), *The River King* (2005), and *Pride and Glory* (2008).

EICHELBERGER, ETHYL (1945–1990). Born James Roy Eichelberger in Pekin, Illinois, this drag performance artist and writer, began his career at **Trinity Repertory Theatre** before moving to New York in 1975 to work with **Charles Ludlam**'s **Ridiculous Theatrical Company**, playing both men and women in various classic and contemporary works (including over 30 of his own creation), often reinventing the plays to challenge sexual stereotypes and traditional views of **sexuality**. Among the real and fictional characters Eichelberger portrayed were Lucrezia Borgia, Jocasta, Medea, Lola Montez, Nefertiti, Clytemnestra, and Empress Carlotta of Mexico. Eichelberger appeared with the Flying Karamazov Brothers in a revival of *The Comedy of Errors* on **Broadway** in 1987. Stricken with **AIDS**, he committed suicide not long after appearing in a revival of *Threepenny Opera* at **Lincoln Center** in 1989. *See also* FEMALE/MALE IMPERSONATION; GAY AND LESBIAN THEATRE.

EIGSTI, KARL (1938–). A native of Goshen, Indiana, Eigsti designed scenery for many regional theatre companies, but developed a long relationship with Washington, D.C.'s **Arena Stage**. Employing two distinct styles, REALISM and symbolism, he has also designed many **Off-Broadway** productions, including *Boesman and Lena* (1969), *The House of Blue Leaves* (1971), *Yentl, The Yeshiva Boy* (1974), and *Losing Time* (1979). He was nominated for a **Tony Award** for *Knockout* (1979) and on **Broadway** he designed scenery and/or lighting for *Inquest* (1970), *Grease* (1972), revivals of *Sweet Bird of Youth* in 1975 and *Once in a Lifetime* in 1978, *Cold Storage* (1977), *Eubie!* (1978), *The American Clock* (1980), *Joseph and the Amazing Technicolor Dreamcoat* (1982), *Amen Corner* (1983), *Alone Together* (1984), and the American premiere of Dario Fo's *Accidental Death of an Anarchist* (1984). Eigsti taught at New York University and is head of the design program at Brandeis University.

EISENHAUER, PEGGY (1962–). Born in New York City, Eisenhauer studied lighting design at Carnegie Mellon University before collaborating with **Jules Fisher** on **Broadway** productions, including *Rags* (1986), *Grand Hotel* (1989), *Death and the Maiden* (1992), and *Angels in America* (1993). She won **Tony Awards** for *Bring in 'Da Noise, Bring in 'Da Funk* (1996) and a revival of *Assassins* in 2004, also winning **Drama Desk Awards** for both, and was nominated for a revival of *Cabaret* in 1998, *Ragtime* (1998), *The Wild Party* (2000), *Marie Christine* (2000), and *Jane Eyre* (2001). Eisenhauer's other Broadway credits include *Tommy Tune Tonight!* (1992), *Twilight: Los Angeles, 1992* (1994), **Elaine Stritch** *At Liberty* (2002), a revival of *Gypsy* in 2003, *Caroline, or Change* (2004), *Laugh Whore* (2004), *Chita Rivera: The Dancer's Life* (2005), a revival of **The Ritz** in 2007, and *9 to 5* (2009). She has also designed lighting for many MUSICAL performers and groups, including The Cars, Billy Ocean, and Lisa Lisa.

EL TEATRO CAMPESINO (ETC). **Luis Valdéz**, a member of **The San Francisco Mime Troupe**, founded this company in 1965 in support of migrant Filipino and Mexican American farm workers striking against the grape farmers of California's San Joaquin Valley. Their first works, in the agit-prop style of the Mime Troupe, were short pieces (*actos*) aimed at exploring and raising consciousness about the plight of the grape pickers. Over time, El Teatro Campesino broadened its themes to include issues of interest to the Chicano population and, at the same time, experimented with varied theatrical techniques, including *commedia dell'arte*, MUSICALS, Mexican folk traditions, and Aztec and Mayan rituals. The group was vocal in opposition to the Vietnam WAR and, in 1971, found a permanent home in a warehouse in San Juan Bautista, although they often took their productions to larger theatres, including their most successful, **Zoot Suit** (1978), which they have frequently revived, *Corridos!* (1981) and *I Don't Have to Show You No Stinking Badges!* (1986). The ETC's *Bandido!* (1981), written by Valdez, was coproduced by the **Mark Taper Forum** in 1994, and the theatre stages an annual Christmas pageant. In recent years, Valdez's three sons, Anáhuac, Kinán, and Lakin, essentially took over operation of the theatre, and also moved the company toward film and video work as well. Annually, the ETC produces two Spanish folk plays, *La pastorela* and *La Virgin of Guadalupe*, at the San Juan Bautista mission. *See also* CHICANO THEATRE.

ELDER, ELDON (1924–2000). Born in Atchison, Kansas, Elder studied scene design with DONALD OENSLAGER at Yale University and worked as Oenslager's assistant on *Second Threshold* (1951), and has amassed a resume of in excess of 200 design credits from **regional theatre** to **Broadway**. He also designed the Delacorte Theatre, the Central Park summer performance space of the **New York Shakespeare Festival**, and served as their resident designer from 1958 to 1961. Elder's Broadway productions include revivals of **Dream Girl** and **Idiot's Delight**, both in 1951, **Time Out for Ginger** (1952), **Take a Giant Step** (1953), *The Girl in Pink Tights* (1954), *Phoenix*

'55 (1955), a revival of *Fallen Angels* in 1956, *Shinbone Alley* (1957), *Of Love Remembered* (1967), *Will Rogers' USA* (1974), *Music Is* (1976), and *Hizzoner!* (1989), among others. He teaches at Brooklyn College, but has also designed numerous productions for the St. Louis Municipal Opera. He was the author of *Will It Make a Theater*, a book about creating theatres from non-traditional spaces, and felt his experiences with **Joe Papp** and the New York Shakespeare Festival taught him that "you had a sense that you were making a contribution to society."

ELDER, LONNE, III (1931–1996). This Americus, Georgia-born playwright was raised in New Jersey and, worked for a time as an actor, including playing Bobo in the original **Broadway** production of *A Raisin in the Sun* (1959). He proved more successful as a writer, most notably with his drama *Ceremonies in Dark Old Men* (1969), which won a **Drama Desk Award** and led to his becoming director of the Playwrights' Unit of the **Negro Ensemble Company**. Much of his subsequent writing was for films, including the acclaimed *Sounder* (1972), for which he received an Academy Award nomination, but he also created a **solo** stage drama, *Splendid Mummer* (1988), on the life of nineteenth century black actor Ira Aldridge. *See also* AFRICAN AMERICAN THEATRE.

ELDRIDGE, FLORENCE (1901–1988). Born Florence McKechnie in Brooklyn, New York, she began her **Broadway** career as a chorus girl in the MUSICAL *Rock-a-Bye Baby* (1918). Numerous subsequent roles during the 1920s included *Ambush** (1921), *The Cat and the Canary** (1922), the American premiere of Luigi Pirandello's *Six Characters in Search of an Author* in 1922, and *The Great Gatsby* (1926), and she toured in THE THEATRE GUILD productions with her husband, actor **Fredric March**. She also appeared in silent films in this era, but following her marriage to March, her stage work was often in partnership with him, including the original productions of *The American Way* (1939), the PULITZER PRIZE-winning *The Skin of Our Teeth* (1942), *Years Ago* (1946), **Arthur's Miller's** adaptation of HENRIK IBSEN's *An Enemy of the People* in 1950, *The Autumn Garden* (1951), and, most notably her last Broadway appearance as the haunted Mary Tyrone in the premiere production of EUGENE O'NEILL's Pulitzer Prize-winning *Long Day's Journey into Night* (1956), for which she received a **Tony Award** nomination. She also appeared in **Lillian Hellman's** *Days to Come* (1936) and in a few later films, including *Mary of Scotland* (1936), *Another Part of the Forest* (1949), *Christopher Columbus* (1949), and *Inherit the Wind* (1960), costarring with her husband and SPENCER TRACY.

ELEPHANT MAN, THE. This two-act play by Bernard Pomerance was first produced at London's Hampstead Theatre, followed by an **Off-Broadway** production, but when it moved to **Broadway** on 19 April 1979, it ran for 916 performances at the Booth Theatre and won a **Tony Award** and **Drama Desk Award** as Best Play. Recounting the life of Joseph Merrick, a nineteenth-century Englishman physically deformed by a genetic disorder, the play explores the nature of human deformity, as Merrick is abandoned by family and hideously exploited by a carnival entrepreneur before he comes to the attention of Dr. Frederick Treves, who cares for Merrick, finds him a permanent home in his hospital, and introduces the brilliant and intellectually curious Merrick to life's finer aspects. **Philip Anglim** and **Kevin Conway** won critical approval as Merrick and Treves, respectively. The play was revived on **Broadway** in 2002 starring **Billy Crudup** and Rupert Graves and was the basis for a 1980 film.

ELIOT, T. S. (1888–1965). Thomas Stearns Eliot was born in St. Louis, Missouri, although he spent much of his life in England. He studied at Harvard University, the Sorbonne, and Oxford before winning acclaim as a poet and sometime playwright. His first major play, *Murder in the Cathedral* (1935), was commissioned for the Canterbury Festival prior to being produced at Yale University and the **Federal Theatre Project.** Eliot's *The Cocktail Party* (1949) won a **Tony Award** and a **New York Drama Critics Circle Award**, but his other plays, *The Family Reunion* (1939), *The Confidential Clerk* (1953), and *The Elder Statesman* (1958), were less successful. Eliot's 1939 collection of poems, *Old Possum's Book of Practical Cats*, provided the source material for the musical *Cats* (1982), which ran for 18 years on **Broadway.**

ELIZABETH THE QUEEN. THE THEATRE GUILD produced the first of MAXWELL ANDERSON's historically based blank verse tragedies, in this case depicting the reign of England's Elizabeth I and her relationship with the Earl of Essex, on 3 November 1930 at the Guild Theatre, where it ran for 147 performances. Directed by PHILIP MOELLER, with scene design by LEE SIMONSON, LYNN FONTANNE and ALFRED LUNT played the leads to critical acclaim, with a supporting cast including Percy Waram, Arthur Hughes, Phoebe Brand, and **Morris Carnovsky.** The play was occasionally revived for tours starring noted actresses, including EVA LE GALLIENNE in 1961 and **Judith Anderson** in 1966. A 1939 film, *The Private Lives of Elizabeth and Essex*, starring **Bette Davis** and Errol Flynn, was loosely adapted from Anderson's play.

ELLIOTT, SCOTT (1963–). A wunderkind director born in Long Island, New York, Elliott (whose name often appears as Elliot) studied music at the Boston Conservatory prior to transferring to New York University to study film and psychology. On **Broadway**, he acted as a replacement in *Les Misérables* (1987) and *Ain't Broadway Grand* (1993), but found greater success as a director and producer. He received **Drama Desk Award** nominations for his **Off-Broadway** direction of *The Monogamist* (1996), *Goose-Pimples* (1998), and a revival of **David Rabe's** *Hurlyburly* in 2005. Off-Broadway, Elliott also directed *End of the Day* (1994), *Ecstasy* (1995), and *Curtains* (1995), for which he and the cast received an **Obie Award**. On Broadway, he has specialized in staging revivals, including *Present Laughter* in 1996, *The Three Sisters* in 1997, *The Women* in 2001, *Barefoot in the Park* in 2006, and *Threepenny Opera* in 2006.

As founding artistic director for the New Group, Elliott helped bring *Avenue Q* (2004) to Broadway, and he directed **Arthur Miller's** *The Ride Down Mt. Morgan* at the **Williamstown Theatre Festival** in 1996. His only foray into film, *A Map of the World* (1999), starred **Sigourney Weaver**. In conversation with Arthur Miller, Elliott talked of the importance of bringing a play's subtext to the surface because "I think audiences want to know the truth behind what's happening to the people in the play. And I really do believe that's because we understand more about what makes people tick than we did fifty years ago."

ELLIS, SCOTT (1957–). Born in Washington, D.C., Ellis began as a performer in regional theatre and appeared on **Broadway** in *Musical Chairs* (1980) and *The Rink* (1984), but made his mark as a director of mostly MU-SICALS, although he has also staged dramas, including revivals of *Picnic* in 1994, *A Month in the Country* in 1995, *A Thousand Clowns* in 1996, *The Rainmaker* in 1999, and *The Man Who Had All the Luck* in 2002, most for the **Roundabout Theatre** where he is artistic director. Ellis won a **Drama Desk Award** for his direction of **Off-Broadway** productions of *And the World Goes 'Round* and a revival of *A Little Night Music* in 1991 and he was subsequently nominated for **Tony Awards** and Drama Desk Awards for a revival of *She Loves Me* in 1994, *Steel Pier* (1997), and revivals of *1776* in 1998 and *12 Angry Men* in 2005. He also garnered a Tony nomination for *Curtains* (2007). In 2007, he received an Emmy Award nomination for his direction of an episode of *30 Rock;* he works frequently in episodic television. He directed a 2008 revival of **David Rabe's** *Streamers* at Boston's **Huntington Theatre** and Off-Broadway, telling an interviewer that "For me, the text and characters and the situations are *it*—I don't try to put something else on top of that."

ELSON, CHARLES (1909–2000). A native of Chicago, Illinois, Elson found his way into theatre through a Hull House* program. His first scene design, for a production of *The Ticket-of-Leave Man* at Whitefield, New Hampshire's Chase Barn Playhouse in 1934, led to a long stint designing 44 productions for the Ogunquit Playhouse in Maine from 1939 to 1945. A graduate of the Yale School of Drama, Elson became a highly prolific scene and lighting designer beginning with his first **Broadway** production, a flop 1945 revival of *As You Like It*. He assisted DONALD OENSLAGER, with whom he studied at Yale, on a revival of *Pygmalion* in 1945, *Born Yesterday* (1946), *Years Ago* (1946), and *The Eagle Has Two Heads* (1947) before branching out on his own with scene and/or lighting designs for such Broadway productions as revivals of *The First Mrs. Fraser* in 1947, *Private Lives* in 1948, *Regina* (1949), *Out of This World* (1950), *The Rose Tattoo* (1951), *The Deep Blue Sea* (1952), *Quadrille* (1954), *Compulsion* (1957), *La Plume de Ma Tante* (1958), *Blue Denim* (1958), *First Impressions* (1959), *Wildcat* (1960), *Photo Finish* (1963), and *Mirele Efros* (1967). Elson taught at Yale, the City University of New York, and Hunter College, and also designed for the Metropolitan Opera and his 1958 designs for *Madame Butterfly* were used for over 20 years. His sole film work, as assistant art director, was for a classic, the Judy Garland *A Star Is Born* (1954).

EMMONS, BEVERLY (1943–). Emmons began her career as an assistant to lighting designer **Jules Fisher**. She has been nominated for **Tony Awards** for her **Broadway** lighting designs for *The Elephant Man* (1979), *A Day in Hollywood/A Night in the Ukraine* (1980), *Les Liasons Dangereuses* (1987), *Passion* (1994), a revival of *The Heiress* in 1995, and *Jekyll & Hyde* (1997), with **Drama Desk Award** nominations for *The Elephant Man, The Dresser* (1981), *Passion, The Heiress,* and *Chronicle of a Death Foretold* (1995). Emmons's first Broadway lighting design for a failed musical, *A Letter for Queen Victoria* (1975), led to many more distinguished productions, including *Amadeus* (1980), *Piaf* (1981), *The Life and Adventures of Nicholas Nickleby* (1981), *Good* (1982), and revivals of *Cat on a Hot Tin Roof* in 1990, *Abe Lincoln in Illinois* in 1993, and *Annie Get Your Gun* in 1999. **Off-Broadway**, she designed lights for *The Vagina Monologues* (1999) and numerous other productions, winning a 1980 Distinguished Lighting Obie Award the year she designed lights for **Sam Shepard**'s *True West*. Emmons has collaborated frequently with **Joseph Chaikin, Meredith Monk, Liviu Chiulei,** and **Robert Wilson,** designing lights for some of his productions, including *Einstein on the Beach* (1976), and designed lighting for dance, including for Trisha Brown, Martha Graham, and Merce Cunningham. Emmons teaches lighting at Columbia University and from 1997 to 2002, she was artistic director of the **Lincoln Center** Institute, an outreach program for New York City schools. In thinking about the use of color in lighting, Emmons has said, "There is not one right answer: everyone thinks about color their own way, and it is important in teaching to defend the non-verbal aspects of the lighting experience."

EMOND, LINDA (1959–). Born in New Brunswick, New Jersey, and raised in Southern California, Emond studied at the University of Washington. She began her career in Chicago, Illinois, winning several Joseph Jefferson Awards and nominations for performances in classics, including **Shakespeare**, for 11 years. She appeared on **Broadway** in the 1997 revival of *1776*, received a **Tony Award** nomination and an **Outer Critics Award** for *Life (x) 3* (2003), and a **Drama Desk Award** nomination for *Nine Armenians* (1997) **Off-Broadway**. Emond acted with **Al Pacino** in the 2002 **National Actors Theatre** revival of **Bertolt Brecht**'s *The Resistible Rise of Arturo Ui* and, in **regional** and Off-Broadway theatres in numerous productions, including the premieres of **Craig Lucas**'s *The Dying Gaul* at the **Vineyard Theatre** in 1998 and John Kander and Fred Ebb's *Over & Over* at the **Signature Theatre** in 1999. Emond won critical acclaim as the title character of **Tony Kushner**'s *Homebody/Kabul* (2001), in which she delivered the play's hour-long first-act monologue, winning an **Obie Award** and a **Lucille Lortel Award** for her performance. She played the role in the play's long gestation process through revised productions at the **New York Theatre Workshop**, the **Mark Taper Forum**, and the **Brooklyn Academy of Music**. Emond again worked with Kushner on the premiere performances of *The Intelligent Homosexual's Guide to Capitalism and Socialism with a Key to the Scriptures* (2009) at the **Guthrie Theatre**. Emond also acts in film, including the screen version of *The Dying Gaul* (2005) and *Julie & Julia* (2009), and television, from soap operas to *Law & Order*.

END OF SUMMER. S. N. BEHRMAN's three-act comedy opened on 17 February 1936 at the Guild Theatre in a THEATRE GUILD production for 152 performances. Directed by PHILIP MOELLER, with scene designs by LEE SIMONSON, the adept cast won plaudits in this witty comedy starring **Ina Claire** as Leonie Frothingham, a wealthy New Englander from "old money" whose snobbish mother (**Mildred Natwick**), continually reminds her of her privileged background while Leonie observes her daughter, Paula, choosing between two suitors. One (Van Heflin) will be able to keep Paula in luxury, while the other, a young political radical (Shepperd Strudwick) promises only a stimulating existence as part of a rapidly changing society. The play's title suggests Leonie's dilemma, realizing her daughter's choice of the radical will change all of their lifes. OSGOOD PERKINS and Minor Watson also appeared in supporting roles.

ENSEMBLE STUDIO THEATRE (EST). A not-for-profit theatre founded in 1969 by Curt Dempster (who led it until his death in 2007), the EST's initial goals were to foster the talents of individual artists and to develop new American plays. Since its founding, a remarkable 6,000 plays have been produced, many new, bringing the operation numerous acknowledgments, including **Obie Award, Outer Critics Circle Awards**, and others. Among the plays developed by EST are **Christopher Durang**'s controversial *Sister Mary Ignatius Explains It All for You* (1979) and Shirley Lauro's *Open Admissions* (1984). EST's Annual Marathon of One-Act Plays was significant in reviving the popularity of short form plays, and the annual Octoberfest presents new scripts. Among its membership, which includes numerous actors and playwrights, are **John Patrick Shanley, Richard Greenberg**, and **David Mamet**. *See also* REPERTORY THEATRE.

ENSLER, EVE (1953–). New York native Ensler was inspired in her work by her childhood experiences of abuse by her father. She attended Middlebury College. As a playwright and performer, Ensler is an antiviolence advocate for **women**. She rose to prominence with *The Vagina Monologues* (1996), a series of monologues recounting the **sexual** experiences and responses to their bodies of women of various ages and backgrounds. Ensler won an **Obie Award** and several CRITICS awards, and her **solo performance** of the piece was filmed for television in 2002. *The Vagina Monologues* has been translated into nearly 50 languages and performed all over the world, often on an annual "V-Day" (Valentine's Day) when many groups perform the play, including with leading actresses (as well as non-professionals) performing the monologues, often to controversial responses resulting from its content. Ensler's other works include *Necessary Targets* (1997), *The Good Body* (2005), and *The Treatment* (2006). Of her work, Ensler has said, "My dream of a good play is that you're laughing, you're hysterical, and then you're suddenly in the middle of hell and you don't know how you got there."

ENTERS, ANGNA (1897–1989). Born in New York City as Anita Enters, she was raised in Milwaukee, Wisconsin, where she graduated high school in 1915 and not long after enrolled at Milwaukee State Normal School intending to teach art. Not long after, she saw performances by Denishawn and Sergei Diaghilev's Les Ballets Russes, which led to a move to New York, where she continued to study art at the Art Students League, beginning in 1919. She turned to dance and MIME, studying with Michio Ito, becoming his stage partner in 1923. Enters created the dance-mime piece *Moyen Age*, developing a singular merger of the two forms, followed by her **solo** program *Theatre of Angna Enters*, first performed in 1939 and which she continued to present until 1960. Much of her work involved political satire and the experiences of **women** and she gained an international reputation with performances in London and Paris. Along with performances, Enters's sketches, set and costume designs, and other art works drew attention. She taught at the STELLA ADLER Studio from 1957 to 1960 and was artist-in-residence at the **Dallas Theatre Center** in 1961–1962. Enters also wrote plays, including *Love Possessed Juana: A Play of the Inquisition in Spain*, cowritten with her husband, Louis Kalonyme (1946) and *The Unknown Lover* (1947), both produced by the Houston Little Theatre. Enters's 1966 book, *On Mime*, chronicled her conceptions of movement, and she wrote three autobiographies.

EPPERSON, JOHN (1955–). Better known by his drag name, Lypsinka, Epperson was born in Hazlehurst, Mississippi, where at age four he lip-synched to his father's collection of show tunes and imitated Ann-Margret from the film version of the MUSICAL *Bye Bye Birdie*. Taunted in school as a "sissy," he studied classical piano prior to attending Belhaven College. Following graduation, he worked as a pianist in Colorado before moving to New York as rehearsal pianist for the American Ballet Theatre. On the side, Epperson appeared in drag in various nightclubs, including Club 51 and the Pyramid Club where he developed a following. He appeared as Lypsinka for the first time in 1988 with performances of **Charles Busch**'s long-running *Vampire Lesbians of Sodom* (1984) before quitting his pianist job in 1991 to devote himself to the character he claimed was based, in part, on singer Dolores Gray. His particular technique is to lip-sync to show-length soundtracks meticulously assembled from diverse bits and pieces of many female performers from stage and screen.

Before developing the character of Lypsinka, he created two musical drag pieces, *Dial "M" for Model* (1987) and *Ballet of the Dolls* (1988), the last based on Jacqueline Susann's *Valley of the Dolls*. As Lypsinka, Epperson appeared to critical acclaim in a variety of solo Off-Broadway shows beginning with *I Could Go on Lip-Synching!* (1988), followed by many variations and sequels, including *Lypsinka! Now It Can by Lip-Synched, Lypsinka! A Day in the Life, Lypsinka Must Be Destroyed, Lypsinka! The Boxed Set,* and *As I Lay Lip-Synching*. In 2004, he appeared as the Wicked Stepmother in the New York City Opera's revival of Rodgers and Hammerstein's *Cinderella* and, also that year, in his autobiographical piece, *Show Trash*. Most recently, Epperson as Lypsinka as Joan Crawford appeared in *The Passion of the Crawford* (2006), a work he had begun developing in 1998. He also developed *My*

Deah (2006), a parody of *Medea* without the Lypsinka persona present. The subject of an Emmy Award-winning PBS documentary, Epperson says of his work, "I don't like the term 'drag queen,' because it describes an amateur. Why not call me an actor? I suppose drag artist would be okay." *See also* FEMALE/MALE IMPERSONATION.

EPSTEIN, ALVIN (1925–). A native New Yorker, Epstein made his stage debut in a United States Army production of *Richard III* in 1945, followed by his first New York appearance at the **Equity Library Theatre** in a small role in a revival of *Ah, Wilderness!* in 1946. His numerous performances in international theatres, with **regional** companies, and **Off-Broadway** seldom made it to **Broadway**, but he appeared with distinction with MIME Marcel Marceau in 1955, in the **Orson Welles** revival of *King Lear* as the Fool in 1956, as Lucky in the original Broadway production of *Waiting for Godot* (1956), beginning a long association with Samuel Beckett's plays, *From A to Z* (1960), *No Strings* (1962), *The Passion of Josef D* (1964), *Postmark Zero* (1965), *A Kurt Weill Cabaret* (1979) with Martha Schlamme, and a revival of *Threepenny Opera* (1989).

An actor with a wide range, Epstein moved comfortably from avant-garde work to mainstream commercial theatre, appearing in straight drama and MUSICALS. From 1953 to 1955, he toured with Israel's Habima Theatre, in productions of *Lost in the Stars, The Living Corpse, The Golem, The Mother, Macbeth, Legend of 3 and 4, The Caine Mutiny Court-Martial, Henry IV,* and *King Lear.* Epstein appeared in the American premiere of *Endgame* (1958) at the Cherry Lane Theatre and in the world premiere of **Sam Shepard** and **Joseph Chaikin**'s *When the World Was Green (A Chef's Fable)* (1996) and in a wide range of classic and contemporary plays in many theatres (with over fifty performances at the **American Repertory Theatre**), winning a 1968 **Obie Award** for *Dynamite Tonight!*, a 1996 Elliot Norton Award for Sustained Excellence, and the IRNE Award for Best Supporting Actor in *Ivanov* in 1999. Epstein appeared Off-Broadway in *Tuesdays with Morrie* (2002) and in numerous films and television shows. He also cofounded the **Berkshire Theatre Festival** in 1967, served as associate director of the **Yale Repertory Theatre** (1973–1977), and as artistic director of the **Guthrie Theatre** (1977–1979).

EQUITY LIBRARY THEATRE (ELT). Founded by actor Sam Jaffe in 1943 with the cooperation of ACTORS' EQUITY ASSOCIATION and the New York Public Library's Theatre Collection, under the supervision of George Freedley,* the theatre's goal was as a showcase for younger talents and to provide theatre at low prices for those unable to afford commercial theatre.

ELT productions were originally presented in libraries, but in 1949 it moved to its own space at the Lenox Hill Playhouse and, later, to other available auditoriums. Actors including **Jason Robards, James Earl Jones, Jean Stapleton, Tony Randall, Ossie Davis, Martin Balsam**, Jack Klugman, Danny DeVito, Rod Steiger, Treat Williams, Jerry Stiller, Anne Meara, **Sidney Poitier**, Harvey Korman, and **Richard Kiley** had their early careers boosted by performances at the ELT, and two of its revivals had brief runs on **Broadway**, *Night Music* in 1951 and *Canterbury Tales* in 1980. The ELT won a special **Tony Award** in 1977 and a **Drama Desk Award** in 1984, but it closed in the midst of its 1989–90 season due to financial constraints.

EQUUS. English playwright **Peter Shaffer**'s acclaimed drama of a psychiatrist's effort to unravel the complex psyche of a young man who has blinded a stable full of horses opened in a **Shubert Organization** production under the direction of **John Dexter** on **Broadway** on 24 October 1974 at the Plymouth Theatre (later moving to the Helen Hayes Theatre) for 1,209 performances following its original run in London's West End. In the years following World W**AR** II, numerous British plays found success in a Broadway transfer, but few won as much acclaim and as long a run as *Equus*. The play also won a **Tony Award** and a **Drama Desk Award** as Best Play. Anthony Hopkins and Peter Firth won approval in the roles of psychiatrist and patient, respectively, but the production's most talked-about element were the horses—actors wearing abstract horse heads and kothurni-like hooves, not to mention full male nudity at the climactic moment of the play's first act. Noted actors took over the leading roles, with **Richard Burton** and **Anthony Perkins** both stepping in for Hopkins and Tom Hulce replacing Firth. A 2008 Broadway revival ran for 156 performances with Richard Griffiths and Daniel Radcliffe playing the leading roles. Burton and Firth both received Academy Award nominations and Golden Globe Awards in the film version, directed by Sidney Lumet.

ESBJORNSON, DAVID (1953–). Following completion of a B.A. in Theatre and English from Gustavus Adolphus College and an M.F.A. in Directing from New York University, Esbjornson began a directing career in which he served as artistic director of New York's **Classic Stage Company** from 1992 to 1999 (a period acknowledged with a **Lucille Lortel Award** for the body of work done by CSC), after which he worked as a freelance and became artistic director of the **Seattle Repertory Company** from 2005 to 2009. His directing credits include plays by such leading contemporary dramatists as **Arthur Miller, Edward Albee, Tony Kushner, Suzan-Lori Parks**, and others. In fact, his directing and producing career vividly reflects the vast changes in American theatre since the 1960s—as one of the most honored and prolific directors working in the first decade of the new millennium, Esbjornson has only three **Broadway** credits, Miller's *The Ride Down Mt. Morgan* (2000), Albee's *The Goat, or Who Is Sylvia?* (2002), and the aborted *Bobbi Boland* (2003), which never officially opened.

Off-Broadway, Esbjornson won an **Obie Award** for a revival of *Thérèse Raquin* in 1997 and was nominated for a **Drama Desk Award** for *Iphigenia and Other Daughters* in 1995. Esbjornson staged Kushner's one-act *Homebody* (1995), the precursor to *Homebody/Kabul*, at London's Chelsea Centre, the world premiere of Parks's *In the Blood* (1999) at the **New York Shakespeare Festival/Public Theatre**, and a 2004 revival of **Larry Kramer**'s *The Normal Heart* for the Public. He also directed the world premieres of Miller's *Resurrection Blues* (2002), Mitch Albom and Jeffrey Hatcher's *Tuesdays with Morrie* (2002), **Neil Simon**'s *Rose and Walsh* (2003), and the New York premieres of Albee's *The Play about the Baby* (2002), and **Israel Horowitz**'s *My Old Lady* (2002), as well as numerous **regional theatre** and Off-Broadway productions. In 2010, Esbjornson directed **James Earl Jones** and Vanessa Redgrave in a Broadway revival of **Alfred Uhry**'s *Driving Miss Daisy*.

ESTERMAN, LAURA (1945–). A native of Lawrence, Long Island, Esterman attended Radcliffe and studied at the London Academy of Music and Dramatic Art and with **Uta Hagen**. She began her **Broadway** career in two revivals, *The Time of Your Life* in 1969 and *The Waltz of the Toreadors* in 1973, subsequently appearing in *God's Favorite* (1974), *Teibele and Her Demon* (1979), *The Suicide* (1980), *Metamorphosis* (1989), and a revival of *The Show-Off** (1992), but has worked more frequently **Off-Broadway**, where she won an **Obie Award** and a **Drama Desk Award** playing a leukemia patient in Scott McPherson's *Marvin's Room* (1992). Her many Off-Broadway credits include revivals of *Ghosts* in 1973 at the **Roundabout Theatre**, *Macbeth* in 1974 at the New York Shakespeare Festival, *Golden Boy** in 1975 at the **Manhattan Theatre Club**, *A Midsummer Night's Dream* in 1981 at the **Brooklyn Academy of Music**, as well as playing Sarah Bernhardt* in *Duet* (2003) at the Greenwich Street Theatre, and in repertory theatres she has appeared notably in the **Goodman Theatre**'s revival of *Mourning Becomes Electra* in 1975 and **Yale Repertory Theatre**'s revival of *Rip Van Winkle** in 1981 and *The Glass Menagerie* in 1999. She has appeared frequently on television, in films, and as won popularity as the title character of the radio drama *Ruby the Galactic Gumshoe*.

ETHAN FROME. Owen Davis,* collaborating with his son Donald Davis, had his last success with this adaptation of Edith Wharton's novel, which opened on 21 January 1936 at the National Theatre for 120 performances. RUTH GORDON, **Raymond Massey**, and Pauline Lord* won critical approval in this **Max Gordon** production directed by GUTHRIE MCCLINTIC and designed by JO MIELZINER. Wharton commented on the "great skill and exquisite sensitiveness" with which Davis and son adapted her New England tale of Mattie Silver (Gordon), who comes to live with her cousin Zenobia (Lord) and her husband, Ethan (Massey). When Ethan and Mattie fall in love, Zenobia orders them to leave and they attempt suicide. Instead, they are seriously and permanently injured and must be cared for by the bitter Zenobia. Wharton's novel was filmed in 1993, but without the Davis adaptation.

ETHNIC THEATRE. The significant influx of European and Asian immigrants into the United States beginning in the mid-nineteenth century somewhat abated by 1930 as immigration laws stiffened in the 1920s. The companies and individual artists nurtured in the theatre companies emerging during this great era of immigration to the United States had radically influenced American drama, but theatre companies with an ethnic character declined by the late 1920s, although the **Federal Theatre Project** of the Works Progress Administration of the New Deal kept YIDDISH, **African American**, and other ethnic performances and performers before American audiences during its short history, as did a few surviving groups, including New York's Folksbiene Theatre* and Chicago's Swedish Folk Theatre.

The World WAR II years produced another fall-off in ethnic productions, but with the war's end, Puerto Rican, European, and Eastern immigrants influenced the development of theatre, as did the rising civil rights movement, which brought black-themed theatre into the mainstream in the late 1950s and 1960s. The Puerto Rican influence was significant in New York City, as Spanish-speaking neighborhoods created their own companies as pre-1930 immigrant groups had done. In the late 1960s and 1970s, the Puerto Rican Traveling Theatre and the **Nuyorican Theatre** were influential, and despite the decline of **Broadway**, a wide range of ethnic performances of various kinds turned up in non-traditional theatre spaces where production expenses could be kept low.

Among Hispanic groups, **Luis Valdez**'s **El Teatro Campesino** (Farm Workers' Theatre) created original plays (actos) and provided a model for politically active theatres. The 1970s saw the emergence of **Native American theatre** with **Hanay Geiogamah**'s **Native American Theatre Ensemble**, which produced plays employing traditional dramatic techniques to present Native American values, issues, and history. After 1980, **Asian American** theatre grew significantly with the appearance of the **East West Players** in Los Angeles standing out in its accomplishment, which included providing a venue for such playwrights as **David Henry Hwang**. In California and Florida, other **Chicano theatre** companies appeared, addressing the concerns of Mexican and Cuban immigrants, respectively. Central and South American immigrants found voice through New York Teatro Cuarto and other groups and, by the mid-1980s, virtually every major ethnic group in the United States could boast a theatrical organization devoted to their concerns. Mainstream regional theatres increasingly found means to encourage new plays and artists emerging from these ethnic companies as even Broadway and **Off-Broadway** made room for more diverse dramas and performers and increasingly made use of multi-ethnic and race-blind casting.

ETTINGER, HEIDI. *See* LANDESMAN, HEIDI ETTINGER.

EUGENE O'NEILL MEMORIAL THEATRE CENTER. Leasing an estate in Waterford, Connecticut, in 1964, George C. White established this center named for America's foremost dramatist, EUGENE O'NEILL, with the goal of providing a working environment for new playwrights away from commercial demands and media CRITICISM. Focused on the work of playwrights and critics, as well as ways to educate and develop an audience, the center established some programs, including the National Playwrights Conference, and annual five-day retreat led after a few formative years by **Lloyd Richards** (James Hougton and Wendy C. Goldberg succeeded Richards), who guided the NPC from 1968 to 1999, leading to a special **Tony Award** in acknowledgment of the success of its new play development. The center also established the **National Theatre of the Deaf** and the National Critics Institute in 1967, the National Theatre Institute in 1970, New Drama for Television in 1976, the National Music Theater Conference in 1978, and the National Puppetry Conference in 1990. The center also oversees operations of the Monte Cristo Cottage, O'Neill's family's summer home in New London, Connecticut, which is a museum and archive for scholars and artists. In 2010, the center received the outstanding **regional theatre** Tony Award.

EUREKA THEATRE COMPANY (ETC). This small not-for-profit San Francisco, California-based theatre, founded in 1972 by **Robert Woodruff** and Chris Silva, served as a collective presenting politically charged plays by such contemporary dramatists as Caryl Churchill, Dario Fo, and **Emily Mann**, whose *Execution of Justice* (1986) was commissioned by the Eureka. In 1981, the ETC's church-basement space was destroyed by fire, but continued to function in various borrowed spaces until 1984 when it established a home base in a 250-seat space in the Mission District. Among its premieres are Anthony Clarvoe's *Pick Up Axe* (1990), but the theatre won particular note when artistic director **Oskar Eustis** commissioned playwright **Tony Kushner** to write his two epic *Angels in America* plays, *Millennium Approaches* and *Perestroika*, which were first performed there in 1991. The two plays premiered at the Eureka prior to subsequent performances at the **Mark Taper Forum**, the National Theatre of Great Britain, and Broadway. Other ETC artistic directors were Richard E. T. White and Tony Taccone.

EUSTIS, OSKAR (1959–). Born in Minnesota, Eustis was educated at New York University before moving to San Francisco, California, where he began his career with the politically radical Red Wing Theatre **collective**. In 1981, he became resident director and dramaturg for the **Eureka Theatre Company** and, five years later, emerged as its artistic director. Eustis actively encouraged politically charged new plays, commissioning **Emily Mann**'s *Execution of Justice* in 1986 and **Tony Kushner**'s *Angels in America* in 1991. He became artistic director of the **Mark Taper Forum** in 1989, where he directed *Angels in America* in its world premiere. He developed a reputation for encouraging new works, including plays by **Philip Kan Gotanda, David Henry Hwang, Suzan-Lori Parks**, and **Eduardo Machado**, among others. In 1994, Eustis became artistic director of Providence, Rhode Island's **Trinity Repertory Company** and moved to **New York Shakespeare Festival/Public Theatre** in 2005, replacing **George C. Wolfe** as artistic director. The Public's 2009 revival of *Hair* scored a major critical and commercial hit and moved to **Broadway**. Under Eustis's leadership, the Public also staged Kushner's adaptation of **Bertolt Brecht**'s *Mother Courage and Her Children* in 2006. He has also taught at Brown University and at Middlebury College.

EVANS, MAURICE (1901–1989). Born in England as Maurice Herbert Evans, he spent 15 years acting in England, making notable appearances as Hamlet for the Old Vic in 1934 and in R. C. Sherriff's *Journey's End* (1929) before moving to the United States, where he became a citizen in 1941. Noted for his **Shakespeare**an performances in the 1930s and 1940s, mostly directed by **Margaret Webster**, Evans also appeared in a range of roles on stage, screen, and television. On **Broadway**, he won a special 1950 **Tony Award** for leading the City Center Theatre Company, and he produced **John Patrick**'s *Teahouse of the August Moon* (1953), which won a Tony, and *No Time for Sergeants* (1955). He was nominated for a Tony as an actor for a revival of GEORGE BERNARD SHAW's *The Apple Cart* in 1957 and for the MUSICAL *Tenderloin* (1961). He also appeared in *Dial "M" for Murder* (1952), *The Aspern Papers* (1962), and in other Shaw plays. He brought

Shakespeare's plays to 1950s' television, appearing in his stage successes, and continued acting into his 80s.

EVE OF ST. MARK, THE. MAXWELL ANDERSON's two-act drama opened on 7 October 1942 at the Cort Theatre for 307 performances in a **Playwright's Company** production. This play was a rarity in that it dealt seriously with the human losses of World WAR II during the war. Anderson's plot centered on a young man, played by William Prince, from a New York farm family who falls in love with a neighbor (Mary Rolfe). When the war begins, the young man enlists and he and his girl face the pain of separation. When he is killed, she and his family must face his death and attempt to understand its significance. Aline McMahon was also in the cast as the young man's mother. A 1944 screen adaptation starred William Eythe and Anne Baxter.

EVELYN, JUDITH (1913–1967). Born in Seneca, South Dakota, this stage and screen actress survived the September 1939 sinking of the *S.S. Athenia* when it was the first liner torpedoed by a German submarine in World WAR II. On **Broadway**, she appeared in major roles in *Angel Street* (1941), *The Rich Full Life* (1945), a 1947 revival of *Craig's Wife,* * *The Ivy Green* (1949), and *The Shrike* (1952). Evelyn's notable film roles include playing Miss Lonelyhearts in Alfred Hitchcock's *Rear Window (*1956), *Giant* (1956), and *The Tingler* (1959), among others, as well as numerous television dramas.

EWELL, TOM (1909–1994). A familiar character actor of stage and screen, Ewell was born Samuel Yewell Tompkins in Owensboro, Kentucky. He made his first stage appearances in STOCK beginning in 1928, followed by his **Broadway** debut in a small role in JOHN WEXLEY's *They Shall Not Die* in 1934. He continued to work in stock and in supporting roles on Broadway, including in *Let Freedom Ring* (1935), *Ethan Frome* (1936), *Stage Door* (1936), and he played Cornelius Hackl in **Thornton Wilder's** *The Merchant of Yonkers* (1938), directed by MAX REINHARDT. Ewell took over the role of Gage in MAXWELL ANDERSON's *Key Largo* (1939) during the run and also appeared in *Liberty Jones* (1941), *Sunny River* (1941), *Apple of His Eye* (1946), *John Loves Mary* (1947), and *Small Wonder* (1948).

Ewell scored a major Broadway success in *The Seven Year Itch* (1952), for which he won a **Tony Award**. He repeated his role as a man imagining an affair with an attractive neighbor, and won a Golden Globe Award, in a 1955 film version directed by Billy Wilder and costarring Marilyn Monroe. Ewell studied at **The Actors Studio** and in a demonstration of versatility he appeared opposite **Bert Lahr** in the American premiere of *Waiting for Godot* (1956) at the **Coconut Grove Playhouse** in Miami, Florida. His subsequent

Broadway appearances were in *The Tunnel of Love* (1957), *Patate* (1958), *A Thurber Carnival* (1960), and *Xmas in Las Vegas* (1965). Ewell appeared frequently in films after 1940, including roles in *Adam's Rib* (1949), *The Girl Can't Help It* (1956), *Tender Is the Night* (1962), and *State Fair* (1962) as well as numerous television shows, including his own situation comedy, *The Tom Ewell Show* (1961–1962) and the drama series *Baretta* (1975–1978) for which he was nominated for an Emmy Award.

EXECUTION OF JUSTICE. Emily Mann's **Drama Desk Award**-nominated ensemble drama examining the case of the *People vs. Dan White* was commissioned by the **Eureka Theatre**. An early version of the play was produced at the **Arena Stage** in 1984, but the play opened on **Broadway** on 13 March 1986 for 12 performances, with a cast including John Spencer as Dan White, with Wesley Snipes, Stanley Tucci, Mary McDonnell, and **Earle Hyman**. **Ming Cho Lee** designed scenery, with lighting by **Pat Collins** (Drama Desk winner) and sound by Tom Morse. The play focuses on events surrounding the trial of Dan White, a San Francisco city supervisor who shot and killed Harvey Milk, the first openly gay supervisor and San Francisco mayor George Moscone, a seminal tragedy in the gay rights movement. White was controversially acquitted using the "Twinkie" defense—claiming his actions were explained by eating an excess of junk food. The play featured many multimedia elements to explore the highly charged events surrounding the trial. A television film was first show in 1999, winning a GLAAD Media Award as Outstanding Television Movie.

EXPERIMENTAL THEATRE, INC. (ET). This New York City-based company was founded in 1940 as a showcase for actors and playwrights, but World WAR II closed it a year later. ET was revived in 1946 with support from the **American National Theatre and Academy (ANTA)** and theatrical **unions** provided concessions to allow a season to proceed at low costs. Success was elusive and despite the concessions the company lost money and shuttered operations following the 1948–1949 season.

F

FALLS, ROBERT (1954–). A native of Ashland, Illinois, Falls was educated at the University of Illinois, Urbana-Champaign prior to studying acting with Edward Kaye-Martin. His directing career commenced with the **Wisdom Bridge Theatre**, where he served as artistic director from 1977 to 1985 and directed over 30 productions. In 1986, Falls became artistic director of the **Goodman Theatre**, where several of his productions have transferred to **Broadway**, including revivals of *Galileo, **The Iceman Cometh, The Night of the Iguana***, and ***Long Day's Journey into Night***, the last bringing him a **Drama Desk Award** and a **Tony Award** nomination. Fall's direction of ***Death of a Salesman*** in 1999 brought him a Tony and a **Drama Desk Award**. He also received Tony and Drama Desk nominations for a 2000 production of ***A Moon for the Misbegotten,*** and the Goodman under Falls's leadership received a 1992 regional theatre Tony Award. Other Broadway productions directed by Falls include *The Speed of Darkness* (1991), a revival of ***The Rose Tattoo*** in 1995, ***The Young Man from Atlanta*** (1997), *Aida* (2000), *Shining City* (2006), *Talk Radio* (2007), and revivals of ***American Buffalo*** in 2008 and *Desire under the Elms** in 2009.

FAT PIG. **Neil LaBute**'s comedy opened 17 November 2004 at New York's Manhattan Class Company with a cast, including Ashlie Atkinson, Andrew McCarthy, Jeremy Piven, and Keri Russell, winning an **Outer Critics Circle Award**. The play returned to a frequent LaBute theme of the overemphasis on physical attractiveness in human relationships, depicting a young businessman, Tom, who is attracted to an overweight librarian, Helen. Both end up heartbroken when Tom acknowledges that he cannot commit to her because he fears what his friends will think. CRITIC David Amsden, writing in *New York Magazine*, applauded LaBute's "cruel wit" and his status as "the most legitimately provocative and polarizing playwright at work today." A 2005 London premiere of the play brought LaBute an Olivier Award nomination for Best New Comedy.

FAY, FRANK (1897–1961). Irish Catholic Francis Anthony Donner was born in San Francisco, California, prior to beginning a vaudeville* career during World WAR I. With the dawn of sound films, he had some success on screen beginning with *The Show of Shows* (1929). Notoriously difficult to work with, Fay's **Broadway** appearances were mostly in MUSICALS and revues,* with Fay often writing sketches and lyrics, including *Girl o'Mine* (1918), *The Passing Show of 1918*, *Oh, What a Girl!* (1919), *Jim Jam Jems* (1920), *Frank Fay's Fables* (1922), *Raymond Hitchcock's Pinwheel* (1922), *Artists and Models* (1923), *Harry Delmar's Revels* (1927), *Tattle Tales* (1933), *Frank Fay Vaudeville* (1939), and *Laugh Time* (1943). Fay had his most notable success late in his career as the gentle tippler Elwood P. Dowd in **Mary Chase**'s PULITZER PRIZE-winning comedy, *Harvey* (1944). Fay was married to actress Barbara Stanwyck from 1928 to 1935.

FAYE, JOEY (1909–1997). Born Joseph Palladino in New York to an Italian immigrant barber, he began his stage career in amateur nights, vaudeville,* and BURLESQUE, becoming one of the last of a breed of stage performers adept in the traditions of burlesque comedy, although Faye survived the death of burlesque by developing himself as a character actor, going "legitimate" in the national tour of *Room Service* in 1937, and as straight man for Phil Silvers, with whom he appeared in two MUSICALS, *High Button Shoes* (1947) and *Top Banana* (1951). Faye appeared in numerous films and television shows with occasional returns to **Broadway** for *Strip for Action* (1942), revivals of *The Milky Way* and *Boy Meets Girl* in 1944, several minor musicals and revues,* *The Tender Trap* (1954), *Little Me* (1962), a revival of *Guys and Dolls* in 1965, *70, Girls, 70* (1971), a revival of *The Ritz* in 1983, *Grind* (1985), and his last, a revival of *Three Men on a Horse* in 1993.

FEDER, ABE (1909–1997). Milwaukee, Wisconsin-born Feder studied at the Carnegie Institute of Technology and became one of the earliest well-known lighting designers beginning with *Trick for Trick* (1932). He designed lighting for numerous **Federal Theatre Project** productions, including the legendary *The Cradle Will Rock* (1938), and many **Broadway** productions, including *Four Saints in Three Acts* (1934), *Angel Street* (1941), *Winged Victory* (1943), *The Immortalist* (1954), *The Flowering Peach* (1954), *Inherit the Wind* (1955), *My Fair Lady* (1956), *A Visit to a Small Planet* (1957), *Orpheus Descending* (1957), *Time Remembered* (1958), *The Cold Wind and the Warm* (1958), *A Loss of Roses* (1959), *Camelot* (1960), *Tiger, Tiger Burning Bright* (1962), *Blues for Mister Charlie* (1964), *On a Clear Day You Can See Forever* (1964), *Scratch* (1971), and numerous revivals between the mid-1930s and the early 1970s. Feder was nominated for a **Tony**

Award and a **Drama Desk Award** for *Goodtime Charley* in 1975, one of his last Broadway productions. He designed lighting as a consultant for the 1964 New York World's Fair and numerous theatres and buildings, including Rockefeller Center and the **Kennedy Center**.

FEDERAL THEATRE PROJECT (FTP). President Franklin D. Roosevelt's "New Deal" intended this project, a Federal One project of the Works Progress Administration, to fund theatre and other live artistic performances throughout the United States. Officially established on 27 August 1935, the FTP provided one of the most intriguing, albeit brief, chapters in the history of American theatre. **Hallie Flanagan**, a theatre professor at Vassar College, was appointed director by Harry Hopkins, who announced that the FTP productions would be "free, adult, and uncensored," a promise that would be compromised almost immediately and ultimately lead to the project's demise. Among its many productions, **Living Newspapers** were among the true innovations and perhaps the first **documentary theatre** in the U.S. Researchers combed daily newspapers to create plays on topical issues, with resulting performances addressing national farm policies, as in *Triple-A Plowed Under* (1935), which assailed the U.S. Supreme Court for halting an aid agency for farmers. Others dealt with such explosive topics as the spread of syphilis (*Spirochete* in 1938), the Tennessee Valley Authority (*Power* in 1937), unions (*Injunction Granted* in 1935), and inequities in housing (***One Third of a Nation*** in 1938), creating controversy despite the fact that the Living Newspaper productions were popular with audiences.

When the U.S. State Department objected to the depiction of foreign heads of state in *Ethiopia* (1936), a Living Newspaper production chronicling that country's battle against Fascist Italy's invading army, playwright ELMER RICE, head of the FTP's New York office, resigned in protest. Another noted dramatist, SUSAN GLASPELL, was the FTP's Midwest director, and among the hundreds of young talents working on FTP productions (at the peak of the FTP over 10,000 artists were employed) were **Orson Welles**, **John Houseman**, Martin Ritt, **Arthur Miller**, **Elia Kazan**, **Canada Lee**, **Howard Bay**, **Joseph Cotten**, **Norman Lloyd**, **Will Geer**, PAUL GREEN, **Mary Chase**, **Arlene Francis**, Virgil Thomson, John Huston, Joseph Losey, **Arthur Arent**, **Abe Feder**, and Marc Blitzstein, whose collaboration with Welles and Houseman on his MUSICAL satire ***The Cradle Will Rock*** (1938) generated more controversy for the FTP when government officials padlocked the theatre where it was to premiere on its opening night. Welles, Houseman, and Blitzstein responded by renting a vacant theatre and opening the play sans scenery and costumes, with Blizstein playing his score and the actors, situated throughout the theatre, performing their roles.

FTP was divided into numerous units, including those devoted to an **African American** theatre, **children's theatre**, foreign-language productions, PUPPETRY, **religious drama**, musicals, CIRCUSES, and dance. The so-called Negro Unit had several notable successes, including the "voodoo" *Macbeth* in 1936, *Haiti* (1938), and *The Swing Mikado* (1939). Other noted FTP productions included Sinclair Lewis's *It Can't Happen Here* (1936), which opened in 20 cities simultaneously, **T. S. Eliot**'s *Murder in the Cathedral* (1936), and Paul Green's enduring **outdoor drama**, *The Lost Colony*, which opened in 1937 in an outdoor theatre in Roanoke, Virginia, built by the WPA. This extraordinary and ambitious attempt at a nationalized theatre met with increasing resistance during its brief existence. Controversy over the content of several productions caused a conservative Congress to challenge its existence, and the FTP was ended officially on 30 June 1939. Flanagan published *Arena*, a 1940 memoir of her experiences leading the FTP, and numerous subsequent studies of the FTP have been published. In 1999, Tim Robbins's film *Cradle Will Rock* offered a view of the FTP through the controversial events surrounding Blitzstein's musical.

FEFU AND HER FRIENDS. **Maria Irene Fornés**'s three-part examination of **women's** issues and **feminism** opened under Fornés's direction on 5 May 1977 at the New York Theatre Strategy prior to an **American Place Theatre** production, which opened on 8 January 1978. Ostensibly set in 1935 in the New England living room of the title character and her husband, Phillip (who is never seen, but presumed to be in the nearby garden), the first part depicts a group of eight women rehearsing a theatre education project. Fefu confesses to the women that she and Phillip play a game in which she fires blanks at him and he pretends to be shot, but ominously adds that Phillips has said that one day he might replace the blanks with live ammunition. In the second part, subsets of the women are seen sharing their individual problems and quests for individuality and liberation from the social and personal constraints they feel. Part Three focuses on the women's hopes for themselves and for the creation of a shared community, despite the revelations of strains behind their seemingly affectionate relationships as they work on their theatre project. When Fefu fires her gun at Phillip in the garden once more, one of the women unexpectedly dies in the living room.

FEIFFER, JULES (1929–). Born Jules Ralph Feiffer in the Bronx, New York, Feiffer learned cartooning as an assistant to Will Eisner in the 1940s prior to creating his own cartoons (eventually winning a PULITZER PRIZE for his editorial cartoons in *The Village Voice* in 1986), **children's** books, and numerous plays and screenplays. Feiffer's films include an animated short

Munro (1961), for which he won an Academy Award. He also contributed screenplays for *Carnal Knowledge* (1971), *Popeye* (1980), *I Want to Go Home* (1989), and an adaption of his own play, **Little Murders** (1971), which had first been performed **Off-Broadway** in 1967, but failed. It was later produced by the Royal **Shakespeare** Company, where it was well-received, and was subsequently staged at the **Circle in the Square** in 1969. Other Feiffer plays include *Knock, Knock* (1976), which was nominated for a Best Play **Tony Award**, and *Grown Ups* (1981), which received a **Drama Desk Award** nomination. His other **Broadway** productions include sketches for *Oh! Calcutta!* (1969), an "E-Mail" for *Short Talks on the Universe* (2002), and the musical *The Apple Tree* (1966), based on Feiffer's 1957 story "Passionella." Off-Broadway, *Jules Feiffer's Hold Me!* (1977) was Drama Desk-nominated. His other plays, all short works, include *Crawling Around* (1961), *Only When I Laugh* (1967), and *The White House Murder Case* (1969).

FEINGOLD, MICHAEL (1945–). Chicago, Illinois-born Feingold attended Columbia University and Yale University prior to become a drama CRITIC for *The Village Voice* in 1971, rising to chief critic in 1974. Recipient of the GEORGE JEAN NATHAN Award in 1996, Feingold has served as literary manager for the **Yale Repertory Theatre**, the **Guthrie Theatre**, and the **American Repertory Theatre**, and as literary advisor to New York's **Theatre for a New Audience**. Feingold is also a playwright and translator of numerous European classics, including works by Molière, HENRIK IBSEN, **Bertolt Brecht**, and others.

FEIST, GENE (1923–). Born Eugene Feist in New York, he graduated from Carnegie Mellon and New York University prior to training at **The Actors Studio** and the **American Theatre Wing**. He married actress Elizabeth Owens in 1957 and together they revived the New Theatre in Nashville, Tennessee, prior to founding the **Roundabout Theatre Company** in 1965, where he served as producing director of over 150 productions that won **Tony Awards** and **Drama Desk Awards** for revivals of *Anna Christie** in 1993, *Nine* in 2003, and *Assassins* in 2004. Drama Desk Awards went to Roundabout productions of *She Loves Me* in 1994, and *12 Angry Men* in 2005. Revivals of *Glengarry Glen Ross* in 2005, *The Pajama Game* in 2006, and *The 39 Steps* (2008) won Tonys. Feist was presented with a lifetime achievement **Lucille Lortel Award** in 1996.

FEMALE/MALE IMPERSONATION. Cross-dressing (or "drag") in theatre is as old as the theatre itself, although its popularity in mainstream theatre ebbs and flows. Gender flipping may suggest androgyny, challenge stereotypes, or provide broad comedy, all evident in nineteenth-century American theatre with such actors as Neil Burgess,* George W. Munroe, Gilbert Sarony, the Russell Brothers, and other **men** playing "dame" roles, often with an ethnic flavor, as did many minstrel* and vaudeville* performers, while actresses, most notably Charlotte Cushman,* continued the long tradition of "breeches roles" for **women** in **Shakespeare** and other plays. Sarah Bernhardt famously played Hamlet in the late nineteenth century, with a few twentieth-century actresses, notably **Judith Anderson** and Diane Venora, playing the melancholy Dane to decidedly mixed critical responses generations later. In the twentieth century, men in drag provided amusement in WARtime MUSICALS and other entertainments during both World Wars, although after World WAR II, most drag performance was relegated to the variety stage and **gay** nightclubs, with a few performers such as T. C. Jones, Craig Russell, Charles Pierce, and Lynn Carter, become well-known, mostly through impersonating female movie and stage stars.

The era of gay liberation that began after World War II and picked up steam in the 1960s brought a more serious exploration of androgyny and gender boundaries which, in rock music, had been evident in the performance styles of Alice Cooper, Boy George, Michael Jackson, and Madonna, among others. Some groups took a more radical approach, described as "gender-fuck," as seen first in San Francisco, California, with such groups as the Cockettes, Angels of Light, the Cycle Sluts, and the Sisters of Perpetual Indulgence, with parodies of gender roles and traditional drag even as groups like the all-male Ballets Trocadero de Monte Carlo continued it.

On New York stages, drag evolved into performance art in the work of **solo** artists like **John "Lypsinka" Epperson**, while playwright and actor **Charles Ludlam** pioneered **Ridiculous Theatre**, a movement of the 1970s which elevated "camp" to a theatrical genre in which performers like Ludlam, Divine, **Ethyl Eichelberger**, and **Charles Busch**, in their highly individual ways, could mix many theatrical genres and devices with cinematic traditions to create plays and performances in which the smashing and reinventing of gender roles, not to mention theatrical styles parodied, was a central component.

Gay men pioneered much of this work, but increasingly after 1990, **lesbian** theatre groups like **Split Britches** and others, brought "dyke noir" to the fore and otherwise assaulted gender stereotypes from their vantage point. Much of this work went on in **Off-Broadway** and **Off-Off Broadway** theatres, nightclubs, and other performance venues, while mainstream **Broadway** plays only occasionally moved into this realm in the drag musical *La Cage aux Folles* (1983) or in **David Henry Hwang**'s *M. Butterfly* (1988), while the cast of five men and three women in **Tony Kushner**'s *Angels in America* (1993) crossed gender lines with each playing both male and female characters in this epic work. In the new millennium, cross-dressing was accepted on Broadway and in regional theatres in both mainstream entertainments and serious drama at the level it had been in Off-Broadway and Off-Off Broadway theatre for decades. The dual 2003 Broadway triumphs of the musical *Hairspray*, with **Harvey Fierstein** in the drag role of Edna Turnblad and **Doug Wright**'s one-person *I Am My Own Wife*, in which Jefferson Mays played German transvestite Charlotte von Mahlsdorf, proved the point. *See also* SEXUALITY.

FEMINIST THEATRE. Since the nineteenth century both male and female dramatists have addressed the issues of gender inequities, **women's** rights, marriage, and **sexuality**, and despite the fact that women playwrights were comparatively scarce until the second half of the twentieth century (although such women as RACHEL CROTHERS, Zona Gale,* SUSAN GLASPELL, **Lillian Hellman, Rose Franken**, and others made significant strides), this situation began to change slowly after World WAR II as more women began to write, direct, and design for the American stage. This activity radically increased in the 1960s as feminism emerged as an organized political and cultural movement over such issues as equal pay and opportunity in all realms of American life, as well as various forms of liberation from social stereotypes about women and sexuality. Much energy centered around the National Organization for Women (NOW), which campaigned for an equal rights amendment to the Constitution of the United States.

More militant forms of feminism emerged in this period based on the notion that patriarchal domination of the American society is systemic, stressing that gender roles are socially constructed, not a matter of nature. Numerous women scholars began to address the subject of feminism within the realms of theatre and drama (and American culture at large). In this period a number of women's theatre groups appeared, including New York's It's Alright to Be a Woman Theatre, the **Magic Theatre**, and the Women's Experimental Theatre, among others, and a number of individual women dramatists emerged between the 1960s and 1980s, including **Megan Terry**, Roberta Sklar, **Adrienne Kennedy, Maria Irene Fornés**, and others, offering plays in which feminist issues, women's history, and the nature of sexual roles were central.

Other theatre groups appeared later in the twentieth century, including some with **ethnic** concerns as well, including **Spider-Woman Theatre** and **At the Foot of the Mountain**, and other groups not overtly identified with feminism increasingly included these concerns in their missions or produced feminist plays with regularity, including **The Open Theatre, The Living Theatre**, and **The Performance Group**. Increased gay and lesbian political activism led to the rise of lesbian theatre **collectives** like **Split Britches** and others, stressing gender-fuck and other issues inherent in challenging traditional sexual roles. During this era, much debate centered around the question of whether assimilation with or separatism from the mainstream theatre was in the best interest of feminist theatre artists.

After 1980, women dramatists writing on feminist issues found more access to mainstream stages on **Broadway** and **Off-Broadway**, including such writers as **Beth Henley**, **Marsha Norman**, **Ntozake Shange**, **Wendy Wasserstein**, and, later, **Paula Vogel**, **Suzan-Lori Parks**, **Naomi Wallace**, and others. Noted performers, from **Lily Tomlin** to **Cherry Jones**, stressed their feminist concerns (and their personal lives as lesbians) through those works with which they associated themselves, and women directors, including **Anne Bogart** and **Tina Landau**, led the way in incorporating feminist principles in their productions as critics and theatre scholars increasingly wrote on the subject, particularly after 1990. *See also* GAY AND LESBIAN THEATRE.

FENCES. **August Wilson**'s PULITZER PRIZE-winning play, directed by **Lloyd Richards** and with a strong cast headed by **James Earl Jones**, premiered at the **Eugene O'Neill Center** in 1983 and was performed elsewhere before opening on **Broadway** on 26 March 1987 at the 46th Street Theatre for 525 performances, winning, along with the Pulitzer, a **Tony Award**, **Drama Desk Award**, and **New York Drama Critics Circle Award**. Set in the 1950s, the play centers on garbage man Troy Maxson (Jones), once a talented baseball player whose career was stunted by racism, and his complex relationship with his son (Courtney B. Vance) and wife (**Mary Alice**). *Fences* is one of the ten decade-by-decade plays Wilson wrote chronicling the experience of **African Americans** in the twentieth century. Richards, Jones, and Alice won Tonys, with nominations for Frankie R. Faison and Vance, with the latter winning a **Theatre World Award**. As of 2010, no film version of *Fences* has appeared, although it has had many productions in **regional** and university theatres. Under Kenny Leon's direction, *Fences* was produced at Boston's **Huntington Theatre** and subsequently revived on Broadway at the Cort Theatre, starring **Denzel Washington**, **Viola Davis**, and Chris Chalk in 2010, and won critical approval, including a Tony and a Drama Desk Award as Best Revival, Tony and **Outer Critics Circle Awards** for Washington and Davis, and a **Theatre World Award** for Chalk.

FERBER, EDNA (1887–1968).[†] A native of Kalamazoo, Michigan, Ferber is best known as author of *Show Boat* (1926), the durable novel of itinerant performers living on the Mississippi River between the 1880s and 1920s that became a celebrated Florenz Ziegfeld*-produced MUSICAL with a score by Jerome Kern and lyrics by Oscar Hammerstein II in 1927. Another Ferber novel, *Saratoga Trunk* (1941), was adapted into a 1959 musical. Despite success as a novelist, Ferber collaborated on several of the most popular plays of the first three decades of the twentieth century. Without a collaborator, Ferber wrote *The Eldest* (1920), but her best works for the stage were created with partners, beginning with her first important collaboration, with George V. Hobart,* which produced *Our Mrs. Chesney** (1915), a sturdy vehicle for ETHEL BARRYMORE, and *$1200 a Year* (1920), written with Newman Levy. Her longest and most successful collaboration was with GEORGE S. KAUFMAN and resulted in *Minick** (1924) and *The Royal Family** (1927). After 1930, Ferber and Kaufman had two of their most enduring successes with *Dinner at Eight* (1932) and *Stage Door* (1936). Both comedy-dramas, the plays garnered critical acclaim, long and profitable runs, and film versions now considered classics. Two subsequent collaborations with Kaufman, *The Land Is Bright* (1941) and *Bravo!* (1948), were less successful.

FERNALD, JOHN (1905–1985). Born in Marin County, California, as John Bailey Fernald, he worked in England as a director before founding the Meadow Brook Theatre in Rochester, Michigan, in 1967 as a not-for-profit operation. The theatre performed on the campus of Oakland University, eventually growing to the largest professional company in Michigan. Under Fernald's direction, the company performed a range of classic and modern revivals before dissolving in 2003. On **Broadway**, Fernald directed *The Affair* (1962) and a 1970 revival of *The Cherry Orchard*. He also authored the textbooks *The Play Produced: An Introduction to the Technique of Producing Plays* (1952) and *Sense of Direction* (1968), and an **award** in his name was established in 1988 to support assistant directors at the start of their careers.

FERRER, JOSÉ (1912–1992). This versatile actor, director, and producer, was born José Vicente Ferrer de Otero y Cintrón in Santurce, Puerto Rico, and graduated from Princeton University in 1933. He began his acting career on **Broadway** in *A Slight Case of Murder* (1935), winning plaudits within a short time in such productions as *Mamba's Daughters* (1939), *Key Largo* (1939), a revival of *Charley's Aunt* in 1940, and as Iago to PAUL ROBESON's Othello in an acclaimed 1943 revival. In this period, he began to direct and produce with some regularity, staging *Strange Fruit* (1945) and producing an acclaimed revival of *Cyrano de Bergerac* in 1946, which brought him a **Tony Award** and which led to his Academy Award-winning performance in a 1950 screen version. Ferrer also received three Tonys as Best Director for *The Fourposter* (1951), *Stalag 17* (1951), and *The Shrike* (1952), for which he also won a Best Actor Tony, and his libretto for the MUSICAL *Oh Captain!* (1958) was Tony-nominated.

As an actor, Ferrer's other Broadway appearances include revivals of *Volpone*, *The Alchemist*, and *Angel Street* in 1948, *Twentieth Century* in 1950, and *Richard III* in 1953, *Edwin Booth** (1958), *The Girl Who Came to Supper* (1963), and he stepped in as a replacement for the title character in *Man of La Mancha* in 1966. On Broadway, Ferrer also directed *As We Forgive Our Debtors* (1947), *The Chase* (1952), *My Three Angels* (1953), *Juno* (1959), *The Andersonville Trial* (1959), and *Carmelina* (1979), among others.

In films, Ferrer was Oscar-nominated for *Joan of Arc* (1948) and *Moulin Rouge* (1952), and also appeared in *The Caine Mutiny* (1954), *The Shrike* (1955), *I Accuse!* (1958), *Ship of Fools* (1965), *Enter Laughing* (1967), *Fedora* (1978), *A Midsummer Night's Sex Comedy* (1982), and *To Be or Not to Be* (1983), and directed several films. On television, Ferrer received two Emmy Award nominations and appeared in many dramatic shows. His three wives were actress/teacher **Uta Hagen**, actress Phyllis Hill, and singer Rosemary Clooney.

FICHANDLER, ZELDA (1924–). Born Zelda Diamond in Boston, Massachusetts, she attended George Washington University and Cornell University prior to marrying Thomas C. Fichandler and with him and Edward Mangum founded Washington, D.C.'s **Arena Stage**. She served at its artistic director for 41 years, until her retirement in 1991. Fichandler staged many of the Arena's productions during her tenure, from great American plays to modern European classics. Under her guidance, the Arena also produced new works, including *The Great White Hope* (1967), *Indians* (1969), *Moonchildren* (1971), *Raisin* (1973), *Zalmen, or The Madness of God* (1976), *A History of the American Film* (1978), and *K2* (1983), and she developed an interest in Russian and Eastern European drama during a trip there in 1973. In 1976, the Arena received the **Tony Award** for Regional Theatre and Fichandler won a Helen Hayes Award for directing a revival of *The Crucible* in 1988, she was awarded the National Medal of the Arts by President Bill Clinton in 1997, and she was inducted into the **Theatre Hall of Fame** in 1999, the first non-New York artist so honored. A theatre enthusiast, Fichandler stated, "There is a hunger to see the human presence acted out. As long as that need remains, people will find a way to do theatre."

FIELD, BETTY (1918–1973). A native of Boston, Massachusetts, this fine but largely unsung actress began her career in the London production of HOWARD LINDSAY's farce, *She Loves Me Not* (1933) and debuted on **Broadway** in a small role in *Page Miss Glory* (1934). She played a wide range of roles on stage, but for a time she was stuck in a range of comic ingénue roles after GEORGE ABBOTT cast her as the naïve secretary in the zany farce *Room*

Service (1937) and similar characters in a series of comedies, including *Angel Island* (1937), *If I Were You* (1938), *What a Life* (1938), *The Primrose Path* (1939), *Ring Two* (1939), *Two on an Island* (1940), *Flight to the West* (1940), *A New Life* (1943), and she replaced **Margaret Sullavan** in the hit comedy *The Voice of the Turtle* in 1944. Field married playwright ELMER RICE in 1942. He wrote the comedy *Dream Girl* (1945) for Field, and she scored a major success. Her subsequent Broadway appearances were in a wide variety of plays, including *The Rat Race* (1949), *Not for Children* (1951), *The Ladies of the Corridor* (1953), *Festival* (1955), a revival of *The Waltz of the Toreadors* (1958), *A Touch of the Poet* (1958), *A Loss of Roses* (1959), a revival of *Strange Interlude** in 1963, *Where's Daddy?* (1966), and *All Over* (1971). She also replaced **Jessica Tandy** in *The Fourposter* in 1952. Field won plaudits in her first important movie role, as Mae in *Of Mice and Men* (1939), appearing in several films including *King's Row* (1942), *Flesh and Fantasy* (1943), *The Southerner* (1945), *The Great Gatsby* (1949), *Picnic* (1955), *Bus Stop* (1956), *Peyton Place* (1957), *Butterfield 8* (1960), and *Birdman of Alcatraz* (1962). Field and Rice were divorced in 1956 and, along with her stage and film work, she also appeared in numerous television dramas.

FIERSTEIN, HARVEY (1954–). Harvey Forbes Fierstein, born in the Bensonhurst section of Brooklyn, New York, as the son of a handkerchief manufacturer and a school librarian began working as a drag performer around 1970. Featured as a 270-pound teenage transvestite specializing in Ethel Merman impersonations, Fierstein made his professional debut at Club 82 and also worked with the **La Mama Experimental Theatre Club** in 1971 prior to attending the Pratt Institute in 1973. He also acted in plays, beginning with Andy Warhol's *Pork* (1971), and while studying at Pratt, began writing plays, including *In Search of the Cobra Jewels* (1972), *Freaky Pussy* (1974), *Cannibals Just Don't Know No Better* (1975), and *Flatbush Tosca* (1975), the last of which was produced by the New York City Theatre Ensemble.

Fierstein's playwriting gained significant attention with *Torch Song Trilogy*, a collection of three **Off-Broadway** one-act plays, *The International Stud* (first produced in 1976), *Fugue in a Nursery* (1979), and *Widows and Children First!* (1979), all held together by a central character, Arnold Beckoff, Fierstein's alter ego, a role he played himself both onstage and in a subsequent 1988 film version. The **Broadway** production brought Fierstein a **Tony Award**, **Theatre World Award**, and **Drama Desk Award** for his performance and a Tony for Best Play. Fierstein followed *Torch Song Trilogy* with *Spookhouse* (1982), which failed to excite critical or commercial approval, but two years later he scored with his libretto for the long-running hit MUSICAL *La Cage aux Folles* (1984), for which he won a Tony.

Turning his attention to the **AIDS** pandemic in the mid-1980s, Fierstein wrote *Safe Sex* (1987), another trilogy connected by topic. Fierstein appeared in *Safe Sex* when it moved to Broadway's Lyceum Theatre, but it closed after a mere nine performances. Fierstein also contributed the libretto for the failed musical *Legs Diamond* (1988), but by the 1990s he devoted much of his attention to acting in films and television, as well as performing in cabarets. Back on the Broadway stage, he scored in the drag role of Edna Turnblad in the musical *Hairspray* (2002), winning a Tony and a Drama Desk Award for his performance, and scripted and performed in the musical *A Catered Affair* (2008). *See also* FEMALE/MALE IMPERSONATION; GAY AND LESBIAN THEATRE; MEN/MASCULINITY; SEXUALITY.

FIFTH COLUMN, THE. Ernest Hemingway made a rare foray into playwriting with his 1937 WAR drama adapted by Benjamin Glazer and directed by **Lee Strasberg** for THE THEATRE GUILD. The play opened at the Alvin Theatre on 6 March 1940 for 87 performances with a cast including **Franchot Tone**, Lenore Ulric,* and **Lee J. Cobb**. Set in Madrid during the Spanish Civil War, *The Fifth Column* involves two mismatched journalists, Philip Rawlings and Dorothy Bridges, who fall into an affair during a major battle. Glazer's doctoring of Hemingway's play stressed antifascist attitudes, but it found scant favor with audiences. New York's **Mint Theatre Company** revived the play in 2008, but otherwise it has only rarely been produced.

FIFTH OF JULY. **Lanford Wilson**'s two-act drama under the direction of Marshall W. Mason was produced by the **Circle Repertory Company** on 27 April 1978 for 158 performances with a cast including **William Hurt**, as Ken Talley, a **gay** paraplegic Vietnam WAR veteran who has returned to his Missouri home to teach, and **Jeff Daniels**, as Jed, Ken's lover. Most of the play's characters, including Gwen, a former schoolmate of Ken's who with her husband, John, wants to buy Ken's house for a recording studio; Ken's sister, June, a former antiwar militant and her precocious adolescent daughter, Shirley; and Ken's ailing, widowed aunt Sally all endeavor to free themselves from the constraints of the past and the impact of the 1960s and the Vietnam era. Confronted with selling his family home, Ken is ultimately gently guided by Jed and Sally to face his current reality and the specters of the past by keeping his home and imagining a new future in it. Critics found this play, like much of Wilson's oeuvre, reminiscent of **Anton Chekhov** and **Tennessee Williams**. A **Broadway** production opened at the New Apollo Theatre on 5 November 1980 for 511 performances and reaped five **Tony Award** nominations and a Tony for **Swoosie Kurtz** as Gwen. **Christopher Reeve** replaced Hurt and Daniels reprised his role for the Broadway production. A PBS-TV film, with **Richard Thomas** stepping in for Reeve, was shown in 1982, with Daniels and Kurtz reprising their roles.

FINLEY, KAREN (1956–). Born in Evanston, Illinois, Finley completed an M.F.A. at the San Francisco Art Institute and, with the assistance of a **National Endowment for the Arts (NEA)** grant, moved to New York and began her work as a **performance artist** and writer collaborating with the Kipper Kids (Brian Routh, Martin von Haselberg, and David Wojnarowicz). Many of her performance pieces reflect her concern with **women's** bodies and **sexuality**, the collapse of the nuclear family (in part, a reaction to her father's 1979 suicide), and society's victimization of the disenfranchised. Among these are *The Constant State of Desire* (1987), *The Theory of Total Blame* (1988), *We Keep Our Victims Ready* (1989), *A Certain Level of Denial* (1993), *The American Chestnut* (1997), for which she won an Obie Award and a Guggenheim Fellowship, *The Return of the Chocolate-Smeared Woman* (1998), *Make Love* (2003), and *George and Martha* (2004). At the height of the Culture Wars, Finley was one of the "NEA Four," artists whose grants were revoked due to charges of obscenity brought by North Carolina Senator Jesse Helms, setting off a controversy about national funding of art. Finley also courted considerable controversy by frequently appearing onstage nude and smeared with chocolate or honey, but with the articulated goal of desexualizing **nudity**. *See also* FEMINIST THEATRE; SEXUALITY; SOLO PERFORMANCES; WOMEN/FEMININITY.

FISHER, JULES (1937–). This noted **Broadway** lighting designer was born in Norristown, Pennsylvania, and graduated from the Carnegie Institute of Technology before becoming one of the leading and most prolific lighting designers on Broadway and **Off-Broadway** (credited with over 200 productions) as well as in film, television, dance, opera, and the concert stage. On Broadway, his numerous **Tony Award**-winning designs include *Pippin* (1972), *Ulysses in Nighttown* (1973), *Dancin'* (1978), *Grand Hotel* (1990), *The Will Rogers Follies* (1991), *Jelly's Last Jam* (1992), *Bring in 'Da Noise, Bring in 'Da Funk* (1996), and a revival of *Assassins* in 2004. He received a **Drama Desk Awards** for his designs for *Chicago* (1975), *Grand Hotel, Bring in 'Da Noise, Bring in 'Da Funk,* and *Assassins.*

Among Fisher's many other Broadway designs are *Anyone Can Whistle* (1964), *High Spirits* (1964), *The Subject Was Roses* (1964), *The Sign in Sidney Brustein's Window* (1964), *You Know I Can't Hear You When the Water's Running* (1967), *The Man in the Glass Booth* (1968), *Hair* (1968), *Butterflies Are Free* (1969), *Jesus Christ Superstar* (1971), revivals of *No, No, Nanette* in 1971, *The Iceman Cometh* in 1973, and *Uncle Vanya* in 1973,

American Buffalo (1977), *La Cage aux Folles* (1983), *Death and the Maiden* (1992), *Angels in America* (1993), *Twilight: Los Angeles, 1992* (1994), and *Caroline, or Change* (2004). Fisher often works in collaboration with **Peggy Eisenhauer** and their joint productions include *Song and Dance* (1985), *Rags* (1986), *Legs Diamond* (1988), *Ragtime* (1998), revivals of *Gypsy* in 2003 and *The Ritz* in 2007, and *9 to 5* (2009). Fisher is married to dancer/choreographer Graciela Daniele and teaches at the New School for Social Research.

FITZGERALD, GERALDINE (1913–2005). Born in Greystones, County Wicklow, Ireland, Fitzgerald was inspired by her aunt, actress and director Shelah Richards. Her first work as an actress in Dublin in 1932 led to London two years later, where she acted in English films before moving to the United States to appear on **Broadway** opposite **Orson Welles** in a **Mercury Theatre** revival of *Heartbreak House* in 1938. That same year, Warner Bros. film producer Hal Wallis offered Fitzgerald a contract and she subsequently divided her time between movies and theatre, appearing on stage in *Sons and Soldiers* (1943), playing Goneril to Welles's Lear in a revival of *King Lear* in 1956, *Hide and Seek* (1957), a revival of *Ah, Wilderness!* in 1975, *The Shadow Box* (1977), and a revival of *A Touch of the Poet* in 1977. Fitzgerald was nominated for a **Tony Award** and a **Drama Desk Award** for her direction of Bill C. Davis's *Mass Appeal* (1981) and Drama Desk-nominated for her *Geraldine Fitzgerald in Streetsongs* (1979). Her appearances **Off-Broadway** include a 1971 revival of *Long Day's Journey into Night*, for which she won a Drama Desk Award. Also in 1971, Fitzgerald became the first **woman** to play the Stage Manager in a production of **Thornton Wilder**'s *Our Town* at the **Williamstown Theatre Festival**.

Fitzgerald's film appearances include her Academy Award-nominated performance in *Wuthering Heights* (1939), *Dark Victory* (1939), *Watch on the Rhine* (1943), *Wilson* (1944), *Ten North Frederick* (1958), *The Pawnbroker* (1964), *Rachel, Rachel* (1968), and *Arthur* (1981). On television, she won a Daytime Emmy Award for *Rodeo Red and the Runaways* in 1979 and was nominated for an Emmy for an episode of *The Golden Girls* in 1988. Fitzgerald was the mother of director Michael Lindsay-Hogg and the great-aunt of actress Tara FitzGerald.

FIVE STAR FINAL. Louis Weitzenkorn's three-act melodrama,* produced by A. H. Woods,* opened at the Cort Theatre on 30 December 1930 for 175 performances. The highly charged plot involves a newspaper editor, Randall (Arthur Byron), compelled by his ruthless producer to dredge up an old story about Nancy Vorhees, a woman accused of killing her lover. Vorhees, now married and preparing for the marriage of her grown daughter Jenny, begs

Randall to kill the story so as not to ruin Jenny's chance for happiness. Under pressure, Randall runs the story, leading to the suicide of Vorhees and her husband. Jenny comes to Randall's office intending to kill him, but she learns he has resigned his post over what has occurred. A 1931 film version was nominated for an Academy Award for Best Picture and starred EDWARD G. ROBINSON.

FLANAGAN, HALLIE (1890–1969). Born in Redfield, South Dakota, as Hallie Ferguson, she was raised in Iowa and attended Grinnell College and studied with George Pierce Baker* at Harvard University. She married Murray Flanagan, but his premature death in 1918 led her to take a job teaching theatre at Vassar College. Her interest in European experimentation in theatre practice and a Guggenheim Fellowship in 1926 provided the impetus for a European tour during which she met with such notables as John Galsworthy, **Constantin Stanislavsky**, Edward Gordon Craig, and Lady Augusta Gregory. Back at Vassar, Flanagan established the Vassar Experimental Theatre and cowrote *Can You Hear Their Voices?* (1931), which won national attention. In 1935, Harry Hopkins, head of the New Deal's Works Progress Administration, selected Flanagan to direct the **Federal Theatre Project (FTP)**, a bold project intended to not only put theatre artists back to work during the Great Depression, but to bring all manner of theatre to American citizens (especially those with little or no access to mainstream theatre) that would be free, adult, and uncensored.

Despite considerable success at meeting the heady goals Flanagan articulated, the FTP met with increasing controversy resulting from the content of various productions, from the topical **"Living Newspapers"** to the **Orson Welles** staging of Marc Blitzstein's satiric MUSICAL *The Cradle Will Rock* (1938). In 1939, a conservative U.S. Congress bent on turning back New Deal programs succeeded in shutting down the FTP. Flanagan returned to her teaching post at Vassar and wrote a memoir of the FTP experience, *Arena* (1940). In 1942, Flanagan became head of the Theatre Department at Smith College, where she worked until her retirement. In Tim Robbins's 1999 film *Cradle Will Rock*, which chronicled the censorship battle over the Blitzstein musical, actress **Cherry Jones** played Flanagan.

FLEA THEATRE, THE. Established by artistic director Jim Simpson, scene designer Kyle Chepulis, and playwright **Mac Wellman** in 1996, partly in an attempt to revive the glory days of **Off-Off Broadway** experimentation, this company operates in two tiny performances spaces (one with 40 seats, the other with 80) and typically stages three productions annually. Their production of Anne Nelson's *The Guys* (2002), which was written in nine days in response to the tragic events of 9/11, won acclaim for its depiction of the experiences of a fireman faced with eulogizing several of his colleagues killed at the World Trade Center. The Flea received a 2004 **Drama Desk Award** for Distinguished Achievement.

FLETCHER, ALLEN (1922–1985). San Francisco, California-born Fletcher was educated at Stanford University, Yale University, the Bristol Old Vic Theatre School, and the London Academy of Music and Dramatic Art prior to beginning a career as a director in 1948 at the **Oregon Shakespeare Festival**, continuing with the festival for eight years. Fletcher directed for the Antioch Shakespeare Festival, the **Old Globe Theatre** in San Diego, California, and the Association of Producing Artists in the 1950s and early 1960s, winning acclaim for his 1963 staging of *King Lear* with **Morris Carnovsky**, after which he took over as director and head of the professional training program for the **American Shakespeare Festival** in 1962. He moved to the **Seattle Repertory Theatre** from 1966 to 1970, after which he established the Actor's Company and served as director of the Conservatory for the **American Conservatory Theatre** until 1984, when he moved to the **Denver Theatre Center** for a brief time prior to his death.

FLETCHER, BRAMWELL (1904–1988). Born in Bradford, Yorkshire, England, Fletcher became a stage, film, and television actor in the U.S. and England beginning in 1927. He debuted on **Broadway** in *Scotland Yard* (1929), after which he appeared in many plays, including *Within the Gates* (1934), revivals of *The Circle* and *Outward Bound* in 1938, *Margin for Error* (1939), *Rebecca* (1945), *The Lovers* (1956), and several revivals of GEORGE BERNARD SHAW's plays during the 1940s and 1950s. He also stepped in as a replacement Henry Higgins in *My Fair Lady* (1956). With the dawn of sound films, he appeared in several early classics, including costarring with John Barrymore* in *Svengali* (1931), as well as *The Mummy* (1932), *The Scarlet Pimpernel* (1934), *White Cargo* (1942), and *Random Harvest* (1942), and also appeared frequently on television in the 1950s and 1960s. Fletcher wed actresses Helen Chandler and Diana Barrymore, but both marriages ended in divorce.

FOLGER SHAKESPEARE LIBRARY AND THEATRE. Established in 1932 with a gift from Henry Clay Folger and his wife Emily Jordan Folger, the library, which is located on Capitol Hill in Washington, D.C. houses the world's largest collection of **Shakespeare** materials, as well as Renaissance books, manuscripts, and art works. For many years, it included a theatre, which left the library in 1992 for larger facilities. The Folger Theatre features a three-play season in a 250-seat Elizabethan-style space reminiscent of an innyard theatre.

FOLKSBIENE YIDDISH THEATRE.† Originally one of many theatres established in New York City during the heyday of YIDDISH THEATRE, the Folksbiene has staged productions annually since 1915, becoming the longest surviving theatre. **Joseph Buloff** and JACOB BEN-AMI were among early directors and the theatre established itself in the Central Synagogue, but lost their home there in 1998 as the result of a fire. After brief periods in other spaces, the theatre settled into the Jewish Community Center in Manhattan and in 2006 changed its name to the National Yiddish Theatre–Folksbiene. *See also* ETHNIC THEATRE.

FONDA, HENRY (1905–1982). One of the great American film stars of mid-twentieth century, Henry Jaynes Fonda was born in Grand Island, Nebraska, and began his theatrical career acting at the Omaha Community Playhouse prior to working in STOCK in New England. Fonda made his **Broadway** debut in a small role in *The Game of Love and Death* (1929), followed by *I Loved You Wednesday* (1932) and *New Faces of 1934* (1934) before a notable success in *The Farmer Takes a Wife* (1934), which led to his long Hollywood career with his 1935 appearance in the film version.

Despite movie stardom, Fonda returned frequently to the Broadway stage, scoring a notable success as the title character in *Mister Roberts* (1948), which brought him a **Tony Award**. He repeated his performance as the self-sacrificing navy office in the 1955 screen version of the play. Fonda also appeared on Broadway in *Point of No Return* (1951), *The Caine Mutiny Court-Martial* (1954), *Two for the Seesaw* (1958), *Silent Night, Lonely Night* (1958), *Critic's Choice* (1960), *A Gift for Time* (1962), *Generation* (1965), a revival of *Our Town* in 1969, *Clarence Darrow* (1974), for which he received a **Drama Desk Award** and a Tony nomination, and *First Monday in October* (1978). In 1979, Fonda was presented with a special Tony.

Fonda appeared in over 100 films, including such classics as *Jezebel* (1938), *Young Mr. Lincoln* (1939), *The Grapes of Wrath* (1940), *Lady Eve* (1941), *The Ox-Bow Incident* (1943), *My Darling Clementine* (1946), *12 Angry Men* (1957), *Advise & Consent* (1962), *The Best Man* (1964), *Fail-Safe* (1964), and he won an Academy Award for *On Golden Pond* (1981), although he had been presented with an honorary Oscar the year before. He also appeared on television, garnering Emmy Award nominations for *The Red Pony* (1973), *Clarence Darrow* (1974), and *Gideon's Trumpet* (1980). In 1980, he appeared in a rare live television presentation of Preston Jones's play *The Oldest Living Graduate*, one of the works in *A Texas Trilogy*.

Fonda was the father of Jane Fonda and Peter Fonda and the grandfather of Bridget Fonda.

FONTANNE, LYNN (1887–1983).† Born in England, Lillie Louise Fontanne debuted at the age of 17 in *Cinderella* (1905), after studying acting with the great Victorian star, Ellen Terry. Fontanne's American debut came five years later in the innocuous *Mr. Preedy and the Countess* (1910). In 1916, she appeared with her future husband, ALFRED LUNT, who she married in 1922, in *A Young Man's Fancy* (1916). Fontanne scored a personal success in *Dulcy** (1921) and several THEATRE GUILD productions, including EUGENE O'NEILL's Pulitzer Prize-winning *Strange Interlude** (1928). She appeared with Lunt in Ferenc Molnar's *The Guardsman* (1924), a triumph for the couple as a team, and after the late 1920s they worked together exclusively. The team won acclaim in *The Second Man** (1927), *The Doctor's Dilemma* (1927), *Caprice* (1928), and *Meteor** (1929).

After 1930, the stature of Lunt and Fontanne grew with each new production, beginning with MAXWELL ANDERSON's historical verse drama, *Elizabeth the Queen* (1930). The Lunts achieved an impressive ability to work as a complementary unit, with Fontanne's beauty, poise, and subtlety balanced by Lunt's more impassioned acting. They were particularly applauded for their well-honed effect of seeming to interrupt each others' lines which, to critics of the time, created a higher level of **naturalism** than had been previously seen. Post-1930, their successes included three ROBERT E. SHERWOOD plays, *Reunion in Vienna* (1931), *Idiot's Delight* (1936), and *There Shall Be No Night* (1940), S. N. BEHRMAN's *Amphitryon 38* (1937) and *The Pirate* (1942), and **Noël Coward**'s *Design for Living* (1933), in which the playwright joined the Lunts onstage in a memorable threesome.

After World WAR II, the vehicles selected by the Lunts, *O Mistress Mine* (1946), *I Know My Love* (1949), *Quadrille* (1954), and *The Great Sebastians* (1956), proved somewhat less worthy of their unique talents than prior plays, although all were well-received. Their final appearance in Friedrich Dürrenmatt's grim drama *The Visit* (1958) once again provided an appropriate challenge met by the greatest acting team in **Broadway** history. They appeared in an acclaimed television production of *The Magnificent Yankee* in the 1960s, but in old age chose to live quietly in Genesee Depot, Wisconsin. Their rare public appearances during their retirement included accepting a joint **Tony Award** for lifetime achievement in 1970.

FOOL FOR LOVE. **Sam Shepard**'s two-act, three-character drama premiered at San Francisco's **Magic Theatre** on 8 February 1983 prior to its **Off-Broadway** production at the **Circle Repertory Theatre** on 26 May

1983. Ed Harris and Kathy Baker played unhappy lovers Eddie and May battling in a Mojave Desert motel where she is attempting to hide in order to get away from Eddie. They are haunted by the specter of an old man whose presence suggests that Eddie may, in fact, be May's half-brother. A 1985 film version directed by Robert Altman with Shepard costarred with Kim Basinger as the ill-starred lovers, and the play also had a major London revival in 2006 and was performed by the Bull and **The Living Theatre** in a coproduction in 2009.

FOOTE, HORTON (1916–2009). Albert Horton Foote, Jr. was born in Wharton, Texas, and studied acting at the **Pasadena Playhouse** in 1931, but by 1940 with his play *Wharton Dance* he embarked on a long career as a playwright and screenwriter, inspired by the plays of **Anton Chekhov.** His nearly 50 plays include his PULITZER PRIZE-winning and **Tony Award**-nominated *The Young Man from Atlanta* (1995) and *The Trip to Bountiful* (1953), which debuted on live television before moving to **Broadway.** Other Foote plays produced on Broadway include *Only the Heart* (1944), *The Chase* (1952), *The Traveling Lady* (1954), and *Dividing the Estate* (2008), which was nominated for a Tony and a **Drama Desk Award.** As a screenwriter, Foote won Academy Awards for *To Kill a Mockingbird* (1962) and *Tender Mercies* (1983). He adapted his play *The Trip to Bountiful* for a 1985 film version and received an Oscar nomination. For television, Foote won a 1997 Emmy Award for *Old Man*, adapted from William Faulkner's story. Foote, the father of actress Hallie Foote, received a 2006 Drama Desk Career Achievement Award. Discussing the themes of his work in 1986, Foote stated, "I believe very deeply in the human spirit and I have a sense of awe about it because I don't know how people carry on. I've known people that the world has thrown everything at to discourage them, to kill them, to break their spirit. And yet something about them retains a dignity. They face life and they don't ask quarters."

FOR COLORED GIRLS WHO HAVE CONSIDERED SUICIDE/WHEN THE RAINBOW IS ENUF. Poetic drama was occasionally offered by American dramatists, but in this unique work **African American** playwright/performer **Ntozake Shange** pioneered a radically new dramatic form, the "choreopoem," a bold mixture of character, poetry, song, and dance which might more accurately be labeled a dramatic/poetic collage, an expression conveying the unique mixture of language, theatre, movement, and music that has become more the rule than the exception in theatrical explorations of the experiences of blacks. In this case, Shange focused on the coming-of-age experiences of contemporary black **women.** *for colored girls* premiered

Off-Broadway at New York's Studio Rivbea on 7 July 1975, where it met with critical approval before transferring to the **New York Shakespeare Festival/Public Theatre** on 1 June 1976, followed by a move to **Broadway**'s Booth Theatre on 15 September 1976. In all, *for colored girls* gave an impressive 867 performances in New York, leading to a cast album and a PBS-TV *American Playhouse* film in 1982. *for colored girls* won numerous honors, including an **Obie Award**, an Outer Critics Award, an Audelco Award, and a Mademoiselle Award, as well as nominations for a **Tony Award**, a Grammy for the cast album, and an Emmy for the television film. In 2010, director/writer Tyler Perry produced and adapted the play as a film starring Janet Jackson, Whoopi Goldberg, Phylicia Rashad, Thandie Newton, Loretta Devine, and Anika Noni Rose. *See also* FEMINIST THEATRE; SEXUALITY.

FORD, PAUL (1901–1976). This character actor of stage, screen, and television was one of those familiar faces audience members could rarely name, despite Ford's ability to move effortlessly from broad comedy to drama. Born Paul Ford Weaver in Baltimore, Maryland, he appeared in four **Broadway** flops, *Decision* (1944), *War President* (1944), *Lower North* (1944), and *Flamingo Road* (1946), and one moderate success, *Kiss Them for Me* (1945), before landing roles in stronger plays, including *Another Part of the Forest* (1946), *As We Forgive Our Debtors* (1947), and *Command Decision* (1947). Generally playing fathers, military officers, and pompous businessmen, Ford demonstrated a particular affinity for comic approaches to such characters, first evident in his **Broadway** performance as Colonel Purdy in *The Teahouse of the August Moon* (1953), a role he repeated in the 1956 film version and, on television, in the hapless Colonel Hall in the *Sgt. Bilko* series. Much sought after for character roles in movies and on TV, Ford returned to Broadway with some regularity, stepping in to replace David Burns as blustering Mayor Shinn in the hit MUSICAL, *The Music Man* (1957), a role he repeated in the 1962 film version. He scored again in the revue *A Thurber Carnival* (1960) and especially in Sumner Arthur Long's comedy *Never Too Late* (1962), garnering a **Tony Award** nomination as a middle-aged expectant father, a role he repeated in the 1965 movie version. His subsequent Broadway roles were less successful, including roles in *3 Bags Full* (1966), *What Did We Do Wrong* (1967), a short-lived revival of *Three Men on a Horse* in 1969, as a replacement in a revival of *The Front Page** (1969), and *Fun City* (1972). In films, Ford's supporting performances in the all-star comedies *It's a Mad, Mad, Mad, Mad World* (1962) and *The Russians Are Coming, The Russians Are Coming* (1966) added considerably to the hilarity of both.

FORD, RUTH (1915–2009). Born in Hazlehurst, Mississippi, to parents in the hotel business in Tennessee, Ford worked as a photographer's model, posing in *Harper's, Town and Country*, and *Mademoiselle* before her 1937 stage debut at the Ivorytown Playhouse in Connecticut, after which she joined **Orson Welles's Mercury Theatre**, where she appeared in *The Shoemaker's Holiday* (1938) and *Danton's Death* (1938), after which she debuted in films with roles in *Murder in the Big House* (1942), *The Devil's Trail* (1942), *The Keys to the Kingdom* (1944), *Circumstantial Evidence* (1945), and *Act One* (1964). On **Broadway**, Ford appeared in such diverse productions as the MUSICAL *Swingin' the Dream* (1939) and Jean-Paul Sartre's existential one-act *No Exit* (1946). Ford's other Broadway appearances include *This Time Tomorrow* (1947), *Clutterbuck* (1949), *The House of Bernarda Alba* (1951), *Island of Goats* (1955), *The Stronger* (1956), *Requiem for a Nun* (1959), revivals of *The Milk Train Doesn't Stop Here Anymore* in 1964 and *Dinner at Eight* in 1966, *The Ninety Day Mistress* (1967), *The Grass Harp* (1967), *Poor Murderer* (1976), and *Harold and Maude* (1980). She also appeared **Off-Broadway**, in STOCK, and **regional theatre**, playing Claire Zachanassian in *The Visit* at Houston's **Alley Theatre** in 1982. Ford's second husband was the actor Zachary Scott.

FOREIGNER, THE. Actor-playwright **Larry Shue**'s farce premiered at the **Milwaukee Repertory Theatre** prior to an **Off-Broadway** production at the Astor Place Theatre where it opened on 1 November 1984 for 686 performances. Under the direction of **Jerry Zaks**, the play received an **Outer Critics Circle Award**, and Zaks and star Anthony Heald won **Obie Awards**. Set in a faded fishing lodge in rural Georgia, the play centers on Charlie Baker and his friend, Englishman Froggy LeSueur. Charlie is so painfully shy that he is unable to speak in front of strangers, so Froggy concocts the idea of telling others that Charlie is from an unnamed exotic country and does not speak English. Unexpectedly, this revelation permits other characters to speak freely in Charlie's presence and he is eventually able to reveal and foil a plot by a local Ku Klux Klansman to oust the owner of the lodge. **Matthew Broderick** and **Frances Sternhagen** appeared in a 2004 **Roundabout Theatre** revival and *The Foreigner* has been widely produced by **regional**, STOCK, and university theatres.

FOREMAN, RICHARD (1937–). New York-born playwright educated at Brown University and the Yale School of Drama, Foreman founded the Ontological-Hysteric Theatre Company in 1968 where most of his plays have been produced, although other companies, most notably the **New York Shakespeare Festival (NYSF)**, the Music Theatre Group, and the **Wooster**

Group have coproduced several. Foreman's avant-garde works have brought him five Best Play **Obie Awards** and five Obies for directing and sustained achievement. He had also received MacArthur, Guggenheim, Rockefeller, **National Endowment of the Arts (NEA)**, and Ford fellowships or grants, a 1990 NEA Distinguished Artist Fellowship for Lifetime Achievement, a 2001 PEN/Laura Pels Master American Playwright Award, and an Officer of the Order of Arts and Letters from France in 2004.

Foreman's plays eschew Aristotelian concepts and instead are driven by disorientation and misunderstanding. Over time, Foreman has moved toward multimedia techniques. His plays include *Total Recall* (1970), *Pandering to the Masses* (1975), *Le Livre de splendeurs* (1976), *Penguin Touquet* (1981), *Egyptology* (1983), *Film Is Evil: Radio Is Good* (1987), *Love and Science* (1990), *Eddie Goes to Poetry City* (1991), *Samuel's Major Problems* (1993), *I've Got the Shakes* (1995), *The Universe, I.E.: How It Works* (1996), *Pearls for Pigs* (1997), *Benita Canova* (1998), *Badboy Nietzsche!* (2000), *King Cowboy Rufus Rules the Universe* (2004), *The Gods Are Pounding My Head!* (2005), *Zomboid!* (2006), *Wake Up Mr. Sleepy! Your Unconscious Mind Is Dead!* (2007), *Deep Trance Behavior in Potatoland* (2008), and *Idiot Savant* (2009).

In 2009, Foreman directed John Zorn's opera *Astronome: A Night at the Opera*. Foreman received a 1976 **Drama Desk Award** nomination for his direction of a revival of *Threepenny Opera* on **Broadway** for the NYSF. His only other Broadway entry, *Stages* (1978), closed after a single performance. Foreman has published a novel, collections of his plays, and essays, including *Unbalancing Acts: Foundations for a Theatre* (1992). In 2009, Foreman publicly announced that his Public Theatre production of *Idiot Savant*, which he wrote and directed, and which *New Yorker* critic Hilton Als described as "elegiac and beautiful," would be his last theatre piece and that in the future he would work in film.

FORNÉS, MARIA IRENE (1930–   ). Born in Havana, Cuba, Fornés moved to the United States and became a naturalized citizen in 1951 and by the 1960s was a fixture of **Off-Broadway** theatre emphasizing Hispanic American themes, gender issues, and others social concerns of that era. Her first produced work was *Tango Palace* (1963) and her numerous plays and MUSICALS have brought her an impressive nine **Obie Awards**, including a 1982 "sustained achievement" award. Fornés's best-known works, *Fefu and Her Friends* (1977) and *Sarita* (1984), emphasize the varied dilemmas of contemporary **women** reaching for self-actualization despite societal oppressions and **sexual** tensions. She has adapted plays by a varied array of writers, including Federico García Lorca, Calderón, and **Anton Chekhov**, and collaborated with various composers. Her most characteristic works make use of cinematic techniques, fantasy, music, and humor with a strong **feminist** perspective. Among her other works are *Promenade* (1965), *The Successful Life of Three* (1965), *Dr. Kheal* (1968), *Lolita in the Garden* (1977), *Mud* (1983), *The Danube* (1984), *The Conduct of Life* (1985), *A Matter of Faith* (1986), *Lovers and Keepers* (1986), *Abingdon Square* (1987), *Hunger* (1988), *And What of the Night?* (1989), *Oscar and Bertha* (1992), *Enter the Night* (1993), *Terra Incognita* (1992), *Summer in Gossensass* (1995), *Manual for a Desperate Crossing* (1996), and *Letters from Cuba* (2000). Fornés's *The Office* (1966), under the direction of Jerome Robbins, closed in previews before an intended **Broadway** production. Fornés had a longtime relationship with Susan Sontag and, as a teacher she championed the work of **Nilo Cruz**. In 2010, **International Arts Relations, Inc. (INTAR)** and New York University staged the New York Fornés Festival to celebrate her 80th birthday. *See also* CHICANO THEATRE; GAY AND LESBIAN THEATRE.

FORSYTHE, HENDERSON (1917–2006). Born in Macon, Missouri, Forsythe worked in his family's gas station and transferred from Culver-Stockton College to the University of Iowa, where he was a classmate of **Tennessee Williams**. Following service in World WAR II, Forsythe acted for several years with Pennsylvania's Erie Playhouse. He had a long career onstage, winning a **Tony Award** for *The Best Little Whorehouse in Texas* (1979), film, with roles in *Silkwood* (1983) and *Chances Are* (1989), and television, where he appeared for 32 years on the soap opera *As the World Turns*, earning a Daytime Emmy Award nomination in 1981. He made his first **Broadway** appearance in the short-lived *The Cellar and the Well* (1950), which he also directed, and *Miss Lonelyhearts* (1957). He replaced **Arthur Hill** as George in *Who's Afraid of Virginia Woolf?* (1962) and his roles improved as he moved into middle age in *The Right Honourable Gentleman* (1965), *Malcolm* (1966), the PULITZER PRIZE-winning *A Delicate Balance* (1966), *The Birthday Party* (1967), a revival of *Harvey* in 1970 playing opposite James Stewart and HELEN HAYES, *The Engagement Baby* (1970), *The Freedom of the City* (1974), *A Texas Trilogy* (1976), and *Some Americans Abroad* (1990). Forsythe also appeared in numerous television dramas and films.

FOSTER, FRANCES (1924–1997). Yonkers, New York-born Frances Helen Brown studied with the **American Theatre Wing** and took the stage name Foster. She was a cofounded of the **Negro Ensemble Company**, acting in more than 25 of their productions, including *The River Niger* (1973), *The First Breeze of Summer* (1975), and *Henrietta* (1985). Foster received a 1985 **Obie Award** for Sustained Excellence in Performance, and she was nominated for a **Drama Desk Award** for *Nevis Mountain Dew* (1979). On **Broadway**, she appeared in *The Wisteria Trees* (1955), understudied the roles of Beneatha and Ruth in *A Raisin in the Sun* (1959) and Miss Sadie Delaney in *Having Our Say* (1995), and was seen in a 1970 revival of **Bertolt Brecht**'s *The Good Woman of Setzuan*. Foster appeared in several films, including three directed by Spike Lee: *Malcolm X* (1992), *Crooklyn* (1994), and *Clockers* (1995), and on television she acted numerous roles from soap operas to *Law & Order*. *See also* AFRICAN AMERICAN THEATRE.

FOSTER, GLORIA (1933–2001). Born in Chicago, Illinois, Foster studied at the University of Illinois and the **Goodman Theatre School** prior to beginning her acting career at the University of Chicago's Court Theatre. **Off-Broadway**, Foster won a **Drama Desk Award** for her debut performance in the documentary theatre production of *In White America* (1964), a **Theatre World Award** in the title role of **Robinson Jeffers**'s adaptation of *Medea* in 1966, and was Drama Desk-nominated for The *Forbidden City* (1989). She appeared in several productions for the **New York Shakespeare Festival/ Public Theatre**, including revivals of *Coriolanus* in 1979, *Mother Courage and Her Children* in 1980, and *Blood Wedding* in 1992. On **Broadway**, Foster began by understudying roles in *Purlie Victorious* (1961) and appeared in *A Hand Is on the Gate* (1966), *Yerma* (1966), and *Having Our Say* (1995). In occasional films, she appeared in *The Cool World* (1964), *The Comedians* (1967), and *The Matrix* (1999), and on television she appeared in several television films, including *The Atlanta Child Murders* (1985) and *Separate but Equal* (1991), and guested on such varied programs as *The Cosby Show* in 1987 and *Law & Order* in 1992 and 1997. *See also* AFRICAN AMERICAN THEATRE.

FOURPOSTER, THE. Jan de Hartog's two-character **Tony Award**-winning play opened on 24 October 1951 at the Ethel Barrymore Theatre for 632 performances under the Tony-winning direction of **José Ferrer** and starring **Hume Cronyn** and **Jessica Tandy**. Cronyn and Tandy played Michael and Agnes, a married couple, and the comedy-drama traced their ups and downs for 35 years, from their wedding night in 1890 to their last in the bedroom that is the play's sole setting. Cronyn and Tandy repeated their performances in a 1955 television production, but a 1952 film version starred **Rex Harrison** and Lili Palmer. In 1966, *The Fourposter* was adapted as the MUSICAL *I Do! I Do!* starring **Robert Preston** and **Mary Martin**.

FOX, FREDERICK (1910–1991). New York-born scene (and sometimes lighting and costume) designer Fox was educated at Yale University and the National Academy of Design and worked at Connecticut's Ivoryton Playhouse before his first **Broadway** design for *Farewell Summer* (1937), amassing an extraordinary 200 designs during a 30-year career, including productions of *Johnny Belinda* (1940), *Junior Miss* (1941), *The Doughgirls* (1942), *Those Endearing Young Charms (1943), The Two Mrs. Carrolls* (1944), *Anna Lucasta* (1944), *The Man Who Had All the Luck* (1944), *Dear Ruth* (1944), *Kiss Them for Me* (1945), *John Loves Mary* (1947), *Light Up the Sky* (1948), *Darkness at Noon* (1951), *The Seven Year Itch* (1952), *King of Hearts* (1954), *Anniversary Waltz* (1954), *The Warm Peninsula* (1959), *The Hostage* (1960), *Send Me No Flowers* (1960), and *From the Second City* (1961), among many others. In the earliest days of television in the 1940s, Fox was one of the first major designers to work in the new medium.

FRANCIS, ARLENE (1907–2001). Born Arline Francis Kazanjian in Boston, Massachusetts, to an Armenian father and American mother, she attended Finch College before beginning a long career on stage, screen, and television. She made her **Broadway** debut in the short-lived *La Gringa* (1928), working steadily through the 1930s in mostly innocuous plays, although she was in the original cast of *The Women* (1936) and by the 1940s, the size and range of her roles improved with *The Doughgirls* (1942), *The Overtons* (1945), *Metropole* (1949), *The Little Blue Light* (1951), and *Late Love* (1953). Francis had a particular success in the comedy *Once More with Feeling* (1958), playing opposite **Joseph Cotten**, and also appeared in *Beekman Place* (1964), *Mrs. Dally* (1965), a revival of *Dinner at Eight* in 1966, and *Don't Call Back* (1975), and she stepped into roles in *Tchin-Tchin* in 1963 and *Gigi* in 1973. Francis appeared in occasional films, including *All My Sons* (1948) and *One, Two, Three* (1961), opposite James Cagney and directed by Billy Wilder. Beginning in the early days of television, she became a popular personality, garnering an Emmy Award nomination for the *Home* series in 1956, and on game shows and talk shows, including a long stint as a panelist on *What's My Line?* from 1950 to 1967. Francis was married twice, the second time to actor/producer **Martin Gabel**.

FRANKEL, GENE (1920–2005). New York-born Eugene Frankel served in the United States Army during World WAR II, after which he was one of the first members of the Actors Studio, but made his mark as a director. Frankel's **Broadway** productions include *Once There Was a Russian* (1961), *A Cry of Players* (1968), *Indians* (1969), *The Engagement Baby* (1970), a revival of *Lost in the Stars* in 1972), *The Lincoln Mask* (1972), and *The Night That Made America Famous* (1975), but it was for his **Off-Broadway** work that he most known. Frankel's directing of revivals of *Volpone* in 1957 and

Machinal* in 1960 won **Obie Awards**, and among his most noted Off-Broadway productions were a revival of JOHN WEXLEY's *They Shall Not Die* (1949), *Nat Turner* (1950), *The Enemy of the People* (1959), *The Blacks: A Clown Show* (1961), which racked up a remarkable 1,400 performance at St. Mark's Playhouse, *Brecht on Brecht* (1962), *The Firebugs* (1963), and *To Be Young, Gifted, and Black* (1969). He also staged the premiere of *Pueblo* (1971) at the **Arena Stage** and worked in other regional and international theatres. Frankel founded the **Berkshire Theatre** and was artistic director of the Gene Frankel Theatre Workshop.

FRANKEN, ROSE (1895–1988). Born Rose Lewin in Fort Worth, Texas, as the daughter of divorced parents, Franken grew up to work out her insecurities in stories and plays about a young and appealingly naïve wife, Claudia. She abandoned her studies at Barnard College to marry Dr. Sigmund Franken, who encouraged her writing. Her first play, *Another Language* (1932), was successfully produced on **Broadway** and in London. Franken remains best known for her Claudia stories, which became the basis for her 1941 play *Claudia*, two motion pictures, and a popular radio series. She wrote nine plays, including *Outrageous Fortune* (1943), *Doctors Disease* (1943), *Soldier's Wife* (1944), and *The Hallams* (1948), and directed most of them on Broadway.

FRANKIE AND JOHNNY IN THE CLAIRE DE LUNE. Terrence McNally's two-character play opened at Stage II of the **Manhattan Theatre Club** **(MTC)** on 2 June 1987 under the direction of Paul Benedict and featuring **Kathy Bates** as Frankie and **F. Murray Abraham** as Johnny. When the play moved to Stage I at MTC in the following October, Kenneth Walsh took over as Johnny. In the play, Frankie, a wisecracking waitress whose tough manner is a cover for a gentler side, and Johnny, a cook and recovering alcoholic, work in a diner where despite being middle-aged and their past heartbreaks they tentatively move toward a relationship. A 1991 film, with the title shortened to *Frankie and Johnny*, starred **Al Pacino** and Michelle Pfeiffer, and a 2002 Broadway production featured Edie Falco and Stanley Tucci (in a **Tony Award**-nominated performance) under **Joe Mantello**'s direction for 243 performances. Joe Pantoliano and Rosie Perez, in her **Broadway** debut, replaced Falco and Tucci during the run.

FRANZ, ELIZABETH (1941–). Born Betty Jean Frankovitch in Akron, Ohio, Franz worked as a secretary after completing high school, saving up enough for tuition to the AMERICAN ACADEMY OF DRAMATIC ART. She made her **Broadway** debut in *Rosencrantz and Guildenstern Are Dead* (1967) and worked intermittently in regional theatre and New York. On Broadway, she received a **Tony Award** nomination for *Brighton Beach Memoirs* (1983) and won a Tony as Linda Loman in a 1999 revival of **Arthur Miller**'s *Death of a Salesman*. She was nominated for a Tony again in 2002 for a revival of **Paul Osborn**'s *Morning's at Seven*. Her other Broadway appearances include a 1977 revival of *The Cherry Orchard*, *The Octette Bridge Club* (1985), *The Cemetery Club* (1990), and revivals of *Getting Married* in 1991 and *Uncle Vanya* in 1995. She also replaced **Linda Lavin** in *Broadway Bound* in 1987. **Off-Broadway** Franz won an **Obie Award** as the title character of **Christopher Durang**'s controversial *Sister Mary Ignatius Explains It All for You* (1979) and appeared to critical plaudits in Julia Cho's *The Piano Teacher* (2007). In London, Franz appeared in **Sam Shepard**'s *Buried Child* at the Royal National Theatre in 2004. Franz has also been a reliable character actress in films and television, appearing on the big screen in *Jacknife* (1989), *School Ties* (1992), *Sabrina* (1995), and *The Substance of Fire* (1996), and on TV in soap operas, made-for-TV films, a recurring role on the *Roseanne* series, and she was nominated for an Emmy Award for reprising her Broadway role in *Death of a Salesman* in 2000 and garnered a Daytime Emmy nomination in 1990 for an *ABC Afterschool Special*.

FREE SOUTHERN THEATRE. A response to the civil rights movement, this New Orleans, Louisiana-based company was founded by John O'Neal, **Gilbert Moses**, and Doris Derby in 1963, with guidance from **Richard Schechner**. The founders articulated a mission of nurturing a theatre as responsive to the black experience as blues or jazz music. The company also devoted itself to bringing theatre to rural and poor audiences, giving free performances, and offering workshops in the black community. The company disbanded in 1980. *See also* AFRICAN AMERICAN THEATRE.

FREEDLEY, GEORGE (1904–1967). Born in Richmond, Virginia, George Reynolds Freedley graduated from the University of Richmond in 1925, after which he studied with George Pierce Baker* at Yale University until 1928, when he worked for THE THEATRE GUILD, including serving as an assistant stage manager for EUGENE O'NEILL's *Dynamo** (1929). As an actor, he appeared in *The Grey Fox* (1928), *The Camel through the Needle's Eye* (2929), and *Everything's Jake* (1930), but in 1931 began to work at the New York Public Library, where in 1938 he took over curatorship of the theatre collection. During his tenure at the library, he established the **Theatre Library Association**, serving as its president from 1937 to 1963. Freedley also served on the Board of the **American National Theatre and Academy (ANTA)** and produced the **Broadway** flop *The Cellar and the Well* (1950). In 1956, the Theatre Collection of the New York Public Library was presented with a special **Tony Award**. Freedley wrote several books, was a columnist for *Playbill*, and a sometime drama CRITIC.

FREEDMAN, GERALD (1927–). This noted director and educator was born in Lorain, Ohio, and educated at Northwestern University, after which he worked as assistant director on **Broadway**, including for several classic MU-SICALS, *Bells Are Ringing* (1956), *West Side Story* (1957), and *Gypsy* (1959). As a director, he staged *The Gay Life* (1961), *Man in the Moon* (1964), revivals of *West Side Story* in 1964 and 1980, a revival of *King Lear* in 1968, *Soon* (1971), *The Incomparable Max* (1971), *The Creation of the World and Other Business* (1972), *The Au Pair Man* (1973), *An American Millionaire* (1974), the 1975 and 1976 productions of *The Robber Bridegroom*, both of which brought him **Drama Desk Award** nominations, a revival of *Mrs. Warren's Profession* in 1976, *The Grand Tour* (1979), and revivals of *Broadway** in 1987 and *The School for Scandal* in 1995. Freedman also directed, and wrote book and lyrics, for *A Time for Singing* (1966) and directed the **New York Shakespeare Festival/Public Theatre** production of *Hair* (1968). He served as artistic director of the Great Lakes Theatre Festival and as Dean of Drama at the University of North Carolina School of the Arts.

FREEMAN, MORGAN (1937–). Born Morgan Porterfield Freeman, Jr. in Memphis, Tennessee, he began acting in school plays in childhood and worked as a mechanic for the United States Air Force. In the mid-1960s, he toured in a production of *The Royal Hunt of the Sun* and debuted **Off-Broadway** in *The Nigger Lovers* (1967) and on **Broadway** in the all-black version of the MUSICAL *Hello, Dolly!* in 1968. He received a **Drama Desk Award** Off-Broadway as Zeke in *The Mighty Gents* (1978) and won **Obie Awards** in revivals of *Coriolanus* in 1979 and *Mother Courage and Her Children* in 1980, *The Gospel at Colonus* (1984), and *Driving Miss Daisy* (1987), a role he repeated in the 1989 film version, garnering an Academy Award nomination and a Golden Globe Award.

Freeman appeared with Tracey Ullman in a Wild West version of *The Taming of the Shrew* for the **New York Shakespeare Festival** in 1990. In 2008, Freeman returned to Broadway in a revival of *The Country Girl* playing opposite Frances McDormand and **Peter Gallagher**. On screen, Freeman won an Academy Award (and Golden Globe and Screen Actors Guild Awards) for his performance in *Million Dollar Baby* (2005), with prior nominations for *Street Smart* (1987), *Driving Miss Daisy*, and *The Shawshank Redemption* (1994). Freeman's other films include *Glory* (1989), *Unforgiven* (1992), *Amistad* (1997), *Deep Impact* (1998), *Batman Begins* (2005), and played

Nelson Mandela in *Invictus* (2009). On television, he had gained his first recognition as the Easy Reader on PBS-TV's *Electric Company*, appearing from
1971 to 1976. In 2008, he was selected for the **Kennedy Center** Honors. *See
also* AFRICAN AMERICAN THEATRE.

FRENCH, ARTHUR (1942–). Born in New York as Arthur Wellesley
French, Jr., he was educated at Brooklyn College and debuted **Off-Broadway**
in 1962 and made an early appearance in *Day of Absence* (1965). He was
involved with the **Negro Ensemble Company** and worked as a versatile
character actor, appearing on **Broadway** in *Ain't Supposed to Die a Natural
Death* (1971), ***The River Niger*** (1973), revivals of ***The Iceman Cometh*** in
1973, *All God's Chillun Got Wings** in 1975, and ***Death of a Salesman*** in
1975, ***The Poison Tree*** (1976), revivals of ***You Can't Take It with You*** in
1983 and *Design for Living* in 1984, ***Ma Rainey's Black Bottom*** (1984),
Death and the King's Horseman (1987), *Mule Bone* (1991), and *Dividing the
Estate* (2008). Off-Broadway, French acted in productions including *A Soldier's Play* (1982), ***Joe Turner's Come and Gone*** (1996), and productions
of *Medea* and *King Lear* in 2002. He has also appeared in supporting roles in
film and television. *See also* AFRICAN AMERICAN THEATRE.

FRIEDMAN, BRUCE JAY (1930–). A native New Yorker born in the
Bronx, Friedman was educated at the University of Missouri in journalism,
after which he served in the United States Air Force from 1951 to 1953. He
wrote for many magazines, several novels, including *A Change of Plan* which,
on screen, became *The Heartbreak Kid* (1972, remade in 2007), screenplays,
and a few whimsically satiric plays, including *Scuba Duba* (1967), sketches
for *Oh! Calcutta!* (1969), *Steambath* (1970), and *Have You Spoken to Any
Jews Lately?* (1995). Friedman's screenplays include *The Lonely Guy* (1984),
adapted from one of his novels, and *Splash* (1984), for which he was nominated for an Academy Award. A television production of his play *Steambath*
in 1973 brought him an Emmy Award nomination. *See also* SEXUALITY.

FROM THE MISSISSIPPI DELTA. Endesha Ida Mae Holland's autobiographical drama in which three actresses play numerous roles, recounts the
journey of Holland's life in Greenwood, Mississippi, from a rape in her tragic
youth, to life as a prostitute, and a rebirth through the civil rights movement
and education when she received a Ph.D. from the University of Minnesota.
The play also focuses on the life of Holland's mother, known as Aint Baby,
who rented rooms to prostitutes. Holland began writing the play in 1981, and
it was first produced at the New Federal Theatre in New York in September
1987, as well as in several **regional theatres (Goodman Theatre, Arena**

Stage, **Hartford Stage**), prior to a production at the **Circle in the Square**, where it opened on 11 November 1991. *See also* AFRICAN AMERICAN THEATRE.

FRYER, ROBERT (1920–2000). A prolific **Broadway** producer, Fryer was born in Washington, D.C., and attended Western Reserve University. His second production, *Wonderful Town* (1953), won a **Tony Award** and his productions would reap numerous Tony and **Drama Desk Award** nominations and wins. Among the wide range of plays and MUSICALS Fryer and his partners in Fryer, Carr & Harris, Inc. produced are *The Desk Set* (1955), *Auntie Mame* (1956), *Redhead* (1959), *Advise & Consent* (1960), *Sweet Charity* (1966), *Mame* (1966), *Abelard and Heloise* (1971), a revival of *A Funny Thing Happened on the Way to the Forum* in 1972, *Chicago* (1975), *The Norman Conquests* (1975), *California Suite* (1976), *Chapter Two* (1977), *On the Twentieth Century* (1978), *They're Playing Our Song* (1979), *Sweeney Todd* (1979), *The West Side Waltz* (1981), *A Little Family Business* (1982), *Brighton Beach Memoirs* (1983), *Noises Off* (1983), *Biloxi Blues* (1985), *Benefactors* (1985), and *Wild Honey* (1986). Fryer also produced several films, including *The Boston Strangler* (1968), *The Prime of Miss Jean Brodie* (1969), *Myra Breckinridge* (1970), *Travels with My Aunt* (1972), *Mame* (1974), *The Boys from Brazil* (1978), and *The Shining* (1980).

FUGARD, ATHOL (1932–). A dramatist, actor, novelist, and director born in Middelburg, Eastern Cape, South Africa, as Harold Athol Lanigan Fugard, his plays, many of which deal with racial strife and related issues in South Africa, have often been produced in the United States, initially in collaboration with **Lloyd Richards** at the **Yale Repertory Theatre**, where his *A Lesson from Aloes* was produced in 1980 before moving to **Broadway**. Yale Rep also produced three other Fugard world premieres, including *"Master Harold". . .and the Boys* (1982), which won a **New York Drama Critics Circle Award** and a **Drama Desk Award** when it transferred to Broadway, *The Road to Mecca* (1984), and *A Place with the Pigs* (1987). Yale also revived other Fugard works, including *The Blood Knot* (1961), *Hell and Goodbye* (1965), and *Boesman and Lena* (1969), during the 1980s.

FULLER, CHARLES (1939–). Philadelphia, Pennsylvania, native Charles H. Fuller, Jr., attended Villanova University, after which he joined the United States Army in 1959. When he left the service in 1962, he continued his education at La Salle University and cofounded the Afro-American Arts Theatre in Philadelphia in 1967. His early plays include *The Village: A Party* (1969), *The Brownsville Raid* (1975), and he won an **Obie Award** for *Zooman and* *the Sign* (1980), all of which deal with **race** tensions. His most noted work, *A Soldier's Play* (1982), won a PULITZER PRIZE and his screenplay, retitled *A Soldier's Story*, was nominated for an Academy Award, a Golden Globe Award, and a Writer's Guild of America Award. Most of Fuller's subsequent writing has been for the screen because, as he explains, "I always wanted to reach the most people with my work. Not enough people go to the theatre." *See also* AFRICAN AMERICAN THEATRE.

FUNICELLO, RALPH (1947–). He studied at New York University prior to working as a scene designer on the West Coast, including as director of design for the **American Conservatory Theatre** from 1988–1990. On **Broadway**, he was assistant scene designer for *Jesus Christ Superstar* (1971) and designed *Division Street* (1980), QED (2001), *Henry IV* in 2003, which brought him **Tony Award** and **Drama Desk Award** nominations, *King Lear* in 2004, *Brooklyn Boy* (2005), and *Julius Caesar* in 2005. His work has been seen in numerous **regional** theatres in the United States, including the **Milwaukee Repertory Theatre**, the **Berkeley Repertory Theatre**, the **Denver Theatre Center**, the **Williamstown Theatre Festival**, and others. Funicello is Powell Chair in Set Design at San Diego State University.

FUNNYHOUSE OF A NEGRO. **Adrienne Kennedy**'s **Obie Award**-winning one-act drama was written in 1960 and first produced **Off-Broadway** at the East End Theatre in 1962. The surreal, semi-autobiographical work is expressed from the nightmarish imaginative world of Sarah, a troubled young black woman. Focused on issues of black identity in America, gender, and history, Kennedy makes use of poetic imagery in her language and attempt to portray the state of mind of her central character. Billie Allen, who played Sarah in the original production, directed a 2006 revival of this much-produced play at the Harlem School of the Arts Theatre. *See also* AFRICAN AMERICAN THEATRE.

FUSCO, COCO (1960–). Born in New York of Cuban American heritage, Fusco was educated at Brown University and Stanford University prior to developing a career as a **performance artist** stressing interdisciplinary concepts and techniques in creating pieces on women's lives, WAR, and race. With **Guillermo Gómez-Peña**, her best-known work is *The Couple in the Cage* (1993), which dealt with Amerindian issues, and she has collaborated with other on *Stuff* (1996), *Dolores from 10 to 10* (2001), and *The Incredible Disappearing Woman* (2003). Her other performances include *Rights of Passage* (1997), *The Last Wish* (1997), and *A Room of One's Own: Women and Power in the New America* (2006). After a stint (1995–2001) at Temple

University, Fusco teaches at Columbia University. *See also* ALTERNATIVE THEATRE; CHICANO THEATRE; FEMINIST THEATRE; NATIVE AMERICANS ON STAGE.

FUTZ. **Rochelle Owens**'s comedy of **sexual** satire was first produced by the **Guthrie Theatre** in Minneapolis, Minnesota, in 1965, prior to a run at **La Mama Experimental Theatre Club** in June 1968. The play, which generated some controversy, centers on a farm boy, Cyrus Futz (John Bakos), who is in love with a pig named Amanda. A parable of non-conformist attitudes and sexual liberation, the play met with mixed reviews, although even naysayers felt it was, as the *Saturday Review* critic wrote, "one of the most original and uninhibited pieces of dramatic poetry ever written." **Tom O'Horgan**'s direction won praise, and he subsequently directed a 1969 film version, adding an exclamation mark to the title.

G

GABEL, MARTIN (1912–1986). Born in Philadelphia, Pennsylvania, Gabel had a varied career as an actor, film director, producer, and television personality. On **Broadway**, Gabel appeared in a range of plays, including *Dead End* (1935) and several plays for **Orson Welles**'s **Mercury Theatre**, including revivals of *Julius Caesar* in 1937 and *Danton's Death* in 1938. He also appeared on **Broadway** in a revival of *King Lear* in 1950, *The Little Blue Light* (1951), *Reclining Figure* (1954), *Will Success Spoil Rock Hunter?* (1955), *The Rivalry* (1959), *Children from Their Games* (1963), *Baker Street* (1965), *Sheep on the Runway* (1970), and *In Praise of Love* (1974), and won a **Tony Award** as Best Featured Actor for *Big Fish, Little Fish* (1961). As a director, Gabel staged *The Cream in the Well* (1941), *The Survivors* (1948), and *Men of Distinction* (1953), and he produced *Café Crown* (1942), *The Hidden River* (1957), *Once More with Feeling* (1958), and *Mrs. Dally* (1965). Gabel occasionally appeared in movie character roles, including *Marnie* (1964), *Divorce American Style* (1967), *Lady in Cement* (1968), *There Was a Crooked Man* (1970), the 1974 remake of *The Front Page,** and *The First Deadly Sin* (1980). He was married to actress/television personality **Arlene Francis**.

GABRIEL, GILBERT W. (1890–1952). Born Gilbert Wolf Gabriel in Brooklyn, New York, he attended Williams College prior to beginning a long career as a CRITIC in 1912 with the *New York Evening Sun*, where he reviewed music. Gabriel switched to reviewing drama in 1924 when he joined the staff of the *New York Telegram-Mail* for a year prior to returning to the *Evening Sun* as theatre critic until 1929. That year, he moved to the *New York American* until 1937, writing for a mainstream audience on theatre and the New York cultural scene. Gabriel also wrote fiction, including novels such as *The Seven-Branched Candlestick* (1917) and stories published in *Munsey's Magazine* and others. Gabriel later served as drama critic for *THEATRE ARTS MONTHLY* and *Cue Magazine*, continuing to his death.

GAHAGAN, HELEN (1900–1980). A native of Boonton, New Jersey, and brought up in a strict Catholic family, Gahagan attended Barnard College prior to appearing in numerous **Broadway** plays during the 1920s, including *Manhattan* (1922), *Fashions for Men* (1922), *Chains* (1923), a revival of *Leah Kleschna** in 1924, *The Enchanted April* (1925), *Young Woodley* (1925), a revival of *Trelawny of the "Wells"* in 1927, *Diplomacy* (1928), *Tonight or Never* (1930), and *Moor Born* (1934), among others. She married **Melvyn Douglas** and continued her career in the 1930s, appearing in one film, *She* (1935). Active in politics from 1940 as Helen Gahagan Douglas, she was a Democratic National Committeewoman from 1940–1944 and elected as a liberal Democratic Congresswoman from California in 1944. In 1950, she ran for the Senate against Richard M. Nixon, who smeared her as a Communist, stating that she was "pink right down to her underwear." Douglas responded by calling him "Tricky Dick," but the damage was done and she lost the election. She and Douglas remained married until her death, although it was rumored that she had long affair with Lyndon B. Johnson beginning during her time in Congress. Douglas returned to Broadway once, in 1952, in a revival of *First Lady*.

GAINES, BOYD (1953–). A versatile actor easily able to move from MUSICALS to dramas, Gaines was born Boyd Payne Gaines in Atlanta, Georgia, and was trained at the Juilliard School. He won a **Theatre World Award** for a 1980 revival of *A Month in the Country* at the **Brooklyn Academy of Music** and **Tony Awards** for *The Heidi Chronicles* (1989), a 1994 revival of *She Loves Me*, *Contact* (2000), and a 2008 revival of *Gypsy*. He also won **Drama Desk Awards** for *She Loves Me, Gypsy*, and a 2007 revival of *Journey's End*. Gaines has appeared in film and television, but found the most success onstage, appearing in numerous regional theatres and **Off-Broadway**, where he won critical approval in *Bach at Leipzig* (2005) at the **New York Theatre Workshop**. His other Broadway appearances include revivals of *The Show Off** in 1992, *Company* in 1995, *12 Angry Men* in 2004, *Pygmalion* in 2007, *The Grand Manner* (2010), playing GUTHRIE MCCLINTIC, and in 1999 he took over the role of Cliff in a revival of *Cabaret*.

GALATI, FRANK (1943–). Born in Highland Park, Illinois, he trained and later taught at Northwestern University and began his career as a devotee of Robert Breen's theories on chamber theatre. Galati joined **Steppenwolf Theatre** in 1986 and was associate director of the **Goodman Theatre** beginning in 1987. Although he occasionally acted, mostly with the **Wisdom Bridge Theatre**, Galati increasingly focused on directing and adapting texts, including his most noted production, *The Grapes of Wrath* in 1990, adapted from John Steinbeck's novel and first produced at the Steppenwolf prior to transferring to **Broadway**, where it won **Tony**

Awards for Best Play and a Best Direction for Galati. His other adapted productions include *She Always Said, Pablo* (1987) from GERTRUDE STEIN, *As I Lay Dying* (1995) from William Faulkner, *After the Quake* (2005) from Haruki Murakami. On **Broadway**, he directed a revival of *The Glass Menagerie* starring **Julie Harris** in 1994, *Ragtime* (1998), for which he received Tony Award and **Drama Desk Award** nominations, and *The Pirate Queen* (2007). He also directed **Tony Kushner**'s *Homebody/Kabul* (2003) at Steppenwolf, was nominated for an Academy Award for his screenplay of *The Accidental Tourist* (1988), and staged the world premiere of the operatic adaptation of **Arthur Miller**'s *A View From the Bridge* at the Chicago Lyric Opera in 1999.

GALLAGHER, HELEN (1926–). This Brooklyn, New York-born actress studied dance at the American Ballet School and began as a dancer on **Broadway** in her late teens, where she labored in such MUSICALS as *Seven Lively Arts* (1944) and *High Button Shoes* (1947). Graduating to supporting roles, she won a **Tony Award** for the 1952 revival of *Pal Joey*. Another revival, *No, No, Nanette*, in 1971, brought Gallagher a Tony as Best Actress, and she also appeared in the musicals *Make a Wish* (1951), *Hazel Flagg* (1953), *Sweet Charity* (1966), for which she received a Tony nomination, and *Cry for Us All* (1970), among others. **Off-Broadway**, Gallagher moved away from musicals in *Hothouse* (1974), *Tickles by Tucholsky* (1976), a revival of **Neil Simon**'s *The Gingerbread Lady* in 1977, *Money Talks* (1980), and *Tallulah* (1983), playing stage legend TALLULAH BANKHEAD. She also won three Emmy Awards for her performance on the soap opera *Ryan's Hope*.

GALLAGHER, PETER (1956–). Born Peter Killian Gallagher in New York, Gallagher attended Tufts University and developed a career encompassing stage, film, and television. On **Broadway**, he began as a replacement in the original production of *Grease* (1972) and won a **Theatre World Award** in the short-lived MUSICAL *A Doll's Life* (1982). He moved comfortably between dramatic and musical roles, reaping a **Tony Award** nomination playing Edmund for the 1986 revival of *Long Day's Journey into Night* opposite **Jack Lemmon** and **Kevin Spacey**, and a **Drama Desk Award** nomination as Sky Masterson in a 1992 revival of *Guys and Dolls*. He also appeared in revivals of *Noises Off* in 2001 and *The Country Girl* in 2008. On film, he shared in a Golden Globe Award with the ensemble of *Short Cuts* (1993), and his many movie appearances include *The Player* (1992), *While You Were Sleeping* (1995), *To Gillian on her 37th Birthday* (1996), *American Beauty* (1999), *Mr. Deeds* (2002), and among his many television roles, his recurring role as Sandy Cohen on *The O.C.* (2003–2007) won critical approval.

GALLO, DAVID (1966–). Born on a navy base in Delaware, Gallo was raised in Spain, Long Island, and New York City prior to attending the State University of New York at Purchase. A prolific scene designer, Gallo has done numerous New York productions, winning a **Tony Award** and a **Drama Desk Award** for his designs for the MUSICAL *The Drowsy Chaperone* (2006). He received a Tony nomination for *Gem of the Ocean* (2005) and Drama Desk nominations for *You're a Good Man, Charlie Brown* (1999), *King Hedley II* (2001), *Thoroughly Modern Millie* (2002), *Radio Golf* (2007), which also brought him a Tony nomination, and *A Catered Affair* (2008). Gallo's other **Broadway** credits include the **Al Pacino** revival of *Hughie* in 1996, *Titanic* (1997), *Jackie* (1997), revivals of *A View from the Bridge* in 1997, *Little Me* in 1998, and *The Lion in Winter* in 1999, *Epic Proportions* (1999), revivals of *Ma Rainey's Black Bottom* in 2003 and *Company* in 2006, *Reasons to Be Pretty* (2009), and *Memphis* (2009). **Off-Broadway**, Gallo won Drama Desk Awards for his designs of *Bunny Bunny* (1997) and *Jitney* (2000), and received Drama Desk nominations for a revival of *Machinal** in 1991, *The Wild Party* (2000), and *Wonder of the World* (2002). He also received an **Obie Award** for sustained excellence in 2000.

GALLO, PAUL (1953–). Bronx, New York-born Gallo graduated from Ithaca College and continued his studies at Yale University before becoming an accomplished lighting designer who has designed more than 200 productions in New York and in **regional theatre**s, beginning on **Broadway** with *Passione* (1980). Gallo has been nominated for **Tony Awards** for *The House of Blue Leaves* (1986), a revival of *Anything Goes* in 1988, *City of Angels* (1990), a revival of *Guys and Dolls* in 1992, *Crazy for You* (1992), revivals of *42nd Street* in 2001 and *The Crucible* in 2002, and *Three Days of Rain* (2006). On Broadway, Gallo won a **Drama Desk Award** for *Guys and Dolls*, and Drama Desk nominations for *The Mystery of Edwin Drood* (1986), *Anything Goes, Lend Me a Tenor* (1989), *City of Angels,* and *The Civil War* (1999). His Broadway credits include the Elizabeth Taylor revival of *The Little Foxes* in 1981, *Come Back to the 5 & Dime Jimmy Dean, Jimmy Dean* (1982), *Beyond Therapy* (1982), a revival of *The Front Page** in 1986, *Six Degrees of Separation* (1990), *I Hate Hamlet* (1991), revivals of *The Man Who Came to Dinner* in 2000 and *The Caine Mutiny Court-Martial* in 2006, *Losing Louie* (2006), *Mauritius* (2007), *A Bronx Tale* (2007), *November* (2008), and a revival of *Pal Joey* in 2008.

Off-Broadway, Gallo received Drama Desk nominations for *Wenceslas Square* (1988), *Miracolo D'Amore* (1989), *Blade to the Heart* (1995), and *Blackbird* (2007). Of his work, Gallo says, "Lighting is very primal. To all of us, it's the most natural thing, more than we realize. When we're born, the first thing we respond to is light. And when we get up and look outside and it's a sunny day, we don't feel the same as when it's a dark day."

GARBER, VICTOR (1949–). Born Victor Joseph Garber in London, Ontario, Canada, he took to acting as a child and worked at the University of Toronto's Hart House in his teens and was in a folk band. In the United States from the early 1970s, Garber appeared **Off-Broadway** in a 1973 revival of *Ghosts* at the **Roundabout Theatre**, which brought him a **Theatre World Award**, *Joe's Opera* (1975), *Cracks* (1976), *Wenceslas Square* (1988), and *Assassins* (1990). He has won consistent acclaim on **Broadway**, reaping **Tony Award** nominations for *Deathtrap* (1978), a revival of *Little Me* in 1982, *Lend Me a Tenor* (1989), and a revival of *Damn Yankees* in 1994. On Broadway, he also appeared in *The Shadow Box* (1977), a 1977 revival of *Tartuffe, Sweeney Todd* (1979), *Noises Off* (1983), revivals of *You Never Can Tell* in 1986 and *The Devil's Disciple* in 1988, *Two Shakespearean Actors* (1992), *Arcadia* (1995), *'Art'* (1998), and revivals of *A Little Night Music* in 2009 and *Present Laughter* in 2010. He has appeared in numerous films, including *Godspell* (1973), *Sleepless in Seattle* (1993), *The First Wives Club* (1996), *Titanic* (1997), *Legally Blonde* (2001), and *Milk* (2008), and has been nominated for six Emmy Awards for *Life with Judy Garland: Me and My Shadows* (2001), for the series *Alias* in 2002, 2003, and 2004, and guest spots on *Frasier* in 2001 and *Will & Grace* in 2005.

GARDENIA, VINCENT (1922–1992). This Italian American actor was born Vincent Scognamiglio in Naples, Italy, but left with his family for the United States when he was a baby. He began acting in 1935. On **Broadway**, this short, rotund actor debuted in *The Visit* (1958) with ALFRED LUNT and LYNN FONTANNE, after which he appeared in many productions, winning a **Tony Award** in 1972 for *The Prisoner of Second Avenue* and a nomination for Best Actor in a MUSICAL for *Ballroom* (1978). His other Broadway credits include *The Cold Wind and the Warm* (1958), *Rashomon* (1959), *Only in America* (1959), *The Wall* (1960), *Daughter of Silence* (1961), *Seidman and Son* (1962), *The Chinese and Dr. Fish* (1970), *God's Favorite* (1974), and he stepped in as a replacement in *California Suite* (1976), *Sly Fox* (1976), and *Glengarry Glen Ross* (1984). **Off-Broadway**, Gardenia won **Obie Awards** for a 1960 revival of *Machinal** and *Passing through Exotic Places* (1969), and he also appeared in *The Man with the Golden Arm* (1956). Gardenia acted in numerous films, receiving Academy Award nominations for his performance in *Bang the Drum Slowly* (1973) and *Moonstruck* (1987), and he also acted in *Little Murders* (1971), *Death Wish* (1974), and *Little Shop of Horrors* (1986). On television, he was a regular on *All in the Family* in 1973–74, won an Emmy Award for a TV movie *Age-Old Friends* (1989), and appeared in many other shows beginning in 1954.

GARDNER, HERB (1934–2003). Born Herbert George Gardner in Brooklyn, New York, he had a unique career as an artist, cartoonist, playwright, and screenwriter. He attended New York's High School for the Performing Arts and Antioch College. He created a popular 1950s' comic strip called *The Nebbishes* prior to scoring a **Broadway** success with his touching, whimsical play *A Thousand Clowns* (1962), in which **Jason Robards** played Murray Burns, an unemployed writer forced to choose between his nonconformist life and gaining custody of his young nephew. Gardner's screenplay for the 1965 film version was nominated for an Academy Award. His most successful play, *I'm Not Rappaport* (1985) won a **Tony Award** as Best Play and was also filmed in 1996 with Gardner directing. His other Broadway plays include *The Goodbye People* (1968), which Gardner directed on film in 1984, *Thieves* (1974), the failed MUSICAL *One Night Stand* (1980), and *Conversations with My Father* (1992). Gardner also wrote the screenplay for *Who Is Harry Kellerman, and Why Is He Saying Those Terrible Things About Me?* (1971).

GARFIELD, JOHN (1913–1952). Born Jacob Julius Garfinkle in New York to Russian Jewish immigrant parents, Garfield spent several years in a school for difficult children following his mother's premature death and became interested in boxing and acting. Because of his own health woes, which had weakened his heart, he had to give up athletics and instead won a scholarship to study acting with **Maria Ouspenskaya** prior to his **Broadway** debut in *Lost Boy* (1932). He also appeared in a revival of *Counsellor-at-Law* in 1932, *Peace on Earth* (1933), and *Gold Eagle Guy* (1934) before joining **The Group Theatre**, where he appeared as Ralph Berger in the original production of *Awake and Sing!* (1935). He also appeared in The Group productions of *Weep for the Virgins* (1935), *Case of Clyde Griffiths* (1936), and *Johnny Johnson* (1936). **Clifford Odets** wrote *Golden Boy* (1937) with Garfield in mind, but he was instead given a secondary role and left The Group for Hollywood, receiving a 1938 Academy Award nomination for his performance in *Four Daughters*. He was nominated again in 1948 for *Body and Soul* and also appeared notably in *Juarez* (1939), *Saturday's Children** (1940), *The Sea Wolf* (1941), *Tortilla Flat* (1942), *The Postman Always Rings Twice* (1946), *Humoresque* (1946), and *Gentlemen's Agreement* (1947).

Garfield's career suffered a blow in the late 1940s when he was blacklisted in *Red Channels* and compelled to testify before the House Un-American Activities Committee (HUAC). Despite the ban on his appearances in films resulting from his appearance before the HUAC, he was able to work on

Broadway, having continued with occasional stage roles during his film career. His later Broadway appearances include *Having a Wonderful Time* (1937), *Heavenly Express* (1940), *Skipper Next to God* (1948), *The Big Knife* (1949), and revivals of *Peer Gynt* in 1951 and *Golden Boy* in 1952, finally having the opportunity to play the role of Joe Bonaparte written by Odets with Garfield in mind. He died of a heart attack a month after the show closed. His daughter, Julie Garfield, is an actress.

GASSNER, JOHN (1903–1967). Born John Waldhorn Gassner in Marajaros-Sziget, Hungary, he emigrated to the United States during childhood and studied at Columbia University. He became a book reviewer for the *New York Herald Tribune* in 1926 and was play editor for THE THEATRE GUILD from 1931 to 1944. He taught theatre **criticism** and playwriting at several universities, including Columbia, Hunter College, the University of Michigan, Queens College, and the New School for Social Research before settling at the Yale School of Drama in 1956 as Sterling Professor of Playwriting. He wrote and edited several theatre books, including *Treasury of the Theatre* (1940), *Form and Idea in Modern Theatre* (1956), and the Best American Plays series.

GAY AND LESBIAN THEATRE. These terms most often refer to plays written by and for homosexuals, mostly since the mid-1960s as various marginalized groups—**women**, **African Americans**, **Chicanos**, among others—sought liberation from the social constraints which denied them opportunity and equality in American life and this struggle was reflected on stages in the United States. Homosexual **men**, lesbians, bisexuals, and transgendered individuals are traditionally grouped together as "gay" within the realm of drama, but in the past few decades the term has also come to refer to a sensibility in which the world is viewed through the lens of gay culture.

With the onset of the **AIDS** pandemic in the early 1980s, gay dramas have more overtly explored serious questions inherent in being homosexual in the United States and, to a significant extent, gay drama has grown extraordinarily on American stages since 1980. Most gay dramas achieving mainstream acclaim have been by and about gay men, with the other subgroups making strides in **Off Broadway**, **Off-Off Broadway**, and **regional theatre**. Alfred Kazin writes, "'The love that dare not speak its name' (in the nineteenth century) cannot, in the twentieth, shut up," but the emergence of a vigorous gay drama demonstrates that there is much to say on a subject about which the stage has been silent for centuries. Perhaps the first American play to deal openly with homosexuality is believed to be Mae West's* *The Drag*, which generated so much controversy that it closed before completing a tumultuous pre-**Broadway** tour in 1927. A few other curiosities appeared in subsequent decades, most notably **Lillian Hellman**'s *The Children's Hour* (1934), in which the question of a lesbian relationship is at the center of the play, or in imported plays such as England's *The Green Bay Tree* (1933) by Mordaunt Shairp, which featured a gay villain. Secondary homosexual characters appear in a few plays of the 1930s and 1940s, but these are rarely identified as such. For example, Simon Stimson, the alcoholic choir master of **Thornton Wilder**'s Pulitzer Prize-winning *Our Town* (1938), is typical in that he is comparatively unimportant to the plot, mostly as a tragic victim, and Wilder makes no overt identification of the character as homosexual (even supplying Stimson with an off-stage wife).

Gay characters became more prevalent after World War II, most overtly in the plays of **Tennessee Williams**, who initially placed gay characters off-stage, as in the case of Blanche DuBois's long-dead closeted husband, Allan Gray, in *A Streetcar Named Desire* (1947) or predatory Sebastian Venable in *Suddenly Last Summer* (1958), but closeted characters appeared with Williams's Brick Pollitt of *Cat on a Hot Tin Roof* (1955) and, after the 1960s, Williams presented openly gay characters in his plays, as in *Small Craft Warnings* (1972) and *Something Cloudy, Something Clear* (1981). In the early 1950s, **Robert Anderson**'s *Tea and Sympathy* (1953) won popularity on stage and screen in its depiction of a sensitive young man viewed by his peers as a homosexual (even though it later becomes clear that he is probably not) and, as such, he should be ostracized, but more fully dimensioned gay characters and themes slowly came out of the shadows in the 1950s. **William Inge**, inspired to become a playwright by Williams's example, did not feature openly homosexual characters in any of his major plays, but in a few lesser-known one-acts he does so, including *The Tiny Closet* (1959) and *The Boy in the Basement* (1962), works making a plea for tolerance.

By the mid-1960s, mainstream theatre in general was catching up with Williams's depictions of homosexuality and a major breakthrough came with the appearance of **Mart Crowley**'s *The Boys in the Band* (1968), a comedy-drama in which a group of varied gay men—some deeply closeted and others "out"—gather to celebrate the birthday of one, but end up confronting their feelings about their sexual orientation. Between 1960 and the early 1980s, however, gay characters were often reduced to peripheral status in the plays—or were seen most vividly in MUSICALS like *La Cage aux Folles* (1983), tolerance plays like *Torch Song Trilogy* (1981), or in broad stereotypes in straight plays. There were a exceptions Off-Broadway, as in the case of **LeRoi Jones**'s (**Amiri Baraka**'s) *The Toilet* (1964) and **Ed Bullins**'s *Clara's Ole Man* (1965) or on Broadway in **Edward Albee**'s *Everything in the Garden* (1967), which flopped, or more overtly in the grotesquerie of drag in **Charles Ludlam**'s **Theatre of the Ridiculous**. The 1970s brought forth more dimensioned portraits of gay characters in **Robert Patrick**'s *Kennedy's Children* (1973), James Kirkwood's *P.S. Your Cat Is Dead* (1975), **Albert Innaurato**'s *Gemini* (1977), **Lanford Wilson**'s *Fifth of July* (1978), Jane Chambers's *Last Summer at Bluefish Cove* (1980), **Martin Sherman**'s *Bent* (1978), and Alan Bowne's *Forty-Deuce* (1981).

In the 1980s, with the appearance of AIDS, homosexual plays became scathing indictments of American society's failure to respond adequately to the crisis, as in **Larry Kramer**'s *The Normal Heart* (1985), works reflecting the fears of AIDS and grieving the tragedies, as in Robert Chesley's *Night Sweat* (1983) or Rebecca Ransom's *Warren* (1984), or darker tolerance pleas as in **William M. Hoffman**'s *As Is* (1981). The continuing AIDS crisis and changes in American attitudes about gay life brought significant changes to gay-themed drama, particularly evident in the PULITZER PRIZE-winning *Angels in America* (1993), in which **Tony Kushner** brought an intense intellectualism, love of language, and complex issues of history, politics, and morality to bear in this two-play epic which depicts gays as central to American life. No plea for tolerance, *Angels* offers a view of homosexuals living with the ramifications of post-World WAR II American history, from McCarthyism to the election of Ronald Reagan as U.S. president and the frightening height of the AIDS pandemic in the mid-1980s, not to mention their own highly charged personal struggles. The play's Broadway production featured a cast of eight (five men, three women) crossing genders to play a multitude of roles. Another Pulitzer Prize-winning gay-themed play, **Terrence McNally**'s *Love! Valour! Compassion!* (1994) proved to be little more than an updating of *The Boys in the Band*, presenting a group of gay friends adding fears of AIDS to negotiating their relationships and other works celebrated life (if somewhat satirically) in the face of the pandemic, as in **Paul Rudnick**'s *Jeffrey* (1993). Gay-themed plays seemed to dominate the selections of the Pulitzer Prize Committee, with awards presented to *Angels in America, Love! Valour! Compassion!*, and either works centrally featuring gay characters and themes or written by openly gay playwrights, as with Albee's *Three Tall Women* (1994), **Horton Foote**'s *Young Man From Atlanta* (1995), Jonathan Larson's musical *Rent* (1996), **Paula Vogel**'s *The Baltimore Waltz* (1992) and *How I Learned to Drive* (1998), **Nilo Cruz**'s *Anna in the Tropics* (2003), and **Doug Wright**'s *I Am My Own Wife* (2004). **Obie Award**-winning gay playwright **Harry Kondoleon** demonstrated promise in 17 plays, most produced Off-Broadway before his career was cut short by AIDS in 1994.

In the late 1990s, some plays addressed grim historical realities of homophobia, as in the **Tectonic Theatre**'s productions of *Gross Indecency* (1997), about the Oscar Wilde trials, and *The Laramie Project* (2001), which gave voice to the town's varied responses in the aftermath of the murder of gay college student Matthew Shepard, employing the techniques of documentary theatre. In the 1980s and beyond, **feminist** writers brought lesbian characters to the fore, as in the work of playwrights like Vogel, **Maria Irene Fornés**, Jane Chambers, and others, and groups like **Split Britches** or **solo** performers like **Holly Hughes**. Minority theatre companies draw a gay and lesbian audiences with works featuring such characters, and the queering of American life was continued in the work of dramatists like **Craig Lucas**, who addressed post-AIDS gay life on a cultural and familial level in *The Dying Gaul* (1998) or *What I Meant Was* (1999), and **Richard Greenberg**, whose *Take Me Out* (2002) found gays (and homophobia) present even in such traditionally macho environments as major league baseball. A storm of controversy arose (including pickets, bomb threats, and the possible withdrawal of the play) when homosexuality met religion in McNally's *Corpus Christi* (1998), which equated Christ's passion with gay lives, although curiously enough, when Rudnick visited the same terrain with *The Most Fabulous Story Ever Told* (1999) a year later, little furor accompanied the production. As the end of the first decade of the new millennium approached, gay and lesbian-themed drama was as prevalent as any other type of play on American stages from Broadway to regional, **academic**, and **community theatres**. *See also* SEXUALITY.

GAZZARA, BEN (1930–). Born Biagio Anthony Gazzara in New York to Italian immigrants, he studied electrical engineering at the City College of New York prior to taking acting classes at the Dramatic Workshop of the New School for Social Research, studying with **Erwin Piscator**. Gazzara joined **The Actors Studio** and appeared on **Broadway**, in films, and on television. He received a 1954 **Theatre World Award** for his performance in *End as a Man* and scored **Tony Award** nominations for *A Hatful of Rain* (1956), *Hughie/Duet* (1975), and a revival of *Who's Afraid of Virginia Woolf?* playing George opposite **Colleen Dewhurst**'s Martha, which also brought him a **Drama Desk Award** nomination. He originated the role of alcoholic athlete Brick Pollitt in **Tennessee Williams**'s PULITZER PRIZE-winning *Cat on a Hot Tin Roof* (1955) and received two additional Drama Desk nominations, one for the Off-Broadway play *Nobody Don't Like Yogi* (2004), as a member of the ensemble of a 2006 revival of *Awake and Sing!* Gazzara's other Broadway appearances include *The Night Circus* (1958), a revival of *Strange Interlude** in 1963, *Traveller without Luggage* (1964), and *Shimada* (1992). Gazzara's notable film appearances include *Anatomy of a Murder* (1959), *A Rage to Live* (1965), *Capone* (1975), *They All Laughed* (1981), and *The Big Lebowski* (1998). On television, Gazzara won an Emmy Award for *Hysteri-*

cal Blindness (2002), and three Emmy nominations, two for his series *Run for Your Life* in 1967 and 1968 (which also brought him three Golden Globe Award nominations), and for the TV film *An Early Frost* (1985).

GEDDES, BARBARA BEL (1922–2005). The daughter of noted scene designer NORMAN BEL GEDDES, she was born in New York and began acting in STOCK in 1940, while still in her teens. Her first **Broadway** roles were as an ingénue* in *Out of the Frying Pan* (1941), *Little Darling* (1942), *Nine Girls* (1943), and *Mrs. January and Mr. X* (1944) before she won critical praise in a key role in *Deep Are the Roots* (1945), winning a 1946 **Theatre World Award**. Her versatility is suggested by the two roles for which she received **Tony Award** nominations: "Maggie the Cat" in **Tennessee Williams**'s PU-LITZER PRIZE-winning *Cat on a Hot Tin Roof* (1955) and in the title role of **Jean Kerr**'s light comedy *Mary, Mary* (1961). Geddes continued to move easily from such popular entertainments to more serious dramas in her other Broadway appearances, including major roles in *Burning Bright* (1950), *The Moon Is Blue* (1941), *The Living Room* (1954), *The Sleeping Prince* (1956), *Silent Night, Lonely Night* (1959), *Everything in the Garden* (1967), and *Finishing Touches* (1973). She also replaced **Anne Jackson** in *Luv* in 1965. Geddes also acted in films, including *I Remember Mama* (1948), *Blood on the Moon* (1948), *Caught* (1949), and *Summertree* (1971), and she appeared in numerous television dramas, including a long stint as matriarch Miss Ellie on the TV drama *Dallas* (1978–1990).

GEDDES, NORMAN BEL (1893–1958).[†] Born Norman Melancton Geddes in Adrian, Michigan, Geddes studied art in Cleveland, Ohio, and Chicago, Illinois, before beginning his distinguished designing career at the Los Angeles Little Theatre* in 1916. Profoundly influenced by the modernist designers of Europe, including Adolphe Appia and Edward Gordon Craig, Geddes abandoned the proscenium for some of his productions and brought current movements in art into his productions, as his art deco designs for MUSICALS demonstrate. He collaborated with MAX REINHARDT on *The Miracle** (1924), for which he converted **Broadway**'s Century Theatre into the interior of a gothic cathedral, and he demonstrated his originality and versatility designing Broadway productions of *Lady, Be Good!* (1924), *Jeanne d'Arc* (1925), *Ziegfeld Follies** (1925), *Julius Caesar* (1927), *The Five O'Clock Girl* (1927), *The Patriot* (1928), and *Fifty Million Frenchmen* (1929), among many others. After 1930, Geddes designed less frequently, but no less notably with productions of Aristophanes' *Lysistrata* (1930), **Raymond Massey**'s *Hamlet* (1931), the musical *Flying Colors* (1932), **Sidney Kingsley**'s gritty drama *Dead End* (1935), *Iron Men* (1936), *The Eternal Road* (1937), *Siege* (1937),

It Happened on Ice (1940), and the musical revue *Seven Lively Arts* (1944). Geddes also worked as an industrial designer, designed a few theatres, pioneered the use of lenses in lighting instruments, and was the father of actress **Barbara Bel Geddes**.

GEER, WILL (1902–1978). A native of Frankfort, Indiana, born William Aughe Ghere, he aimed to be a botanist and completed a master's degree at the University of Chicago before switching to theatre, debuting as an actor on show boats* and tent shows before his 1928 **Broadway** debut in a revival of *The Merry Wives of Windsor* with Otis Skinner,* Henrietta Crosman,* and Minnie Maddern Fiske.* Very active in political and social causes during the Great Depression, he joined the Communist Party in 1934, and many of his Broadway roles reflected his political beliefs. He stepped into the role of Jeeter Lester in *Tobacco Road* (1933) as a replacement and appeared in productions of *Let Freedom Ring* (1935), *Bury the Dead* (1936), *200 Were Chosen* (1936), *A House in the Country* (1937), and *Of Mice and Men* (1937). For the **Federal Theatre Project (FTP)**, he played Mr. Mister in Marc Blitzstein's *The Cradle Will Rock* (1938), the famous production directed by **Orson Welles** that was shut down by the government on opening night, but performed without sets and costumes in another theatre in defiance of the attempted **censorship**.

Geer's subsequent Broadway credits include *Journeyman* (1938), *Washington Jitters* (1938), *Sing Out the News* (1938), *The More the Merrier* (1941), *Johnny on a Spot* (1942), *Comes the Revelation* (1942), revivals of *Tobaaco Road* in 1942 and *The Cradle Will Rock* in 1947, *On Whitman Avenue* (1946), *The Wisteria Trees* (1955), *The Vamp* (1955), *The Ponder Heart* (1956), *We, Comrades Three* (1966), and *Scratch* (1971), among others. Geer received a **Tony Award** nomination for the MUSICAL *110 in the Shade* (1963). He appeared with the **American Shakespeare Festival** and the **Association of Producing Artists,** and in 1933 founded the Folksay Theatre in Los Angeles. Geer was blacklisted from films during the McCarthy era, but by the 1960s he was working again in such films as *Advise & Consent* (1962), *Seconds* (1966), *In Cold Blood* (1967), and others, and he won a 1975 Emmy Award (and five additional nominations) playing Grandpa Walton on the hit television series *The Waltons* from 1972 until his death in 1978, despite having been blacklisted during the McCarthy era.

GEIDT, JEREMY (1933–). This English-born actor and teacher trained at the Old Vic Theatre School with Michel Saint-Denis and George Devine prior to touring to the United States in 1954 in an Old Vic production of *A Midsummer Night's Dream* and, later, in the satiric cabaret *The Establish-*

ment in 1962. He remained in the United States, acting on **Broadway** in *Alfie!* (1964), **Off-Broadway** and in television prior to becoming a founding member of the **Yale Repertory Theatre** in 1966, appearing in numerous productions before helping **Robert Brustein** found the **American Repertory Theatre** at Harvard University in 1980, where he has appeared in nearly 100 productions, from the classics to new works, earning the **Elliot Norton** Award in 1992. *See also* REGIONAL THEATRE.

GEIOGAMAH, HANAY (1945?–). Born in Lawton, Oklahoma, of **Native American** and Irish heritage, Geiogamah studied at the University of Oklahoma, after which he worked as an intern for Senator Edward M. Kennedy of Massachusetts. In the early 1970s, he conceived the idea of an all-Indian acting company and founded the Native American Theatre Ensemble with their first production, his own play *Body Indian* (1972), which was staged at New York's **La MaMa Experimental Theatre Club**. The play toured the United States and Germany. Geiogamah's subsequent play, *Foghorn* (1973), premiered in Berlin. Geiogamah returned to school at Indiana University to complete a major in theatre and continued to write, including the musical *49* (1982). In 1987, he became director of the American Indian Dance Theatre and Teaches at the University of California at Los Angeles. Of his work, Geiogamah has said, "For decades American Indians have been portrayed in films and on television in a manner entirely derogatory to their cultural and mental well-being. Who wants to see themselves and their race depicted as fiendish savages and murderers?"

GELBART, LARRY (1928–2009). Son of Jewish immigrant parents, Larry Simon Gelbart was born in Chicago, Illinois, and he began writing comedy for Danny Thomas's radio program at the age of 16, and later writing for Bob Hope, Red Buttons, and Jack Paar. Gelbart moved to television writing in the 1950s, most notably as part of the extraordinary team writing for Sid Caesar's live variety show, which included **Neil Simon**, **Woody Allen**, Mel Brooks, and Carl Reiner. By the 1960s, Gelbart was writing for **Broadway** and films. He shared a **Tony Award** with Burt Shevelove for their book for the MUSICAL *A Funny Thing Happened on the Way to the Forum* (1962), and he later wrote *Sly Fox* (1976), *Mastergate: A Play on Words* (1989), and the libretto for the musical *City of Angels* (1989), which also brought him a Tony and a **Drama Desk Award**. Gelbart's play *Power Failure* (1991) was performed by the **American Repertory Theatre**, he won a Peabody Award and an Emmy Award for his writing of the long-running television series *M*A*S*H* (1972–1983), and he was twice nominated for Academy Awards for his screenplays of *Oh, God!* (1977) and *Tootsie* (1982).

GEMINI. **Albert Innaurato**'s two-act comedy-drama of a dysfunctional South Philadelphia Italian family premiered at **Playwrights Horizons** in December 1976, followed by a March 1977 production at the **Circle Repertory Company**. The play moved to **Broadway**'s Little Theatre on 21 May 1977 for 1,819 performances under the direction of **Marshall W. Mason**. The Geminiani family has gathered in the summer of 1973 to celebrate the 21st birthday of their son, Francis, a recent Harvard University graduate. Two of Fran's college friends, Judith and Randy, are present for the party, a stressful situation for Fran since Judith has romantic feelings for him, but he is drawn to Randy, uncertain of his own **sexual** orientation. Fran's outrageously dysfunctional extended family and neighbors add to his stresses. *Gemini* was adapted as a film by Richard Benner with the title *Happy Birthday, Gemini* (1980). *See also* GAY AND LESBIAN THEATRE.

GENTLE PEOPLE, THE. This three-act "Brooklyn fable" by **Irwin Shaw**, produced by **The Group Theatre**, opened on 5 January 1939 at the Belasco Theatre for 141 performances under **Harold Clurman**'s direction, with scene design by BORIS ARONSON. The plot involves two middle-aged cronies, Jonah Goodman and Philip Anagnos (played by Sam Jaffe and Roman Bohnen), who enjoy fishing and their otherwise simple life. When they fall under the control of a gangster, Goff (**Franchot Tone**), who extorts money and attempts to steal the affections of Goodman's daughter, Stella (Sylvia Sidney), Goodman and Anagnos realize they have no choice and take Goff out in their boat, kill him, dump his body in the sea, and return to their simple life. The cast also included **Lee J. Cobb**, **Elia Kazan**, Karl Malden, and Martin Ritt. A film version, renamed *Out of the Fog* (1941), starred **John Garfield**, Ida Lupino, and THOMAS MITCHELL.

GEORGE WASHINGTON SLEPT HERE. Produced by SAM H. HARRIS, GEORGE S. KAUFMAN and **Moss Hart**'s three-act comedy opened on 18 October 1940 at the Lyceum Theatre for 173 performances under Kaufman's direction. ERNEST TRUEX, as Newton Fuller, persuades his wife, played by Jean Dixon, to join him in purchasing a ramshackle old country house where, he has been told, George Washington once slept. The house proves largely uninhabitable and family problems, from their daughter's affair with a married actor from a STOCK company and the arrival of boorish Uncle Stanley (DUDLEY DIGGES), who was once rich, but is now broke and needing to live with the Fullers. Adding insult to injury, the Fullers discover that Washington did not sleep in the house, but Benedict Arnold did. Percy Kilbride, later Pa Kettle in the movies, added to the hilarity as a local character, Mr. Kimber.

Kilbride repeated his role in the 1942 film version starring Jack Benny, Ann Sheridan, and CHARLES COBURN.

GÉRARD, ROLF (1909–). Born in Berlin, Germany, Gérard became a British citizen and worked in the United States and Europe. In theatre, Gérard became known for his glamorized approach in costume designs, and he was nominated for a **Tony Award** for his costumes for the musical *Irma La Douce* (1960). His other **Broadway** credits include *That Lady* (1949), a revival of *Caesar and Cleopatra* in 1949, *An Evening with Beatrice Lillie* (1952), *The Love of Four Colonels* (1953), *The Strong Are Lonely* (1953), *The Fighting Cock* (1959), and *Tovarich* (1963). Gérard also designed for films, including *The Silver Chalice* (1954), *Invitation to the Dance* (1956), and *The Honey Pot* (1967), and he designed a television production of *The Merry Widow* in 1983. Gérard is also an accomplished painter and, in celebration of his 100th birthday, an exhibit of his work was in Locarno, Switzerland, near where he resides in Ascona.

GETTING OUT. **Marsha Norman**'s two-act drama was first produced at **Actors Theatre of Louisville** by the **Phoenix Theatre** on 19 October 1978 at the Marymount Manhattan Theatre for 22 performances. It reopened at the Theatre de Lys on 15 May 1979 for 237 performances. Norman's first play, it received an **American Theatre Critics Award** for its unique story of Arlene (Susan Kingsley), a woman recently released from prison who plans to find a better life. Holed up in a decrepit flat, she grapples with specters from her past, including her own former persona, played by Pamela Reed, as well as her former pimp, a jailer who tried to seduce her, and her mother. With the help of a kind neighbor, Arlene determines that she can face her past and restart her life. A 1994 film version starred Rebecca De Mornay and **Ellen Burstyn**.

GIBBS, WOLCOTT (1902–1958). Born Oliver Wolcott Gibbs in New York, he attended and was expelled from the Hill School, after which he attended another prep school, but did not go to college. Over the course of his long and varied career as a writer and CRITIC, Gibbs was embarrassed about his lack of formal education. He joined the staff of the *New Yorker* in 1927 as a copyreader, moving through the ranks to editorial writer and, in 1940, succeeding Robert Benchley* as theatre critic, a post he held until his death. Gibbs was admired for the quality of his writing, but was feared for his sarcasm and walked out of performances at the end of first acts if he did not like the show. Despite this, he had a timid persona. He also wrote a comedy, *Season in the Sun* (1950), but it ran only one month on **Broadway**.

GIBSON, MELISSA JAMES (1970?–). Gibson moved to New York to study at the AMERICAN ACADEMY OF DRAMATIC ART in hopes of an acting career, which she soon abandoned. Further study at Columbia University and the Yale School of Drama led Gibson to playwriting and an **Obie Award** and the **Joseph Kesselring** Prize for *[sic]* (1997), a work commissioned by **Steppenwolf Theatre** and first produced in New York at Soho Repertory in November 2001. Gibson's other plays, many of which have been produced **Off-Broadway** and in **regional theatre**, include *Nuda Veritas* (1994), *Given Fish* (1995), *Six Fugues* (1995), *God's Paws* (1996), *Brooklyn Bridge* (2001), a children's play, *Suitcase, or Those That Resemble Flies from a Distance* (2003), *Current Nobody* (2007), and *This* (2009). Gibson has won a Whiting Award, a Guggenheim Fellowship, and a **Lucille Lortel Award**.

GIBSON, WILLIAM (1914–2008). Born in New York, Gibson lived in Topeka, Kansas, in his youth, and his first plays were produced at the Topeka Civic Theatre. He studied at the City College of New York before becoming a playwright and novelist. He was nominated for a **Tony Award** for *Two for the Seesaw* (1958), which was later adapted as the MUSICAL *Seesaw* (1973), and he won a Tony for *The Miracle Worker* (1959), a drama focused on Annie Sullivan, the devoted teacher of Helen Keller. Gibson scripted the 1962 film version, earning an Academy Award nomination. The stars of both the play and the film, **Anne Bancroft** and Patty Duke, won Tonys on stage and Academy Awards for the film.

Gibson also received a Tony nomination for his libretto for the musical *Golden Boy* (1964). His other plays include *I Lay in Zion* (1947); *Dinny and the Witches* (1948); *A Cry of Players* (1968); *A Mass for the Dead* (1968); *John and Abigail* (1969); *The Body and the Wheel* (1974); *The Butterfingers Angel* (1974); *Golda* (1977); *Goodly Creatures* (1980); *Monday After the Miracle* (1982), a sequel to *The Miracle Worker*; *Handy Dandy* (1984); the libretto for the musical *Raggedy Ann and Andy* (1986); and *Golda's Balcony* (2003), a revision of *Golda* that became the longest-running **solo performance** in the history of **Broadway**.

Gibson also wrote non-fiction, most notably *The Seesaw Log*, his account of the preparations for the Broadway production of *Two for the Seesaw*. For films, Gibson adapted his novel *The Cobweb* as a screenplay in 1955, but otherwise only wrote screenplays for film versions of his own plays. Late in his long life, speaking about writing, he said "that's the thing where I feel most alive—at least while I'm doing it. I started out to be a writer and I'm still a writer. Not bad."

GIDEON. Paddy Chayefsky's two-act play about man and divinity opened on 9 November 1961 at the Plymouth Theatre for 236 performances under

Tyrone Guthrie's direction. God (Fredric March), in the guise of an Angel, appears to simple farmer Gideon (Douglas Campbell), whom He wishes to lead the Israelites against the Midianties. Gideon takes some convincing, but eventually does so with God's help, although he later resists orders from God to kill the elders of Succoth. Gideon's pride distresses God, who recognizes that man cannot seem to rise above human circumstances and recognize the divine. The play was nominated for several **Tony Awards**, including Best Play. A 1971 television production starred **Peter Ustinov** and **José Ferrer**. *See also* RELIGIOUS DRAMA.

GILDER, ROSAMUND (1891–1986).† Born Janet Rosamond de Kay Gilder in Marion, Massachusetts, she grew up in an artistic milieu, exposed to literature, art, and music, and socializing with such cultural leaders as Mark Twain, Jacob Riis, and Eleonora Duse.* After contributing articles to THEATRE ARTS MONTHLY during the 1920s, she joined its staff in 1936 and, in 1946, succeeded founding editor EDITH ISAACS to the editorship. In 1947, Gilder was one of the founders of the International Theatre Institute (ITI). Under its auspices, she promoted international cultural exchanges, sending American theatre companies to tour abroad. Elected president of the American center of ITI, she served from 1963 to 1969. She launched a number of theatre publications and published her own articles and books on theatre.

GILFORD, JACK (1908–1990). Born Yankel Gellman in Brooklyn, New York, this seemingly gentle, mild-mannered character actor carved out a long career in a wide range of roles. He began as a master of ceremonies in nightclubs and was "discovered" by Milton Berle. On **Broadway**, he was nominated twice for **Tony Awards** as Hysterium, the nervous Roman slave, in the MUSICAL *A Funny Thing Happened on the Way to the Forum* (1962), and the gentle Herr Schultz in *Cabaret* (1966). His other Broadway credits include *Meet the People* (1940), *They Should Have Stood in Bed* (1942), *Alive and Kicking* (1950), *The Live Wire* (1950), *The Diary of Anne Frank* (1955), *Romanoff and Juliet* (1957), *Drink to Me Only* (1958), *Look After Lulu* (1959), *Once Upon a Mattress* (1958), *The Tenth Man* (1959), revivals of *Three Men on a Horse* in 1969 and *No, No, Nanette* in 1971, *Sly Fox* (1976), *The Supporting Cast* (1981), and *The World of Sholom Aleichem* (1982).

Gilford replaced **Jack Albertson** in the Broadway production of *The Sunshine Boys* in 1973. He had appeared with frequency in films and on television, despite his career being damaged in the early 1950s during the McCarthy era when his left-leaning politics led to his blacklisting, although he worked steadily in theatre and his career had a major resurgence in the early 1960s. In films, Gilford was nominated for an Academy Award and a Golden Globe Award for his performance in *Save the Tiger* (1973), and he recreated his Broadway performance in the film version of *A Funny Thing Happened on the Way to the Forum* (1966). Gilford also appeared in such films as *Enter Laughing* (1967), *Catch-22* (1970), and *Cocoon* (1985). On television, he received two Emmy nominations in one year in 1989, for guest roles on *The Golden Girls* and *"thirtysomething"* and he won a Daytime Emmy Award for *The Big Blue Marble* (1974).

GILL, BRENDAN (1914–1997). The erudite writer and CRITIC of theatre, film, and architecture, was born in Hartford, Connecticut. He attended Yale University and he began writing books and contributing to periodicals, most particularly the *New Yorker*, after graduating, eventually becoming film critic in 1961 and theatre critic in 1968, continuing in that post until 1987. He wrote well-received biographies of Frank Lloyd Wright, TALLULAH BANKHEAD, and Cole Porter, edited a collection of eight PHILIP BARRY plays, and his book *The Day the Money Stopped* (1957) was adapted as a play by MAXWELL ANDERSON in 1958.

GILLMORE, MARGALO (1897–1986).[†] London, England-born actress Margaret Lorraine Gillmore, spent much of her career on the **Broadway** stage, beginning in *A Scrap of Paper* (1917) and continuing to the 1960s. Among Gillmore's numerous credits are a range of plays from the classics to new works, including *Alias Jimmy Valentine** (1921), *He Who Gets Slapped* (1922), *Outward Bound** (1924), *The Green Hat* (1925), *Ned McCobb's Daughter** (1926), *The Silver Cord** (1926), *The Second Man** (1927), *Marco Millions** (1928), *Berkeley Square** (1929), *The Dark Tower* (1933), **Valley Forge** (1934), *The Women* (1936), *No Time for Comedy* (1939), *Outrageous Fortune* (1943), *State of the Union* (1945), *Kind Sir* (1953), *Peter Pan** (1954), and *Sail Away* (1961). She also stepped in as a replacement in *The Barretts of Wimpole Street* in 1931 and *The Diary of Anne Frank* in 1956. Late in her career, Gillmore also appeared in films, including *Perfect Strangers* (1950), *Cause for Alarm!* (1951), *Gaby* (1956), and *High Society* (1956), and television productions, most notably as Mrs. Darling in the 1955, 1956, and 1960 broadcasts of the **Mary Martin** *Peter Pan,** recreating her Broadway role.

GILMAN, REBECCA (1964–). Born in Trussville, Alabama, Gilman attended Middlebury College, Birmingham-Southern College and the University of Iowa. She moved to Chicago, Illinois, and began writing plays, a number of which have been produced at the **Goodman Theatre**. Her best known play, *Spinning into Butter* (1999), is typical of her work in addressing sociopolitical concerns, in this case political correctness and racial strife. Her other works include *The Glory of Living* (1999) and *Boy Gets Girl* (2000), both of which examine contemporary **sexual** issues, and *The Crime of the Century* (1999), *The American in Me* (1999), *Speech Therapy* (1999), *Heaven and Hell on Earth* (2001), *Blue Surge* (2002), *Bill of (W)rights* (2004), *The Sweetest Swing in Baseball* (2004), *The Boys Are Coming* Home (2007), and *A True History of the Johnstown Flood* (2010). Gilman's adaptation of **Carson McCullers**'s novel *The Heart Is a Lonely Hunter* was produced by the **New York Theatre Workshop** in 2009.

GILMAN, RICHARD (1923–2006). Brooklyn, New York-born Gilman was a writer and **critic** with particular interest in European drama and literature. He wrote theatre and literary criticism for *Commonweal* (1961–1964), *Newsweek* (1964–1967), and the *New Republic* (1968–1970), and taught at Yale University from 1967 to 1999. He received the GEORGE JEAN NATHAN Award for Drama Criticism in 1971. Among his several books on drama are *The Making of Modern Drama* (1974), **Chekhov's Plays: An Opening into Eternity** (1996), and *The Drama Is Coming Now: The Theatre Criticism of Richard Gilman* (2005).

GILROY, FRANK D. (1925–). Born Frank Daniel Gilroy in New York, son of a coffee salesman, he studied at Dartmouth College and the Yale School of Drama. He won an **Obie Award** for his first play, *Who'll Save the Plowboy?* (1962), and his first **Broadway** production, *The Subject Was Roses* (1964), won the PULITZER PRIZE, **Tony Award**, and **New York Drama Critics Circle Award** for this three-character play featuring **Jack Albertson**, Martin Sheen, and Irene Dailey about a returning World WAR II soldier and the troubled marriage of his seemingly happy parents. Patricia Neal replaced Dailey in a much-honored 1968 film version. Gilroy's subsequent plays, including *Any Given Day* (1993), found scant approval, but he worked as a successful film and television writer. For the movies, he scripted *The Gallant Hours* (1960) and *The Only Game in Town* (1970), and for TV he wrote many scripts for episodic shows. He also directed several films and TV films.

GIN GAME, THE. D. L. Coburn's PULITZER PRIZE-winning two-act, two-character play premiered at American Theatre Arts in Hollywood, California, in September 1976, followed by a run at **Actors Theatre of Louisville** prior to opening on Broadway on 6 October 1977 at the John Golden Theatre for 517 performances under **Mike Nichols**'s direction. Set in a home for the aged, Weller Martin and Fonsia Dorsey become acquainted and play gin rummy, revealing their life stories as the gin game, which Fonsia persistently wins, escalating into a pitched battle. Weller finally explodes in rage, ending the game. **Hume Cronyn** and **Jessica Tandy** played the leads, with Tandy winning a **Tony** and **Drama Desk Award**. Cronyn and Tandy appeared in a 1981 television production of the play and were replaced by **E. G. Marshall** and **Maureen Stapleton** during the **Broadway** run. The play was revived on Broadway in 1997 with **Charles Durning** and **Julie Harris** under the direction of **Charles Nelson Reilly**. A West End production starred Joss Ackland and Dorothy Tutin in 1999.

GIOVANNI, PAUL (1933–1990). This New York-born playwright, actor, director, and musician, won notice for his music for the horror film *The Wicker Man* (1973), and he wrote and directed the successful Sherlock Holmes* play, *The Crucifer of Blood* (1978), reaping a **Tony Award** nomination for his direction. The play was produced as a TV film in 1991 starring Charlton Heston. In 1981, he directed Edward Sheehan's *Kingdoms* on **Broadway**. He completed an unproduced MUSICAL, *Shot Through the Heart*, but he succumbed to the effects of **AIDS**.

GISH, DOROTHY (1898–1968).[†] The younger sister of LILLIAN GISH was born in Massillion, Ohio, and first performed on stage at age four as Little Willie in the melodrama* *East Lynne*. She played child roles on the road* and in New York until 1912. That year, she and her sister joined D. W. Griffith's motion picture company, for which Dorothy made 61 films prior to obtaining her first star contract in 1915, after which she appeared in one of her most popular films, *Hearts of the World* (1917). Gish returned to legitimate theatre in 1928 to perform in *Young Love* on **Broadway**, followed by a London engagement. Among her other Broadway credits are four revivals in 1930–1931, *The Inspector General*, *Getting Married*, *The Streets of New York*, and *Pillars of Society*. She also appeared in *The Bride the Sun Shines On* (1931), *Foreign Affairs* (1932), *Autumn Crocus* (1932), *By Your Leave* (1934), *Brittle Heaven* (1934), in which she played Emily Dickinson, *Mainly for Lovers* (1936), *Missouri Legend* (1938), and *Morning's at Seven* (1939). Gish was also one of the numerous mature "name" actresses to take over from **Dorothy Stickney** as Vinnie in the long-running *Life With Father* (1939). Her final Broadway appearances included a revival of *Love for Love* (1940), *The Great Big Doorstep* (1942), *The Magnificent Yankee* (1946), *The Story of Mary Surratt* (1947), and *The Man* (1950).

GISH, LILLIAN (1896–1993).[†] Born in Springfield, Ohio, Gish, the elder sister of DOROTHY GISH, made her stage debut as "Baby Lillian" in a touring melodrama* in 1902. Occasionally during childhood she toured apart from her protective mother and sister. After she was hired by D. W. Griffith to star in motion pictures in 1912, Gish devoted most of her acting career to film, including such silent classics as *The Birth of a Nation* (1915), *Intolerance* (1916), *Broken Blossoms* (1919), *Way Down East* (1920), *Orphans of the Storm* (1921), *La Boheme* (1926), *The Scarlet Letter* (1926), and *The Wind* (1928). She appeared on **Broadway** once in this period, in *A Good Little Devil (1913)*. Her work on the legitimate stage included appearances in revivals of *Uncle Vanya* in 1930 and *Camille* in 1932, *Nine Pine Street* (1933), *The Joyous Season* (1934), *Within the Gates* (1934), as Ophelia opposite John Gielgud in *Hamlet* (1936), *The Star-Wagon* (1937), *Dear Octopus* (1939), *Mr. Sycamore* (1942), *Crime and Punishment* (1947), *The Curious Savage* (1950), *The Trip to Bountiful* (1953), *The Family Reunion* (1958), *All the Way Home* (1960), a revival of *Too True to Be Good* in 1963, *Anya* (1965), *I Never Sang for My Father* (1968), an all-star **Circle in the Square** revival of *Uncle Vanya* in 1973, and *A Musical Jubilee* (1975). After the silent film days, Gish continued to act in films, garnering an Academy Award nomination for *Duel in the Sun* (1946), and she also appeared in *Portrait of Jennie* (1948), *The Night of the Hunter* (1955), *The Unforgiven* (1960), *The Comedians* (1967), which brought her a Golden Globe Award nomination, and *The Whales of August* (1987). Gish was presented with an Honorary Oscar in 1971 and she appeared in several television dramas. Her autobiography, *The Movies, Mr. Griffith, and Me*, was published in 1973.

GLASPELL, SUSAN (1882–1948).[†] A native of Davenport, Iowa, Glaspell was educated at Drake University and the University of Chicago before embarking on a career writing novels and plays. She was one of the founders of the Provincetown Players* along with her husband George Cram Cook,* with whom she wrote one-act plays including *Suppressed Desires** (1914; coauthored by Cook) and *Trifles** (1916). A committed **feminist**, Glaspell's intellectualism and literary skill are evident in her plays and when she began writing full-length works with *Bernice* (1919), she found critical approval for subsequent plays, including *The Inheritors** (1921), *The Verge** (1921), and *Alison's House* (1930), a fictionalization of Emily Dickinson's life, for which she won the PULITZER PRIZE. Like EUGENE O'NEILL, another dramatist whose career was launched by the Provincetown Players, Glaspell merged contemporary themes with dramatic techniques emerging from modernist European playwrights. Expressionistic* and symbolist elements are found in her plays, which often depict the "new woman." In collaboration with her second husband, Norman Matson, Glaspell wrote *The Comic Artist*, which met with success in Europe, but failed in its 1933 New York production. During the Great Depression, Glaspell headed the Midwest bureau of the **Federal Theatre Project (FTP)**.

GLASS MENAGERIE, THE. **Tennessee Williams**'s first **Broadway** play was recognized as a masterpiece by many critics when it premiered in the midst of a blizzard in Chicago, Illinois, on 26 December 1944, followed by a Broadway production beginning on 31 March 1945. The performance received 24 curtain calls and a rhapsodic response from critics, both for the play and the performance of legendary actress LAURETTE TAYLOR in her last role, playing Amanda Wingfield in what Williams labeled as a "memory play." The four-character cast also included **Eddie Dowling**, **Julie Haydon**, and **Anthony Ross**.

As a self-avowed "stage magician," Tom Wingfield (Dowling) reflects back on his life with his mother (Taylor) and sister (Haydon), conjuring scenes from the past. At the height of the Great Depression, the sensitive Tom aspires to be a writer, but financial exigencies force him to work in a St. Louis factory. His mother, Amanda, is an unhappy woman who was deserted by her husband years before and is ill-equipped to cope with the hard realities of her reduced circumstances. Amanda struggles to make ends meet and worries about the future of her deeply repressed daughter, Laura. Amanda pressures Tom to bring home a "gentleman caller" for Laura in a desperate hope that she might find security in a marriage. Despite practical pressures, Amanda frequently retreats into either real or imagined memories of herself as a romantic Southern belle receiving 17 gentlemen callers. Laura, too, frequently escapes into a fantasy world, listening to old Victrola records her father left behind and collecting glass figurines. Among these, a unicorn is her favorite; as a unique and fragile creature herself, she relates to the symbolism of its distinguishing horn. Amanda's browbeating finally convinces Tom to bring Jim O'Connor (Ross), his factory coworker, home to dinner. Laura and Jim discover they were high school classmates and, alone with Jim, Laura touchingly recalls the crush she had on him, remembering his good-humored teasing and revealing that her feelings for him have remained unchanged. Jim apologizes, making a hasty departure after confessing his engagement to another girl. Amanda angrily turns on Tom for his blunder and they argue bitterly. Tom, as Amanda has predicted and feared, storms out the door never to return. As the play ends, Tom is again seen in the present reflecting with sadness on the past, explaining that despite geographic distance and the intervening years he has been unable to extinguish the memory of his sister and her plight.

The Glass Menagerie has been filmed no less than four times, first in a 1950 Hollywood adaptation with **Gertrude Lawrence**, **Arthur Kennedy**, Jane Wyman, and Kirk Douglas. Other versions include a 1966 television production featuring **Shirley Booth**, Barbara Loden, **Hal Holbrook**, and **Pat Hingle**, another television production in 1973 starring **Katharine Hepburn** in her first small-screen appearance as Amanda, with **Sam Waterston**, Joanna Miles, and Michael Moriarty in support, and a 1987 big-screen version with Joanne Woodward, Karen Allen, **John Malkovich,** and **James Naughton**, under the direction of **Paul Newman**. *The Glass Menagerie* has been revived on Broadway five times, starring **Maureen Stapleton**, Piper Laurie, **George Grizzard**, and **Pat Hingle** in 1965; Stapleton again in 1975, costarring with Paul Rudd, Pamela Payton-Wright, and **Rip Torn**; **Jessica Tandy** played Amanda in 1983, supported by **Amanda Plummer**, Bruce Davison, and John Heard; **Julie Harris** took on the role of Amanda in 1994, costarring with Calista Flockhart, Zeljko Ivanek, and Kevin Kilner; and Jessica Lange, Josh Lucas, Sarah Paulson, and Christian Slater appeared in a 2005 revival. The play has also been revived **Off-Broadway**, including a 2010 **Lucille Lortel Award**-winning production at the **Roundabout Theatre**. HELEN HAYES played Amanda in the original London production in 1948, drawn to a character within whom both tragic and comic aspects are richly represented.

GLEASON, JOANNA (1950–). Born Joanne Hall in Winnipeg, Manitoba, Canada, the daughter of television personality Monty Hall, Gleason was educated at the University of California at Los Angeles and Occidental College before winning a **Theatre World Award** for her performance in *I Love My Wife* (1977) and **Tony** and **Drama Desk Awards** for *Into the Woods* (1987). Much of her work has been in MUSICALS, including *Dirty Rotten Scoundrels* (2005), which brought her Tony and Drama Desk nominations, and *Nick & Nora* (1991). She has also been lauded in dramatic roles, including winning Drama Desk Awards for *It's Only a Play* (1986) and *Social Security* (1986), and she was nominated for Tony and Drama Desk Awards for a revival of *A Day in the Death of Joe Egg* (1985). She married actor Chris Sarandon in 1994 and has appeared in such films as *Crimes and Misdemeanors* (1989), *Mr. Holland's Opus* (1995), *Boogie Nights* (1997), and *Sex and the City* (2008).

GLEASON, JOHN (1941–2003). Brooklyn, New York-born Gleason studied at Hunter College and as a lighting designer worked on over 100 **Broadway** productions, including *We Bombed in New Haven* (1968), *Lovers and Other Strangers* (1968), *The Great White Hope* (1968), *A Cry of Players* (1968), *In the Matter of J. Robert Oppenheimer* (1969), *Two by Two* (1970), *The Love Suicide at Schofield Barracks* (1972), *Veronica's Room* (1973), *Over Here!* (1974), *All Over Town* (1974), and numerous classics and revivals. Gleason was also resident designer for the **Repertory Theatre of Lincoln Center** and the **Mark Taper Forum**. He also taught at New York University from 1972 to 1997.

GLENGARRY GLEN ROSS. **David Mamet**'s PULITZER PRIZE and **Tony Award**-winning two-act drama depicting the dark side of American-style capitalism premiered in England, at London's Royal National Theatre, where it opened on 23 September 1983, and was well-received. The **Broadway** production opened on 25 March 1984 at the John Golden Theatre, where it ran for 378 performances under the direction of **Gregory Mosher**. The cast of seven actors, **Joe Mantegna** (Tony winner), Mike Nussbaum, **Robert Prosky** (Tony nominee), Lane Smith, James Tolkan, Jack Wallace, and J. T. Walsh, won a **Drama Desk Award** as outstanding ensemble. They played present-day Chicago real estate agents or their clients in a savage portrait of the moral decadence inherent in selling, as the agents, under intense pressure to make unrealistic quotas selling what may be bogus condominiums, abandon ethics to employ any tactic in order to prevail. The play was revived on Broadway in 2005, winning the Tony for Best Revival and a Tony for actor **Liev Schreiber**, a **Theatre World Award** for Gordon Clapp, and a Drama Desk Award for the ensemble cast and **Santo Loquasto**'s scene design. A 1992 screen version, starring **Jack Lemmon, Kevin Spacey, Alan Arkin**, Ed Harris, Alec Baldwin, Jonathan Pryce, and **Al Pacino**, who was nominated for an Academy Award and a Golden Globe Award, won critical approval.

GLENVILLE, PETER (1913–1996). Born Peter Patrick Brabazon Browne in Hampstead, London, Glenville came from a family of actors. He was educated at Oxford University and became director of the Old Vic in 1944. Continuing to work in England, he also directed frequently on **Broadway**, scoring **Tony Award** nominations for *Separate Tables* (1957), *Rashomon* (1959), *Take Me Along* (1959), and *Tchin-Tchin* (1963). His other Broadway productions include such American and British plays and MUSICALS as *The Browning Version* (1949), *The Innocents* (1950), *The Curious Savage* (1950), *Island of Goats* (1951), *Hotel Paradiso* (1957), *Silent Night, Lonely Night* (1959), *Becket* (190), *Tovarich* (1963), *Dylan* (1964), *Everything in the Garden* (1957), *A Patriot for Me* (1969), and *Out Cry* (1973), as well as a revival of *Romeo and Juliet* in 1951 starring screen actress Olivia de Havilland in her Broadway debut.

GOAT, THE; or WHO IS SYLVIA? **Edward Albee** won a **Tony Award** and a **Drama Desk Award** for this two-act play about sexual taboos. It opened at the JOHN GOLDEN Theatre on 10 March 2002 for 309 performances under the direction of **David Esbjornson** with scene design by **John Arnone**. Bill Pullman played Martin, a middle-aged architect, comfortably married and middle class, who falls in love with a goat. This revelation sets off a family crisis and allows Albee to explore cultural taboos, including bestiality, incest, infidelity, and **homosexuality** as he questions the boundaries of a liberal society. **Mercedes Ruehl** (Tony-nominated) played Stevie, Martin's wife. During the Broadway run, **Bill Irwin** and Sally Field stepped into the roles of Martin and Stevie. *See also* GAY AND LESBIAN THEATRE; SEXUALITY.

GOLDEN, JOHN (1874–1955).[†] Born in New York, Golden grew up in Ohio before returning to New York in his teens to become an actor. He was not successful, so he spent a dozen years as a salesman, during which time he wrote sketches, short plays, and songs, some of which were performed on **Broadway** as early as 1900, including his most enduring song, "Poor Butter-fly." In 1918, Golden abandoned his sales career to produce *Turn to the Right*. He produced more than 150 shows and gained a reputation for emphasizing family entertainments. His Broadway productions include *Lightnin'** (1918), *Three Wise Fools** (1918), *The First Year** (1920), *Seventh Heaven** (1922), *Let Us Be Gay** (1929), *As Husbands Go* (1931), *When Ladies Meet* (1932), *The Bishop Misbehaves* (1935), *Susan and God* (1937), *Skylark* (1939), *Claudia* (1941), *Made in Heaven* (1946), and Maurice Chevalier in concert (1948). Golden was also centrally involved in founding the Stage Relief Fund and the **Stage Door Canteen**.

GOLDEN BOY. **Clifford Odets**'s three-act drama, one of the biggest hits produced by **The Group Theatre** and one of its most quintessential works, opened at the Belasco Theatre on 4 November 1937 for 250 performances under the direction of **Harold Clurman**, with scene designs by MORDECAI GORELIK. Despite the fact that Odets wrote the play with **John Garfield** in mind (Garfield appeared in a 1952 **Broadway** revival), **Luther Adler** appeared as Joe Bonaparte, a young man torn between a career as a violinist and boxing, which might raise him, his family, and his girl, Lorna, from the tenements at the height of the Great Depression. Joe's struggle between his idealistic artistic pursuits and the practical realities of survival made for compelling drama as performed by Adler, **Morris Carnovsky** as his father, and Frances Farmer as Lorna. Garfield appeared in a supporting role, as did such Group Theatre luminaries as **Lee J. Cobb**, Phoebe Brand, Roman Bohnen, **Howard Da Silva**, **Elia Kazan**, **Robert Lewis**, Art Smith, and Martin Ritt, among others. *Golden Boy* was filmed in 1939 with William Holden and Barbara Stanwyck. The play has had numerous revivals **Off-Broadway** and in **regional theatres** and Odets later collaborated with **William Gibson** on a successful (568 performances) **Tony Award**-nominated musical version starring Sammy Davis, Jr. in 1964.

GOLDMAN, JAMES (1927–1998). Born in Chicago, Illinois, Goldman wrote a few plays and screenplays of note, including *Blood, Sweat, and Stanley Poole* (1961) and, more notably, **The Lion in Winter** (1966), which he adapted for a 1968 film version, winning an Academy Award. He also contributed libretti for two **Broadway** MUSICALS, *A Family Affair* (1962), with music by John Kander, and *Follies* (1971), with music and lyrics by **Stephen Sondheim**, which brought Goldman a **Tony Award** nomination. In collaboration with Sondheim, Goldman also wrote another musical for television, *Evening Primrose* (1966). Goldman's other plays include **They Might Be Giants** (1961), which was produced in England and later adapted as a 1971 film, adaptations of *Oliver Twist* (1982) and *Anna Karenina* (1985), *Anastasia: The Mystery of Anna* (1986), and *Tolstoy* (1996). Goldman's screenplays include *Nicholas and Alexandra* (1971), *Robin and Marian* (1976), and *White Nights* (1985). Goldman was also the author of several novels and a few television films.

GÓMEZ-PEÑA, GUILLERMO (1955–). This Mexican-born **performance artist**, writer, and teacher moved to the United States in 1978. His themes emphasize the intersections of American and Mexican cultures with emphasis on issues of the border between the countries, immigration, assimilation, cultural identity, and racial and linguistic concerns. Gómez-Peña employs multimedia elements, including radio, video, photographs, and visual art elements. Among his best-known works, sometimes created in collaboration with others, are *Border Brujo* (1988), *The Couple in the Cage* (1992), *The Crucifiction Project* (1994), *The Temple of Confessions* (1995), *The Mexterminator Project* (1997), *The Living Museum of Fetishized Identities* (1999), and *The Mapa-Corpo Series* (2004–2008). Among his frequent collaborators are **Coco Fusco**, James Luna, Maria Estrada, and Demián Flores, among others. *See also* CHICANO THEATRE.

GOODBYE AGAIN. Allan Scott and George Haight's three-act comedy opened at the Masque Theatre on 28 December 1932 for 216 performances. The play featured **Osgood Perkins** as Kenneth Bixby, a famous writer confronted by Julia, an ex-lover anxious to restart the relationship. When her husband shows up the situation becomes complicated, but Bixby's loyal assistant, Anne, helps restore order. Future movie star **James Stewart** appeared in a small role as a chauffeur. A 1943 revival flopped, as did a 1956 revival starring **Donald Cook**. A 1933 film version starred Warren William and Joan Blondell.

GOODBYE, MY FANCY. Fay Kanin's three-act comedy, which starred film actress Madeleine Carroll, opened at the Morosco Theatre on 17 November

1948 for 446 performances. Agatha Reid, a liberal Congresswoman, returns to Good Hope College for Women to receive an honorary degree. Her past engagement to the college's conservative president, James Merrill (Conrad Nagel) creates some awkwardness. When they were students at Good Hope, she had been expelled for covering up his misdeeds, but now he falls in love with her again. Unable to abide his politics, and annoyed at his attempts to prevent his liberal-minded daughter from pursuing her own dreams, she threatens to reveal the truth of her expulsion. Merrill relents and Agatha finds happiness with a magazine photographer. **Shirley Booth** was among the supporting cast, and she won a **Tony Award** as Best Supporting Actress. **Sam Wanamaker**, who was also in the cast, directed and DONALD OENSLAGER designed the settings and lights. Joan Crawford and Robert Young starred in a 1951 film version.

GOODMAN THEATRE AND SCHOOL.† Founded in 1925 as a memorial to Kenneth Sawyer Goodman,* a promising playwright of Chicago's art and literary renaissance of the 1910s who died of influenza while serving in the United States Navy in 1918, the theatre was built on Lake Shore Drive behind Chicago's Art Institute. The theatre, which also housed a drama school, was constructed underground, but its resident company thrived in productions of original plays and classics, opening its doors with the U.S. premiere of John Galsworthy's *The Forest*. The Great Depression forced the termination of the company in 1930, and the Goodman remained a drama school until the resident company was re-established in 1969. Led by **Robert Falls** and **Gregory Mosher**, the Goodman focused on new works and provided an early platform for the plays of Chicago dramatists **David Mamet** and **David Rabe**.

The Goodman school was uncoupled from the theatre in 1978 and shifted to DePaul University and the old theatre at the Art Institute was abandoned for a new state-of-the-art facility on N. Dearborn Street. Numerous Goodman productions have shifted from Chicago to **Broadway**, most notably their 1999 revival of **Arthur Miller's** *Death of a Salesman* starring **Brian Dennehy** in an acclaimed performance as Willy Loman. In recent years, the Goodman's annual season has included pre-Broadway tryouts for new works, including **Stephen Sondheim's** MUSICAL *Bounce* (2003).

GOODRICH, FRANCES (1890–1984) and **ALBERT HACKETT (1900– 1995).** This married team of playwrights and screenwriters collaborated for over 50 years. Goodrich was born in Belleville, New Jersey, and attended Vassar College, after which she pursued an acting career, appearing on **Broadway** in *Daddy Long Legs** (1918) and several other plays. After two failed marriages (including actor Robert Ames), Goodrich married Albert

Maurice Hackett, who had been born in New York and began his career as a child actor, continuing into adulthood, appearing on Broadway in *The Happy Marriage* (1909), *The Nervous Wreck** (1923), *Twelve Miles Out* (1925), and the MUSICAL *Whoopee!* (1928). They embarked on a long writing career in the 1920s, prior to their 1931 marriage. Hackett also appeared in their first writing collaboration on *Up Pops the Devil* (1930), after which both abandoned their acting careers to pursue their writing.

More frequently writing for films, Goodrich and Hackett occasionally wrote for Broadway, most notably **The Diary of Anne Frank** (1956), which brought them a PULITZER PRIZE and a **Tony Award**. They adapted the play for film in 1959, winning a Writers Guild Award. Their other Broadway plays include the libretto for *Everybody's Welcome* (1931), the musical version of *Up Pops the Devil*, *Bridal Wise* (1932), and *The Great Big Doorstep* (1942). For the movies, Goodrich and Hackett were nominated for Academy Awards for *The Thin Man* (1934), *After the Thin Man* (1936), *Father of the Bride* (1950), and *Seven Brides for Seven Brothers* (1954). They received Writers Guild Awards for *Easter Parade* (1948) in collaboration with Sidney Sheldon, *Father's Little Dividend* (1951), and *Seven Brides for Seven Brothers*. Their other screenplays include *Lady in the Dark* (1944), *It's a Wonderful Life* (1946), **The Pirate** (1948), *In the Good Old Summertime* (1949), and *Five Finger Exercise* (1962).

GORDON, MAX (1892–1978). This noted **Broadway** producer was born Mechel Salpeter in New York. In partnership with Albert Lewis, he began producing plays with the hit comedy *The Nervous Wreck** (1923). Among the other Lewis and Gordon productions, *The Jazz Singer** (1925) scored a hit. Gordon branched out on his own, becoming one of Broadway's most prolific producers from the mid-1920s to the mid-1950s. He produced a few films, but Gordon's taste associated him with some of the most successful and critically applauded plays and MUSICALS of the era, including among many others, *The Band Wagon* (1931), *Roberta* (1933), **Dodsworth** (1934), *The Great Waltz* (1934), *The Farmer Takes a Wife* (1934), *Pride and Prejudice* (1935), **Ethan Frome** (1936), **The Women** (1936), *Sing Out the News* (1938), *The American Way* (1939), *Very Warm for May* (1939), **My Sister Eileen** (1940), *The Land Is Bright* (1941), **Junior Miss** (1941), **The Doughgirls** (1942), **Over 21** (1944), **The Late George Apley** (1944), **Born Yesterday** (1946), **Years Ago** (1946), and **The Solid Gold Cadillac** (1953). Cole Porter, whose *Jubilee* (1935) Gordon produced, immortalized him in the lyrics of the song "Anything Goes": "When Rockefeller can still hoard enough/money to let Max Gordon/produce his shows, Anything Goes!"

GORDON, RUTH (1896–1985). Born Ruth Gordon Jones in Wollaston, Massachusetts, as the only child of a former ship captain and his wife, Gordon completed high school and saw actress Hazel Dawn in *The Pink Lady*. When Gordon received a letter from Dawn in reply to one she had written the star, it inspired Gordon to pursue an acting career. She attended the AMERICAN ACADEMY OF DRAMATIC ARTS and appeared in some silent films before debuting on **Broadway** as Nibs, a lost boy, in a 1915 revival of *Peter Pan** starring Maude Adams.* She scored a personal success in *Seventeen** (1918), costarring Gregory Kelly, whom she married in 1921 (they divorced in 1926). She subsequently appeared in numerous plays, initially in *Hotel Universe* (1930), *A Church Mouse* (1931), *Three-Cornered Moon* (1933), *They Shall Not Die* (1934), and *A Sleeping Clergyman* (1934). Gordon's acting career achieved distinction with her performances in *Ethan Frome* (1936), revivals of *The Country Wife* in 1936, *A Doll's House* in 1937, and *The Three Sisters* in 1942, costarring with KATHARINE CORNELL and **Judith Anderson** in the latter.

Gordon married playwright/director **Garson Kanin** in 1942, and she began writing scripts for stage and screen, sometimes with Kanin's collaboration. Her two hit plays, *Over 21* (1944), in which she appeared, and the autobiographical *Years Ago* (1946), in which **Fredric March** (who won a **Tony Award**) and **Florence Eldridge** played her parents, slowed her acting career, as she spent increasing amounts of time writing. She made periodic returns to Broadway, most notably as Dolly Gallagher Levi in **Thornton Wilder**'s *The Matchmaker* (1955), which brought her a Tony nomination, and *My Mother, My Father, and Me* (1963), her own play *A Very Rich Woman* (1965) in which she starred, *The Loves of Cass McGuire* (1966), *Dreyfus in Rehearsal* (1974), and a revival of *Mrs. Warren's Profession* in 1976.

On screen, Gordon was nominated for an Academy Award and won a Golden Globe Award for *Inside Daisy Clover* (1965) and won an Oscar and a Golden Globe for *Rosemary's Baby* (1968). Her other film appearances include playing Mary Todd Lincoln in *Abe Lincoln in Illinois* (1940), *Dr. Ehrlich's Magic Bullet* (1940), *Edge of Darkness* (1943), *Where's Poppa?* (1970), and her most memorable role, Maude, in the cult classic *Harold and Maude* (1971). She won a 1979 Emmy Award for a guest appearance on *Taxi* and was nominated three additional times. Among the film scripts she collaborated on with Kanin, Gordon was nominated for Academy Awards for *A Double Life* (1948), *Adam's Rib* (1949), and *Pat and Mike* (1952), the last two with her close friends, SPENCER TRACY and **Katharine Hepburn**. Tracy played Gordon's father in the film version of *Years Ago*, retitled *The Actress* (1953).

GORDONE, CHARLES (1925–1995). The first **African American** to win a PULITZER PRIZE for Drama, Gordone was born Charles Edward Fleming in Cleveland, Ohio. He studied at Los Angeles City College, California State University, New York University, and Columbia University. Following service in the United States Air Force, Gordone settled in New York and began acting in **Off-Broadway** productions, including a 1953 all-black revival of *Of Mice and Men* for which he won an **Obie Award**. During the 1950s, he continued acting, adding directing experiences, and he performed in Jean Genet's *The Blacks* (1961), after which he began to write, completing his first play *A Little More Light Around the Place* (1964). His play *No Place to Be Somebody* (1969), won the Pulitzer, a **Drama Desk Award**, the Los Angeles Drama Critics Circle Award, and the American Academy of Arts and Letters Award. None of Gordone's subsequent plays met with similar critical acclaim, but these include *Worl's Champeen Lip Dansuh an' Watah Mellon Jooglah* (1969), *Chumpanzee* (1970), *Willy Bignigga* (1970), *Gordone Is a Muthah* (1970), *Baba-Chops* (1975), *Under the Boardwalk* (1976), *The Last Chord* (1977), *A Qualification for Anabiosis* (1978), *The Block* (1983), and *Anabiosis* (1983). He also acted in a few films, including *Coonskin* (1975) and *Angel Heart* (1987).

GORELIK, MORDECAI (1899–1990).[†] Born in Russia, Gorelik came to the United States in his youth to study at the Pratt Institute and with several American designers, most notably ROBERT EDMOND JONES, NORMAN BEL GEDDES, and SERGE SOUDEIKINE. His first designs were on a modest scale for the **Provincetown Players** beginning in 1920, but he became one of **Broadway**'s most important scenic artists. He won attention for his design of *Processional** in 1925 and his work with the **Neighborhood Playhouse**, and when he joined **The Group Theatre** he designed **Sidney Kingsley**'s PULITZER PRIZE-winning drama *Men in White* (1933), as well as **Clifford Odets**'s *Golden Boy* (1937), *Rocket to the Moon* (1938), and *Night Music* (1940). After World WAR II, Gorelik's most notable designs were for **Arthur Miller**'s *All My Sons* (1947), **Michael Gazzo**'s *A Hatful of Rain* (1957), and others. Inspired by Adolphe Appia and Edward Gordon Craig, as well as **Bertolt Brecht**'s epic theatre, Gorelik also taught and wrote several books on theatrical art, including *New Theatres for Old* (1940).

GOTANDA, PHILIP KAN (1951–). Born in Stockton, California, this Japanese American playwright and filmmaker graduated from Hastings College with a degree in law and training in music, but has been a significant force in the evolution of **Asian American** theatre since the 1980s. His plays have been performed by Asian American companies and at the **New York Shakespeare Festival/Public Theatre, Manhattan Theatre Club,** and **Mark Taper Forum**. Gotanda's most acclaimed plays include *The Wash* (1987), which he also adapted for film, concerns a divorcing Japanese American couple. His most-produced work, *Yankee Dawg You Die* (1987), assails Hollywood stereotyping of Asians. He has written MUSICALS, including *Bullet Headed Birds (1981)*, family dramas such as *Fish Head Soup* (1991), and historical works such as *After the War* (2007), performed by the **American Conservatory Theatre**, which focused on the plight of Japanese Americans following their release from World WAR II internment camps. Other Gotanda plays include *Song of a Nisei Fisherman* (1980), *Day Standing on Its Head* (1993), *Ballad of Yachiyo* (1995), *Under the Rainbow* (2005), and *Yohen* (2006).

GOTTFRIED, MARTIN (1933–). New York-born and educated at Columbia University, Gottfried has had a long career as a drama CRITIC and author. He began writing music criticism for *The Village Voice* in 1961, followed by a long stint as theatre critic for *Women's Wear Daily* beginning in 1962. He ultimately moved in 1974 to the *New York Post* as senior drama critic, while also contributing to other periodicals. Gottfried has written a score of books on theatre, beginning with *A Theatre Divided* (1967), a study of post-World WAR II American drama, which won the George Jean Nathan Award, and he has written biographies of such theatre luminaries as **Arthur Miller,** JED HARRIS, **Stephen Sondheim**, Danny Kaye, **Angela Lansbury**, and Bob Fosse. His other books include *Opening Night* (1969) and *Broadway* MUSICALS (1979).

GOTTLIEB, MORTON (1921–2009). A native of Brooklyn, New York, Morton Edgar Gottlieb studied drama at Yale University prior to beginning his career as a press agent, moving up to production manager in STOCK. He began on **Broadway** as company manager of *Edward, My Son* (1948), moving up to the producing with *His and Hers* (1954). His many productions included *Enter Laughing* (1963), *The Killing of Sister George* (1966), *Lovers* (1968), *We Bombed in New Haven* (1968), *Sleuth* (1970), *Veronica's Room* (1973), *Same Time, Next Year* (1975), *Tribute* (1975), *Faith Healer* (1979), *Romantic Comedy* (1979), *Special Occasions* (1982), and *Dancing in the End Zone* (1985). Commenting on his own career, Gottlieb said, "The Broadway theatre is the only place in the world where the easiest way to break in is by starting at the top. You don't need experience, you don't need a license, you don't need money. All you need is chutzpah."

GRAND HOTEL. W. A. Drake's translation/adaptation of Vicki Baum's German novel opened on 13 November 1930 at the National Theatre for 459 performances in a **Herman Shumlin** production. Set in the Grand Hotel in Berlin, this 18-scene drama featured Eugenie Leontovich as Grusinskaia, a heartsick ballerina, and followed her story and those of a dying clerk (Sam Jaffe), a secretary, a ruthless businessman, and a jewel thief, among others. The play is rarely performed, but *Grand Hotel* has endured. It was famously adapted to the screen in 1932, winning the Academy Award as Best Picture, with an all-star cast including Greta Garbo, John Barrymore,* Lionel Barrymore,* Joan Crawford, and Wallace Beery. In 1989, it was adapted as a **Tony Award**-nominated **Broadway** MUSICAL by Luther Davis (libretto), Robert Wright (music and lyrics), and George Forrest (music) and ran for 1,017 performances.

GRAND MANNER, THE. **A. R. Gurney**'s semi-autobiographical play about a stagestruck schoolboy meeting legendary **Broadway** actress KATHARINE CORNELL and her theatrical inner circle, opened on 27 June 2010 at the Mitzi E. Newhouse Theatre at **Lincoln Center**. **Kate Burton** starred as "Kit" Cornell, dubbed by CRITIC Alexander Woollcott* as "The First Lady of the Theatre," seen here at a transition moment in her life and career, contending with her closeted **gay** husband and theatre director **Guthrie McClintic (Boyd Gaines)**, her own lesbian lover (Brenda Wehle), and an admiring schoolboy (Bobby Steggert) to whom she reveals more about her conflicted feelings about life, **sexuality**, and theatrical art than she initially intends. Gurney's play was based on his own meeting with Cornell when she was appearing in a 1947 revival of *Antony and Cleopatra*; his audience with the star was brief, but in the play, Gurney imagines what might have transpired if he had stayed longer. Directed by **Mark Lamos**, with scene designs by **John Arnone** and costumes by **Ann Hould-Ward**, the play opened to mixed reviews.

GRANDAGE, MICHAEL (1962–). Born in Yorkshire, England, Grandage was trained as an actor at the Central School of Speech and Drama and worked as an actor for a dozen years before turning to directing in 1996. Most of his work has been done in England, where he is artistic director of the Donmar Warehouse. Grandage won Olivier Awards for his directing of *Caligula* (2004), *Grand Hotel* (2004), and a 2006 revival of *Guys and Dolls*. On Broadway, he received a **Drama Desk Award** and a **Tony Award** nomination for *Frost/Nixon* (2007), and won the Tony for **John Logan**'s *Red* (2010). His other **Broadway** productions include revivals of *Mary Stuart, The Philanthropist*, and *Hamlet*, all in 2009.

GRAPES OF WRATH, THE. **Frank Galati** adapted and directed **John Steinbeck**'s 1939 PULITZER PRIZE-winning novel at **Steppenwolf Theatre** in 1988, with stops at San Diego's **La Jolla Playhouse** in 1989 and the Royal National Theatre in London prior to opening on **Broadway** at the Cort Theatre on 22 March 1990 for 188 performances, winning a **Tony Award** as Best Play and another for Galati's direction (he also won a **Drama Desk Award**), as well as a slew of nominations for cast members (Terry Kinney, **Gary Sinise, Lois Smith**) and designers (Kevin Rigdon, Erin Quigley). This much-honored production featured a cast of 41, a live band, and spare, evocative settings to recreate the story of the Joad family's struggle to survive the Great Depression, the Dust Bowl, and prejudice. Under Galati's direction, the production was filmed for television in 1991.

GRAY, SPALDING (1941–2004). Born Spalding Rockwell Gray in Providence, Rhode Island, this noted writer, monologist, and actor was educated at Emerson College before working as an actor. Joining **The Performance Group** in 1970, he worked with **Richard Schechner** until 1980, when he became a founding member of **The Wooster Group**. Influenced by the poetry of Allen Ginsberg, he wrote the autobiographical *Three Places in Rhode Island* between 1975 and 1978, with collaboration from **Elizabeth LeCompte**, and between 1979 and 2000 he wrote and performed 18 monologues also drawn from his own life experiences, most notably *Swimming to Cambodia* (1985), *Monster in a Box* (1991), *Gray's Anatomy* (1993), *It's a Slippery Slope* (1996), and *Morning, Noon, and Night* (1999), several of which he performed on **Broadway**. As an actor, he won acclaim playing the Stage Manager in the Wooster Group's revival of *Our Town* in 1988, appeared in a Broadway revival of *The Best Man* in 2000, and acted in numerous films. Gray battled depression for his entire life and following serious injuries in an auto accident that seemed to exacerbate his problems, he committed suicide.

GREAT WHITE HOPE, THE. **Howard Sackler**'s drama based on the life of **African American** boxer Jack Johnson won the **Tony Award** as Best Play when, following an initial 1967 run at Washington, D.C.'s **Arena Stage**, it opened on 3 October 1968 at the Alvin Theatre for 546 performances. Directed by **Edwin Sherin** with scene design by **Robin Wagner**, it won Tony and **Drama Desk Awards** for **James Earl Jones** and **Jane Alexander**. The play examined the rise and fall of the first black world heavyweight boxing champion as a result of racism and his relationship with a white woman in the 1910s. Jones and Alexander recreated their performances, and garnered Academy Award nominations, in a 1970 film version directed by Martin Ritt.

GREEN, ABEL (1900–1973). New York-born and educated at New York University, Green was hired by Sime Silverman* as a cub reporter for *VA-RIETY*, the theatrical trade newspaper, in 1918 and he rose to editor in 1933. In collaboration with Joe Laurie, Jr., Green wrote *Show Biz: From Vaude to Video* (1951), a chronicle of the stage, screen, and television era he knew intimately. His other books include *Inside Stuff on Popular Songs* (1927) and *The Spice of Variety* (1952). Green is credited with creating the short, pithy headlines ("Hix Nix Stix Pix") and slang typical of *Variety* in its mid-twentieth-century heyday. *See also* CRITICISM; PERIODICALS.

GREEN, PAUL (1894–1981).[†] Paul Eliot Green was born in Lillinton, North Carolina, and wrote many one-act plays beginning during his school-ing at the University of North Carolina, where he studied with Frederick Koch, and Cornell University. In 1926, Green's drama of racial conflict in the South, *In Abraham's Bosom,** received the PULITZER PRIZE. Green's leftist politics, evident in his plays, often focused on racial issues. From the mid-1920s to World WAR II, he wrote several critically applauded works, including *The Field God* (1927), **The House of Connelly** (1931), *Roll, Sweet Chariot* (1934), *Hymn to the Rising Sun* (1936), the libretto and lyrics for the antiwar MUSICAL **Johnny Johnson** (1936; with music by Kurt Weill), and a collaboration with **Richard Wright** on a stage adaptation of Wright's novel **Native Son** (1941). From 1937, when he wrote the first **outdoor drama** (or symphonic drama), the historical pageant *The Lost Colony* set on Roanoke Island, North Carolina), Green wrote others, including *The Common Glory* (1947), *The Founders* (1957), and *Cross and Sword* (1965), and taught drama at the University of North Carolina.

GREEN PASTURES, THE. Marc Connelly won a PULITZER PRIZE for this "fable" in 18 scenes, adapted from Roark Bradford's folk tales of **African American** life. It opened on 26 February 1930 for 644 performances at the Mansfield Theatre. Connelly also directed the original production, mixing traditional spiritual music with the story of a black minister in a small South-ern church teaching biblical history to a Sunday school class. Employing images of black life (much now deemed stereotypical), *The Green Pastures* pleased Depression-era audiences with its simple, childlike depiction of fa-miliar Bible tales and Christian values. Featuring an all-black cast, a rarity on **Broadway** in 1930, Rex Ingram starred as "De Lawd," whose entrance was announced by the angel Gabriel shouting, "Gangway! Gangway for de Lawd God Jehovah!" With the assistance of De Lawd, the minister recounted numerous Old Testament legends, including the stories of Adam and Eve in the Garden of Eden, Cain and Abel, Noah, and Moses, all leading to the climactic crucifixion of Jesus Christ. *The Green Pastures* was revived successfully in 1935, made into a hit film in 1936 (with Ingram repeating his role), and revived again in 1951, although its short run suggests that changing attitudes about race deemed images in the play as racist. *See also* RELIGIOUS DRAMA.

GREENBERG, RICHARD (1958–). Born in East Meadow, New York, Greenberg grew up on Long Island before attending Princeton University and completing an M.F.A. in Playwriting at the Yale School of Drama. A prolific and imaginative writer, Greenberg won a **Tony Award, New York Drama Critics Circle Award, Drama Desk Award,** and **Lucille Lortel** Award for *Take Me Out* (2003), a comedy-drama about the ramifications resulting from a major league baseball player announcing his **homosexuality.** Some of his early plays, including *The Bloodletters* (1984), *Life Under Water* (1985), *Vanishing Act* (1986), *The Author's Voice* (1987), *The Hunger Artist* (1987), *The Maderati* (1987), *Eastern Standard* (1988), *Neptune's Hips* (1988), *The American Plan* (1990; revised 2009), *The Extra Man* (1991), and *Jenny Keeps Talking* (1992), were produced in **regional theatres**. He revised the book of the MUSICAL *Pal Joey* for a 1992 revival, and his *Three Days of Rain* (1997), was nominated for a PULITZER PRIZE and won acclaim in a **Manhattan Theatre Club (MTC)** production. His subsequent plays, which have been produced at such theatres as the MTC and the **Roundabout Theatre,** including *Hurrah at Last* (1998), *The Dazzle* (2000), *Everett Beekin* (2000), *The Dance of Death* (2003), *The Violet Hour* (2003), *A Naked Girl on the Appian Way* (2005), *Bal Masque* (2006), *The Well-Appointed Room* (2006), *The House in Town* (2006), *The Injured Party* (2008), and *Our Mother's Brief Affair* (2009). Among the honors for his work, he is a recipient of the Oppenheimer Award and the first PEN/Laura Pels Award for a mid-career playwright. *See also* GAY AND LESBIAN THEATRE.

GREENSPAN, DAVID (1956–). This actor and playwright was educated at the University of California at Irvine, moved to New York in 1978, and studied at New Dramatists. He won **Obie Awards** for his performances in a revival of *The Boys in the Band* in 1996, *Some Men* in 2007, and *Faust, Parts I and II* in 2007. He has acted in a range of plays, classic and contemporary, at such theatres as the **New York Shakespeare Festival/Public Theatre, Second Stage, Classic Stage Company, Playwrights Horizons,** and **Primary Stages,** and **regional theatres** including **Hartford Stage.** He has received numerous foundation grants and fellowships, including a Guggenheim Foundation grant, for his playwriting, with such works as *The Horizontal and the Vertical* (1986), *Jack* (1987), *Dig a Hole and Bury Your*

Father (1987), *The Home Show Pieces* (1988), *Principia* (1988), *2 Samuel 11, Etc.* (1989), *Dead Mother, or Shirley Not All in Vain* (1991), *Dog in a Dancing School* (1993), *Trains Passing* (1993), *Son of an Engineer* (1993), *Start from Scratch* (1993), *Something's Gotta Give* (1993), *Them* (1999), *The Myopia* (2003), *She Stoops to Comedy* (2003), which won an Obie, *The Argument* (2007), *Aristophanes' The Frogs* (2008), and the MUSICAL *Coraline* (2009). *New York Times* critic **Charles Isherwood** described Greenspan as one of contemporary theatre's "glorious freaks."

GREENWOOD, JANE (1934–   ). This British-born costume designer whose designs have brought her 17 **Tony Award** nominations, was born in Liverpool and educated at London's Central School of Arts and Crafts. After designing for the Oxford Playhouse, she moved to Canada, but ultimately found her way to New York. Her first **Broadway** costume design, *The Ballad of the Sad Café* (1963), introduced her to her future husband, scene designer **Ben Edwards**. Her diverse credits include numerous classics and revivals, as well as *Incident at Vichy* (1964), *Where's Daddy?* (1966), *The Prime of Miss Jean Brodie* (1968), *The Seven Descents of Myrtle* (1968), *More Stately Mansions* (1968), *Les Blancs* (1970), *Wise Child* (1972), *Same Time, Next Year* (1975), *A Matter of Gravity* (1976), *California Suite* (1976), *A Texas Trilogy* (1976), *Vieux Carré* (1977), *Romantic Comedy* (1979), *The West Side Waltz* (1981), *Plenty* (1983), *Lillian* (1986), *The Secret Rapture* (1989), *I Hate Hamlet* (1991), *Park Your Car in Harvard Yard* (1991), *The Sisters Rosensweig* (1993), *Passion* (1994), *Master Class* (1995), *The Last Night of Ballyhoo* (1997), *An American Daughter* (1997), *The Dinner Party* (2000), *The Violet Hour* (2003), and *Thurgood* (2008).

Among the many revivals she has designed, Greenwood won particular praise for *Hay Fever* in 1971, *Medea* in 1982, *Heartbreak House* in 1984 and 2007, *The Iceman Cometh* in 1986, *Our Town* in 1989, *She Loves Me* in 1994, *The Heiress* in 1995, *A Delicate Balance* in 1996, *Morning's at Seven* in 2002, *Who's Afraid of Virginia Woolf?* in 2005, and *Waiting for Godot* and *Brighton Beach Memoirs* in 2009. Greenwood was presented with the **Irene Sharaff** Lifetime Achievement Award in 1998, and she was inducted into the **Theatre Hall of Fame** in 2004. She had also designed several films, including *The Four Seasons* (1981), *Arthur* (1981), *Sweet Liberty* (1986), *Glengarry Glen Ross* (1993), and *Oleanna* (1994), and television productions, including the **Richard Burton** *Hamlet* in 1964, which she had designed on Broadway.

GREGORY, ANDRE (1934–   ). Born in New York and educated at Harvard University, Gregory has had a successful career as an actor, director, and producer in both avant-garde and mainstream theatre and film circles, beginning **Off-Broadway** in the late 1950s. He spent time in Poland studying the techniques of Jerzy Grotowski. Gregory's directing won critical attention at The Writer's Stage in the early 1960s, after which he established The Manhattan Project (TMP), winning an **Obie** and **Drama Desk Award** for his direction of *Alice in Wonderland* (1970). At TMP, which was made up of six actors, he also directed the company's radically staged revivals of *Endgame* (1973) and *The Seagull* (1975), and *Jinx's Bridge* (1976). These productions inspired critical debate and Gregory largely left the theatre in 1975 for film work, but he has occasionally returned to the stage, most notably for a production of **David Mamet**'s adaptation of *Uncle Vanya*, which he spent nearly four years (1990–1994) developing, a process subsequently filmed as *Vanya on 42nd Street* by Louis Malle. Gregory also directed **Wallace Shawn**'s *The Designated Mourner* (2002). As an actor, Gregory appeared on Broadway in *Rumors* (1988) and the following year played Prospero in *The Tempest* with Boston's **Shakespeare** & Company. In films, he notably costarred with Shawn in *My Dinner With Andre* (1981) playing himself, but has also appeared in *Protocol* (1984), *The Mosquito Coast* (1986), *The Last Temptation of Christ* (1988), and *Celebrity* (1998).

GREIF, MICHAEL (1958–). Born in Brooklyn, New York, Greif completed an M.F.A. in directing at the University of California, San Diego in 1985 and began his career as assistant director of the **Broadway** production of *Sleight of Hand* (1987). In 1991, Greif won an **Obie Award** directing a revival of *Machinal** **Off-Broadway** and he staged the 1994 premiere of Jonathan Larson's MUSICAL *Rent* for the **New York Theatre Workshop**, winning another Obie and, ultimately, a **Tony Award** nomination when *Rent* moved to Broadway in 1996. From 1995–1999, Greif served as artistic director of **La Jolla Playhouse**, bringing their 1995 revival of *How to Succeed in Business without Really Trying* and 2000 productions of a musical version of *Jane Eyre* and *The Green Bird* to Broadway, as well as staging the premieres of **Tony Kushner**'s *Slavs!* (1995) and Diana Son's *Boy* (1996). He won a third Obie for *Dogeaters* (2001) after leaving La Jolla, and has also directed *Never Gonna Dance* (2003), the musical *Grey Gardens* (2006), which brought him a Tony nomination, and *Next to Normal* (2009), which brought him another Tony nomination. In 2009, he directed the premiere of Kushner's *The Intelligent Homosexual's Guide to Capitalism and Socialism with a Key to the Scriptures* (2009) at the **Guthrie Theatre**.

GRIEBLING, OTTO (1896–1972). This much-loved clown was born in Koblenz, Germany, and had a long career in American CIRCUS from his arrival in the United States in 1910. He began his career as an equestrian, but an injury in 1930 forced him to reinvent himself as a silent clown. He performed with the Hagenbeck-Wallace Circus and the Cole Brothers Circus, but ultimately joined Ringling Bros. and Barnum & Bailey Circus in 1951. His popularity rivaled the most famous American clown of the period, tramp-clown **Emmet Kelly**. While Kelly played the sad clown in the tradition of Pierrot, Griebling, also adopting the persona of a tramp, was a happy clown and made use of props from a steadily melting block of ice to a plant that grows into a tree to amuse his audiences. Griebling made his last appearance at Madison Square Garden in 1970, little more than a year before his death.

GRIFFIES, ETHEL (1878–1975). Born Ethel Woods in Sheffield, England, Griffies had a remarkably long career on stage and in films and television, making her debut as a child in 1881 and continuing to 1967. On **Broadway**, Griffies appeared in such plays as *Old English* (1924) with George Arliss,* *The Criminal Code** (1929), *The Druid Circle* (1947), *The Hallams* (1948), *The Leading Lady* (1948), *The Shop at Sly Corner* (1949), the Irving Berlin musical *Miss Liberty* (1949), *Legend of Sarah* (1950), a revival of *The Royal Family** in 1951, ***The Autumn Garden*** (1951), *Write Me a Murder* (1961), *A Very Rich Woman* (1965), a 1966 revival of *Ivanov* with John Gielgud and Vivien Leigh, and *The Natural Look* (1967). She acted in over 90 films, including two with Arliss, *Old English* (1930) and *The Millionaire* (1931), *Waterloo Bridge** (1931 and 1940), *Love Me Tonight* (1932), *Alice in Wonderland* (1933), *Anna Karenina* (1935), *A Yank in the R.A.F.* (1941), *How Green Was My Valley* (1941), *Saratoga Trunk* (1945), *The Birds* (1963), and *Bus Riley's Back in Town* (1965). From its earliest days, Griffies occasionally appeared on TV.

GRIMES, TAMMY (1934–). Born in Lynn, Massachusetts, as Tammy Lee Grimes, this versatile actress studied at Stephens College and THE NEIGH-BORHOOD PLAYHOUSE. She began her **Broadway** career as **Kim Stanley**'s understudy in ***Bus Stop*** (1955) and **Off-Broadway** in *The Littlest Revue* (1956). When **Noël Coward** saw her perform in a nightclub, he cast her in his play *Look After Lulu* (1959), which won her a **Theatre World Award**. A **Tony Award** followed for the MUSICAL *The Unsinkable Molly Brown* (1960). She won a second Tony and a **Drama Desk Award** for a revival of Coward's *Private Lives* (1969) and costarred in the musical adaptation of Coward's *Blithe Spirit*, renamed *High Spirits* (1964), with Beatrice Lillie. On Broadway, Grimes has also appeared in *Rattle of a Simple Man* (1963), *The Only Game in Town* (1968), *A Musical Jubilee* (1975), *California Suite* (1976), a revival of *Tartuffe* in 1977, *Trick* (1979), *42nd Street* (1980), and a 1989 revival of *Orpheus Descending*. Off-Broadway and in **regional theatre**, Grimes appeared in *Father's Day* (1979) and *Paducah* (1985) at the **American Place Theatre**, Simon Gray's *Molly* in 1982 at the **Long Wharf Theatre**, *A Month in the Country* in 1979 at the **Roundabout Theatre**, and *Over My Dead Body* in 1984 at the Hartman Theatre. She also appeared for several years with the Stratford Festival of Canada and in 2003 was inducted into the **Theatre Hall of Fame**. Grimes also appeared in films, including *The Runner Stumbles* (1979), *Can't Stop the Music* (1980), *Mr. North* (1988), *High Art* (1998), and television, including her own short-lived TV series in 1966. Grimes was married to **Christopher Plummer** and is the mother of actress **Amanda Plummer**.

GRIZZARD, GEORGE (1928–2007). This versatile **Broadway**, film, and television actor was born in Roanoke Rapids, North Carolina, and studied at the University of North Carolina at Chapel Hill and, once in New York following a brief advertising career, he studied acting with **Sanford Meisner**. He debuted on Broadway in *The Desperate Hours* (1955). Grizzard won a **Theatre World Award** for *The Happiest Millionaire* in 1957 and was nominated for **Tony Awards** for *The Disenchanted* (1959), *Big Fish, Little Fish* (1961), and won a Tony for a 1996 revival of **Edward Albee**'s *A Delicate Balance*. He demonstrated a particular affinity for Albee's plays, appearing in *Who's Afraid of Virginia Woolf?* (1962) and a 2005 revival of *Seascape* as well.

Grizzard also appeared on Broadway in *Face of a Hero* (1960), a revival of *The Glass Menagerie* in 1965, *You Know I Can't Hear You When the Water's Running* (1967), *Noël Coward's Sweet Potato* (1968), *The Gingham Dog* (1969), *Inquest* (1970), a revival of *The Country Girl* in 1972, *The Creation of the World and Other Business* (1972), *Crown Matrimonial* (1973), a revival of *The Royal Family** in 1975, *California Suite* (1976), a revival of *Man and Superman* in 1978, and *Judgment at Nuremberg* (2001). **Off-Broadway**, Grizzard acted in *The Gingham Dog* (1969) and *Regrets Only* (2006), and appeared in numerous repertory productions, including playing Hamlet in the **Guthrie Theatre**'s first production in 1963. Grizzard acted in many films, including *Advise & Consent* (1962), *Happy Birthday, Wanda June* (1971), *Comes a Horseman* (1978), *Seems Like Old Times* (1980), and *Flags of Our Fathers* (2006), and numerous television programs, winning an Emmy Award for *The Oldest Living Graduate*, one of the plays in *A Texas Trilogy*, in 1980.

GROSBARD, ULU (1929–). Born in Antwerp, Belgium, Grosbard, a theatre and film director, lived in Cuba beginning in 1942 before moving to the United States in 1948, where he studied at the University of Chicago and the Yale School of Drama prior to entering the U.S. Army and becoming a naturalized American citizen in 1954. As a director, he debuted **Off-Broadway** with *The Days and Nights of Beebee Fenstemaker* (1962). On **Broadway**, he was **Tony Award**-nominated for *The Subject Was Roses* (1964), which he also directed in its 1968 film version, and he won an **Obie Award** and a **Drama Desk Award** for an Off-Broadway revival of **Arthur Miller**'s *A View from the Bridge* in 1965. Grosbard directed Miller's *The Price* (1968) and received Tony and Drama Desk nominations for *American Buffalo* (1977). His other Broadway directing credits include Peter Weiss's *The Investigation* (1966), which he also translated, *That Summer—That Fall* (1967), *The Floating Light Bulb* (1981), *The Wake of Jamey Foster* (1982), and a revival of *The Tenth Man* (1989). Off-Broadway, Grosbard also staged *Weekends Like Other People* (1982). Grosbard also served as assistant director on several films in the 1960s prior to directing several himself, including *Who Is Harry Kellerman and Why Is He Saying Those Terrible Things about Me?* (1971), *Straight Time* (1978), *True Confessions* (1981), *Falling in Love* (1984), *Georgia* (1995), and *The Deep End of the Ocean* (1999).

GROUP THEATRE, THE. This profoundly influential theatre company, founded in 1931 by **Harold Clurman**, **Lee Strasberg**, and **Cheryl Crawford**, responded to the social issues of the 1930s and the Great Depression as no other American theatre entity managed with the exception of the **Federal Theatre Project**. Its most lasting impact has been the widespread acceptance of acting techniques based in those of the Moscow Art Theatre* and its director, **Constantin Stanislavsky**. The Group would ultimately splinter in part over disagreements in interpreting Stanislavsky's principles, with the result that several of The Group's members taught their own individual approaches based in Stanislavsky, including most notably Strasberg and **Stella Adler**, a leading actress with The Group.

Its membership and those involved with individual Group productions, included **Morris Carnovsky**, Phoebe Brand, **Sanford Meisner**, Art Smith, Ruth Nelson, **Luther Adler**, **Lee J. Cobb**, **Robert Lewis**, Roman Bohnen, Margaret Barker, **John Garfield**, **Elia Kazan**, **Franchot Tone**, Sam Jaffe, Frances Farmer, Sidney Lumet, J. Edward Bromberg, **Burgess Meredith**, Martin Ritt, Sylvia Sidney, Karl Malden, Charles Bickford, **Howard Da Silva**, Russell Collins, Leif Erickson, Van Heflin, designers MORDECAI GORELIK and BORIS ARONSON, and playwright **Clifford Odets**, whose finest plays were written for The Group, including *Awake and Sing!* (1935), *Waiting for Lefty* (1935), *Till the Day I Die* (1935), *Paradise Lost* (1935), *Golden Boy* (1937), *Rocket to the Moon* (1938), and others.

Between The Group's founding in 1931 and its demise in 1940, it generated 22 new American plays, including among them PAUL GREEN's *The House of Connelly* (1931), **Maxwell Anderson**'s *Night Over Taos* (1932), **Sidney Kingsley's** PULITZER PRIZE-winning *Men in White* (1933), **John Howard Lawson**'s *Success Story* (1932), **Erwin Piscator** and Lena Goldschmidt's adaptation of Theodore Dreiser's *The American Tragedy* renamed *Case of Clyde Griffiths* (1936), Green and Kurt Weill's *Johnny Johnson* (1937), **Irwin Shaw**'s *The Gentle People* (1939), and **William Saroyan**'s *My Heart's in the Highlands* (1939).

GUARE, JOHN (1938–). A New York-born playwright educated at Georgetown University and Yale School of Drama, Guare won an **Obie Award** for one of his earliest plays, *Muzeeka* (1968). He also won the **New York Drama Critics Circle Award** for *The House of Blue Leaves* (1971)— and its revival in 1986 won four **Tony Awards**. Guare also won Tony, **Drama Desk Award**, and the New York Drama Critics Circle Award for his libretto for the MUSICAL *Two Gentlemen of Verona* (1971) and an Obie, New York Drama Critics Circle Award, and England's Olivier Award for *Six Degrees of Separation* (1990).

Guare's other plays include *Cop-Out* (1969), *Rich and Famous* (1974), *Landscape of the Body* (1977), which was Drama Desk-nominated, *Marco Polo Sings a Solo* (1977), *Bosoms and Neglect* (1979), *Lydie Breeze* (1982), *Gardenia* (1982), *Women and Water* (1990), *Four Baboons Adoring the Sun* (1992), which was nominated for a Tony, *Lake Hollywood* (1999), *Chaucer in Rome* (2001), *A Few Stout Individuals* (2002), and the libretto for *Sweet Smell of Success* (2002), which was nominated for a Tony and a Drama Desk Award. New York's **Signature Theatre** devoted a season to honoring Guare's work in 1998–1999 and, in 2010, **Jeffrey Wright** was announced for the leading role in Guare's *Free Man of Color*, a play set in 1801 New Orleans, in its **Broadway** premiere.

Guare was elected to membership in the American Academy and Institute of Arts and Letters in 1989, inducted into the **Theatre Hall of Fame** in 1993, and won a PEN/Laura Pels Foundation Award in 2003. Guare has written for film, most notably the screenplay for Louis Malle's *Atlantic City* (1980), which brought him an Academy Award nomination and a New York Film Critics Association Award. Of Guare's work, Malle wrote that Guare "practices a humor that is synonymous with lucidity, exploding genre and clichés, taking us to the core of human suffering: the awareness of corruption in our own bodies, death circling in. We try to fight it all by creating various mythologies, and it is Guare's peculiar aptitude for exposing these grandiose lies of ours that makes his work so magical."

GUERNSEY, OTIS LOVE, JR. (1918–2001). This drama critic and editor was born in New York and studied at Yale University. He worked at the *New York Herald Tribune* from 1941–1960, sometimes as drama or film CRITIC. He edited and was theatre critic for *Show Magazine* (1963–1964), edited the *Dramatists Guild Quarterly* from 1964–1994, and was a founding member of the **American Theatre Critics Association**. His most significant contribution was taking over from **Henry Hewes** as editor of the *Best Play* Series from 1965–2000. Guernsey also wrote several books, including *Directory of the American Theatre* (1971), *Playwrights, Lyricists, Composers on Theatre* (1974), ***Broadway: Song & Story*** (1986), and *Curtain Time* (1987).

GUNN, MOSES (1929–1993). A St. Louis, Missouri, native, Gunn left his family at age 12 following his mother's death. He enlisted in the United States Army in 1954, after which he attended Tennessee State University and the University of Kansas before teaching and Grambling College and beginning an acting career. He was a cofounder of the **Negro Ensemble Company**, winning a 1968 **Obie Award** for his **Off-Broadway** work, which included Jean Genet's *The Blacks* (1962), *In White America* (1963), and *Sky of the Blind Pig* (1971), among others. Gunn was nominated for a **Tony Award** for *The Poison Tree* (1976). Gunn played Othello on **Broadway** for the **American Shakespeare Festival** in 1970. His other Broadway appearances were in *A Hand in on the Gate* (1966), as Orsino in **Ellis Rabb**'s production of *Twelfth Night* (1972), *The First Breeze of Summer* (1975), and he stepped into the role of Martin Luther King, Jr. in *I Have a Dream* (1976). In film, Gunn appeared in ***The Great White Hope*** (1970), *Shaft* (1971), *Remember My Name* (1978), *Ragtime* (1981), and *Heartbreak Ridge* (1986). On television, Gunn was nominated for an Emmy Award for his performance in the mini-series *Roots* (1977). *See also* AFRICAN AMERICAN THEATRE.

GURNEY, A. R., JR. (1930–). Born in Buffalo, New York, as Albert Ramsdell Gurney, Jr., he was educated at Williams College and the Yale School of Drama. He took a job teaching humanities at the Massachusetts Institute of Technology and began writing novels and plays. Among Gurney's plays, ***The Dining Room*** (1981) and *Love Letters* (1988), which was nominated for a PULITZER PRIZE, are best known. His over 40 other plays include *Love in Buffalo* (1958), *The Rape of Bunny Stuntz* (1966), *The Golden Fleece* (1968), *Scenes from American Life* (1970), *What I Did Last Summer* (1975), *Who Killed Richard Cory?* (1976), *The Middle Ages* (1977), *The Golden Age* (1981), *Another Antigone* (1987), *The Cocktail Hour* (1988), *Sylvia* (1995), *Ancestral Voices* (1999), *Buffalo Gal* (2001), *Screen Play* (2005), *Post Mortem* (2006), *Indian Blood* (2006), *Crazy Mary* (2007), and *A Light Lunch*

(2008). In 2010, Gurney's *The Grand Manner*, directed by **Mark Lamos,** played a limited engagement at **Lincoln Center,** with a cast including **Kate Burton** as KATHARINE CORNELL and **Boyd Gaines** as GUTHRIE MCCLINTIC. Gurney has written of his hometown (also Cornell's) that "I was bitten by the theatre bug in Buffalo at an early age and have remained infected ever since."

GUSSOW, MEL (1933–2005). A New York native of Jewish Lithuanian heritage, he was born Melvyn Hayes Gussow and educated at Middlebury College and Columbia University, where he received an M.A. in journalism. After a stint in the United States Army, he became a theatre and film CRITIC for *Newsweek* in 1962. He joined the staff of the *New York Times* in 1969 and continued until shortly before his death, writing in excess of 4,000 reviews and articles for the paper. He won particular praise for his astute writing about twentieth-century American and European drama. Gussow wrote a biography of **Edward Albee** and published books of his interviews with **Arthur Miller,** Samuel Beckett, Harold Pinter, and **Tom Stoppard**. In 2008, he was posthumously inducted into the **Theatre Hall of Fame**.

GUTHRIE THEATRE. Named for Sir **Tyrone Guthrie**, who directed the theatre's first production, *Hamlet*, in 1963, the Guthrie Theatre was established by Oliver Rea, **Peter B. Zeisler**, and Guthrie with the goal of creating a permanent **repertory** company away from New York City, until that time the center of American theatre. In 1959, with the support of the Walker Art Center in Minneapolis, Minnesota, who supplied a $400,000 grant, Guthrie and designer **Tanya Moiseiwitsch** planned an asymmetrical arena/thrust space seating over 1,400 people completed in time for the 1963 opening. Guthrie seasons were typically a mix of classics, modern European and American drama, and occasional new works. Ultimately, the company mounted tours, offered educational programs, and grew in size and scope, also providing a **regional theatre** model followed by many other companies forming after the mid-1960s. In 2006, under the guidance of artistic director Joe Dowling, the Guthrie moved to a new multistage complex on the Mississippi River. In 2009, the Guthrie staged a festival in honor of playwright **Tony Kushner**, which included a premiere of Kushner's latest play, *The Intelligent Homosexual's Guide to Capitalism and Socialism with a Key to the Scriptures*, and included productions of Kushner's other plays, symposia and speakers, including Kushner himself.

GUTHRIE, TYRONE (1900–1971). This celebrated British director, born in Tunbridge Wells, Kent, studied at Oxford University and began his career at the Oxford Playhouse. After a long, distinguished career in England and

Canada, in 1953, he helped establish the Stratford Festival of Canada, working closely with **Tanya Moiseiwitsch** to design a **Shakespeare** Theatre for the festival, a process they repeated in founding (along with **Peter B. Zeisler** and Oliver Rea) the **Guthrie Theatre** in Minneapolis, Minnesota, a repertory theatre that became a prototype for the **regional theatre** movement in the United States. In 1963, Guthrie directed *Hamlet* as the Guthrie Theatre's first production. The theatre has thrived. He authored two books, *Theatre Prospect* (1932) and *A Life in the Theatre* (1959), largely based on lectures he had given. Guthrie was knighted in 1961.

GUTIERREZ, GERALD (1950–2003). Born in Brooklyn, New York, Gutierrez trained at the Juilliard School and developed a successful directing career, although he acted on **Broadway** in **The Acting Company** revivals of *Edward II, The Time of Your Life*, and *The Three Sisters* (in which he understudied two roles) in 1975. Following some initial experiences directing for the **McCarter Theatre** and other **regional theatres**, he staged **Off-Broadway** productions of *Geniuses* (1982), *The Rise and Rise of Daniel Rocket* (1983), and he was nominated for a **Drama Desk Award** for *Isn't It Romantic?* (1984). On Broadway, Gutierrez was Drama Desk-nominated for a 1992 revival of *The Most Happy Fella*, a **Tony Award** for a 1993 revival of *Abe Lincoln in Illinois*, and won Tony and Drama Desk Awards for revivals of *The Heiress* in 1995 and *A Delicate Balance* in 1996. He directed the original works *The Curse of the Aching Heart* (1982) and *Honour* (1998), but the remainder of his Broadway productions were intelligently interpreted, lovingly staged revivals, including *Little Johnny Jones* in 1982, *White Liars & Black Comedy* in 1993, *Once Upon a Mattress* in 1996, *Ivanov* in 1997, *Ring Round the Moon* in 1999, and *Dinner at Eight* in 2002. Gutierrez also directed a few television movies.

H

HACKETT, ALBERT (1900–1995). *See* GOODRICH, FRANCES.

HAGAN, JAMES P. (1888–1947). After a successful career in journalism in St. Louis, Hagan (sometimes billed as Hagen) decided to write for the stage. To learn the craft, he did some acting, including appearing on **Broadway** in *The Faith Healer** (1910), a revival of *If I Were King* (1916), *The Great Divide** (1917), *Molière* (1919), *The Letter of the Law* (1920), in a season of **Shakespeare**an roles with E. H. Sothern* and Julia Marlowe,* *Fashions for Men* (1922), *The Potters** (1923), and *Collision* (1932). Hagan also stage-managed for producer ARTHUR HOPKINS and his best-known plays were *Guns* (1928), one of Broadway's earliest gangster plays, *One Sunday Afternoon* (1933), *Mid-West* (1936), and *Here Come the Clowns* (1938).

HAGEDORN, JESSICA (1949–). A Filipino American born in Manila as Jessica Tarahata Hagedorn studied at the **American Conservatory Theatre** and settled in New York in the 1970s as a playwright and actor. Inspired by historical questions of the relationship of **race** and gender/**sexuality**, she makes use of poetry, dialogue, music, and multimedia visual images to explore these themes. Hagedorn's style was influenced by playwright/actress **Ntozake Shange** during Hagedorn's time in the original cast of *for colored girls who have considered suicide/when the rainbow is enuf* in 1974. With Shange and Thulani Davis, she created *When the Mississippi Meets the Amazon* (1977), which was performed at the **New York Shakespeare Festival/ Public Theatre**. Her other works include *Tenement Lover* (1981), *Airport Music* (1994), and *Dogeaters* (1998), which was staged at San Diego's **La Jolla Playhouse**. *See also* ASIAN AMERICAN THEATRE.

HAGEN, UTA (1919–2004). This German American acting legend and teacher was born in Göttingen, Germany, emigrated to the United States in childhood, and began her career at the age of 17 playing Ophelia to EVA LE GALLIENNE's Hamlet in 1937 on tour as a result of writing the great actress a letter asking for an audition. Hagen had an equally auspicious **Broadway**

debut in 1938 as Nina in *The Seagull* playing opposite ALFRED LUNT and LYNN FONTANNE, with *New York Times* critic BROOKS ATKINSON enthusing that Hagen was "grace and aspiration incarnate." Her next appearance in Charlotte Armstrong's flop, *The Happiest Days* (1939), did not advance her career, but it freed her to appear in MAXWELL ANDERSON's *Key Largo* (1939). Following a brief run in the farce *Vickie* (1942), Hagen was cast as Desdemona to PAUL ROBESON's Othello and **José Ferrer**'s Iago in an acclaimed 1943 revival of *Othello*, continuing in it until the summer of 1945. Hagen and Ferrer had married in 1938, but she had an affair with Robeson and she and Ferrer were divorced a decade later.

Hagen acted in the short-lived *The World Over* (1947) prior to taking on the role of Blanche DuBois opposite **Anthony Quinn**'s Stanley Kowalski in the national tour of *A Streetcar Named Desire* from 1947 to 1950, with an interruption of several months in 1948 when she returned to **Broadway** to play Mrs. Manningham in **Angel Street** (1948). In 1947, Hagen began teaching at the HB Studio in New York, which was founded by **Herbert Berghof** (a decade later, they married and remained so until his death in 1990).

Despite continuing her acting career, Hagen became a devoted teacher of acting, utilizing her own approach to the theories of **Constantin Stanislavsky**, as was true of the other major American acting teachers of her time, including **Lee Strasberg**, STELLA ADLER, **Robert Lewis, Sanford Meisner**, and others. She especially rejected Strasberg's dependence on emotional memory and became one of the most admired and sought-after teachers of acting in New York. While teaching, Hagen worked sporadically as an actor, including originating the role of Georgie Elgin in **Clifford Odets**'s *The Country Girl* (1950), which brought her a **Tony Award**, and other Broadway productions, including revivals of *Saint Joan* in 1951 and *Tovarich* in 1952, three short-lived original plays, *In Any Language* (1952), *The Magic and the Loss* (1954), and *Island of Goats* (1955), and two 1956 revivals: *A Month in the Country* and *The Good Person of Setzuan*.

As foul-mouthed, alcoholic Martha in **Edward Albee**'s *Who's Afraid of Virginia Woolf?* (1962), Hagen won critical acclaim and a Tony in what was regarded as one of the finest performances of her career. She only returned to Broadway for three brief runs, in revivals of *The Cherry Orchard* in 1968 and *You Never Can Tell* in 1986 and the short-lived *Charlotte* (1980), directed by Berghof. **Off-Broadway**, Hagen received a 1996 **Drama Desk Award** nomination for her performance in *Mrs. Klein* and appeared in *Collected Stories* (1998).

In 2001, she appeared at Los Angeles's Geffen Playhouse in *Six Dance Lessons in Six Weeks*. Due to the McCarthy-era blacklist, Hagen's film work was limited to the last phase of her career with character roles in *The Other* (1972), *The Boys from Brazil* (1978), *A Doctor's Story* (1984), *Reversal of Fortune* (1990), and she narrated *Limón: A Life beyond Words* (2001). On television, Hagen appeared occasionally, including receiving two Daytime Emmy Award nominations, in 1986 for the soap opera *One Life to Live* and in 1988 for the *ABC Afterschool Special: Seasonal Differences*. She also appeared in an episode of *Oz* in 1999. Hagen was elected to the **Theatre Hall of Fame** in 1981, received a **Lucille Lortel Award** (1995) and a Tony (1999) for lifetime achievement, and President George W. Bush presented her with the National Medal of the Arts in 2002. Hagen published two books on her theories on acting, *Respect for Acting* (1973) and *A Challenge for the Actor* (1991), widely considered essential reading.

HAILEY, OLIVER (1932–1993). A native of Pampa, Texas, Hailey worked as a journalist for the *Dallas Morning News* before becoming a playwright and television writer. He won a **Drama Desk Award** for his play *Hey You, Light Man!* (1963), but all of his **Broadway** efforts, *First One Asleep, Whistle* (1966), *Father's Day* (1971), and *I Won't Dance* (1981), folded after a single performance. His other plays include *Child's Play: A Comedy for Orphans* (1962), *Home By Hollywood* (1964), *Animal* (1965), *Picture* (1965), *Kith and Kin* (1966), *Who's Happy Now?* (1967), *Crisscross* (1969), *Orphan* (1970), *Continental Divide* (1970), *For the Use of the Hall* (1974), *And Furthermore* (1977), *Red Rover, Red Rover* (1977), *Triptych* (1978), *I Can't Find It Anywhere* (1979), *And Baby Makes Two* (1981), *About Time* (1982), and *Round Trip* (1984). In collaboration with Marilyn Cantor Baker, he won a Writers Guild of America Award for *Sidney Shorr: A Girl's Best Friend* (1981), which also brought an Emmy nomination and led to a short-lived television series, the first to feature an openly **gay** man, played by **Tony Randall**, as the central character. He also wrote for episodic television, and his only theatrical film was *Just You and Me, Kid* (1979).

HAIMES, TODD (1956–). Manhattan-born Haimes attended Yale University and came armed with an M.B.A. to the **Roundabout Theatre Company** in 1986 where he reversed the company's financial woes, becoming its artistic director in 1990. By the end of the decade, Haimes had led the Roundabout to its status as the second-largest theatre operation in the United States. Under Haimes's leadership, the Roundabout has reaped **Tony Awards** and **Drama Desk Awards**, as well as nominations, for a number of revivals (such as *Cabaret* in 1998) and new works (*Side Man* [1999]) of classics, MUSICALS, and occasional original works. *See also* REPERTORY THEATRE.

HALL, ADRIAN (1928–). Born in Van, Texas, Hall studied at the Texas State Teacher's College, **Pasadena Playhouse**, and with **Lee Strasberg** prior to directing **Off-Broadway** and in **regional theatre**. He was a founder of the **Trinity Repertory Theatre** in Providence, Rhode Island, in 1964, serving as its artistic director until 1989, during which the theatre won the 1981 **Tony Award** Regional Theatre Award. In 1983, he also took over artistic directorship of the **Dallas Theatre Center**. The plays and innovative production approaches he presented have often generated controversy, whether the choices involve using cross-gender and cross-racial casting or presenting plays in non-traditional spaces or styles. His Off-Broadway revival of *As You Like it* in 1993 brought him a **Drama Desk Award** nomination, and he also directed Off-Broadway and regional theatre productions of *Orpheus Descending* in 1959, *The Grass Harp* in 1966, *Two Gentlemen of Verona* in 1994, **F. Murray Abraham** in *King Lear* in 1996, and, for New York's 29th Street Repertory, *In the Belly of The Beast* (2004). On **Broadway**, Hall has directed *Wilson in the Promised Land* (1970), *The Suicide* (1980), *The Hothouse* (1982), and *On the Waterfront* (1995). Hall also teaches at the University of Delaware.

HALL, PETER (1930–). Born in Bury St. Edmunds, Suffolk, England, as Peter Reginald Frederick Hall, he founded the Royal **Shakespeare** Company in 1960 and took over the artistic directorship of the National Theatre of Great Britain from **Laurence Olivier** in 1973, continuing in that position until 1988. Most of his work as a director has been done in England, but he has either exported productions or staged a few directly for **Broadway**, most notably winning **Tony Awards** for *The Homecoming* (1967) and *Amadeus* (1981), and Tony nominations for *The Rope Dancers* (1958), *Old Times* (1972), *Bedroom Farce* (1979), *The Merchant of Venice* (1990), *Four Baboons Adoring the Sun* (1992), and *An Ideal Husband* (1996). Hall also won **Drama Desk Awards** for *Old Times* and *Amadeus* and Drama Desk nominations for *Saturday Sunday Monday* (1975) and *Bedroom Farce*. In 2009, Hall remained at work directing *Pygmalion* for the Hong Kong Arts Festival.

HALLIDAY, JOHN (1880–1947). The actor was born in Brooklyn, New York, and was educated in London. He went prospecting for gold in Nevada; after losing everything, he joined a touring company. With T. Daniel Frawley's company, he traveled to the Far East. On **Broadway**, Halliday appeared in *The Whip* (1912), *The Ware Case* (1915), *A Place in the Sun* (1918), *The Circle* (1921), *East of Suez* (1922), *Two Fellows and a Girl* (1923), *Dancing Mothers* (1924), *The Spider* (1927), *Jealousy* (1928), *The Humbug* (1929),

Damn Your Honor (1929), *Rain from Heaven* (1934), and *Tovarich* (1936). He has appeared in numerous silent films, but he switched permanently to films in the early sound era, appearing in *The Dark Angel* (1935), *Peter Ibbetson* (1935), *Desire* (1936), *Intermezzo* (1939), and most notably as **Katharine Hepburn**'s father in *The Philadelphia Story* (1940). Actress Eva Lang was the second of his three wives.

HAMBLETON, T. EDWARD (1911–2005). A native of Baltimore, Maryland, where he was born to a wealthy family, Hambleton was educated at Yale University, where he studied chemistry, but gave it up for the theatre. Inspired by **Orson Welles** and **John Houseman**, Hambleton began producing on **Broadway** and, with **Norris Houghton** (and later **Ellis Rabb**'s **Association of Producing Artists**), established and operated the **Phoenix Theatre** from 1953–1983. Among the over 100 productions of ancient and modern classics, American plays, and new works he produced in New York, both on Broadway and **Off-Broadway**, was the premiere of **Bertolt Brecht**'s *Galileo* (1947). The APA-Phoenix was presented with a special **Tony Award** in 1968 and Hambleton was presented with a 2000 lifetime achievement Tony.

HAMPDEN, WALTER (1879–1955).[†] One of the last prominent actors of the nineteenth-century romantic style, Brooklyn-born and Harvard-educated Walter Dougherty Hampden received his theatrical training in **Shakespeare** and the classics as an apprentice in F. R. Benson's British stage company. Hampden's 1907 American debut was as ALLA NAZIMOVA's leading man and his long career vacillated between popular contemporary plays and the classics. Much of his reputation was built in Shakespearean roles and Hampden made a particularly noteworthy Cyrano de Bergerac in a 1923 **Broadway** revival (revived again in 1932 and 1936). During the 1940s, Hampden was a member of the **American Repertory Theatre (ART)** and won plaudits in the ART's productions of *Henry VIII* (as Cardinal Wolsey) and *What Every Woman Knows*, both in 1946. On Broadway, he also played Hamlet in 1934, appeared in a revival of *Seven Keys to Baldpate** in 1935, *Achilles Had a Heel* (1935), revivals of *An Enemy of the People* in 1937, *Love for Love* in 1940, and *The Rivals* in 1942, *The Strings, My Lord, Are False* (1942), *The Patriots* (1943), *And Be My Love* (1945), *The Traitor* (1949), and *The Velvet Glove* (1949). Hampden's career extended well into the 1950s, when he appeared in a few films, most notably as the old actor in *All About Eve* (1950) and as Humphrey Bogart's crotchety father in *Sabrina* (1954). His final stage appearance was in the role of Governor Danforth in **Arthur Miller**'s *The Crucible* (1953).

HANDMAN, WYNN (1922–). A New Yorker educated at City College and Columbia University, he served in the United States Navy during World WAR II, after which he joined THE NEIGHBORHOOD PLAYHOUSE and studied with **Sanford Meisner**. As cofounder and artistic director of the not-for-profit **American Place Theatre**, Handman remained in that post until 2002. He was praised for his interest in non-traditional casting, which brought him the **Rosetta LeNoire** Award from ACTORS' EQUITY ASSOCIATION in 1994.

HANLEY, WILLIAM (1931–). Born in Lorain, Ohio, he became a playwright best known for his **Broadway** drama, *Slow Dance on the Killing Ground* (1964). Hanley also won two **Drama Desk Awards** for the **Off-Broadway** *Mrs. Dally* (1962), which moved to Broadway in 1965, and *Whisper into My Good Ear* (1962). His other plays include *Conversations in the Dark* (1963), *Today Is Independence Day* (1963), *Flesh and Blood* (1968), and *No Answer* (1968). Hanley also wrote novels, the screenplays for *The Gypsy Moths* (1969) and *Too Far to Go* (1982), and won two Emmy Awards, for the television films *Something About Amelia* (1984) and *The Attic: The Hiding of Anne Frank* (1988), and was Emmy-nominated for several other TV films.

HANSBERRY, LORRAINE (1930–1965). Born into a well-to-do **African American** family of civil rights activists in Chicago, Illinois, Hansberry was exposed to some of the luminaries of pre-World WAR II black life, including LANGSTON HUGHES, PAUL ROBESON, Duke Ellington, and W. E. B. DuBois. Educated in Chicago schools prior to entering the University of Wisconsin in 1948, Hansberry spent two years studying drama before leaving school for New York City in 1950. After working for a time as a reporter for a black newspaper, the experiences of her early life inspired the outstanding achievement of Hansberry's playwriting career, *A Raisin in the Sun* (1959), a drama concerning the frustrated hopes and dreams of a South Side Chicago family in the period. It was the first play by a black woman produced successfully on **Broadway**. Hansberry followed *A Raisin in the Sun* with *The Sign in Sidney Brustein's Window* (1964), which dealt with the turbulent lives of Greenwich Village intellectuals. It failed to equal the success of *Raisin,* and during its preparations Hansberry learned she was suffering from cancer.

Following her death, Hansberry's husband, writer and producer Robert Nemiroff, whom she had married in 1953, pieced together three plays taken from Hansberry's unfinished writings, *What Use Are Flowers?, To Be Young, Gifted, and Black,* and *Les Blancs,* and he encouraged frequent revivals of *A Raisin in the Sun.* Ultimately, other bits and pieces of previously unproduced Hansberry works emerged, including an unproduced script commissioned by

CBS-TV for the centennial of the Civil War. Entitled *The Drinking Gourd*, it deals with the harsh conditions of slavery and its effects on a young black couple. In 1973, Nemiroff and Charlotte Zaltzberg adapted *A Raisin in the Sun* into the musical *Raisin*, which won a **Tony Award** as Best MUSICAL and was successfully revived in 1981.

HAPPY BIRTHDAY. ANITA LOOS's two-act comedy provided a light respite for dramatic actress HELEN HAYES, who was applauded for her performance in this otherwise slight play which opened on 31 October 1946 at the Broadhurst Theatre for 563 performances in a Rodgers and Hammerstein production directed by **Joshua Logan**. Hayes played Addie Bemis, a shy Newark, New Jersey, librarian, frustrated by her feelings for a young man named Paul (Louis Jean Heydt). She follows him to the Jersey Mecca Bar and loses her inhibitions with her first drinks, including the notorious "Pink Lady," described as the "tart's drink." Addie finds the courage to express her feelings, which include singing for the bar's patrons. Critics, while acknowledging the play's slight plot, and **Broadway** audiences clearly enjoyed seeing Hayes have a comic field day, for which she won a **Tony Award**, as did costume designer **Lucinda Ballard**.

HAPPY TIME, THE. **Samuel Taylor**'s three-act comedy sent in Ottawa, Canada, in 1920, opened on 24 January 1950 at the Plymouth Theatre for 614 performances in a Rodgers and Hammerstein production directed by **Robert Lewis**. A young man, Bibi (Johnny Stewart), is coming of age, and his mother (Leora Dana) worries that the carousing brothers of his father (Claude Dauphin) will lead him astray. A 1952 film version starred **Charles Boyer** and a 1968 musical adaptation by **N. Richard Nash**, with music by John Kander and lyrics by Fred Ebb, was **Tony Award**-nominated as Best MUSICAL.

HARDWICK, ELIZABETH (1916–2007). Born in Lexington, Kentucky, and educated at the University of Kentucky, Hardwick wrote novels, but ultimately became a noted dramatic and literary CRITIC. She wrote theatre reviews for the *New York Review of Books* from 1963–1983 and was the first woman to receive the GEORGE JEAN NATHAN Award in 1967. Hardwick was married to poet Robert Lowell from 1949 to 1972.

HARDY, JOSEPH (1929–). A native of Carlsbad, New Mexico, Hardy has had a varied career as a director of theatre and film. He won a **Drama Desk Award** for his direction of *You're a Good Man, Charlie Brown* (1967), a **Tony Award** nomination for *Play It Again, Sam* (1969), and won both

Tony and Drama Desk Awards for *Child's Play* (1970), credits suggesting the range of his work. Hardy's other **Broadway** credits include *Johnny No-Trump* (1967), *Bob and Ray: The Two and Only* (1970), *Children! Children!* (1972), *Gigi* (1972), a 1976 revival of *The Night of the Iguana*, *Diversions and Delights* (1978), and *Romantic Comedy* (1979). Hardy's film work includes his direction of television productions of numerous literary classics, including *Shadow of a Gunman* in 1972, *A Tree Grows in Brooklyn* in 1974, and *Great Expectations* in 1974, and episodes of the television series *The Paper Chase* (1978). He most recently directed Lynn Redgrave in her one-woman play *Nightingale* (2009) for the **Manhattan Theatre Club** and has directed *Grace* (2008) **Off-Broadway** and in **regional theatres**.

HARE, DAVID (1947–). English-born playwright, screenwriter, and director, Hare has worked mostly in Great Britain, but his plays have been produced with some frequency on **Broadway**. He won a 1983 **New York Drama Critics Circle Award** for his play *Plenty*, which also received a **Tony Award** nomination, as did *Racing Demon* (1996) and *Skylight* (1997). He won a **Drama Desk Award** for *Via Dolorosa* (1999) and Drama Desk nominations for *The Secret Rapture* (1990), which he also directed, and *Stuff Happens* (2006). Other Hare works on Broadway included his adaptation of **Anton Chekhov**'s *Ivanov* in 1997, *The Judas Kiss* (1998), *The Blue Room* (1998), which caused a stir when film actress Nicole Kidman appeared **nude** in a scene, and *The Vertical Hour* (2006). Hare also directed Vanessa Redgrave in the Broadway production of *The Year of Magical Thinking* (2007). Hare has received two Academy Award nominations for screenplays for *The Hours* (2002) and *The Reader* (2008) and has adapted several of his plays for the screen.

HARRIET. Produced by GILBERT MILLER, this three-act play by husband-and-wife playwrights Florence Ryerson and Colin Clements opened on 3 March 1943 at Henry Miller's Theatre for 377 performances under **Elia Kazan**'s direction. HELEN HAYES played Harriet Beecher Stowe who discovers that her marriage to Calvin Stowe, played by Rhys Williams, and her writing are a means of escaping family pressures. None of her family approved of her writing *Uncle Tom's Cabin*, but its success encourages Stowe to support abolitionist movement and the Civil WAR as a means of ending slavery.

HARRIGAN, WILLIAM (1893–1966). Son of actor/playwright Edward Harrigan,* this stage and screen actor appeared in films beginning in 1915, but had begun earlier on stage, appearing on **Broadway** in one of his father's plays, *Old Lavender* (1906). Among his many Broadway roles, Harrigan appeared in *The Chaperone* (1908), *The Melody of Youth* (1916), *Bought and Paid For** (1921), *Polly Preferred** (1923), *The Great God Brown** (1926), *The Moon in the Yellow River* (1932), *The Dark Tower* (1933), *Paths of Glory* (1935), *Days to Come* (1936), *In Time to Come* (1941), and won plaudits as the tyrannical Captain in ***Mister Roberts*** (1948). He often played military personnel, but also appeared as Charlie Chan in the play *Keeper of the Keys* (1933). His final Broadway appearances were in *The Wayward Saint* (1955) and *A Shadow of My Enemy* (1957).

HARRIS, AURAND (1915–1996). Born in Jamesport, Missouri, this pioneer of **children's theatre** studied at the University of Kansas City and Northwestern University. He wrote over 50 plays for young audiences between his first success, a *commedia dell'arte*-style *Androcles and the Lion* (1963), and his last, *The Orphan Train* (1996). Harris also wrote *Steal Away Home* (1972), *Yankee Doodle* (1975), *A Toby Show* (1978), and *The Arkansas Bear* (1980). He was the first playwright to receive the **National Endowment for the Arts** Creative Writing Fellowship and the New England Theatre Conference established an annual **award** in Harris's name in 1997.

HARRIS, JED (1899–1979).[†] Born Jacob Horowitz in Vienna, Austria, Harris arrived in America as a child and attended Yale University before working as a newspaper reporter for the *New York Clipper*. Often described as the "wonder boy" of **Broadway**, many coworkers found his near-mythical eccentricities, ruthless business practices, and cutting sarcasm unpleasant. GEORGE ABBOTT called him the "Little Napoleon" of the American stage, an apt description that captures Harris's brilliance, flamboyance, and dictatorial style (GEORGE S. KAUFMAN joked that after his death he wished to be cremated and have his ashes thrown in Harris's face).

Most of Harris's greatest successes were in the 1920s, including the original productions of *Broadway** (1926), *Coquette** (1927), *The Royal Family** (1927), and *The Front Page** (1928), but his staging of *Uncle Vanya* (1930) starring LILLIAN GISH was well-received and his production of the early **gay**-themed melodrama* *The Green Bay Tree* (1933) provided **Laurence Olivier** with one of his first Broadway appearances. The same year, Harris presented **Katharine Hepburn** in *The Lake*, a failure that nearly ended Hepburn's career. More important later productions included **Thornton Wilder**'s *Our Town* (1938), also directed by Harris, and *The Heiress* (1947), adapted by **Albert Hackett** and **Frances Goodrich** from Henry James's *Washington Square*, but his productions of *Dark Eyes* (1943) and *The Traitor* (1949) were only mildly successful. Harris directed **Arthur Miller**'s ***The Crucible*** in 1953, but his final production, Guy Bolton's *Child of Fortune*, which he also directed, failed in 1956.

Two Harris memoirs, *Watchman, What of the Night?* (1963), which offered his point of view on the backstage squabbles during the production of *The Heiress*, and an autobiography, *A Dance on the High Wire* (1979), were rare moments in the spotlight for Harris, who became increasingly reclusive after the mid-1950s, but who also appeared on Dick Cavett's television show for a rare extended interview shortly before his death.

HARRIS, JULIE (1925–). This much-honored actress was born Julia Ann Harris in Grosse Point, Michigan, and was educated at the Yale School of Drama. She debuted on **Broadway** in *It's a Gift* (1945), beginning a distinguished stage career that lasted half a century. She won a **Theatre World Award** for *Sundown Beach* (1949) and **Tony Awards** for **John Van Druten**'s *I Am a Camera* (1952), *The Lark* (1956), *Forty Carats* (1969), *The Last of Mrs. Lincoln* (1973), and *The Belle of Amherst* (1977), garnering Tony nominations for *Marathon '33* (1964), *Skycraper* (1966), her only MUSICAL, *The Au Pair Man* (1974), *Lucifer's Child* (1991), and a 1997 revival of *The Gin Game*. She also received a **Drama Desk Award** for *The Last of Mrs. Lincoln*, and a Drama Desk nomination for *The Belle of Amherst*. Her many other Broadway credits include **Carson McCullers**'s *The Member of the Wedding* (1950), a revival of *The Country Wife* in 1957, *The Warm Peninsula* (1959), *Little Moon of Alban* (1960), *A Shot in the Dark* (1961), *Ready When You Are, C.B.!* (1964), *And Miss Reardon Drinks a Little* (1971), *Voices* (1972), *In Praise of Love* (1974), *Break a Leg* (1979), *Mixed Couples* (1980), and a revival of **Tennessee Williams**'s *The Glass Menagerie* in 1994, among many others on Broadway, in **regional theatres**, and on tour.

The slight, slim Harris suggests fragility, but her performances in a wide range of characters and genres reveals a strength of body and voice, and a stage technique that ranks her among the greatest twentieth-century American stage actors. Her love of her art has encouraged her to continue her work even in her 80s, and after suffering a stroke in 2001. In 2008, the intrepid Harris appeared as Nanny in a production of **Paul Zindel**'s *The Effect of Gamma Rays on Man-in-the-Moon Marigolds,* and she continued to appear in films.

Harris was nominated for an Academy Award in her debut appearance in the film version of *The Member of the Wedding* (1952) and also appeared in *East of Eden* (1955), *I Am a Camera* (1955), *The Haunting* (1963), *Harper* (1966), *Reflections in a Golden Eye* (1967), *The Hiding Place* (1975), and *The Bell Jar* (1979). On television, Harris won three Emmy Awards for *Little Moon of Alban* (1951), *Victoria Regina* (1961), and for her voice-over performance in *Not for Ourselves Alone* (1999). She also received eight other Emmy nominations. Harris was inducted into the **Theatre Hall of Fame**, received a **Kennedy Center** Honor, a 1994 National Medal of Arts, and lifetime achievement awards: Tony Award (2002) and Drama Desk Award (2005).

HARRIS, ROSEMARY (1930–). Born in Ashby, Suffolk, England, Rosemary Ann Harris attended convent schools, worked in **repertory** theatres, and studied at the Royal Academy of Dramatic Art. Since debuting on **Broadway** in *Climate of Eden* (1951), for which she won a **Theatre World Award**, Harris has worked frequently in New York and London's West End, as well as in films and television. In England, her many performances included playing Ophelia to Peter O'Toole's Hamlet in the debut production of the National Theatre of Great Britain. Exuding elegance and authority on stage, Harris often plays upper-class characters or royalty, but has demonstrated diversity in a wide range of roles. On Broadway, she won a **Tony Award** playing Eleanor of Aquitaine in *The Lion in Winter* (1966) and **Drama Desk Awards** for *Old Times* (1972), in revivals of *A Streetcar Named Desire* (1973) and *The Merchant of Venice* (1973), and *Pack of Lies* (1985). Harris also won an **Obie Award** for an **Off-Broadway** revival of *All Over* in 2002.

Harris's other notable Broadway appearances include *Troilus and Cressida* (1956), *Interlock* (1958), *The Disenchanted* (1958), *The Tumbler* (1960), revivals of *The School for Scandal* and *Right You Are If You Think You Are* in 1966, *We, Comrades Three* (1966), revivals of *The Wild Duck* and *You Can't Take It With You* in 1967, *War and Peace* (1967), revivals of *The Royal Family** in 1975, *Heartbreak House* in 1983, and *Hay Fever* in 1985, she replaced **Irene Worth** in *Lost in Yonkers* in 1991, revivals of *An Inspector Calls* in 1994 and *Waiting in the Wings* in 1999, and *Oscar and the Pink Lady* (2008). On screen, Harris was nominated for an Academy Award in *Tom & Viv* (1994) and has appeared in *The Boys from Brazil* (1978), *Crossing Delancey* (1988), *Looking for Richard* (1996), *Hamlet* (1996), and she plays Aunt May in *Spider-Man* (2002) and its sequels. She won Emmy awards for *Notorious Woman* (1976) and *Holocaust* (1978), the latter bringing her a Golden Globe Award as well. Harris is the mother of actress **Jennifer Ehle**. *See also* SHAKESPEARE ON U.S. STAGES.

HARRIS, SAM H. (1872–1941).[†] A native of New York's Lower East Side, Samuel Henry Harris became manager of boxer Terry McGovern, who appeared in a touring BURLESQUE show between bouts. When Harris bought a piece of the show, his producing career began and it expanded in 1900 when he embarked on a four-year partnership with A. H. Woods* and P. H. "Paddy" Sullivan to mount touring melodramas.* In 1904, Harris formed a legendary **Broadway** producing partnership with GEORGE M. COHAN, staging innumerable productions, including virtually all of Cohan's works until they amicably dissolved their partnership in 1920. On his own, Harris kept up a prodigious and diverse producing schedule that included *The Music Box Revues* and many of the most successful MUSICALS and plays of the 1920s and 1930s, including the PULITZER PRIZE-winning *Icebound** (1923), a rare foray into serious drama for Harris.

Harris's prestige only expanded in the 1930s with productions of the Pulitzer Prize-winners *Of Thee I Sing!* (1933) and **You Can't Take It with You** (1936), and a reunion with Cohan, who starred in the Harris-produced Richard Rodgers-Lorenz Hart musical satire *I'd Rather Be Right* (1937). His other 1930s' productions include **Once in a Lifetime** (1930), *Face the Music* (1932), **Dinner at Eight** (1932), *As Thousands Cheer* (1933), *Let 'Em Eat Cake* (1933), **Merrily We Roll Along** (1934), *Jubilee* (1935), **Room Service** (1935), **Stage Door** (1936), *Of Mice and Men* (1937), **The Man Who Came to Dinner** (1939), **George Washington Slept Here** (1940), and *Lady in the Dark* (1941). Harris was well-respected for his taste, attention to every detail, and his genial manner.

HARRISON, BERTRAM (1877–1955). Harrison began his career as a journeyman actor and stage manager for Henry Miller's* company, with Miller ultimately casting him in important roles. On **Broadway**, Harrison appeared in *Zira** (1905) and *The Great Divide** (1906), and worked successfully as a director and production manager for many Broadway shows. He directed both MUSICALS and comedies, including *Little Women** (1912), *Parlor, Bedroom, and Bath** (1917), *Up in Mabel's Room** (1919), *Ladies' Night** (1920), *Getting Gertie's Garter** (1921), *Lawful Larceny* (1922), *Partners Again* (1922), *The Kiss in the Taxi* (1925), *Potash and Perlmutter,* Detectives* (1926), *Treasure Girl* (1928), *Singin' the Blues* (1931), *Hot Money* (1931), *The Red Cat* (1934), *Say When* (1934), *Swing Your Lady!* (1936), *Around the Corner* (1936), *Miss Quis* (1937), *Sea Legs* (1937), and *30 Days Hath September* (1938).

HARRISON, REX (1908–1990). Born Reginald Carey Harrison in Huyton, Lancashire, England, and studied at Liverpool College. He began acting in 1924, but his career was interrupted by his service in the Royal Air Force in World WAR II. Following the war, he found stardom onstage in London and New York, and in films. He was often associated with the plays of GEORGE BERNARD SHAW, **Noël Coward**, and Terence Rattigan, but other than **Shakespeare** (he was the only major English actor of his generation to avoid Shakespeare's plays) he played diverse roles in dramas, comedies, and a MUSICAL. On **Broadway**, Harrison won **Tony Awards** for his performances playing Henry VIII in MAXWELL ANDERSON's *Anne of the Thousand Days* (1948) and Henry Higgins in Alan Jay Lerner and Frederick Loewe's *My Fair Lady* (1956, 1981), the musical adaptation of Shaw's *Pygmalion* in which he famously talked-sang the songs, including "I've Grown Accustomed to Her Face." Harrison was presented with a special Tony in 1969, nominated for a Tony and a **Drama Desk Award** for a 1983 revival of *Heartbreak House*, and he received a 1985 Drama Desk Special Award for his career achievement.

Harrison also appeared notably on Broadway in **T. S. Eliot**'s *The Cocktail Party* (1950), **John Van Druten**'s *Bell, Book and Candle* (1950), Christopher Fry's *Venus Observed* (1952), **Peter Ustinov**'s *The Love of Four Colonels* (1953), which he also directed, Jean Anouilh's *The Fighting Cock* (1959) directed by Peter Brook, a revival of Luigi Pirandello's *Henry IV* in 1973, Rattigan's *In Praise of Love* (1974), a 1977 revival of Shaw's *Caesar and Cleopatra*, William Douglas Home's *The Kingfisher* (1978), Frederick Lonsdale's *Aren't We All?* (1985), and Somerset Maugham's *The Circle* (1989). Harrison was nominated for an Academy Award for *Cleopatra* (1963) and won an Oscar and the New York Film Critics Circle Award for the film version of *My Fair Lady* (1964).

Harrison's varied film roles reflected his theatrical tastes, including his appearances in film versions of *Major Barbara* (1941), *Blithe Spirit* (1945), *Anna and the King of Siam* (1946), and *The Fourposter* (1952). Harrison was married six times and among his wives were the actresses Lili Palmer and Rachel Roberts. An affair with Hollywood starlet Carole Landis during Harrison's marriage to Palmer ended in Landis's suicide, which caused a front-page scandal. However his career was not harmed by the tragedy. Harrison was the father of actor Noël Harrison, named for his father's friend, Noël Coward.

HARRISON, RICHARD B. (1864–1935). Born in London, Ontario, Canada, Richard Berry Harrison was the son of fugitive slaves who had escaped the United States via the Underground Railroad. He studied at the Detroit Training School of Dramatic Art and with Edward Weitzel, touring as a dramatic reader of **Shakespeare** and poetry prior to working with the **Lafayette Theatre**. His most noted roles, as De Lawd in MARC CONNELLY's PULITZER PRIZE-winning play *The Green Pastures,* (1930) kept him on **Broadway** and the road* for a few years, including a 1935 revival, and he taught speech and drama at North Carolina A&T University and other schools prior to his death. *See also* AFRICAN AMERICAN THEATRE.

HART, MOSS (1904–1961). New York-born playwright and director, Hart was interested in theatre from childhood thanks to an aunt who took him to plays. He worked on amateur productions, as entertainment director at a summer resort, and as an actor, appearing on **Broadway** in a revival of *The Emperor Jones** in 1926. He convinced veteran playwright/director GEORGE S. KAUFMAN to collaborate with him. Their first play, *Once in a Lifetime* (1930), was a hit and during the 1930s they wrote several successful works, including their PULITZER PRIZE-winning comedy *You Can't Take It with You* (1936), as well as *Merrily We Roll Along* (1934), the libretto for the MUSICAL *I'd Rather Be Right* (1937), *The Fabulous Invalid* (1938), *The American Way* (1939), *The Man Who Came to Dinner* (1939), and *George Washington Slept Here* (1940). During his partnership with Kaufman, Hart also wrote the books for the musicals *Face the Music* (1932), *As Thousands Cheer* (1933), *The Great Waltz* (1934), *Jubilee* (1935), and *The Show Is On* (1936).

After the end of his partnership with Kaufman, Hart continued to write and increasingly turned his attention to directing, sometimes combining the two, as he did with *Lady in the Dark* (1941), *Winged Victory* (1943), *Christopher Blake* (1946), *Light Up the Sky* (1948), and *The Climate of Eden* (1952). He directed *Junior Miss* (1941), *Dear Ruth* (1944), *The Secret Room* (1945), *Miss Liberty* (1949), *Anniversary Waltz* (1954), *My Fair Lady* (1956), and *Camelot* (1960). Hart's screenplays include his Academy Award-nominated condemnation of anti-Semitism, *Gentlemen's Agreement* (1947), *Hans Christian Andersen* (1952), and the Judy Garland version of *A Star Is Born* (1954). Hart also wrote *Act One* (1959), one of the most admired autobiographies of a Broadway personality, although the book only covers his life up to beginning his partnership with Kaufman. He was married to actress Kitty Carlisle from 1946 until his death, despite being bisexual.

HARTFORD STAGE COMPANY (HSC). Jacques Cartier founded this theatre in 1963 in a grocery warehouse where it opened with a 1964 production of *Othello*. In 1968, operations moved to a permanent theatre designed by architect Robert Venturi. The HSC gained national recognition after 1980 under the artistic leadership of **Mark Lamos**, who stressed a mixture of classics, great American plays, and new works. To date, the HSC has staged over 260 productions, established the annual **Tennessee Williams** Marathon, and various education and **community** programs. Michael Wilson replaced Lamos in 1998.

HARVEY. **Mary Coyle Chase**'s seemingly innocuous comedy about a genial tippler who imagines a six-foot rabbit as his drinking companion improbably won a PULITZER PRIZE and ran for 1,775 performances at the 48th Street

Theatre in its original **Broadway** production which opened on 1 November 1944. Chase, whose subsequent plays did not find either critical or commercial success, originally named this pleasing comedy *The Pooka*, an ancient Celtic term for a fairy spirit in animal guise.

The aforementioned pooka is Harvey, the imaginary rabbit friend of whimsical drunk Elwood P. Dowd (played in the original production by vaudevillian* **Frank Fay**), who causes unending distress for Dowd's social-climbing sister, Veta Louise Simmons (JOSEPHINE HULL), and Veta's unmarried daughter, Myrtle Mae (Jane Van Duser). When Elwood shows up at home unexpectedly during a gathering of local society matrons, Myrtle is humiliated when the invisible Harvey is introduced to one and all. Pressuring the conflicted Veta, Myrtle wants to send Elwood to the "booby hatch," Chumley's Rest, fearing that future social gaffs will prevent her from finding a husband and social position. At Chumley's a series of misunderstandings leads to the accidental incarceration of Veta as a patient, as well as other comical confusions. Although it seems only Elwood can see and converse with Harvey, those around him, including Dr. Chumley, slowly begin to feel the pooka's presence. Elwood's benign, friendly philosophy, reflected by his relationship with Harvey, calls into question what it means to be sane and Veta, realizing she likes Elwood as he is, takes him—and Harvey—home.

Fay won critical plaudits, but film star **James Stewart** subsequently replaced him during the run and also played Elwood in a 1950 screen version for which he was Academy Award-nominated (along with Hull in an Oscar-winning performance), a 1970 Broadway revival (costarring with HELEN HAYES) filmed for television in 1972, and became permanently identified with the character. A film version to be directed by Steven Spielberg was planned for 2011.

HATFUL OF RAIN, A. Actor **Michael V. Gazzo**'s three-act drama on the impact of a Korean WAR veteran's drug addiction and its impact on his family opened on 9 November 1955 at the Lyceum Theatre for 389 performances under Frank Corsaro's direction and with scene designs by MORDECAI GORELIK. **Ben Gazzara** and Anthony Franciosa were both nominated for **Tony Awards** and the strong cast also included **Shelley Winters**, Frank Silvera, Harry Guardino, and Henry Silva in this **naturalistic** treatment of a largely taboo subject in **Broadway** drama up to that time. Franciosa repeated his performance in a 1957 screen version directed by Fred Zinnemann and garnered Academy Award and Golden Globe Award nominations.

HAVING WONDERFUL TIME. MARC CONNELLY produced and directed this three-act comedy by Arthur Kober at the Lyceum Theatre, where it opened on 20 February 1937 for 372 performances. Katherine Locke played Teddy Stern, a young secretary vacationing at a Berkshire resort to escape an unhappy relationship with an older man. She meets Chick Kessler (**John Garfield**, then billed as Jules), a young waiter. Teddy vacillates for a time, but when she is heavily courted by a vulgar ladies' man, Pinkie Aaronson (Sheldon Leonard), she decides to turn to Chick. *Having Wonderful Time* was the source material for the MUSICAL *Wish You Were Here* (1952).

HAVOC, JUNE (1913–2010). Born Ellen Evangeline Hovick in Vancouver, British Columbia, Canada, Havoc began in theatre as a child vaudevillian* billed as "Baby June" under the guidance of her mother Rose and with her sister, Rose Louise Hovick, later known as the BURLESQUE "ecdysiast" **Gypsy Rose Lee**. Havoc's childhood in vaudeville became a theatrical legend in the fictionalized musical *Gypsy* (1959), based on Lee's memoirs. Beginning with her **Broadway** debut in *Forbidden Melody* (1936), Havoc worked on stage and screen until the 1990s. On Broadway, she was nominated for a **Tony Award** for the direction of her own play, *Marathon '33* (1963), based on her memoirs, which starred **Julie Harris**. Havoc also received a **Drama Desk Award** nomination for her performance in *Habeas Corpus* (1975), and she also appeared in *Pal Joey* (1940), *Mexican Hayride* (1944), *Sadie Thompson* (1944), *The Ryan Girl* (1945), *Dunnigan's Daughter* (1945), *The Infernal Machine* (1958), a revival of *The Beaux Strategem* in 1959, *The Warm Peninsula* (1959), a revival of *Dinner at Eight* in 1966, and she stepped in as a replacement Miss Hannigan in the long-running musical *Annie* in 1982.

HAYDON, JULIE (1910–1994). A native of Oak Park, Illinois, the small, ethereal Haydon was born Donella Lightfoot Donaldson and began her career in her teens touring with Minnie Maddern Fiske* in *Mrs. Bumpstead-Leigh.* She made her **Broadway** debut in PHILIP BARRY's flop *Bright Star* (1935) and, in less than a decade, appeared in three legendary performances, as Brigid the maid caught in a love triangle with a conservative churchman and a liberal school master in Ireland in Paul Vincent Carroll's *Shadow and Substance* (1938), as the despairing prostitute Kitty Duval in **William Saroyan**'s *The Time of Your Life* (1939), and as the fragile recluse Laura Wingfield in **Tennessee Williams**'s *The Glass Menagerie* (1945). Haydon's rare other Broadway appearances included *Magic/Hello Out There* (1942), *The Patriots* (1943), *Miracle in the Mountains* (1947), and *Our Lan'* (1947). Haydon appeared in a few films after 1931, most notably in *The Age of Innocence* (1934), *The Scoundrel* (1935) playing opposite **Noël Coward**, and the first Andy Hardy film, *A Family Affair* (1937), and she later appeared in a few television dramas. She married CRITIC GEORGE JEAN

N<small>ATHAN</small> in 1955 and when he died in 1958, Haydon taught acting and gave readings of Nathan's books.

HAYES, HELEN (1900–1993).† Born Helen Brown in Washington, D.C. to an actress and a salesman, Hayes debuted at the age of five with a S<small>TOCK</small> company before appearing in Lew Fields's **Broadway** M<small>USICAL</small>, *Old Dutch* (1909). After appearing in other musicals, she acted opposite William Gillette* in *Dear Brutus* (1918). Beginning with *Clarence** (1919), her demure, natural acting, which departed from the more histrionic approach typical in the 1920s, elevated her stature. In 1926, she assayed her favorite role, Maggie, in a revival of *What Every Woman Knows*, which she followed with an acclaimed performance in *Coquette** (1927). After 1930, and throughout her long career, Hayes appeared with distinction in a range of classic and contemporary roles almost all of which enhanced her title as one of the "First Ladies of the American Theatre," along with contemporaries L<small>YNN</small> F<small>ONTANNE</small> and K<small>ATHARINE</small> C<small>ORNELL</small>.

Hayes gave standout performances in M<small>AXWELL</small> A<small>NDERSON</small>'s *Mary of Scotland* (1933), a well-liked revival of **Shakespeare**'s *Twelfth Night* in 1940, *Candle in the Wind* (1941), as Harriet Beecher Stowe in *Harriet* (1943), in **Anita Loos**'s *Happy Birthday* (1946), in **Joshua Logan**'s adaptation of **Anton Chekhov**'s *The Cherry Orchard* retitled *The Wisteria Trees* (1950), in **Mary Chase**'s *Mrs. McThing* (1952), Jean Anouilh's *Time Remembered* (1957), in the first production of E<small>UGENE</small> O'N<small>EILL</small>'s *A Touch of the Poet* (1958), revivals of G<small>EORGE</small> K<small>ELLY</small>'s *The Show-Off** (1967), *The Front Page** (1969), which was cowritten by her late husband, C<small>HARLES</small> M<small>AC</small>A<small>RTHUR</small>, and her last New York appearance in Mary Chase's *Harvey* (1970) opposite **James Stewart**. Her signature performance in Laurence Housman's *Victoria Regina* (1935) was a virtuosic turn in which she played Queen Victoria from youth to old age. Hayes also appeared in films periodically, winning Academy Awards as Best Actress in 1931 for *The Sin of Madelon Claudet* and again in the supporting category for *Airport* (1970). On television, she was nominated nine times for an Emmy Award, winning once in 1953.

HAYS, DAVID (1930–). This multi-**Tony Award**-nominated scene and lighting designer was born in New York City as David Arthur Hays and graduated from Harvard University. Inspired by the work of J<small>O</small> M<small>IELZINER</small>, he became a successful **Broadway** designer and founded the **National Theatre of the Deaf** in 1967. He was also a cofounder of the **Eugene O'Neill Memorial Theatre Center**. On Broadway, he received Tony nominations for his designs of *The Tenth Man* (1960), *All the Way Home* (1961), *No Strings* (1962), a revival of *Marco Millions** in 1964, and *Drat! The Cat!*

(1965). His other notable designs include the original Broadway production of *Long Day's Journey Into Night* (1956), *Gideon* (1961), *Sunday in New York* (1961), *A Family Affair* (1962), a revival of *Strange Interlude** in 1963, *UTBU* (1966), *A Cry of Players* (1968), *The Goodbye People* (1968), *Two By Two* (1970), *The Gingerbread Lady* (1970), *Bring Back Birdie* (1981), and *Kingdoms* (1981).

HAYWARD, LELAND (1902–1971). Born in Nebraska City, Nebraska, Hayward studied at Princeton University, but quit to work as a journalist and press agent, ultimately developing his own talent agency and managing some of the top Hollywood stars, including Fred Astaire, **Katharine Hepburn** (with whom he was romantically involved), Greta Garbo, **Henry Fonda**, Judy Garland, and others. In 1945, he sold his talent agency and became a **Broadway** producer responsible for several major hits, including two PULITZER PRIZE-winners, *State of the Union* (1945) and *South Pacific* (1949), as well as *A Bell for Adano* (1945), *Mister Roberts* (1948), *Anne of the Thousand Days* (1948), *Call Me Madam* (1950), *Wish You Were Here* (1952), *Gypsy* (1959), *The Sound of Music* (1959), *Goodbye, Charlie* (1959), *A Shot in the Dark* (1961), *Mr. President* (1962), and *The Trial of the Catonsville Nine* (1971). He was married to actress **Margaret Sullavan** and was the father of actress Brooke Hayward.

HECHT, BEN (1894–1964).[†] Born in New York and reared in Wisconsin, Hecht is often thought of as a Chicagoan since his best-known play, coauthored with CHARLES MACARTHUR, is *The Front Page** (1928), a scathing and hilarious melodrama* of 1920s yellow journalism in the Windy City. Also in partnership with MacArthur, Hecht wrote the farce *Twentieth Century* (1932), and on his own he wrote the Richard Rodgers-Lorenz Hart MUSICAL *Jumbo* (1935), *Ladies and Gentlemen* (1939), *Swan Song* (1946), and *A Flag Is Born* (1946). He collaborated with Gene Fowler on *The Great Magoo* (1932), but Hecht spent most of his career writing novels and particularly screenplays. He wrote (credited or uncredited) over 150 films, including *Scarface* (1932), *Viva Villa!* (1934), *Nothing Sacred* (1937), *Wuthering Heights* (1939), *Spellbound* (1945), *Notorious* (1946), *A Farewell to Arms* (1957), as well as screen adaptations of his plays.

HECHT, JESSICA (1965–). Born in Princeton, New Jersey, Hecht was educated as an actor at New York University's Tisch School of the Arts. On **Broadway**, her credits include *Last Night of Ballyhoo* (1997) and revivals of *After the Fall* in 2004, *Julius Caesar* in 2005, *Brighton Beach Memoirs* in 2009, and *A View from the Bridge* in 2010. **Off-Broadway**, she has appeared in *Plunge* (1997), *Stop Kiss* (1998), and *Lobster Alice* (1999). She has appeared in several films, including *Sideways* (2004) and *Calling It Quits* (2009), and many television programs, most notably in the recurring role of the lesbian lover of Ross's ex-wife on the comedy series *Friends* from 1994 to 2000.

HECKART, EILEEN (1919–2001). A Columbus, Ohio, native born Anna Eileen Heckart, she attended Ohio State University before beginning a long and successful career as a character actress on **Broadway** and in movies and television. Her Broadway debut was as understudy and assistant stage manager of ***The Voice of the Turtle*** (1943). After appearing in a few flops, she won critical praise as Rosemary Sydney in **William Inge's** PULITZER PRIZE-winning *Picnic* (1953), winning a **Theatre World Award**. She received **Tony Award** nominations for ***The Dark at the Top of the Stairs*** (1957), *Invitation to a March* (1960), ***Butterflies Are Free*** (1969), and she was presented with a special Tony in 2000. She was nominated for a **Drama Desk Award** for her **Off-Broadway** performance in *Northeast Local* (1996) and won an **Obie Award**, a **Lucille Lortel** Award, and a Drama Desk Award for *The Waverly Gallery* (2000). On Broadway, Heckart's other notable appearances included ***The Bad Seed*** (1954), ***A View from the Bridge*** (1955), *Everybody Loves Opal* (1961), *A Family Affair* (1962), a revival of *Too True to Be Good* in 1963, *And Things That Go Bump in the Night* (1965), ***You Know I Can't Hear You When the Water's Running*** (1967), *The Mother Lover* (1969), *Veronica's Room* (1973), *Ladies at the Alamo* (1977), and *The Cemetery Club* (1990).

In **regional theatres**, Heckart played such varied roles as **Mother Courage** and Daisy Werthan in ***Driving Miss Daisy***, and she toured as Eleanor Roosevelt in *Eleanor* (1976). Heckart won an Academy Award reprising her Broadway role as the controlling mother Mrs. Baker in *Butterflies Are Free* (1972) and was nominated repeating another stage role, as Mrs. Daigle, the mother of a murdered child, in *The Bad Seed* (1956), for which she won a Golden Globe Award. On television, she won an Emmy Award for *Love & War* in 1994 and was nominated five other times, as well as garnering a Daytime Emmy Award nomination for the soap opera *One Life to Live* in 1987.

HEDGEROW THEATRE. Jasper Deeter founded this **repertory** theatre in Rose Valley, Pennsylvania, in 1923. In its first three decades, the theatre operated as a true repertory, performing a rapidly changing bill of fare year-round. In the 1950s, the theatre abandoned the repertory approach and continued until 1985, when a fire destroyed Hedgerow's facility. However, it was rebuilt and opened in 1990 under artistic director Penelope Reed, staging two dozen plays a year and operating a school and mounting **children's theatre** productions.

HEIDI CHRONICLES, THE. Wendy Wasserstein's PULITZER PRIZE, **Tony Award**, and **Drama Desk Award**-winning play opened **Off-Broadway** at **Playwrights Horizons** on 18 November 1988 before transferring to **Broadway** on 9 March 1989 at the Plymouth Theatre for 622 performances under the direction of Tony nominee **Daniel Sullivan.** Tony nominee **Joan Allen** played Heidi Holland, a woman in search of her identity set against the cultural background of the era between the 1960s and the 1980s, depicting the changes in women's lives and expectations in American life. Heidi is a committed **feminist** in the 1970s, but her attitudes evolve over the course of the play. Joanne Camp, playing several of Heidi's friends, was Tony-nominated, and **Boyd Gaines** won a Tony as Heidi's gay best friend. A 1995 television film version featured Jamie Lee Curtis and Tom Hulce and a 2006 revival was staged at the **Berkshire Theatre Festival. Mel Gussow**, writing in the *New York Times* of the original production, praised Wasserstein as a "clever writer of comedy," adding that in this case "she has been exceedingly watchful about not settling for easy laughter, and the result is a more penetrating play." *See also* WOMEN/FEMININITY.

HEIFNER, JACK (1946–   ). Born in Corsicana, Texas, and educated at Southern Methodist University, Heifner started his theatre work as an actor, but moved toward playwriting following the success of his first produced work, *Vanities* (1976), which brought him a **Drama Desk Award** nomination, ran **Off-Broadway** for over 1,700 performances, and was widely produced in **regional**, university, and **community theatres**. *Vanities* tracked the lives of three **women** who are first seen as high school cheerleaders on the day of President John F. Kennedy's assassination and follows them into adulthood. In the aftermath of the success of *Vanities*, Heifner's *Patio/Porch* (1978) was produced unsuccessfully on **Broadway** and he provided material for the MUSICAL *Leader of the Pack* (1985). Heifner's other plays, none of which have matched the success of *Vanities*, include *Casserole* (1975), *Star Treatment* (1980), *America Was* (1982), *Running on Empty* (1982), *Smile* (1983), *Natural Disasters* (1985), *American Beauty* (1988), *Boy's Play* (1989), *Home Fires* (1990), *Jumping for Joy* (1994), *Dwarf Tossing* (1999), *Key West* (1999), *Earth to Bucky* (2001), *China Dolls* (2002), and *Seduction* (2004). A musical version of *Vanities*, with music by David Kirshenbaum, was produced in 2009 at New York's **Second Stage.** Heifner is playwright-in-residence at Stephen F. Austin State University.

HEILPERN, JOHN (1942–). Born in Manchester, England, Heilpern studied law at Oxford University prior to writing for *The Observer* in London, where his profiles of major figures in the arts led to work as a dramaturg for **Peter Hall** on a 1976 National Theatre of Great Britain production of *Tamburlaine*. After 1980, when he moved to New York, Heilpern wrote theatre **criticism** for the *New York Observer* and the "Out to Lunch" feature in *Vanity Fair*, and books on theatre, including *Conference of the Birds: The Story of Peter Brook in Africa* (1977), *How Good Is David Mamet, Anyway?* (1999), and *John Osborne: The Many Lives of the Angry Young Man* (2006).

HEIRESS, THE. Ruth and Augustus Goetz adapted Henry James's 1880 novel *Washington Square* to the stage and, under JED HARRIS's direction, it opened on **Broadway** at the Biltmore Theatre on 29 September 1947 for 410 performances. The stellar cast featured Wendy Hiller, **Basil Rathbone**, who was nominated for a **Tony Award**, Peter Cookson, and PATRICIA COLLINGE. Costume designer Mary Percy Schenck won a **Tony Award** for her lavish nineteenth-century costumes. Set in 1850, the play follows the novel's plot involving a repressed daughter, a domineering father, a meddling aunt, and a gold-digging suitor. Rathbone repeated his performance in a short-lived 1950 revival with Margaret Phillips, John Dall, and Edna Best and a 1976 revival starring **Jane Alexander**, **Richard Kiley**, David Selby, and Jan Miner also flopped, but an acclaimed 1985 revival, starring **Cherry Jones** and **Frances Sternhagen**, both of whom won Tonys, with **Philip Bosco** and Jon Tenney, won a Tony and **Drama Desk Award** as Best Revival. An acclaimed 1949 film version, directed by William Wyler, starred Olivia de Havilland in an Academy Award-winning performance, with Ralph Richardson, Montgomery Clift, and Miriam Hopkins. **Julie Harris**, Barry Morse, Farley Granger, and Muriel Kirkland appeared in a 1961 television adaptation. A 1997 film version of *Washington Square* did not make use of the Goetz adaptation.

HELBURN, TERESA (1887–1959).[†] Born in New York, Helburn was educated at Bryn Mawr College, studied with George Pierce Baker* and at the Sorbonne in Paris before briefly pursuing an acting career. She worked briefly as theatre CRITIC for *The Nation* before serving as literary manager of THE THEATRE GUILD from its founding in 1919. She became casting director and ultimately executive director. Under her leadership, the Guild achieved some financial stability and she developed strong relationships with American (EUGENE O'NEILL) and European (GEORGE BERNARD SHAW) dramatists, as well as talented actors, including ALFRED LUNT and LYNN FONTANNE. She left the Guild in 1933 for Hollywood, but returned within a year as administrative director with LAWRENCE LANGNER. Among the Guild's many successes under her leadership were the **Broadway** productions of most of O'Neill's plays of the late 1920s and early 1930s, *Oklahoma!* (1943), and the PAUL ROBESON *Othello* in 1943. Helburn completed her memoirs of her time with the Guild, *A Wayward Quest* (1960), shortly before her death.

HELLMAN, LILLIAN (1905–1984). Born into a Jewish family in New Orleans, Louisiana, Hellman spent much of her childhood dividing her time between New York City, where she attended public school, and a boarding house in New Orleans run by her aunts, a place populated with family members and boarders who inspired characters in many of her works. Hellman studied at New York University and Columbia University, never completing a degree, before marrying writer Arthur Kober in 1925 (they divorced in 1932). She worked as a press agent and play reader for **Broadway** producer **Herman Shumlin**, as well as screenplay reader for MGM. Discouraged about her own writing, she considering quitting until writer Dashiell Hammett encouraged her to continue. The two met in 1931 and began a 30-year off-and-on-again love affair. Hammett, the author of *The Maltese Falcon, The Thin Man,* and other detective novels, is believed to have modeled *The Thin Man*'s central female character, Nora Charles, on Hellman.

Hellman's first Broadway play, *The Children's Hour* (1934), produced by her old boss Shumlin, generated both controversy and acclaim through its story of a schoolgirl's defamation of two **women** teachers. Despite hints of **lesbianism**, the play had a long Broadway run and most CRITICS heralded Hellman as a major talent and as a standout among a small group of women playwrights. Hellman's follow-up play, *Days to Come* (1936), was a disappointment, but her third play, *The Little Foxes* (1939), was admired by critics for its scalding melodrama* exposing the dark side of capitalism in the Old South and was a resounding commercial hit.

With the outbreak of World WAR II, Hellman wrote two plays in response to the crisis. The first, *Watch on the Rhine* (1941), is an anti-Nazi drama implying America's ultimate commitment to defeating fascism, and it won the **New York Drama Critics Circle Award** and became a successful film. Hellman's next play, *The Searching Wind* (1944), also championed antifascist efforts and offered blunt criticism of American failures to halt the aggressions of Adolf Hitler and Benito Mussolini. Following the war, Hellman's *Autumn Garden* (1951) drew on childhood memories of the New Orleans boarding house run by her aunts. Critics expressed disappointment that the play offered little of the ferocity of her earlier dramas and seemed more inspired by **Anton Chekhov** than HENRIK IBSEN, whose REALISTIC social problem plays seemed a more likely precursor to Hellman's earlier plays.

Hellman's *Toys in the Attic* (1960) also drew on her New Orleans childhood, offering a harrowing depiction of possessive love. It was awarded a New York Critics Circle Award. Her final play, *My Mother, My Father, and Me* (1963), was a rare departure from realism in its seriocomic depiction of Jewish family life drawn, once again, from her own past. Despite a cast including **Ruth Gordon**, Lili Darvas, and **Walter Matthau**, it closed after a mere 17 performances. During her career, Hellman also contributed to the troubled libretto of the 1956 MUSICAL version of Voltaire's *Candide*, and adapted two plays, *Montserrat* (1949) and Jean Anouilh's *The Lark* (1956). She also occasionally worked on films, including the first screen version of *The Children's Hour*, renamed *These Three* (1936), and the cinematic adaptation of *The Little Foxes* (1942), as well as *The Dark Angel* (1935), ***Dead End*** (1937), and *The North Star* (1943). After *Toys in the Attic*, Hellman devoted her attention to three acclaimed memoirs, *An Unfinished Woman: A Memoir* (1969), *Pentimento* (1973), and *Scoundrel Time* (1976).

Hellman's plays ensure her place in American theatre history, but her actions during the early 1950s House Un-American Activities Committee (HUAC) Communist "witch hunt" era guaranteed a place in American history. Hammett had been a Communist Party member for a time in the 1930s; called by HUAC to testify in 1952, Hellman was pressed to name acquaintances with Communist Party affiliations. Although some historians dispute the claim, Hellman is believed to have responded with a prepared statement in which she refused to do the "inhuman and indecent and dishonorable" act of hurting former friends to "save myself" and insisted that "I cannot and will not cut my conscience to fit this year's fashions" by naming names. Hellman frequently battled publicly and privately with her critics, including Diana Trilling and, most famously, Mary McCarthy, who challenged her veracity. Hellman has been the subject of films (*Julia*) and plays (*Imaginary Friends*, *Cakewalk*) and, despite controversies, is an essential character in American cultural life. *See also* FEMINIST THEATRE.

HEMSLEY, GILBERT (1936–1983). A native of Bridgeport, Connecticut, Hemsley studied history at Yale University prior to earning an M.F.A. at the Yale School of Drama, after which he worked as assistant to lighting designer **Jean Rosenthal**. He designed for and managed tours of opera and ballet companies and served as production manager for the inaugurations of President Richard M. Nixon and Jimmy Carter. Hemsley designed many operas for the New York City Opera Company, for the American Ballet Theatre, the Bolshoi Ballet, and Martha Graham. He also oversaw the premiere of Leonard Bernstein's *Mass* at the **Kennedy Center** and the Philip Glass opera *Einstein* *at the Beach* (1976) at the Metropolitan Opera. On **Broadway**, Hemsley was nominated for **Drama Desk Awards** for his designs of a 1977 revival of *Porgy and Bess* and *The Mighty Gents* (1978) and, among his Broadway designs are *We, Comrades Three* (1966), revivals of *The Wild Duck* and *You Can't Take It with You* in 1967, *War and Peace* (1967), *Cyrano* (1973), *Jumpers* (1974), *Your Arms Are Too Short to Box With God* (1976), *I Love My Wife* (1977), and *Sugar Babies* (1979). Hemsley also taught at the University of Wisconsin at Madison.

HENDERSON, MARK (1950?–). The British-born lighting designer from Nottinghamshire, England, began at Opera North and has designed over 50 productions in London, winning four Olivier Awards, as well as designs for opera and dance productions. Henderson has also frequently provided designs on **Broadway**, where he won a **Tony Award** for *The History Boys* (2006) and nominations for *Indiscretions* (1995), a 1999 revival of *The Iceman Cometh*, *Chitty Chitty Bang Bang* (2005), and *Faith Healer* (2006). Henderson's other Broadway designs include revivals of *The Merchant of Venice* in 1989, *Cat on a Hot Tin Roof* in 1990, and *Hamlet* in 1995, *Racing Demon* (1995), *The Judas Kiss* (1998), *Amy's View* (1999), *Copenhagen* (2000), revivals of *The Real Thing* in 2000 and *A Moon for the Misbegotten* in 2007, and *Deuce* (2007). Of his design process, Henderson says, "I normally come in relatively late to a production. I read a script, talk to the director, and I see the designer's model. Then you start putting the pictures together in your head, from what you've talked to the director about and what the script is telling you."

HENLEY, BETH (1952–). Born Elizabeth Becker Henley in Jackson, Mississippi, she was educated at Southern Methodist University and the University of Illinois before beginning a career as a playwright and actress. Her writing became her dominant pursuit when her 1978 play, *Crimes of the Heart*, premiered at the **Actors Theatre of Louisville** prior to a **Broadway** production that brought her a PULITZER PRIZE, **New York Drama Critics Circle Award**, and a **Tony Award** nomination. Henley's 1986 screenplay for this comedy-drama about three Southern sisters was nominated for an Academy Award. Henley adapted her own *The Miss Firecracker Contest* (1979) into a film starring Holly Hunter in 1989, and *The Wake of Jamey Foster* (1981), which starred Hunter on Broadway but only lasted a dozen performances. Henley's other plays include *Am I Blue* (1972), *The Debutante Ball* (1985), *The Lucky Spot* (1986), *Abundance* (1990), *Control Freaks* (1992), *Signature* (1995), *L-Play* (1996), *Impossible Marriage* (1998), *Family Week* (2000), and *Ridiculous Fraud* (2006). *Family Week* was revised for Broadway in

2010, but met with predominantly negative reviews. Henley has also written screenplays for *True Stories* (1986) and *Nobody's Fool* (1986).

HENRY, WILLIAM ALFRED, III (1950–1994). South Orange, New Jersey-born Henry studied at Yale University and for a time acted in STOCK and at the **Yale Repertory Theatre** before going into journalism, writing for the *Boston Globe* and shared a PULITZER PRIZE for his 1975 coverage of desegregation in Boston. In the 1980s he became theatre CRITIC for *Time Magazine* and won an Emmy Award for a documentary on Bob Fosse. Among his books, he wrote a 1992 biography of Jackie Gleason and *In Defense of Elitism* (1994), which argued for renewed interest in education, multiculturalism, and the arts in the United States.

HEPBURN, KATHARINE (1907–2003). Born in Hartford, Connecticut, to a doctor father and suffragette mother, Katharine Houghton Hepburn attended Bryn Mawr and debuted in a STOCK production of *The Czarina* in 1928 in Baltimore. She spent a few years being hired, fired, and rehired by **Broadway** producers of *Night Hostess* (1928), *These Days* (1928), and *Art and Mrs. Bottle* (1930), among others, before she scored a Broadway success in as an Amazon princess in *The Warrior's Husband* (1932). This performance led to a Hollywood contract and the start of a legendary 62-year screen career that brought her four Best Actress Academy Awards and 12 nominations.

Hepburn, who exuded confidence, but played as many vulnerable **women** as strong ones, was drawn to films with a theatrical source and she returned to the stage with some frequency, including a disastrous performance in *The Lake* (1934), which inspired DOROTHY PARKER to write, "Miss Hepburn runs the gamut of emotions from A to B." Undaunted, Hepburn appeared with great success in *Jane Eyre* (1936) and triumphed in ***The Philadelphia Story*** (1938), which playwright PHILIP BARRY had written for her (Hepburn had previously appeared in a 1938 film version of Barry's *Holiday**). Hepburn returned to Broadway in Barry's ***Without Love*** (1942) and acclaimed revivals of *As You Like It* in 1950 and GEORGE BERNARD SHAW's *The Millionairess* in 1952. In 1955, she toured Australia with the Old Vic in productions of *The Merchant of Venice, Measure for Measure*, and *The Taming of the Shrew*, following by two seasons with the Shakespeare Theatre in Stratford, Connecticut, appearing in *The Merchant of Venice* and *Much Ado About Nothing* in 1957 and *Antony and Cleopatra* and *Twelfth Night* in 1960. In 1969, she took on the challenge of a Broadway MUSICAL, appearing for a year in *Coco*, playing celebrated French designer Coco Chanel, which brought her a **Tony Award** nomination. She toured with *Coco* and in 1976 returned to Broadway in Enid Bagnold's *A*

Matter of Gravity. Her final Broadway appearance, in Ernest Thompson's *The West Side Waltz* (1981), brought her a Tony nomination.

On screen, Hepburn won Oscars for her performances in *Morning Glory* (1933), *Guess Who's Coming to Dinner* (1967), *The Lion in Winter* (1968), and *On Golden Pond* (1981), and was Academy Award-nominated for *Alice Adams* (1935), *The Philadelphia Story* (1940), *Woman of the Year* (1942), *The African Queen* (1951), *Summertime* (1955), *The Rainmaker* (1956), *Suddenly Last Summer* (1959), and *Long Day's Journey into Night* (1962). Hepburn's Emmy Award-nominated television appearances included *The Glass Menagerie* in 1973 and *The Corn Is Green* in 1979, as well as *Mrs. Delafield Wants to Marry* (1986), and she appeared opposite **Laurence Olivier** in *Love among the Ruins* (1975), winning an Emmy Award. Hepburn had been briefly married to Ludlow Ogden Smith, but in the 1930s had relationships with such notable men as John Ford, **Leland Hayward**, and Howard Hughes, but after working with SPENCER TRACY in *Woman of the Year*, they began a close relationship that survived until his death in 1967. Following Hepburn's death, the town of Old Saybrook, Connecticut, where she had lived her entire life, constructed the state-of-the-art Katharine Hepburn Cultural Arts Center and Theatre, and it opened in 2009.

HER MASTER'S VOICE. Based on her vaudeville* sketch, "The Choir Boy," this two-act comedy by Clare Kummer* opened in a **Max Gordon** production on 23 October 1933 at the Plymouth Theatre for 224 performances. Roland Young* starred as feckless Ned Farrar, an aspiring singer, whose wife, Queena, and meddling mother-in-law are frustrated by his inability to hold a job. When Queena's pretentious aunt (Laura Hope Crews*) arrives, she mistakes Ned for a servant. Ultimately, Ned is a success as a radio singer, and he and Queena are reconciled following a temporary break-up. A 1964 revival **Off-Broadway** flopped. A 1936 film version featured Edward Everett Horton as Ned, with Crews repeating her stage role.

HERBERT, F. HUGH (1897–1958). Vienna, Austria, was the birthplace of this playwright, novelist, and screenwriter who studied at the University of London prior to moving to the United States. He wrote several screenplays for MUSICALS and light comedies in the 1930s and 1940s and directed a few of them. On **Broadway**, his first play, *Quiet, Please!* (1940) flopped, but he scored long-running hits with *Kiss and Tell* (1943) and *The Moon Is Blue* (1951). Herbert adapted both to the screen, but *The Moon Is Blue*, for which Herbert received a Writers Guild of America nomination, caused a scandal when the Motion Picture Production Code refused its seal of approval because of the frank **sexual** themes in the film. The uproar only helped the movie's box office and as such *The Moon Is Blue* contributed to the weakening of the code. Herbert's other Broadway plays, *For Keeps* (1944), *Oh, Brother!* (1945), *For Love or Money* (1947), *A Girl Can Tell* (1953), and *The Best House in Naples* (1956), had short runs. Herbert won a Writers Guild of America Award for his screenplay for *Sitting Pretty* (1948) and he wrote episodic television as well.

HERLIE, EILEEN (1920–2008). Born in Glasgow, Scotland, this versatile actress of stage and screen equally at home in the classics and MUSICALS began her career with the Scottish National Theatre before moving to London, where she won critical plaudits in Jean Cocteau's *The Eagle Has Two Heads* (1944) before an eventual move to New York. On **Broadway**, Herlie made her debut as Irene Molloy in **Thornton Wilder**'s *The Matchmaker* (1955) and was nominated for a **Tony Award** for *Take Me Along* (1959), the musical adaptation of EUGENE O'NEILL's *Ah, Wilderness!* She also appeared in *Makropoulos Secret* (1957), *Epitaph for George Dillon* (1958), *All American* (1962), *Photo Finish* (1963), as Gertrude in the **Richard Burton** *Hamlet* in 1964, *Halfway Up the Tree* (1967), a 1973 revival of *Emperor Henry IV* with **Rex Harrison**, and *Crown Matrimonial* (1973). In films, Herlie played Gertrude in **Laurence Olivier**'s *Hamlet* (1948) and appeared in *The Story of Gilbert and Sullivan* (1953), *Freud* (1962), and others. On television, Herlie appeared in the long-running soap opera *All My Children*, garnering four Daytime Emmy Award nominations.

HERLIHY, JAMES LEO (1927–1993). A native of Detroit, Michigan, Herlihy joined the United States Navy after high school and the G. I. Bill allowed him to study at Black Mountain College where he became interested in the arts. He became a playwright, novelist, and sometime actor until the 1980s, when he increasingly spent his time teaching. His 1958 play, *Blue Denim*, had a moderately successful run on **Broadway** under **Joshua Logan**'s direction. His other plays include *Streetlight Sonata* (1950), *Moon in Capricorn* (1953), *Crazy October* (1959), and *Stop, You're Killing Me: Three Short Plays* (1969). Herlihy acted in **Edward Albee**'s *The Zoo Story* in Boston and Paris in 1963 and appeared in the film *Four Friends* (1981) and is perhaps best known for his novels, *All Fall Down* (1960), *Midnight Cowboy* (1965), and *The Season of the Witch* (1971), the first two of which were successfully adapted to the screen.

HERNE, CHRYSTAL (1882–1950).[†] Daughter of nineteenth-century playwright/actor James A. Herne,[*] she was born Katherine Chrystal Herne in Dorchester, Massachusetts. She debuted on **Broadway** in her father's play, *Sag Harbor** (1900), and had a long career ranging from ingénue roles to character parts in such plays as *Major Andre* (1903), the first American production of GEORGE BERNARD SHAW's *Mrs. Warren's Profession* in 1905 (and several other Shaw plays), *The Melting Pot* (1909), *As a Man Thinks** (1911), and *Polygamy* (1915). In her later roles, including Somerset Maugham's *Our Betters* (1917) and RACHEL CROTHERS's *Expressing Willie** (1924), she moved toward playing haughty society women. She scored a notable success in the title role of GEORGE KELLY's PULITZER PRIZE-winning *Craig's Wife** (1925). Her later appearances in *These Modern Women* (1928), *Mayfair* (1930), *Ladies of Creation* (1931), and *A Room in Red and White* (1936) were less successful.

HERRMANN, EDWARD (1943–). Born Edward Kirk Herrmann in Washington, D.C., he attended Bucknell University and studied at the London Academy of Music and Dramatic Art. Successful as an actor in theatre, film, and television, Herrmann made his first **Off-Broadway** appearance in *The Basic Training of Pavlo Hummel* in 1971 and debuted on **Broadway** in *Moonchildren* (1972). He won a **Tony Award** in a revival of *Mrs. Warren's Profession* in 1976. Herrmann also appeared on Broadway in a revival of *The Philadelphia Story* in 1980 and garnered another Tony nomination for *Plenty* (1983). He also returned to Broadway in a revival of *The Deep Blue Sea* in 1998. Herrmann received a **Drama Desk Award** nomination for **John Patrick Shanley**'s *Psychopathia Sexualis* (1997), and his other noted Off-Broadway appearances include *Tom and Viv* (1985) and *Life Sentences* (1993), and he played opposite Alec Guinness in *A Walk in the Woods* in London in 1988. He has also appeared in **regional theatres**, including the **Williamstown Theatre Festival** and the **Huntington Theatre**. In films, Herrmann has appeared in *The Great Gatsby* (1974), *Reds* (1981), *Annie* (1982), *The Purple Rose of Cairo* (1985), *Born Yesterday* (1993), *Nixon* (1995), *The Cat's Meow* (2001), and *The Aviator* (2004). Herrmann has been nominated for five Emmy Awards, winning one for a guest appearance on *The Practice* in 1999. Two of his nominations for were *Eleanor and Franklin* (1976) and *Eleanor and Franklin: The White House Years* (1977), two acclaimed television films in which he played Franklin D. Roosevelt. Herrmann appeared in a recurring role on the television series, *The Gilmore Girls* beginning in 2007.

HEWES, HENRY (1917–2006). The scion of a wealthy Massachusetts family, Hewes was born in Boston, and educated at Harvard University, Carnegie Mellon University, and Columbia University. He served in the United States Army-Air Corps during World WAR II and later became drama CRITIC, writing first for the *New York Times* before settling in at the *Saturday Review* in 1954. He edited the annual Best Plays volumes from 1961 to 1964, created the **Drama Desk Awards**, and was founded of the **American Theatre Critics Association** in 1974. The **American Theatre Wing** named its design awards in Hewes's honor in 1999.

HEYWARD, DUBOSE (1885–1940) AND DOROTHY (1890–1961). With his wife, Dorothy Hartzell Kuhns, Edwin Dubose Heyward crafted two of his novels into important folk dramas* of **African American** life in the early twentieth century. A native of South Carolina, Heyward was an insurance man who published short stories and poetry in the early 1920s. With his wife's collaboration, he crafted his novel *Porgy** into a 1927 PULITZER PRIZE-winning drama depicting a crippled beggar's doomed love for a faithless woman. Heyward collaborated when George Gershwin composed a folk opera, *Porgy and Bess* (1935), from this work. In 1931, Heyward's drama *Brass Ankle*, written specifically for the stage and recounting the tale of a woman who plans suicide when she learns she has Negro blood, managed 44 performances, but another Heyward novel, *Mamba's Daughters* (1939), a tragic melodrama* of three generations of a black family, was well-received in a production directed by GUTHRIE McCLINTIC, in part due to the compelling performance of **Ethel Waters** in the leading role, a first for a black woman in a **Broadway** drama. The play's respectful reception and Waters's breakthrough performance opened the door to greater opportunity for black writers and actors on the New York stage.

HICKEY, WILLIAM (1928–1997). Born in Brooklyn, New York, of Irish American descent, Hickey became a successful stage, and later film and television actor, and began teaching at the HB Studio in 1953. He made his **Broadway** debut in 1951 in a revival of *Saint Joan*, followed by character roles in a revival of *Tovarich* in 1952, *Miss Lonelyhearts* (1957), *The Body Beautiful* (1958), *Make a Million* (1958), *Moonbirds* (1959), *Step on a Crack* (1962), *Happy Birthday, Wanda June* (1970), a revival of *Mourning Becomes Electra* in 1972), *Thieves* (1974), and a revival of *Arsenic and Old Lace* in 1986. He also appeared frequently **Off-Broadway**, most notably in **Tennessee Williams's** *Small Craft Warnings* (1972). Hickey received an Academy Award nomination for his performance as a wizened Mafia don in *Prizzi's Honor* (1985), and he also appeared memorably as a drunk in *The Producers* (1968), as well as *The Boston Strangler* (1968), *Little Big Man* (1970), *Wise Blood* (1979), and *Da* (1988). Among his many television appearances, Hickey was nominated for an Emmy Award for his performance in *Tales from the Crypt* in 1990.

HIGGINS, JOHN MICHAEL (1963–). A native of Boston, Massachusetts, Higgins attended Amherst College. Both an actor and director, Higgins acted on **Broadway** in David Hirson's *La Bête* (1991) and won acclaim for his **Off-Broadway** performance in the title role of **Paul Rudnick**'s comedy *Jeffrey* (1994) playing a **gay** man in the age of **AIDS**. He also appeared in a 2000 **Second Stage** revival of **Edward Albee**'s *Tiny Alice*, was nominated for a **Drama Desk Award** for **A. R. Gurney**'s *Big Bill* (2003), and appeared at the **Mark Taper Forum** as Donald Rumsfeld in **David Hare**'s *Stuff Happens* in 2004. In films, Higgins has appeared in *Wag the Dog* (1997), *Best in Show* (2000), *A Mighty Wind* (2003), *For Your Consideration* (2006), *Evan Almighty* (2007), and numerous television shows.

HIGH TOR. MAXWELL ANDERSON's three-act blank-verse fantasy opened at the Martin Beck Theatre on 9 January 1937 for 171 performances, winning the **New York Drama Critics Circle Award** for its story of Van Van Dorn, a young man disillusioned with contemporary life, who quarrels with his girlfriend, Judith. He retreats to a piece of property he owns overlooking the Hudson River, where he runs afoul of land speculators wanting his property, thieves, and ghosts of Dutch-era sailors. Ultimately, he sells his land for a profit and reconciles with Judith. Anderson adapted the play as a television MUSICAL with music by Arthur Schwartz in 1956.

HIKEN, GERALD (1927–). A native of Milwaukee, Wisconsin, Hiken first appeared **Off-Broadway** in a 1955 revival of *The Cherry Orchard* and made his **Broadway** debut in *The Lovers* (1956). He was nominated for a **Tony Award** and a **Drama Desk Award** for his performance in *Strider* (1979) and also appeared on Broadway in *The Good Woman of Setzuan* (1956), *The Cave Dwellers* (1957), *The Nervous Set* (1959), *The Fighting Cock* (1959), *The 49th Cousin* (1960), *Foxy* (1964), a revival of *The Three Sisters* in 1964, *Golda* (1977), and *Fools* (1981). He also took over the title role in **Gideon** from Douglas Campbell in 1962, but Hiken appeared more frequently Off-Broadway and became best known for his performances in the plays of **Anton Chekhov**, including revivals of *Uncle Vanya* and *The Seagull* in 1956. He also appeared Off-Broadway in the 1957 revival of EUGENE O'NEILL's *The Iceman Cometh* and in **Tony Kushner**'s *Slavs!* (1994). He was artistic director of the Stanford Repertory from 1966 to 1968.

HILFERTY, SUSAN (1953–). Born in Massachusetts, Hilferty studied at Syracuse University and the Yale School of Drama, as well as St. Martin's School of Art. Her work as a costume designer has included theatre, opera, and film. On **Broadway**, she won a **Tony Award**, **Drama Desk Award**, and

Outer Critics Circle Award for *Wicked* (2003). She received Tony nominations for a 2002 revival of *Into the Woods, Lestat* (2006), and *Spring Awakening* (2006), and her other Broadway designs include *A Lesson from Aloes* (1980), a 1985 revival of *Blood Knot, Coastal Disturbances* (1987), revivals of *The Comedy of Errors* in 1987, *How to Succeed in Business without Really Trying* in 1995, and ***The Night of the Iguana*** in 1996, *Sex and Longing* (1996), *Dirty Blonde* (2000), revivals of *"Master Harold". . .and the Boys* in 2003 and *Assassins* in 2004, *The Good Body* (2004), and ***Radio Golf*** (2007). **Off-Broadway** and in regional theatre, Hilferty's designs have been seen in numerous productions, and she has designed for the ballet troupes of Eliot Feld, Alvin Ailey, and Jennifer Muller. Hilferty won a 2000 **Obie Award** for Sustained Excellence in costume design, and she heads the Graduate Department of Design at New York University's Tisch School of the Arts.

HILL, ARTHUR (1922–2006). A native of Melfort, Saskatchewan, Canada, Arthur Edward Spence Hill studied law at the University of British Columbia and served in the Royal Canadian Air Force during World War II before taking up acting. He debuted on **Broadway** in a 1957 revival of ***The Matchmaker*** and won a **Tony Award** as George in ***Who's Afraid of Virginia Woolf?*** (1962). Hill also appeared in ***Look Homeward, Angel*** (1957), *The Gang's All Here* (1959), ***All the Way Home*** (1960), *Something More!* (1964), and *More Stately Mansions* (1967), but concentrated on a successful film and television career after the early 1960s, including roles on the big screen in *Harper* (1966), *Petulia* (1968), *The Chairman* (1969), *The Andromeda Strain* (1971), and *A Little Romance* (1979), and nearly 100 television programs.

HINGLE, PAT (1924–2009). Born Martin Patterson Hingle in Miami, Florida, he studied at the University of Texas, but dropped out to enlist in the United States Navy at the start of World War II. Following the war, he completed his degree in broadcasting at the University of Texas before beginning his acting career. He debuted on **Broadway** in *End as a Man* (1953) and played a range of roles, including reaping a **Tony Award** nomination as Rubin Flood in ***The Dark at the Top of the Stairs*** (1957). His other notable appearances include playing Gooper in ***Cat on a Hot Tin Roof*** (1955), the title character in ***J.B.*** (1958), and Victor Franz in ***The Price*** (1968), and he also appeared in *Festival* (1955), *Girls of Summer* (1956), *The Deadly Game* (1960), a revival of *Strange Interlude** in 1963, ***Blues for Mister Charlie*** (1964), *A Girl Could Get Lucky* (1965), a 1965 revival of ***The Glass Menagerie***, *Johnny No-Trump* (1967), *Child's Play* (1970), *The Selling of the President* (1972), a revival of *The Lady from the Sea* in 1976, *A Life* (1980), and he made his last appearance as Benjamin Franklin in a 1997 revival of the

MUSICAL *1776*. Hingle also replaced **Walter Matthau** as Oscar in *The Odd Couple* in 1966 and Richard A. Dysart as the coach in *That Championship Season* in 1973. Hingle appeared in many films, including *Splendor in the Grass* (1961), *The Ugly American* (1963), *All the Way Home* (1963), *Hang 'Em High* (1968), *Norma Rae* (1979), and *Batman* (1989), as well as over 100 television appearances.

HIRSCH, JUDD (1935–). Born Judd Seymore Hirsch in the Bronx to a Russian Jewish family, Hirsch studied physics at the City College of New York before beginning an acting career that has encompassed theatre, film, and television. He debuted on **Broadway** in *Barefoot in the Park* as the telephone man replacing Herb Edelman in 1966. He won a 1976 **Drama Desk Award** for his performance in **Jules Feiffer**'s *Knock, Knock* and a nomination for **Neil Simon**'s *Chapter Two* (1977). He was nominated for a **Tony Award** and a Drama Desk Award as Jewish immigrant Matt Friedman in **Lanford Wilson**'s *Pulitzer Prize*-winning *Talley's Folly* (1980). He won Tonys for two **Herb Gardner** plays, *I'm Not Rappaport* (1985), appearing in the title role again in the 2002 revival, and *Conversations with My Father* (1992). He also appeared in a 1996 revival of *A Thousand Clowns*, stepped into the role of Marc in *Art* in 1998, and acted in *Sixteen Wounded* (2004). He also appeared in several **Off-Broadway** productions, most notably *The Hot L Baltimore* (1973) and a **Circle Repertory Company** revival of *The Seagull* in 1983. On screen, Hirsch was nominated for an Academy Award for *Ordinary People* (1980), and won two Emmy Awards for leading roles in the television series *Taxi* (1978–1983) and a Golden Globe Award for another series, *Dear John* (1988–1992).

HIRSCHFELD, AL (1903–2003). Few individuals captured **Broadway**'s Golden Age by any means more memorably than one man whose career lasted a remarkable 75 years. Born Albert Hirschfeld in St. Louis, Missouri, he studied art in New York and Paris before moving into doing drawings of theatre personages for several New York newspapers, settling at the *New York Times* in 1925. Until shortly before his death at age 100, Hirschfeld provided the *Times* with illustrations to accompany theatre and film reviews and articles about the latest plays and stage personalities of the era. Hirschfeld published several collections of his illustrations. He was presented with two special **Tony Awards** (1975, 1984) and shortly after his death, the Martin Beck Theatre was renamed the Al Hirschfeld Theatre. *See also* CARICATURES; PERIODICALS.

HISPANIC THEATRE. *See* CHICANO THEATRE.

HOCH, DANNY (1970–). Brooklyn-born Hoch began as a break dancer, rapper, and writer in his teens, but in the 1990s won acclaim for his **solo Off-Broadway** shows in which he captured a range of characters and dialects drawn from his childhood on the streets of Brooklyn, including *Some People* (1994), which brought him an **Obie Award**. Especially adept at recreating a range of accents and attitudes, Hoch's subsequent works, including *Pot Melting* (1991), *Clinic Con Class* (1997), *Jails, Hospitals, & Hip Hop* (1997), *Up Against the Wall* (1999), *Till the Break of Dawn* (2007), and *Taking Over* (2008), reflected the rapidly changing landscape of city life.

HOFFMAN, DUSTIN (1937–). Born in Los Angeles, California, as Dustin Lee Hoffman, he studied medicine at Santa Monica College, but quit to join the **Pasadena Playhouse**. After moving to New York with his roommate Gene Hackman, he joined **The Actors Studio** and began working **Off-Broadway**, debuting in **Ronald Ribman**'s *Harry, Noon, and Night* (1965) followed by Ribman's *The Journey of the Fifth Horse* (1966). He also had a small role on **Broadway** in the short-lived *A Cook for Mr. General* (1961) and was Martin Sheen's standby for *The Subject Was Roses* (1964). Hoffman won critical acclaim in Harry Livings's *Eh?* (1966), which brought him a **Theatre World Award** and a **Drama Desk Award**. He was cast the following year as Benjamin Braddock in the film *The Graduate* (1967), which brought him his first Academy Award nomination and established him as a major movie star. He occasionally returned to the stage, winning a Drama Desk Award for the MUSICAL *Jimmy Shine* (1968), and he appeared in **Murray Schisgal**'s *All Over Town* (1974).

For a decade, Hoffman devoted himself to films, but he returned to Broadway as Willy Loman in an acclaimed revival of *Death of a Salesman* in 1984, winning a Drama Desk Award. His only other return brought him **Tony Award** and Drama Desk Award nominations as Shylock in a revival of *The Merchant of Venice* in 1989. On screen, Hoffman has appeared in nearly 50 films and been nominated for the Academy Award seven times, winning twice for *Kramer vs. Kramer* (1979) and *Rain Man* (1988), both of which also brought him Golden Globe Awards, as did his performance in *Tootsie* (1982). He also won an Emmy Award and a Golden Globe Award reprising his stage performance in *Death of a Salesman* in 1985.

HOFFMAN, PHILIP SEYMOUR (1967–). A native of Rochester, New York, Hoffman trained at New York University's Tisch School of the Arts prior to beginning an acting career on stage, film, and television. His two **Broadway** appearances, in revivals of **Sam Shepard**'s *True West* in 2000 and **Eugene O'Neill**'s *Long Day's Journey into Night* in 2003, brought him

Tony Award nominations and he received a Theatre World Award for the former. Off-Broadway, Hoffman has appeared in *Defying Gravity* (1997), *Shopping and Fucking* (1998), *The Author's Voice* (1999), and a revival of *The Seagull* in 2001. Also a director, Hoffman has staged Labyrinth Theatre productions of *Our Lady of 121st Street* (2003), *Jesus Hopped the A-Train* (2004), *The Last Days of Judas Iscariot* (2005), and *The Little Flower of East Orange* (2008), and, for the Manhattan Class Company, he directed *The Glory of Living* (2001).

On screen, Hoffman won an Academy Award for *Capote* (2005) and has been nominated for *Charlie Wilson's War* (2007) and *Doubt* (2008), and his other films include *Nobody's Fool* (1994), *Twister* (1996), *Boogie Nights* (1997), *The Big Lebowski* (1998), *Magnolia* (1999), *The Talented Mr. Ripley* (1999), *Punch-Drunk Love* (2002), *Cold Mountain* (2003), and *Synecdoche, New York* (2008). On television, Hoffman was nominated for an Emmy Award for the mini-series *Empire Falls* (2005).

HOFFMAN, WILLIAM M. (1939–). New York-born dramatist who began writing for Off-Off-Broadway theatres in the mid-1960s, Hoffman rose to prominence with his AIDS-themed play, *As Is* (1985), one of the first to respond to the mounting pandemic and its impact on the gay community. The play won a Drama Desk Award and a Tony Award nomination and was filmed for television the following year. Hoffman's other plays include *Thank You, Miss Victoria* (1965), *Good Night, I Love You* (1966), *Saturday Night at the Movies* (1966), *Incantation* (1967), *xxx (aka Nativity Play)* (1969), *Luna* (1970), *From Fool to Hanged Man* (1972), *Children's Crusade* (1972), *Giles De Rais* (1975), and *The Cherry Orchard, Part II* (1983). Hoffman teaches at the City University of New York, worked as an editor at Hill and Wang, and was Emmy Award-nominated for writing the TV soap opera *One Life to Live* in the 1990s.

HOGAN'S GOAT. William Alfred's two-act play opened Off-Broadway at the American Place Theatre on 11 November 1965 for 607 performances and won a Drama Desk Award for Alfred and Theatre World Awards for actors Faye Dunaway and Richard Mulligan. Set in the world of New York's Irish Americans in 1890, the play depicts a mayoral candidate, Matthew Stanton (Ralph Waite), attempting to defeat a corrupt mayor, Ned Quinn (Tom Ahearne), who uncovers Stanton's secret, that he and his wife, Kathleen (Dunaway), were not married in the Catholic Church and that he was once a kept man (a "goat") of Agnes Hogan, now Quinn's mistress. Cliff Gorman and Conrad Bain played supporting roles. Alfred wrote lyrics and cowrote the book for a MUSICAL version of the play called *Cry for Us All* (1970), but it flopped on **Broadway**. A 1971 PBS television version featured Dunaway, Robert Foxworth, **George Rose**, **Philip Bosco**, **Kevin Conway**, and Rue McClanahan.

HOLBROOK, HAL (1925–). Born Harold Rowe Holbrook, Jr. in Cleveland, Ohio, he began his acting career in 1942 with a local STOCK company, where he stayed for four years before touring in classical scenes and developing his **solo** show *Mark Twain Tonight!* (1955), which he has played throughout his career, including **Off-Broadway** in 1959, winning a **Drama Desk Award**, and on **Broadway** in 1966, winning a **Tony Award**. Holbrook's other Broadway credits include *Do You Know the Milky Way?* (1961), *After the Fall* (1964), a revival of *Marco Millions** (1964), *Incident at Vichy* (1964), a revival of *Tartuffe* in 1965, *I Never Sang for My Father* (1968), *Does a Tiger Wear a Necktie?* (1969), and *An American Daughter* (1997). He also stepped in to replace leads in a revival of *The Glass Menagerie* in 1965, *The Apple Tree* in 1967, and *Man of La Mancha* in 1968. On screen, Holbrook was nominated for an Academy Award for *Into the Wild* (2007) and appeared in numerous films, including *The Great White Hope* (1970), as "Deep Throat" in *All the President's Me*n (1976), *Julia* (1977), *The Firm* (1993), *Judas Kiss* (1998), and *The Majestic* (2001). On television, he won Emmy Awards for an episode of *The Bold Ones* in 1970, *Pueblo* (1973), *Lincoln* (1974), and *Portrait of America* (1983).

HOLLIDAY, JUDY (1923–1965). The daughter of Russian Jewish parents, she was born Judith Tuvim in New York and worked as a switchboard operator for **The Mercury Theatre** following school. She partnered with Betty Comden, Adolph Green, Leonard Bernstein, Alvin Hammer, and John Frank to form a nightclub act called "The Revuers" in 1938 and the worked together until 1944. Holliday made her **Broadway** debut in *Kiss Them for Me* (1945), winning a **Theatre World Award**. When screen star Jean Arthur withdrew from the cast of **Garson Kanin**'s *Born Yesterday* (1946), Holliday took over the role of Billie Dawn, a role she repeated on screen in an Academy Award and Golden Globe Award-winning performance. Holliday also appeared in a 1951 revival of *Dream Girl* and starred in the MUSICAL *Bells Are Ringing* (1956), winning a **Tony Award**. She made her final Broadway appearance in the short-lived musical *Hot Spot* (1963). On screen, Holliday appeared in Golden Globe Award-nominated performances in *Adam's Rib* (1949), *The Solid Gold Cadillac* (1956), and *Bells Are Ringing* (1960). Her early death from breast cancer robbed theatre and film of one of its most unique performers.

HOLM, CELESTE (1917–   ). Born in New York, this versatile actress studied at the University of Chicago. She appeared with LESLIE HOWARD and in STOCK productions prior to her earliest **Broadway** appearance in the late 1930s. Following the flop *Gloriana* (1938), she played the mysterious Mary L. in **William Saroyan**'s PULITZER PRIZE-winning *The Time of Your Life* (1939), followed by *Another Sun* (1940), *The Return of the Vagabond* (1940), *Eight O'Clock Tuesday* (1941), *My Fair Ladies* (1941), *Papa Is All* (1942), *All the Comforts of Home* (1942), and *The Damask Cheek* (1942) before delivering a memorable performance as Ado Annie in her first MUSICAL, *Oklahoma!* (1943).

Holm followed *Oklahoma!* with another musical, this time starring as Evalina in *Bloomer Girl* (1944), and she pursued a film career beginning in 1946. She returned to Broadway with some frequency, including *Affairs of State* (1950), she replaced an ailing **Gertrude Lawrence** in *The King and I* in 1952, a revival of *Anna Christie** in 1952, *His and Hers* (1954), *Interlock* (1958), *Third Best Sport* (1958), *Invitation to a March* (1960), she was one of a long series of actresses playing the title role in *Mame* (1966), a revival of *Candida* in 1970, *Habeas Corpus* (1975), *The Utter Glory of Morrissey Hall* (1979), and *I Hate Hamlet* (1991). In the movies, Holm won an Academy Award and a Golden Globe Award for *Gentlemen's Agreement* (1947) and was nominated for Oscars for *Come to the Stable* (1949) and *All About Eve* (1950), and appeared in *The Snake Pit* (1948), *The Tender Trap* (1955), *High Society* (1956), and *Tom Sawyer* (1973). On television, Holm was nominated for Emmy Awards for an episode of *Insight* in 1968 and *Backstairs at the White House* (1979).

HOLY GHOSTS. **Romulus Linney**'s 1971 drama was first staged at Eastern Carolina University prior to two **Off-Off Broadway** productions and several **regional theatre** staging before it opened at New York's Theatre 890 in a **San Diego Repertory Theatre** production in August 1987. Set in a makeshift church, the play depicts the motley congregation of Rev. Obediah Buckhorn, Sr., and the failed lives to some extent redeemed by their bedrock and occasionally blind faith. The play is frequently produced in regional and university theatres.

HOME OF THE BRAVE. **Arthur Laurents**'s three-act drama opened at the Belasco Theatre in a Lee Sabinson production on 27 December 1945 for 69 performances. An uncommonly REALISTIC examination of anti-Semitism in the United States military and the problem of battle fatigue, the play centered on the loss of speech of a soldier whose trauma is ultimately revealed and leads to his cure. The cast included Eduard Franz and Russell Hardie and was directed by Michael Gordon, with scene and lighting design by **Ralph Alswang**. A 1949 film version dropped the Jewish protagonist in favor of a black hero, played by James Edwards. *See also* ETHNIC THEATRE.

HOMEBODY/KABUL. **Tony Kushner**'s **Obie Award**-winning three-act epic drama of a British family's encounter with Afghanistan under Taliban rule premiered at the **New York Theatre Workshop** on 19 December 2001 under the direction of Declan Donnellan. Kushner continued to revise the play through a **Trinity Repertory Company** production in 2002 directed by **Oskar Eustis** and a 2004 production at the **Brooklyn Academy of Music** directed by **Frank Galati**. The play begins with an hour-long monologue by The Homebody, an unhappy middle-class British woman fascinated with Afghanistan who journeys to that country and disappears. The remainder of the play deals with her daughter's search for her mother and for answers. Unwilling to believe the Taliban's official account of her mother's death, the daughter takes to the streets of the mysterious and frightening city of Kabul, seeking answers. Kushner originally wrote The Homebody's monologue for English actress Kika Markham, who performed it at London's Chelsea Theatre Centre in 1999.

HOMOSEXUALITY. *See* GAY AND LESBIAN THEATRE.

HOOKS, ROBERT (1937–   ). Washington, D.C.-born Robert Dean "Bobby" Hooks is a pioneering **African American** actor who won a **New York Drama Critics Circle Award** for his debut **Broadway** performance in **Lorraine Hansberry**'s *A Raisin in the Sun* (1959). Hooks was a founder of two of the most important black companies of the period: New York's **Group Theatre** Workshop and Washington's Black **Repertory** Company. He also was among the cofounders of the **Negro Ensemble Company**. He appeared in the original productions of *Dutchman* (1964) and *Where's Daddy?* (1966), which brought him a **Theatre World Award**. He was nominated for a **Tony Award** for the musical *Hallelujah, Baby!* (1967). Hooks also appeared in *Tiger, Tiger Burning Bright* (1962) and *Day of Absence* (1966). In films, Hooks appeared in *Sweet Love, Bitter* (1967) and *Hurry Sundown* (1967), and in numerous television shows. He was the first black actor to play a lead on a television drama in *N.Y.P.D.* (1967–1969).

HOPKINS, ARTHUR (1878–1950).[†] Born in Cleveland, Arthur Melancthon Hopkins worked as a newspaper reporter covering President William McKinley's assassination before becoming a vaudeville* press agent, doing publicity for Vernon and Irene Castle, and beginning his producing work as a booking AGENT. His first **Broadway** producing effort, *Poor Little Rich Girl* (1913), was successful and he followed it with *On Trial** (1914) and *Redemption* (1918) starring John Barrymore.* Hopkins produced two notable **Shakespeare**an productions, *Richard III* (1920) and *Hamlet* (1922), starring Barrymore. When he directed EUGENE O'NEILL's PULITZER PRIZE-winning *Anna Christie** (1921) and *The Hairy Ape** (1922), Hopkins began a decade of producing and/or directing many of the most important plays of the era, including *What Price Glory** (1924), *Paris Bound** (1927), *Burlesque* (1927; which he coauthored), *Holiday** (1928), *Machinal** (1928), and his own play *Conquest* (1933), a retelling of *Hamlet*. Hopkins worked closely with designer ROBERT EDMOND JONES for several of these productions, and he is credited with discovering Pauline Lord* and **Katharine Hepburn**.

Hopkins produced and directed with less frequency after 1930, but he was associated with a few more important plays, most notably ROBERT E. SHERWOOD's ***The Petrified Forest*** (1935), which starred LESLIE HOWARD and provided Humphrey Bogart with his first significant role, SIDNEY HOWARD's *Paths of Glory* (1935), Sophie Treadwell's* *Plumes in the Dust* (1936), PHILIP BARRY's ***Without Love*** (1942; Hopkins took over the direction when original director Robert B. Sinclair joined the army), Emmet Lavery's *The Magnificent Yankee* (1946), and a hit 1946 revival of *Burlesque* starring **Bert Lahr**. Hopkins believed it was the role of the producer to introduce new talent to the theatre. His polished productions did just that, not only introducing new stars and playwrights, but also providing support to those already established.

HORNER, HARRY (1910–1994). Born in Holitz, Czechoslovakia, designer, art director, architect, and director Horner worked as an assistant director for MAX REINHARDT in Vienna and moved to the United States with Reinhardt in 1936 to work on the **Broadway** production of *The Eternal Road*. Horner designed scenery (and sometimes lighting) for such Broadway plays and MUSICALS as *Reunion in New York* (1940), *Lady in the Dark* (1941), *Banjo Eyes* (1941), *In Time to Come* (1941), a revival of *A Kiss for Cinderella* in 1942, **Winged Victory** (1943), *Christopher Blake* (1946), *Me and Molly* (1948), and *Hazel Flagg* (1953), among others. Horner's art director for films brought him Academy Awards for ***The Heiress*** (1949) and *The Hustler* (1961), and an Oscar nomination for *They Shoot Horses, Don't They?* (1969).

HOROVITZ, ISRAEL (1939–). A native of Wakefield, Massachusetts, Horovitz attended Harvard University and spent two years (1961–1963) at London's Royal Academy of Dramatic Art. He was resident playwright with the Royal **Shakespeare** Company and is the author of more than 70 plays. In the United States, his first successes were in **Off-Broadway** theatres, including one-act plays examining the increasingly violent and isolating cityscape: *It's Called the Sugar Plum* (1968), *The Indian Wants the Bronx* (1968), which won him an **Obie Award** and a **Drama Desk Award**, *Rats* (1968), and *Line*, which opened in 1974 and was still running in 2010. His *North Shore Fish* (1987) was Drama Desk-nominated. On **Broadway**, Horovitz contributed the one-act *Morning* to a bill called *Morning, Noon, and Night* (1968), which also included plays by **Terrence McNally** and Leonard Melfi. His 1991 play, *Park Your Car in Harvard Yard*, directed by **Zoe Caldwell**, starred **Jason Robards** and **Judith Ivey** in a **Tony Award**-nominated performance. Among his numerous other plays are *The Wakefield Plays* (1974–1979), *The Good Parts* (1982), *Henry Lumper* (1985), *The Chopin Playoffs* (1986), *A Rosen by Any Other Name* (1987), *Unexpected Tenderness* (1994), *Lebensraum* (1996), *My Old Lady* (1996), *Stations of the Cross* (1998), and *What Strong Fences Make* (2009). Horovitz has also written for films, including *The Strawberry Statement* (1970), the semi-autobiographical *Author! Author!* (1982), and *Sunshine* (1999).

HOTEL UNIVERSE. Philip Barry's one-act drama was produced by The Theatre Guild at the Martin Beck Theatre, where it opened on 14 April 1930 for 81 performances under the direction of Philip Moeller. Katherine Alexander played Ann Field, a wealthy woman who has invited several friends to her estate where her mystical father, Stephen (**Morris Carnovsky**), causes the guests to reveal the frustrations preventing fulfillment of their hopes and dreams. As the gathering ends, all depart with new hope unaware that Stephen has died. Among the cast for this intermissionless play were **Ruth Gordon**, Glenn Anders, **Franchot Tone**, Earl Larimore,* and Phyllis Povah.

HOT L BALTIMORE. Lanford Wilson's three-act comedy-drama opened in an **Off-Off Broadway** production of the **Circle Repertory Company** on 27 January 1973, prior to a move to the **Circle in the Square** where it opened on 22 March 1973 for 1,166 performances, winning an **Obie Award**, **New York Drama Critics Circle Award**, and the **Outer Critics Circle Award**. Directed by **Marshall W. Mason**, Wilson's play depicts the misfit residents of a rundown New York hotel, all of whom imagine better lives but are unable to rise above their circumstances. The original cast featured **Judd Hirsch**, Conchata Ferrell, Jonathan Hogan, and Trish Hawkins. Ferrell was in the cast of a short-lived 1975 half-hour television series of the same name inspired by the play.

HOUGHTON, NORRIS (1909–2001). A **Broadway** producer and designer born in Indianapolis, Indiana, Houghton attended Princeton University as a classmate of **Joshua Logan** and **James Stewart**. He took a job in stage management for the University Players on Cape Cod, where he worked with **Henry Fonda** and **Margaret Sullavan**. In 1934, on a Guggenheim Fellowship, Houghton toured the theatres of the Soviet Union, where he met with and observed the productions of **Constantin Stanislavsky** and Vsevolod Meyerhold. Houghton wrote *Moscow Rehearsals* (1936) when he returned to the United States, a book about Russian theatre. He designed and directed **Broadway** productions, most notably staging a production of *Macbeth* starring Michael Redgrave in 1948. In partnership with T. Edward Hambleton in 1953, Houghton founded the **Phoenix Theatre**, one of the first not-for-profit **Off-Broadway** theatres, keeping production costs and ticket prices low and offering a **repertory** of important classical and modern plays.

HOULD-WARD, ANN (1951–). Born in Glasgow, Montana, Hould-Ward studied at Mills College, the University of Virginia, and the Art Students League with the aim of becoming a costume designer. She worked as an assistant to **Rouben Ter-Arutunian** and **Patricia Zipprodt**, with whom she collaborated on her first **Broadway** production, **James Lapine** and **Stephen Sondheim**'s PULITZER PRIZE-winning MUSICAL *Sunday in the Park with George* (1984), which brought them a **Tony Award** nomination. Hould-Ward also received Tony nominations for a revival of *Into the Woods* in 1988, and she won a Tony for her design of *Beauty and the Beast* (1994). Among her other Broadway productions are *Falsettos* (1992), revivals of *Saint Joan*, **Three Men on a Horse, In the Summer House**, and *Timon of Athens*, all in 1993, *The Molière Comedies* (1995), *On the Waterfront* (1995), *Dream* (1997), *More to Love* (1998), a revival of *Little Me* in 1998, *Dance of the Vampires* (2002), a revival of *Company* in 2006, *A Catered Affair* (2008), which brought her a **Drama Desk Award** nomination, and *The Grand Manner* (2010). Hould-Ward has designed costumes for numerous regional theatres, including **La Jolla Playhouse**, the Goodspeed Opera House, and San Diego's **Old Globe Theatre**, and **Off-Broadway**, where she designed *Lobster Alice* (2000) for **Playwrights Horizons** and *A Midsummer Night's Dream* (2007) and *Road Show* (2008) at the **New York Shakespeare Festival/Public Theatre**.

HOUSE OF BLUE LEAVES. **John Guare**'s two-act comedy-drama opened on 10 February 1971 at the Truck and Warehouse Theatre under the direction of **Mel Shapiro**. Harold Gould played Artie Shaughnessy, an aspiring songwriter who works for the zoo. Artie's disturbed wife, Bananas (Katherine Helmond), thinks she's a dog and his hard-boiled mistress, Bunny (Anne Meara), sleeps with him but refuses to do housework until he divorces Bananas and marries her. Artie's son, Ronnie, shows up with a bomb in an attempt to kill the pope, who is visiting New York, but accidentally kills his girlfriend instead. The play won significantly more attention in a **Lincoln Center** production, which opened on 29 April 1986 at the Vivian Beaumont Theatre for 398 performances under the direction of **Jerry Zaks**. *House of Blue Leaves* was nominated for a **Tony Award** for Best Play and actors John Mahoney and **Swoosie Kurtz**, along with scene design **Tony Walton** and Zaks, won Tonys, with Julie Hagerty winning a **Theatre World Award**.

HOUSE OF CONNELLY, THE. **Paul Green**'s two-act play was produced by **The Group Theatre** at the Martin Beck Theatre, where it opened on 28 September 1931 for 91 performances under the direction of **Lee Strasberg** and **Cheryl Crawford**. The large cast, including **Morris Carnovsky**, **Stella Adler**, Phoebe Brand, **Franchot Tone**, **Clifford Odets**, Rose McClendon,* Mary Morris,* **Robert Lewis**, and Art Smith, appeared in this moody **Chekhovian** drama set in the American South in 1905 on a plantation where issues of family ties, class distinctions, and **race** control the lives of Connelly family members. A film version, retitled *Carolina* (1934), starred Janet Gaynor, Lionel Barrymore,* and Robert Young, but won little attention. *See also* AFRICAN AMERICAN THEATRE.

HOUSEMAN, JOHN (1902–1988). Born Jacques Haussmann in Bucharest, Hungary, Houseman studied at Clifton College in England and worked in the grain business there prior to emigrating to the United States in 1925. He produced many **Broadway** plays and also directed *Four Saints in Three Acts* (1934), a revival of *The Lady from the Sea* in 1934, *Valley Forge* (1934), *The Devil and Daniel Webster* (1939), *Lute Song* (1946), a 1950 revival of *King Lear, Pantagleize* (1967), revivals of *The Country Girl* in 1972 and *Don Juan in Hell* in 1973, and others. Houseman rose to prominence and faced controversy working with the **Federal Theatre Project (FTP)**, first overseeing the FTP's Negro unit and working in partnership with **Orson Welles** staging an acclaimed all-black production of *Macbeth* in 1936 that became known as the "Voodoo Macbeth."

Controversy came to Houseman and Welles with their production of Marc Blitzstein's *The Cradle Will Rock* (1937), a satirical MUSICAL about **unions** set in a fictional Steeltown. Government officials padlocked the theatre where the production was being prepared and Houseman and Welles responded by inviting the audience to join them at the Venice Theatre, which they had hastily rented, where the show was performed without scenery and costumes.

With the end of the FTP in 1939 and the start of World War II, Houseman worked for the Voice of America, produced films, and acted with increasing frequency, winning an Academy Award for his performance in *The Paper Chase* (1973), and he also received two Golden Globe Award nominations for a TV series based on the film. Houseman taught at the Juilliard School, where he established a touring **repertory** group ultimately known as **The Acting Company**. *See also* AFRICAN AMERICAN THEATRE; CENSORSHIP.

HOW I LEARNED TO DRIVE. Paula **Vogel**'s PULITZER PRIZE-winning drama opened on 16 March 1997 at New York's **Vineyard Theatre** for 400 performances, also winning an **Obie Award**, a **Lucille Lortel Award**, a **Drama Desk Award**, a **New York Drama Critics Circle Award**, and an **Outer Critics Circle Award**. Directed by **Mark Brokaw**, the play examines the relationship of adolescent Li'l Bit, played by **Mary-Louise Parker**, and her aunt's husband, Peck (David Morse), who begins molesting her at age 11 while ostensibly teaching her to drive. The play tracks their interaction until Li'l Bit leaves for college and reflects on what has transpired, leading to her complete rejection of Peck, who has waited for her 18th birthday so they might marry. Controversy was aroused by the fact that Peck is a sympathetic pedophile and the inherent issues of incest and misogyny troubled some critics who, nonetheless, admired the play's artistry. *How I Learned to Drive* was produced by many **regional** and university theatres, and firmly established Vogel as a major American dramatist. *See also* SEXUALITY.

HOWARD, KEN (1944–). Born Kenneth Joseph Howard, Jr. in El Centro, California, he studied at Amherst College and the Yale School of Drama, after which he proved himself a versatile actor, winning a **Tony Award** for the drama *Child's Play* (1970), but also starring in MUSICALS, including *1776* (1969), which brought him a **Theatre World Award**, *Seesaw* (1973), and *1600 Pennsylvania Avenue* (1976). On **Broadway**, Howard also appeared in *Promises, Promises* (1968), *Little Black Sheep* (1975), *The Norman Conquests* (1975), and *Rumors* (1988). Howard also appeared in the national tour of *Equus* in 1976, and **Off-Broadway** in *Camping with Harry and Tom* (1995), *In the Moonlight Eddie* (1996), and *According to Tip* (2007). Howard has also appeared in films, including *Tell Me That You Love Me, Junie Moon* (1970), *Such Good Friends* (1971), *1776* (1972), *Mastergate* (1992), *In Her Shoes* (2005), *Michael Clayton* (2007), and *Rambo* (2008). On television, he received an Emmy Award nomination for *Grey Gardens* (2009), he won a Daytime Emmy for *The Body Human: Facts for Boys* (1980), and he starred in television series, including *Adam's Rib* (1973) with Blythe Danner and *The White Shadow* (1978–1981).

HOWARD, LESLIE (1893–1943).[†] British-born Leslie Stainer, who changed his name to Howard, made his first appearance in the United States in *Just Suppose* (1920) and although he appeared on stage and in films in England, by the mid-1920s he was performing more frequently in America. He acted notably in *Outward Bound* (1924), *The Green Hat* (1925), *Her Cardboard Lover* (1927), and *Berkeley Square* (1929), but his greatest stage successes came in three important post-1930 productions, PHILIP BARRY's *The Animal Kingdom* (1932), ROBERT E. SHERWOOD's *The Petrified Forest* (1935), and his last appearance in his own staging of *Hamlet* in 1936. That same year, his own play, *Elizabeth Sleeps Out*, had a short run at the Comedy Theatre. On screen, Howard notably repeated his role as the disillusioned poet in *The Petrified Forest* (1936) and he directed and starred in the film *Intermezzo* (1939), which introduced **Ingrid Bergman** to American audiences. He also had cinematic successes in *The Scarlet Pimpernel* (1934), *Pygmalion* (1938), and *Gone with the Wind* (1939). Howard, who was admired for his sensitive, intellectual acting, died in a plane crash while serving in the British military during World WAR II.

HOWARD, SIDNEY (1891–1939).[†] Born Sidney Coe Howard in Oakland, California, the eminent playwright studied under George Pierce Baker* in 1915–1916. He served in Europe during World WAR I, before writing for *Life* magazine (1919–1922). He was married to actress Clare Eames from 1922 to 1930. In 1938, he was a founding member of the **Playwrights' Company**. His 25 or so plays include the PULITZER PRIZE-winning *They Knew What They Wanted* (1924) as well as *Lucky Sam McCarver* (1925), *Ned McCobb's Daughter* (1926), *The Silver Cord* (1926), *The Late Christopher Bean* (1932), and *Alien Corn* (1933), which starred KATHARINE CORNELL. Despite occasional turgid sequences, his plays hold up well as REALISTIC treatments of ordinary people in emotionally fraught situations. Howard, who also wrote for motion pictures (most notably, *Gone With the Wind* [1939]), died as a result of a tractor accident on his farm.

HOWE, TINA (1937–). New York-born Howe was educated at Sarah Lawrence College and received a **Tony Award** nomination for her play *Coastal Disturbances* (1986). Howe's other plays, *The Art of Dining* (1979), *Painting Churches* (1983), which won an **Outer Critics Circle Award**, and *Pride's Crossing* (1997), won critical plaudits. Howe was awarded a 1983 **Obie Award** for her body of work, which also includes *The Nest* (1969), *Museum* (1976), *Approaching Zanzibar* (1989), *One Shoe Off* (1993), her translation of Eugene Ionesco's *The Bald Soprano* in 1994, *Birth and After Birth* (1995), *Rembrandt's Gift* (2002), *Skin Deep* (2007), and *Chasing Manet* (2008).

Howe, who claims the Marx Brothers* as an influence on her early plays, blends a comic touch with darker issues that explore the discordance between public expectations and private pain.

HOYLE, GEOFF (1945–). English-born performer known as a "new vaudevillian,"* who appeared with **Bill Irwin** in the **Pickle Family Circus** in the late 1970s, working ultimately as a **solo** artist in performances he has created, including *Boomer* (1986), *Feast of Fools* (1988), *Don Quixote de La Jolla* (1990), *The Convict's Return* (1991), *Geni(us)* (1995), and *The First 100 Years* (1999), among others. He has also appeared with **Cirque du Soleil** and originated the role of Zazu in *The Lion King* (1997), receiving a **Drama Desk Award** nomination.

HSIEH, TEHCHING (1950–). A native of Nanjhou, Taiwan, he joined the Merchant Seamen for the Republic of China, but jumped ship and arrived in the United States in 1974, emerging as a **performance artist** known as Sam Hsieh. A painter and performer influenced by a range of inspirations from Asian martial arts to Nietzsche and Kafka, he staged a series of body-art works in New York in 1976–1977 and a series of ordeal performances between 1978 and 1986. In 1986, he began his "Thirteen-Year Plan," which ran until 2000 during which time he made art but did not show it until after 2000. He has since retired from performance art work. *See also* ASIAN AMERICAN THEATRE.

HUDSON GUILD THEATRE. Established in 1896 during the settlement house movement, the aim of this theatre was to involve the poor **children** of the Chelsea neighborhood in New York in theatrical endeavors. It continued until World War II, when it sank into a dormant period before being revived by David Kerry Heefner in 1975, who moved the operation to the Neighborhood House on West 26th Street, in the midst of a housing project populated with poor, multiracial families, but with a professional agenda. In 1990, the Hudson Guild withdrew support and the theatre closed. *See also* COMMUNITY THEATRE.

HUGHES, BARNARD (1915–2006). Born Bernard Aloysius Kiernan Hughes in Bedford Hills, New York, Hughes was the son of Irish immigrants. He studied at the LaSalle Academy and Manhattan College. Hughes began his career with the **Shakespeare** Fellowship **Repertory** Company and is believed to have played over 400 roles in theatre during his long life, including his **Tony Award** and **Drama Desk Award**-winning performance in the title role of Hugh Leonard's *Da* (1978), a part he played again in the 1988 film version. He had previously been Tony-nominated for a 1973 revival of *Much Ado about Nothing,* and in 2000 he was presented with a lifetime achievement Drama Desk Award. Among his many **Broadway** credits are such plays as *A Majority of One* (1959), *Advise & Consent* (1960), *Nobody Loves an Albatross* (1963), the **Richard Burton** *Hamlet* in 1964, *How Now, Dow Jones* (1967), *Sheep on the Runway* (1970), the **Circle in the Square** revival of *Uncle Vanya* in 1973, *The Good Doctor* (1973), *All Over Town* (1974), *Angels Fall* (1983), a revival of *The Iceman Cometh* in 1984, *Prelude to a Kiss* (1990), and *Waiting in the Wings* (1999). Hughes's many film appearances include *Midnight Cowboy* (1969), *Oh, God!* (1977), *Doc Hollywood* (1991), *The Fantasticks* (1995), and *Cradle Will Rock* (1999). Hughes appeared in over 100 television programs and won an Emmy Award for a guest performance on *Lou Grant* in 1978. He was married to actress Helen Stenborg and had two children, including director **Doug Hughes**.

HUGHES, DOUG (1950?–). Son of actors **Bernard Hughes** and Helen Stenborg, Hughes has discussed his desire to avoid acting as a career, but did not stray far from his roots when he turned to directing. He won a **Tony Award** and a **Drama Desk Award** for his direction of **John Patrick Shanley**'s *Doubt* (2005) and was nominated for a Tony for *Frozen* (2004) and reaped Drama Desk Award nominations for *The Grey Zone* (1996) **Off-Broadway** and the 2007 **Broadway** revival of *Inherit the Wind*. He has also directed *A Naked Girl on the Appian Way* (2005), a revival of *A Touch of the Poet* in 2005, *Mauritius* (2007), and revivals of *A Man for All Seasons* in 2008, *The Royal Family** in 2009, *Oleanna* in 2009, and *Mrs. Warren's Profession* in 2010. Hughes has also directed for many **regional theatres**.

HUGHES, HOLLY (1955–). Born in Saginaw, Michigan, Hughes studied painting at Kalamazoo College and moved to New York in 1979. She managed the WOW Café in the East Village until 1983, where she encouraged performances in which artists were able to show and discuss their work. As a self-avowed lesbian **performance artist**, she first gained critical attention with *The Well of Horniness* (1983), among others, and worked closely with Peggy Shaw and Lois Weaver on *Dress Suits to Hire* (1987). Her other **solo performances** have included *The Lady Dick* (1984), *World Without End* (1988), *Dead Meat* (1990), *Clit Notes* (1993), and *Preaching to the Perverted* (2000), the last a response to Hughes's experiences as part of the NEA Four (also including **Karen Finley**, John Fleck, and **Tim Miller**), a 1990 controversy in which their grants were revoked by the **National Endowment for the Arts** on obscenity grounds at the height of the "Culture Wars." As the winner of two **Obie Awards**, Hughes intends her work, which is often satiric, to create controversy, exploring issues of **feminism**, **sexuality**, and she has explored the boundaries between eroticism and pornography, which has generated critical controversy. Hughes teaches at the Michigan School of Arts and Design. *See also* CENSORSHIP; GAY AND LESBIAN THEATRE; WOMEN/FEMININITY.

HUGHES, LANGSTON (1902–1967).[†] James Mercer Langston Hughes, one of the most celebrated **African American** poets of the first half of the twentieth century, was among the few black writers to present serious dramas on **Broadway** prior to the 1960s. Raised in Cleveland, Ohio, by his grandmother, who had lost her first husband in John Brown's Harpers Ferry raid, Hughes grew to love literature through her encouragement. His first published play, *The Gold Piece*, appeared in 1921, but his first Broadway success was *Mulatto* (1935), a melodramatic* work focusing on racial strife in the South. His previously unproduced 1930 play, *Mule Bone*, coauthored with Zora Neale Hurston, was produced at **Lincoln Center** in 1991. Many of his pre-World WAR II dramatic works, including *Little Ham* (1936), *Troubled Island* (1936), *Joy to My Soul* (1937), and *Front Porch* (1938) premiered at the KARAMU THEATRE in Cleveland, but by the late 1940s his contributions, including the book and lyrics for Kurt Weill's MUSICAL drama *Street Scene* (1947), were seen more frequently on New York stage. *Street Scene* was a critical and commercial success, but another musical, *The Barrier* (1950), failed. He established three theatre companies, the Harlem Suitcase Theatre, where his *Don't You Want to Be Free?* (1938) played for a substantial run, Los Angeles's New Negro Theatre in 1939, and Chicago's Skyloft Players in 1949, although none lasted for long. Hughes's folk musical *Simply Heavenly* (1957; music by David Martin) and *Tambourines to Glory* (1963; music by Jobe Huntley) had short New York runs and a Hughes poem inspired **Lorraine Hansberry**'s 1959 drama *A Raisin in the Sun*.

HUGHIE. EUGENE O'NEILL completed this 1942 one-act character study of a down-on-his-luck **Broadway** gambler as part of an intended eight-play cycle of one-acts with the all-encompassing title of *By Way of Obit. Hughie* was the only play for the cycle that O'Neill completed. It was not published until after his death in 1959. Its first Broadway production, directed by **José Quintero**, opened at the Royale Theatre on 22 December 1964 for 51 performances and starred **Jason Robards** in a **Tony Award**-nominated performance as Erie Smith, returning to his rundown hotel room following a bender in the aftermath of the death of the night clerk, Hughie, his only friend whose romanticizing of Erie's exploits gave the small-time gambler the confidence he needed. Erie discovers a new night clerk on the job whose name, Hughes

(Jack Dodson), intrigues Erie and a new friendship is born. Robards and Dodson repeated their performances for a 1984 Showtime-TV production. **Ben Gazzara** played Erie in a 1975 Broadway revival, and **Al Pacino** starred in and directed a 1996 revival. In 2010, **Brian Dennehy** played the role on a double-bill with Samuel Beckett's *Krapp's Last Tape*.

HULL, HENRY (1890–1977).† Brother of actor Shelley Hull,* this durable stage and screen actor was born in Louisville, Kentucky. During the first decade of his career, Hull played leading roles in *The Man Who Came Back** (1916), *The Cat and the Canary** (1922), *The Youngest* (1924), *Lulu Belle** (1926), and *Grand Hotel* (1930), among others. He occasionally appeared on stage after 1930, including roles in John Galsworthy's *The Roof* (1931), Will Cotton's *The Bride the Sun Shines On* (1931), Denis Johnston's *The Moon in the Yellow River* (1932), Paul Hervey Fox and George Tilton's *Foreign Affairs* (1932), Benn W. Levy's *Springtime for Henry* (1933), MAXWELL ANDERSON's *The Masque of Kings* (1936), and PHILIP BARRY's *Foolish Notion* (1945), but his major triumph was as sharecropper Jeeter Lester in *Tobacco Road* (1933), after which he spent much of his career as a respected character actor in Hollywood films.

HULL, JOSEPHINE (1886–1957).† Josephine Sherwood, a native of Newtonville, Massachusetts, was educated at Radcliffe and studied with nineteenth-century actress Kate Reingolds* before gaining practical experience in several STOCK companies and in a few minor **Broadway** offerings. She retired from acting in 1910 when she married actor Shelley Hull,* but when he died in 1919, his wife, now billed as Josephine Hull, returned to the theatre and achieved success as a character actress on both stage and screen. In the 1920s, she won strong reviews in *Neighbors* (1923), *Fata Morgana* (1924), *Craig's Wife** (1925), and *Daisy Mayme** (1926), but her greatest successes came after 1930, first in GEORGE S. KAUFMAN and **Moss Hart**'s PULITZER PRIZE-winning comedy *You Can't Take It with You* (1936) in which she played the mother-playwright Penny Sycamore. This role typecast the small, rotund actress as flighty, lovable little old ladies, but she was fortunate in playing the type in significant plays.

In 1941, Hull played Abby Brewster, one of two elderly New England spinsters who sweetly murder lonely old men, in *Arsenic and Old Lace* (1941), repeating her performance in Frank Capra's 1944 film version. That year, Hull also scored another success as the confused social climber Veta Louise Simmons in Mary Chase's Pulitzer Prize-winner, *Harvey*, also repeating this role (and winning an Academy Award) in the 1950 film starring **James Stewart**, who had succeeded comedian **Frank Fay** as Elwood P. Dowd in the stage production. Following *Harvey*, she appeared in three failures, *Minnie and Mr. Williams* (1948), *The Golden State* (1950), and *Whistler's Grandmother* (1952). Hull's last stage role as Lucy Patridge, a minor stockholder who takes on a corporation in Howard Teichmann and George S. Kaufman's *The Solid Gold Cadillac* (1953), won her plaudits and a long run.

HULL-HOUSE THEATRE.† From the beginning, Jane Addams made the arts integral to her social work at Chicago's Hull-House, which she founded with Ellen Gates in 1889. There were play readings, concerts, and art exhibits offered with the aim of inculcating good values among the laboring poor through "recreation and education." Addams shunned the cheap appeals of the popular melodrama* of the day and instead fostered theatre through a **Shakespeare** Club. The first fully staged production at Hull-House—indeed, the first settlement house theatrical performance in the United States—was *The Sleeping Car* by William Dean Howells,* presented in 1896 on a platform in the gymnasium. Others followed, and the success of Shakespeare's *As You Like It* in 1897 resulted in the hiring of Walter Pietsch as director of drama for Hull-House. A new theatre was completed in 1899. After a group of Greek immigrants performed a dramatization of *The Odyssey* in Greek, other ethnic groups mounted plays in their own languages. In 1900, retired actress Laura Dainty Pelham became director and brought the theatre to a new level of professionalism, eventually changing the name from Hull-House Dramatic Association to Hull-House Players. Because of Addams's insistence on producing plays of literary merit, Hull-House was recognized as a leading proponent of the art theatre movement. Maurice Browne* credited the Hull-House Players as the true origin of the Little Theatre* movement in America. *See also* COMMUNITY THEATRE; ETHNIC THEATRE.

HUNT, HELEN (1963–   ). This Academy Award-winning film actress born in Culver City, California, to a film director and a photographer, has occasionally appeared in theatre, beginning her **Broadway** career replacing **Penelope Ann Miller** as Emily in a 1988 revival of *Our Town*. Hunt also appeared as Viola in **Shakespeare**'s *Twelfth Night* with Paul Rudd, **Philip Bosco**, and Kyra Sedgwick in a 1998 **Lincoln Center** revival directed by **Nicholas Hytner** (Hunt also appeared in a television version of this production). In 2003, Hunt appeared in Yasmina Reza's *Life (x) 3* in a **Circle in the Square** production directed by **Matthew Warchus**, costarring with **Linda Emond**, Brent Spiner, and John Turturro. In 2010, Hunt stepped into the role of the Stage Manager, usually played by a male actor, in the **Off-Broadway** revival of *Our Town* directed by **David Cromer**. Hunt won her Oscar (as well as a Golden Globe Award and Screen Actors Guild Award) for *As Good as*

It Gets (1997) and has appeared in numerous films and in the long-running television situation comedy, *Mad About You* (1992–1999), for which she won an Emmy Award.

HUNT, LINDA (1945–). Born in Morristown, New Jersey, to a prosperous family, Hunt attended the Interlochen Arts Academy. As an actress, she debuted on **Broadway** in 1975, playing the Irish maid in a revival of *Ah, Wilderness!* and on film in 1980 in Robert Altman's *Popeye*, but rose to prominence with her performance as a male Indonesian dwarf (Hunt is 4'9" tall) in *The Year of Living Dangerously* (1983), which brought her an Academy Award as Best Supporting Actress and a New York Film Critics Circle Award. Her theatre work includes the **Off-Broadway** productions of the **Obie Award**-winning *Metamorphosis in Miniature* (1982), and she was part of the Obie-winning ensemble of *Top Girls* (1983). Continuing to act in films, Hunt also pursued a series of challenging stage roles, including her **Tony Award**-nominated performance in **Arthur Kopit**'s *End of the World* (1984). Off-Broadway, Hunt won critical plaudits for **Wallace Shawn**'s *Aunt Dan and Lemon* (1984), **Emily Mann**'s *Annulla* (1988), a 1988 revival of *The Cherry Orchard*, and others. In **regional theatres**, she has played the title role in *Mother Courage and Her Children*, Olga in *The Three Sisters*, Dolly Levi in *The Matchmaker*, and Sister Aloysius in *Doubt*, among others. Hunt also directs and in the movies has appeared in *Dune* (1984), *She-Devil* (1989), *Prêt-à-Porter* (1994), and *Stranger than Fiction* (2006), and was a regular on the television series *The Practice* (1997–2002), *Carnivàle* (2003–2005), and *NCIS: Los Angeles* beginning in 2009.

HUNTER, KIM (1922–2002). As Janet Cole, Hunter was born in Detroit, Michigan, and, after completing high school, began acting in 1939. Her **Broadway** debut was an auspicious one, as Stella Kowalski, the tragic Blanche DuBois's sister, in the original production of **Tennessee Williams**'s *A Streetcar Named Desire* (1947). Hunter reprised her performance in the 1951 film version, winning an Academy Award and a Golden Globe Award. Blacklisted during the McCarthy era, Hunter only sporadically appeared in movies, but she acted more consistently on television from the late 1940s and she was nominated for a Daytime Emmy Award for the soap opera *The Edge of Night* in 1980. By the 1960s, she appeared occasionally in films again, including *Planet of the Apes* (1968) and its sequels. Hunter's other Broadway appearances include *Darkness at Noon* (1951), *The Chase* (1952), a 1952 revival of *The Children's Hour*, *The Tender Trap* (1954), *Write Me a Murder* (1961), *Weekend* (1968), *The Penny Wars* (1969), an all-star revival of *The Women* in 1973, *To Grandmother's House We Go* (1981), and she stepped into the role of Lady Markby during the run of a revival of *An Ideal Husband* in 1996. She also toured with **Julie Harris** in the national company of *And Miss Reardon Drinks a Little* and acted with the **Shakespeare** Festival Theatre and **Off-Broadway**, appearing in *The Eye of the Beholder* (1993).

HUNTINGTON THEATRE COMPANY, THE. Boston University founded this theatre in 1982 and established it as a not-for-profit company in 1986. Its productions have ranged from American and European classics to world premieres, including 2009 productions of Richard N. Goodwin's *Two Men of Florence* and David Grimm's *The Miracle at Naples*. The company's first artistic director was Peter Altman, followed in 2000 by Nicholas Martin who, in turn, was replaced by Peter DuBois in 2008. The company has three performances spaces, two of which are located at the Boston Center for the Arts.

HURLYBURLY. **David Rabe**'s drama about the drug-riddled Hollywood scene of the 1980s had its first performances at Chicago's **Goodman Theatre** in April 1984 before opening **Off-Broadway** in June 1984, after which it transferred to **Broadway**'s Ethel Barrymore Theatre on 7 August 1984, where it ran for 343 performances and received a **Tony Award** nomination as Best Play. Directed by **Mike Nichols** on Broadway, the stellar cast included **William Hurt**, **Ron Silver** (replaced by **Christopher Walken** who had played the role earlier), **Sigourney Weaver**, Harvey Keitel, Cynthia Nixon, Jerry Stiller, and **Judith Ivey**, who won a Tony and a **Drama Desk Award** for her performance. The play emphasized male relationships in the cutthroat environment of contemporary Hollywood, emphasizing the characters' self-destructiveness.

Rabe had been dissatisfied with the Broadway production and changes made to the play, so it was performed in 1986 at the **Trinity Repertory Theatre** and under **David Wheeler**'s direction the cuts were restored. Rabe himself directed a later production in Los Angeles at the Westwood Playhouse, and in 1998 a film version was released with a cast including Sean Penn, **Kevin Spacey**, Robin Wright Penn, Chazz Palminteri, Garry Shandling, Anna Paquin, and Meg Ryan. The play was revived Off-Broadway by the New Group Theatre in 2005 to considerable critical acclaim under the direction of **Scott Elliott** with a cast including Ethan Hawke, Josh Hamilton, Parker Posey, and **Wallace Shawn**. *New York Magazine* critic **John Simon** wrote that this revival of *Hurlyburly* "confirms it as a major play."

HURT, MARY BETH (1948–). Born Mary Beth Supinger in Marshalltown, Iowa, after studying at the University of Iowa and New York University's Tisch School of the Arts, Hurt began her stage career in 1974. She was nominated for **Tony Awards** in a 1976 revival of *Trelawny of the "Wells"*, as Meg in **Beth Henley**'s *Crimes of the Heart* (1981), and in Michael Frayn's *Benefactors* (1986). On **Broadway**, her credits include revivals of *Love for Love* and *The Rules of the Game* in 1974, ***The Member of the Wedding*** in 1975, *Secret Service** and ***Boy Meets Girl*** in 1976, *The Cherry Orchard* in 1977 and *The Misanthrope* in 1983, *The Secret Rapture* (1989), a revival of ***A Delicate Balance*** in 1996, and *Top Girls* (2008). Hurt won an **Obie Award** for the **Off-Broadway** production of *Crimes of the Heart* prior to its Broadway run and was nominated for a **Drama Desk Award** for her Off-Broadway performance in Don DeLillo's *The Day Room* (1988). Hurt's film roles include *Interiors* (1978), *The World According to Garp* (1982), *The Age of Innocence* (1993), ***Six Degrees of Separation*** (1993), and *Lady in the Water* (2006), and she has appeared in television films and series. Hurt was married to actor **William Hurt** for a decade; following their divorce, she married writer/director Paul Schrader.

HURT, WILLIAM (1950–). A native of Washington, D.C., he attended Tufts University to study theology, but chose to pursue acting and attended the Juilliard Drama School. Hurt debuted **Off-Broadway** in the **New York Shakespeare Festival** production of *Henry V* in 1977. He won a 1978 **Theatre World Award** for his performances with the **Circle Repertory Theatre**, an **Obie Award** for **Corinne Jacker's** *My Life* (1977), and a Tony Award nomination for *Hurlyburly* (1984), his only **Broadway** appearance to date. In film, Hurt emerged as a major leading man, won an Academy Award for *Kiss of the Spider Woman* (1985) and was nominated for Oscars for ***Children of a Lesser God*** (1986), *Broadcast News* (1987), and *A History of Violence* (2005), for which he also won a New York Film Critics Award. He also appeared in the films *Altered States* (1980), *Body Heat* (1981), *The Big Chill* (1983), *The Accidental Tourist* (1988), *Alice* (1990), *Michael* (1996), *Sunshine* (1999), *A.I.: Artificial Intelligence* (2001), *Syriana* (2005), and *Into the Wild* (2007).

HUSTON, WALTER (1884–1950).† Canadian-born Walter Huston spent most of his career on U.S. stages and in films following his 1902 stage debut in Toronto. Huston's first **Broadway** appearance in the melodrama* *In Convict Stripes* (1905) led to a long and varied career on vaudeville* stages between 1909 and 1924 before he scored major successes in EUGENE O'NEILL's *Desire under the Elms** (1924) and *The Fountain* (1925). With the advent of sound films, Huston shifted his attention to screen work with D. W. Griffith's *Abraham Lincoln* (1930), but he made periodic returns to the stage, most notably in the title role of SIDNEY HOWARD's *Dodsworth* (1934), repeating his performance in a lavish 1936 screen adaptation. Huston's 1937 performance as Othello was respectfully received, but he scored a personal triumph as Peter Stuyvesant in Kurt Weill and MAXWELL ANDERSON's MUSICAL, *Knickerbocker Holiday* (1938), in which he introduced "The September Song." During the 1940s, Huston became one of the screen's most versatile character actors, appearing as GEORGE M. COHAN's vaudevillian* father in *Yankee Doodle Dandy* (1942) and winning a Best Supporting Actor Oscar as Howard, the grizzled prospector, in *Treasure of the Sierra Madre* (1948), written and directed by his son John. Huston made his final Broadway appearance in the unsuccessful *Apple of His Eye* (1946).

HWANG, DAVID HENRY (1957–). Born in Los Angeles, California, to Chinese parents, Hwang studied at Stanford University and the Yale School of Drama prior to studying playwriting with **Sam Shepard** and **Maria Irene Fornés**. He has written for stage (including MUSICALS, for which he writes music and lyrics) and screen. Hwang's early plays include *FOB* (1980), *Dance and the Railroad* (1981), *Family Devotions* (1981), which brought him a **Drama Desk Award** nomination, and *Rich Relationship* (1986), which deal with the **Asian American** experience, but he rose to prominence, the first Asian American playwright to do so, with *M. Butterfly* (1988), which won a **Tony Award** as Best Play and which he later adapted to the movies (1993). Hwang subsequently received Tony nominations for *Golden Child* (1998), the revised book he wrote for the 2003 revival of *Flower Drum Song*. His own musical, *Face Values* (1993), failed to open on **Broadway**, but he provided the librettos for *Aida* (2002) and *Tarzan* (2008). His other full-length plays include *Tibet Through the Red Box* (2004) and *Yellow Face* (2007), and he has written several short plays, including *The Dance and the Railroad* (1981), *The House of Sleeping Beauties* (1983), *The Sound of a Voice* (1983), *As the Crow Flies* (1986), *Bondage* (1992), *Trying to Find Chinatown* (1996), *Bang Kok* (1996), *Merchandising* (1999), and *Jade Flowerpots and Bound Feet* (2001). While artist-in-residence at the **Trinity Repertory Theatre**, Hwang completed a 1998 adaptation of HENRIK IBSEN's *Peer Gynt* in collaboration with Stephan Muller.

HYDRIOTAPHIA, OR THE DEATH OF DR. BROWNE. An early play by **Tony Kushner**, this "epic farce about death and primitive capital accumulation" was first performed in June 1987 at HOME for Contemporary Theatre and Art in New York with **Stephen Spinella** in the cast prior to revisions by Kushner and an April 1997 production at New York University's Tisch School of the Arts, after which the play was staged in a joint production by

Houston's **Alley Theatre** and the **Berkeley Repertory Theatre** in 1998. The cast, led by Jonathan Hadary as seventeenth-century scientist and writer Sir Thomas Browne, presents a behind-the-scenes scramble of family and sycophants vying for Browne's wealth as he lay on his sickbed. Kushner views Browne as a seminal capitalist, interested only in accumulating a bigger fortune despite the ramifications on family and community.

HYMAN, EARLE (1926–). Born in Rocky Mount, North Carolina, he grew up in Brooklyn, New York and when he attended a performance of HENRIK IBSEN's *Ghosts* starring ALLA NAZIMOVA at age 13, he decided to pursue acting. On **Broadway**, he debuted in *Run, Little Chillun* (1943) and became a member of the **American Negro Theatre**. He appeared for two years as Rudolf in *Anna Lucasta* (1944). Hyman won a **Theatre World Award** in 1956 and appeared on Broadway in *The Climate of Eden* (1952), a revival of *The Merchant of Venice* in 1943, *No Time for Sergeants* (1955), *Mister Johnson* (1956), revivals of *Saint Joan* in 1956, *Waiting for Godot* (an all-black cast) in 1957, *The Duchess of Malfi* in 1957, *The Infernal Machine* (1958), *Les Blancs* (1970), and he was nominated for a **Tony Award** for his performance in *The Lady from Dubuque* (1980). Hyman's later Broadway appearances include *Execution of Justice* (1986), *Death and the King's Horseman* (1987), and a revival of *The Master Builder* in 1992. On tours, in England, and on university campuses, he has frequently acted in **Shakespeare**'s plays, including multiple appearances in *Othello* and in several other roles with the **American Shakespeare Theatre** in the late 1950s. He won the State Award in Oslo, Norway, for the title role of EUGENE O'NEILL's *The Emperor Jones** in 1965. **Off-Broadway,** he replaced **Morgan Freeman** as Hoke in *Driving Miss Daisy* in 1988 and appeared in a **New York Shakespeare Festival/ Public Theatre** production of *East Texas Hot Links* in 1994, among other roles. *See also* AFRICAN AMERICAN THEATRE.

HYTNER, NICHOLAS (1956–). An English-born director and producer, he was born in Manchester and attended Trinity Hall, Cambridge University before working as associate director of Manchester's Royal Exchange Theatre prior to become artistic director of the National Theatre of Great Britain in 2003. On **Broadway**, Hytner was nominated for **Tony Awards** for his direction of *Miss Saigon* (1991) and *Jumpers* (2004), and he won Tony and **Drama Desk Awards** for his acclaimed revival of *Carousel* in 1994 and for *The History Boys* (2006). Hytner was also Drama Desk-nominated for *The Sweet Smell of Success* (2002), and he also staged a Broadway revival of *Twelfth Night* in 1998 starring Helen Hunt.

I

I AM A CAMERA. **John Van Druten**'s three-act drama based on Christopher Isherwood's *The Berlin Stories* opened on 28 November 1951 for 214 performances at the Empire Theatre. The play won the **New York Drama Critics Circle Award** and plaudits for leading lady **Julie Harris** as Sally Bowles, an eccentric young singer in a Berlin café. A young writer, Christopher Isherwood, resides in a Berlin rooming house run by Fräulein Schneider in the early 1930s as the Nazis rise to power, terrorizing the city. Christopher and the amoral Sally become seriously involved with each other, but Christopher realizes he cannot close his eyes to what is going on about him and leaves Berlin, while the apolitical Sally remains in Berlin ignoring the mounting terror. Harris and supporting actress Marian Winters won **Tony Awards** for their performances. In 1966, John Kander and Fred Ebb adapted Isherwood's stories and Van Druten's play into the groundbreaking MUSICAL *Cabaret*.

I AM MY OWN WIFE. This unique **solo** show by **Doug Wright** opened on 3 December 2003 at the Lyceum Theatre for 360 performances, winning a PULITZER PRIZE, **Tony Award**, and **Drama Desk Award**. Directed by **Moisés Kaufman** with Tony-winning actor Jefferson Mays, the play focuses on the real-life character Charlotte von Mahlsdorf, an East German transvestite. Mays played Charlotte, but also 40 other characters needed to recount an extraordinary life that involved surviving the Nazi and Communist eras. Mays took the play to London, but it met with a disappointing reception there.

I NEVER SANG FOR MY FATHER. **Robert Anderson**'s drama of a middle-aged man facing the mortality of his aging parents opened on 25 January 1968 for 124 performances at the Longacre Theatre in a Shubert production. Directed by **Alan Schneider**, with scene design by JO MIELZINER, the cast included **Hal Holbrook** as Gene Garrison, a college professor who has been unable to connect with his remote and domineering father Tom, played by Alan Webb, although he has a more sympathetic relationship with his mother (LILLIAN GISH). Gene feels guilt about his desire to move on with his life despite the demands and needs of his parents. In 1970, a film version featured Gene Hackman, **Melvyn Douglas**, and **Estelle Parsons**.

I REMEMBER MAMA. Facile **Broadway** dramatist and adaptor **John Van Druten** adapted Kathryn Forbes's stories, *Mama's Bank Account*, into this two-act drama produced by Richard Rodgers and Oscar Hammerstein II. It opened on 19 October 1944 at the Music Box Theatre for an impressive 713 performances. **Mady Christians** played Mama with a young **Marlon Brando** in his Broadway debut as the family's son, Nels. The play depicts the lives of a large immigrant family in 1910 San Francisco remembered by the family's eldest daughter Katrin, played by Joan Tetzel, a budding writer. A warmly sentimental glimpse of a close-knit Norwegian clan, Van Druten leavened *I Remember Mama*'s sentimentality by setting its inherent optimism against an undercurrent of family strife, illness, and death as Mama, the play's title character, emerges as an iconic representation of familial love, compassionate tolerance, and self-sacrifice. The long run of *I Remember Mama* is explained, in part, by its timing. As World WAR II drew to a close, audiences sought escape into a rose-colored vision of the past. *I Remember Mama* proved remarkably durable, spawning a 1948 film starring Irene Dunne as Mama, a long-running 1950s television series featuring Peggy Wood as Mama, and a failed 1979 MUSICAL with a score by Richard Rodgers starring Liv Ullmann as Mama. A staple of STOCK and **community theatres**, *I Remember Mama* was frequently performed in the decades following its premiere.

IBSEN ON THE U.S. STAGE.[†] The social problem plays of Norwegian dramatist Henrik Ibsen (1828–1906) inspired American writers and actors in the first three decades of the 20th century, but between 1882 and 1930 only a small group of actors and companies produced Ibsen's plays in the United States. Audiences and some CRITICS were hostile to Ibsen's plays for their un-precedented frankness and for what was perceived as the author's promotion of **women's** rights. From Helena Modjeska's 1882 production of *A Doll's House*, retitled *Thora*, to BLANCHE YURKA's production of *The Vikings*, which she both directed and starred in, the most important Ibsen productions appeared through the willingness of particular actresses to risk critical scorn. These included Minnie Maddern Fiske, ETHEL BARRYMORE, Nance O'Neil, Mary Shaw, and ALLA NAZIMOVA, some of whom continued to appear in Ibsen's plays throughout their careers. Perhaps the most significant effort came from EVA LE GALLIENNE, who made Ibsen's plays, along with other modernist classics, central to her CIVIC REPERTORY THEATRE, which opened its first season in 1925 with productions of *The Master Builder* and *John Gabriel Borkman*. Throughout the 1930s and 1940s, Le Gallienne was the most visible presence in Ibsen's plays via her productions of *The Master Builder* (1934, 1939), *Hedda Gabler* (1934, 1939, 1948), *A Doll's House* (1934), *Rosmersholm* (1935), *John Gabriel Borkman* (1946), and *Ghosts* (1948). As late as the 1960s, Le Gallienne staged a national tour of *Hedda Gabler* starring Signe Hasso.

In the post-World WAR II era, Ibsen's plays were more frequently seen on university stages as the result of increasing scholarly interest, which led to a range of new translations. In the 1950s, **Arthur Miller** adapted Ibsen's *An Enemy of the People* (1950) and **Lee Strasberg** staged *Peer Gynt* (1951). **The Phoenix Theatre** also produced *Peer Gynt* (1960), following their earlier production of *The Master Builder* (1955). In this period, occasional adaptations of Ibsen's plays were presented on television, including a notable 1959 live hour-long production of *A Doll's House* with **Julie Harris, Christopher Plummer, Jason Robards, Hume Cronyn**, and **Eileen Heckart**. As had always been the case with Ibsen's plays in the United States, actresses propelled productions of his masterworks. Along with several English-language film versions of Ibsen's plays, important European actresses brought successful productions of the plays to **Broadway**. **Claire Bloom** appeared in acclaimed productions of *A Doll's House* and *Hedda Gabler* in 1971, Liv Ullmann starred in *A Doll's House* in 1975 and *Ghosts* in 1981, Glenda Jackson played Hedda in 1975 and Susannah York in 1981, and Vanessa Redgrave assayed *The Lady from the Sea* in 1976. More importantly, Ibsen became a staple for **regional repertory theatres** around the country from the early 1960s as those theatres sprang up in most major cities.

The founding of the Ibsen Society of America in 1979 encouraged interest in Ibsen's work and from the 1980s experimentation and new production concepts were frequently seen, from *A Doll's Life*, a 1982 MUSICAL sequel to *A Doll's House* written by Adolph Green and Betty Comden to **Charles Ludlam**'s transgender performance as *Hedda Gabler* at the **American Repertory Theatre** in 1984. Post-1980, **Austin Pendleton** directed a **Circle in the Square** production of *John Gabriel Borkman* starring **E. G. Marshall** and **Irene Worth** in 1980, **Tony Randall**'s **National Actors Theatre** presented **Earle Hyman** in *The Master Builder* in 1992, the **Roundabout Theatre** staged *Hedda Gabler* with Kelly McGillis, English actress Janet McTeer won plaudits in *A Doll's House* in 1997, **Kate Burton** appeared in *Hedda Gabler* for the Shubert organization in 2001, and the Roundabout Theatre produced *Hedda Gabler* with **Mary-Louise Parker** and **Michael Cerveris** in 2009. *See also* FEMINIST THEATRE; INTERNATIONAL STARS AND COMPANIES IN THE UNITED STATES; WOMEN/FEMININITY.

ICEMAN COMETH, THE. The last new play by EUGENE O'NEILL produced on **Broadway** during his lifetime, this towering drama probing the human need for illusion in an isolating modern world was completed by the reclusive and ailing O'Neill in 1939, but it was not produced until 9 October 1946 at the Martin Beck Theatre for a disappointingly short run of 136 performances. Weaknesses in the production, particularly the leading performance of **James Barton**, caused reviewers to find the lengthy play inferior to O'Neill's earlier achievements. CRITICAL rejection and audience apathy obscured its merits until an acclaimed 1956 revival at New York's **Circle in the Square Theatre** directed by **José Quintero**, who had scored a notable success directing O'Neill's PULITZER PRIZE-winning *Long Day's Journey into Night* shortly before. *The Iceman Cometh* has come to be regarded as an O'Neill masterpiece, and it has been revived on Broadway in 1973, 1985, and 1999, and was filmed twice, for television in 1960 (with cast members from the 1956 **Off-Broadway** revival) and on the big screen in 1973.

Set in Harry Hope's "last chance" saloon in New York City in the summer of 1912, the down-and-out habitués of the bar delude themselves about their past failings and the possibility of restoring lost fortunes, dreams, relationships, and shattered confidence. In the meantime, the lost souls drink to oblivion and are only aroused by the imminent arrival of Theodore Hickman, known to all as "Hickey," a fifty year-old hardware salesman who regales them with tall stories and buys endless rounds of drinks. This time, however, Hickey arrives with a missionary's zeal to force them to face the hard truths of their lives and give up their "pipe dreams." Ultimately, the misfits all fail to face their fears, Hickey's own hypocrisies are revealed and the tragedy of his life shocks all, and, in the end, the characters are able to go on living only when some shard of their individual illusions survive. O'Neill's intense drama undoubtedly seemed too desperate in outlook for Broadway audiences in the immediate aftermath of World WAR II. O'Neill, deeply disappointed in what he considered the play's failure, was further disappointed by the out-of-town closing of his last play, *A Moon for the Misbegotten* (1943), the following year, and there were no further Broadway productions of his plays during the remaining years of his life.

IDIOT'S DELIGHT. ROBERT E. SHERWOOD's three-act comedy opened on 24 March 1936 for 299 performances at the Shubert Theatre, winning the PULITZER PRIZE and critical approval for the play and its stars, ALFRED LUNT and LYNN FONTANNE. Set in the Hotel Monte Gabrielle in a once-Austrian mountain town ceded to Italy after World WAR I, a group of guests face uncertainties about the possibility of another war. A third-rate vaudevillian, Harry Van (Lunt), arrives with a group of chorus girls. Van realizes that a Russian Countess (Fontanne), who is married to a munitions manufacturer, is actually a former stage performer with whom he had an affair in Omaha. As the dreaded war begins, Van and the Countess reignite their old affair and plan a new mind-reading act. A lavish 1939 film version starred Clark Gable and Norma Shearer, and a 1951 **Broadway** revival starring LEE TRACY and RUTH CHATTERTON, flopped.

I'M NOT RAPPAPORT. **Herb Gardner**'s **Tony Award**-winning comedy opened on 19 November 1985 for 891 performances at the Booth Theatre, following its original presentation at the **Seattle Repertory Theatre**. Directed by **Daniel Sullivan**, with scene design by **Tony Walton**, the cast featured **Judd Hirsch** as an elderly Jewish radical, Nat, and Cleavon Little as his aging **African American** friend, Midge. The two old men share a park bench, where they battle the infirmities of age and explore the subjects of society's treatment of the aged, relationships of the elderly with their adult children, the troubled urban landscape, and the eternal struggles of politics. Hirsch returned in a 2002 **Broadway** revival, this time costarring with Ben Vereen, but this production managed only 53 performances. A 1996 film version, directed by Gardner, starred **Walter Matthau**, **Ossie Davis**, and Amy Irving.

IMPOSSIBLE YEARS, THE. Bob Fisher and Arthur Marx collaborated on this two-act comedy for comedian Alan King which opened on 13 October 1965 for 670 performances at the Playhouse Theatre. King played Dr. Kingsley, a renowned psychiatrist writing a book on raising children, but in his own home he has difficulty managing his two strong-willed, precocious daughters. King won praise for his performance and the play mildly reflected the changing values of the 1960s. A 1968 film version starred David Niven.

IN THE COMPANY OF MEN. **Neil LaBute**'s first important play premiered at his alma mater, Brigham Young University, in 1993, establishing his often disturbing depictions of human nature. In this case, two misogynist businessmen, Chad and Howard, collaborate to woo and reject a deaf woman, Christine. Actor Aaron Eckhart, a former classmate of LaBute's, appeared in the play, which LaBute adapted into a film in 1997, directed by LaBute and featuring Eckhart, Matt Malloy, and Stacy Edwards. The film won LaBute the Independent Spirit Award and nominations for several other awards.

IN THE SUMMER HOUSE. Jane Bowles's two-act drama opened on 29 December 1953 for 55 performances at the Playhouse Theatre produced by the **Playwrights' Company** and **Oliver Smith**. The play featured **Judith Anderson** as Gertrude, an oppressively demanding mother focused on controlling her daughter's life. **Mildred Dunnock** played an alcoholic who has been abandoned by her family. She finds comfort in her drinking, while Gertrude is lost when ultimately abandoned by her daughter who musters the will to leave. The play was revived in 1993 with **Dianne Wiest** and **Frances Conroy**, but failed to fine an audience.

INDIAN WANTS THE BRONX, THE. **Israel Horovitz**'s one-act play opened **Off-Broadway** at the Astor Place Theatre on 17 January 1968 for 177 performances. The play focuses on Gupta, a young man who arrives in New York City from his native India. While waiting at a bus stop, Gupta, who barely speaks English, is accosted by two street toughs whose taunts turn violent. The original cast included **Al Pacino** and John Cazale, and the play won **Obie Awards** for them and the play. **John Malkovich** directed a **Steppenwolf Theatre** production in Chicago in 1976 starring Terry Kinney and **Gary Sinise**.

INDIANA REPERTORY THEATRE (IRT). The Athenaeum, established in Indianapolis in the 1850s as a center for encouraging German American culture, and was used for a variety of performances (German-language and otherwise), became the first home of the IRT when it was established in 1972. Founded by Benjamin Mordecai, Edward Stern, and Gregory Poggi, the IRT presents annual seasons of plays (their first production was the 1890s' farce *Charley's Aunt*). The goal of producing a range of classic and contemporary plays was enhanced when Tom Haas became artistic director in 1980. Haas oversaw the move into the renovated Indiana Theatre, which provided two stages: a 610-seat proscenium space and a 314-seat thrust. A small cabaret was also included. When Haas died after being struck by a car in 1991, Libby Appel had a brief tenure as artistic director before being succeeded by Janet Allen, who had been the theatre's business manager. *See also* REGIONAL THEATRE MOVEMENT.

INDIANS. The Nederlander organization produced **Arthur Kopit**'s **Tony Award**-nominated play on 13 October 1969 for 96 performances at the Brooks Atkinson Theatre, featuring **Stacy Keach**. Set in Buffalo Bill* Cody's Wild West Show, the play explores the contradictions of Cody's—and America's—interaction with **Native Americans**. Keach won a **Drama Desk Award** and a Tony nomination for his performance, and the supporting cast included Manu Tupou, **Tom Aldredge**, **Kevin Conway**, **Charles Durning**, **Raúl Juliá**, and **Sam Waterston**. A 1976 film adaptation directed by Robert Altman retitled *Buffalo Bill and the Indians, or Sitting Bull's History Lesson*, starred **Paul Newman**.

INGE, WILLIAM (1913–1973). Born William Motter Inge in Independence, Kansas, Inge was a gentle and sensitive child taunted by bullies. He retreated into artistic and literary pursuits with his mother's encouragement. He received a B.A. degree from the University of Kansas at Lawrence in 1935. His theatrical career essentially began when he acted in tent shows in rural Kansas beginning in 1932. He completed an M.A. in English at George Peabody College for Teachers before taking a job teaching English at Stephens College in Columbia, Missouri, in 1938. His interest in theatre was heightened when he became a close friend of legendary stage actress Maude Adams,* who also taught at Stephens.

Attempting to confront his **homosexuality** and struggle with alcoholism, Inge began Freudian analysis, a foundation on which Inge constructed his characters when he began writing plays and, coupled with his admiration for **Tennessee Williams**, who encouraged him, Inge wrote his first play, *Farther Off from Heaven* (1945), which, with Williams's help, was produced by **Margo Jones**'s Theatre 47 in Dallas, Texas. Inge's major theatrical breakthrough came with *Come Back, Little Sheba* in a 1950 **Broadway** production starring **Shirley Booth** and **Sidney Blackmer**, winning Inge the George Jean Nathan Award. His next play, *Picnic,* about the unsettling impact of a virile drifter on three generations of women living in a small Kansas town, was directed by **Joshua Logan** and won the PULITZER PRIZE, **New York Drama Critics Circle Award**, and a **Donaldson Award**. Inge followed *Picnic* with *Bus Stop* (1955), a comedy-drama featuring **Kim Stanley** as the "chanteuse" Cherie, who spends a night trapped in a roadside café in Kansas with a group of travelers, improbably finding love with a rowdy cowboy. Inge's *The Dark at the Top of the Stairs* (1957), directed by **Elia Kazan** and featuring a cast including Teresa Wright, **Pat Hingle**, and **Eileen Heckart**, focused on a 1920s' Oklahoma family, especially the young son who is afraid of the closed, dark attic in the family home.

Inge's impressive string of successes ended with *A Loss of Roses* (1959), which closed after a mere 25 performances on Broadway. Inge won acclaim for his screenplay for his drama *The Dark at the Top of the Stairs*, released in 1960, followed by *Splendor in the Grass*, a hugely popular movie scripted by Inge which won him an Academy Award for Best Original Screenplay. *Come Back, Little Sheba*; *Picnic*; and *Bus Stop* were all filmed in the 1950s and were popular with audiences and well-received by most critics.

In the 1960s, Inge continued to battle his demons through psychoanalysis, but found only occasional success with screen versions of his plays, including *The Stripper* (1963; adapted from *A Loss of Roses*) and *Bus Riley's Back in Town* (1965; adapted from an Inge one-act play of the same name), as well as adaptations of works by other writers, including *All Fall Down* (1962), adapted from James Leo Herlihy's novel. Inge's later plays, *Natural Affection* (1963) and *Where's Daddy?* (1966), were met by a chorus of critical disapproval. Beginning in 1968, Inge began occasional stints teaching theatre arts at the University of California, Irvine, while working on two unsuccessful novels, *Good Luck, Miss Wyckoff* (1970) and *My Son Is a Splendid Driver* (1971). Depression over the failures of his recent plays and novels, his continuing struggle with alcoholism, and inner conflicts about his **sexuality** led him to take his own life.

INHERIT THE WIND. This three-act historical drama by **Jerome Lawrence** and **Robert E. Lee**, based on the famous 1925 Scopes "Monkey" Trial, opened on 21 April 1955, at the National Theatre for 806 performances. Produced by **Herman Shumlin** and **Margo Jones**, the play explored the collision between faith and science inherent in the Scopes trial, in which a small-town Tennessee school teacher, Bertram Cates, was charged for violating state law prohibiting teaching Darwin's theory of evolution. PAUL MUNI played Chicago lawyer Henry Drummond, based on Clarence Darrow, who arrives to defend Cates with the help of journalist E. K. Hornbeck, a character inspired by H. L. Mencken* and played by **Tony Randall**, while the prosecution is carried out by Matthew Harrison Brady, based on William Jennings Bryan and portrayed by **Ed Begley**. Cates's trial devolves into a media carnival, and Drummond and Brady indulge in a fierce debate. Cates is found guilty, but only fined $100, which Brady feels is a defeat, and he dies from the strain of the trial. Drummond has truly prevailed over the religious fundamentalist Brady who, in Drummond's words, sought "God too high up and far away."

A 1960 screen version memorably starred SPENCER TRACY and **Fredric March**, with Gene Kelly in support, and the film was nominated for four Academy Awards, while **Broadway** has seen two revivals. The first, in 1996, starred **George C. Scott** and **Charles Durning**, but despite excellent reviews was cut short when Scott became ill, and the second, in 2007, starred **Christopher Plummer** and **Brian Dennehy**. Scott appeared opposite **Jack Lemmon** in a television film version in 1999, which followed two previous television adaptations (1965, 1988). *See also* RELIGIOUS DRAMA.

INNAURATO, ALBERT (1947–). Born in Philadelphia, Pennsylvania, Innaurato graduated from the California Institute of the Arts and the Yale School of Drama. At Yale, he collaborated with **Christopher Durang** on three plays, *I Don't Normally Like Poetry But Have You Read Trees* (1972), *Gyp, The Real-Life Story of Mitzi Gaynor*, and *The Idiots Karamazov* (1974). His first important play, *Gemini* (1976), was staged at **Playwrights Horizons**, winning an **Obie Award** before transferring to **Broadway** for a remarkable 1,819 performances, especially since the play's subjects included

homosexuality and expressed the tensions between generations of an Italian American family. The play became a musical in 2006 called *Gemini: The Musical*. Innaurato's *The Transfiguration of Benno Blimpie* (1973) won an Obie and praise for its star, James Coco. Other Innaurato plays include *Ulricht* (1971), *Earth Worms* (1974), *Ulysses in Traction* (1977), *Passione* (1980), *Coming of Age in Soho* (1984), *Gus and Al* (1987), *Magda and Callas* (1988), and *Dreading Thekla* (1997). Innaurato adapted Puccini's *La Rondine* at Lincoln Center and has written for television and films. *See also* ETHNIC THEATRE.

INTELLIGENT HOMOSEXUAL'S GUIDE TO CAPITALISM AND SO-CIALISM WITH A KEY TO THE SCRIPTURES, THE. **Tony Kushner**'s three-act drama, inspired, in part, by the plays of **Arthur Miller**, premiered at the **Guthrie Theatre** in Minneapolis, Minnesota, in May 2009 during a Guthrie-sponsored festival celebrating Kushner's work. Set mostly in the home of a retired New York longshoreman, Gus Marcantonio, played by **Michael Cristofer**, who struggles with his past, his grown children, including a **gay** son, and their significant others, and a sister, while grappling with the importance of belonging, whether it be to a family, a set of beliefs, a relationship, and/or life itself. The Guthrie cast, under the direction of **Michael Grief**, included **Linda Emond**, **Stephen Spinella**, and **Kathleen Chalfant**. The **Signature Theatre** and the **New York Public Theatre** in a joint production expect to give the play its New York premiere during the 2010–2011 season.

INTERART THEATRE. A theatre program established by the not-for-profit Women's Interart Center in 1971 by Marjorie De Faxio, Alice Rubenstein, Jane Chambers, and Margot Lewitin. Presenting both innovative and traditional theatre under the guidance of artistic director Lewitin, Interart Theatre also encourages dance, music, visual art, and video work created by women or on women's issues. *See also* FEMINIST THEATRE; WOMEN/FEMININITY.

INTERNATIONAL ARTS RELATIONS, INC. (INTAR). One of the longest-running **Latino theatre** companies producing in English in the United States, International Arts Relations, Inc. (INTAR) has made a priority of providing Latino artists a forum, nurturing the growth and development of plays and performing arts. Under the artistic directorship of playwright **Eduardo Machado**, INTAR stresses "theatre without borders," and has been instrumental in the development of such dramatists as **José Rivera** and **Nilo Cruz**. Founded in the mid-1960s, INTAR had commissioned over 175 new works by Latino writers by 2010. *See also* CHICANO THEATRE; ETHNIC THEATRE.

INTERNATIONAL STARS AND COMPANIES IN THE UNITED STATES. During and after World WAR I, and through the 1920s, many foreign companies appeared in New York and, at times, in other cities across the United States, including Israel's Habimah, England's D'Oyly Carte, Russia's Moscow Art Theatre* and Chauve-Souris, Ireland's Abbey Theatre, Austrian director MAX REINHARDT's company, and France's Théâtre du Vieux Colombier. A serious decline in such visits occurred with the beginning of the Great Depression until the 1960s, although individual actors and directors from various countries appeared or emigrated to the United States permanently. Beginning in the 1960s, such foreign theatres as the Moscow Art Theatre, the Royal **Shakespeare** Company, the D'Oyly Carte, the Comédie-Française, the Piraikon Theatre of Athens, the Schiller Theatre, the Bavarian State Theatre, the Bunraku **Puppet** Theatre of Japan, the Grand Kabuki, the Jewish Theatre of Poland, the Vienna Burgtheater, the Compagnie due Théâtre de la Cité Villeurbanne, and the Polish Laboratory Theatre have performed residencies in the United States, and numerous plays by foreign authors have been produced in New York, often on **Broadway**, and in theatres throughout the United States and many international directors and designers have worked in the United States. Various arts festivals around the country have adopted an international approach, attracting various foreign companies and performers to participate.

ACTORS' EQUITY ASSOCIATION and other theatrical unions resisted international incursions on the American stage, and after 11 September 2001 (9/11), the government occasionally blocked entry to the country by troupes and individual artists from what were considered unfriendly nations. This was not a new problem—for example, Nobel Prize-winning Italian playwright and actor Dario Fo, whose leftist politics were deemed dangerous, was blocked by President Ronald Reagan's conservative administration from traveling to the United States for a visit in the early 1980s. Only a significant outpouring of protests from the artistic community permitted Fo to eventually come to America. *See also* CENSORSHIP.

INTIMAN THEATRE. Founded in Seattle, Washington, by Margaret Booker in 1972 and established as a not-for-profit theatre in 1973, the Intiman (Swedish for "intimate") was modeled on August Strindberg's small Stockholm theatre. The company performed in various theatres prior to 1987 when it found a permanent space in the Seattle Center Playhouse. Under several artistic directors, the Intiman emerged in the mid-1990s as a major **regional theatre**, producing Robert Schenkkan's PULITZER PRIZE-winning *The Kentucky Cycle* (1992) and was the first regional theatre to stage both parts of **Tony Kushner**'s *Angels in America* in 1994–1995. The Intiman received the **Tony Award** as outstanding regional theatre in 2006.

INTIMATE APPAREL. **Lynn Nottage** first gained notice as a dramatist with this play set in 1905 concerning a young **African American** woman who gains independence through work as a seamstress. Commissioned by Baltimore's **Center Stage** and California's **South Coast Repertory Theatre (SCR)**, the play opened at Center Stage on 2 February 2003 under Kate Whoriskey's direction. The play moved to the SCR in April of that year and opened **Off-Broadway** at the **Roundabout Theatre** on 17 March 2004 under **Daniel Sullivan**'s direction with a cast, including **Viola Davis**, who won a **Drama Desk Award** for her performance as Esther, the central character. *Intimate Apparel* won the 2004 Steinberg Play Award.

IRISH REPERTORY THEATRE, THE (IRT). Founded by Ciarán O'Reilly and Charlotte Moore in 1988, this company established since 1995 in Chelsea in a renovated warehouse, states its mission as bringing Irish and Irish American classics and contemporary plays to the stage, providing background on the Irish American experience, and encouraging the development of new plays focusing on the Irish American experience. The theatre has received a special **Drama Desk Award**, **Jujamcyn** Theatre Awards, and a **Lucille Lortel Award** for its body of work. Works by such diverse Irish playwrights as Sean O'Casey, William Butler Yeats, Samuel Beckett, Brian Friel, GEORGE BERNARD SHAW, Edna O'Brien, and others have been presented on the IRT stage. *See also* ETHNIC THEATRE; REGIONAL THEATRE MOVEMENT.

IRON CLAD AGREEMENT, THE. Founded in Pittsburgh, Pennsylvania, by Wilson Hutton and Julia Swoyer in 1976 on leaves from the Carnegie Mellon Drama School, this theatre group embarked on *Out of This Furnace*, a three-act play aimed at mill towns. Later the group produced a cycle of seven original plays about inventors called *The Gilded Age of Invention* using a minimalist style and aimed at a working-class audience, which was their typical approach. Their final work, *Virgins and Dynamos*, was produced shortly before the group disbanded in 1983.

IRVING, GEORGE S. (1922–). One of **Broadway**'s most versatile character actors since the late 1940s, Irving was born in Springfield, Massachusetts, as George Irving Shelasky. He made his first Broadway appearance in a small role in the original production of *Oklahoma!* (1943). He left the show when he was drafted into the service during World WAR II. Particularly adept in MUSICALS, he nevertheless appeared in all manner of theatre. His most notable Broadway appearances in musicals include *Can-Can* (1953), *Me and Juliet* (1953), *Bells Are Ringing* (1956), *Tovarich* (1963), **The Happy Time** (1968), *So Long, 174th Street* (1976), revivals of *The Pirates of Penzance* in 1981 and *On Your Toes* in 1983, *A Wonderful Life* (2005), and a 2007 revision of *So Long, 174th Street* renamed *Enter Laughing* at **Off-Broadway**'s York Theatre Company. He won a **Tony Award** for his featured role in *Irene* (1973), was nominated again for *Me and My Girl* (1987), and won a **Drama Desk Award** for his acclaimed portrayal of Richard Nixon in **Gore Vidal**'s *An Evening with Richard Nixon and . . .* (1972). Other non-musical roles for Irving included *The Good Soup* (1960), *Romulus* (1962), *A Murderer among Us* (1964), *Alfie!* (1964), a revival of **Bertolt Brecht**'s *Galileo* (1967), *Four on a Garden* (1971), *Who's Who in Hell* (1974), and a revival of **Once in a Lifetime** in 1978. Irving also appeared in occasional film and television roles and received the Oscar Hammerstein Award for Lifetime Achievement in 2008. He frequently worked with his wife, actress Maria Karnilova, and they were married for 53 years.

IRVING, JULES (1924–1979). Best known as director of the **Repertory Theatre of Lincoln Center** in the 1960s and 1970s, Irving was born in New York City. He married actress Priscilla Pointer and they had three children, including actress Amy Irving. With Pointer, **Herbert Blau**, and Beatrice Manley, Irving founded the San Francisco **Actor's Workshop**. Among his productions for the **Repertory Theatre of Lincoln Center**, Irving directed revivals of *The Caucasian Chalk Circle* in 1966, *The Alchemist* in 1966, *An Enemy of the People* in 1971, *Mary Stuart* in 1971, and *A Streetcar Named Desire* in 1973, among others. He also staged the American premieres of Harold Pinter's *Landscape* and *Silence* in 1971.

IRWIN, BILL (1950–). Born in Santa Monica, California, this entertainer, director, and actor emerged as part of the New Vaudeville movement following his education at the University of California at Los Angeles, Oberlin College, the Ringling Bros. Clown College, and working with the **Pickle Family Circus**. His postmodern approach to clowning incorporated the existential foundation of plays by Samuel Beckett and Eugene Ionesco, as well as silent film comedians (Charlie Chaplin, Buster Keaton, Harold Lloyd), CIRCUS, vaudeville,* various aspects of popular culture, and his own extraordinary physical dexterity. He made his **Broadway** debut in Dario Fo's *Accidental Death of an Anarchist* (1984), but won critical acclaim (and a **Tony Award**

nomination) with his own work, *The Regard of Flight* (1987), *Largely New York* (1989), and *Fool Moon* (1993). He made a seemingly effortless transition to non-physical roles, stepping into **Edward Albee's** *The Goat, or Who Is Sylvia?* in 2002, and was nominated for **Drama Desk Awards** for an acclaimed revival of Albee's *Who's Afraid of Virginia Woolf?* in 2005, which also brought him a Tony, and a 2009 Broadway revival of Beckett's *Waiting for Godot* (he had previously appeared in this play at **Lincoln Center** in 1988). In late 2009, he played the role originated by Paul Lynde in a **Roundabout Theatre** revival of the MUSICAL *Bye Bye Birdie*.

ISAACS, EDITH (1878–1956).[†] Born in Milwaukee, Wisconsin, as Edith Juliet Rich Isaacs, she attended Downer College. This American theatre CRITIC and editor wrote for the literary section of the *Milwaukee Sentinel* until 1904, when she began freelancing in New York before becoming drama critic for *Ainslee's Magazine* in 1913. She went to work for THEATRE ARTS in 1918 and from 1922–1946 edited the publication, guiding it to seminal status to theatre professionals and theatergoers and converting it from a quarterly publication to a monthly. She actively promoted the idea of an American national theatre and was involved in the **Federal Theatre Project (FTP)** (1935–1939) and other organizations. She also edited *Theatre: Essays on the Arts of the Theatre* (1927), *Plays of American Life and Fantasy* (1929), and wrote *The Negro in the American Theatre* (1947). *See also* PERIODICALS.

ISRAEL, ROBERT (1939–). A scene and costume designer who studied fine arts, Israel has worked mostly in opera and ballet, designing over 70 productions at **Lincoln Center**, the Metropolitan Opera, the national operas in London and Tokyo, the Paris Opera, and others. He also designed four premieres of operas by Philip Glass and collaborated with **Martha Clarke** on *Vienna: Lusthaus* (1986) and *Vienna: Lusthaus (Revisited)* (2002) and designed *King Lear* (2009) for Baltimore's **Center Stage** and several productions for the **American Repertory Theatre**.

ISHERWOOD, CHARLES (1964–). California-born and educated at Stanford University, Isherwood began his career writing for VARIETY as its West Coast CRITIC. He rose to senior editor and chief theatre critic in 1998 before moving to the *New York Times* in 2004 to replace **Margo Jefferson** as the second-string drama critic.

IT CAN'T HAPPEN HERE. This **"Living Newspaper"** production of the **Federal Theatre Project (FTP)**, written by John C. Moffitt and Sinclair Lewis, had the unique distinction of opening simultaneously in 20 or more locations on 27 October 1936, including **Broadway**'s Adelphi Theatre, where it ran for 95 performances. Based on Lewis's novel, the play imagines the rise of a dictator in America, inspiring both sides of the political divide to imagine the play as either pro or con on President Franklin D. Roosevelt's New Deal. Among the productions of the play there were demonstrations of variety, including an all-black cast and a YIDDISH THEATRE production. Vincent Sherman, later a noted film director, staged the Broadway production of a work that would contribute to the debate over the political leanings of the FTP.

ITALIAN ACTORS UNION (IAU). Established in 1937 in affiliation with the AFL-CIO, the IAU (also known as the Guild of Italian American Actors) continues with goals typical of most **unions**, to protect the interests of their membership in the profession. In this case, the IAU also lobbies to end stereotypical casting of Italian actors and actively promotes a positive image of Italian American culture. *See also* ETHNIC THEATRE.

IVES, DAVID (1950–). This Chicago-born playwright who studied theatre at Northwestern University and Yale School of Drama found success with collections of absurdly comic one-act plays, *Mere Mortals* (1990), *Long Ago and Far Away* (1993), and *All in the Timing* (1993), the last presented at **Primary Stages** and ultimately running for a remarkable 600 performances. Among his other works are *Don Juan in Chicago* (1995), *Polish Joke* (2003), *Roll Over, Beethoven* (2005), and *Venus in Fur* (2010), which *New Yorker* CRITIC Hilton Als described as "wildly intelligent and sometimes frightening" when it opened in a **Classic Stage Company** production under Walter Bobbie's direction. Ives has adapted MUSICALS for the City Center *Encores!* Series and adapted the script of *Wonderful Town* for its 2003 revival.

IVEY, DANA (1941–). A native of Atlanta, Georgia, Ivey studied at Rollins College and the London Academy of Music and Dramatic Art before appearing in notable Canadian productions. She developed a reputation for versatility and received **Drama Desk Award** nominations for *Present Laughter* (1982), *Quartermaine's Terms* (1983), and ***Driving Miss Daisy*** (1987), winning one for ***The Last Night of Ballyhoo*** (1997). She received **Obie Awards** for *Driving Miss Daisy* and *Quartermaine's Terms* and was also nominated for **Tony Awards** for her performances in *Heartbreak House* (1983), *Sunday in the Park with George* (1984), *The Last Night of Ballyhoo*, *The Rivals* (2005), and *Butley* (2007). She made her **Broadway** debut as a witch in the Philip Anglim *Macbeth* (1981) and appeared in *Pack of Lies* (1985) and revivals of *The Marriage of Figaro* (1985), *Waiting in the Wings* (1999), *Major Barbara* (2001), *A Day in the Death of Joe Egg* (2003), and

Henry IV (2003). Ivey has also appeared in many films, including *The Color Purple* (1985), and many television shows, including *Ugly Betty* (2010). In 2008, she was inducted into the **Theatre Hall of Fame**.

IVEY, JUDITH (1951–). Born in El Paso, Texas, as Judith Lee Ivey, she studied at Illinois State University before beginning a distinguished career as an actress and occasional director. She won two **Tony Awards** and **Drama Desk Awards** for *Steaming* (1983) and *Hurlyburly* (1985) and was nominated for a Tony for *Park Your Car in Harvard Yard* (1992). Ivey's other **Broadway** credits include *Piaf* (1981), *Precious Sons* (1986), a revival of *Blithe Spirit* in 1987, *Voices in the Dark* (1999), and a revival of *Follies* (2001). In 2009, she appeared in *The Glass Menagerie* at the **Long Wharf Theatre**, winning plaudits for her performance. Ivey has also appeared in numerous films, including *Brighton Beach Memoirs* (1986) and *Washington Square* (1997), and numerous television shows, including a recurring role on *Designing Women* in 1992–1993 and she was nominated for an Emmy Award for the TV movie *What the Deaf Man Heard* (1997).

IZENOUR, GEORGE (1912–2007). A native of New Brighton, Pennsylvania, Izenour attended Wittenburg College, after which **Hallie Flanagan** tapped him to be lighting director for the **Federal Theatre Project (FTP)**. In 1939, he designed the theatre at the Golden Gate International Exposition in San Francisco. Following military service during World WAR II, Izenour worked closely with Ed Kook on designing lighting innovations for Century Lighting. He consulted on designs for numerous American and international theatre structures, pioneering multipurpose designs for spaces to be used for drama and music with adjustable acoustics, taught at Yale University, and authored three books, *Theater Design* (1977), *Theater Technology* (1988), and *Roofed Theaters of Classical Antiquity* (1992).

J

J.B. God played Broadway when poet **Archibald MacLeish's** two-act drama opened at the **American National Theatre and Academy (ANTA)** Theatre on 11 December 1958 for 364 performances, winning the PULITZER PRIZE and a **Tony Award** as Best Play. Directed by **Elia Kazan**, the distinguished cast included **Raymond Massey, Christopher Plummer**, and **Pat Hingle** as the title character based on Job. The allegorical plot set in a CIRCUS ring essentially followed the Bible tale of Job's refusal to deny God despite the loss of everything dear to him. In 1974, **Neil Simon** revisited the Job story on **Broadway** in his farcical comedy, *God's Favorite. See also* RELIGIOUS DRAMA.

JACKER, CORINNE (1933–). A Chicago native, Jacker began writing plays in her childhood, claiming to have adapted **Anton Chekhov**'s *The Seagull* by age 12. Her plays, many of which have first been staged by the **Circle Repertory Theatre**, include *Project Omega: Lillian* (1971), *Taking Care of Harry* (1974), *Harry Outside* (1975), *Bits and Pieces* (1975), *My Life* (1977), *Terminal* (1977), *Night Thoughts* (1977), *Later* (1978), *The Chinese Restaurant Syndrome* (1979), *Rites of Passage* (1983), and *Domestic Issues* (1983). She has also written for film and television. Of her work, Jacker has said, " I really believe if I wasn't a playwright, I'd be called a schizophrenic— I keep hearing voices. I hear the characters talking in my head."

JACKSON, ANNE (1926–). Anna June Jackson was born in Allegheny, Pennsylvania, before seeking theatrical training at New York's **Neighborhood Playhouse** and **The Actors Studio**. Her performance in **Paddy Chayefsky**'s *Middle of the Night* (1956) brought her a **Tony Award** nomination. Her numerous **Broadway** credits since her 1944 debut include several revivals, including *The Cherry Orchard* in 1945, *John Gabriel Borkman* in 1946, *Yellow Jack* (1947), *Major Barbara* in 1956, *The Waltz of the Toreodors* in 1973, *Café Crown* in 1989, and *The Flowering Peach* in 1994, as well as *Summer and Smoke* (1948), *Oh, Men! Oh, Women!* (1953), *Rhinoceros* (1961), *Luv* (1964), and *Inquest* (1970). Jackson also replaced **Irene Worth**

in the Broadway production of *Lost in Yonkers* (1991). **Off-Broadway**, she appeared in *Brecht on Brecht* (1961), a double bill of *The Tiger* and *The Typist* (1962), and *Twice Around the Park* (1982). She teaches at New York's HB Studio, has appeared in films and television, and since 1948 she has been married to actor **Eli Wallach**, with whom she frequently acts.

JACOBI, LOU (1913–2009). Often cast as Jewish Americans, this familiar character actor of stage, film, and television was born in Toronto, Canada. His **Broadway** credits include *The Diary of Anne Frank* (1955), *The Tenth Man* (1959), *Come Blow Your Horn* (1961), *Fade Out-Fade In* (1964), *Don't Drink the Water* (1966), *Norman, Is That You?* (1970), *Unlikely Heroes* (1971), *Cheaters* (1978), and he replaced **Sam Levene** in **Neil Simon**'s *The Sunshine Boys* (1972) and appeared in London revivals of *Guys and Dolls* (1953) and *Pal Joey* (1954). Jacobi's many film appearances include *The Diary of Anne Frank* (1959), *Irma La Douce* (1963), *Everything You Always Wanted to Know About Sex (But Were Afraid to Ask)* (1972), and *My Favorite Year* (1982).

JACOBS, LOU (1904–1992). Born Ludwig Jacob in Bremerhaven, Germany, he moved to America in 1923 to work as a tumbler in CIRCUS, carnival, and vaudeville.* He made his mark with the Ringling Bros. and Barnum & Bailey Circus as a white-faced clown in a colorfully gaudy costume and tiny hat on a pointed, cone-shaped head. From 1926 to 1988, he often partnered with his dog, Knucklehead, adding a tiny car to his act in 1946.

JAMPOLIS, NEIL PETER (1943–). A New York-born scene and lighting designer and director, Jampolis made his first mark designing lights on **Broadway** for *Borstal Boy* (1970), but gained prominence when he won the **Tony Award** and a **Drama Desk Award** for his lighting of the Royal **Shakespeare** Company's revival of *Sherlock Holmes** in 1975. He was subsequently Tony-nominated three more times, for *The Innocents* (1977), *Black and Blue* (1989), and a revival of *Orpheus Descending* (1990). Along with his designs for several opera companies, Jampolis has created sets and/ or lighting designs for over 40 Broadway productions, including *Les Blancs* (1970), *Wise Child* (1972), *Don't Bother Me, I Can't Cope* (1972), *Butley* (1972), *Crown Matrimonial* (1973), *Brief Lives* (1974), *The American Clock* (1980), *The Life and Adventures of Nicholas Nickleby* (1981), *The Search for Signs of Intelligent Life in the Universe* (1985), and the **Dustin Hoffman** revival of *The Merchant of Venice* (1989), among others. Off-Broadway, he designed *One Flew Over the Cuckoo's Nest* (1971), among others.

JANIE. This innocuous three-act comedy by Josephine Bentham and Herschel Williams opened at Henry Miller's Theatre on 10 September 1942 in a BROCK PEMBERTON production under ANTOINETTE PERRY's direction for a whopping 642 performances. The title character, an impulsive, scatter-brained teenager (Gwen Anderson) with a high school boyfriend, becomes infatuated with a soldier, the son of her mother's friend. While her parents are away, Janie allows a party of soldiers to take place at the family home. The soldiers ship out and Janie makes amends with her boyfriend. Even more remarkable than the play's runaway success was the fact that Warner Bros. released a popular 1944 film version that spawned a sequel, *Janie Gets Married* in 1946.

JANUS. Carolyn Green's three-act comedy opened on 24 November 1955 at the Plymouth Theatre in an **Alfred de Liagre, Jr.**, production for 251 performances. A slight comedy, it was elevated by an expert cast including **Margaret Sullavan**, Claude Dauphin, and **Robert Preston**. Even though they are married to others, Jessica and Denny spend every summer at a New York apartment where they secretly write novels under the pen name, Janus. This well-guarded secret is revealed when intrusions from Jessica's husband, Denny's agent, and a tax collector cause chaos.

JAY, RICKY (1948–). Born Richard Jay Potash in Brooklyn, New York, he is an actor, writer, and magician. Some of his own stage shows, including *Ricky Jay and His 52 Assistants* (1994), which won an **Obie Award**, and *Ricky Jay: On the Stem* (2002), for which he was nominated for a **Drama Desk Award**, have been staged at New York's **Second Stage** by **David Mamet**. Jay has also appeared in several of Mamet's films. He is considered a scholar of unique forms of entertainment and has written several books on the subject since his first, *Cards as Weapons* (1977).

JEAN COCTEAU REPERTORY. Eve Adamson founded this company as an **Off-Off-Broadway** theatre in 1971. Its earliest performances were given in a Lower East Side storefront before the company established itself at the Bouwerie Lane Theatre in 1974. Initially, the theatre articulated a goal of producing classics, and although the company continues to do so, the emphasis has shifted over the years to a focus on ensemble acting. In 2002, the theatre became an Equity company and in 2006, due to financial issues and internal problems, the company merged with New Orleans's EgoPo Productions after the latter lost its theatre in Hurricane Katrina. Following this merger, under the guidance of resident director Ernest Johns, the theatre has renewed its mission to produce classics. *See also* REPERTORY THEATRE.

JEFFERS, ROBINSON (1887–1962). Born John Robinson Jeffers in Allegheny, Pennsylvania, he attended Occidental College and the University of Southern California before winning acclaim as a poet in the 1920s. His most enduring theatrical work is his modern adaptation of Euripides' *Medea* (1947), which won **Broadway** kudos for **Judith Anderson** in the title role and **Zoe Caldwell** in a 1983 revival. He also adapted elements from Aeschylus's *The Oresteia* and Euripides' *Electra* for *The Tower beyond Tragedy* (1950), again starring Anderson, but with less success. Washington's **Arena Stage** produced Jeffers's retelling of the Phaedra legend, *The Cretan Woman*, in 1954.

JEFFERSON, MARGO (1947–). Chicago, Illinois-born CRITIC of postmodern theatre and American culture, Jefferson attended Brandeis University and Columbia University before becoming an associated editor at *Newsweek* in 1973. She has written for numerous publications, including *Vogue* and *7 Days*, and has taught at New York University and Columbia. Since 1993, she became cultural critic for the *New York Times*, serving briefly as Sunday theatre critic before becoming critic-at-large in 1996, which permits her to write about theatre, books, and other arts. **Charles Isherwood** replaced her as the *Times's* second-string drama critic in 2004.

JEFFREY. **Paul Rudnick**'s satiric play opened at the WPA Theatre on 31 December 1992 under the direction of Christopher Ashley and featuring **John Michael Higgins** as the title character, an optimistic thirty-something **gay** man whose varied experiences in present-day America satirize attitudes about homosexuality, moral values, and love. Widely heralded as the first **AIDS**-era gay comedy, *Jeffrey* was filmed in 1995 with Steven Weber in the lead. *See also* SEXUALITY.

JENKIN, LEN (1941–). Dramatist, director, novelist, screenwriter, and educator often praised for his experimentation with language and form in his plays, Jenkin was educated at Columbia University. His more than 20 plays, most produced **Off-Broadway** under his direction include *Kitty Hawk* (1972), *Grand American Exhibition* (1973), *The Death and Life of Jesse James* (1974), *Mission* (1975), *Gogol: A Mystery Play* (1976), *Kid Twist* (1977), *Limbo Tales* (1980), *Five of Us* (1981), *Dark Ride* (1981), *My Uncle Sam* (1983), *American Notes* (1986), *Poor Folk's Pleasure* (1987), *Pilgrims of the Night* (1991), *Careless Love* (1993), *Ramona Quimby* (1994), *Like I Say* (2003), *The Dream Express (Out Takes)* (2004), *Margo Veil* (2005), and *Port Twilight, or The History of Science* (2007). He has also written several films and television shows, and three novels. He is a three-time **Obie Award** winner.

JENKINS, GEORGE (1908–2007). A native of Baltimore, Maryland, born George Clarke Jenkins, he attended the University of Pennsylvania before working with scene designer JO MIELZINER in the late 1930s. Beginning with *Early to Bed* (1943), Jenkins designed many **Broadway** productions and was nominated for **Tony Awards** for *The Happiest Millionaire* (1957), *Too Late the Phalarope* (1957), *The Miracle Worker* (1960), and *13 Daughters* (1961), and received a **Drama Desk Award** nomination for *Sly Fox* (1977). Other Broadway shows for which he designed sets and/or lighting include *Mexican Hayride* (1944), *I Remember Mama* (1944), *Dark of the Moon* (1945), *Lost in the Stars* (1949), *The Curious Savage* (1950), *Bell, Book and Candle* (1950), *The Bad Seed* (1954), *Two for the Seesaw* (1958), *Tall Story* (1959), *Jennie* (1963), and *Wait Until Dark* (1966). He also did art direction for films, including *The Best Years of Our Lives* (1946), *The Miracle Worker* (1962), *1776* (1972), and *Sophie's Choice* (1982), winning an Academy Award for *All the President's Men* (1976).

JESURUN, JOHN (1951–). Born in Battle Creek, Michigan, he studied sculpture at Yale University before establishing himself as a playwright, director, and designer. He merges narrative and visual elements (including film) in his work, most notably in his groundbreaking *Chang in a Void Moon* (1982), a "serial" play that has had over 60 episodes at the Pyramid Club on New York's Lower East Side. He won a 1986 **Obie Award** for his media trilogy *Deep Sleep* and has directed and/or designed over 25 productions, including *Faust/How I Rose* (2004), *Philoktetes* (2005), and *Firefall* (2006). Early in his career, he worked in television, an experience that has greatly influenced his work, and in 1996 he won a MacArthur Fellowship.

JEWISH REPERTORY THEATRE (JRT). Ran Avni founded this company in 1974 with the goal of producing Jewish classics and new works, making use of various performance venues in New York. Their production of *Kuni-Leml* (1984) won three **Outer Critics Circle Awards**, and the JPT won another in 1989 for continued outstanding productions. Financial concerns have undermined the JRT's work since 2003 and the theatre has no permanent venue. A similarly named group in Buffalo, New York, established in 2002, pursues similar goals. *See also* ETHNIC THEATRE; REPERTORY THEATRE; YIDDISH THEATRE.

JILLETTE, PENN (1955–) AND TELLER, RAYMOND (1948–). As the magic/comedy team Penn & Teller, these two performers have spent much of their career on Las Vegas stages, but also **Off-Broadway**, where in 1985 their stage show won critical kudos. Jillette is the speaking member of the act, adopting the persona of a cynical raconteur and con man, while Teller is more akin to a silent MIME and is often the butt of Jillette's barbs and tricks. Penn and Teller have twice appeared on **Broadway** (1987 and 1991) and appear frequently on television and occasionally in films. The duo first performed together in the 1970s as part of a threesome (with Weir Chrisimer) called Asparagus Valley Cultural Society. Penn Fraser Jillette was born in Greenfield, Massachusetts, and studied at the Ringling Brothers and Barnum & Bailey Clown College. Raymond Joseph Teller was born in Philadelphia, Pennsylvania, and was educated at Amherst College before teaching high school English and Latin.

JITNEY. An early entry in **August Wilson**'s decade-by-decade 10-play "Pittsburgh Cycle," *Jitney* was written in 1979 and first performed in 1982 at Pittsburgh's Allegheny Repertory Theatre. Set in 1977 in Pittsburgh, the plot focuses on Becker, owner of a jitney/car service, and his relationship with his son, Booster, recently released from a 20-year prison sentence for killing a wealthy white girl after she falsely accused him of rape. The play has had numerous productions in **regional theatre** and was revived **Off-Broadway** at the **Second Stage** in 2000 and won the **New York Drama Critics Circle Award**. *Jitney* was revived at the **Kennedy Center** in 2008. *See also* AFRICAN AMERICAN THEATRE.

JOAN OF LORRAINE. MAXWELL ANDERSON's blank verse historical drama, which opened on 18 November 1946 at the Alvin Theatre for 199 performances, won a **Tony Award** for **Ingrid Bergman** in the title role. Directed by **Margo Jones**, with designs by LEE SIMONSON, this play-within-a-play finds an acting troupe staging a play about Joan of Arc, rife with conflict between the leading lady and the director. As their work moves forward, Joan's story is revealed and the actress and director resolve their differences. Bergman repeated her performance in the 1948 film version, retitled *Joan of Arc*, which abandoned the play-within-a-play device.

JOE TURNER'S COME AND GONE. An entry in **August Wilson**'s decade-by-decade 10-play "Pittsburgh Cycle," this play was directed by **Lloyd Richards** when it opened on 27 March 1988 at the Ethel Barrymore Theatre for 105 performances, following an initial run at the **Yale Repertory Theatre**. Set in a Pittsburgh boarding house for blacks in 1911, the play examines issues of **race**, including discrimination, migration, and identity as seen in the everyday encounters of the boarders. Music features strongly in the play, as is typical of Wilson's cycle, and the language of the play reflects its period.

The original production was nominated for a **Tony Award** and a **Drama Desk Award** and a **Broadway** revival opened on 19 March 2009. *See also* AFRICAN AMERICAN THEATRE.

JOHN F. KENNEDY CENTER FOR THE PERFORMING ARTS. Following President John F. Kennedy's assassination in 1963, plans were made to honor his memory with the construction of a performing arts center, housing several theatre spaces of various sizes. The "living memorial" to Kennedy, who was a vocal advocate for the arts, opened in 1971 on the banks of the Potomac, very near the Lincoln Memorial. Since its opening, it has become a center of cultural activity in Washington, presenting new plays by the finest American dramatists, from **Tennessee Williams** to **August Wilson**, and music and dance events as well. The Kennedy Center hosts visits from international companies, American troupes, and also is the home to the **American College Theatre Festival**. In 2003, a $650 million dollar budget was established for a 10-year plan of renovations and additions to the center and the former American Film Institute space was converted into the Family Theatre for **children's** shows in 2005.

JOHN LOVES MARY. Produced by Richard Rodgers and Oscar Hammerstein II, this farcical three-act wartime comedy by **Norman Krasna** opened on 4 February 1947 at the Booth Theatre for 423 performances. The lightweight plot turns on John, a soldier returning from World War II with an English bride. He has only married her to help her get to the United States, causing complications with Mary, his true love, and her family, especially her father, a senator. John tries various deceptions, but eventually the situation is resolved with John and Mary united. A popular 1949 film version, adapted by Henry and Phoebe Ephron from Krasna's play, starred Ronald Reagan and Patricia Neal.

JOHNNY BELINDA. Elmer Harris's three-act drama opened on 18 September 1940 at the Belasco Theatre for 321 performances. Harris, who had been a playwright and librettist since 1909, had his greatest success with this play, which focused on Belinda, an abused and ostracized deaf mute, who is treated kindly by a newcomer doctor, Jack Davidson, who teaches her sign language. Belinda cares for the doctor, but she is pregnant by Locky McCormick, a local bully. When McCormick attempts to take the child from Belinda, she kills him. A trial follows, but Davidson provides her defense and she is acquitted and marries him. A 1948 film version won Jane Wyman an Academy Award in the role Helen Craig played on **Broadway**.

JOHNNY JOHNSON. This antiWAR play in three acts with music, with text by PAUL GREEN and music by Kurt Weill, opened on 19 November 1936 in a **Group Theatre** production at the 44th Street Theatre for 68 performances. Despite his pacifist beliefs, a young soldier, Johnny Johnson, is wounded in World War I. In a bold gesture, he attacks his commanders with laughing gas and is institutionalized. With fellow inmates, he forms his own League of Nations and once again embraces his pacifism. The extraordinary cast under **Lee Strasberg**'s direction included **Sanford Meisner, Lee J. Cobb, Elia Kazan, Luther Adler**, and **Morris Carnovsky**, along with Russell Collins in the title role. At the height of the Vietnam War, in 1971, the play was revived on BROADWAY under **José Quintero**'s direction, but managed only a single performance.

JOHNSON, ALBERT R. (1910–1967). Born in La Crosse, Wisconsin, as Albert Richard Johnson, this innovative scene designer began as a scene painter and studied with NORMAN BEL GEDDES. Most of the first decade of his career was spent designing MUSICALS and revues,* and over 30 productions for Radio City Music Hall. Some of his most noted early productions were *The Band Wagon* (1931), *As Thousands Cheer* (1933), *The Great Waltz* (1934), *Jumbo* (1935), *Leave It to Me!* (1938), but by the 1940s, he also designed non-musical works, including *The Skin of Our Teeth* (1942), *Proof Through the Night* (1942), *Dear Judas* (1947), *Two Blind Mice* (1949), *Fancy Meeting You Again* (1952), *Stockade* (1954), *Cloud 7* (1958), *Night Life* (1962), and *What Did We Do Wrong?* (1967).

JONES, CHERRY (1956–). Born in Paris, Tennessee, this versatile actress of stage, film, and television is a graduate of the Carnegie Mellon School for Drama. She won an **Obie Award** for *The Baltimore Waltz* in 1991. On **Broadway**, Jones has won **Tony Awards** for a 1995 revival of *The Heiress* and *Doubt* (2005), and was nominated for *Our Country's Good* (1991) and a revival of *A Moon for the Misbegotten* in 2000. She won **Drama Desk Awards** for *The Heiress* and *Doubt*, and nominations for *Pride's Crossing* (1998) and *The Faith Healer* (2006). Other Broadway credits include *Stepping Out* (1987), **Christopher Plummer**'s *Macbeth* (1988), revivals of *The Night of the Iguana* in 1996 and *Major Barbara* in 2001, and *Imaginary Friends* (2002). In 2010, she appeared in a revival of *Mrs. Warren's Profession* for the **Roundabout Theatre Company**. Jones also replaced **Ellen McLaughlin** in the cast of *Angels in America* (1993). In film, she has appeared in *Cradle Will Rock* (1999), *Divine Secrets of the Ya-Ya Sisterhood* (2000), and *Ocean's Twelve* (2004), and on television she had a continuing role on *24*.

JONES, JAMES EARL (1931–). Known for his deep, resonant voice by film and television audiences, Jones, who was born in Arkabutla, Mississippi, is better known to theatergoers for his extraordinary stage performances in a wide range of roles spanning more than 50 years. The son of an actor, Robert Earl Jones, Jones made his **Broadway** debut in a small part in *Sunrise at Campobello* (1958), followed by roles in several flops on Broadway and impressed critics with **Shakespeare**an roles for the **New York Shakespeare Festival** before scoring a personal triumph in *The Great White Hope* (1968), winning a **Tony Award** and a **Drama Desk Award** for his powerful performance as Jack Jefferson, the first black heavyweight champion of the world. He repeated the role on screen to acclaim, essentially beginning a successful movie and television career, although he has frequently returned to the stage.

Jones's other Broadway credits include *Les Blancs* (1970), revivals of *The Iceman Cometh* in 1973 and *Of Mice and Men* in 1974, the **solo** piece PAUL ROBESON (1978), *A Lesson from Aloes* (1980), a revival of *Othello* in 1982 (he had first played this role Off-Broadway in 1965 and won a Drama Desk Award), and revivals of *On Golden Pond* in 2005 and *Cat on a Hot Tin Roof* in 2008. He won another Tony as Troy Maxson in *Fences* (1987), picking up a Drama Desk Award for this performance as well. He also won Drama Desk Awards for *Les Blancs*, **Off-Broadway** performances in *Hamlet* and *The Cherry Orchard* in 1973, and he was nominated for *Paul Robeson* and was presented with a special Drama Desk Award for career achievement in 2008. In 2005, Jones was nominated for a Tony for *On Golden Pond*. Despite nearly 200 film and television performances, Jones is most often identified as the voice of Darth Vader from the *Star Wars* films of the 1980s. *See also* AFRICAN AMERICAN THEATRE.

JONES, MARGO (1913–1955). A producer-director whose name became associated with some of the most important American plays and playwrights of the middle of the twentieth century, Margaret Virginia Jones was born in Livingston, Texas, and attended Texas State College for **Women**. Her love of theatre led her to the **Pasadena Playhouse**, where she worked for a time, and found work during the late 1930s in Houston, Texas, as an assistant director for the **Federal Theatre Project (FTP)**. She taught at the University of Texas where she experimented with arena-style staging techniques and later secured a Rockefeller Foundation grant to start a **repertory theatre** in Dallas utilizing an arena approach. Jones's 1949 book, *Theatre-in-the-Round*, offers the arena style as a viable option for staging.

While awaiting the construction of her theatre, Jones assisted in directing the original production of **Tennessee Williams**'s *The Glass Menagerie* (1945) and MAXWELL ANDERSON's *Joan of Lorraine* (1946). Her Theatre

'47 opened that same year and among the productions she staged were **William Inge**'s *Farther Off from Heaven* (ultimately renamed *The Dark at the Top of the Stairs*), Williams's *Summer and Smoke*, and **Jerome Lawrence** and **Robert E. Lee**'s *Inherit the Wind*, among others. Lawrence and Lee ultimately established the **Margo Jones** Award in her memory to support producing managers committed to new works. Other plays produced or directed by Jones on Broadway were Maxine Wood's *On Whitman Avenue* (1946) and Owen Crump's *Southern Exposure* (1950).

JONES, ROBERT EDMOND (1887–1954).[†] A native of Milton, New Hampshire, and educated at Harvard University, Jones commenced a career as a scene designer in 1911 after spending a year observing MAX REINHARDT's Deutsches Theatre. Perhaps more than any other artist of the first half of the twentieth century, Jones influenced the evolution of American scene design by introducing techniques emerging in modernist Europe. Influenced by the theories of Adolphe Appia and Edward Gordon Craig, Jones designed his first **Broadway** production, *The Man Who Married a Dumb Wife* (1915). Jones aimed for simplified and symbolic visual images, rejecting both photographic REALISM as well as the painted realism typical to that time. Jones's influence grew after 1920 with his acclaimed productions of *Richard III* (1920) and *Hamlet* (1922), both starring John Barrymore.* In the early 1920s, Jones began a long association with EUGENE O'NEILL, first as part of the **Provincetown Players**, and later designing many of O'Neill's dramas on Broadway, including *The Fountain* (1925) and *The Great God Brown** (1926), both of which he also directed, and *Desire under the Elms** (1924).

Firmly established as the dean of American scene designers by 1930, Jones continued to innovate with a wide range of productions, including O'Neill's *Mourning Becomes Electra* (1931), *Ah, Wilderness!* (1933), and *The Iceman Cometh* (1946), as well as *The Green Pastures* (1930), *Mary of Scotland* (1933), *Dark Victory* (1934), *The Devil and Daniel Webster* (1939), and a revival of *Juno and the Paycock* (1940). He adapted and designed *Camille* (1932) for LILLIAN GISH, although the production failed, as did *Othello* (1937) starring WALTER HUSTON. Jones also designed the controversial English drama *The Green Bay Tree* (1933), a revival of *The Sea Gull* with ALFRED LUNT and LYNN FONTANNE, **Philip Barry**'s *The Philadelphia Story* (1940) and *Without Love* (1942), and the MUSICAL *Lute Song* (1946). Jones wrote several important books, including *Continental Stagecraft* (1922; with KENNETH MACGOWAN) and the highly influential *The Dramatic Imagination* (1941).

JONES, SIMON (1950–). Born in Charlton Park, Wiltshire, England, this actor and director works regularly in both Great Britain and the United States.

Along with serving as coartistic director of **The Actors Company** Theatre, for whom he directed productions of *Widower's House* and *Flare Path*, Jones made his **Broadway** debut as a replacement actor in *The Real Thing* in 1984, subsequently appearing in *Benefactors* (1985), revivals of *Getting Married* in 1991, *The Real Inspector Hound* in 1992 and *The School for Scandal* in 1995, *The Herbal Bed* (1998), a revival of *Ring Round the Moon* (1999), and revivals of **Noël Coward**'s *Waiting in the Wings* (1999) and *Blithe Spirit* (2009). **Off-Broadway**, he was nominated for a **Drama Desk Award** for *Privates on Parade* (1990) and appeared in the premiere of Coward's *Long Island Sound* (2002). He also has many credits as actor and director in **regional theatre**, including his performance in the U.S. premiere of Brian Friel's *The Home Place* in 2007, and is well-known to television audiences as Arthur Dent in *The Hitchhiker's Guide to the Galaxy.*

JORDAN, JULIA (1970–). This Chicago, Illinois-born playwright and director graduated from Barnard College and Dublin's Trinity College before moving to New York to work as a painter. Switching to theatre, she studied acting at **The Neighborhood Playhouse** and playwriting under **Christopher Durang** and **Marsha Norman** at the Juilliard School. Her output of plays include *St. Paul* (1999), *Nightswim* (2002), *St. Scarlet* (2003), *Summer of the Swans* (2003), *Boy* (2004), *Tatjana in Color* (2004), *Walk Two Moons* (2005), and *Dark Yellow* (2006). She has written a film, *The Hat* (2000), and wrote for the television soap opera, *As the World Turns.*

JORY, JON (1938–). The son of character actor Victor Jory, Jory founded the **Long Wharf Theatre** in 1964 with Harlan Kleiman following their graduation from the Yale School of Drama. From 1969 to 2000, Jory served as producing director of the **Actors Theatre of Louisville**, where he directed over 125 plays, and where he eventually founded the annual Festival of New American Play Festival (later called ATL's Humana New Play Festival). It realized Jory's goal of encouraging new playwrights and experimentation from established dramatists. Under the pseudonym **Jane Martin**, Jory has written a number of successful plays, including *Talking With . . .* (1981), ***Keely and Du*** (1993), *Jack and Jill* (1996), *Anton in Show Business* (1999), *Back Story* (1999), *Flaming Guns of the Purple Sage* (2001), *Heaven and Hell (On Earth): A Divine Comedy* (2001), *Bill of (W)Rights* (2004), and *Flags* (2007). Jory has directed in many of the finest **repertory theatres** in the United States and, after leaving ATL, he joined the faculty of the University of Washington and authored *Tips: Ideas for Actors* (2000, *Tips: Ideas for Directors* (2002), and *Tips II for Actors* (2005).

JOURNEY OF THE FIFTH HORSE. Produced at the **American Place Theatre (APT)**, this **Obie Award**-winning play by **Ronald Ribman** opened in 1965 in a production directed by Larry Arrick. Based on Ivan Turgenev's *Diary of a Superfluous Man*, Ribman focuses his play around a Russian, Mr. Zorditch, a reader at a publishing firm whose study of literature has led him to examine the power of language and his own worth in the world. **Dustin Hoffman** had one of his first important roles in the APT production, which was filmed for television in 1966.

JUDSON POETS' THEATRE. For 20 years (1961–1981), this **Off-Off Broadway** company provided a venue for poets, musicians, and other artists. Beginning in 1958, Rev. Howard Moody made the Judson Memorial Church a haven for the artistic **community**, allowing such artists as Allen Ginsberg, Claes Oldenburg, Robert Rauschenberg, and **Allan Kaprow**, among others, to create work in the space. In 1961, when Al Carmines became assistant minister, **alternative theatre**, **performance art**, and other experimental works with strong sociopolitical viewpoints were developed and performed there during a turbulent era in American culture. Among its most noted theatre events were **Maria Irene Fornés** and Carmines's *Promenade* (1965) and **Ronald Tavel**'s *Gorilla Queen* (1967).

JUJAMCYN THEATRES. William L. McKnight, CEO of 3M, established this producing organization in 1956, creating its peculiar name by conflating the names of his three grandchildren, Judy, James, and Cynthia. Jujamcyn owns several **Broadway** theatres (St. James, **Al Hirschfeld**, Eugene O'Neill, Virginia, and **Walter Kerr**) and, at times, managed theatres in other major cities. The organization has presented the annual Jujamcyn Award to resident theatre developing new talent and, in 1986, Jujamcyn collaborated in establishing the American Playwrights Project to further encourage new work. Among Jujamcyn's many major producing credits are *Big River* (1985), *Into the Woods* (1987), *M. Butterfly* (1988), the **Steppenwolf Theatre** production of *The Grapes of Wrath* (1990), *The Piano Lesson* (1990), *Angels in America* (1993), *The Who's Tommy* (1993), *Love! Valour! Compassion!* (1995), *Proof* (2000), *The Producers* (2001), *Take Me Out* (2003), *Caroline, or Change* (2004), *Gem of the Ocean* (2004), *Grey Gardens* (2006), *Radio Golf* (2007), and *33 Variations* (2009), as well as several notable revivals. In 2005, **Rocco Landesman** bought ownership of Jujamcyn's interest and produced **John Patrick Shanley**'s Pulitzer Prize-winning play, *Doubt* (2005).

JULIÁ, RAÚL (1940–1994). Born into a family of musicians and a restaurant owner father in San Juan, Puerto Rico, as Raúl Rafael Juliá y Arcely, Juliá was educated at the Jesuit Colegio San Ignacio de Loyola. He attended Fordham University for a year, but completed his education at the University of Puerto Rico. He moved to New York in 1964 and worked in **Off-Broadway** and **alternative theatre** on the city's streets. By 1966, he was in the company of the **New York Shakespeare Festival** under **Joseph Papp**'s guidance and appeared as Edmund in *King Lear* in 1973, and opposite **Meryl Streep** in *The Taming of the Shrew* and *Othello* in 1979. He received a **Tony Award** nomination and a **Drama Desk Award** for *Two Gentlemen of Verona* (1972) on **Broadway**, followed by notable performances in revivals of *Where's Charley?* in 1975, *Threepenny Opera* in 1976, as well as *Nine* (1982). His other **Broadway** credits include *The Cuban Thing* (1968), *Indians* (1969), *The Castro Complex* (1970), *Via Galactica* (1972), a revival of *The Cherry Orchard* in 1977, *Betrayal* (1980), and revivals of *Design for Living* in 1984, *Arms and the Man* in 1985, and *Man of La Mancha* in 1992. He also took over the title role in a revival of *Dracula** in 1977, replacing **Frank Langella**. Juliá also appeared in many films and television shows, most notably *Kiss of the Spider Woman* (1985), until into the early 1990s, when he was diagnosed with cancer. He continued to work until shortly before his death.

JUNIOR MISS. A slight three-act domestic comedy by **Jerome Chodorov** and Joseph A. Fields, *Junior Miss*, produced by **Max Gordon**, opened on 18 November 1941 at the Lyceum Theatre for a staggering 710 performances under **Moss Hart**'s direction. The play centers on precocious Judy Graves (Patricia Peardon), a 13-year-old with a wild imagination. Convinced that her uncle is a criminal and her father is having an affair with his boss's daughter, Judy and her sidekick, Fuffy (Lenore Lonergan), set out to put the world in order, instead causing mild chaos that ends with Judy preparing for her first date. Considered by CRITICS to be representative of the light situation comedies popular on the commercial **Broadway** stage during World WAR II, *Junior Miss* was deemed one of the better efforts in the genre. A 1945 film version was similarly popular.

K

KACZOROWSKI, PETER (1956–). A Buffalo, New York, native, Kaczorowski began his career as a lighting designer as assistant to several designers, including John Bury, Beverly Emmons, **Thomas Skelton**, and **Neil Peter Jampolis**. Kaczorowski won a **Tony Award** for *The Producers* (2001) and received Tony nominations for a 2000 revival of *Kiss Me, Kate* and *Grey Gardens* (2006). He won a **Drama Desk Award** for *Contact* (2000). His other **Broadway** credits include a 1991 revival of *The Homecoming, A Small Family Business* (1992), *On the Waterfront* (1995), *Steel Pier* (1997), *Honour* (1998), ***Anna in the Tropics*** (2003), a 2005 revival of ***Who's Afraid of Virginia Woolf?***, *A Naked Girl on the Appian Way* (2005), *Curtains* (2007), *Young Frankenstein* (2007), *Is He Dead?* (2007), and a 2009 revival of *Waiting for Godot*, and he has designed **Off-Broadway**, including the 2009 PULITZER PRIZE-winner, ***Ruined***, at the **Manhattan Theatre Club**, and for **Lincoln Center** Theatre, the **New York Shakespeare Festival**, and **Playwrights Horizons**, among others, and many **regional theatres**. Kaczorowski has also designed lighting for numerous opera productions with companies throughout the United States, including the Metropolitan Opera, New York City Opera, and others, as well as international companies.

KAHN, MADELINE (1942–1999). A versatile actress and singer born Madeline Gail Wolfson in Boston, Massachusetts, Kahn is most remembered for her broad, quirky performances in Mel Brooks's film comedies, *Blazing Saddles* (1974), for which she received an Academy Award nomination, *Young Frankenstein* (1974), *High Anxiety* (1977), and *History of the World, Part I* (1981), as well as the wacky farce *What's Up, Doc?* (1972), the period comedy *Paper Moon* (1973), which also brought her an Oscar nomination, and as Martha Mitchell in Oliver Stone's *Nixon* (1995). On **Broadway**, Kahn had more opportunity to demonstrate her range with performances in *Leonard Sillman's New Faces of 1968* (1968), *Two by Two* (1970), ***In the Boom Boom Room*** (1973), which brought her a **Drama Desk Award** and a **Tony Award** nomination, *On the Twentieth Century* (1978), for which she was nominated for a Tony, a 1989 revival of ***Born Yesterday*** for which she garnered a Tony nomination, and **Wendy Wasserstein**'s *The Sisters Rosensweig* (1993), for which she won a Tony and Drama Desk Award. Kahn won a Daytime Emmy Award in 1987 for an *ABC Afterschool Special*.

KAHN, MICHAEL (1937–). A Brooklyn, New York, native educated at the High School for the Performing Arts and Columbia University, Kahn began his directing career in **Off-Off Broadway** theatres, including a production of **Jean-Claude van Itallie**'s *American Hurrah* (1966) and *The Rimers of Eldritch* (1976). On **Broadway**, Kahn has directed *Here's Where I Belong* (1968), *The Death of Bessie Smith/The American Dream* (1968), revivals of *King Henry V* in 1969, *Othello* in 1970, *Cat on a Hot Tin Roof* in 1974, and *The Royal Family** in 1975, for which he won a **Drama Desk Award**. His other Broadway credits include *The Night of the Tribades* (1977), *Whodunnit* (1982), and a 1983 revival of *Show Boat* for which he was nominated for a **Tony Award**. Kahn was artistic director of the **American Shakespeare Theatre** and Festival from 1969 to 1974, the **McCarter Theatre** from 1974 to 1979, **The Acting Company** from 1978 to 1988, was Richard Rodgers Director of the Drama Division at the Julliard School from 1992 to 2006 and is artistic director of the Shakespeare Theatre Company in Washington, D.C., a post he took on in 1986.

KALEM, T. E. (1919–1985). Born Theodore Eustace Kalem in Malden, Massachusetts, he had a long career as drama CRITIC at *Time* magazine, beginning in 1961, following completion of his education at Harvard University. Kalem's writing was much admired and among the most oft-quoted of his lines are "He sometimes ran a purple ribbon through his typewriter and gushed where he should have damned" and "The heart is the only broken instrument that works."

KALFIN, ROBERT (1933–). As Robert Zangwill Kalfin, he was born in the Bronx, New York, to Russian Jewish parents. He studied at Alfred University and the Yale School of Drama before beginning a directing career **Off-Broadway** with a 1959 revival of *The Golem*. Among his Off-Broadway credits are Henry Zeiger's *Five Days* (1965), Gordon Porterfield's *The Universal Nigger* (1970), and Allen Ginsberg's *Kaddish* (1972). Kalfin staged Mark Rozovsky's *Strider* Off-Broadway in 1979, after which its success led to a **Broadway** production in 1980 for which he was nominated for a **Drama Desk Award**. Kalfin's 1977 revival of *Happy End* brought him **Tony Award** and Drama Desk nominations. He founded the Chelsea Theatre Center (CTC) in 1965, serving as its artistic director until CTC's closing in 1983, after which he freelanced as a director, including the **Broadway** MUSICAL, *Truly Blessed* (1990).

KANIN, FAY (1917–). Born Fay Mitchell in New York, Kanin is best known for her work in films as a screenwriter, producer, and as president of the Academy of Motion Picture Arts and Sciences from 1979 to 1983. Raised in Elmira, New York, she attended all-women Elmira College and was inspired with a love of the theatre after seeing ALFRED LUNT and LYNN FONTANNE in *Idiot's Delight*. She married writer Michael Kanin in 1942, and they collaborated on various film projects, including their Academy Award-nominated *Teacher's Pet* (1959). Kanin's **Broadway** work, which emphasizes her interest in **women's** rights, achieved its pinnacle with her first play, *Goodbye, My Fancy* (1948), which was a hit comedy and, in 1951, a successful film. Kanin had less success with subsequent plays, including *His and Hers* (1945) and *Rashomon* (1959), which both had relatively short runs, and her book for the MUSICAL *The Gay Life* (1961). Kanin was nominated for a **Tony Award** for her book for the musical *Grind* (1985). She won Emmy Awards for *Tell Me Where It Hurts* (1974) and *Friendly Fire* (1978) and has received numerous honors from literary and women's organizations. *See also* WOMEN/FEMININITY.

KANIN, GARSON (1912–1999). Born in Rochester, New York, Kanin began his long career as a playwright, screenwriter, and director as an actor, appearing in vaudeville* and in such plays as *Little Ol' Boy* (1933), *Spring Song* (1934), *Ladies' Money* (1934), *Three Men on a Horse* (1935), *The Body Beautiful* (1935), and *Star Spangled* (1936). He turned to directing on **Broadway** in 1937 with *Hitch Your Wagon*, followed by *Too Many Heroes* later that year. He left the stage for Hollywood after working as GEORGE ABBOTT's assistant director, but returned to direct his close friend SPENCER TRACY in ROBERT E. SHERWOOD's *The Rugged Path* (1945). As a Broadway director and writer, he scored his greatest hit with *Born Yesterday* (1946), which was adapted to the screen in 1950. Kanin frequently collaborated with his wife, **Ruth Gordon**, on various projects, and directed her plays, including *Years Ago* (1946), *The Leading Lady* (1948), and *A Very Rich Woman* (1965). He also directed his own, including *The Smile of the World* (1949), *The Rat Race* (1949), *The Live Wire* (1950), *The Good Soup* (1960), *A Gift of Time* (1962), *Come on Strong* (1962), and *Dreyfus in Rehearsal* (1974), as well the MUSICAL *Do Re Mi* (1960), for which he wrote the libretto and garnered **Tony Award** nominations for Best Musical and Best Direction. Among Kanin's other Broadway directing credits, the most notable include *The Diary of Anne Frank* (1955), for which he received a Tony nomination, *A Hole in the Head* (1957), *Sunday in New York* (1961), and *Funny Girl* (1964). In collaboration with Gordon, Kanin was nominated for the Academy Award three times, for *A Double Life* (1947), *Adam's Rib* (1949), and *Pat and*

Mike (1952), but they gave up writing together, they noted, for the sake of their marriage. Kanin also wrote novels, stories, and a memoir of their friendship with Tracy and **Katharine Hepburn**.

KANSAS CITY REPERTORY THEATRE (KCRT). Founded in 1964 as a summer **repertory** by **Patricia McIlrath**, the theatre, named the Missouri Repertory Theatre, grew in its first decade to a year-round operation on the campus of the University of Missouri-Kansas City (although a separate entity) producing up to eight productions annually. McIlrath retired in 1985 and was succeeded by George Keathley, who served as artistic director for 15 years. Keathley was succeeded by Peter Altman in 2000 who, in turn, was succeeded by Eric Rosen in 2007. In 2004, the MRT changed its name to the Kansas City Repertory Theatre and opened a second space, Copaken Stage, in downtown Kansas City in 2007.

KAPROW, ALLAN (1927–2006). An Atlantic City, New Jersey, native, Kaprow was an early **performance artist** most often credited with pioneering "Happenings" during the 1960s. He studied at New York University and Columbia University, first as a painter. He then studied music with John Cage prior to developing his first "Happenings" in 1959. He ultimately staged over 200 productions with an emphasis on a merger of art and theatre, influenced by figures including Marcel Duchamp, Jackson Pollock, and others, as well as aesthetic elements from Asian art and theatre.

KARAMU HOUSE.[†] Founded in Cleveland by Rowena* and Russel Jelliffe,* graduates of Oberlin College, Karamu (Swahili for "a place of enjoyment for all") House remains the oldest active **African American** theatre in the United States, although it began its life as a multiracial theatre. Established in 1915, the original facility was destroyed by fire in 1939, but a larger space was built and opened after World War II. Initially called the Gilpin Players in honor of noted black actor Charles Gilpin,* Karamu House focused its efforts around inner-city black life in Cleveland, presenting an annual season of as many as 11 productions, including straight drama, MUSICALS, and occasional operas. During the 1920s and 1930s, six LANGSTON HUGHES plays premiered there, and in 1981 there was a movement to establish an African American Equity unit, but it provided impossible.

KASZNAR, KURT (1913–1979). Born Kurt Servischer in Vienna, Austria, Kasznar emigrated to America in 1937 to appear in MAX REINHARDT's **Broadway** production of Franz Werfel's *The Eternal Road*. After being drafted into the United States Army in 1941, Kasznar received training as a cinematographer and was part of a team that filmed the Japanese surrender in 1945. After World WAR II, Kasznar returned to a successful acting career in theatre, films, and television. On Broadway, he was nominated for a **Tony Award** for his performance as Max Detweiler in *The Sound of Music* (1959). His other Broadway appearances include *Crazy with the Heat* (1941), *Army Play-by-Play* (1943), *Joy to the World* (1948), *Make Way for Lucia* (1948), *Montserrat* (1949), *The Happy Time* (1950), *Seventh Heaven* (1955), a 1955 revival of *Six Characters in Search of an Author*, and *Look After Lulu* (1959). He also originated the roles of Pozzo in *Waiting for Godot* (1956) and Victor Velasco in *Barefoot in the Park* (1963). Kasznar was married to actress Leora Dana, and he appeared in numerous films and television shows.

KAUFFMANN, STANLEY (1916–). New York-born drama and film CRITIC, Kauffmann was educated at New York University before beginning his work as a film critic with several publications, most notably *The New Republic* since 1958, serving as their theatre critic from 1969 to 1979. Among his numerous books, most of which are on movies, are a few related to the stage, including *Persons of the Drama* (1976), *Theatre Criticisms* (1984), and *Distinguishing Features* (1994). An erudite critic, Kauffmann raised hackles with a 1966 article in the *New York Times* in which he anonymously "outed" **gay** American dramatists **Tennessee Williams**, **William Inge**, and **Edward Albee**, positing that their dramatic depictions of women were actually acts of "transference," a means by which the playwrights represented homosexual attitudes in the guise of women characters. Kauffmann taught at several schools, including Yale University, Adelphi University, and the City University of New York, and he was honored with the GEORGE JEAN NATHAN Award for Dramatic Criticism in 1972.

KAUFMAN, GEORGE S. (1889–1961).[†] This man of the theatre was born George Simon Kaufman in Pittsburgh, Pennsylvania, and worked for newspapers in Washington, D.C. and New York before teaming with playwright MARC CONNELLY. Their first play *Dulcy** (1921) was a hit and they subsequently collaborated on *To the Ladies** (1922), *Merton of the Movies** (1922), and *Beggar on Horseback** (1924), among others. Throughout his career, Kaufman worked with writing partners. In the late 1920s, he collaborated with EDNA FERBER on *Minick** (1924), *The Royal Family** (1927), *Dinner at Eight* (1932), and *Stage Door* (1936). Kaufman also directed **Broadway** plays, most notably *The Front Page** (1928), and was widely regarded for his varied talents as writer, director, and play doctor, and his barbed wit as a member of the fabled Algonquin Hotel roundtable. In the 1920s, Kaufman cowrote two Marx Brothers* MUSICALS, *The Cocoanuts**

(1925; with music and lyrics by Irving Berlin) and *Animal Crackers** (1928; with Morrie Ryskind*), and with Ryskind, wrote librettos for three musicals in collaboration with George and Ira Gershwin. *Strike Up the Band* (1930) and *Let 'Em Eat Cake* (1933) were successful, but their *Of Thee I Sing* (1931) was the first musical to win a PULITZER PRIZE.

Kaufman cowrote *June Moon** (1929) with Ring Lardner* and the libretto for the musical *The Band Wagon* in 1931, but in 1930 Kaufman's most enduring partnership, with playwright and director **Moss Hart**, began with *Once in a Lifetime*. Their *You Can't Take It with You* (1936) won a Pulitzer Prize and their other works include *Merrily We Roll Along* (1934), *I'd Rather Be Right* (1937), *The Fabulous Invalid* (1938), *The Man Who Came to Dinner* (1939), *The American Way* (1939), and *George Washington Slept Here* (1940). From 1930 to the end of World WAR II, he directed *Flying Colors* (1932), Irving Berlin's *Face the Music* (1933), *Dark Tower* (1933, coauthored with Alexander Woollcott*), *First Lady* (1935; coauthored with Katharine Dayton), *Of Mice and Men* (1937), *Mr. Big* (1941), *The Land Is Bright* (1941; coauthored with Ferber), *The Doughgirls* (1942), *The Naked Genius* (1943), *Over 21* (1944), and *While the Sun Shines* (1944).

After World War II, Kaufman continued to write and direct with distinction. Among his directing credits, *My Sister Eileen* (1940), *Guys and Dolls* (1950), and *Romanoff and Juliet* (1957) were standouts. No longer working with Hart, he wrote *The Late George Apley* (1944; with J. P. Marquand), *The Solid Gold Cadillac* (1953; with Howard Teichmann), and librettos for the musicals, *Seven Lively Arts* (1944; coauthored with BEN HECHT), *Hollywood Pinafore* (1945), a revival of *Of Thee I Sing* (1952), and *Silk Stockings* (1955). A witty raconteur, Kaufman also became a television personality on various talk and game shows in the early 1950s.

KAUFMAN, MOISÉS (1963–). Born and raised in Caracas, Venezuela, Kaufman moved to New York in 1987 and founded the **Tectonic Theatre Company** for whom he directed and cowrote *Gross Indecency: The Three Trials of Oscar Wilde* (1997), *33 Variations* (2007), and most notably *The Laramie Project* (2000), this last focused on the hate-crime murder of **gay** University of Wyoming college student Matthew Shepard in Laramie, Wyoming. The Tectonic troupe, under Kaufman's leadership, went to Laramie and interviewed a cross-section of the local citizenry to create the play from their own words. HBO released a film based on the play in 2002. The play won international acclaim and, in October 2009, *The Laramie Project: Ten Years Later*, a "sequel" created by the Tectonic Company following a return visit to Laramie, was performed simultaneously by theatres across the United States on the anniversary of the Shepard murder. Kaufman also directed the

PULITZER PRIZE-winning play, *I Am My Own Wife* by **Doug Wright**, in 2004, for which he won an **Obie Award** and a **Tony Award** nomination. Among other projects, Kaufman also adapted and directed **Tennessee Williams**'s short story *One Arm* in 2004 at Chicago's **Steppenwolf Theatre**.

KAZAN, ELIA (1909–2003). This much-honored, and ultimately controversial, director, actor, and writer, was born Elias Kazanjoglou in Kayseri, Turkey, and emigrated to the United States. As an actor with **The Group Theatre** during the 1930s, Kazan appeared in *Men in White* (1933), *Waiting for Lefty* (1935), *Johnny Johnson* (1936), and *Golden Boy* (1937). When he turned to directing, Kazan was associated with some of the most important **Broadway** dramas of the 1940s through 1960s, including *The Skin of Our Teeth* (1942), *A Streetcar Named Desire* (1947), *All My Sons* (1947), *Death of a Salesman* (1949), *Cat on a Hot Tin Roof* (1955), and *Sweet Bird of Youth* (1960), winning **Tony Awards** for the last two. Kazan's Broadway credits also include *Casey Jones* (1938), *Thunder Rock* (1939), *One Touch of Venus* (1943), *Jacobowsky and the Colonel* (1944), *Harriet* (1944), *Deep Are the Roots* (1945), *Dunnigan's Daughter* (1945), *Truckline Café* (1946), *Love Life* (1948), *Camino Real* (1953), *Tea and Sympathy* (1953), *The Dark at the Top of the Stairs* (1957), *J.B.* (1958), *After the Fall* (1964), and *But for Whom Charlie* (1964).

Kazan brought several of his stage projects to the screen, most notably *A Streetcar Named Desire* in 1951. He won two Academy Awards as Best Director for *Gentlemen's Agreement* (1947) and *On the Waterfront* (1954), and received Oscar nominations for *A Streetcar Named Desire*, *East of Eden* (1955), and *America, America* (1963). When he cooperated with the House Un-American Activities Committee (HUAC) by "naming names" in his testimony in 1952, he met with scorn from some members of his profession, including close colleagues like **Arthur Miller**. When Kazan received an honorary Oscar in 1999, there were protesting voices in the Academy membership, although his work was widely admired.

KEACH, STACY (1941–). Born Walter Stacy Keach, Jr. in Savannah, Georgia to parents in the theatre profession, Keach studied at the University of California, Berkeley, before completing an M.F.A. at the Yale School of Drama and a Fulbright scholarship at the London Academy of Music and Dramatic Art. As an actor, Keach scored his first success in the title role of the **Off-Broadway** production of *MacBird!* (1966), winning an **Obie Award** and a **Drama Desk Award**, and in *The Niggerlovers* (1967). In 1969, he debuted on **Broadway** as Buffalo Bill Cody in **Arthur Kopit**'s *Indians*, winning a Drama Desk Award and a **Tony Award** nomination. He won Obies in

1971 and 1973, the latter for his first performance as Hamlet (he played the role in two subsequent productions), which also brought him a Drama Desk Award. He received plaudits for his 1971 performance as Jamie Tyrone in a revival of *Long Day's Journey into Night* at the Promenade Theatre, for which he won a Drama Desk Award, and in several **Shakespeare**an roles, including *Macbeth* in 1995 at Washington, D.C.'s Shakespeare Theatre and *King Lear* at Chicago's **Goodman Theatre** in 2006.

Keach's other Broadway performances include revivals of *Danton's Death* and *The Country Wife* in 1965, *The Caucasian Chalk Circle* (1966), and as Edmund in *King Lear* in 1968. He took on the role of Sidney Bruhl as a replacement in *Deathtrap* in 1978 and also appeared in *Solitary Confinement* (1992) and *The Kentucky Cycle* (1993). In films, he has appeared in *Fat City* (1972), *Luther* (1974), *That Championship Season* (1982), and *American History X* (1998), and on television he won a Golden Globe Award in the title role of *Hemingway* (1988), which also brought him an Emmy Award nomination. Keach appeared to critical acclaim as the outrageous alcoholic, womanizing father in the situation comedy *Titus* from 2000 to 2002 and he is a frequent narrator of PBS-TV and other documentary programs.

KEELY AND DU. This controversial and much-produced abortion-themed drama by **Jane Martin** (**Jon Jory**'s pseudonym) premiered at the **Actors Theatre of Louisville** Humana Festival of New American Plays in March 1993, featuring Anne Pitoniak as Du and Julie Boyd as Keely, under Jory's direction. Written as a long one-act play, the multiscene play tracks the relationship of Keely, a young woman seeking an abortion, who is imprisoned by a fundamentalist Christian antiabortion advocate, who aims to prevent Keely from succeeding at her goal. A 1994 production at the George Street Playhouse in New Brunswick, New Jersey, inspired *New York Times* critic Alvin Klein to describe the play as a "sizzling" and "joltingly real play" on the divisive topic. *See also* FEMINIST THEATRE; SEXUALITY.

KELLOGG, MARJORIE BRADLEY (1946–). A talented scene designer born in Cambridge, Massachusetts, Kellogg attended Vassar College. She began her **Broadway** career as an assistant to **Ming Cho Lee**, **Santo Loquasto**, and **Robin Wagner** before designing **Circle in the Square** revivals of *Where's Charley?* in 1974 and *Death of a Salesman* in 1975. She has been nominated for four **Drama Desk Awards** for *Steaming* (1983), a revival of *Present Laughter* in 1983, *Extremities* (1983), and *Requiem for a Heavyweight* (1985). Her numerous Broadway credits include *Da* (1978), *The Best Little Whorehouse in Texas* (1978), *Spokesong* (1979), a revival of *The Father* in 1981, *Solomon's Child* (1982), a revival of *The Misanthrope* in 1983, *Moose*

Murders (1983), revivals of ***American Buffalo*** and *Heartbreak House* in 1983, *A Day in the Death of Joe Egg* in 1984, and ***Arsenic and Old Lace*** in 1986, *A Month of Sundays* (1987), *Lucifer's Child* (1991), revivals of ***On Borrowed Time*** in 1991, *The Seagull* in 1992, *Saint Joan* in 1993, and ***Three Men on a Horse*** (1993), and *Any Given Day* (1993). **Off-Broadway**, Kellogg designed *Everybody's Ruby* (1999), *A Lesson before Dying* (2000), and *Thief River* (2001). Kellogg has also designed scenery for many **regional theatres**, teaches design at Colgate University, and has written several science fiction and fantasy novels. She has adapted a **children's** play, and her original MUSICAL, *Livin' in the Garden,* was produced by Atlanta's **Alliance Theatre** in 1997.

KELLY, EMMETT (1898–1979). Born Emmett Leo Kelly in Sedan, Kansas, this iconic, legendary CIRCUS clown whose "Weary Willie" character was inspired by the hobos of the Great Depression, began his career as an aerial artist before switching to clowning in the 1920s, developing his silent, unsmiling clown in the tradition of Charlie Chaplin's "Little Tramp." His most famous routine of attempting to sweep up an uncooperative spotlight enhanced the persona he created of a semi-tragic figure facing life's vicissitudes with resignation and a touch of hope. After appearing with other circuses, he became a star with the Ringling Bros. and Barnum & Bailey Circus in the 1940s and made appearances in films, including Cecil B. DeMille's *The Greatest Show on Earth* (1952) and television.

KELLY, GEORGE (1887–1974).[†] George Edward Kelly, born in Philadelphia, Pennsylvania, began his theatrical life as an actor and vaudevillian.* His brother, Walter C. Kelly (1873–1939), was a popular variety performer, and while following in his footsteps, Kelly wrote and acted his own sketches. He shifted permanently to playwriting with *The Torch-Bearers** (1922), a satire of amateur theatre, which led to three more satiric comedies, *The Show-Off** (1924), the PULITZER PRIZE-winning *Craig's Wife** (1925), and *Daisy Mayme** (1926), all among the most popular plays of the era with both audiences and CRITICS who responded to his solid craftsmanship and keen observation of human foibles. After Kelly wrote sketches for a revue, *A la Carte* (1927), his plays failed to find favor. These include *Behold the Bridegroom** (1927), *Maggie the Magnificent* (1929), *Philip Goes Forth* (1931), *The Deep Mrs. Sykes* (1945), and *The Fatal Weakness* (1946). Kelly's *Reflected Glory** (1936) served as a successful vehicle for TALLULAH BANKHEAD. Kelly was the uncle of actress **Grace Kelly**.

KELLY, GRACE (1929–1982). The niece of PULITZER PRIZE-winning playwright George Kelly,* she was born in Philadelphia, Pennsylvania, to a wealthy family who resisted her desire to be an actress. She gained her first notice in a 1949 **Broadway** revival of August Strindberg's *The Father*, starring **Raymond Massey** and **Mady Christians**, for which she won a **Theatre World Award**. She next appeared on Broadway in William Marchant's *To Be Continued* (1952), a short-lived comedy directed by **Guthrie McClintic**. She had appeared in numerous television dramas in the early 1950s and a few film roles, including the part of the Quaker wife of Gary Cooper in *High Noon* (1952). She was nominated for an Academy Award for *Mogambo* (1953) and won an Oscar for *The Country Girl* (1954). She made a few other films, including three classics for director Alfred Hitchcock—*Dial M for Murder* (1954), *Rear Window* (1954), and *To Catch a Thief* (1955)—and a MUSICAL version of *The Philadelphia Story* called *High Society* (1956)—before she retired from acting to become Princess Grace of Monaco when she married Prince Rainier in 1956.

KELLY, JOHN (1954–). A New Jersey-born **performance artist** who began his career in New York's East Village clubs in the early 1980s, Kelly trained as a dancer with the American Ballet Theatre and as a visual artist at the Parson School of Design and the Boston's Museum of the Fine Arts School. Kelly also studied MIME in Paris and aerial work with the **Pickle Family Circus**, as well as voice with Peter Elkus at the Academia Musicale Ottorino Respighi in Assisi, Italy. Kelly has created over 20 performance art pieces since 1984, including *The Skin I'm In* (2004), which featured elements inspired by Egon Schiele, Maria Callas, Jean Cocteau, expressionistic* films, and mythology. Kelly appeared on **Broadway** in *James Joyce's The Dead* (2000) and played Cupid in the **American Repertory Theatre**'s production of Christopher Marlowe's *Dido, Queen of Carthage* in 2005. He won **Obie Awards** in 1987 for *Pass the Blutwurst, Bitte* and 1991 for *Love of a Poet*, as well as numerous grants and fellowships. Kelly's most recent works include *caraViaggio* (2007), *Dargelos at Bar 13* (2008), *Songs for a Shiny Hot Night* (2009), *Paved Paradise Redux* (2008), and *The Escape Artist* (2009).

KELTON, PERT (1907–1968). Born in Great Falls, Montana, this Irish American character actress of stage and screen appeared first in vaudeville,* but ultimately in both MUSICALS and comedies on **Broadway** beginning in the 1920s. She was nominated for **Tony Awards** for *Greenwillow* (1960) and *Spofford* (1968) late in her career, which had begun in a supporting role in the Marilyn Miller musical *Sunny* (1925). Her other Broadway appearances include *The Five O'Clock Girl* (1927), *The Dubarry* (1932), *All in Fun* (1940), *Guest in the House* (1942), *Lady, Behave!* (1943), *The Music Man* (1957), *Come Blow Your Horn* (1961), *I Was Dancing* (1964), and *Minor Miracle*

(1965). In the movies, Kelton made her first appearance in *Sally* (1929), again with Miller, and recreated her Broadway role as Widow Paroo in *The Music Man* in 1962. She appeared regularly on radio and was briefly the original Alice Kramden in *The Honeymooners* on television, but the McCarthy-era blacklisting of her husband, Ralph Bell, cost her the role.

KENNEDY, ADRIENNE (1931–). A native of Pittsburgh, Pennsylvania, Kennedy was born Adrienne Hawkins and she grew up in Cleveland, Ohio, prior to attending Ohio State University, Columbia University, and the **American Theatre Wing**. Her first play, ***Funnyhouse of a Negro*** (1962), is perhaps her best-known work and won an **Obie Award** when produced at the **Circle in the Square** in 1964. Like much of Kennedy's work, *Funnyhouse of a Negro* merges REALISTIC and surreal elements to create a nightmarish sphere depicting a character's inner turmoil, in this case a young woman contemplating suicide because she cannot accept her mixed **racial** identity. Kennedy's subsequent works, many of which are semi-autobiographical and focus on questions of identity for **African American women** and racial and cultural politics, include *The Owl Answers* (1965), *A Rat's Mass* (1966), *The Lennon Play: In His Own Write* (1967), *A Movie Star Has to Star in Black and White* (1976), *A Lancashire Lad* (1980), *Ohio State Murders* (1992), *The Alexander Plays . . . Suzanne in Stages* (1995). *Sleep Deprivation Chamber* (1995), coauthored with her son Adam, won an Obie. Also with her son she wrote *Mom, How Did You Meet the Beatles* (2008).

At the time of Kennedy's emergence as a dramatist, *New York Times* critic **Clive Barnes** wrote, "While almost every black playwright in the country is fundamentally concerned with REALISM—**LeRoi Jones [Amiri Baraka]** and **Ed Bullins** at times have something different going on but even their symbolism is straightforward stuff—Miss Kennedy is weaving some kind of dramatic fabric of poetry."

KENNEDY, ARTHUR (1914–1990). Born John Arthur Kennedy in Worcester, Massachusetts, he studied at the Carnegie Mellon School of Drama. He was "discovered" by screen star James Cagney, who encouraged his casting in the film *City for Conquest* (1940), and subsequently Kennedy built a long career in films and theatre. On **Broadway**, Kennedy had a long association with the works of **Arthur Miller**, winning a **Tony Award** as Biff Loman in the original production of ***Death of a Salesman*** (1949), and appearing as Chris Keller in ***All My Sons*** (1947), John Proctor in ***The Crucible*** (1953), and Walter Franz in ***The Price*** (1968). His other Broadway roles include *Everywhere I Roam* (1938), *Life and Death of an American* (1939),

An International Incident (1940), *See the Jaquar* (1952), *Time Limit!* (1956), *The Loud Red Patrick* (1956), *Becket* (1961), and *Veronica's Room* (1973).

Among his more than 70 films, Kennedy was nominated for Academy Awards for *Champion* (1949), *Bright Victory* (1951), which brought him a New York Film Critics Circle Award, *Trial* (1955), for which he won a Golden Globe Award, *Peyton Place* (1957), and *Some Came Running* (1958), and he also appeared in *High Sierra* (1941), *They Died with Their Boots On* (1941), **The Glass Menagerie** (1950), **The Desperate Hours** (1955), *Elmer Gantry* (1960), *Lawrence of Arabia* (1962), *Fantastic Voyage* (1966), and *Nevada Smith* (1966). Kennedy also appeared in numerous television dramas. He was the father of actress Laurie Kennedy.

KENNEDY CENTER FOR THE PERFORMING ARTS. *See* JOHN F. KENNEDY CENTER FOR THE PERFORMING ARTS.

KENNEDY'S CHILDREN. **Robert Patrick**'s two-act drama, which began its stage life at **Playwrights Horizons** on 30 May 1973, opened on **Broadway** on 3 November 1975 at the John Golden Theatre for 72 performances under the direction of Clive Donner, with scene design by **Santo Loquasto**. Set in 1974 in a bar in New York's Lower East Side, the six-character play is essentially a series of loosely connected monologues in which the characters express their dashed hopes and dreams in the decade following President John F. Kennedy's 1963 assassination, capturing a lost generation including a drug-addled Vietnam WAR veteran, a political radical, a vulnerable blonde, and others. Shirley Knight won a **Tony Award** for her performance, but the play was not fully appreciated in its original production, although it has come to be recognized as a vivid depiction of the turbulence of the 1960s.

KENTUCKY CYCLE, THE. **Robert Schenkkan**'s cycle of nine related one-act plays tracking three Appalachian families between 1775 and 1975 began its stage life with workshops at the **Mark Taper Forum (MTF)** in 1988 and 1989 prior to a staging at Seattle, Washington's **Intiman Theatre** in 1991 and a revised version, again at the MTF, in 1992, where it won the Los Angeles Drama Critics Award and a PULITZER PRIZE, the first ever given to a play staged outside New York. Following a run at the **Kennedy Center**, *The Kentucky Cycle* moved to **Broadway** on 14 November 1993 for a mere 33 performances at the Royale Theatre. Despite a strong cast including **Stacy Keach** and **Tony Award** and **Drama Desk Award** nominations as Best Play, along with Tony nominations for cast members Gregory Itzin and Jeanne Paulson, the play failed to find an audience in New York.

KERR, JEAN (1922–2003). Born Bridget Jean Collins in Scranton, Pennsylvania, she attended Marywood College before seeking a Master's degree at the Catholic University of America, where she met her future husband, **Broadway** drama CRITIC **Walter Kerr**. They married in 1943 and raised a family in Larchmont, New York, where in collaboration with her husband she wrote a few unsuccessful plays, including *The Song of Bernadette* (1946) and *Jenny Kissed Me* (1948), as well as sketches for MUSICAL revues,* including *Touch and Go* (1949) and *John Murray Anderson's Almanac* (1953). Kerr had a modest success with the farcical satire *King of Hearts* (1954), which was directed by her husband, and wrote a highly popular semi-autobiographical book lampooning life in the suburbs, *Please Don't Eat the Daisies* (1957), which was subsequently adapted to the screen starring Doris Day and David Niven in 1960. The following year, Kerr collaborated again with her husband on the libretto for the MUSICAL *Goldilocks* (1958) before branching out on her own to write several successful Broadway plays, most notably the comedy *Mary, Mary* (1961), which became the longest-running non-musical of the time. Her other less successful plays include *Poor Richard* (1964), *Finishing Touches* (1973), and *Lunch Hour* (1980).

KERR, WALTER (1913–1996). This admired drama CRITIC was born Walter Francis Kerr in Evanston, Illinois, where he received both B.A. and M.A. degrees from Northwestern University. While teaching speech and drama at the Catholic University of America, he met his future wife, Bridget Jean Collins, later known as **Jean Kerr**, and they married in 1943, later collaborating on several theatrical projects including writing sketches for the MUSICAL revue* *Touch and Go* (1949) and the libretto for the musical *Goldilocks* (1958). Kerr also directed several productions, including his wife's play, *King of Hearts* (1954). Kerr wrote dramatic criticism for *Commonweal* before becoming critic for the *New York Herald Tribune* in 1951, moving to the *New York Times* in 1966. He won a PULITZER PRIZE for criticism in 1978 and continued at the *Times* until 1983. In 1990, Broadway's Ritz Theatre was renamed in Kerr's honor. His tastes were largely those of the mainstream **Broadway** audience of his generation during the post-World WAR II era, and he was slow to accept changes; for example, he dismissed **Stephen Sondheim**'s early works. He published several books, including collections of his criticism, such as *Journey to the Center of the Theatre* (1979).

KERZ, LEO (1912–1976). Born in Berlin, Germany, Kerz became a scene and lighting designer after studying with **Bertolt Brecht** and working as an assistant designer for **Erwin Piscator**. He fled Berlin at the rise of Adolf Hitler in the early 1930s and ultimately emigrated to the United States in

1942 after working in several European capitals and founding the Pioneer Theatre in Johannesburg, South Africa. Once in America, he again worked with Piscator and began designing lighting on **Broadway** for *Flamingo Road* (1946) and *Christopher Blake* (1946), among others, before designing all aspects of *Open House* (1947). His scenic, lighting, and occasionally costume designs were seen in productions, including KATHARINE CORNELL's revival of *Antony and Cleopatra* in 1947, *A Long Way from Home* (1948), *Me and Molly* (1948), *Bravo!* (1948), *For Heaven's Sake, Mother!* (1948), *The Biggest Thief in Town* (1949), *Edwina Black* (1950), *The Sacred Flame* (1952), *Whistler's Grandmother* (1952), *Hit the Trail* (1954), *Moonbirds* (1959), a flop he also produced and directed), *Rhinoceros* (1961), which he also produced, *Hidden Stranger* (1963), *Dance of Death* (1971), and *Children of the Wind* (1973). He also worked as production designer for several films, including *The Goddess* (1958) and **Middle of the Night** (1959).

KEY LARGO. MAXWELL ANDERSON's realistic two-act blank-verse play with a prologue, a departure from a string of Anderson's historical dramas, set a battle of good against evil in Spain and in a Key West, Florida, resort, where a gangster and his henchman hold several people hostage during a hurricane. The play opened on 27 November 1939 at the Ethel Barrymore Theatre, where it ran for 105 performances under GUTHRIE MCCLINTIC's direction, with scene designs by JO MIELZINER. The play starred **Paul Muni** as a veteran of the Spanish Civil WAR who deserted under fire and redeems himself by sacrificing his life to defend the family of a true war hero, with **José Ferrer**, **Uta Hagen**, and Karl Malden in the large supporting cast. A 1948 film version, starring EDWARD G. ROBINSON, Humphrey Bogart, **Lauren Bacall**, Claire Trevor, and Lionel Barrymore* significantly changed Anderson's play in a rewrite by director John Huston and Richard Brooks, focusing on the post-World War II era.

KILEY, RICHARD (1922–1999). Chicago, Illinois, native Richard Paul Kiley attended Loyola University of Chicago and the Barnum Dramatic School, after which he worked as a radio announcer in New York. Following service in the United States Navy during World WAR II, Kiley toured as Stanley Kowalski in *A Streetcar Named Desire* (1947) prior to appearing on **Broadway** in a revival of GEORGE BERNARD SHAW's *Misalliance* in 1953, winning a **Theatre World Award**. He demonstrated his versatility appearing that same year in the MUSICAL *Kismet* (1953). He won two **Tony Awards** for his performances in the musicals *Redhead* (1959) and *Man of La Mancha* (1965), in which he introduced "The Impossible Dream." Kiley was also nominated for Tonys for Richard Rodgers's *No Strings* (1962) and in a 1987 revival of *All My Sons*, as well as a **Drama Desk Award** nomination for a 1976 revival of *The Heiress*. Kiley's other Broadway credits include *Time Limit!* (1956), *Advise & Consent* (1960), *I Had a Ball* (1964), *Her First Roman* (1968), *The Incomparable Max* (1971), *Voices* (1972), and *Absurd Person Singular* (1974). Kiley appeared in numerous films, including *The Little Prince* (1974), *Looking for Mr. Goodbar* (1977), and *Patch Adams* (1998), and on television he won Emmy Awards and Golden Globe Awards for *The Thorn Birds* (1983) and *A Year in the Life* in 1988 and an Emmy for *Picket Fences* in 1994, as well as several nominations, and he frequently narrated TV documentaries.

KILLER JOE. Tracy Lett's two-act comedy-drama about a trailer park family mixed up with a hired killer, opened at Chicago's Next Lab Theatre in 1993 prior to a 1998 SoHo Playhouse production starring **Amanda Plummer** and Scott Glenn. The play's Gothic horror mixed with humor reminded CRITICS of *Tobacco Road* and the full-frontal **nudity** and over-the-top violence disturbed some critics and audiences. Despite the controversial elements, the play has been widely produced in the United States and Europe.

KILTY, JEROME (1922–). Born Jerome Timothy Kilty on the Pala Indian Reservation in California, he worked successfully as an actor, director, and playwright, often with his wife, Cavada Humphrey. As an actor, Kilty's **Broadway** credits include revivals of *The Relapse* in 1950, *Love's Labour's Lost* in 1953, and *Misalliance* in 1953, *A Pin to See the Peepshow* (1953), *The Frogs of Spring* (1953), *Quadrille* (1955), a revival of *A Moon for the Misbegotten* in 1984, and *Mastergate* (1989). As a dramatist, his best-known work, *Dear Liar* (1957), is a two-character play drawn from the correspondence of GEORGE BERNARD SHAW and Mrs. Patrick Campbell. Kilty and his wife had toured in the play, but when it came to Broadway Kilty directed KATHARINE CORNELL (in her last stage appearance) and **Brian Aherne** in the roles. Also for Broadway, Kilty adapted Jean-Claude Carrière's *The Little Black Book* (1972) and wrote *Look Away* (1973), based on a book about Mary Todd Lincoln, but both flopped. In 1991, Kilty won a Joseph Jefferson Award for a revival of *The Iceman Cometh* at Chicago's **Goodman Theatre,** and he appeared in several television dramas during the 1950s.

KIM, WILLA (1930?–). Los Angeles, California-born Kim studied at the California Institute of the Arts and became a celebrated costume designer after working as an assistant to Raoul Pène du Bois, winning **Tony Awards** for *Sophisticated Ladies* (1981) and *The Will Rogers Follies* (1991) and Tony nominations for *Goodtime Charley* (1975), *Dancin'* (1978), *Song and Dance*

(1986), and *Legs Diamond* (1989). Kim also won **Drama Desk Awards** for *Operation Sidewinder* (1970), the **Off-Broadway** productions of *Promenade* (1970) and *The Screens* (1972). Although many of her designs have been for MUSICALS and ballet (including the American Ballet Theatre, Elliot Feld Ballet, and the Joffrey Ballet), she designed a range of plays on **Broadway**, including *Have I Got a Girl for You!* (1963), *Malcolm* (1966), *Hail Scrawdyke!* (1966), a 1972 revival of *Lysistrata*, *Jumpers* (1974), *Bosoms and Neglect* (1979), revivals of **Long Day's Journey into Night** and *The Front Page** in 1986, *Four Baboons Adoring the Sun* (1992), *Tommy Tune Tonight!* (1992), a 1994 revival of *Grease*, and *Victor/Victoria* (1995). Kim was inducted into the **Theatre Hall of Fame**, received the **Irene Sharaff** Lifetime Achievement Award in 1999, and won a 1981 Emmy Award for *Great Performances: Dance in America*.

KING, BRUCE (195?–). A **Native American** of the Turtle clan of the Haudenosaunee-Oneida Nation in Wisconsin, King studied at Northwestern University, the University of Illinois, NAES College in Chicago, the Institute of American Indian Arts, and Santa Fe Community College. He turned to playwriting following three years in the United States Army in Vietnam. His semi-autobiographical play *Dustoff* (1982), which premiered at the Westside Mainstage in New York, depicts a young man drafted from an Indian reservation who recounts the atrocities he observed in the Vietnam WAR but was unable to stop. In more recent years, King has premiered his newest works at the Thunderbird Theatre at the Haskell Indian Nations University in Lawrence, Kansas, including *Evening at the Warbonnet* (1990) and *Threads* (2001).

KING, DENNIS (1897–1971). Born in Coventry, Warwickshire, England as Dennis Pratt, King appeared in London productions beginning with *Monsieur Beaucaire* in 1919, but emigrated to the United States in 1921. On **Broadway**, he appeared in a range of dramas, operettas,* and MUSICALS, often as aristocratic heroes or villains, including *Claire de Lune* (1921), *Back to Methuselah* (1922), revivals of *Romeo and Juliet* in 1923 and *Antony and Cleopatra* in 1924, *Rose-Marie* (1924), *The Vagabond King* (1925), *The Three Musketeers* (1928), revivals of *Peter Ibbetson* in 1931 and *Show Boat* in 1932, *Richard of Bordeaux* (1934), *Petticoat Fever* (1935), *Parnell* (1936), *Frederika* (1937), a 1937 revival of *A Doll's House* opposite **Ruth Gordon**, *I Married an Angel* (1938), *Lorelei* (1938), a 1942 revival of *The Three Sisters* with KATHARINE CORNELL, Ruth Gordon, and **Judith Anderson**, *The Searching Wind* (1944), *Dunnigan's Daughter* (1945), a 1946 revival of *He Who Gets Slapped*, and *The Haven* (1946). He replaced John Gielgud in the

Robinson Jeffers's adaptation of *Medea* in 1948, and appeared in a 1950 revival of *The Devil's Disciple, Billy Budd* (1951), a 1951 revival of *Music in the Air, The Strong Are Lonely* (1953), *Lunatics and Lovers* (1954), *A Day By the Sea* (1955), *Affair of Honor* (1956), *Shangri-La* (1956), *The Hidden River* (1957), *The Greatest Man Alive* (1957), *Love and Libel* (1960), *Photo Finish* (1963), *Minor Miracle* (1965), *The Loves of Cass McGuire* (1966), *Portrait of a Queen* (1968), in which he played Benjamin Disraeli, and *A Patriot for Me* (1969), which brought him a **Tony Award** nomination.

On screen, the suave King debuted in 1930 recreating his stage role in the operetta *The Vagabond King* and also appeared with Stan Laurel and Oliver Hardy in *The Devil's Brother* (1933), but his appearances were infrequent, including *Between Two Worlds* (1944), *The Miracle* (1959), and *Some Kind of a Nut* (1969). King appeared frequently in television dramas beginning in the late 1940s. He was the father of actors Dennis King, Jr. and John Michael King.

KING, WOODIE, JR. (1937–). A native of Baldwin Springs, Alabama, King graduated from high school in Detroit, Michigan, after which he worked for the Ford Motor Company before founding the Concept East Theatre in Detroit in 1960. He later moved to New York and founded the New Federal Theatre in 1970, producing and directing over 180 productions by black dramatists, including **Amiri Baraka**, **Ed Bullins**, and **Ntozake Shange**. King also established the National Black Touring Circuit in 1974. King received a 1997 **Obie Award** for sustained achievement, the 2003 PAUL ROBESON Award, and the 2005 **Rosetta LeNoire** Award, and he wrote several books on black drama in the United States. *See also* AFRICAN AMERICAN THEATRE.

KINGSLEY, SIDNEY (1906–1995). Born in Philadelphia, Pennsylvania, Kingsley was educated at Cornell University where his interests in theatre inspired him to write one-act plays for the campus dramatic society. He began his professional career as an actor, but within a few years his first major **Broadway** play, *Men in White* (1933), a three-act drama about the conflict between an idealistic intern and his wealthy fiancée who fails to appreciate his dedication, was produced by **The Group Theatre** at the Broadhurst Theatre where it scored a critical and commercial hit. *Men in White* won a PULITZER PRIZE, but it was two years before the methodical, thoughtful Kingsley offered another play. *Dead End* (1935), which proved to be his most enduring work and is one of the most emblematic plays of the Great Depression. Its highly naturalistic depiction of the impact of the socioeconomic strains of the era on the lives of both rich and poor, *Dead End*, like much of Kingsley's work, springs from his left-wing political sentiments and his compassionate interest in human intimacies set against the unstoppable flow of cultural change.

Kingsley revisited these dominant themes later in his career in the hit drama *Detective Story* (1949), a realistic portrait of a day in a police station depicting the human toll of a policeman's overzealous pursuit of justice. Among Kingsley's subsequent works, he had two costly failures he produced and directed: *Ten Million Ghosts* (1936), a pacifist drama pitting an idealistic poet against a munitions salesman, and *The World We Make* (1939), adapted from Millen Brand's novel, *The Outward Room*, which focused on the attempts of a mentally ill man to pursue a normal existence. Kingsley's dramatic fortune recovered with his acclaimed drama, *The Patriots* (1943), which focused on the political differences of Thomas Jefferson and Alexander Hamilton in the formative years of the United States. It won the **New York Drama Critics Circle Award** and was lauded for its exploration of the rise of Jeffersonian democratic values in the midst of World WAR II. Kingsley won another New York Drama Critics Circle Award for *Darkness at Noon* (1951), an anti-Communist melodrama* adapted from an Arthur Koestler novel about the execution of a party loyalist for "political divergences." The character recalls his involvement in Josef Stalin's purges and, as he goes to his execution, apologizes to those murdered in the name of Communism and repudiates his belief in Marxist principles. Produced by the **Playwrights' Company** at the height of anti-Communist fervor in the United States, *Darkness at Noon* won critical and audience approval.

Surprisingly, Kingsley's next play, *Lunatics and Lovers* (1954), was a broad comedy about a Broadway operator, and it won modest approval, but his final play, *Night Life* (1962), which he produced and directed, was a return to naturalistic drama in its presentation of an assortment of characters in a café who reflect on the complications of their lives. Kingsley, a longtime president of the **Dramatists Guild**, remained active in theatrical matters until late in his life, and although few of his plays are revived, he is remembered as one of the socially conscious dramatists who best captured the collisions of high-minded idealism and the sociopolitical realities of the 1930s.

KIRBY, MICHAEL (1931–1997). Born in California, Kirby studied at Princeton University, Boston University, and New York University, becoming a professor of drama at the latter with a deep interest in **alternative** theatre. He edited *The Drama Review* from 1969 to 1986, stressing that theatre events, no matter how temporal or visual, should be documented. He authored major books on the avant-garde theatre of the 1960s, including *Happenings* (1965), *The Art of Time* (1969), and *Futurist Performance* (1971).

KIRKLAND, JACK (1902–1969). Born in St. Louis, Missouri, Kirkland was a Broadway producer and writer. Among his 10 productions, Kirkland had his greatest success with his adaptation of Erskine Caldwell's novel *Tobacco Road* (1933), which, in its original production, ran for an extraordinary 3,182 performances (eight years) on **Broadway**. He had a moderate success with *I Must Love Someone* (1939), coauthored by Leyle Georgie, which fictionalized the phenomenon of the Florodora Girls, a famous double sextet of singing beauties from the 1899 British **musical**, *Florodora*. Kirkland was less successful with his other written works, including his adaptation of **John Steinbeck**'s *Tortilla Flat* (1938), *Suds in Your Eye* (1944), *Mr. Adam* (1949), and *Mandingo* (1961). Kirkland also supplied Hollywood with several stories and screenplays, none of particular note.

KISS AND TELL. **F. Hugh Herbert**'s three-act comedy opened on 17 March 1943 at the Biltmore Theatre for 956 performances under GEORGE ABBOTT's direction. In the play, two teenage girls, Corliss Archer and Mildred Pringle, set their families at odds because they have been selling kisses for charity. When Corliss's brother, Lenny, a soldier, elopes with Mildred, he compels his sister to keep the secret. When Mildred becomes pregnant, Corliss tries to be helpful and is seen leaving the doctor's office by Mildred's mother, who jumps to the wrong conclusion. The comparatively innocent family conflicts amused critics and audiences during the war years. Joan Caulfield and Richard Widmark had their first successes in *Kiss and Tell*. Shirley Temple played Corliss in the 1945 film version of the play, which proved so popular that it inspired a sequel, *A Kiss for Corliss* (1949).

KISS THE BOYS GOOD-BYE. **Clare Boothe**'s three-act comedy opened in a BROCK PEMBERTON production on 28 September 1938 at Henry Miller's Theatre for 286 performances under the direction of ANTOINETTE PERRY. The satiric comedy lampooned Hollywood's highly publicized search for an actress to play Scarlett O'Hara in *Gone with the Wind*. In the play, movie producers are seeking a new face to play Velvet O'Toole in a Civil War novel, with attention centering on a Georgia Southern belle, Cindy Lou Bethany, played by Helen Claire. In a 1941 film version a young **Mary Martin** played Cindy Lou.

KISSEL, HOWARD (1942–). Born Howard William Kissel in Milwaukee, Wisconsin, this drama CRITIC and author was educated at Columbia University and Northwestern University prior to writing for several newspapers, most notably *Women's Wear Daily*, for whom he wrote about the arts, including reviews of music, films, books, and theatre beginning in the

1970s and continuing to 1986, when he became drama critic for the *New York Daily News*. He compiled and edited *Stella Adler: The Art of Acting* (2000) and authored *David Merrick: The Abominable Showman, The Unauthorized Biography* (2000) and *New York Theatre Walks: Seven Historical Tours from Times Square to Greenwich Village and Beyond* (2007).

KITCHEN, THE. Woody and Steina Vasulka founded this not-for-profit arts organization with an interdisciplinary mission in 1971 with the goal of providing a performance space housed originally in the kitchen of New York's Mercer Arts Hotel for avant-garde and **alternative theatre** writers, actors, dancer, and **performance artists**, among whom at various times were **Laurie Anderson**, **Meredith Monk**, Vito Acconci, Constance de Jong, Gary Hill, Kiki Smith, Charles Atlas, Lucinda Childs, Elizabeth Streb, and Bill T. Jones.

KLINE, KEVIN (1947–). Born in St. Louis, Missouri, as Kevin Delaney Kline, he attended Indiana University and the Juilliard School, where, along with **Patti LuPone** and David Ogden Stiers, they formed the nucleus of the City Center Acting Company (later known as **The Acting Company**), which traveled the United States with a **repertory** of plays, including revivals of *The Three Sisters, The Beggar's Opera, Measure for Measure, Scapin*, all in 1973, and the original MUSICAL *The Robber Bridegroom* (1975), and revivals of *Edward II* and *The Time of Your Life*, both in 1975, all of which brought him and his fellow players significant acclaim. Branching out on his own beginning in 1976, Kline won a **Tony Award** and a **Drama Desk Award** in the musical *On the Twentieth Century* (1978). He won both awards again in 1981 for a revival of *The Pirates of Penzance,* and in 2004 he won a Drama Desk Award and was Tony-nominated for a **New York Shakespeare Festival (NYSF)** production of *Henry IV*. Kline was also nominated for a Drama Desk Award twice for *Hamlet* in 1986 and 1991 (he also directed the 1991 production, garnering a Drama Desk nomination for his direction), *The Tempest* in 1996, and *Cyrano de Bergerac* in 2008 (a PBS-TV broadcast brought him an Emmy Award nomination). Kline's other **Broadway** appearances include *Loose Ends* (1979), revivals of *Arms and the Man* in 1985 and *Ivanov* in 1997.

Among his performances for the NYSF, Kline appeared in **Tom Stoppard**'s adaptation of **Anton Chekhov**'s *The Seagull* in 2001, costarring with **Meryl Streep**, with whom he also appeared in **Tony Kushner**'s adaptation of **Bertolt Brecht**'s *Mother Courage and Her Children* for the NYSF, and in 2007 he was acclaimed in a NYSF revival of *King Lear*. In films, Kline won an Academy Award for *A Fish Called Wanda* (1988), and he was nominated for Golden Globe Awards for *Sophie's Choice* (1982), *Soapdish* (1991), *Dave* (1993), *In & Out* (1997), and *De-Lovely* (2004). His other movies include *The Big Chill* (1983), *Cry Freedom* (1987), *I Love You to Death* (1990), *Chaplin* (1992), *French Kiss* (1995), *The Ice Storm* (1997), *Wild Wild West* (1999), *A Prairie Home Companion* (2006), and *As You Like It* (2006). Kline, who is married to actress Phoebe Cates, was inducted into the **Theatre Hall of Fame** in 2004.

KLOTZ, FLORENCE (1920–2006). Born Kathrina E. Klotz in Brooklyn, New York, she attended the Parsons School of Design and took a job painting fabrics for Brooks Costumes. In 1951, Klotz began to work as assistant to costume designer **Irene Sharaff** on the MUSICAL *The King and I*. On her own, she won six **Tony Awards**, all for **Broadway** musicals, including *Follies* (1971), *A Little Night Music* (1973), *Pacific Overtures* (1976), *Grind* (1985), *Kiss of the Spider Woman* (1993), and a 1995 revival of *Show Boat*, but she designed all manner of plays, including **Never Too Late** (1962), *Nobody Loves an Albatross* (1963), **The Owl and the Pussycat** (1964), *Paris Is Out!* (1970), *Norman, Is That You?* (1970), *Dreyfus in Rehearsal* (1974), *Harold and Maude* (1980), *Goodbye Fidel* (1980), a revival of **The Little Foxes** (1981), as well as the musicals *Side by Side by Sondheim* (1977), *A Doll's Life* (1982), *Jerry's Girls* (1985), *Rags* (1986), and *City of Angels* (1989), the last bringing Klotz a Tony nomination, among others. Klotz was the domestic partner of producer Ruth Mitchell.

KOMISARJEVSKY, THEODORE (1882–1954). As Fyodor Fyodorovich Komissarzhevsky, he was born in Venice, Italy, the son of an opera singer. His sister, Vera, became a major Russian actress and he turned to the study of architecture, although he was lured to the theatre by his sister to stage productions at her theatre. He worked closely with theatrical visionary Nikolai Evreinov and evolved a notion of a "theatre of all the arts"—a synthetic approach aimed at merging the play's "inner rhythm, spirit and ideology." In 1910, Komisarjevsky established his own studio in Moscow and after the Russian Revolution was appointed director of the Bolshoi Theatre, but within a short time he left Russia for England, where he won acclaim staging **Anton Chekhov**'s plays. He married actress Peggy Ashcroft and lectured at the Royal Academy of Dramatic Art, winning further acclaim for his staging of **Shakespeare**'s plays in the 1930s, most notably *Macbeth* in 1933 and *King Lear* in 1936. As early as the 1920s, he worked in the United States, directing three THEATRE GUILD productions, *The Lucky One* (1922), *The Tidings Brought to Mary* (1922), and a revival of *Peer Gynt* in 1923, and his other **Broadway** productions included *Maitresse De Roi* (1926), *Revenge with Music* (1934), *Escape Me Never* (1935), which he also designed, *Russian Bank* (1940), *Andrea Chenier* (1947), and his acclaimed revival of *Crime and Punishment* in 1947, starring John Gielgud and LILLIAN GISH.

Komisarjevsky also directed the 1928 film *Yellow Stockings*. He emigrated permanently to the United States in 1939 and established the Komisarjevsky Theatre Studio in New York, taught at Yale University, directed productions for the New York City Opera Company in the late 1940s, and he wrote *Theatrical Preludes* (1916), *Costume of the Theatre* (1931), and *The Theatre and a Changing Civilization* (1935). *See also* INTERNATIONAL STARS AND COMPANIES IN THE UNITED STATES.

KONDOLEON, HARRY (1955–1994). Winner of an **Obie Award** as the "most promising young playwright" in 1983, Kondoleon's promising career was cut short due to his death from **AIDS** at age 39. Born in Forest Hills, New York, he attended Hamilton College and the Yale School of Drama. Kondoleon won several fellowships and his highly imaginative plays, sometimes compared to those of Luigi Pirandello, include *The Brides* (1980), *The Cote d'Azur Triangle* (1980), *Rococco* (1981), *Self-Torture and Strenuous Exercise* (1982), *Andrea Rescued* (1982), *Clara Toil* (1982), *The Fairy Garden* (1982), *Christmas on Mars* (1983), *Slacks and Tops* (1983), *Linda Her* (1984), *The Vampires* (1984), *Anteroom* (1985), *Play Yourself* (1988), *The Poet's Corner* (1988), *Zero Positive* (1988), *Love Diatribe* (1990), *The Houseguests* (1992), which won an **Obie Award**, *Half Off* (1993), and *Saved or Destroyed* (1994). Kondoleon also wrote two novels, *The Whore of Tjampuan* (1988) and *Diary of a Lost Boy* (1994), and a collection of poetry, *The Death of Understanding* (1987). At his death, *Village Voice* CRITIC Charles McNulty wrote that Kondoleon "was a playwright constitutionally incapable of playing by the rules."

KOPIT, ARTHUR (1937–). As Arthur Lee Kopit, he was born in New York and attended Harvard University, where he wrote his first plays. His **Off-Broadway** production, ***Oh Dad, Poor Dad, Mama's Hung You in the Closet and I'm Feelin' So Sad*** (1962) won a Vernon Rice Award. Subsequent plays reflecting the versatility of his writing include three works nominated for **Tony Awards**: *Indians* (1969), **Wings** (1979), and the libretto for the MUSICAL *Nine* (1982). Kopit's other plays include *Don Juan in Texas* (1957), *Gemini* (1957), *The Questioning of Nick* (1957), *On the Runway of Life, You Never Know What's Coming Off Next* (1957), *Across the River and Into the Jungle* (1958), *Aubade* (1958), *Sing to Me Through Open Windows* (1959), *Chamber Music* (1962), *Asylum* (1963), *The Conquest of Everest* (1964), *The*

Hero (1964), *The Day the Whores Came Out to Play Tennis* (1964), *What's Happened to the Thorne's House* (1972), *Louisiana Territory* (1975), *Secrets of the Rich* (1976), *Good Help is Hard to Find* (1981), an adaptation of Henrik Ibsen's *Ghosts* in 1982, *End of the World with Symposium to Follow* (1984), *Bone-the-Fish* (1989), *Road to Nirvana* (1991), *Success* (1991), *Phantom* (1992), *High Society* (1998), *Y2K* (1999), *Chad Curtis, Lost Again* (2001), *Because He Can* (2006), and *Myth America* (2007). Kopit has taught at Wesleyan University, Yale University, and the City College of New York.

KORDER, HOWARD (1957–). New York-born playwright and screenwriter Korder studied at the State University of New York at Binghamton before beginning his writing career. In theatre, he is best known for his play *Boy's Life* (1988), a cynical coming-of-age drama about contemporary **men** compared to the works of **David Mamet** and nominated for a **Drama Desk Award** and a Pulitzer Prize. His subsequent plays include *Search and Destroy* (1990), which had a brief **Broadway** run. Korder's other plays have been produced **Off-Broadway** or in **regional theatres**, including full-length and one-act works such as *Night Maneuver* (1982), *The Middle Kingdom* (1985), *Lip Service* (1985), *Episode 26* (1985), *Fun* (1987), *Nobody* (1987), *The Lights* (1993), which was nominated for a Drama Desk Award and won an **Obie Award**, and *Sea of Tranquility* (2004). Korder has also written for film, including *The Passion of Ayn Rand* (1999), *Stealing Sinatra* (2003), and *Lakeview Terrace* (2008), as well as several television scripts, including episodes of the TV series *Kate & Allie* in 1987.

KRAMER, LARRY (1935–). Born in Bridgeport, Connecticut, Kramer attended Yale University, where he struggled with a painful "coming out" experience, including a suicide attempt. Upon graduating with an English degree, Kramer began his career rewriting scripts for Columbia Pictures and, later, United Artists, garnering an Academy Award nomination for his script for *Women in Love* (1969) and he also wrote the screenplay for the musical adaptation of *Lost Horizon* (1973). Increasing engaged in political activism in the **gay** community, Kramer's 1978 novel, *Faggots*, met with controversy due to its condemnation of what Kramer depicted as the shallow promiscuity of the homosexual community.

Kramer's political activism grew tenfold with the appearance of the **AIDS** pandemic in the early 1980s, and he was a founder of the Gay Men's Health Crisis (GMHC), a major organization with the goal of assisting those stricken with AIDS. Kramer denounced the government and the media for apathy and bureaucratic paralysis, and was equally critical of the gay community for denial of the seriousness of the disease and its potential for worldwide catastrophe. His attitudes were expressed vividly in his semi-autobiographical drama *The Normal Heart* (1985), which won both critical acclaim and controversy for militant attacks on government, media, and the medical profession. Kramer founded the AIDS Coalition to Unleash Power (ACT UP) in 1987 to continue his protest of the slow pace of response to AIDS and other gay issues. Kramer's satire, *Just Say No: A Play about a Farce* (1988), which assailed President Ronald Reagan and his family, New York mayor Ed Koch, and other government officials Kramer accused of failing to respond to AIDS, met with critical derision, but Susan Sontag said of it, "Larry Kramer is one of America's most valuable troublemakers. I hope he never lowers his voice."

Kramer published a collection of his writings on the AIDS crisis called *Reports from the Holocaust: The Story of an AIDS Activist* (1989; expanded in 1994) and his *The Normal Heart* sequel, *The Destiny of Me* (1992), similarly focused on Kramer the activist. It was nominated for a PULITZER PRIZE and continued the story of Kramer's dramatic alter ego, Ned Weeks, on a personal journey to understand his own past and the roots of his activism. The play won two **Obie Awards**. More recently, Kramer published *The Tragedy of Today's Gays* (2004) in response to his anger at the reelection of President George W. Bush, and he continues work on a massive study, *The American People*, as yet unpublished. Since *The Destiny of Me*, Kramer has not written again for the theatre, but he was presented with an Award in Literature from the American Academy of Arts and Letters.

KRAPP, HERBERT J. (1887–1973). This New York-born theatre architect and designer began his career as an apprentice with Herts* & Tallant, where he was involved in designing plans for several **Broadway** theatre buildings, including the Lyceum, Booth, New Amsterdam, and Longacre theatres before he left the firm in 1915. He had begun working for the Shubert Brothers* in 1912, becoming their primary architect and designing the Shubert Theatre. Krapp's influence on Broadway architecture is incalculable. He was involved in redesigning the Winter Garden Theatre and the Helen Hayes Theatre and designed such theatres known in 2009 as the Ambassador, the Brooks Atkinson, the Ethel Barrymore, the Biltmore, the Bernard B. Jacobs, the Broadhurst, the John Golden, the Imperial, the Majestic, the Eugene O'Neill, the Richard Rodgers, the Gerald Schoenfeld, and the Neil Simon. He also designed the Morosco Theatre, which was torn down in 1982, and the Ed Sullivan Theatre (previously known as Hammerstein's Theatre), the Forest Theatre in Philadelphia, Pennsylvania, and the Folly Theatre in Kansas City, Missouri, as well as the building housing **Sardi's Restaurant** on 44th Street in New York.

KRASNA, NORMAN (1909–1984). Born in Corona, Queens, New York, Krasna completed his education at New York University, Columbia University, and Brooklyn Law School before writing for various newspapers and doing publicity work for Warner Bros. Krasna's first **Broadway** play, *Louder, Please* (1931), won mostly approving response from CRITICS and audiences and it was followed by another moderate success, *Small Miracle* (1934). Krasna also began writing screenplays in this period and received an Academy Award nomination for Fritz Lang's *Fury* (1936) starring SPENCER TRACY. Krasna's other 1930s films include *The Richest Girl in the World* (1934) and *The Devil and Miss Jones* (1941), both of which garnered him Academy Award nominations for Best Screenplay. Despite other screen successes, Krasna frequently returned to the stage and in 1941 he directed his play *The Man with Blonde Hair*, which was a moderate success. Two years later he scripted and directed the film *Princess O'Rourke* (1943), for which he won an Academy Award for Best Original Screenplay. He continued to write numerous plays and screenplays after World WAR II, achieving his greatest stage successes with *Dear Ruth* (1944), a wartime comedy about a teenager who writes letters to a lonely soldier using her older sister's name and photo, and *John Loves Mary* (1947), another lighthearted wartime comedy about a soldier marrying his best friend's English girlfriend in order to bring her to the United States, with the resultant romantic complications. Both plays were also made into popular films scripted by Krasna. His subsequent plays include *Kind Sir* (1953), *Sunday in New York* (1961), *Love in E Flat* (1967), and *We Interrupt This Program* (1975).

KRASS, MICHAEL (1955–). Connecticut native Krass attended William and Mary College and began his **Broadway** career as a costume designer with a 1996 **Roundabout Theatre** revival of *The Rehearsal*, which brought him a **Drama Desk Award** nomination, as did his 1996 **Off-Broadway** designs for a revival of *Entertaining Mr. Sloane*. Krass received a 2006 **Tony Award** nomination for his costumes for a **Broadway** revival of *The Constant Wife*, and his other Broadway designs include a revival of *A View from the Bridge* in 1997, *Getting and Spending* (1998), revivals of *You're a Good Man, Charlie Brown* in 1999, *The Lion in Winter* in 1999, and *Hedda Gabler* in 2001, *An Almost Holy Picture* (2002), revivals of *The Man Who Had All the Luck* in 2002 and *After the Fall* in 2004, *Match* (2004), *Reckless* (2004), revivals of *12 Angry Men* and *'night, Mother* in 2004, *After the Night and the Music* (2005), and *After Miss Julie* (2009). Krass also designed for the **Williamstown Theatre Festival** over a 10-year period and has worked closely with particular directors, including **Michael Mayer**, **Mark Brokaw**, **Scott Ellis**, and Nicholas Martin.

KROLL, JACK (1926–2000). A noted drama critic, Kroll was born in New York as John Kroll, son of a radio personality and an Earl Carroll* showgirl. He graduated from City College of New York and served in the United States Army during the Korean War. He worked as a copy editor for Benton & Bowles Advertising and as an art CRITIC for *Art News*, which led to his move to *Newsweek* magazine in 1963, first as art critic and editor before he moved into reviewing drama. He championed certain playwrights, most notably **Sam Shepard**, and applauded experimentation. Kroll was instrumental in convincing *Newsweek* to include bylines on arts reviews, which had not been their policy. He won a National Magazine Award in 1973 for an issue of *Newsweek* devoted to "Arts in America," which he edited, and he won the George Jean Nathan Award for Dramatic Criticism in 1980. Near the end of his life, Kroll raised hackles with his insistence that video games were not art. His style was simple and direct. On the passing of dancing legend Fred Astaire, Kroll memorably wrote, "Wrap up the 20th century; Fred Astaire is gone."

KRON, LISA (1961–). Born in Ann Arbor, Michigan, Kron attended Kalamazoo College before becoming a founding member of the **Five Lesbian Brothers** in 1989. As a solo performer/writer, Kron established herself after 1984 and won CRITICAL approval with such works as *101 Humiliating Stories* (1993) and *2.5 Minute Ride* (1996), semi-autobiographical monologues marked by witty humor, as is her play, *Well* (2004), which premiered at the **New York Shakespeare Festival/Public Theatre** prior to a 2006 **Broadway** run, which brought Kron a **Tony Award** nomination. Her dramatic philosophy may be best summed up in her explanation of *2.5 Minute Ride*, which merges a trip she took with her German-born father to Auschwitz, where his parents were exterminated, and the annual family trip to a theme park: "Humor and horror are juxtaposed and you might not know for a second whether you are at Auschwitz or an amusement park. The show does not tell you when to laugh and when to become solemn. The response is up to you."

KRONENBERGER, LOUIS (1904–1980). A respected drama CRITIC, Kronenberger was born in Cincinnati, Ohio, and studied at the University of Cincinnati. He moved to New York in 1924 and worked as an editor at Boni and Liveright, Alfred A. Knopf, and *Fortune* magazine before becoming drama critic for *Time* magazine in 1938, continuing in the post until 1961, and for *PM* magazine from 1940 to 1948. Noted for his stylish writing, Kronenberger also adapted Jean Anouilh's *Mademoiselle Colombe* (1954), which was produced on **Broadway**. He edited the Best Play series from 1952 to 1961, and he taught at Brandeis University from 1951 to 1970. He wrote or edited numerous books, including his own memoir, *No Whippings, No Gold Watches*

(1970), as well as *The Thread of Laughter* (1952) and edited collections of the plays of Richard Brinsley Sheridan and GEORGE BERNARD SHAW and a *Cavalcade of Comedy* (1953) and a 1976 study of Oscar Wilde.

KRUTCH, JOSEPH WOOD (1893–1970).† A native of Knoxville, Tennessee, Krutch was educated at the University of Tennessee and completed a Ph.D. at Columbia University. He served in the United States Army during World WAR I and spent a year traveling in Europe before taking a position teaching at Brooklyn Polytechnic. In 1924, he became drama CRITIC for *The Nation*, remaining in that position until 1952, and he taught at Columbia University from 1937 to 1953, when he moved to Arizona for his health, ultimately becoming a respected naturalist and conservationist. He called for an American drama of greater profundity and style, but felt that during his time only EUGENE O'NEILL achieved such heights. Krutch wrote several books, including *Comedy and Conscience after the Restoration* (1924) and *The American Drama Since 1918* (1939, revised 1957).

KUCHWARA, MICHAEL (1947–2010). Born in Scranton, Pennsylvania, the son of an airline pilot, and he was attracted to the theatre as a child. He was educated at Syracuse University and the University of Missouri, where he completed a master's degree in journalism, Kuchwara began working for the Associated Press around 1970. He rose to the position of theatre CRITIC in 1984 and endeared himself to the **Broadway** and **Off-Broadway** theatre **community** for the fairness and insightfulness of his reviews, although his inclinations were toward MUSICALS and lighter fare. He served a stint as president of the **New York Drama Critics Circle**.

KULICK, BRIAN (1963–). A major force among early twenty-first-century New York City directors, Kulick became artistic director of the **Classic Stage Company (CSC)** in 2003 after serving as artist-in-residence at the **Mark Taper Forum** and as associate artistic director at **Trinity Repertory Theatre** from 1994 to 1996 and as artistic associate at the **New York Shakespeare Festival/Public Theatre (NYSF/PT)** from 1996 to 2003, for whom he directed critically lauded productions of *Twelfth Night*, *The Winter's Tale*, and *Timon of Athens*. He received a **Drama Desk Award** nomination for his staging of *The Mysteries* (2004) at CSC and has also staged *Death and the Ploughman* (2004), *The False Servant* (2005), and in collaboration with actor Michael Cumpsty, a modern-dress *Hamlet* in 2005, *Richard II* in 2006, and *Richard III* in 2008, *The Tempest* in 2008, and *Agamemnon* and *Elektra* codirected with Gisela Cardenas in 2009. Kulick directed the 1995 NYSF/PT production of **Tony Kushner**'s adaptation of *A Dybbuk* and several new works by **Charles L. Mee** and **Nilo Cruz**. He teaches at Columbia University and has directed productions in numerous **regional theatres**. Of his achievement at CSC, a *Village Voice* critic wrote that he "has brought a fresh feeling and energy to CSC . . . banishing any doubts about resurrecting adventurous classical theatre in New York."

KURTZ, SWOOSIE (1944–). A native of Omaha, Nebraska, Kurtz attended the University of Southern California and the London Academy of Music and Dramatic Art and made her television debut introducing her father, a highly decorated World WAR II pilot, on the *To Tell the Truth* television show. Kurtz made her stage debut at the **Cincinnati Playhouse** in the Park and **Off-Broadway** in *The Effect of Gamma Rays on Man-in-the-Moon Marigolds* (1970) prior to her **Broadway** debut in a 1975 revival of *Ah, Wilderness!* Kurtz won **Tony Awards** for *Fifth of July* (1980) and *The House of Blue Leaves* (1986), and was nominated for a 1978 revival of *Tartuffe*, *Frozen* (2004), and a 2007 revival of *Heartbreak House*. She also won **Drama Desk Awards** for *A History of the American Film* (1978) and *Fifth of July*, and garnered Drama Desk Award nominations for *Uncommon Women and Others* (1977), *The House of Blue Leaves*, and *The Mineola Twins* (1999). Kurtz's other Broadway credits include playing **Lillian Hellman** in *Imaginary Friends* (2002). Off-Broadway, Kurtz's credits include *Lips Together, Teeth Apart* (1991) and *The Guys* (2002). On screen, Kurtz has appeared in *Slap Shot* (1977), *Oliver's Story* (1978), *The World According to Garp* (1982), *Dangerous Liaisons* (1988), *Reality Bites* (1994), *Citizen Ruth* (1996), *Cruel Intentions* (1999), and *Bubble Boy* (2001), and she won an Emmy Award in 1990 for *Carol & Company*, as well as Emmy nominations for the television series *Love, Sidney* in 1982 and 1983, *The Image* (1990), *Sisters* in 1993 and 1994, *And the Band Played On* (1993), *ER* in 1998, and *Huff* in 2005 and 2006. Kurtz also received a Golden Globe nomination for the TV movie *Baja Oklahoma* (1988).

KUSHNER, TONY (1956–). Born in New York City, Kushner spent his childhood in Lake Charles, Louisiana, the son of classically trained musicians who named him after Tony Bennett. During his childhood, Kushner's mother appeared in semi-professional theatre productions, leaving an indelible impression on her precocious literature, music, and history-loving son. Kushner moved to New York City to study at Columbia University and the Tisch School of the Arts at New York University, where he trained as a stage director under the mentorship of **Bertolt Brecht** specialist Carl Weber and where he confronted his **homosexuality**. During this period, he also began to write plays. He adapted Goethe's romantic tragedy *Stella*, wrote several

children's plays, and completed other original plays, including *Hydrio-taphia, or The Death of Dr. Browne* (1987), and a free adaptation of Pierre Corneille's *L'illusion comique*, retitled *The Illusion* (1988).

Kushner's first important play, *A Bright Room Called Day* (1987), viewed the rise of the Nazis as seen through the eyes of a group of artists and film-makers in Berlin during the years 1932–1933. CRITICAL response to the first New York production of the play **Off-Broadway** in 1991 was largely nega-tive, with many reviewers finding the Hitler-Reagan comparison extreme. Critics did a complete about face the following year with Kushner's *Angels in America. A Gay Fantasia on National Themes.* Comprised of two long plays, *Angels* confronted the **AIDS** crisis, the lives and losses of gay men, and a range of issues regarding politics and history, spirituality and **religion**, popular culture, and other major issues in American life. *Part One: Millen-nium Approaches* opened on **Broadway**. *Millennium Approaches* was the most acclaimed American play of the 1990s, winning Kushner the PULITZER PRIZE for Drama, as well as a **Tony Award** for Best Play, an Olivier Award for Best Play (during its run at the Royal National Theatre of Great Britain), and virtually every critical award. *Perestroika*, the second Angels play, and like *Millennium Approaches*, nearly four hours, also won a Tony as Best Play. In 2003, both parts of *Angels* were filmed for a six-hour film for HBO directed by **Mike Nichols** and with a stellar cast led by **Al Pacino**, **Meryl Streep**, and Emma Thompson, winning multiple Emmy and Golden Globe Awards.

Kushner's next play, *Slavs! Thinking about the Longstanding Problems of Virtue and Happiness* (1994), is constructed out of characters and two scenes originally intended for *Perestroika*. In late 2001, Kushner's *Home-body/Kabul*, a drama about an English family caught up in the tragedies of Afghanistan under the Taliban, seemed prescient when it was already in rehearsals at the **New York Theatre Workshop** when the attacks of 11 Sep-tember 2001 occurred. *Homebody/Kabul* won the **Obie Award** for Best Off-Broadway Play and several critics' prizes, but Kushner continued to revise it in preparation for a production at Chicago's **Steppenwolf Theatre** in the summer of 2003, under **Frank Galati**'s direction.

In 2003, Kushner adapted libretti for two chamber operas, *Brundibar* and *The Comedy on the Bridge*, both designed by Kushner's close friend Maurice Sendak and produced by the Chicago Opera Theatre in the spring of 2003. He also published a one-act play, *Only We Who Guard the Mystery Shall Be Unhappy* (2004) in *The Nation* and presented it as a reading in a number of venues. Kushner wrote the libretto for an original opera, *Caroline, or Change*, which, with music by Jeanine Tesori, opened to good reviews at the **New York Shakespeare Festival/Public Theatre** (**NYSF/PT**) under the direction of **George C. Wolfe** in late 2003. The production, with slight changes, moved to Broadway in early 2004 where it received six Tony Award nominations. Kushner adapted Brecht's *Mother Courage and Her Children* in 2005 for a production by the NYSF/PT, starring Meryl Streep and **Kevin Kline**. Kushner's *The Intelligent Homosexual's Guide to Capitalism and Socialism with a Key to the Scriptures* (2009) premiered at the **Guthrie Theatre** in Minneapolis, Minnesota, during a festival of Kushner's work which included a production of *Caroline, or Change* and a bill of Kushner one-acts. Writing for the screen, Kushner received an Academy Award nomination for *Munich* (2005).

L

LA JOLLA PLAYHOUSE. Film actors Gregory Peck, **Dorothy McGuire**, and Mel Ferrer founded this theatre in 1947 with an emphasis on actor involvement, but in its current state, La Jolla found its footing as a not-for-profit professional theatre under the leadership of **Des McAnuff**, who served as artistic director from 1983 to 1994, followed by **Michael Greif** (1995–1999) and Christopher Ashley, who in 2009 continues to lead the theatre. Many La Jolla productions have transferred to **Broadway**, reaping over 20 **Tony Awards**, including the 1993 Tony for outstanding **regional theatre**. Among the Broadway transfers are *Big River* (1985), *A Walk in the Woods* (1988), *The Who's Tommy* (1993), *How to Succeed in Business without Really Trying* (1995), *Thoroughly Modern Millie* (2002), and *Jersey Boys* (2006). The Playhouse is housed on the campus of the University of California, San Diego.

LA MAMA EXPERIMENTAL THEATRE CLUB. Founded by **Ellen Stewart** at the dawn of the **Off-Off Broadway** theatre movement in 1961, La MaMa has presented numerous avant-garde plays as a result of its mission to develop new and original performance work with a commitment to diversity and international work. La MaMa productions have won more than 30 **Obie Awards**, among others. La MaMa, under Stewart's leadership, was also significant in nurturing full-time resident companies, including **Mabou Mines**, the **Pan Asian Repertory**, and numerous others, as well as such artists as **Sam Shepard**, **Harvey Fierstein**, **Lanford Wilson**, **Julie Bovasso**, **Adrienne Kennedy**, **Tom O'Horgan**, **Rochelle Owens**, **Megan Terry**, Elizabeth Swados, **Andrei Serban**, **Ping Chong**, **Tisa Chang**, **Hanay Gelogamah**, **Tom Eyen**, Robert Babb, Lee Shapiro, and others. La MaMa has also offered a venue to international artists, including Peter Brook, Jerzy Grotowski, Tadeusz Kantor, Eugenio Barba, and others. *See also* ALTERNATIVE THEATRE.

LA TURISTA. **Sam Shepard**'s two-act drama (his first move away from the one-act form and only his second play to be published) opened at the **American Place Theatre** on 4 March 1967 for 29 performances with a cast including **Sam Waterston**, Joyce Aaron, and Michael Lombard under Jacques Levy's direction. The play's title, inspired by the common illness that befalls travelers, begins in Mexico, where a couple, Kent and Salem, suffer from dysentery, which some CRITICS viewed as an allegorical representation of America's involvement in the Vietnam WAR. The play is most notable in introducing prototypes of the characters, themes, and style explored more fully in Shepard's later work.

LABUTE, NEIL (1963–). Raised in Spokane, Washington, LaBute was born in Wayne, Michigan, and studied theatre at Brigham Young University where, while a student, he joined The Church of Jesus Christ of Latter-day Saints. His theatre productions at Brigham Young were often controversial and sometimes closed by university officials. LaBute later studied at the University of Kansas, New York University, and the Royal Academy of London before teaching at Indiana University-Purdue University in Fort Wayne, Indiana. In 1993, Brigham Young University provided the venue for LaBute's first important play, *In the Company of Men*, which he subsequently adapted into a film, winning several movie CRITICS awards and nominations. LaBute's subsequent plays, most of which have been produced **Off-Broadway**, include *Bash* (1999), *The Shape of Things* (2001), *The Distance from Here* (2002), and *The Mercy Seat* (2002), one of the first plays set in the aftermath of 11 September 2001 (9/11). Other LaBute works, some of which premiered at the **Manhattan Theatre Club**, include *Autobahn* (2003), *Fat Pig* (2004), *This Is How It Goes* (2005), *Some Girls* (2005), *Wrecks* (2005), *In a Dark Dark House* (2007), *reasons to be pretty* (2008), *Helter Skelter/Land of the Dead* (2008), and *Some White Chick* (2009), among others. His films include adaptation of *Bash* (2001) and *The Shape of Things* (2003), as well as *Your Friends & Neighbors* (1998), *Tumble* (2000), *Nurse Betty* (2000), *Possession* (2002), *The Wicker Man* (2006), and *Lakeview Terrace* (2008). LaBute's plays and films have won admirers, but many critics have criticized the misanthropic viewpoints reflected in his work.

LACY, SUZANNE (1945–). A noted figure in public art, Lacy has established herself in Oakland, California, where she was born, but works with arts organizations around the United States as a **performance artist**, writer, teacher, and sometime public servant. She emerged in the 1970s, combining political activism with performance art in *Three Weeks in May*, an event staged on the steps of the Los Angeles City Hall addressing rape and other forms of violence against **women**. Her emphasis is often on the use of public spaces for performance art works, a viewpoint emphasized when she edited an anthology titled *Mapping the Terrain: New Genre Public Art* (1994). Her most noted work, *The Crystal Quilt* (1987), which featured over 400 older women talking about their life experiences, was filmed live in performance in Minneapolis by PBS-TV. Lacy was Dean of Fine Arts at California College of the Arts (1987–1997) and was a founding faculty member at California State University, Monterey Bay, in 1997. Since 2002, she has been at Otis College of Art and Design, where she established a Master of Fine Arts curriculum in Public Practice in 2007. *See also* FEMINIST THEATRE; SEXUALITY.

LADIES OF THE CORRIDOR, THE. Directed by **Harold Clurman** with designs by **Ralph Alswang**, this DOROTHY PARKER and **Arnaud D'Usseau** play opened on 21 October 1953 at the Longacre Theatre for 45 performances with a cast including Edna Best, Vera Allen, Margaret Barker, **Betty Field**, JUNE WALKER, **Walter Matthau**, and Shepperd Strudwick. The play is set in the fictional Hotel Marlowe in New York and spans a year in the lives of the widows and divorcées residing there. Although the original **Broadway** production was short-lived, a 2005 **Off-Broadway** production by the Peccadillo Theatre Company won critical approval.

LAHR, BERT (1895–1967). This legendary rubber-faced comedian born Irving Lahrheim in New York is most remembered as the Cowardly Lion in the classic film *The Wizard of Oz* (1939), but he appeared in vaudeville,* BURLESQUE, and MUSICALS, including *Delmar's Revels* (1927), *Hold Everything!* (1928), *Flying High* (1930), *Hot-Cha!* (1932), *George White's Music Hall Varieties* (1932), *Life Begins at 8:40* (1934), *George White's Scandals* (1935), *The Show Is On* (1936), *Du Barry Was a Lady* (1939), and *Seven Lively Arts* (1944). He branched out and won critical praise as the down-and-out burlesque comic in a revival of *Burlesque** in 1946, before appearing in the national tour of the revue* *Make Mine Manhattan* (1948) and starring on **Broadway** in *Two on the Aisle* (1951), another revue.

Stepping away from the musical stage once again, Lahr won critical acclaim as Estragon in the American premiere of Samuel Beckett's tragicomic *Waiting for Godot* in 1956. He subsequently appeared in several notable plays and musicals, including a Broadway revival of *Hotel Paradiso* in 1957 and toured in *Romanoff and Juliet* in 1959 and as Bottom in *A Midsummer Night's Dream* in 1960. He won acclaim playing a variety of roles in *The Beauty Part* (1962) and made his last Broadway appearance in the short-lived musical, *Foxy* (1964), although he appeared on television and in movies, including a small role as an aging burlesque comic in his last film, *The Night They Raided Minsky's* (1968). He was the father of critic **John Lahr**.

LAHR, JOHN (1941–). Son of beloved stage and film comedian/actor **Bert Lahr**, this much-admired CRITIC for the *New Yorker* (as senior drama critic since 1992) and author of several books on theatre and film, was born in Los Angeles, California. He studied at Yale University and Worcester College, Oxford, prior to beginning his career as a writer. In 1969, he wrote a highly praised biography of his father, *Notes on a Cowardly Lion*, and another on the British playwright Joe Orton, *Prick Up Your Ears* (1978). He has also written books about Frank Sinatra, Barry Humphries (Dame Edna Everage), and, as of 2010, was working on a major biography of **Tennessee Williams**. Lahr has also published six collections of his dramatic essays, as well as collections of his *New Yorker* profiles of major cultural figures. Lahr has been married to British actress/writer Connie Booth since 2000.

LAHTI, CHRISTINE (1950–). Born in Birmingham, Michigan, Lahti studied at Florida State University and the University of Michigan before touring Europe as part of a MIME troupe. In New York, she studied with **Uta Hagen** and William Esper, and appeared in some films, including *...And Justice for All* (1979) the same year she appeared as a replacement playing Susan in the **Broadway** production of *Loose Ends* (1979). She won a **Theatre World Award** that year for her appearance **Off-Broadway** in *The Woods* (1979). Her Broadway appearances include *Division Street* (1980), *Scenes and Revelations* (1981), a revival of *Present Laughter* in 1982, and she stepped into the title role in *The Heidi Chronicles* on Broadway in 1989. In 1993, she received a **Drama Desk Award** nomination for her performance in *Three Hotels* (1993). In late 2009, she played the role of Veronica in the Broadway production of *God of Carnage* (2009). Lahti is married to director/writer Thomas Schlamme. Lahti was nominated for a Supporting Actress Academy Award and won a New York Film Critics Circle Award for *Swing Shift* (1984) and shared an Academy Award with Jana Sue Memel for directing the short film *Lieberman in Love* (1995). She also won a 1998 Emmy Award (and three other nominations) for her performance on the television series *Chicago Hope*. Lahti also won a Golden Globe Award for *Chicago Hope* in 1997 and for the television film *No Place Like Home* (1989).

LAMOS, MARK (1946–). A native of Chicago, Illinois, Lamos studied the violin and ballet as a child and pursued his education in music at Northwestern University prior to becoming an actor at the **Guthrie Theatre**. He appeared in a few short-lived **Broadway** productions, including *The Love Suicide at Schofield Barracks* (1972), *The Creation of the World and Other Business* (1972), *Cyrano* (1973), and a revival of *Man and Superman* in

1978, before switching to directing as artistic director of the **Hartford Stage** in 1980, leading that theatre to a 1989 **Tony Award** as outstanding **regional theatre**. He was subsequently nominated for a Tony for his direction of *Our Country's Good* in 1991. For Broadway, he also directed a revival of *The Deep Blue Sea* in 1998, *The Gershwins' Fascinating Rhythm* (1999), revivals of *The Rivals* in 2004, *Seascape* in 2005, and *Cymbeline* in 2007, and **A. R. Gurney**'s *The Grand Manner* (2010). Lamos also acted in the film *Longtime Companion* (1990).

LANDAU, TINA (1962–). New York-born Landau was raised in Beverly Hills, California, and educated at Yale University and the **American Repertory Theatre** Institute for Advanced Theater Training at Harvard University. She won some early success writing the book for and directing the MUSICAL *Floyd Collins* (1996), garnering **Drama Desk Award** nominations for writing and directing. She joined the **Steppenwolf Theatre** in Chicago, Illinois, in 1997, where she directed acclaimed revivals of *The Time of Your Life* in 2002, *The Cherry Orchard* in 2004, and *The Diary of Anne Frank* in 2006, as well as *Time to Burn* (1996), *Berlin Circle* (1998), *The Ballad of Little Jo* (2000), and *Theatrical Essays* (2003). Landau directed the **Broadway** revival of *Bells Are Ringing* in 2001 and her Steppenwolf production of **Tracy Letts**'s *Superior Donuts* (2007) moved to Broadway in 2009. She has also directed for the **Vineyard Theatre**, the **New York Shakespeare Festival/ Public Theatre**, and **Playwrights Horizons**. Landau also teaches at Yale University and the Tisch School of the Arts.

LANDESMAN, HEIDI ETTINGER (1951–). Born Heidi Prentice Ettinger in San Francisco, California, she attended Occidental College and the Yale School of Drama. She was married to producer **Rocco Landesman** when she debuted as a scene and costume designer with *'night, Mother* (1983). Ettinger won **Tony Awards**, **Drama Desk Awards**, and **Outer Critics Circle Awards** for the MUSICALS *Big River* (1985) and *The Secret Garden* (1991) for her scenic designs. She designed the settings and coproduced **Ken Ludwig**'s *Moon Over Buffalo* (1995) and her other **Broadway** credits include *Into the Woods* (1987), *The Red Shoes* (1993), *Smokey Joe's Café* (1995), *Triumph of Love* (1997), a revival of *The Sound of Music* in 1998, *The Adventures of Tom Sawyer* (2001) for which she was nominated for a Tony and a Drama Desk Award, *Dracula,* the Musical* (2004), and *Good Vibrations* (2005). **Off-Broadway**, she was Drama Desk-nominated for *One Shoe Off* (1993).

LANDESMAN, ROCCO (1947–). Born in St. Louis, Missouri, Landesman studied at Colby College and the University of Wisconsin before completing a doctorate in dramatic literature at the Yale School of Drama, where he taught for four years after completing his degree. In 1987, after a decade operating a private investment fund, he became president of **Jujamcyn Productions** (purchasing the company in 2005). He was a major **Broadway** producer before and after assuming control of Jujamcyn, sometimes coproducing with his then-wife, scene designer **Heidi Ettinger Landesman**. Among Landesman's most noted productions are *Big River* (1985), *The Grapes of Wrath* (1990), *The Piano Lesson* (1990), *The Secret Garden* (1991), *Jelly's Last Jam* (1992), *Angels in America* (1993), *Love! Valour! Compassion!* (1995), *Titanic* (1997), *The Full Monty* (2000), *The Producers* (2001), *Take Me Out* (2003), *Caroline, or Change* (2004), *Doubt* (2005), *Grey Gardens* (2006), *Spring Awakening* (2006), and *33 Variations* (2009), as well as numerous revivals of MUSICALS and plays. In 2009, Landesman became chairman of the **National Endowment for the Arts**, appointed by President Barack Obama.

LANDSCAPE OF THE BODY. **John Guare**'s two-act play opened on 12 October 1977 at the **New York Public Theatre** following an earlier production that year at the Academy Festival Theatre in Illinois. Directed by John Pasquin, the cast included **Shirley Knight** and **F. Murray Abraham**. An episodic work inspired by absurdist theatre, the play moves indiscriminately in time as it focuses on Betty Yearn, the mother of a murdered son. *Landscape of the Body* was revived at New York's **Second Stage** in 1984 under the direction of **Gary Sinise** and a 2006 **Signature Theatre** revival was staged by **Michael Greif**.

LANE, NATHAN (1956–). Born Joseph Lane in Jersey City, New Jersey, this versatile actor has appeared in drama, comedy, and MUSICALS on stage and screen, but with his most notable success on **Broadway**. When he was unable to afford to stay at college, he moved to New York and began to work as a stand-up comic with a partner, Patrick Stack, prior to acting in **Off-Broadway** and **Off-Off Broadway** productions at **Second Stage**, **Roundabout Theatre**, and the **Manhattan Theatre Club (MTC)** before his first Broadway appearance in a 1982 revival of *Present Laughter* starring **George C. Scott**, for which he received a **Drama Desk Award** nomination. Lane also appeared in *Merlin* (1983), *The Wind in the Willows* (1985), *Some Americans Abroad* (1990), and the national tour of *Broadway Bound*.

A long association with playwright **Terrence McNally** brought Lane a Drama Desk Award in McNally's *The Lisbon Traviata* (1990), and he appeared in McNally's *Lips Together, Teeth Apart* (1991) at the MTC. He was back on Broadway in a revival of *On Borrowed Time* in 1991, again with Scott, and Lane received a **Tony Award** nomination and Drama Desk and

Outer Critics Circle Awards as Nathan Detroit in a revival of *Guys and Dolls* in 1992. In 1993, Lane appeared in **Neil Simon**'s *Laughter on the 23rd Floor* and he won another Drama Desk Award in 1995 for McNally's *Love! Valour! Compassion!* A 1996 revival of *A Funny Thing Happened on the Way to the Forum* brought him Tony and Drama Desk Awards, and he starred in another revival, *The Man Who Came to Dinner*, in 2000.

Lane costarred with **Matthew Broderick** in Mel Brooks's musical, *The Producers* (2001), winning Tony and Drama Desk Awards for his performance as unscrupulous Broadway producer Max Bialystock in one of the biggest Broadway hits in years, reprising the role in a 2005 film version. Lane also appeared on Broadway in **Stephen Sondheim**'s *The Frogs* (2004), revivals of *The Odd Couple* in 2005 and *Butley* in 2006, *November* (2008), a revival of *Waiting for Godot* in 2009, and the musical *The Addams Family* (2010). Lane has been nominated for Golden Globe Awards twice, for the films *The Birdcage* (1996) and *The Producers* (2005) and was nominated for Emmy Awards guest starring on the series *Frasier* in 1995 and *Mad About You* in 1998, and also appeared in such films as *The Boys Next Door* (1996), *Love's Labour's Lost* (2000), and *Swing Vote* (2008).

LANGELLA, FRANK (1938–). Born in Bayonne, New Jersey, as Frank A. Langella, Jr., he studied at Syracuse University. He has acted in **regional theatre**, including a revival of *Sherlock Holmes** in 1981 filmed for HBO-TV. He debuted **Off-Broadway** in *The Immoralist* (1963) and made his first **Broadway** appearance in a revival of *Yerma* in 1966. He scored a major success in **William Gibson**'s *A Cry of Players* (1968), playing William Shakespeare opposite **Anne Bancroft** as Anne Hathaway. Langella's Off-Broadway and regional appearances (more than 50) include playing Cyrano de Bergerac in 1971 at the **Wiliamstown Theatre Festival**, where he also appeared in revivals of *The Seagull* in 1974 and *Ring Round the Moon* in 1975, among numerous others. He also appeared in films, scoring successes in *The Twelve Chairs* (1970) and *Diary of a Mad Housewife* (1970), which brought him a Golden Globe nomination. Langella won a **Tony Award** and a **Drama Desk Award** in **Edward Albee**'s *Seascape* (1975), but gave a highly acclaimed and Tony-nominated performance in the title role in a revival of *Dracula** in 1977, a production memorably designed by artist Edward Gorey. Langella subsequently reprised the role in a 1979 film version, playing opposite **Laurence Olivier**.

Langella's subsequent Broadway roles include *Passione* (1980), taking over the role of Salieri in *Amadeus* in 1982, a revival of *Design for Living* (1984), *Hurlyburly* (1984), *Sherlock's Last Case* (1987), and he won a Drama Desk Award for a revival of August Strindberg's *The Father* in

1996. Langella was Drama Desk-nominated for a revival of **Noël Coward**'s *Present Laughter* in 1996 and won a Tony and a Drama Desk Award for *Fortune's Fool* (2002), was nominated for both awards for *Match* (2004), and won both again for *Frost/Nixon* (2007), playing the disgraced 37th president of the United States. Langella also appeared in the title role of a 2008 revival of *A Man for All Seasons*. In films, Langella was nominated for an Academy Award and a Golden Globe Award reprising the role of Richard Nixon in *Frost/Nixon* (2008) and also appeared in *Those Lips, Those Eyes* (1980), *Dave* (1993), *Lolita* (1997), *Good Night, and Good Luck* (2005), and *Superman Returns* (2006). On television, he was nominated for an Emmy Award for *I, Leonardo: A Journey of the Mind* (1983).

LANGHAM, MICHAEL (1919–2011). Born in Bridgewater, England, he studied law at the University of London and served in the British Army beginning in 1939. He was a prisoner of WAR for five years during World War II, after which he worked in **repertory** in England and Canada, including a stint as artistic director of the Stratford Festival in Canada from 1956 to 1967 prior to serving in the same capacity at the **Guthrie Theatre** from 1971 to 1977. Langham became director of the Juilliard School from 1979 to 1982, returning to this post again from 1987 to 1992. On **Broadway**, Langham was nominated for a **Tony Award** for his direction of a revival of *Timon of Athens* for the **National Actors Theatre**, directed several revivals, including *Two Gentlemen of Verona* in 1958, *The Seagull* in 1992, *Saint Joan* in 1993, *The Government Inspector* in 1994, *The Flowering Peach* in 1994, *The Molière Comedies* in 1995, and *Waiting in the Wings* in 1999, as well as such plays as *The Broken Jug* (1958), *Andorra* (1963), and ***The Prime of Miss Jean Brodie*** (1968).

LANGNER, LAWRENCE (1890–1962).[†] A native of Wales, Langner worked in London theatre as a young man prior to moving to the United States in 1911. He was a founder of The Washington Square Players* in 1914 and worked with them until the troupe disbanded in 1917. Langner then became one of the founders of THE THEATRE GUILD in 1918, which he co-managed with THERESA HELBURN during its most important and productive period. He is credited with supervising as many as 200 Guild productions. Langner pushed for productions of European classics, and he admired the plays of EUGENE O'NEILL, prevailing upon the Guild to produce O'Neill's *Strange Interlude** (1928), which won the PULITZER PRIZE. In collaboration with his wife, Armina Marshall, Langner built the **Westport Country Playhouse** in 1931, establishing a theatre company there, and he also founded the **American Shakespeare Festival** at Stratford, Connecticut, in the 1950s. In

1961, he accepted a **Tony Award** on behalf of The Theatre Guild, acknowledging its importance to the development of the American theatre.

LANSBURY, ANGELA (1925–). As Angela Brigid Lansbury, she was born in London, England, the daughter of actress Moyna MacGill and businessman and politician Edgar Lansbury. After her father's death and as the Nazis began the blitz and Britain entered World WAR II, Lansbury and her mother emigrated to the United States, where still in her teens she found almost immediate success in Hollywood films, reaping Academy Award nominations for two of her first three films, *Gaslight* (1944) and *The Picture of Dorian Gray* (1945). Demonstrating an extraordinary versatility that would be evident throughout her long career, Lansbury continued to play a range of roles on screen, garnering another Oscar nomination for *The Manchurian Candidate* (1962). However, when Lansbury turned her attention to the **Broadway** stage in the late 1950s, beginning with a revival of *Hotel Paradiso* in 1957, costarring with **Bert Lahr**, and continuing with *A Taste of Honey* (1960), she found even greater success. When Lansbury switched from drama to MUSICALS, she scored a series of remarkable triumphs following an initial failure in **Stephen Sondheim**'s *Anyone Can Whistle* (1964). Jerry Herman's hit *Mame* (1966) brought Lansbury her first **Tony Award**, followed by wins for Herman's *Dear World* (1969), a revival of *Gypsy* (1974), and Sondheim's *Sweeney Todd* (1979). She was also nominated for a **Drama Desk Award** when she took over the lead in a revival of *The King and I* in 1977 and reaped another Tony nomination for **Terrence McNally**'s two-character play *Deuce* (2007).

Remarkably, in her 80s, Lansbury won Tony and Drama Desk Awards as the eccentric Madame Arcati in a revival of **Noël Coward**'s *Blithe Spirit* in 2009 and was also nominated for both playing Madame Armfeldt in a revival of Sondheim's *A Little Night Music* in late 2009, costarring with Catherine Zeta-Jones. Lansbury was nominated for numerous Emmy Awards for television appearances, many for her long-running series, *Murder, She Wrote* (1984–1996) for which she won four Golden Globe Awards. Lansbury also won Golden Globes for the films *The Picture of Dorian Gray* and *The Manchurian Candidate*, and she was presented with a Lifetime Achievement Award from the Screen Actors Guild in 1997.

LAPINE, JAMES (1949–). This notable director and librettist was born in Mansfield, Ohio, and studied at Franklin and Marshall College before working as a photographer, graphic designer, and in architecture. He moved into teaching scene design at Yale University and ultimately moved into writing and directing with *Photography of Gertrude Stein* (1977). He won the PULITZER PRIZE, a **Tony Award** nomination, and a **Drama Desk Award** for coauthoring with **Stephen Sondheim** the MUSICAL *Sunday in the Park with*

George (1984), which he also directed, winning a Drama Desk Award and a Tony nomination for that contribution. Lapine collaborated again with Sondheim on *Into the Woods* (1987), winning Tony and Drama Desk Awards for his libretto and repeated this feat, once again in collaboration with Sondheim, for *Passion* (1994). Lapine also won a Drama Desk Award for his direction of *The 25th Annual Putnam County Spelling Bee* (2005). Lapine wrote the plays *Table Settings* (1978), *Twelve Dreams* (1978), *Luck, Pluck, and Virtue* (1994), *The Moment When* (2000), and *Fran's Bed* (2005), and received several award nominations for his direction of a revival of **The Diary of Anne Frank** in 1997, *Dirty Blonde* (2000), and *Amour* (2003).

LARAMIE PROJECT, THE. Written by **Moisés Kaufman** and the members of his **Tectonic Theatre Project (TTP)**, this play culled from dozens of interviews and contemporary reports about the 1997 hate crime murder of **gay** University of Wyoming college student Matthew Shepard in Laramie, Wyoming, it opened at the Ricketson Theatre in a **Denver Theatre Center** production in February 2000 before moving to New York's Union Square Theatre in May 2000. It was subsequently performed in Laramie in November 2002. The Tectonic troupe, under Kaufman's leadership, had traveled to Laramie and interviewed a cross-section of the local citizenry to create the play as much as possible from the words of the Laramie citizens and from the responses of the TTP actors themselves. HBO released a film based on the play in 2002. The play won international acclaim and, in October 2009, *The Laramie Project: Ten Years Later*, a "sequel" also created by the Tectonic Company following a return visit to Laramie, was performed simultaneously by theatres across the United States on the anniversary of the Shepard murder.

LARKIN, PETER (1926–). Born in Boston, Massachusetts, and following education at Deerfield Academy and Yale University, Larkin moved to New York to work as a scene and lighting designer. He won **Tony Awards** for his scenic designs for **The Teahouse of the August Moon** (1953), *Ondine* (1954), **No Time for Sergeants** (1955), and **Inherit the Wind** (1955), and was nominated for Tonys for *Miss Isobel* (1957), *Compulsion* (1957), *Good as Gold* (1957), *Blue Denim* (1958), *Greenwillow* (1960), and *The Rink* (1984). Larkin's other important Broadway designs include **Dial "M" for Murder** (1952), *Peter Pan** (1954), *Goldilocks* (1958), *Wildcat* (1960), revivals of **The Crucible** and *The Seagull* in 1964, *Les Blancs* (1970), *Twigs* (1971), *Wise Child* (1972), *Dancin'* (1978), and *Doonesbury* (1983), among many others. In the 1980s, Larkin moved into production design for movies, including such films as *Tootsie* (1982), *3 Men and a Baby* (1987), *Everybody Wins* (1990), *Get Shorty* (1995), *The First Wives Club* (1996), *Miss Congeniality* (2000), and **Dinner with Friends** (2001).

LAST MILE, THE. A **naturalistic** prison drama, *The Last Mile* opened on 13 February 1930 at the Sam H. Harris Theatre, starring a young SPENCER TRACY in the dynamic leading role of John "Killer" Mears, a tough inmate on death row who leads his fellow prisoners in a riot to protest prison conditions. JOHN WEXLEY's play won critical acclaim and ran for 289 performances, with subsequent touring productions (including one starring Clark Gable) and film versions in 1932 and 1959. The sensation caused by *The Last Mile* led to a spate of prison-themed plays and films and, more importantly, to prison reform and heightening debate over the viability of the death penalty.

LAST NIGHT OF BALLYHOO, THE. Alfred Uhry's **Tony Award** and **Outer Critics Circle Award**-winning comedy-drama premiered at the Helen Hayes Theatre on 27 February 1997 for 556 performances. Set in 1939 on the brink of World WAR II, the play focuses on the Freitag family in Atlanta, Georgia, an assimilated Jewish family who are excited about the upcoming Ballyhoo, an annual cotillion at their exclusive country club, and the local premiere of the film *Gone with the Wind*. The family and their Jewish friends are forced to confront their own denial of prejudice within their city and their own Jewish American community. Directed by Ron Lagomarsino, with scene design by **John Lee Beatty** and costumes by **Jane Greenwood**, the cast featured **Dana Ivey**, Paul Rudd, **Jessica Hecht**, Celia Watson, Terry Beaver, Stephen Largay, and Arija Bareikis. *See also* ETHNIC THEATRE.

LAST OF THE RED HOT LOVERS. **Neil Simon**'s three-act comedy about a dissatisfied fish market owner contemplating an affair brought acclaim to James Coco in the title role when it opened on 28 December 1969 at the Eugene O'Neill Theatre for 706 performances. Directed by **Robert Moore**, with scene design by **Oliver Smith** and costume design by Donald Brooks, Coco was supported by **Linda Lavin**, Doris Roberts, and Marcia Rodd as the three **women** his character, Barney Cashman, attempts, unsuccessfully, to have an affair with, making use of his mother's apartment while she is away. Barney confronts his dissatisfactions with life with a hard-bitten cynic, a marijuana-smoking girl, and a middle-aged customer from his fish market. The play, Coco, Lavin, and Moore were all nominated for **Tony Awards**. A 1972 film version, directed by **Gene Saks**, starred Alan Arkin, Sally Kellerman, Paula Prentiss, and Renée Taylor.

LATE GEORGE APLEY, THE. John P. Marquand and GEORGE S. KAUFMAN collaborated on this three-act (plus epilogue) comedy based on Marquand's Pulitzer Prize-winning novel. It was produced by **Max Gordon** at the Lyceum Theatre, where it opened on 21 November 1944 for 385 performances. Set in Boston in 1912, the play focuses on a well-established Boston snob, George Apley, played by **Leo G. Carroll**, whose comfortable arid life is upset by his daughter's relationship with a Greenwich Village intellectual radical and his son's broken engagement with the daughter of a wealthy businessman. The daughter, Eleanor (Joan Chandler), marries her bohemian boyfriend, to George's consternation, but in the play's epilogue, set in 1924, George has died and his son has replaced him as a rigid snob. The cast also included Janet Beecher,* Percy Waram, Margaret Phillips, and Howard St. John. Ronald Colman starred in a 1947 film version directed by Joseph L. Mankiewicz.

LATINO THEATRE. *See* CHICANO THEATRE.

LAUGHTON, CHARLES (1899–1962). This much-admired actor of stage and screen was born in Scarborough, Yorkshire, England, and educated at Stonyhurst College. Following military service during World WAR I, he appeared in amateur theatre and attended the Royal Academy of Dramatic Art. He acted in several London productions, impressing CRITICS in both classical and contemporary roles before debuting on **Broadway** in the thriller *Payment Deferred* (1931), followed by *The Fatal Alibi* (1932). For 15 years, Laughton appeared in a range of Hollywood film classics, not returning to Broadway until a short-lived production of **Bertolt Brecht**'s *Galileo,* which Laughton had adapted himself. He also appeared in a revival of **Anton Chekhov**'s *The Cherry Orchard* in 1950, the same year he became an American citizen, and he scored a major success in *Don Juan in Hell* (1951), which he directed and was taken from GEORGE BERNARD SHAW's *Man and Superman.*

Laughton subsequently adapted and directed *John Brown's Body* (1953), directed ***The Caine Mutiny Court-Martial*** (1954), appeared in and directed Shaw's *Major Barbara* (1956), and played the title character in *King Lear* in 1959 at Stratford-upon-Avon. Although he was bisexual (or possibly **gay**) Laughton was married to actress Elsa Lanchester from 1929 until his death, and they frequently appeared together in films. Among his most notable screen appearances are his Academy Award-winning performance in *The Private Life of Henry VIII* (1933), followed by subsequent Oscar nominations for *Mutiny on the Bounty* (1935) and *Witness for the Prosecution* (1957), and noted appearances in *The Old Dark House* (1932), *The Sign of the Cross* (1932), ***The Barretts of Wimpole Street*** (1934), *Ruggles of Red Gap* (1935), *Les Misérables* (1935), *Rembrandt* (1936), *The Hunchback of Notre Dame* (1939), *The Canterville Ghost* (1944), *The Paradine Case* (1947), *Hobson's Choice* (1954), *Spartacus* (1960), and *Advise & Consent* (1962). *See also* INTERNATIONAL STARS AND COMPANIES IN THE UNITED STATES.

LAURENTS, ARTHUR (1918–). Playwright, librettist, and director Laurents was born in Brooklyn, New York, and educated at Cornell University. He was drafted into the United States Army during World WAR II and wrote training films and radio broadcasts. After the war, Laurents wrote his first major play, *Home of the Brave* (1945), an exposé of anti-Semitism in the military, which had a brief **Broadway** run. Laurents's next play, *The Bird Cage* (1950), failed, but he scored a success with *The Time of the Cuckoo* (1952), which ran a season with **Shirley Booth** as star. Laurents garnered **Tony Award** nominations for his books for the MUSICALS *West Side Story* (1957) and *Gypsy* (1959), and won a Tony for his libretto for *Hallelujah, Baby!* (1967). He won a **Drama Desk Award** and a Tony nomination for his direction of a 1974 revival of *Gypsy*. Laurents contributed librettos for *Anyone Can Whistle* (1964), which he also directed, *Do I Hear a Waltz?* (1965), based on his play *The Time of the Cuckoo*, *The Madwoman of Central Park* (1979), which he also directed, and *Nick & Nora*, which he also directed. Laurents won a Best Director Tony for staging *La Cage aux Folles* (1983) and was Tony-nominated directing the 2008 revival of *Gypsy*. His other plays include *The Enclave* (1973), *Jolson Sings Again* (1995), *The Radical Mystique* (1995), *My Good Name* (1996), *Claudia Lazlo* (2001), *Attacks on the Heart* (2003), and *2 Lives* (2003). At age 91, Laurents directed a 2009 revival of *West Side Story*. Laurents also received Academy Award and Golden Globe nominations for his screenplay for *The Turning Point* (1977), and wrote screenplays for *Rope* (1948), *Anastasia* (1956), *The Way We Were* (1973), and his own play, *Home of the Brave* in 1949.

LAVIN, LINDA (1937–). Born in Portland, Maine, Lavin graduated from the College of William and Mary and began an acting career with the Compass Players in the late 1950s. On **Broadway**, she debuted in bit roles in the MUSICAL *A Family Affair* (1962), won a 1965 **Theatre World Award** for the **Off-Broadway** production of *Wet Paint*, but scored a personal success singing "You've Got Possibilities" in the musical *"It's a Bird . . . It's a Plane . . . It's Superman* (1966). She also scored Off-Broadway in *The Mad Show* (1966) and fluctuated between Broadway and Off-Broadway for a series of plays and musicals, including *On a Clear Day You Can See Forever* (1967), *Little Murders* (1969), which brought her a **Drama Desk Award**, *Last of the Red Hot Lovers* (1969), for which she was nominated for a **Tony Award**, *Paul Sills' Story Theater* (1970), and *The Enemy Is Dead* (1973), among others.

From 1976 to 1985, Lavin starred in the title role of the situation comedy *Alice* on CBS-TV, appeared in several films, and did not return to the Broadway stage until 1986 in *Broadway Bound* (1986), winning a Tony and a

Drama Desk Award. She was Drama Desk-nominated for the Off-Broadway production of *Death Defying Acts* (1995) and reaped Tony and Drama Desk nominations for a revival of *The Diary of Anne Frank* in 1998 and *The Tale of the Allergist's Wife* (2000). Lavin's other Broadway appearances include taking over the lead from Tyne Daly in a revival of *Gypsy* in 1990, *The Sisters Rosensweig* (1993), *Hollywood Arms* (2002), and a 2010 revival of **Donald Margulies'** *Collected Stories*, which brought her a Tony nomination. Off-Broadway, Lavin won a Drama Desk Award for **Paul Rudnick**'s *The New Century* (2008). In 2004, Lavin began performing in cabaret in a show called *Songs to Remember When*. Lavin has been married three times, including to actors **Ron Liebman** and Kip Niven.

LAWRENCE, GERTRUDE (1898–1952). A native of London, England, the now-legendary actress and singer was born Gertrud Alexandra Dagman Klasen. As a child performer, Lawrence toured with her mother, debuting in the West End in *Babes in the Wood* (1910). In this period, she developed a lifelong friendship with actor-playwright-composer **Noël Coward**, frequently performing with him throughout her career. Lawrence made her first New York appearance in *Charlot's Revue* (1924) and followed this success with several notable performances in both MUSICALS and straight plays, including appearing with Coward in one of her most emblematic roles, Amanda Prynne, in Coward's comedy *Private Lives* (1931). She also appeared with Coward in his revue *Tonight at 8:30* (1936) and scored dramatic successes in **Samson Raphelson**'s *Skylark* (1939) and **Rachel Crothers**'s *Susan and God* (1943). She appeared in a 1948 revival of *Pygmalion* and a revival of *Tonight at 8:30* that same year, although this time without Coward. Lawrence's appearances in musicals include originating the roles of Liza Elliott in *Lady in the Dark* (1941) and Anna Leonowens in *The King and I* (1951), winning a **Tony Award** in the latter. Unfortunately, Lawrence fell ill with cancer during the run of *The King and I* and died shortly thereafter.

Lawrence made very few films, including about a half-dozen at the dawn of the sound era, but made notable appearances in two movies: *Rembrandt* (1936) and as Amanda Wingfield in the first film version of **Tennessee Williams**'s *The Glass Menagerie* (1950). Lawrence also appeared in a few early live television performances, including reprising her role in *Skylark* in 1951. Late in life, Lawrence was married to producer **Richard Stoddard Aldrich**, who wrote a laudatory biography of her, but to balance the scales, it has long been believed that Lawrence was the inspiration for the predatory, amoral Lorraine Sheldon in GEORGE S. KAUFMAN and **Moss Hart**'s comedy *The Man Who Came to Dinner* (1939). *See also* INTERNATIONAL STARS AND COMPANIES IN THE UNITED STATES.

LAWRENCE, JEROME (1915–2004) AND ROBERT E. LEE (1918–1994). This team of playwrights created several **Broadway** successes beginning in the 1950s. Lawrence was born Jerome Schwartz in Cleveland, Ohio, and worked as a journalist before partnering with Lee, who was born in Elyria, Ohio, to write the radio show *Favorite Story*. Ultimately collaborating on nearly 40 works, Lawrence and Lee had major successes with *Inherit the Wind* (1955), a drama based on the Scopes "Monkey Trial" of the 1920s, and which starred **Paul Muni** and **Ed Begley** (and was filmed in 1960 starring Spencer Tracy and **Fredric March**). They also adapted Patrick Dennis's *Auntie Mame* into a notable 1956 Broadway hit starring **Rosalind Russell** (who also appeared in the 1958 screen version) and serving as the source for the musical *Mame* (1966). Among their other works were the books for the musicals *Look Ma, I'm Dancin'* (1948) and *Shangri-La* (1956), *The Gang's All Here* (1959), *Only in America* (1959), *A Call on Kuprin* (1961), *Diamond Orchid* (1965), *The Incomparable Max* (1969), the book for the musical *Dear World* (1969), *The Night Thoreau Spent in Jail* (1970), and *First Monday in October* (1978). Lawrence and Lee founded the American Playwrights' Theatre in 1965 with the intention of aiding playwrights in circumventing the commercial nature of Broadway in developing new plays, and they established the Jerome Lawrence and Robert E. Lee Theatre Research Institute at Ohio State University, Lawrence's alma mater, in 1986.

LAWSON, JOHN HOWARD (1895–1977). A New York native, Lawson attended Williams College, where he began writing plays with a strong Marxist bent. His leftist politics led him to develop a dramatic approach he labeled "political vaudeville,"* a style first seen on **Broadway** in his short-lived *Roger Bloomer** (1923), but Lawson's next play, *Processional** (1925), was produced by The Theatre Guild and won critical kudos. His next three plays failed, but *Success Story* (1932), produced by **The Group Theatre**, won approval. His subsequent works, *The Pure in Heart* (1934), *Gentlewoman* (1934), and *Marching Song* (1937), eked out short runs, although a 1937 **Federal Theatre Project (FTP)** revival of *Processional* managed 81 performances. Lawson wrote a book, *Theory and Technique of Playwriting* (1936), but when sound films began he spent much of his time writing screenplays until he was blacklisted as one of the "Hollywood Ten" during the McCarthy era.

LE GALLIENNE, EVA (1899–1991).† A distinguished actress and director, Eva Le Gallienne was the daughter of noted writer Richard Le Gallienne. Born in London, she was trained for the stage at the Royal Academy of Dramatic Arts. After a few years in undistinguished roles, she scored a triumph in *Liliom* (1921). Le Gallienne's most significant achievement was the founding of the CIVIC REPERTORY THEATRE (CRT), a bold attempt to establish the **repertory** system on **Broadway** with the goal of bringing the classics of international drama to American audiences at bargain prices. Founded in 1926, the CRT ran for six seasons before financial strains exacerbated by the Great Depression ended the experiment, although Le Gallienne herself gave well-received performances (and direction) in a range of CRT productions. She continued acting in New York and on tour, most successfully as Lettie in Thomas Job's *Uncle Harry* (1942).

After World WAR II, in partnership with **Cheryl Crawford** and **Margaret Webster**, Le Gallienne attempted once again to establish a New York repertory company. Their **American Repertory Theatre** began operations in 1946, but like the CRT, it failed commercially. Her last major triumph came in 1975 as Fanny Cavendish, matriarch of an eccentric theatrical clan modeled on the BARRYMORES, in a lavish revival of *The Royal Family*.* Her final stage appearance was in a 1982 revival of her adaptation of *Alice in Wonderland*, which had first been done at the CRT. Le Gallienne appeared in occasional films, but her true métier was the stage. She might easily have rivaled KATHARINE CORNELL or HELEN HAYES had she chosen to pursue a more commercial career, but she preferred experimenting with the classics and serious modern drama, especially the plays of HENRIK IBSEN, **Anton Chekhov**, and GEORGE BERNARD SHAW.

LEACH, WILFORD (1929–1988). Born Carson Wilford Leach in Petersburg, Virginia, he made his first theatrical mark as artistic director of New York's **La MaMa Experimental Theatre Club**. He was nominated for **Drama Desk Awards** for his scene designs for revivals of *All's Well That Ends Well* in 1979 and *The Pirates of Penzance* in 1981, for which he won a **Tony Award** for Best Direction. He also won Tony and Drama Desk Awards for his direction of *The Mystery of Edwin Drood* (1985). He also directed *The Human Comedy* (1984) at the **New York Shakespeare Festival/Public Theatre (NYSF/PT)**, and it transferred to **Broadway**. Leach's eclectic approach to directing drew on multimedia influences, opera, **puppetry**, and vaudeville,* elements seen in his NYSF/PT production of *Mandragola* in 1977, *The Taming of the Shrew* in 1978, *Othello* in 1979, and *Mother Courage and Her Children* in 1980. Leach taught theatre at Sarah Lawrence beginning in 1958 and, collaborating with Brian DePalma and Cynthia Munroe, he wrote and directed the film *The Wedding Party* (1969).

LEAGUE OF AMERICAN THEATRES AND PRODUCERS. The League of New York Theatres was established in 1930, but changed its name in 1985. Among its functions as a trade organization, the League operates the annual ANTOINETTE PERRY **Tony Awards**. The League's director, **Harvey B. Sabinson**, was presented with a special Tony Award in 1995 for his long service and was replaced by Jed Bernstein and, more recently, by Charlotte St. Martin. In recent years, the League has been known as the Broadway League.

LEAGUE OF HISTORIC AMERICAN THEATRES (LHAT). Established by 42 charter theatre members in 1976, LHAT serves as a network of over 250 operating historic theatres in the United States and Canada, emphasizing the preservation, restoration, and use of iconic theatres. Since 2005, LHAT has worked toward increasing **community** engagement with historic theatres and developing means to sustain these spaces.

LEAGUE OF RESIDENT THEATRES (LORT). This administration body for major not-for-profit theatres in the United States has 76 member theatres and arranges contracts with the major theatrical **unions**, ACTORS' EQUITY ASSOCIATION, the **Society of Stage Directors & Choreographers**, and **United Scenic Artists**. LORT, which was founded in 1965 by **Peter Zeisler** of the **Guthrie Theatre**, is also a clearinghouse for information for member theatres with the goal of promoting the welfare of **regional theatres** in the United States.

LECOMPTE, ELIZABETH (1944–). Born Elizabeth Alice LeCompte in New Jersey, she studied at Skidmore College, and worked in a coffeehouse where she began performing in plays with **Spalding Gray**. They moved together to New York and worked with **The Performance Group** beginning in 1970, with LeCompte serving as designer. She eventually became involved with actor **Willem Dafoe** and she took over the company in 1979, renamed **The Wooster Group**, an experimental acting troupe considered at the forefront of the New York avant-garde of the period. Among the productions she cowrote and/or directed are a trilogy, *Three Places in Rhode Island*, including *Sakonnet Point* (1975), *Rumstick Road* (1977), and *Nayatt School* (1978), as well as *Route 1 & 9* (1981), *L.S.D. (. . . Just the High Points . . .)* (1984), *The Temptation of St. Anthony* (1987), *Brace Up!* (1991), and a radical reinterpretation of EUGENE O'NEILL's *The Emperor Jones** in 1997 in collaboration with Kate Valk (this production was revived in 2006), and featuring the controversial use of blackface* and cross-gender casting. Among many awards and grants, LeCompte received a 1995 MacArthur Fellowship, a 2007 Rockefeller Foundation Fellowship, and a grant from United States Artists. She is also the recipient of several **Obie Awards** and a **National Endowment of**

the **Arts** Distinguished Artists Fellowship for Lifetime Achievement, among other acknowledgments. *See also* ALTERNATIVE THEATRE.

LEE, CANADA (1907–1952). New York native Lionel Cornelius Canegata was born to West Indian parents and studied music, but changed his name when he became a professional boxer. An eye injury ended his work in the fight ring and after a stint as a nightclub orchestra leader and as a laborer, he was cast in a Central Park production of *Brother Moses* (1934). He became a member of the Negro Unit of the **Federal Theatre Project (FTP),** and he was cast as Banquo in **Orson Welles**'s celebrated FTP production of the "Voodoo" *Macbeth* (1936), as it became known, which eventually led to his being cast in *Mamba's Daughters* (1939), *Big White Fog* (1940), and **Richard Wright**'s *Native Son* (1941), also directed by Welles, winning Lee plaudits from critics who labeled him the finest black actor of the era. He developed a strong passion for socially relevant theatre, and most of his stage roles reflected his politics. Among his subsequent **Broadway** roles, Lee appeared in *Anna Lucasta* (1944), a revival of *The Tempest* in 1945, *On Whitman Avenue* (1946), a revival of *The Duchess of Malfi* (1946), and *Set My People Free* (1948). Lee also appeared in films, including Alfred Hitchcock's *Lifeboat* (1944) and his last, *Cry, the Beloved Country* (1952), and had been called to appear before the House Un-American Activities Committee (HUAC) during the McCarthy era, but died of a heart attack before he could testify. *See also* AFRICAN AMERICAN THEATRE.

LEE, EUGENE (1939–). Prior to becoming one of **Broadway**'s leading scene designers, Lee was born in Beloit, Wisconsin, and studied at the Art Institute of Chicago, Carnegie Mellon University, and the Yale School of Drama. He won a **Drama Desk Award** for an **Off-Broadway** design for *Alice in Wonderland* (1971) and another, as well as a **Tony Award**, for a 1974 revival of *Candide*. Lee also won Tonys for *Sweeney Todd* (1979) and *Wicked* (2004) and was nominated for *Ragtime* (1998). He also designed non-MUSICALS, including a revival of *The Skin of Our Teeth* in 1975, *Some of My Best Friends* (1977), *Agnes of God* (1982), *The Hothouse* (1982), *On the Waterfront* (1995), revivals of *A Moon for the Misbegotten* in 2000 and *The Homecoming* in 2007. He also frequently designed for **Trinity Repertory Theatre** and was head of design at the **Dallas Theatre Center** for seven years. Lee married and often worked with costume designer **Franne Lee**, but they divorced.

LEE, FRANNE (1941–). Born Franne Newman (and known as "Bud") in the Bronx, New York, she studied art at the University of Wisconsin at

Madison. She won a **Tony Award** and **Drama Desk Award** for her costume designs for a revival of *Candide* in 1974 and won a Tony for *Sweeney Todd* (1979). On **Broadway**, Lee also designed costumes for revivals of *Love for Love* in 1974 and *The Skin of Our Teeth* in 1975, *Some of My Best Friends* (1977), *Gilda Radner: Live from New York* (1979), *The Moony Shapiro Songbook* (1981), *Rock'N'Roll! The First 5,000 Years* (1982), and a revival of *Camelot* in 1993. Lee was also costume designer for the television series *Saturday Night Live* from 1975–1979, garnering two Emmy Award nominations for her work. For a time, Lee was married to and frequently worked with scene designer **Eugene Lee**.

LEE, GYPSY ROSE (1911–1970). Born in Seattle, Washington, as Rose Louise Hovick, this BURLESQUE performer, actress, and television host began her career in vaudeville* as a child, performing with her sister Ellen June, later known as **June Havoc**, under the management of her mother, Rose. When her sister left the act during the declining days of vaudeville, Lee began performing as a stripper ("ecdysiast," as H. L. Mencken* famously described her) in burlesque, emerging as a major star at Minsky's Burlesque by combining striptease with humor, adding witty repartee to her act. She also appeared in secondary roles in a few Hollywood films and appeared in small parts in the **Broadway** shows *Hot-Cha!* (1932) and *Melody* (1933). She was a featured performer in the *Ziegfeld* Follies of 1936,* replaced Ethel Merman in *Du Barry Was a Lady* (1939), and starred in *Star and Garter* (1942), a revue.* In 1941, she wrote *The G-String Murders*, a mystery set behind the scenes of a burlesque theatre, and it became a film, *Lady of Burlesque* (1943), starring Barbara Stanwyck. Lee also wrote a shot-lived play, *The Naked Genius* (1943), and published a memoir, *Gypsy*, in 1957 that became the basis for a classic Broadway MUSICAL of the same name starring Ethel Merman as Lee's mother in 1959. Lee became a host of a television talk show in the late 1960s, but died of cancer soon afterward.

LEE, MING CHO (1930–). A native of Shanghai, China, Lee moved to the United States in 1949 and attended Occidental College. Five years later, he became the assistant of **Broadway**'s leading scene designer, JO MIELZINER. Lee's own minimalist, symbolic style departed from Mielziner's more REALISTIC approach, and he branched out on his own with a revival of *Electra* at the **New York Shakespeare Festival/Public Theatre (NYSF/PT)** in 1964. Lee won **Drama Desk Awards** for the Broadway production *Billy* (1969), which also garnered him a **Tony Award** nomination, and **Off-Broadway** for *Invitation to a Beheading* (1969). Other Broadway credits include *La Strada*

(1969), *Gandhi* (1970), *Two Gentlemen of Verona* (1971), a revival of *All God's Chillun Got Wings** in 1975, *for colored girls who have considered suicide/when the rainbow is enuf* (1976), revivals of *Romeo and Juliet* and *Caesar and Cleopatra* in 1977, *The Shadow Box* (1978), and *Angel* (1978). Lee won Tony and Drama Desk Awards for *K2* (1983) and was Drama Desk-nominated for *Execution of Justice* (1986). Lee also designed *The Grand Tour* (1979) and 1975 and 1983 revivals of *The Glass Menagerie*, among others. He has designed over 20 productions of **Shakespeare**'s plays for the NYSF/PT and his designs for *Annie Warbucks* (1993) and *A Perfect Ganesh* (1993) appeared in New York, but much of Lee's work since the mid-1980s has been in regional theatre, opera, and university theatre. Lee has taught at the Yale School of Drama since 1969 and was inducted into the **Theatre Hall of Fame** in 2002. Lee was also awarded a Sustained Achievement **Obie Award**.

LEE, ROBERT E. *See* LAWRENCE, JEROME.

LEFT BANK, THE. ELMER RICE's three-act drama, which he also produced and directed, opened on 5 October 1931 at the Little Theatre for 242 performances with a cast headed by Katherine Alexander. The play dealt with American expatriates in Europe and reflected Rice's disaffection with materialistic attitudes in the United States.

LEGUIZAMO, JOHN (1964–). Born to a Puerto Rican father and Colombian mother in Bogotá, Colombia, Jonathan Alberto Leguizamo emigrated to the United States as a small child and was educated at New York University. After some experience as a stand-up comic, and in bit roles in film and television, Leguizamo wrote *Mambo Mouth* (1991), a **solo performance** in which he also appeared as seven different characters to critical acclaim. The show brought him an **Obie Award** and, in 1993, he created another one-person show, *Spic-O-Rama*. Leguizamo's first **Broadway** show, *Freak* (1998), reaped two **Tony Award** nominations and an Emmy Award for the television adaptation of it, and he returned to the solo approach for the fourth time with *Sexaholix . . . A Love Story* (2001). He began to appear more frequently in movies and television in the 1990s, reaping a Golden Globe nomination for his performance in the film *To Wong Foo, Thanks for Everything, Julie Newmar* (1995). Leguizamo's other film roles include *Carlito's Way* (1993), *Romeo + Juliet* (1996), *Moulin Rouge!* (2001), and *Love in the Time of Cholera* (2007), and also starred in a recurring role on the television series *ER*. *See also* CHICANO THEATRE.

LEIGHT, WARREN (1957–). A New York-born playwright and screenwriter, Leight majored in journalism at Stanford University prior to writing the horror film *Mother's Day* (1980) and a 1982 documentary on the silent filmmaker Edwin S. Porter. He won a Best Play **Tony Award** for his play *Side Man* (1999), about the lives of jazz musicians, and his other plays include the book for the MUSICAL *Mayor* (1985), *Glimmer, Glimmer and Shine* (2001), and *No Foreigners beyond This Point* (2005), which brought him a **Drama Desk Award** nomination. Leight writes many television scripts, including for the series *Law & Order: Criminal Intent* (2008–2009) and *In Treatment* (2009).

LEIGHTON, MARGARET (1922–1976). An actress noted for a refined and sophisticated demeanor on stage and screen, Leighton was born in Barnt Green, Worcersteshire, England, and made her British stage debut in *Laugh with Me* (1938) and joined the Old Vic, acting with **Laurence Olivier** and Ralph Richardson, with whom she appeared in a 1946 **Broadway** production of *Henry IV*, her American debut. In between numerous film roles, Leighton appeared on stage in London and on Broadway. She won two Best Actress **Tony Awards**, for two roles in Terence Rattigan's *Separate Tables* (1957) and as Hannah Jelkes in **Tennessee Williams**'s *The Night of the Iguana* (1961), as well as Tony nominations for a 1960 revival of *Much Ado about Nothing* and Sidney Michaels's *Tchin-Tchin* (1963). Leighton's other Broadway appearances include revivals of *Uncle Vanya, Oedipus Rex*, and *The Critic* on tour with the Old Vic in 1946, *The Chinese Prime Minister* (1964), *Slapstick Tragedy* (1966), and a revival of *The Little Foxes* in 1967. She was nominated for an Academy Award for *The Go-Between* (1970), and her other films include *Under Capricorn* (1949), *The Astonished Heart* (1950), *Waltz of the Toreadors* (1962), *The Best Man* (1964), *7 Women* (1966), *The Madwoman of Chaillot* (1969), and *Galileo* (1975). Leighton also won a 1970 Emmy Award for a *Hallmark Hall of Fame* production of *Hamlet. See also* INTERNATIONAL STARS AND COMPANIES IN THE UNITED STATES.

LEMMON, JACK (1925–2001). One of the most respected film actors of the post-World WAR II era who occasionally appeared on **Broadway**, John Uhler Lemmon III was born in Newton, Massachusetts, and graduated from Harvard University. Following service in the United States Navy, he studied acting with **Uta Hagen** and began to work as an actor on stage, films, and early television. He won a Best Supporting Actor Academy Award for *Mister Roberts* (1955) and a Best Actor Oscar for *Save the Tiger* (1973), as well as Oscar nominations for *Some Like It Hot* (1959), *The Apartment* (1960), *Days* *of Wine and Roses* (1962), *The China Syndrome* (1979), *Tribute* (1980), and *Missing* (1982), among his many screen appearances. Lemmon also appeared on television, winning Emmy Awards for *'S Wonderful, 'S Marvelous, 'S Gershwin* (1972) and *Tuesdays with Morrie* (1999), and four other nominations. His first Broadway appearance in a revival of **Room Service**, in 1953, brought him little attention, and he had a flop with *Face of a Hero* (1960), but his other two appearances, in Bernard Slade's *Tribute* (1978) and in a revival of **Long Day's Journey Into Night** in 1986, reaped him **Tony Award** nominations.

LEND ME A TENOR. **Ken Ludwig**'s popular farce premiered in London on 6 March 1986 at the Globe Theatre for a successful run, followed by a **Broadway** production, directed by **Jerry Zaks** with scene design by **Tony Walton** and costumes by **William Ivey Long**, at the Royale Theatre, where it opened on 2 March 1989 and ran for 476 performances. The expert cast featured veteran actors **Philip Bosco** (who won a **Tony Award**), **Victor Garber**, Ron Holgate, Tovah Feldshuh, and Jane Connell. The plot focuses on egomaniacal tenor Tito Merelli, known to his fans as "Il Stupendo," who is scheduled to sing *Otello* at a Cleveland Opera Company benefit in 1934. When Merelli's tempestuous wife thinks (incorrectly) that he is having an affair, she angrily leaves, causing him to accidentally overdose on tranquilizers, with the result that several characters become engaged in trying either to revive Merelli or go onstage in his place. In the long tradition of farce, *Lend Me a Tenor* is filled with mistaken identities, wild coincidences, **sexual** innuendo, and surprise plot twists. The play received a Tony nomination as Best Play prior to seemingly endless productions by **regional**, university, and **community theatres**. *Lend Me a Tenor* was revived in 2010 at Broadway's Music Box Theatre starring Anthony LaPaglia, Tony Shalhoub, and Justin Bartha under Stanley Tucci's direction.

LENOIRE, ROSETTA (1911–2002). This highly respected **African American** stage and film actress, producer, and casting AGENT, was born in New York as Rosetta Olive Burton. As a child suffering from rickets, she strengthened her legs by dancing with the encouragement of her godfather, Bill "Bojangles" Robinson. She debuted on **Broadway** in support of Robinson in *The Hot Mikado* (1939) before becoming a familiar face (if not a well-known name) on stage, in films, and later in television. On Broadway, she appeared in *Anna Lucasta* (1944), a revival of *Finian's Rainbow* in 1955, *Destry Rides Again* (1959), *Sophie* (1963), *Tambourines to Glory* (1963), **Blues for Mister Charlie** (1964), *I Had a Ball* (1964), *The Great Indoors* (1966), *A Cry of Players* (1968), revivals of *Lost in the Stars* in 1972 and *A Streetcar Named*

Desire in 1973, *God's Favorite* (1974), and revivals of *The Royal Family** in 1975 and *You Can't Take It With You* in 1983. LeNoire founded the AMAS Repertory Theatre Company in 1968, an early interracial company with the goal of encouraging multi-**ethnic** productions. The company's success led to ACTORS' EQUITY ASSOCIATION establishing the Rosetta LeNoire Award for those contributing to the diversification of theatre casting. She was presented with a special **Theatre World Award** in 1993.

LENYA, LOTTE (1898–1981). Born in Vienna, Austria, as Karoline Blamauer, Lenya performed as a singer and actress in Berlin, where she met and married Kurt Weill and appeared in his and **Bertolt Brecht**'s *Threepenny Opera* (1928). With the rise of the Nazis, Lenya and Weill emigrated to the United States and she debuted on **Broadway** in Franz Werfel's *The Eternal Road* (1937). She won a **Tony Award** for a revival of *Threepenny Opera* and was nominated for another for the MUSICAL *Cabaret* (1966). She also appeared on Broadway in *Candle in the Wind* (1941), *The Firebrand of Florence* (1945), and *Barefoot in Athens* (1951), as well as **Off-Broadway** productions, including *Brecht on Brecht* (1961).

LEONARD, ROBERT SEAN (1969–). A native of Jersey City, New Jersey, and born Robert Lawrence Leonard, he attended Fordham University and Columbia University prior to winning critical plaudits in the film *Dead Poets Society* (1989), as well as *Much Ado About Nothing* (1993), *The Age of Innocence* (1993), *In the Gloaming* (1997), and others, but also devoted considerable attention to the stage. He won a **Tony Award** as Best Featured Actor in **Tom Stoppard**'s *The Invention of Love* (2001) and was nominated for revivals of *Candida* in 1993 and *Long Day's Journey into Night* in 2003. Leonard's other **Broadway** appearances include replacing **Matthew Broderick** in *Brighton Beach Memoirs* (1983), *Breaking the Code* (1987), *The Speed of Darkness* (1991), a revival of *Philadelphia, Here I Come!* in 1994, *Arcadia* (1995), a revival of *The Iceman Cometh* in 1999, replacing Craig Bierko in a revival of *The Music Man* in 2000, and *The Violet Hour* (2003). He has continued to appear in movies and on television where, since 2004, he has been a regular on the series *House*.

LESBIAN THEATRE. *See* GAY AND LESBIAN THEATRE.

LETTS, TRACY (1965–). Born in Tulsa, Oklahoma, as the son of an actor/ teacher father and a writer mother, Letts was educated at Southern Methodist University and moved to Chicago, Illinois, where he began his career as an actor in 1988 working at **Steppenwolf Theatre**, Famous Door, and as the founder of Bang Bang Spontaneous Theatre. His 1991 play, *Killer Joe*, was acclaimed in productions in Chicago, **Off-Broadway**, and international theatres. Letts's subsequent plays, *Man from Nebraska* (2003) and *Bug* (2004), were well-received, but his searing family comedy-drama, *August: Osage County* (2007), won a PULITZER PRIZE, **Tony Award**, and **Drama Desk Award** for Best Play, and a film version was in development in late 2009. *Superior Donuts* (2008), Letts's next play, dealt with the subject of contemporary **race** relations and premiered at the Steppenwolf before moving to Broadway in 2009. He also adapted **Anton Chekhov**'s *The Three Sisters* in 2009. His acting resume includes leading roles in Steppenwolf productions of *Three Days of Rain* in 1999, *Glengarry Glen Ross* in 2001, *Homebody/ Kabul* in 2003, and *The Pillowman* in 2006, among others. Letts has also appeared in film and television roles. As an actor, Letts won kudos in 2010 as George in a production of *Who's Afraid of Virginia Woolf?* at the Steppenwolf Theatre.

LEVE, SAMUEL (1908–1999). Born in Russia, Leve emigrated to the United States with his family in 1920, settling in New York City. He began his career as a scene and lighting designer with the **Federal Theatre Project (FTP)**'s **Mercury Theatre** unit, designing, among other productions, **Orson Welles**'s acclaimed 1937 FTP revival of *Julius Caesar*. On **Broadway**, Leve also designed revivals of *The Shoemaker's Holiday* in 1938 and three Gilbert and Sullivan operettas* (*The Gondoliers, The Mikado*, and *The Pirates of Penzance*) in 1940, and *The Beautiful People* (1941). He also designed for Maurice Schwartz's* Yiddish Art Theatre* and designed the 1941 **Maurice Evans** and **Judith Anderson** *Macbeth*. Leve's numerous other Broadway credits include *Wallflower* (1944), *It's a Gift* (1945), a revival of *The Madwoman of Chaillot* in 1948, *Clutterbuck* (1949), *The Fifth Season* (1953), and Jack Benny's Broadway stage show in 1963.

LEVENE, SAM (1905–1980). Born Samuel Levine in Russia, he debuted on **Broadway** in the melodrama* *Wall Street* (1927) and had an over 50-year career on stage and screen, often playing gamblers, hoods, and New York Jewish characters. His Broadway appearances include leading roles in the original productions of *Dinner at Eight* (1932), *Three Men on a Horse* (1935), *Room Service* (1937), *Light Up the Sky* (1948), and as Nathan Detroit in *Guys and Dolls* (1950). He also acted in *Make a Million* (1958), a 1959 revival of *Heartbreak House*, *The Devil's Advocate* (1961), for which he received his sole **Tony Award** nomination, *Let It Ride* (1961), *Seidman and Son* (1962), *Café Crown* (1964), *The Last Analysis* (1964), *Paris Is Out!* (1970), and played Al Lewis in **Neil Simon**'s *The Sunshine Boys* (1972).

Levene stepped into the lead of *The Impossible Years* (1965) during its run and appeared in the all-star Broadway revival of *The Royal Family** in 1975. Shortly before his death, he appeared in the flop *Horowitz and Mrs. Washington* (1980). Levene also appeared opposite **Ruth Gordon** in the London production of *The Matchmaker*. In films, Levene played numerous character roles, including reprising his stage performance in *Three Men on a Horse* (1936), *Golden Boy* (1939), *Crossfire* (1947), *Designing Woman* (1957), . . . *And Justice for All* (1979), and numerous television shows, including a 1977 broadcast of *The Royal Family*.

LEVIN, IRA (1929–2007). A playwright and novelist, Levin was born in New York and had a successful stage career writing diverse plays, including the comedies *No Time for Sergeants* (1955) and *Critic's Choice* (1960), the MUSICAL *Drat! The Cat!* (1965), and the thrillers *Dr. Cook's Garden* (1967), *Veronica's Room* (1973), and *Deathtrap* (1978), which was nominated for a Best Play **Tony Award**, had a long run, and was filmed in 1982. His last play produced on **Broadway**, the comedy *Break a Leg* (1979), was a flop, but many of his novels made successful films, including *Rosemary's Baby* (1968), *The Stepford Wives* (1975), *The Boys from Brazil* (1978), and *A Kiss before Dying* (1991), as well as his plays *No Time for Sergeants* in 1958 and *Critic's Choice* in 1963.

LEWIS, ROBERT (1909–1997). A native of Brooklyn, New York, Lewis, often billed as Bob Lewis as a young actor, emerged as a leading actor, director, and teacher of acting during his long career. He began barely out of his teens as an actor with EVA LE GALLIENNE's CIVIC REPERTORY THEATRE in a production of *The Living Corpse* (1929), appeared in the ensembles of several MUSICALS, and became a member of **The Group Theatre** in 1931, appearing in Group productions *Night Over Taos* (1932), *Men in White* (1933), *Waiting for Lefty* (1935), *Till the Day I Die* (1935), *Paradise Lost* (1935), *Case of Clyde Griffiths* (1936), *Johnny Johnson* (1936), and *Golden Boy* (1937), directing the tour of the last.

Lewis shifted more toward directing in the 1940s, staging the Group's production of **William Saroyan**'s *My Heart's in the Highlands* (1939). During World WAR II, Lewis spent time as a character actor in Hollywood films, but in 1947 he returned to New York and cofounded **The Actors Studio** with **Elia Kazan** and **Cheryl Crawford**. Unresolved differences with Kazan and Crawford led Lewis to break away from the Studio and he directed a series of major **Broadway** plays and musicals, including *Brigadoon* (1947), *Regina* (1949), *The Happy Time* (1950), a 1950 revival of *An Enemy of the People*,

The Grass Harp (1952), **The Teahouse of the August Moon** (1953), *Witness for the Prosecution* (1954), *Jamaica* (1957), revivals of *The Shadow of a Gunman* in 1958 and *Strange Interlude** in 1963, *Foxy* (1964), and *On a Clear Day You Can See Forever* (1965). In 1957, Lewis delivered a series of lectures in New York expressing his ideas of "method acting" as based on concepts of **Constantin Stanislavsky** and challenging the views of other acting teachers of the time. He established the Robert Lewis Theatre Workshop and taught several generations of actors.

LIE OF THE MIND, A. **Sam Shepard**'s searing three-act drama of two families joined by an unhappy marriage opened **Off-Broadway** on 5 December 1985 at the Promenade Theatre under Shepard's direction and with a cast, including Harvey Keitel, **Amanda Plummer**, Aidan Quinn, **Geraldine Page**, James Gammon, Ann Wedgeworth, Will Patton, and Karen Young. The play begins in the aftermath of a tragic incident of domestic abuse when Jake beats his wife, Beth, to the point of brain damage and hospitalization. The play explores issues of deep family dysfunction and the nature of love as the two families cope with their individual issues and face Beth's uncertain future. The MUSICAL group the Red Clay Ramblers memorably provided live music to accompany the play. A London production of *A Lie of the Mind* opened on 14 October 1987 at the Royal Court Theatre and a New York revival appeared in January 2010, produced by the New Group under the direction of Ethan Hawke, who acted in it as well, along with Keith Carradine, Laurie Metcalf, Frank Whaley, Marin Ireland, and Karen Young from the 1985 cast.

LIFE AND ADVENTURES OF NICHOLAS NICKLEBY. David Edgar's nine-hour stage adaptation of Charles Dickens's 1838 comic novel opened in a Royal Shakespeare Company (RSC) production in London at the Aldwych Theatre on 5 June 1980 to enthusiastic reviews and won the Olivier Award as Best Play under the direction of **Trevor Nunn**. The production met with a similarly rhapsodic response when it opened on **Broadway** on 4 October 1981 at the Plymouth Theatre. The production won the **Tony Award** as Best Play and director Nunn, scene designers John Napier and Dermot Hayes, and leading actor **Roger Rees** also won Tonys. Rees played the title character who is forced, by circumstance, to support his mother and sister following the death of his father and vying with his Uncle Ralph, who believes Nicholas is worthless. A 1982 television film of the production was show on British and American television, winning an Emmy Award for Best Miniseries. The RSC revived the play in 1986, and it again transferred to Broadway and was nominated for a Tony for Best Revival.

LIFE WITH FATHER. Howard Lindsay and **Russel Crouse** based this warm family comedy, produced by Oscar Serlin, on Clarence Day's serialized stories of Gilded Age New York first published in the *New Yorker*. The play opened on **Broadway**, with Lindsay in the title role, on 8 November 1939 at the Empire Theatre and became Broadway's longest-running play racking up an unprecedented 3,224 performances (the production was moved to the Bijou Theatre and the Alvin Theatre during its long run). The nostalgic comedy, directed by **Bretaigne Windust**, depicted a rosy American past and seemed to soothe World War II-era audiences who enjoyed the affectionate efforts of Mother, played by Lindsay's wife, Dorothy Stickney, to temper the autocratic ways and short-temper of her husband. The play became a popular film starring William Powell and Irene Dunne in 1947, the same year the play finally closed on Broadway. Lindsay and Crouse were inspired to write a sequel, *Life with Mother* (1948), which did not find the success of the original play, although it ran a season. A television series based on the play ran for three seasons, beginning in 1953, starring Leon Ames and Lurene Tuttle.

LIGHT UP THE SKY. **Moss Hart**'s witty comedy of the out-of-town tryouts of a new cutting-edge play opened on 18 November 1948 at the Royale Theatre for 214 performances. Hart directed the comedy, which featured a cast of seasoned actors including **Sam Levene, Barry Nelson**, Glenn Anders, **Audrey Christie**, and Phyllis Povah. The play, which has found frequent productions in STOCK, **community theatres**, and university theatres, involves the chaos in a Ritz-Carlton Hotel suite in Boston as the production of a new allegorical play meets with the egos and commercial considerations of a pre-**Broadway** tryout. The producer, director, playwright, and leading actress, along with their entourages, comically struggle toward the play's ultimately successful opening.

LIGHTING DESIGN. *See* DESIGN/DESIGNERS.

LINCOLN CENTER FOR THE PERFORMING ARTS. Constructed on over 16 acres in the Lincoln Square area of New York City, this arts complex was begun under the initiative of John D. Rockefeller III during an era of urban renewal spearheaded by Robert Moses. President Dwight D. Eisenhower broke ground for the complex in 1959, and it was completed during the early 1960s after nearly a decade of fund-raising and planning. The center includes three theatres, the David H. Koch Theatre (originally called the New York State Theatre), the Vivian Beaumont Theatre, and the Mitzi E. Newhouse Theatre, as well as venues for music, dance, and film, including the Metropolitan Opera House, Alice Tully Hall, Avery Fisher Hall, the Walter Reade

Theatre, and other spaces, with a number of organizations using the facilities. Over the years, several theatre organizations have taken up residence at the center and **Broadway** productions are now frequently featured in the major theatre spaces.

LINDSAY, HOWARD (1889–1968).† Born in Waterford, New York, Lindsay proved to be a versatile theatre man, with notable successes as a playwright, actor, director, and producer. Educated at Harvard University, he also attended the AMERICAN ACADEMY OF DRAMATIC ARTS, after which he worked as an actor and wrote his first play, *Billeted* (1917). During the 1920s, Lindsay directed and acted in numerous **Broadway** plays, including *Dulcy** (1921). After 1930, Lindsay's prolific output included directing Cole Porter's MUSICAL *Gay Divorcee* (1932), Daniel Kussel's *The Party's Over* (1933), his own comedy *She Loves Me Not* (1933), and the flop *By Your Leave* (1934). That same year, he collaborated with **Russel Crouse** for the first time on the libretto for Porter's hit musical *Anything Goes*, which he also directed. Lindsay also collaborated with Damon Runyon on *A Slight Case of Murder* (1935) and had another hit with Crouse with Porter's musical *Red, Hot, and Blue* (1936) and a moderate success with *Hooray for What!* (1937).

In 1939, Lindsay and Crouse adapted Clarence Day's popular stories about a late-nineteenth-century New York family into one of the longest-running comedies in Broadway history, *Life with Father* (1939), which starred Lindsay as the lovably irascible patriarch, and Lindsay's wife DOROTHY STICKNEY, whom he had married in 1927, played opposite him. *Life with Father* ran for over 3,200 performances, became a staple of STOCK and **community theatres**, and spawned a successful sequel, *Life with Mother* (1948). Lindsay and Crouse produced another long-running hit, **Joseph Kesselring**'s *Arsenic and Old Lace* (1941), with rumors circulating that the team "doctored" Kesselring's play into a hit. Lindsay and Crouse continued to collaborate through the 1940s and their output includes *Strip for Action* (1942) and the PULITZER PRIZE-winning *State of the Union* (1945), a comedy about a presidential candidate and his estranged wife. The team also wrote *Remains to Be Seen* (1951), *The Prescott Proposals* (1953), and *The Great Sebastians* (1956) starring ALFRED LUNT and LYNN FONTANNE, produced several important plays including **John Patrick**'s *The Hasty Heart* (1945) and **Sidney Kingsley**'s *Detective Story* (1949), and returned to writing musicals with Irving Berlin's *Call Me Madam* (1950), *Happy Hunting* (1956), Richard Rodgers and Oscar Hammerstein's *The Sound of Music* (1959), and Berlin's last musical, *Mr. President* (1962). Lindsay and Crouse were given a special **Tony Award** in 1959 and also won a Tony for *The Sound of Music* in 1960.

LINDSAY-ABAIRE, DAVID (1969–). The son of a blue-collar family from South Boston, Massachusetts, born as David Abaire, he majored in theatre at Sarah Lawrence College and studied playwriting at the Juilliard School with **Christopher Durang** and **Marsha Norman**. He first drew CRITICAL attention with *Fuddy Mears* (1999), a play about an amnesiac, and his other plays include *The L'il Plays* (1997), *A Devil Inside* (1997), *Dotting and Dashing* (1999), *Snow Angel* (1999), *Kimberly Akimbo* (2000), *Wonder of the World* (2000), and the book for the MUSICAL *High Fidelity* (2006). Lindsay-Abaire won the PULITZER PRIZE and a **Tony Award** nomination for his play *Rabbit Hole* (2006), about a married couple dealing with the accidental death of their child. He also wrote screenplays for *Robots* (2005), *Inkheart* (2008), and *Spider-Man 4* (2011), as well as *Rabbit Hole* (2010).

LINNEY, LAURA (1964–). The daughter of celebrated dramatist **Romulus Linney** and Miriam Perse, a nurse, she was born Laura Leggett Linney in New York. This dignified, patrician actress was educated at Brown University and the Juilliard School before embarking on an acting career on stage and screen. Much acclaim has accompanied her film work, for which she is best known, but she has consistently appeared on New York stages, making her **Broadway** debut as a replacement in *Six Degrees of Separation* (1990). Linney won CRITICAL approval in *Sight Unseen* (1992), which brought her a **Theatre World** Award in its **Off-Broadway** production, as well as **Tony Award** and **Drama Desk Award** nominations for its 2005 Broadway staging. She was also Tony-nominated for a revival of *The Crucible* in 2002. Her other appearances include revivals of *The Seagull* in 1992, *Hedda Gabler* in 1994, and *Holiday** in 1995, *Honour* (1998), revivals of *Uncle Vanya* in 2000 and *Les Liaisons Dangereuses* in 2008, and *Time Stands Still* (2010). Linney has been nominated for three Academy Awards, for *You Can Count on Me (*2000), *Kinsey* (2004), and *The Savages* (2007), among many other film appearances, and she won an Emmy Award, Golden Globe Award, and Screen Actors Guild Award playing Abigail Adams in the HBO-TV miniseries, *John Adams* (2008), as well as the TV-movie *Wild Iris* (2001 and for a guest appearance on the situation comedy *Frasier* in 2004.

LINNEY, ROMULUS (1930–2011). Born in Philadelphia, Pennsylvania, as Romulus Zachariah Linney IV, he was educated at Oberlin College and the Yale School of Drama. A prolific writer whose work has been produced mostly in **regional theatres**, universities, and occasionally **Off-Broadway**, where he won an **Obie Award** for his play, *Tennessee* (1979), Linney has written numerous full-length plays, including *The Sorrow of Frederick* (1967), *The Love Suicide at Schofield Barracks* (1972), **Holy Ghosts**

(1976), *Childe Byron* (1978), *Laughing Stock* (1984), *Woman without a Name* (1985), *Pops* (1986), *Three Poets* (1989), *Unchanging Love* (1991), *2: Göring at Nuremberg* (1992), *Oscar Over Here* (1995), *Gint* (1998), *A Lesson before Dying* (2000), *Klonsky and Schwartz* (2005), and others, as well as numerous one-act plays. He was the first playwright-in-residence at the **Signature Theatre** in 1991 (where a season of his plays were produced), and he was presented with an Obie for Sustained Excellence in 1992. Linney was the father of actress **Laura Linney**.

LION IN WINTER, THE. **James Goldman**'s comedy-drama set at the court of England's King Henry II opened under the direction of Noel Willman on 3 March 1966 at the Ambassador Theatre for 92 performances starring **Robert Preston** as the King and **Rosemary Harris** (who won a Best Actress **Tony Award**) as his wife, Eleanor of Aquitaine. Set in 1183, intrigue abounds as Henry and Eleanor match wits over which of their three sons, Richard the Lionhearted, Geoffrey, or John, will succeed Henry to the throne of England. The play's short run belied its durability; it was successfully filmed in 1968 starring Peter O'Toole, **Katharine Hepburn** (who won an Academy Award), and Anthony Hopkins (a second film, in 2003, starred Patrick Stewart and **Glenn Close**), and it has had frequent revivals, including a 1999 staging at Criterion Center Stage Right starring Laurence Fishburne and **Stockard Channing** (in a Tony-nominated performance).

LIPS TOGETHER, TEETH APART. **Terrence McNally**'s play about two straight couples spending the 4th of July weekend in the **gay** enclave of Fire Island opened at the **Manhattan Theatre Club (MTC)** on 25 June 1991 under the direction of **John Tillinger**. The **Drama Desk Award**-nominated play starred **Christine Baranski** (who won a Drama Desk Award), **Nathan Lane**, Anthony Heald, and **Swoosie Kurtz**. In the MTC production, Kurtz played Sally Truman, whose brother has recently died of **AIDS**, and the two couples spend a weekend of isolation during which they reveal their attitudes and fears about gay life, the times in which they live, and their relationships. A revival, directed by **Joe Mantello**, and featuring Megan Mullally, Patton Oswalt, Lili Taylor, and David Wilson Barnes, opened at the **Roundabout Theatre** in 2010.

LITHGOW, JOHN (1945–). Born in Rochester, New York, as John Arthur Lithgow to an actress mother and a father who ran New Jersey's **McCarter Theatre**, he studied at Harvard University and at the London Academy of Music and Dramatic Art on a Fulbright Scholarship. His **Broadway** debut in David Storey's *The Changing Room* (1973) brought him a **Tony Award**

and a **Drama Desk Award**. Lithgow's theatre work has been sporadic, interrupted by many film and television appearances. Lithgow's other Tony nominations came for *Requiem for a Heavyweight* (1985), which won him a Drama Desk Award, *M. Butterfly* (1988), and *Dirty Rotten Scoundrels* (2005) and he won a Tony for the MUSICAL *Sweet Smell of Success* (2002). He was also nominated for Drama Desk Awards for *M. Butterly* and the **Off-Broadway** production, *Mrs. Farnsworth* (2004). His other Broadway credits include *My Fat Friend* (1974), revivals of *Trelawny of the "Wells"* in 1975, *A Memory of Two Mondays* in 1976, *Secret Service** in 1976, and *Boy Meets Girl* in 1976, *Comedians* (1976), revivals of *Anna Christie** in 1977 and *Once in a Lifetime* in 1978, *Spokesong* (1979), *Division Street* (1980), *Beyond Therapy* (1982), a revival of *The Front Page** in 1986, *The Retreat from Moscow* (2003), and a revival of *All My Sons* in 2008. On screen, Lithgow has been nominated for Academy Awards for *The World According to Garp* (1982) and *Terms of Endearment* (1983), and has won four Emmy Awards, three for his long-running television comedy series, *3rd Rock from the Sun* (1996–2001), which also brought him a Golden Globe Award and two Screen Actors Guild Awards. In 2006, Lithgow was inducted into the **Theatre Hall of Fame**.

LITTLE FOXES, THE. The frequently revived *The Little Foxes*, which opened on **Broadway** on 15 February 1939 at New York's National Theatre for an impressive 410 performance run, is, on its surface, a cautionary tale of unchecked capitalism and the avariciousness created by an American dream of materialism. Author **Lillian Hellman**'s title is taken from the biblical Song of Solomon: "Take us the foxes, the little foxes, that spoil the vines; for our vines have tender grapes," and it reflects the dilemma of the extended Hubbard family. Producer **Herman Shumlin** directed, with scenery by **Howard Bay** and costumes by **Aline Bernstein**.

Regina Giddens (TALLULAH BANKHEAD), a Southern aristocrat, struggles to gain her own wealth in early twentieth-century America, where a daughter sees her father's fortune left to the sons, in this case Regina's greedy, manipulative brothers, Ben (Charles Dingle) and Oscar (Carl Benton Reid). She is also attempting to break free of a loveless marriage to ailing Horace Giddens (Frank Conroy)—her dream is the high life in fashionable Chicago, but Horace prevents her from participating in Ben and Oscar's deal-making with a Northern businessman. Hellman's depiction of Regina's mounting desperation—and her willingness, and ability, to do anything it takes to have her way—is the evocation of the metaphorical title—foxes like Regina (and Ben and Oscar) spoil the vines (the family and **community**) and the vines have produced tender grapes, namely Regina and Horace's daughter, Alexandra

(Florence Williams), a lovely, gentle girl in her father's mold, and Leo (Dan Duryea), the amoral son of Oscar and his unhappy, alcoholic wife, Birdie (PATRICIA COLLINGE), who he has only married in order to acquire her family's vast cotton fields.

Hellman devotes most of the play's attention to the machinations of Regina, at various times in highly charged conflicts with Horace or Ben and Oscar, but it is Alexandra whose soul is at risk. Oscar would like to see Leo and Alexandra wed, an appalling thought even to Regina, and once Horace dies (when Regina stoops even to murder, standing silently by while he struggles out of his wheelchair to get his medicine), Alexandra becomes the only morally sound member of this rapacious family. Without subtlety, Hellman emphasizes the human cost of the family's unbridled greed—and when Regina succeeds in prevailing financially, the cost for her is the loss of her daughter's love and respect. Regina cannot be redeemed, but Alexandra, Hellman hopefully posits, can rid herself of the spoiled vines threatening her salvation. As she pointedly notes near the play's end, "There are people who eat earth and eat all the people on it like in the Bible with the locusts. And other people who stand around and watch them eat."

The flamboyant Bankhead scored a major personal success as Regina, although a 1941 film version replaced her with **Bette Davis**, but featured most of the original cast. The much-revived play was adapted as an opera in 1949 by composer Marc Blitzstein, retitled *Regina*, and other Broadway revivals featured noted actresses, including **Anne Bancroft** in 1967, Elizabeth Taylor in 1981, and **Stockard Channing** in 1997. In 2010, the **New York Theatre Workshop** staged a revival **Off-Broadway** directed by Ivo van Hove. The critical and commercial success of *The Little Foxes* led Hellman to return to its characters and its indictment of capitalism in *Another Part of the Forest* (1946), a prequel of sorts examining the previous generation of the rapacious Hubbard family, with Regina, Ben, Oscar, and Birdie seen as their youthful selves.

LITTLE MURDERS. **Jules Feiffer**'s absurdist black comedy opened on 25 April 1967 at New York's Broadhurst Theatre in an **Alexander H. Cohen** production for a mere seven performances. A July 1967 **Royal Shakespeare** Company (RSC) staging of the play was more successful, as was a 1969 **Off-Broadway** production at the **Circle in the Square** directed by **Alan Arkin** for a 400 performance run. *Little Murders* is a bitter and often touching satiric work on the tribulations of urban life in the 1960s, exploring the nature of marriage, violence and law, and morality through the experiences of the family of Carol Newquist and his wife, whose daughter is killed on her wedding day by a bullet fired randomly. Arkin also directed a 1971 screen version starring Elliot Gould and Marcia Rodd, and the play has had numerous **re-gional** and university theatre productions.

LIVING NEWSPAPER. A **documentary theatre** employed most notably by the **Federal Theatre Project (FTP)** during the 1930s, these productions focused on a single newsworthy issue (international, national, or local) using a variety of stage techniques to present factual material on the central topic. Several Living Newspaper productions by FTP's "805" unit included *Ethiopia* (1936), dealing with the war in Abyssinia, which never officially opened due to pressures from the State Department fearing offending Benito Mussolini's Italy. Other productions included *Triple-A-Plowed Under* (1936), *1935* (1936), *Injunction Granted* (1936), *It Can't Happen Here* (1936), *Power* (1937), *One Third of a Nation* (1938), and *Life and Death of an American* (1939).

LIVING THEATRE, THE (LT). Established by **Julian Beck** and **Judith Malina** in 1948, The Living Theatre initiated the **Off-Off-Broadway** movement of the post-World WAR II era. Many similar theatres were relatively short-lived, but The Living Theatre had a long life and became a significant force in New York theatre during the turbulent 1960s. Beck and Malina stressed that the experimentation with avant-garde work done by the Living Theatre was intended to reflect a changing American society. Among their most noted works were plays by GERTRUDE STEIN, Federico García Lorca, Luigi Pirandello, Paul Goodman, Jean Cocteau, and **Bertolt Brecht**. Until 1959, The Living Theatre performed in a variety of spaces, but that year they scored one of their earliest successes with **Jack Gelber**'s *The Connection* (1959), followed by Brecht's *Man Is Man* in 1962 and Kenneth Brown's *The Brig* (1963).

From 1964 to 1968, the LT performed in European cities, experimenting with improvisation and **collective** techniques, a period that culminated in their most emblematic production, *Paradise Now* (1968). After a period of performing again in the United States, Beck and Malina returned to Europe, then to Brazil, continuing experimentation with collective theatre creation. The LT reestablished itself in New York in 1984, but Beck died the following year. Malina continues to direct LT in collaboratin with Hanon Reznikov and, in 2007, they revived *The Brig*. *See also* ALTERNATIVE THEATRE.

LLOYD, NORMAN (1914–). A native of Jersey City, New Jersey, Lloyd began his stage career as a member of EVA LE GALLIENNE'S CIVIC REPERTORY THEATRE, after which he joined **Orson Welles**'s **Mercury Theatre** unit of the **Federal Theatre Project (FTP)**, appearing notably as Cinna, the poet, in Welles's production of **Shakespeare**'s *Julius Caesar* in 1937. He also appeared in FTP productions of *Power* (1937) and *The Shoemaker's Holiday* (1938). Lloyd's other **Broadway** roles include playing the Fool to Welles's Lear in a 1950 revival of *King Lear, Medicine Show* (1940), *Liberty Jones* (1941), *Village Green* (1941), *Ask My Friend Sandy* (1943), *Madam, Will You Walk* (1953), which he also directed, and revivals of *Measure for Measure* in 1957 and *The Taming of the Shrew*, both in 1957. Lloyd directed the Broadway MUSICAL *The Golden Apple* (1954) and worked more frequently in films beginning in the early 1940s, appearing most memorably in Alfred Hitchcock's *Saboteur* (1942) and *Spellbound* (1945). He produced, directed, and acted in television with regularity after 1950 and was a regular on the TV drama series, *St. Elsewhere*, from 1982–1988, and was twice nominated for Emmy Awards for producing the series *The Name of the Game* (1968) and the special presentation of the play *Steambath* (1973). At age 90, Lloyd appeared in the film *In Her Shoes* (2005).

LOBEL, ADRIANNE (1955–). Daughter of **children's** book author Arnold Lobel, she graduated from the Yale School of Drama, where she trained with **Ming Cho Lee**. Lobel has won recognition as a cutting-edge scene designer, working often on radically postmodern operatic productions with **Peter Sellars** in major international opera houses. Lobel also designed the Royal National Theatre's revival of *Lady in the Dark* in 1997, and for many **regional theatres**, where she has designed premiere works by many leading American dramatists. Her **Broadway** career began when she assisted scene designer Tom Lynch on *Tintypes* (1980) and she won a 1984 **Obie Award** for her designs of *The Vampires* and *All Night Long*, before being nominated for a **Drama Desk Award** for *Passion* (1994) and receiving a **Tony Award** nomination for *A Year with Frog and Toad* (2003), which was based on her father's books. Her other Broadway designs include *My One and Only* (1983), and revivals of *The Diary of Anne Frank* in 1997 and *On the Town* in 1998. Lobel is married to actor Mark Linn-Baker.

LOGAN, JOHN (1961–). A native of San Diego, California, who also spent part of his youth in New Jersey, John David Logan was the son of Irish immigrants. His plays have tended to focus on historical persons or incidents, as in the case of his earliest plays, *Hauptman* (1992), about the executed kidnapper of the Lindbergh baby, and *Never the Sinner* (1998), about the Leopold and Loeb case; the latter brought Logan an **Outer Critics Circle Award**. He scored his most noted stage success with *Red*, a drama about the artist Mark Rothko, which won kudos in its initial production at

London's Donmar Warehouse in 2009, and a **Tony Award** and a **Drama Desk Award** when the production moved to **Broadway** in 2010. For television, Logan wrote *RKO 281* (1999), for which he garnered an Emmy Award nomination, and for films, he contributed screenplays for *Gladiator* (2000), *The Time Machine* (2002), *Star Trek Nemesis* (2002), *The Aviator* (2004), for which he was nominated for an Academy Award, *Sweeney Todd* (2007), and *Coriolanus* (2011).

LOGAN, JOSHUA (1908–1988). Born in Texarkana, Texas, as Joshua Lockwood Logan III, he studied at Princeton University, befriending several noted actors, including **James Stewart** and **Henry Fonda**, while working with Princeton's Triangle Club and University Players. Logan began his distinguished **Broadway** career as an actor in the flop *Carry Nation* (1932) and followed up with several others until 1938 when he had a hit as a director, staging the original production of *On Borrowed Time* (1938). From there he directed numerous successful plays and MUSICALS, including *I Married an Angel* (1938), *Knickerbocker Holiday* (1938), *Stars In Your Eyes* (1939), *Morning's at Seven* (1939), *Higher and Higher* (1940), a revival of *Charley's Aunt* in 1940, *By Jupiter* (1942), and *This Is the Army* (1942). During World WAR II, Logan's career was interrupted by his time in the service, but at the war's end, he returned to Broadway more successful than he had been before. In collaboration with Thomas Heggen, Logan wrote and directed *Mister Roberts* (1948), winning **Tony Awards** for Best Play, Best Author, and Best Direction.

In 1949, Logan collaborated with Richard Rodgers and Oscar Hammerstein II to adapt James A. Michener's *Tales of the South Pacific* into the musical *South Pacific*, sharing in a PULITZER PRIZE and Tonys in multiple categories, including for his direction. He won another Tony directing **William Inge**'s Pulitzer Prize-winning play *Picnic* (1953). He was nominated again as director for *All American* (1962). On Broadway, Logan also directed *Annie Get Your Gun* (1946), *Happy Birthday* (1946), *The Wisteria Trees* (1950), which he adapted from **Anton Chekhov**'s *The Cherry Orchard, Wish You Were Here* (1952), *Kind Sir* (1953), *Fanny* (1954), *Middle of the Night* (1956), *Blue Denim* (1958), *The World of Suzie Wong* (1958), *There Was a Little Girl* (1960), *Mr. President* (1962), *Tiger, Tiger Burning Bright* (1962), *Ready When You Are, C.B.!* (1964), *Look to the Lilies* (1970), and *Horowitz and Mrs. Washington* (1980), the last two being rare flops for Logan, one of the most astute showmen of Broadway's post-World War II era. Logan also directed several notable films and garnered Academy Award nominations for *Picnic* (1955), for which he won a Golden Globe Award, *Sayonara* (1957), and *Fanny* (1961). For the movies, his directing was centered on moving stage plays and musicals to the screen with **Bus Stop** (1956), *South Pacific* (1958), *Tall Story* (1960), *Ensign Pulver* (1964), a sequel to *Mister Roberts, Camelot* (1967), and *Paint Your Wagon* (1969). Logan was married twice, to actresses Barbara O'Neil and Nedda Harrigan, the daughter of Edward Harrigan.*

LONERGAN, KENNETH (1962–   ). A New York native trained as a playwright and director at Wesleyan University and New York University, Lonergan joined the **Naked Angels**, a theatre troupe willing to produce his first plays and he also began writing for the screen, which brought him his first major success, *You Can Count On Me* (2000), followed by the movies *Analyze This* (1999), *The Gangs of New York* (2002), which was nominated for an Academy Award, and *Margaret* (2007). **Off-Broadway**, Lonergan scored a critical success with *This Is Our Youth* (1998), which brought him a **Drama Desk Award** nomination, followed by *The Waverly Gallery* (2000) and *Lobby Hero* (2001), which was nominated for a Drama Desk Award, **Outer Critics Circle Award**, and Olivier Award, and *The Starry Messenger* (2009). He is married to actress J. Smith-Cameron.

LONG, WILLIAM IVEY (1947–   ). A native North Carolinian, Long studied at the College of William and Mary, the University of North Carolina at Chapel Hill, and the Yale School of Drama prior to embarking on a distinguished career as a costume designer on **Broadway**, in films, and in **regional theatre**. He won a **Tony Award** and a **Drama Desk Award** for his costumes for *Nine* (1982), *The Producers* (2001), and *Hairspray* (2003), Drama Desk Awards for **Lend Me a Tenor** (1989) and a 1992 revival of *Guys and Dolls*, and Tonys for *Crazy for You* (1992) and *Grey Gardens* (2007), as well as numerous other nominations for both. For Broadway, he has also designed *Mass Appeal* (1981), *Eastern Standard* (1989), **Six Degrees of Separation** (1990), *Laughter on the 23rd Floor* (1993), *Smokey Joe's Café* (1995), *The Civil War* (1999), *Swing!* (1999), *Contact* (2000), *Seussical* (2000), *45 Seconds from Broadway* (2001), *The Boy from Oz* (2003), *The Frogs* (2004), *Curtains* (2007), *Young Frankenstein* (2007), and *9 to 5* (2009), as well as many Broadway revivals of plays and MUSICALS. Long has also designed **Off-Broadway** (winning an **Obie Award** for Sustained Excellence), in regional theatres, and for rock artists and dance companies.

LONG DAY'S JOURNEY INTO NIGHT. This play is the fullest realization of EUGENE O'NEILL's autobiographical proclivities, although much of the play is fiction, and the recurrent themes of the final phase of his work as a dramatist. Written between 1939 and 1941, this four-act play was neither published nor produced until three years after O'Neill's death in 1953, although his stated desire was that this intense, deeply personal drama be held back until 25 years after his passing. The original **Broadway** production opened on 7 November 1956 at the Helen Hayes Theatre for 390 performances, and was directed by **José Quintero**, and featured **Fredric March**, **Florence Eldridge**, **Jason Robards, Jr.**, and Bradford Dillman. The play reaped a posthumous PULITZER PRIZE for O'Neill (his fourth) and initiated a CRITICAL reassessment of his work. After nearly two decades of neglect, his reputation was restored by this production and revivals of his earlier plays, insuring his predominance among twentieth-century American playwrights. With this grim, realistic family tragedy, O'Neill abandoned the bold experimentation of his plays of the 1920s–1930s to focus intently on the complexities and contradictions within the psyches of his central characters, the "four haunted Tyrones." A stark, unrelenting exorcism of his own family's dynamics, but woven with compassion by a playwright at the peak of his estimable abilities, *Long Day's Journey into Night* is considered by many critics and scholars to be the greatest American play to date.

Set in the summer of 1912, the play focuses on celebrated romantic actor James Tyrone (March), his wife Mary (Eldridge), and their adult sons Jamie (Robards) and Edmund (Dillman), summering at the family's modest Connecticut cottage. Mary is convalescing from a battle with morphine addiction that began when she gave birth to Edmund. The men exude hope that Mary is finally free of drugs, the source of a long family nightmare that has deeply affected all of them. However, Mary's precarious "recovery" is threatened by the illness of Edmund, who has been unable to shake what she stubbornly refers to as a "summer cold." Nervously awaiting the results of a medical tests, the men are ruefully convinced that Edmund has tuberculosis, and they endeavor to keep the truth from Mary for as long as possible. Mary's deep fears for Edmund, coupled with the demons of her life, slowly erode her resolve. To escape her profound fears, she secretly begins taking morphine again as the men continue to hope. As the agonizing day wears on, James, Jamie, and Edmund realize that their hopes for Mary are dashed, and they sink into alcoholic despair and a cycle of guilt, accusations, and misery.

Long Day's Journey into Night won recognition as O'Neill's greatest achievement in the aftermath of its original production, and it is frequently revived, including a notable British staging in 1971 starring **Laurence Olivier** as Tyrone and **Constance Cummings** as Mary, subsequently filmed for television in 1973, and in an acclaimed 1962 screen version featuring Ralph Richardson, **Katharine Hepburn**, Dean Stockwell, and Robards reprising his stage performance as Jamie. Robards also appeared in a 1988 revival as Tyrone, costarring with **Colleen Dewhurst** as Mary (with the play in **reper-**

tory with O'Neill's rose-colored family comedy, *Ah, Wilderness!* [1933]). An all-black cast starring **Earle Hyman** as Tyrone and **Ruby Dee** as Mary was filmed for television in 1982, and a 1986 Broadway revival starred **Jack Lemmon** as Tyrone and **Kevin Spacey** as Jamie (this version was filmed for television in 1987). In 2003, a revival brought critical accolades to Vanessa Redgrave as Mary, costarring with **Brian Dennehy** as Tyrone, **Philip Seymour Hoffman** as Jamie, and **Robert Sean Leonard** as Edmund.

LONG TIME SINCE YESTERDAY. P. J. Gibson's play opened on 10 October 1985 at the Henry Street Settlement in a **Woodie King, Jr.**, production directed by Bette Howard. The play examines the relationships of five diverse **African American women**, former college friends, who come together for the funeral of a sixth member of their group who has killed herself. The women variously express their individual problems in a variety of confrontations. **Mel Gussow**, writing in the *New York Times*, described the play as "a black, female, lesser version of *The Big Chill.*"

LONG WHARF THEATRE (LWT). Established by two Yale School of Drama alumni, **Jon Jory** and Harlan Kleiman, in 1965, to serve the New Haven, Connecticut, **community** as a professional resident theatre company, the LWT opened its doors with a revival of **Arthur Miller**'s *The Crucible*. The theatre has emerged as one of the outstanding **regional theatres** in the United States. Particularly under the leadership of **Arvin Brown** (1967–1996), the LWT functions in two performance spaces and emphasizes American and international plays focused on human relationships. Over 30 LWT productions have transferred to **Broadway** or **Off-Broadway**, including *The Changing Room* (1972), *Sizwe Banzi Is Dead* (1974**)**, *Streamers* (1976), *The Shadow Box* (1977), *The Gin Game* (1977), *Broken Glass* (1994), and *Wit* (1999), along with revivals of *Ah, Wilderness!* in 1975, *Watch on the Rhine* in 1980, *A View From the Bridge* in 1983, *American Buffalo in* 1983, *All My Sons* in 1987, and *Hughie* in 1996. The Long Wharf won a 1978 Regional Theatre **Tony Award**.

LOOK BACK IN ANGER. **John Osborne**'s realistic "kitchen sink" drama, a seismic event in the history of the British stage ushering in the era of the "angry young man" playwright, opened at London's Royal Court Theatre on 8 May 1956 in an English Stage Company production directed by Tony Richardson, generating controversy over its disaffected, abusive title character.

Jimmy Porter (Kenneth Haigh), a young man from the mean streets of London, is married to an upper-class wife, Alison (Mary Ure), and lives with her and their lodger, the easygoing Cliff, a young Welshman. Jimmy rants about life, politics, and other matters, attempting, often cruelly, to prod reactions from the impassive Alison. Jimmy becomes involved with Alison's best friend, Helena, whose arrogance and air of superiority both attract and repel him. Alison leaves and Helena moves in with Jimmy and Cliff. Eventually, Helena faces her moral lapse, leaves Jimmy, and reconciles with Alison, who in turn reconciles with Jimmy who is surprised to learn of Alison's pregnancy and subsequent loss of the baby.

The **Broadway** production of *Look Back in Anger*, also directed by Richardson and produced by **David Merrick**, opened with most of its English cast at the Lyceum Theatre on 1 October 1957 for 407 performances. It garnered a **Tony Award** nomination for Best Play, and Ure was nominated for her acting as well. A 1958 film version, featuring Ure with **Richard Burton** as Jimmy, was also directed by Richardson; Malcolm McDowell and Lisa Banes appeared in a 1980 remake, and Judi Dench directed Kenneth Branagh and Emma Thompson in a 1989 television film version.

LOOK HOMEWARD, ANGEL. Ketti Frings adapted Thomas Wolfe's novel into a three-act drama, winning the 1958 PULITZER PRIZE for Drama. The play opened on 28 November 1957 at the Ethel Barrymore Theatre for 564 performances. The production received several **Tony Award** nominations, including Best Play. Set in Altamont, North Carolina, in 1916, *Look Homeward, Angel* is a tense family drama focused on young Eugene Gant, a sensitive young man seeking intellectual and artistic fulfillment within the stifling confines of his mother Eliza Gant's boarding house. Eliza rules with an iron hand and battles persistently with Eugene's alcoholic father, W. O., and Eugene's dissolute, dying brother, Ben. The strong cast included Hugh Griffith, Jo Van Fleet, **Anthony Perkins**, and **Arthur Hill**. The play was filmed for television in 1972, and a 1978 MUSICAL, retitled *Angel*, had a brief **Broadway** run.

LOOKINGGLASS THEATRE COMPANY (LTC). Founded in Chicago, Illinois, in 1988 by a group of university students, LTC has devoted itself to a development process for new works (with the core values of collaboration, transformation, and invention guiding their practices) and in slightly over 20 years, produced 50 world premieres. Their first production, *Through the Looking Glass* (1988), was adapted from *Alice in Wonderland*, and many of their productions similarly adapted literary and theatrical works. These include *The Odyssey* (1989), *Eurydice* (1991), *The Arabian Nights* (1992), *The Idiot* (1997), and their most successful production, **Mary Zimmerman**'s *Metamorphosis* (1999), which has had numerous revivals at LTC and moved to **Broadway**. More recent productions include *Hard Times* (2002), *Hillbilly*

Antigone (2004), *The Old Curiosity Shop* (2005), *Around the World in 80 Days* (2007), and *Fedra: Queen of Haiti* (2009).

LOOSE ENDS. **Michael Weller**'s satiric play of the changing times of the 1970s opened on 6 June 1979 at the **Circle in the Square Theatre** for 270 performances under the direction of **Alan Schneider** and with a cast including **Kevin Kline** and Roxanne Hart. Kline's character, Paul, seeks to find his place in the world, and in his relationship with Susan, which begins on a beach in Bali, but his quest is largely defeated by his own passivity and the disillusioning times in which he lives. Approving critics found the play **Chekhovian,** and it was revived in 1988 at **Second Stage**, directed by Irene Lewis.

LOQUASTO, SANTO (1944–). A native of Wilkes-Barre, Pennsylvania, Loquasto studied at the Yale School of Drama prior to beginning a prolific career as a scene and costume designer for **Broadway** and films. He won a **Drama Desk Award** for his design of **David Rabe**'s *Sticks and Bones* (1972) and was **Tony Award**-nominated for **Jason Miller**'s PULITZER PRIZE-winning *That Championship Season* (1972) at the start of his career, which has included over 60 Broadway designs. He has impressed CRITICS with his skills at highly realistic designs, as well as more theatrical, symbolic approaches, and he has moved easily between straight plays and MUSICALS. Loquasto won a Tony for *Café Crown* (1989), and *Grand Hotel* (1989), and his other Tony nominations include *What the Wine-Sellers Buy* (1974), *American Buffalo* (1977), *The Suicide* (1981), *Ragtime* (1998), revivals of *Long Day's Journey Into Night* in 2003 and *Glengarry Glen Ross* in 2005, *Three Days of Rain* (2006), and revivals of *A Touch of the Poet* in 2006 and *Inherit the Wind* in 2007. Loquasto also won Drama Desk Awards for a revival of *The Cherry Orchard* in 1977, *American Buffalo*, *Café Crown*, *Italian American Reconciliation* (1989), *Grand Hotel*, and *Glengarry Glen Ross*, and numerous Drama Desk nominations. Loquasto has worked closely with filmmaker **Woody Allen** and his art direction and costumes for Allen's movies have earned him three Academy Award nominations for *Zelig* (1983), *Radio Days* (1987), and *Bullets over Broadway* (1994).

LORTEL, LUCILLE (1900–1998). A New Yorker by birth, Lortel was educated at the AMERICAN ACADEMY OF DRAMATIC ARTS before traveling to Germany, where she studied under MAX REINHARDT. Upon her return to the United States, she acted in STOCK and appeared in small roles on **Broadway** in four short-lived productions, *Two By Two* (1925), *The Dove* (1925), *One Man's Woman* (1926), *The Man Who Reclaimed His Head* (1932). In the early 1930s, Lortel married Louis Schweitzer and abandoned her career until 1947 when she established the White Barn Theatre at her Westport, Connecticut, home, which, until 2002, provided young performers and playwrights with a venue for summer work. In 1955, Lortel acquired New York's Theatre de Lys where she produced a revival of **Bertolt Brecht** and Kurt Weill's *The Threepenny Opera,* starring Weill's widow, **Lotte Lenya,** and it scored a surprise hit, running for 2,611 performances (until late 1961). Lortel expressed affection for lesser-known works by major international dramatists and new works by young talents with current themes, including such playwrights as **David Mamet, Sam Shepard, Marsha Norman, Larry Kramer, Lanford Wilson, William M. Hoffman,** and others.

Lortel's nickname as the "Queen of **Off-Broadway**" amply demonstrated her varied and essential contributions, but she also aided several Broadway productions, including a 1973 revival of *A Streetcar Named Desire, Angels Fall* (1983), *As Is* (1985), a 1985 revival of *Blood Knot, Sarafina!* (1988), and *A Walk in the Woods* (1988). In 1986, the Off-Broadway community established the **Lucille Lortel Awards** to recognize excellence. Lortel herself was the recipient of numerous **awards** recognizing her contributions, including the first Margo Jones Award in 1961, a special 1985 **Theatre World Award**, and a 1993 **Drama League** Unique Contribution to Theatre Award.

LOS ANGELES THEATRE CENTER (LATC). Established by Ralph Waite and Diane White in 1975 as the Los Angeles Actors' Theatre, the LATC aimed to provide the West coast with a venue not unlike New York's **Public Theatre**. After a decade and over 200 premiere productions, in 1985 with a name change and new spaces in downtown Los Angeles, the theatre began to regularly produce a season of 14 plays, including new works by **Luis Valdéz, Anna Deavere Smith,** and **David Henry Hwang**. LATC expanded its mission to include greater diversity, supporting special wings such as the **Latino** Theatre Lab, the Black Theatre Artists Workshop, the **Asian American Theatre** Project, the **Women's** Project, and the Young Conservatory. The organization closed in 1991, but the Latino **Theatre** Lab struggled to save the facilities at 514 S. Spring Street and raise the necessary funds to keep it afloat. In 2008, they reestablished the theatre with a full season of multi-disciplinary programs. *See also* AFRICAN AMERICAN THEATRE; CHICANO THEATRE; ETHNIC THEATRE; FEMINIST THEATRE.

LOST IN YONKERS. **Neil Simon** won a PULITZER PRIZE, **Tony Award,** and **Drama Desk Award** for this comedy-drama that also brought Tonys and Drama Desk Awards to the play's leading actors, **Irene Worth, Mercedes Ruehl,** and **Kevin Spacey**. The play opened at the Richard Rodgers Theatre on 21 February 1991 for 780 performances. Set in 1942, the progeny of stern, bitter Grandma Kurnitz (Worth) are a troubled lot. One of her sons is a small-time hood on the lam and the other, a struggling widower, comes to her as a last resort, to plead with her to care for his two young sons while he accepts a job far away. The boys are terrified of Grandma, but find an unlikely protector in their mentally challenged Aunt Bella (Ruehl), who ultimately finds courage in herself to stand up to her domineering mother. Worth and Ruehl repeated their performances in a 1993 screen version also starring Richard Dreyfuss and directed by Martha Coolidge.

LOUDON, DOROTHY (1933–2003). A versatile singer, actress, and comedian, Loudon was born in Boston, Massachusetts, and spent more than a decade performing in all manner of show business prior to winning a **Theatre World Award** in the short-lived **Broadway** MUSICAL *Nowhere to Go But Up* (1962). This led to a stint (1962–1964) on television's *The Garry Moore Show*, a variety hour which showcased Loudon's versatility. She also appeared frequently in nightclubs, STOCK, and Broadway shows, including *Noël Coward's Sweet Potato* (1968), *The Fig Leaves Are Falling* (1969), which brought her a **Drama Desk Award** and a **Tony Award** nomination, and revivals of *Three Men on a Horse* in 1969 and *The Women* in 1973.

Loudon scored a major triumph as the comically evil orphanage matron Miss Hannigan in the musical *Annie* (1977), winning a Tony and a Drama Desk Award. Loudon starred in the musical *Ballroom* (1979), which brought her Tony and Drama Desk nominations, although the production had a comparatively brief run. She replaced **Angela Lansbury** in *Sweeney Todd* (1979) and starred with **Katharine Hepburn** in *The West Side Waltz* (1981). She shared in a Drama Desk Award for Best Ensemble for the British farce *Noises Off* (1983), and also appeared on Broadway in *Jerry's Girls* (1985) and a revival of *Dinner at Eight* in 2002. Loudon starred in a short-lived television situation comedy, *Dorothy* (1979), but other than variety shows, she made relatively few television appearances and only a couple of films, although she won critical plaudits as Serena Dawes in *Midnight in the Garden of Good and Evil* (1997).

LOUISVILLE CHILDREN'S THEATRE. Sara Spencer Campbell, founder of Anchorage Press, and Mary Tyler Dick established this theatre in 1946 with Anne Gordon Brigham, associate director of THE NEIGHBORHOOD HOUSE, which had performed **children's theatre** in Louisville, Kentucky, prior to World WAR II. The LCT incorporated in 1948 and hired its first professional director, Katherine Kollmer, in 1950. In 1956, the LCT took up residence at the Belknap Playhouse at the University of Louisiville, but moved to Spalding College in 1967. The LCT changed its name to Stage One and became an EQUITY Theatre in 1980 with a resident acting company and continues its mission of producing high-quality children's theatre and developing new works for young audiences.

LOVE! VALOUR! COMPASSION! **Terrence McNally**'s **Tony Award**, **Drama Desk Award**, and **Obie Award**-winning comedy-drama opened in a **Manhattan Theatre Club** and **Jujamcyn Theatres** production under the direction of **Joe Mantello** on 14 February 1995 for 248 performances at the Walter Kerr Theatre. Set in the mid-1990s at a Dutchess County lakeside house owned by a **gay** choreographer Gregory, who invites a group of close gay friends for relaxing weekends during which the characters struggle with personal relationships, the specter of **AIDS**, and other vicissitudes of life. The characters include two English brothers, John and James (both played by John Glover in a Tony-winning performance), a **Broadway** MUSICAL fanatic, Buzz, played by **Nathan Lane** in a star-making and Drama Desk Award-winning performance, and assorted others, including a young **Latino** dancer who threatens Gregory's longtime relationship with a young blind man, Bobby, played by Justin Kirk. A 1997 screen version, also directed by Mantello, featured Jason Alexander stepping into Lane's role and most of the other cast members from Broadway. A 1995 London production won the Evening Standard Award for Best Play.

LUBIN, BARRY (1953–). One of the rare American clowns to break through from CIRCUS to mainstream show business, Lubin was born in Atlantic City, New Jersey, where he aimed to become a television director. He attended the Ringling Bros. and Barnum & Bailey Clown College and developed the character "Grandma," inspired by his own grandmother and elderly women he observed walking Atlantic City's boardwalk. He joined the Ringling Bros. and Barnum & Bailey Circus, "The Greatest Show on Earth," in 1974. He later teamed with Dick Monday and performed variety comedy shows on tour and Off-Broadway, including *A Couple of Guys Who Gotta Do a Show* and *Pass the Popcorn*. Lubin joined the **Big Apple Circus**, a New York-based one-ring circus, in 1982.

LUCAS, CRAIG (1951–). Adopted by a Pennsylvania family (after he was found in an abandoned car in Atlanta, Georgia), Lucas attended Boston University, where he was encouraged as a writer by Anne Sexton. Lucas appeared as an actor in the **Broadway** MUSICALS *Shenandoah* (1975), *Rex* (1976), *On the Twentieth Century* (1978), and *Sweeney Todd* (1979), but turned to playwriting with *Blue Window* (1984), followed by *Three Post-*

cards (1987), and *Marry Me a Little* (1988), a musical featuring songs by **Stephen Sondheim.** Lucas rose to prominence as a dramatist with *Prelude to a Kiss* (1990), which brought him **Tony Award** and **Drama Desk Award** nominations. His subsequent plays include *Missing Persons* (1995), which was nominated for a Drama Desk Award, *God's Heart* (1997), *The Dying Gaul* (1998), *Stranger* (2001), *The Thing of Darkness* (2002), written in collaboration with David Schulner, *Reckless* (2004), *Small Tragedy* (2004), *The Singing Forest* (2004), the libretto for *The Light in the Piazza* (2005), which brought him a Tony nomination, and *Prayer for My Enemy* (2007). For films, Lucas wrote the **AIDS**-themed *Longtime Companion* (1990), adapted his own *Prelude to a Kiss* (1992), *Reckless* (1995), and *The Dying Gaul* (2005), which he also directed, and *The Secret of Dentists* (2002), for which he was awarded a New York Film Critics Circle Award. Lucas also directed the film *Birds of America (*2008). Lucas is artistic director of the **Intiman Theatre** in Seattle, Washington, and won an **Obie Award** for directing Harry Kondoleon's *Saved or Destroyed* in 2001. *See also* GAY AND LESBIAN THEATRE.

LUCE, CLARE BOOTHE. *See* BOOTHE, CLARE.

LUCE, WILLIAM (1941–). Portland, Oregon, native Luce has developed his own unique corner of contemporary American drama as the author of a series of **solo** plays about celebrated historical figures, beginning with *The Belle of Amherst* (1976), in which **Julie Harris** (in a **Tony Award**-winning performance) portrayed Emily Dickinson. None of Luce's subsequent single-actor shows has been quite as successful, but all have had a stage life, often due to the presence of a major actor. His plays, four of which have appeared on **Broadway**, include *Lillian* (1986), with **Zoe Caldwell** as **Lillian Hellman**, *The Last Flapper* (1987; Zelda Fitzgerald), *Brontë* (1988; Charlotte Brontë), *Bravo, Caruso!* (1991; Enrico Caruso), *Lucifer's Child* (1991; Isak Dinesen), *Barrymore* (1997; John Barrymore*), which brought **Christopher Plummer** a Tony, *Nijinsky* (2000), and *Baptiste: The Life of Molière* (2001).

LUCILLE LORTEL AWARDS. *See* LORTEL, LUCILLE.

LUDLAM, CHARLES (1943–1987). Born in New York City and raised in Northport, Long Island, Ludlam received a degree in dramatic literature from Hofstra University in 1964. When he became a member of John Vaccaro's Play-House of the Ridiculous, a small **Off-Off-Broadway** company, Ludlam found his unique theatrical style. With Vaccaro's company, Ludlam saw his earliest plays, *Big Hotel* (1967) and *Conquest of the Universe* (1967), produced, introducing the theatrical flamboyance, outrageous camp humor, and

gay-themed travesties and popular culture satires that made him a fixture of New York's **Off-Broadway** theatre scene for 20 years. Despite his initial successes with Vaccaro, artistic differences led Ludlam to form his own troupe, **The Ridiculous Theatre Company**, and under this banner, and for the remainder of his career, Ludlam perfected his style as both a playwright and an actor, combining elements of high camp, art, Grand Guignol, melodrama,* and classic movies with often shocking humor in a range of plays inspired by opera, literature, and mainstream American theatrical and cinematic forms. A particularly characteristic touch was Ludlam's use of **female impersonation** as he usually took on the leading role in his own plays, portraying such diverse fictional characters as Marguerite Gautier and Hedda Gabler, as well as genuine icons, including Greta Garbo and Maria Callas.

From among Ludlam's canon of over 20 plays, the most critically appreciated are *Bluebeard* (1970), *Camille* (1973, revived 1990), *Stageblood* (1975), *Professor Bedlam's Punch and Judy Show* (1975), *Der Ring Gott Farblonjet* (1977), *Le Bourgeois Avant-Garde* (1982), and *The Mystery of Irma Vep* (1984), the last being perhaps the most enduring of his numerous stage works. As both leading actor and dramatist, these plays brought Ludlam six **Obie Awards**, a **Drama Desk Award**, and the Rosamund Gilder Award. Ludlam also made a few film appearances, the most significant of which were released in the year he died: *The Big Easy* (1987) and *Forever, Lulu* (1987), and he also improbably made a few television guest appearances. Ludlam also made two silent films with the Ridiculous Theatrical Company called *The Sorrows of Dolores* and *Museum of Wax*; these were thought unfinished at the time of his death, but were pieced together and shown in a Queer/Art/ Film series at the IFC Center in New York in 2010.

Ludlam was also an important theatrical theorist and, five years after his death, publication of his diverse essays on theatrical art, *Ridiculous Theatre: Scourge of Human Folly—The Essays and Opinions of Charles Ludlam,* brought a fuller appreciation of his achievement as an actor and playwright. At the time of Ludlam's death, he was preparing a play called *A Piece of Pure Escapism* in which he intended to portray the legendary early twentieth-century magician Harry Houdini. The Ridiculous Theatre Company dealt openly with homosexuality well before the subject became commonplace in American drama, a fact that gained poignance when Ludlam died of complications from **AIDS**.

LUDWIG, KEN (1950–). Playwright and librettist with a penchant for farce, Ludwig was born in York, Pennsylvania, and studied at Haverford College, Cambridge, and Harvard University Law School. He abandoned law to write for the theatre, scoring a success with his broad backstage farce *Lend*

Me a Tenor (1989), which was nominated for a Best Play **Tony Award**, and has continued in a similar vein with *Moon Over Buffalo* (1995), *Shakespeare in Hollywood* (2003), *Leading Ladies* (2004), and *Be My Baby* (2005). He also revised the **Ben Hecht** and CHARLES MACARTHUR comedy *Twentieth Century* when it was revived on **Broadway** in 2004. Ludwig has also written the books for the musicals *Crazy for You* (1992), which brought him a Tony nomination, and *The Adventures of Tom Sawyer* (2001).

LUNT, ALFRED (1892–1977).[†] Born in Milwaukee, Wisconsin, Alfred David Lunt attended Carroll College with plans of becoming an architect, but instead he became an actor, appearing in STOCK with the Castle Square Theatre in Boston and touring with Lillie Langtry* and Margaret Anglin.* He won acclaim in *Clarence** (1919). When he married LYNN FONTANNE in 1922, they began working together almost exclusively, appearing in a revival of *Sweet Nell of Old Drury* (1923), but scoring their first dual triumph in Ferenc Molnár's *The Guardsman* (1924). Lunt was also well-received in a few **solo** efforts, including *Outward Bound** (1924), *Ned McCobb's Daughter** (1926), and *Marco Millions** (1928). In the mid-1920s, Lunt and Fontanne began a long string of CRITICAL and commercial successes establishing them as the greatest acting couple of their generation in the American theatre, admired for their individual gifts and the skill with which they worked together. Their major joint appearances in the 1920s included *Arms and the Man* (1925), *At Mrs. Beam's* (1926), *The Brothers Karamazov* (1927), *The Second Man** (1927), *The Doctor's Dilemma* (1927), *Caprice* (1928), and *Meteor** (1929).

After 1930, the reputations of the Lunts, individually and together, only grew with distinguished performances in MAXWELL ANDERSON's *Elizabeth the Queen* (1930), ROBERT E. SHERWOOD's *Reunion in Vienna* (1931), **Noël Coward**'s *Design for Living* (1933) and *Point Valaine* (1935), **Shakespeare**'s *The Taming of the Shrew* (1935), Sherwood's PULITZER PRIZE-winning *Idiot's Delight* (1936), Jean Giraudoux's *Amphitryon 38* (1937), **Anton Chekhov**'s *The Seagull* (1938), Sherwood's *There Shall Be No Night* (1940), S. N. BEHRMAN's *The Pirate* (1942), Terrence Rattigan's *O Mistress Mine* (1946), Behrman's *I Know My Love* (1949), Coward's *Quadrille* (1954), HOWARD LINDSAY and **Russel Crouse**'s *The Great Sebastians* (1956), and Friedrich Dürrenmatt's *The Visit* (1958).

Lunt also directed some of their vehicles and won a **Tony Award** as Best Director for *Ondine* (1954), after which he won another as Best Actor for *Quadrille*. Lunt also directed *Candle in the Wind* (1941) and *First Love* (1961). Lunt and Fontanne were respected for their exacting professionalism and for the exhausting tours they did of many of their productions, bringing the finest plays and acting of the period to all corners of the United States. Jointly, the Lunts were presented with a special Tony in 1970.

LUPONE, PATTI (1949–). Born in Northport, New York, LuPone was trained for the stage at the Juilliard School and, with classmate **Kevin Kline**, was instrumental in the establishment of **John Houseman**'s **The Acting Company**, a touring troupe of young Juilliard actors. She appeared in a variety of classical, MUSICAL, and contemporary roles for the Company between 1972 and 1976, She debuted on **Broadway** in the Company's production of **Anton Chekhov**'s *The Three Sisters* in 1973. Her most honored work has been in musical theatre, but LuPone has had an uncommonly varied career, including film and television work, as well as the stage. On Broadway, she has won **Tony Awards** and **Drama Desk Awards** for *Evita* (1979) and a revival of *Gypsy* in 2008, and was nominated for Tonys for *The Robber Bridegroom* (1976) and revivals *Anything Goes* in 1988 and *Sweeney Todd* in 2006. LuPone also won a Drama Desk Award for *Anything Goes* and was Drama Desk-nominated for *The Robber Bridegroom, The Old Neighborhood* (1998), and *Sweeney Todd.* She also appeared on Broadway in *The Water Engine/Mr. Happiness* (1978), *Working* (1978), a revival of *Oliver!* in 1984, *Accidental Death of an Anarchist* (1984), and a revival of *Noises Off* in 2001. She also replaced **Zöe Caldwell** in *Master Class* (1995).

LuPone was nominated for an Emmy Award for a guest appearance on the television situation comedy *Frasier* in 1998 and a Daytime Emmy for *The Song Spinner* (1995). LuPone appeared as Libby Thacher on the TV drama series *Life Goes On* from 1989–1993 and her films include *1941* (1979), *Driving Miss Daisy* (1989), *Summer of Sam* (1999), and *State and Main* (2000).

LUV. **Murray Schisgal**'s two-act, three-character comedy opened on 11 November 1964 in a **Shubert Organization** production at the Booth Theatre for an impressive 901 performances. Directed by **Mike Nichols**, who won a **Tony Award**, and starring Peter Falk, **Eli Wallach**, and **Anne Jackson**, *Luv* was nominated for a Best Play Tony. **Oliver Smith**'s set was a bridge (with lighting by **Jean Rosenthal** and costumes by **Theoni V. Aldredge**) where a wacky threesome battles out their complicated relationships. Tinged with absurdist elements mixed with broad comedy, Schisgal's satiric edge reveals the absurdities of love and marriage. *Luv* was adapted as a MUSICAL, *Love*, in 1984, and revised as *What about Luv?* in 1991.

LYNCH, THOMAS (1953–). An Asheville, North Carolina, native, he studied at the Yale University and has done much of his work as a scene designer in **regional theatres**, most notably Chicago's **Goodman Theatre** and the **Seattle Repertory Theatre**, and with various opera companies, including the Metropolitan Opera. Lynch has been nominated for **Tony Awards** for his **Broadway** designs of *The Heidi Chronicles* (1989) and a 2000 revival of *The Music Man* and **Drama Desk Award** nominations for both Broadway and **Off-Broadway** designs for *Little Footsteps* (1986), *The Heidi Chronicles, Contact* (2000), *Old Money* (2001), *See What I Wanna See* (2006), and *Happiness* (2009). Lynch's Broadway designs also include *Tintypes* (1980), *Rose* (1981), *The Speed of Darkness* (1991), *My Favorite Year* (1992), *The Rise and Fall of Little Voice* (1994), *Having Our Say* (1995), **The Young Man from Atlanta** (1997), *Swing!* (1999), *Thou Shalt Not* (2001), and several revivals. He also worked on the television drama *Six Feet Under* (2003–2005).